Flyfisher's Guide to™
ALASKA
~ Includes Light Tackle ~

Titles Available in This Series

Flyfisher's Guide to™
ALASKA
~ Includes Light Tackle ~

Scott Haugen

with contributions from
Dan Busch and Will Rice

Flyfisher's Guide to™ Series

Wilderness
Adventures
Press, Inc.™

Belgrade, Montana

Flyfisher's Guide to™

Published by Wilderness Adventures Press, Inc.™
45 Buckskin Road
Belgrade, MT 59714
866-400-2012
Website: www.wildadvpress.com
email: books@wildadvpress.com

First edition

Printed in the USA

Library of Congress Cataloging-in-Publication Data

Haugen, Scott.
  Flyfisher's guide to Alaska : includes light tackle / by Scott Haugen; with contributions from Dan Busch and Will Rice.
    p. cm.
  ISBN 1-932098-02-X (pbk. : alk. paper)
  1. Fly fishing--Alaska--Guidebooks. 2. Alaska--Guidebooks. I. Busch, Dan II. Rice, Will (Wilson) III. Title.
  SH467.H28 2003
  799.12'4'09798--dc22
                                                                              2003018928

Table of Contents

SOUTHEAST ALASKA—267

FISHING THE ARCTIC—427

Acknowledgments

SCOTT HAUGEN

The creation of such a comprehensive book would not have been possible without the concerted effort of many individuals. Though too numerous to mention each by name, first and foremost I would like to thank the Alaska Department of Fish and Game for all their assistance. I spent hundreds of hours on the phone with more than 30 ADF&G employees from around the state. These devoted people were my window to the many Alaskan streams I've forever yearned to see.

For the insight and wisdom provided by all the fly and tackle shop owners and close friends and lifelong Alaskan residents who've spent decades exploring the state's many fishing hotspots I am eternally grateful. I would also like to extend a formal thank you to the Alaska Department of Tourism, Alaska Department of Natural Resources, U.S. Forest Service, National Parks Service, United States Geological Survey, and the many Chamber of Commerce affiliates, all of whom had a hand in the crafting of this book.

Most of all, I would like to thank my wife, Tiffany, for the continued support, repeated proofing, and words of encouragement that kept me motivated during the time it took to complete this work. I also want to thank my two sons, Braxton and Kazden, for their understanding and patience during all those times I couldn't break away from the computer to play catch.

Finally, I'd like to thank the traveling angler. Were it not for you, this book would not have come to fruition. Your desire to learn about Alaska—and travel to places most only dream of seeing—is what ultimately motivated me in the creation of this work.

WILL RICE

The author would like to thank the following guides and lodge owners for their invaluable assistance. They all displayed an extensive knowledge of their respective areas and a deep commitment to protecting the resource. Without their help, writing about the fishing available in southwestern Alaska would have been impossible.

Nanci Morris (Katmai Fishing Adventures), Mark Emery (Wet Waders), John Kent (Painter Creek Lodge), Mel Gillis (Sandy River Lodge), John Holman (No-See-Um Lodge), George Riddle (Blueberry Island Lodge), Bill Sims (Newhalen Lodge), Brian Kraft (Alaska Sportsman's Lodge), Dan Michels (Crystal Creek Lodge), Ty Johnson (Bear Bay Lodge), Brian Richardson (Northern Rim Adventures), Chuck Ash (Brightwater Adventures), Bud Hodson (Tikchik Narrows Lodge), Marty Decker (Frontier River Adventures), and John McDonald (Kuskokwim River Adventures).

DAN BUSCH

Several publications from the Kodiak Historical Society, Kodiak Island Convention and Visitors Bureau, Alaska Department of Fish and Game, Alaska Department of Natural Resources, and the Kodiak National Wildlife Refuge were used for descriptive and statistical information.

The following individuals also provided information and assistance: Tony Chatto, Fisheries Management Biologist/Pilot with the Kodiak National Wildlife Refuge (retired); Len Schwarz, Kodiak Area Sport Fish Biologist with the Alaska Department of Fish and Game; Donn Tracy, Assistant Kodiak Area Sport Fish Biologist with the Alaska Department of Fish and Game; Wayne Biessel, Kodiak District State Park Ranger; and Pam Foreman, Executive Director of the Kodiak Island Convention and Visitors Bureau.

Introduction

Alaska! The way the word rolls off the tongue elicits images of nature in its purest sense—raw and demanding, yet unparalleled in beauty and tranquility. No words can truly describe everything that makes Alaska special; it must be experienced firsthand.

Once you've traveled to Alaska, you'll discover how easy it is to get there. And once there, you'll see how simple it is to get around. Between modern air taxi services and extensive road systems, anglers can explore virtually every corner of the state. The only constraints are time and money (and maybe weather).

Accessing remote fishing grounds in Alaska can be a pricey proposition, but then again, if you've budgeted for such a trip, it's attainable. And exploring the state on your own can be accomplished at a surprisingly low cost. The options are endless.

With nearly 34,000 miles of coastline—more than the entire contiguous United States—and six distinct geographic regions, capturing all Alaska has to offer in one book is impossible. Nonetheless, what you will find within these pages is the most comprehensive flyfishing guide ever assembled for Alaska. Of course, it does not cover every fishable water in the state. The authors who combined their extensive knowledge to create this book have spent decades in the state and still haven't seen it all.

Yet from the Arctic to the panhandle the *Flyfisher's Guide to Alaska* will introduce you to more rivers, streams, and lakes than can realistically be explored in a lifetime. Rather than following the regions defined by the Alaska Department of Fish and Game (ADF&G), the text is broken into sections that loosely radiate outward from Anchorage, the primary travel hub for anglers visiting Alaska.

Waters large and small are covered in great detail, along with maps, run-timing charts, extensive information for traveling anglers, pattern and tackle recommendations, and a wealth of other great information.

Whether you're planning your first trip to the Last Frontier or your fiftieth, the information in this book will help you.

—*Scott Haugen*

Legend

═══ Primary Highway

──── Access Roads

1. Glenn Highway
2. Alaska Highway
3. George Parks Highway
4. Richardoon Highway
6. Steese Highway
8. Denali Highway
9. Seward Highway
11. James Dalton Highway

Alaska

0   100   200   300   400   500 MILES

Chukchi Sea

Noatak National Preserve NP

Cape Krusenstern NM

Bering Land Bridge Preserve NP

Nome

Yukon R.

Bethel

Bering Sea

Unalaska

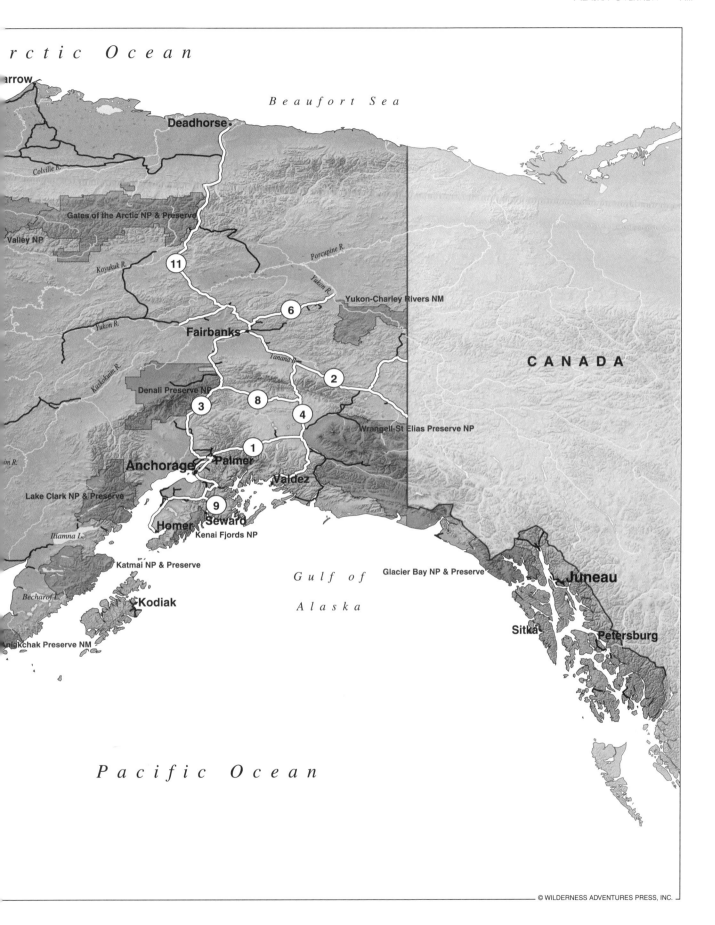

Arctic Ocean

Barrow

Beaufort Sea

Deadhorse

Colville R.

Gates of the Arctic NP & Preserve

Valley NP

Porcupine R.

Koyukuk R.

⑪

Yukon R.

⑥

Yukon-Charley Rivers NM

Yukon R.

Fairbanks

Kuskokwim R.

Tanana R.

CANADA

Denali Preserve NP

②

③ ⑧

④

Wrangell-St Elias Preserve NP

im R.

① Palmer

Anchorage Valdez

Lake Clark NP & Preserve

⑨ Seward

Homer

Iliamna L.

Kenai Fjords NP

Katmai NP & Preserve

Gulf of

Glacier Bay NP & Preserve

Juneau

Becharof L.

Alaska

Kodiak

Sitka

Petersburg

Aniakchak Preserve NM

Pacific Ocean

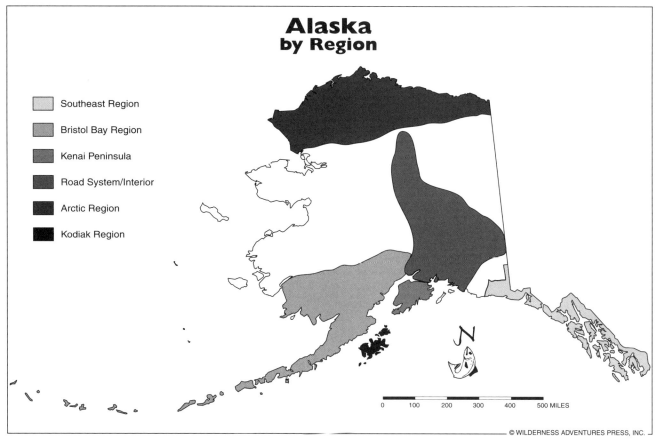

Alaska
by Region

Southeast Region

Bristol Bay Region

Kenai Peninsula

Road System/Interior

Arctic Region

Kodiak Region

0   100   200   300   400   500 MILES

© WILDERNESS ADVENTURES PRESS, INC.

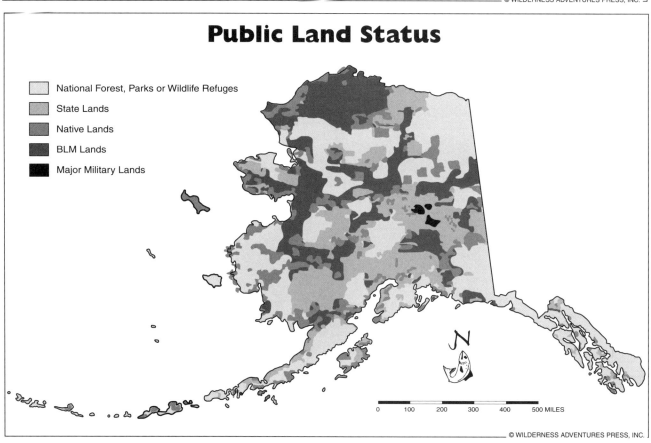

Public Land Status

National Forest, Parks or Wildlife Refuges

State Lands

Native Lands

BLM Lands

Major Military Lands

0   100   200   300   400   500 MILES

© WILDERNESS ADVENTURES PRESS, INC.

Size Comparison

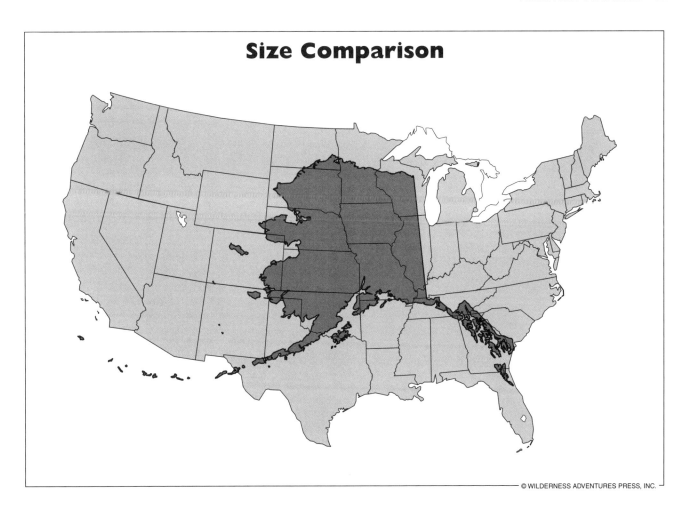

Dolly Varden are native to many Anchorage-area waters.

Pink salmon are Alaska's most neglected gamefish.

Alaska's Game Fish

By Scott Haugen

King (Chinook) Salmon
Oncorhynchus tshawytscha

The mighty king salmon heads the popularity list of most Alaska anglers using conventional tackle. No other fish attracts such huge crowds of anglers from the Lower Forty-Eight and across the world. Surprisingly few fly anglers actively pursue king salmon for the simple reason that they don't like battling one 40- or 50-pound fish for hours. But latching into a mighty king is an awe-inspiring event; one that any devout fisherman knows he must experience at least once. When you've felt the overpowering strength of a king, you'll either be turned off or inspired to make pursing these worthy beasts a lifelong endeavor.

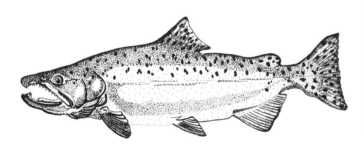

But don't think trophy kings come easy, especially on a fly rod. While many streams in the lower two-thirds of Alaska harbor excellent salmon fishing, convincing fish to take a fly can be a frustrating ordeal. I once tried over a half-dozen patterns on a pool of salmon, before one finally decided to take a shrimp pattern.

Size 2, 1/0, 2/0, and 3/0 weighted flies such as an Egg-Sucking Leech, Hula, and Wiggletail are popular king choices. Though the real challenge lies in getting the fly of choice down deep, in front of the salmon's nose. This usually requires a high-density, sink-tip line, something in the 500-grain class. The T-300 and T-400 series lines are also excellent choices. Ten-weight fly rods are the minimum for big kings, with an 11 or 12 even better.

If you're determined to take a realistic crack at a world-record king, you'll need to fish rivers that carry genetically superior fish. Working a fly rod on the fast-moving, shoulder-to-shoulder Kenai during peak runs will not make you many friends. This is the time to turn to drift-fishing gear—something that will produce more fish and hold the big one once hooked.

The Kenai River is home to the current world-record king salmon, which weighed in at 97 pounds, 4 ounces and succumbed to sport tackle. The largest king salmon ever recorded, however, was one taken in a fish trap near Petersburg, Alaska in 1949. That fat, ocean-fed king buried the scales to 126 pounds.

In addition to the world famous Kenai River runs, major populations of kings return annually to the Yukon, Kuskokwim, Nushagak, Susitna, Copper, Taku, and Stikine Rivers. The Togiak, Karluk, Alagnak, and Goodnews are just a few of the other popular king fisheries, though prime fishing can be had throughout the king's entire range.

Like all salmon of the Pacific, king, or chinook, salmon live an anadromous lifestyle. Anywhere from 3,000 to 14,000 eggs may be deposited into a gravel nest by a mature female in early fall. The males then fertilize the eggs, and by late winter or early spring—depending on the time of spawning and water temperature—the alevins, complete with yolk sac, hatch and remain in the gravel for several weeks. When the yolk sac dissolves, the fry then wriggle their way up through the gravel. Juveniles will remain in the river for a year before migrating to sea as smolt.

In the ocean, chinook salmon are efficient predators, foraging on squid, shrimp, herring, and various crustaceans. Due to their high-protein diets, these salmon grow rapidly, often doubling their weight in a single year at sea. A mature three-year-old chinook may weigh only 4 pounds, while a seven-year-old fish can exceed 50 pounds. Catching any chinook in the 30- to 40-pound class is a thrill.

The spawning colors of chinook greatly vary from the deep silver bodies they exhibit when in the ocean. Once they hit the rivers, chinook quit actively feeding, and their bodies begin deteriorating as they live off reserves in preparation for the spawn. As a result, chinook color may range from copper to red to even black as spawning kicks off.

Mid-June to the end of July marks prime king fishing time, and rivers are often choked with anglers from around the globe during these weeks. Kings are without doubt the most highly prized sport fish in the state—and one of the best eating of all fish. Every time I glance at the 70-pound king gracing the wall of my den, I get the urge to head north once again to the greatest salmon fishing the world has to offer.

Silver (Coho) Salmon
Oncorhynchus kisutch

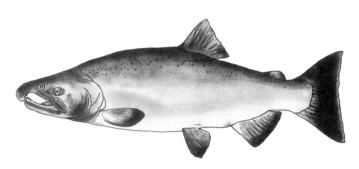

The silver, or coho, salmon is a favorite target for fly anglers heading to Alaska. No other salmon attracts more flyfishers to the Last Frontier. The action they provide on a fly rod and the abundance of 10- to 12-pound fish make silvers exciting to fish for.

Silvers will attack a multitude of bright, flashy flies, with size 2 or 4 Egg-Sucking Leeches, Flash Flies, and Deer-Hair Pollywogs among the most common patterns. Dark Woolly Buggers also perform well, as do pink patterns. As a good friend and Alaskan guide has always said, "When fishing silvers, try pink, if that doesn't work, switch to pink."

Because silvers can be tenacious fighters, a 9- or 10-weight fly rod is a good choice. A strong 12-pound leader (1X tippet) is the minimum many anglers will use on these feisty fish. The choice of fly line depends on the waters being fished. A floating line is ideal for pulling silvers from shallow, slack water where migrating salmon stop to rest. A sinking line may be necessary in fast, deep water, with Teeny T-200 and T-300 lines often very effective.

Silver salmon frequent many of Alaska's coastal rivers from Point Hope all the way down through the Panhandle. The Alaska Peninsula and Kodiak Island are home to some of the state's largest silvers, and the Ugashik, Situk, Togiak, Alagnak, Kasilof, and Kenai Rivers—just to name a few—are also famous silver fisheries. Countless silver streams exist around the state, though the state record came from Southeast Alaska in 1976 and weighed in at 26 pounds.

The life cycle of the coho is truly amazing. As adults enter rivers, their bright silver bodies—with small black spots along the back and upper portion of the tail—help set them apart from chinook. The white gum lines of silver salmon and the absence of black spots on the lower lobe of the tail further distinguish silvers from chinook. But as spawning approaches, both sexes of coho develop dark backs with deep reddish hues along their sides. The

bucks develop the distinctive kype and large teeth indicative of salmon.

From mid-July all the way into November coho salmon make their way into rivers, but water temperatures at the spawning grounds dictate when the fish arrive at the precise spot where they were born. Adults will typically reside in pools until their biological clock moves them onto the spawning beds. The hen digs a nest and deposits up to 4,500 eggs, which are then fertilized by the male.

The eggs develop over the winter and are ready to hatch early in the spring. Once the yolk sac has been depleted, fry emerge from the gravel around May and June. As the fry grow, they take up residence in protected, shallow stream fringes, ponds, pools, and sloughs. As they grow, young silvers are often territorial around other salmonids. This innate aggression is what makes adult silvers so popular among the flyfishing fraternity.

Young silvers spend one to three winters in streams, thriving in habitats void of main channel floods. In lake systems, smolt may stay up to five years prior to migrating to sea. Most silvers remain in the ocean for one to three years before returning to rivers as healthy adults.

Because silvers often congregate and travel through estuaries in large numbers, they can be caught in these environments. Flying out to a secluded bay or river inlet in a floatplane is what many silver salmon fans yearn for. And in the month of September, when Alaska silver fishing is at its best, the sky above Anchorage is often dotted with air taxis heading across Cook Inlet. It's an experience you won't want to miss.

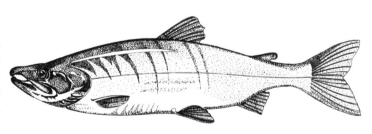

Sockeye (Red) Salmon
Oncorhynchus nerka

One of Alaska's most famous fishing scenes is the shoulder-to-shoulder angling where the Russian River joins the Kenai River. Here anglers from around the globe gather by the hundreds to test their luck on Alaska's sockeye, or red, salmon.

The sockeye is one of Alaska's most important game fish on a commercial, sport, and subsistence level. They range throughout rivers on the Kenai Peninsula, with the Kenai and Kasilof Rivers the most popular with anglers. Several rivers in the Bristol Bay region also yield astounding numbers of sockeyes, as does the Kvichak River, the outlet of Lake Illamna, which likely hosts the largest run of reds in the world.

From a sport-fishing perspective, the beauty of sockeye salmon fishing is in the fish's abundance and accessibility. The annual runs of these fish are measured in the millions, and the fact that you can fly to Alaska, rent a car, drive a couple hours, and be battling fish makes them very popular.

Upon entering rivers in early July, sockeye salmon are silver with deep-blue backs—thus the local name "blueback" salmon—that exude an almost phosphorescent appearance when held in natural light. Oddly, these fish feed on plankton, only nipping at fly patterns presented in front of them. As they travel with their mouths agape much of the time, placing a fly on their lips can trigger a reflex response.

Because sockeyes don't actively feed, many people believe the fly pattern you use makes little difference. I've experienced my best success on purple and brown Coho patterns, though combinations of these patterns in red/white, purple/white, and green/white have also yielded many fish. The key is getting your fly down quickly to where these salmon hug the bottom while traveling. A 2-foot leader often suffices, and using a sink-tip line on a 7- to 8-weight rod or a floating line with split shot placed on the leader is essential. If anglers around you are nailing fish while you're getting skunked, you're likely fishing above the fish.

Sockeyes travel in large schools very close to shore. And if these fish are in the river, there will be anglers pursuing them, leaving no question as to where to start your search. If heading to the Kenai, don't come thinking you'll have the place to yourself, no matter where you go. Public access ramps and fishing docks have been established along many area rivers, making for easy, safe access by bank anglers. Hiking up the Russian River may get you a bit more solitude. And the farther you walk, the fewer anglers you'll see.

Sockeye salmon average 4 to 8 pounds, though 10- and 12-pound fish are taken each summer. The state record of 16 pounds was taken on the Kenai in 1974 and will be tough to break.

After hatching in rivers, juvenile sockeye salmon spend up to four years in the ocean before returning to their natal streams. By the time sockeyes have returned to their spawning grounds, they have covered thousands of miles. Like all Pacific salmon, they use their olfactory senses to guide them to their parent streams.

Spawning normally takes place in rivers, streams, and places of upwelling near lakeshores. The hen selects a site and digs a nest with her tail. As she deposits her eggs, one or more males simultaneously fertilize the eggs as they drop into the nest. This process will be repeated up to five times, with between 2,000 and 4,500 eggs deposited. The female covers the nest with gravel and remains in the area until death.

Like all salmon, sockeyes perish after spawning. If you find yourself in Alaska during mid-August, locate a small stream and observe the courtship and spawning rituals of these incredible fish. As they reach spawning time, the once silvery salmon undergo a color transformation unlike any other salmon, turning a brilliant red with deep green heads. Though it's not sporting to catch the fish at this stage, observing them in their final stages of life is an enthralling experience.

Sockeye eggs hatch during the winter, and the alevins, or sac-fry, remain in the gravel to live off nutrients stored in their yolk sacs until early spring. Juveniles will emerge and seek protective areas, where they will remain for one to three years before heading to sea in the spring as smolts. In systems without lakes, however, many fry move to the sea soon after emerging from the gravel.

In some areas, sockeye salmon are landlocked, spending their entire lives in lakes. This captive form of sockeye is called a kokanee, and though it rarely exceeds 15 inches, it's a popular fish in many lakes outside Alaska.

Due to their rich reddish-orange meat, sockeye are ideal for canning, and many folks claim they are the tastiest of the five salmon species. I feel they lack the oil content that makes kings and coho so delectable, though red salmon are indeed extremely good eating.

Chum (Dog) Salmon
Oncorhynchus keta

One summer I tied a bunch of fly patterns for my dad, who was heading to Kodiak for some early August fishing. Positioning himself where the mouth of a gently sloping stream entered a bay, he caught numerous Dolly Varden without moving a step. He eventually replaced his tattered Black Ghost with a fresh one, and this time his cast made it through the char to the bottom.

It was there that Dad first tied into one of Alaska's chum salmon—and when he gave up char fishing in favor of these powerful salmon. Pound for pound, chum salmon could well be the hardest fighting of the five salmon species. Fresh from salt, these metallic, greenish-blue salmon pull hard and deep, yet can flail and cartwheel over the surface in a way that will impress any steelheader.

Chum, or dog, salmon are the most widely distributed of the Pacific salmon, ranging from the Sacramento River in the south, over to Japan, up to Siberia, and across the Arctic Ocean into Canada's Mackenzie River. In Alaska's Arctic, interior, and northwestern zones, chum salmon are an important food source for subsistence peoples. Their popularity as a sport fish continues to grow in the state.

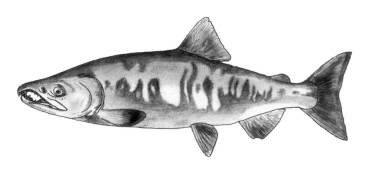

By late July and early August, the chum spawn is usually well underway, depending on geographic locale. Chums prefer spawning in small side channels and upwelling springs, where conditions maximize egg survival. They are also known to spawn in intertidal zones. Some, however, will travel over 2,000 miles to spawn.

Females will deposit as many as 4,000 eggs in a redd. Upon hatching, fry don't hang out in rivers like kings, silvers, and sockeyes; rather, they form schools in salt water, moving into the Bering Sea and Gulf of Alaska by fall. Chum salmon will remain at sea for up to six years, though the fish in Southeast Alaska typically move into rivers after four years. Age and size greatly vary among the state's wide distribution of chums, with an average weight being 7 to 15 pounds. The state record is a stunning 32 pounds.

Like all Pacific salmon, adult chums undergo an impressive metamorphosis as the spawning period nears. Their silvery bodies darken, with reddish, purple, and green vertically broken ribbons painting their sides. The hooked kype, or snout, of the buck becomes very pronounced, as do the enlarged teeth, thus earning it the appellation dog salmon.

Eight- to 10-weight rods are wise choices for chum, as there's always the chance of tying into an especially large fish. A high-density, sink-tip line is ideal, as it will get you down to where these salmon live. A 3- to 4-foot leader in the 2X to 0X range is fine. Size 2 and 4 Popsicles, Egg-Sucking Leeches, and Flashabous in purple or pink or a combination of the two are real chum-getters. Flash Flies

are also good when stripped quickly through the water. Because chum salmon begin to deteriorate upon entering rivers, it's to the angler's advantage to hit these fish as early in their migration as possible.

No longer are chum looked upon as a secondary species. They are finally earning the respect they deserve as one of Alaska's premier species to battle on a fly rod.

Pink (Humpback) Salmon
Oncorhynchus gorbusc

Pink salmon will eat just about any fly placed in front of them, and given their wide range and mind-boggling abundance in most of the streams they frequent, hooking a fish is likely with every cast. This is the one fish you're likely to tire of catching, calling it a day before the bite even wanes.

Pink salmon (or humpbacks, as they are called due to the large, sharp hump that develops on the back of spawning bucks) are found in most intertidal regions of Alaska. I've caught numerous little humpies from the remote Utukok and Kokolik Rivers near Point Lay all the way down to the Kenai Peninsula. They could well be Alaska's most valued salmon, both on a commercial and subsistence basis, and they are very popular among sport fishers.

At adulthood, humpies average 3 to 4 pounds and measure 20 to 25 inches. Seven- and 8-pound pinks are not uncommon, but the state record of 12 pounds, 9 ounces has stood since 1974 and was taken from the Kenai River.

Pinks spend only one year at sea before reentering rivers, and most of Alaska's runs make their way into rivers on even-numbered years, although you'll occasionally see fish in odd years. In some drainages there may be cyclical shifts of dominant runs, meaning a previously weak odd-year run may become plentiful.

Upon entering rivers, pink salmon are silver-bright with a blue back and pronounced black spots, making them difficult to distinguish from other anadromous species. In males, the silvery appearance gives way to yel-

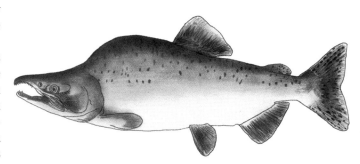

lowish-brown or even black skin above a white belly. Hens turn olive green with obscure patches or bars running above their pale bellies.

Pink salmon enter streams from late June into mid-October and travel very few miles before starting to spawn. They commonly spawn in intertidal zones and at the mouths of streams. Preferred spawning habitat consists of areas where running water breaks over coarse gravel or at the bottom ends of large pools, where quality gravel has filled in.

Depending on a female's size, around 2,000 eggs are deposited into the nest she digs out with her tail. Upon extrusion of the eggs, one or more males quickly fertilize them. Once fertilized, the hen covers the redd by digging and fanning gravel over top. This ritual may be carried out several times before the female is rid of all her eggs. Within a couple weeks of spawning, both the males and females perish.

Life carries on, however, with the hatching of eggs in early to mid-winter. The young fry live off the reserves in their yolk sac until spring, when they emerge from the gravel and move to sea. The out-migration of fry is most common after nightfall and may last several weeks until all the fry have made it out.

Once in salt water, juvenile pink salmon move in large schools, hugging beach lines near the surface, where they feed on plankton, larval fishes, and the infrequent insect. Young pinks grow surprisingly fast, measuring up to 6 inches by one year of age. The following year, at age two, pinks begin their death swim into rivers, where their life cycle carries on.

To gain a better understanding of how important the pink salmon is to Alaska, in 1991 the commercial harvest in the state accounted for 96 percent of the entire North American harvest. From 1983 to 1992, an annual average of 77.4 million pink salmon were harvested in Alaska, not including subsistence- and sport-caught fish. At some point in your flyfishing career, you should make a conscious effort to pursue these special fish.

Steelhead
Salmo gairdneri

Fly anglers would be hard pressed to find a fish offering more excitement than the steelhead. Exuding sheer power, tailwalking across the water's surface, and darting and twisting amid roiling waters, the steelhead is one of the flyfisher's premier quarry. Bridging the gap between trout and salmon, the steelhead is nothing more than a rainbow trout that has lived a large portion of its life in the ocean. Due to the increased availability of oceanic food, these voraciously feeding fish amass considerable weight while at sea.

While steelhead are more slender than resident rainbows—they must be to carry out a predatory, fast-moving lifestyle at sea—the bluish-green back pocked with regularly spaced black spots remains the same. The darker coloration along the back fades to silver as it approaches the lateral line, turning to white near the stomach. A silvery sheen dominates the bodies of steelhead as they start entering rivers, though their bodies darken and the red side stripe more fully emerges as spawning nears. After spawning, steelhead typically lose their spawning colors, reverting back to the silver hues for which they are famous.

Steelhead lead complex lifestyles in comparison to resident rainbows. Depending on age, adult hens (female steelhead) may carry anywhere from 2,000 to 5,000 eggs. Steelhead usually begin spawning between mid-April and early June. Bucks (male steelhead) may spawn with several females, which explains their higher mortality rate. Unlike salmon, steelhead don't die after spawning. The bucks that expire usually do so from exhaustion and stress resulting from their demanding lifestyle.

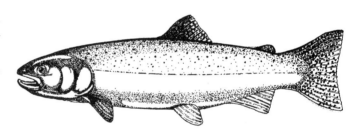

Once a steelhead spawns, it slowly makes its way back to sea where it will feed and replenish lost body fats. Normally, these fish will remain in the ocean another year before heading back into the river to spawn, though some steelhead do return for consecutive spawning runs.

Eggs are deposited in gravel-dug redds, and by mid-summer the alevins have absorbed their yolk sacs and emerged from the rocks. The young steelhead hold near protected stream margins and structure in an attempt to retain ample food to get them through their first winter. Before making their first migration to sea, young steelhead usually hold in their natal streams for three years.

Steelhead then remain at sea from one to five years, feeding on small fish, crustaceans, and insects. They are often caught by commercial net fishers off the Aleutian Islands and as far away as the coast of Japan. Nearly all growth takes place from the time when a steelhead enters the ocean to when it returns to its smolting waters. On average, steelhead that spend two years in the ocean return to their natal waters at four years of age and weigh 6 to 11 pounds. These two-salt steelhead can vary in size depending on ocean diet, distance traveled upriver, river conditions, and obstacles such as dams and ladders that they must contend with, all of which add stress.

The same is true for growth potential among three-salt fish (steelhead that spend three years in the ocean, returning to natal streams at five years of age). These are the big fish that anglers yearn for, ranging from 12 to 20 pounds.

An interesting aspect of Alaska's steelhead is that known populations make their way into rivers in the spring, summer, and fall. While they may enter the rivers at different times of year, they all spawn at the same time—some in the same rivers. This is likely nature's way of preserving the species should floods or other natural catastrophes affect a river.

Steelhead like to hold in broken water, at the heads of riffles, in slicks along tailouts, and amid boulder patches. Glo-Bugs and egg flies like the Babine Special and Two Egg Sperm Fly are good bets. Purple and black Egg-Sucking Leeches in size 2 or 4, Woolly Buggers in purple, black, or brown and black, and the Hair Skykomish and Skykomish Sunrise are also good choices for steelhead.

Due to a steelhead's strength, their tenacity when hooked, and the type of rivers they frequent, a stout fly rod in the 8- to 9-weight class is advised. The type of water you'll be fishing will determine what lines you'll use, so it's a good idea to bring floating and sink-tip lines, as well as a supply of split shot. Leader tippets of 1X and 2X are ideal. Fish them shorter on sink-tip lines than beneath floating lines, where snapping on a split shot or two may be essential. Due to some river-specific gear restrictions, steelhead anglers should be familiar with the latest laws before taking to the water.

Steelhead occupy Alaska's coastal streams, from Dixon Entrance northward around the Gulf of Alaska and westward down to the Cold Bay region of the Alaskan Peninsula. Southeast Alaska is most famous for steelhead, with the Yakutat region seeing its share of big fish. While Alaska's steelhead average 9 to 11 pounds, those in the 15-pound class, and even the coveted 20-pound range, are taken from the Yakutat area.

Prince of Wales Island is home to many prime steelhead streams, several of which receive little pressure. The Situk and Thorne Rivers are two popular Southeast steelhead rivers, with some giant fish in the mid-20-pound class occasionally taken. The state record steelhead is 42 pounds, 3 ounces and came from Bell Island in 1970. Some rivers on the Kenai Peninsula also hold steelhead, with the Anchor River perhaps best known for its fall run of steelies.

Due to the state's incredible salmon and rainbow trout fisheries, Alaska's steelhead are often overshadowed. Many streams throughout Southeast Alaska and along the Kenai Peninsula remain virtually untapped, largely because they are a challenge to access. But there are some fine steelheading waters here, with the Situk River near Yakutat, Kodiak Island's famous Karluk River, and several streams on Prince of Wales leading the way.

Wherever you choose to go for steelhead, plan ahead. They are not usually a species you happen upon while pursuing other fish. Given their acrobatic tendencies when hooked, it won't take long for you to ask yourself why these awesome steelhead are so overlooked when it comes to fishing Alaska.

Rainbow Trout
Oncorhynchus mykiss

Despite the excitement of salmon fishing, it's the mighty rainbow trout that receives much of the attention from fly anglers in Alaska. In fact, many anglers believe the Last Frontier has the best opportunities in the world for catching these giant trout.

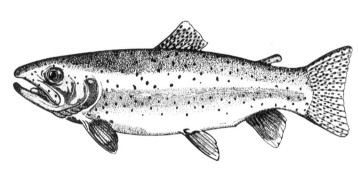

Rainbow trout are native to lakes, rivers, and streams throughout the lower third of Alaska. From the western fringes of the state at Kuskokwim Bay through Southeast Alaska, rainbow trout abound. The Bristol Bay region holds what is regarded as the premier trout habitat, and thus the state's largest rainbows. Wild rainbows are also found on Kodiak Island, the Kenai Peninsula, along the Copper River drainage, and in the fresh waters of upper Cook Inlet. Hatchery releases have extended the range of these fish into waters as far north as the Tanana River drainage.

Not all of Alaska's rainbow trout look alike, which is why the state record of 42 pounds, 3 ounces may never be broken. This record fish was likely a sea-run rainbow (steelhead). Any rainbow over 30 inches is a real trophy.

The coloration and body shape of Alaska's rainbows are reflective of their age, habitat, sex, and the time of year. Body shape may vary from slender to thick, with the color of the back ranging from bluish-green to olive. The shade of red on the side may vary from pinkish to deep red. The bellies of these trout are typically white, giving way to silver before meeting the red sides.

Small black spots are evident above the lateral line, over the back, and on the upper fins and tail. In some geographic locales, the spots may extend well below the lateral line, covering the entire lower side of the trout. The Kenai River's "leopard" rainbows are one example, heralded by many trout fanatics as the most striking trout in the state. Trout in rivers and streams seem to display heavier spotting and more pronounced stripes than those found in lakes.

When water temperatures begin to rise in late winter or early spring, mature rainbows seek out shallow riffles with good spawning conditions. Clear water with clean gravel constitutes the ideal spawning bed, or redd. Depending on location and the intensity of the winter, rainbow trout normally spawn from March through early July. Like with salmon species, the female uses her tail to prepare the redd, creating a depression ranging from 4 to 12 inched in depth and 10 to 15 inches in diameter. A mature female will deposit anywhere from 200 to 8,000 eggs, which are then externally fertilized by the male and covered with gravel.

Depending on the water temperature, the eggs will hatch anywhere from 21 to 120 days after being deposited. A few more weeks may pass before the fry emerge from their gravel domain. Once they do, the small trout gather in groups along sheltered shores to feed on crustaceans, plant material, and aquatic insects. These trout will remain in this protected environment for the next two or three years before moving into larger waters and adopting a more predatory diet of fish, flesh, roe, and even decaying mammals.

The fertility of their aquatic environment, population densities, and genetic makeup all factor into when trout become sexually mature. While trout as young as three and as old as seven have been observed spawning, the mean spawning age is more around six or seven. The frequency of when rainbow trout spawn ranges from annually to once ever few years.

Resident trout living in or migrating to large lakes with sockeye salmon appear to grow faster and larger than those remaining year-round in streams. No doubt, the high-protein diet these fish eat year after year enhances their size.

Rainbows have ravenous appetites and are willing to aggressively approach and strike a wide selection of flies put in front of them. Egg and flesh flies and a variety of streamers are favorite patterns among rainbow anglers,

with time of year and color combinations factoring in. Overall, a #2 Egg-Sucking Leech or a natural color flesh fly may get the nod. Purple or black leeches and black sculpin patterns are also effective.

Alaska's wild rainbow trout are managed to maintain the health of the species and for recreational use, so bag limits, size restrictions, and even seasons can vary greatly across the state and in individual bodies of water at any given time. For instance, many of the classic rainbow rivers are closed to trout fishing during the spawn, while others are designated catch-and-release only to promote a trophy fishery.

Anglers serious about catching a 15-pound, trophy-class rainbow should concentrate on the western part of the state during the fall. The fishing can be phenomenal for big, voracious trout that follow migrating salmon upstream. I've had more success in the fall for large rainbows than in all other seasons combined. If you're timing is right, you'll discover why Alaska's rainbows are so revered by anglers the world over.

Lake Trout
Salvelinus namaycush

Alaska's biggest freshwater fish is the lake trout, the largest representative of the group of fish referred to as char. Lake trout inhabit deep lowland lakes along the central Arctic Coastal Plain, ranging well into the Brooks Range. Oddly, lake trout are not found in the Yukon-Kuskokwim drainages or the southeastern region of the state, though they do appear in turbid glacial lakes on the north side of the Chugach Range and Kenai Peninsula.

There is very good lake trout fishing to be had in the Bristol Bay and Katmai regions, especially in the fall when trout move into shallows. Waters extending into the southwestern fringes of the Alaska Peninsula also hold lake trout, as do a few sparse regions along the western panhandle.

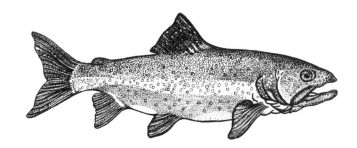

Lake trout thrive best in large, deep, cold lakes, where they spend their entire life. Lake trout spawn from September through November, seeking out clean, rocky bottoms. Before the females make their way to the spawning beds, the males have already prepared a site for egg deposition by creating a clean substrate with their nose and fins.

Lake trout eggs hatch the following spring, and the young are thought to feed on plankton their first few years of life. Lake trout are mature after seven or eight years, at which time they begin to spawn. Typically, lake trout spawn every other year—even less frequently in northern waters—though under ideal conditions like those found on the Kenai Peninsula they'll spawn annually.

The growth rates of lake trout vary from region to region and depend on water temperature, altitude, diet, and genetics. These trout can live more than 40 years, with the average being closer to half that. While the average size for these trout ranges between 6 to 8 pounds, there are monsters lurking in big lakes that would bury the scales to 50 pounds. The state record weighed in at 47 pounds and was taken in 1970.

The coloration of lake trout can also vary between populations, but generally they carry small, irregularly shaped spots on a silvery to darkish back. Lake trout can be distinguished from other char by the absence of pink spots and their deeply forked tail.

The lake trout's diet may include zooplankton, insect larvae, small crustaceans, leeches, snails, and even mice and young birds. Lake trout will gorge themselves on other fish species when given the opportunity. Surprisingly, lake trout can sometimes be seen feeding on the surface, which should excite any fly angler.

In the spring, when lakes are cold, these trout can be found feeding near the surface and cruising shorelines. As temperatures warm, lakers head to deeper water, taking up residence beneath the thermocline. When they're on top, dry flies can elicit a strike. More typically, leech, minnow, and sculpin imitations, along with Zonkers, are good bets for luring lakers. These flies, fished near a lake's outlet or where a river enters, can be effective when fished with a sink-tip line. Fast-sinking and sink-tip shooting heads and streamer patterns that resemble small fish can also be productive on these carnivores.

Lake trout inhabit some of Alaska's most serene, isolated waters. If anglers practice sound conservation ethics solid populations of these unique fish will be around for future generations.

Cutthroat Trout
Oncorhynchus clarkii

Sea-run and/or resident cutthroat trout range from lower Southeast Alaska to Prince William Sound, where they are the most common trout species in the area. Resident cutthroat can be found anywhere from small beaver ponds to bogs to small headwater tributaries. South of Frederick Sound, sea-run cutthroat are associated with rivers and streams connecting the ocean to lakes.

Beginning in late April and running through early June, cutthroat spawn in isolated headwater streams. A month or two later young trout emerge from the gravel and take up secluded lifestyles in protected ponds, sloughs, and lakes, away from predatory fish. After three or four years, when they've reached about 8 inches, many cutthroat make their first migration to sea during the month of May.

Cutthroat will remain at sea anywhere from a few days to more than a hundred prior to returning to the streams in which they hatched. Rarely will cutthroat travel more than 45 miles from their natal stream. They spend the winter months in their home waters.

Maturity is reached in as little as five years, with a ten-year-old fish not uncommon. Approximately 40 percent of the fish survive winter and their journey to the sea, and the fact that some 60 percent of the migrants are sexually mature means reproduction rates can be slow with this species.

Cutthroat have two unique feeding strategies that seem to change with age. Prior to reaching 14 inches or so, they tend to sit and let food come their way. As they grow, they'll become more aggressive, and this is when these trout can really put on the pounds. Cutthroat can live in excess of 12 years, weigh up to 9 pounds, and grow to around 28 inches.

Sea-run cutthroat are typically smaller than localized populations of this species. Ocean-going cutthroat are silver, with faint black spots and bluish backs (thus the locally adopted name "blueback"). Sea-runs also possess a slight slash under their jaw, as opposed to the bright red markings usually associated with this species. Small resident cutthroat are the most colorful of all, with vibrant throat slashes, golden bodies, and distinct black spotting.

Large cutthroat feed very aggressively, which is why flyfishers love them. Minnow and sculpin patterns on fast-sinking lines are productive along shorelines with submerged cover or in deeper holes. A variety of dry flies fished off inlet streams are also effective.

Due to their slow reproduction rates, low population densities, and meager growth rate, overfishing of Alaska's cutthroats is a growing concern. Practicing catch and release for these beautiful fish will ensure their future.

Brook Trout
Salvelinus fontinalis

Between 1917 and 1950, several of Southeast Alaska's lakes, streams, and rivers were stocked with brook trout, which aren't native to the state. Oddly, no fish reportedly survived the introduction into rivers and streams, and very few survived in lakes connecting to the sea.

But brook trout did survive in some of the lakes and today provide excellent angling opportunities. Surprisingly, brook trout did well in subalpine lakes that maintained a relatively low year-round temperature, harbored a scant food supply, and had questionable spawning conditions.

The following bodies of water contain the most healthy, fishable populations of brook trout: Rustabach Lake near Haines; Upper and Lower Dewey Lakes near Skagway; Salmon Creek Reservoir near Juneau; Long, Heart, Thimble, and Green Lakes near Sitka; Crystal Lake near Petersburg, Grace, Shelokum, Perseverance, and Ketchikan Lakes around the Ketchikan area; and Emerald Lake near Hyder.

Brook trout are members of the char family, distinguished from most trout and salmon by their lack of black spots. Brook trout have dark green marbling marks on their backs and dorsal fin, with bluish halos around some

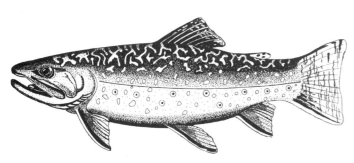

of the red spots appearing on their sides. They spawn in the fall, when temperatures and daylight hours are reduced. The fact that brook trout can spawn in a variety of less than ideal substrates in Alaska makes them highly valued as a sport fish.

However, due to their isolated distribution, anglers only catch a couple of thousand fish each year. Egg patterns, white bucktails, and minnow imitations can be productive, especially on a sinking line or with a weighted leader. Brook trout are also fine-eating fish.

Dolly Varden
Salvelinus malma Walbaum

The Dolly Varden is a fish many Alaska flyfishers believe deserves more respect. The tenacity with which these trout will take a fly, and the hard, twisting fight they put up, sets them apart from other trout. Their infamous reputation for consuming valuable salmon spawn is the reason some anglers scorn them, but it's also why flyfishers thrive on these fast-moving, aggressive fish.

As with many members of the char family, Dolly Varden are easily fooled with a variety of egg patterns. The famous Polar Shrimp and Babine Special egg patterns are tough to beat, while Glo-Bugs should also be in every fly vest. Nymphs and wet flies are also good choices when venturing to Dolly water. Fishing along the bottom of fast-moving water—typically done by placing small split shot a foot or so above the fly under a floating line—is the best way to get at these fish.

Dolly Varden have light spots on their sides, which sets them apart from most other trout and salmon who usually carry dark spots. Alaska's Dolly Varden exist in two forms. The southern form ranges from lower Southeast Alaska on up to the tip of the Aleutian Chain, while the northern form lives primarily along the north slope drainages of the Aleutian Range, northward along the Arctic coast all the way over to Canada. Both types include anadromous and freshwater resident fish that thrive in lakes and rivers.

Sea-run fish are bright silver with olive-green to brown colored backs and abundant reddish or orange spots marking their sides. As they mature and near the spawn, adult males take on a striking coloration; their lower body becomes bright red, their fins and lower body darken, and the leading edges of their fins turn ivory.

Dolly Varden spawn from mid-August to November. Depending on her size, a female drops anywhere from 600 to 6,000 eggs in a redd she has prepared with her caudal fin in a stream. Males usually play no role in nest construction, devoting most of their time to warding off intrusive bachelors. When the female is ready to spawn, the male moves in and fertilizes her eggs.

The eggs hatch four to five months later. And another month later, once their yolk sacs have been absorbed, the young will emerge from the gravel. In northern waters, where mature females have been known to deposit as many as 10,000 eggs, the young may not emerge until well into June.

Young Dollys remain in a protected, secluded habitat, feeding off stream bottoms, before heading to sea for the first time three to four years after being born. The smolt are only about 5 inches long when they head to the ocean, a reflection of how slow their growth rate truly is. Dollys in the southern portion of the state often overwinter in lakes, while those in northern waters overwinter in rivers. Dollys reared in lakes annually migrate to sea, where they feed on rich oceanic life, only to return to lakes in winter. Interestingly, southern Dolly Varden originating in rivers or streams will randomly seek out lakes in which to winter. In the spring, these fish will often migrate out to sea, sometimes entering other stream systems in their quest for food.

Mature Dolly Varden return to their natal streams to spawn. At five to six years of age, and between 12 to 16 inches in length, most southern Dollys are mature, and weigh ½ to 1 pound. Northerly Dollys mature between five and nine years, measuring between 16 to 24 inches. It's believed that not much more than 50 percent of Dolly Varden live to spawn a second time, due to their age and the fact that so many males die as a result of their intense level of fighting during the spawn. A good-sized Dolly Varden weighs up to 4 pounds, with trophies up to 12 pounds being taken.

The fact that Dollys have adapted to so many of Alaska's small to medium non-lake streams that feed into salt water makes them a unique fish. Because sea-run Dollys migrate to sea in the spring, anglers hitting outlet streams and stream mouths should find success from April into June. In estuaries, May through July are the prime months for taking Dollys, and stripping streamers can be effective. From August through September, when mature fish return to streams, fishing can be at its zenith.

Not only are Dolly Varden worthy of utmost respect for the awesome fight they provide, they are some of the best-eating fish you'll find. Their pink, firm flesh is flavor-packed and tasty just about any way it's prepared.

Arctic Char
Salvelinus alpinus Linnaeus

The arctic char, one of Alaska's most striking fish, provides good opportunities for sport fishers. Ranging across the North Slope, in the Kigluaik and Kuskokwim Mountains, along the Kenai and Alaska Peninsulas, on Kodiak Island and near Denali Park, Alaska's arctic char are primarily lake residents. Walker and Selby Lakes in the Kobuk River drainage also carry good numbers of arctic char, as do several unnamed lakes throughout the northern foothills of the Brooks Range. But the largest arctic char are often found in the larger lakes of the Bristol Bay area.

From May through early July, fishing for arctic char is typically best when these fish congregate to feed on salmon smolt migrating out to sea. Arctic char reach sexual maturity between six and nine years of age and are thought to spawn every other year. The spawn usually occurs from August well into October and takes place over steep, broken substrates of gravel shoal at an adequate depth to avoid the buildup of winter ice. In some of Alaska's lakes, char gather in shallow water near the mouths of inlet streams, then move to deeper areas in the lake to spawn.

Arctic char exceeding 10 pounds are not uncommon, although some fish may never grow beyond 2 pounds. Their size and growth rates greatly depend on the availability of quality food and predatory fish residing in the same waters. Many of the same fly patterns used to take Dolly Varden also work on arctic char.

The arctic char is the most northerly-distributed member of the char group and closely resembles the Dolly Varden. In fact, many scientists, biologists, and anglers are not convinced that these two species are totally distinct from one another. However, there are some external characteristics that can be used to distinguish the arctic char from the Dolly Varden. Generally speaking, arctic char have a shorter head and snout, which is most apparent in spawning males. Their tails are a bit more forked, with the base of the tail narrower than that of a Dolly's.

Like other char members, arctic char carry light spots on a dark back. Their overall color is largely dependent on the surrounding environment and time of year. Darker colors on the back become lighter on the sides of the fish, with a pale belly the norm. When spawning time approaches, the belly, spots, and fins of arctic char take on a gold, yellow, orange, or even a bright red hue. The entire body exudes a golden or orange cast, with striking, snow-white leading edges on the fins.

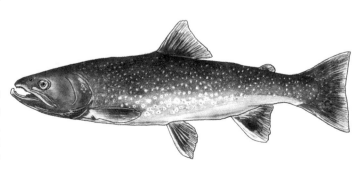

Arctic Grayling
Thymallus arcticus

Without question, one of the most enthralling salmonids is the arctic grayling. The large dorsal fin captures the eye of novice and seasoned line-whippers alike. Many specimens carry black spots along their gray, sleek sides, while some fish are lacking in spots altogether.

Arctic grayling are renowned for their voracious appetites, which explains the high level of success enjoyed by fly anglers. With a diet consisting largely of insects in all stages of development, they will feed on most invertebrate species that become available. Woolly Worms, Beadhead Woolly Buggers, a variety of caddis patterns, and Parachute Adams should be in the vest of all flyfishers. When the salmon spawn commences, Polar Shrimp and Glo-Bugs and other egg patterns can be the ticket. Bringing a selection of dry and wet flies is smart, for even though arctic grayling are aggressive feeders, they can switch off and on the feed for no apparent reason.

Larger grayling typically hold in deeper waters and pools of streams and rivers. When nymphing, pinching a split shot or two on the leader will get you through small and mid-sized grayling, down to where the big ones are holding. Arctic grayling are not aggressive feeders in the sense that they will pursue their quarry with a vengeance. Instead, grayling hold in narrow lanes and wait for food to come their way. This is why flyfishers often have better success than lure-tossers; grayling won't chase spinners like trout will. Grayling can also be finicky eaters at times, preferring a natural, headfirst presentation.

Alaska's largest arctic grayling come from Bristol Bay's river systems, the Lake Clark region, and Ugashik Lake. In fact, the state record grayling of 23 inches and 4 pounds, 13 ounces came from the Ugashik Narrows, considered to be the prime place for trophy grayling. The Nome area is also famous for its classic grayling fishery, and with plenty of roads, offers many opportunities to serious anglers. The Kenai Peninsula's Crescent Lake offers excellent fly-in and hike-in grayling fishing, as do many road systems heading north out of Anchorage.

The Chatanika River along the Steese Highway is a favorite grayling destination for many road-bound anglers, as are many creeks and lakes along the Glenn Highway and Lake Louise Road. The Tanana and Chena Rivers near Fairbanks are also famous for their grayling.

Though tough to access, many rivers and lakes on the North Slope hold incredible grayling fishing. The largest grayling I ever caught stretched the tape to 20 inches and came from the Anaktuvuk River, north of the Inupiat Eskimo village of Anaktuvuk Pass. There are many fish of this caliber in the Far North, but they typically lack the girth of grayling ranging farther south.

Arctic grayling are slow growers, with a five-year-old fish usually measuring 12 inches under ideal conditions. One that's 19 inches will likely be 10 years old, and it's the old ones that are the key to spawning success. At the age of four or five, grayling spawn for the first time. Arctic grayling don't create a redd as do other salmonids, rather the female lays 4,000 to 5,000 eggs on loose gravel, where a sticky membrane holds them in place. The male completes the external fertilization process, and the fry hatch three weeks later.

Grayling may travel many miles during the course of the year or remain in one small locale their entire life. After spring breakup, soon after the eggs have been deposited, adult grayling residing in river systems begin migrating to post-spawn, summer feeding grounds. They may travel 100 miles or more to reach these insect-rich waters. By midsummer, grayling become somewhat segregated based on age, with the older fish congregating in the upper stretches of rivers, sub-adults in midsections, and younger fish in the lower ends.

Because grayling can tolerate such low oxygen content, they survive in waters where other salmonids would perish. Their gluttonous feeding style sustains them through winter, when they hold beneath the surface of ice-covered streams, rivers, and lakes. Not only do grayling need enough body fat to get them through the winter, they must have enough energy stored to commence spawning immediately after breakup. Such a taxing schedule explains why shrews, voles, lemmings, and even salmon smolt have been found in the stomachs of grayling.

While over 70 percent of the trophy grayling registered with the ADF&G came from Ugashik Lake and the river systems of Bristol Bay, the road systems also yield outstanding fishing. Matching the hatch can be critical on these piggish fish, so be prepared.

Arctic grayling occupy some of Alaska's clearest, most pristine waters. In the fall, I've seen them stacked in holes exceeding 10 feet in depth, but with water so clear that it seemed I could reach out and touch them. When you do lift a grayling from the water for the first time, smell the fish; it often exudes a scent of thyme, hence its Latin name, *Thymallus arcticus*.

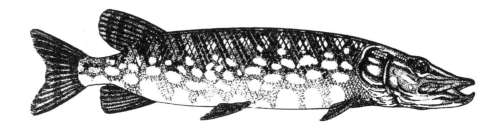

Northern Pike
Esox lucius Linnaeus

A fish with a vicious attitude, northern pike don't usually top the most wanted list of Alaska fly anglers. Much maligned in the early days, pike are now becoming a bit more popular.

Some 80 percent of Alaska holds northern pike, ranging from the Arctic coast to the interior and the Seward Peninsula east all the way to the Canadian border and the southwestern region of the state, amid Bristol Bay's drainages. But the most famous trophy pike fishing lies in the hundreds of square miles of interconnected lakes, sloughs, and rivers that constitute the Minto Flats region west of Fairbanks. Good-sized pike can also be taken from clear-water tributaries and sloughs of the Yukon and Kuskokwim Rivers. Lakes of the Tanana River system also hold pike but receive considerable fishing pressure. Fly-out trips into northern waters, as well as Nome, can put you into solid pike fishing, as well.

During the summer months of June, July, and August, pike will eat just about anything put in front of them. Many anglers prefer large streamers similar to gaudy and colorful saltwater patterns. Fishing on top (or slightly beneath the surface on a sink-tip line) is effective, especially when casting into reed beds. Big mouse patterns are also good producers.

The Alaskan state record for northern pike was taken back in 1978 and weighed 38 pounds. Pike weighing 20 pounds are not uncommon, with 30-pounders landed annually. Rumors of fish seen in the 40- and even 50-pound class occasionally surface, and I don't doubt their authenticity. Many native residents residing in remote northern villages talk of their ancestors taking monster pike, and I've seen early pictures that confirm such reports.

Alaska's northern pike are the same species so famous throughout the upper Midwest. Their soft-rayed dorsal fin sits well back on the body, and combined with a broad snout and bill, gives the fish a streamlined torpedo appearance. Pike have sharp teeth on the roof of the mouth and on the jaws, tongue, and gillrakers. These teeth are in constant renewal, so handle these fish with extreme caution.

A white or yellowish belly is common among all pike, though the sides and back can vary from light to very dark green. Irregular rows of goldish/yellow spots appear on the sides of both male and female pike. The female, however, grows to larger proportions and lives longer than the male.

Soon after the spring thaw, pike initiate spawning. A 25-pound female may carry a half-million eggs, which she drops along the grassy fringes of lakes, sloughs, and slower moving streams.

As the eggs trickle to the bottom, they adhere to rocks, grass, and other structures. They hatch approximately 30 days later, and the young commence feeding on insects and small crustaceans. By the time they reach 2 inches in length, predatory pike may already begin preying on smaller fish.

A pike's diet consists almost entirely of fish. There are several stories out there of 12- to 25-pound pike with fish weighing one-third their body weight entombed in their stomachs. Muskrats, small ducks, mice, and shore birds are also preyed upon by pike.

Though relatively little is known about the wintertime habits of Alaska's pike, it is common knowledge that these fish overwinter in deep, slow waters associated with larger rivers, where the oxygen content is maximized. Pike will also winter in some of the state's deeper lakes. In the spring, the upstream migration toward the spawning and summer feeding grounds is relatively short.

The firm, white meat of pike is very tasty and serves as an important food source among bush villages. While some anglers adhere to the belief that wire leaders are the only way to go when pike fishing, I've heard of anglers doing well with 25- to 40-pound straight monofilament.

Sheefish
Stendous leucichthys nelma

I've been fortunate to taste a wide variety of fish from around the globe, and one whose flavor always makes my mouth water is the sheefish. I tasted my first sheefish, from the Kobuk River, while living in Anaktuvuk Pass. To this day, it ranks among the best-tasting fish ever to touch my pallet.

Without a doubt, sheefish are one of the least pursued freshwater species in Alaska. Their Far North habitat, seasonal movements, and the unpredictable weather conditions where they live make them tough for anglers to target—particularly flyfishers.

A member of the whitefish family, sheefish are most abundant in the Yukon and Kuskokwim River drainages and the Kobuk and Selawik drainages of Kotzebue Sound. Some of the smaller rivers of Norton Sound harbor sheefish, though the most popular stream from which to take trophy sheefish is without doubt the Kobuk River. However, tributaries of the mighty Yukon and the river down to its mouth contain perhaps the greatest density of sheefish. At both Hughes and Allakaket, the Koyukuk River offers the best sheefish angling on the Yukon system.

The streamlined, silvery body and protruding lower jaw of the sheefish earn it the nickname "tarpon of the North." With dark colors accenting the back, it's the velvety, purple sheen it exhibits when lifted from the water that most captures the eye. Males and females of the species look similar, with females living longer and weighing more than males. The Alaska state record, taken in 1986, stands at 53 pounds, though sheefish in the 60-pound class may be lurking in the Selawik-Kobuk area. In their interior range, sheefish rarely exceed 25 pounds.

There are some small, local populations of sheefish in the Porcupine River, as well as in the Black and Nowitna Rivers. Fish in the Selawik-Kobuk area winter in brackish waters and are considered estuarine anadromous fish. The Minto Flats and Upper Yukon River populations of sheefish remain in the area year-round.

Sheefish begin their upstream migration from wintering grounds as soon as the ice breaks up. Some fish will move directly to spawning grounds, while others remain in waters rich in food. Depending on their range, sheefish can migrate up to 1,000 miles upstream to spawn, as they do in the Alatna River. This means that fish may be on the move for four consecutive months, which is why anglers can have a tough time finding them. During the latter stages of the migration, as spawning time nears, sheefish quit feeding, relying instead on built-up body reserves.

A 50-pound spawning female may hold up to 400,000 eggs, while an average 12-pound female will contain around 100,000. But it's the strict spawning regiment that makes sheefish so interesting. They require fast water between 4 and 8 feet deep that rushes over a river bottom composed of a variety of gravel sizes. In late September and early October, in waters that are 40 degrees or colder, the act of spawning occurs during the late afternoon and early evening hours.

Spawning sheefish don't create redds. Instead, the females spawn on the surface of the water, with the males swimming underneath, fertilizing the eggs as they drift. In this act of free-floating egg deposition, females can be heard splashing at the surface. As the fertilized eggs fall to the bottom, an adhesive surface anchors them. After spawning, sheefish quickly migrate back downstream to the wintering grounds to start feeding again. Sheefish can live for many years, spawning several times.

It may take up to six months for sheefish eggs to fully develop and hatch. With the high waters of spring, the young travel downriver into vast delta areas within large river systems. Here, they start feeding on plankton, though their menu quickly changes to insect larvae and small fish. By the age of two, sheefish feed almost exclusively on fish.

Compared to other freshwater fish dwelling in Arctic waters, sheefish exhibit a surprisingly rapid growth rate. For instance, studies have shown the Kuskokwim and Minto Flats populations of sheefish to grow most rapidly, reaching 16 inches at two years of age. By age eight they may measure 30 inches and weigh up to 14 pounds. By comparison, Sheefish in the Selawik-Kobuk region weigh only 10 pounds after as many years, but because they live more than 20 years they can reach impressive sizes.

Because flyfishers must get their flies down quickly, often in fast water, casting a high-density sink-tip fly line is recommended. A floating line with spit shot pinched on a long leader can also be effective. As sheefish are highly predatory, fly patterns that resemble baitfish are popular. Large streamer and leech patterns are also must-haves for sheefish water.

Due to the isolated regions that sheefish occupy, anglers should do their research well and make sure they are armed with a complete arsenal of flies that will enhance their opportunities. It might not be a bad idea to tote a spinning rod with 15- or 20-pound test, as deep-running lures usually out-produce flies.

Catching sheefish in the treeless land above the Arctic Circle is something few anglers have experienced, but it's worth the effort just to fish in such a remote, tranquil environment.

Burbot
Lota lota

Though not a fish targeted by flyfishers, the burbot is a unique species you may wish to pursue, particularly as these fine-tasting fish occupy many Arctic waters, along with interior lakes and rivers. If you tire of catching grayling, pike, or sheefish, these members of the cod family can provide a thrilling alternative.

The peculiar design of the burbot makes it easy to recognize. A thin, elongated body tapering off near the tail and dorsal and anal fins running from its midsection to the base of the tail set this fish apart from other species that occupy the same water. In addition, a single barbel, or chin whisker, dangles from its lower lip, a rudimentary sensing device similar to those found on sturgeon. Burbot are not without scales; their sleek, mottled olive-black to brown skin is laced with yellow spotting and is actually covered in nearly microscopic scales.

An exceptionally large mouth that contains several rows of small teeth leaves no doubt that burbot lead predatory lifestyles. They feed primarily at night, mostly on sculpins, whitefish, lampreys, and other burbot, but they will also dine on plankton, insects, crustaceans, and roe.

Burbot living in excess of 20 years are not uncommon in Alaska, but they are slow-growing fish. At the age of six or seven, burbot stretch about 18 inches and are ready for spawning. During February and March, burbot commence spawning beneath the ice, often gathering in large schools. Eggs are broadcast and fertilized over a wide area, and a single female can produce over one million eggs.

While ice fishing is a common practice among burbot anglers, summer fishing can also be productive. The most efficient way to consistently take burbot is with bait. A size 2/0 to 4/0 hook tipped with a chunk of frozen fish is the way to go. A 2-foot leader tied below a couple ounces of lead will swing around on the bottom, spreading scent and attracting burbot.

Many of Alaska's lakes have new restrictions on burbot harvest due to declining populations, so check local regulations before fishing. In rivers, concentrate your efforts near the mouths of clear tributaries, in back eddies, and around rock bluffs. Glacial rivers such as the Tanana and Yukon have strong burbot fisheries.

SALMON KEY

These terms are often used interchangeably.

King Salmon	=	Chinook
Silver Salmon	=	Coho
Sockeye Salmon	=	Red
Chum Salmon	=	Dog
Pink Salmon	=	Humpback

Small-stream opportunities exist around the big city.

If looking to take salmon home, target the plentiful coho runs from late August into October.

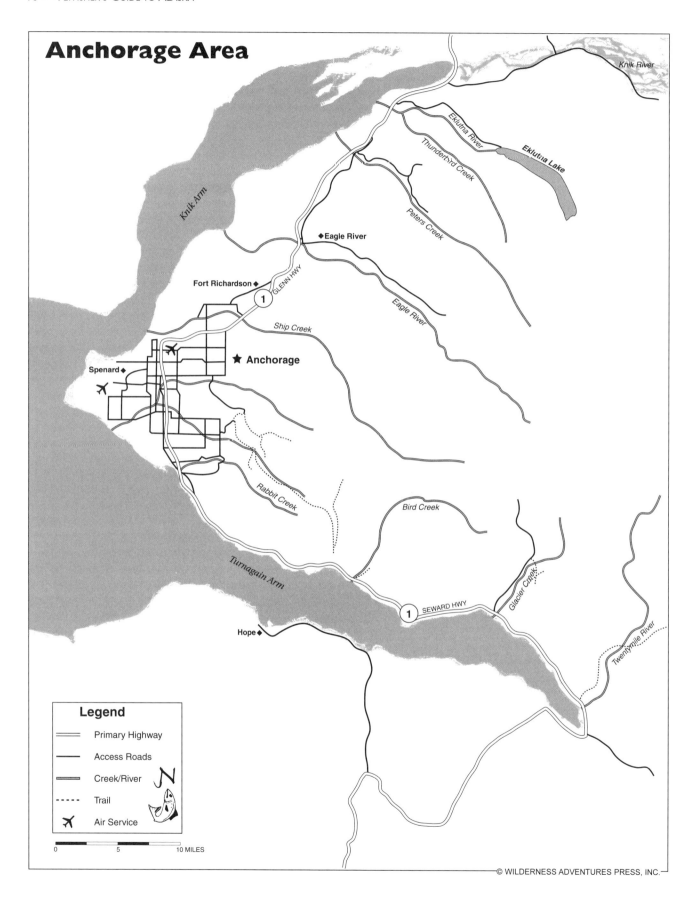

Anchorage Area

Knik River

Eklutna River

Eklutna Lake

Thunderbird Creek

Peters Creek

Knik Arm

◆Eagle River

Fort Richardson ◆

GLENN HWY

1

Eagle River

Ship Creek

✈

★ Anchorage

Spenard ◆

✈

Rabbit Creek

Bird Creek

Glacier Creek

Turnagain Arm

SEWARD HWY

1

Hope ◆

Twentymile River

Legend

Primary Highway
Access Roads
Creek/River
Trail
✈ Air Service

N

0   5   10 MILES

Anchorage—Travel and Fishing

By Scott Haugen

GETTING FROM YOUR HOUSE TO ANCHORAGE

Flying is the way most people choose to reach the Last Frontier. No matter where in the country you live, Alaska is accessible by plane, although this often includes a redeye flight. The redeye is aptly named, for after flying all night you arrive at your destination groggy but excited, with eyes as bloodshot as they get.

Sleep deprived or not, once you see Alaska, catching up on your sleep will be the least of your concerns. Remember, during the prime fishing months of June through August, daylight dominates the clock. You may land in Anchorage at 3:00 in the morning, but because it will still be light, you can have your license in hand and be fishing by 4:00 a.m. if that's your goal.

From the continental U.S., Alaska Airlines, American Airlines, America West, Continental Airlines, Delta Airlines, Northwest Airlines, TWA, and United Airlines are some of the major airlines making their way into Anchorage. You can book your trip yourself or go through a travel agent. There are some great deals to be had by booking your own flight on the Internet, but it's buyer beware and you need to do your homework. Some airlines offer incredible deals on their websites, and if you regularly check their listings you may find a real bargain.

When packing to go to Alaska, I take the biggest carryon allowed by the airline I'm traveling with. Ask for the dimensions of these bags when you book your flight. In the carryon bag I pack my essentials: fly reels, extra spools, lines, one change of fishing clothes, camera gear, spotting glasses, sunscreen, a fishing rod, and a toothbrush. When I leave home, I'm usually wearing the clothes I'll be fishing in when I land in Alaska. By packing my fishing gear and a rod in my carryon bag, I'm assured of being able to fish right away, even if something happens to my checked baggage. I always take a 4-piece fly rod as a carryon. (New terrorist-inspired regulations may make this difficult, so be sure to check with your airline.)

Because excess clothing can be cumbersome and may take up valued space, I wear a few layers on the plane, complete with a bulky, warm jacket. If I get too warm, I just take them off and store them in the overhead storage compartment above the seat. The more room you can make for necessary items the better.

If you're going to do Alaska by car, make sure you've reserved a car or RV in Anchorage before you leave home.

Many people are taken by surprise when they show up at the height of the tourist season, only to learn that nothing is available. By booking ahead, there will be no surprises.

Once your plane arrives in Anchorage, the next step is to get your rental car or RV. The majority of anglers, myself included, get a rental car at the airport. When my plane touches down, I immediately follow the signs to the rental car sector and locate the agency with which I've already reserved a car. I quickly fill out the paperwork and grab the key. Then I get my baggage. If you're a bit late collecting your bags, don't worry, attendants will have set them off to the side of the carousel.

However, if I'm stuck in the back of the plane and it's slow unloading, I'll usually gather my bags before picking up the rental car. Since the 9-11 incident, airline regulations are tight, and you may not want to risk having expensive bags sitting around. Speaking of being stuck in the rear of the plane, this can be avoided during check-in at your hometown airport. Ask to be seated as close to the front of the craft as possible. If you're tall, request a seat on an emergency exit row. The extra legroom can be mighty nice, especially on long flights across the country. You may also want to get a window seat; no matter how often I fly into Anchorage, I never tire of the stunning view.

Now, with the rental car and luggage secured, the next item of business is acquiring a nonresident fishing license. You may also need a king salmon harvest tag, depending on where you're going and what species you're targeting.

There are several locations in Anchorage where you can buy a fishing license late at night. There are six Carrs Quality Center stores in Anchorage that are open 24/7, as is Wal-Mart. Carrs is a large chain that sells licenses at the help desks up front. And if you're looking to pick up some food for the trip, this is the place to go, as well. Wal-Mart has a good, basic tackle supply, and someone there may be able to tip you off to the latest fishing hotspots.

Fred Meyer is open from 7:00 a.m. to 11:00 p.m. and sells fishing licenses at their help counter, not in the sporting goods section. Fred Meyer is a complete one-stop shopping source. If you're outfitting your journey from Anchorage—gathering food, toiletries, and whatever else you need for your stay—you can get it at

Anchorage

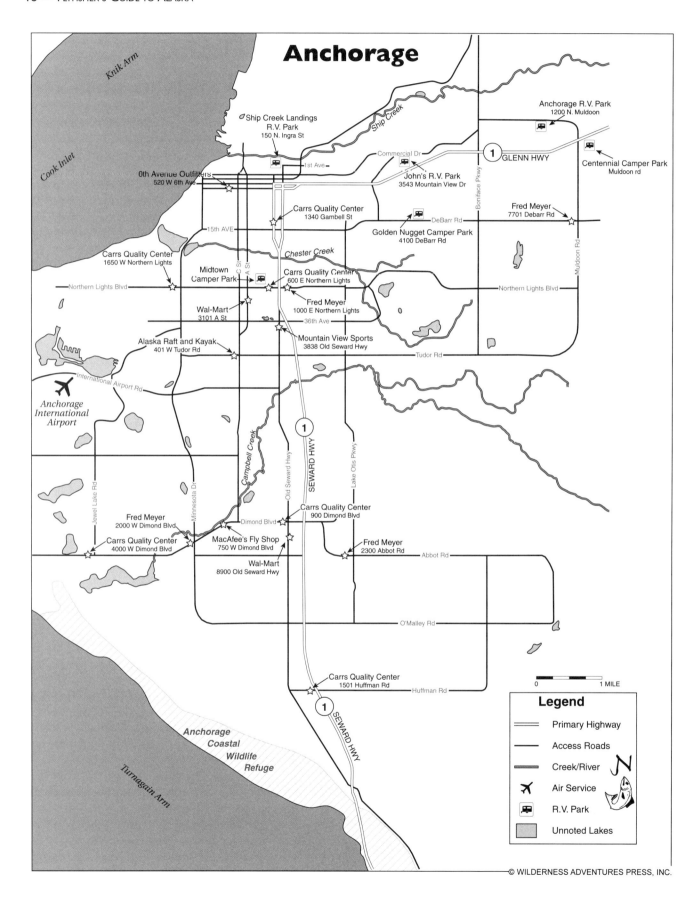

Knik Arm

Cook Inlet

Ship Creek

Anchorage R.V. Park
1200 N. Muldoon

Ship Creek Landings
R.V. Park
150 N. Ingra St

Commercial Dr

1 GLENN HWY

Centennial Camper Park
Muldoon rd

1st Ave

6th Avenue Outfitters
520 W 6th Ave

John's R.V. Park
3543 Mountain View Dr

Boniface Pkwy

Fred Meyer
7701 Debarr Rd

Carrs Quality Center
1340 Gambell St

15th AVE

DeBarr Rd

Golden Nugget Camper Park
4100 DeBarr Rd

Muldoon Rd

Chester Creek

Carrs Quality Center
1650 W Northern Lights

Midtown
Camper Park

C St
A St

Carrs Quality Center
600 E Northern Lights

Northern Lights Blvd

Northern Lights Blvd

Wal-Mart
3101 A St

Fred Meyer
1000 E Northern Lights

36th Ave

Alaska Raft and Kayak
401 W Tudor Rd

Mountain View Sports
3838 Old Seward Hwy

Tudor Rd

International Airport Rd

Anchorage
International
Airport

Campbell Creek

Old Seward Hwy

SEWARD HWY

Lake Otis Pkwy

1

Jewel Lake Rd

Minnesota Dr

Fred Meyer
2000 W Dimond Blvd

Dimond Blvd

Carrs Quality Center
900 Dimond Blvd

Carrs Quality Center
4000 W Dimond Blvd

MacAfee's Fly Shop
750 W Dimond Blvd

Fred Meyer
2300 Abbot Rd

Abbot Rd

Wal-Mart
8900 Old Seward Hwy

O'Malley Rd

0   1 MILE

Carrs Quality Center
1501 Huffman Rd

Huffman Rd

1 SEWARD HWY

Legend

	Primary Highway
	Access Roads
	Creek/River
✈	Air Service
🚐	R.V. Park
	Unnoted Lakes

N

Anchorage
Coastal
Wildlife
Refuge

Turnagain Arm

© WILDERNESS ADVENTURES PRESS, INC.

Freddy's. Some, though not all, of the Tesoro gas stations around the area also sell fishing licenses.

For a complete listing of locations for the six Anchorage-area Carrs, the four Fred Meyer stores, and Wal-Mart, refer to the "Fishing License Vendors" section in the Anchorage hub city information and map on previous page. While several sporting good stores sell fishing licenses, they may not be open if you arrive at an odd hour.

With your rental car crammed with luggage and food, your license in your vest pocket, and a city roadmap sitting next to this book on the front seat, you're on your way to good fishing. If you keep the errands to a minimum, you can honestly be fishing within an hour after your plane lands.

DRIVING AND FISHING BEYOND ANCHORAGE

Let's say you want to drive farther down the road, to fishing holes farther from the big city. What can you expect to spend on such a journey? Your plane just touched down in Anchorage and the intent of your trip is to fish as many waters as possible. Or, rather than try and see it all, you want to head straight to the Kenai River for big rainbows. Or go south to Seward and explore small-stream Dolly fishing at its finest. Maybe you wish to head north, fishing roadside streams and lakes as you make your way to Fairbanks. In this section, we'll take a look at costs involved in renting a car or RV and traveling/fishing on your own.

There are many RV and car rental agencies to choose from in the Anchorage area. The easiest way to rent a car is through an agency operating from within the airport itself. In this case, all you have to do is gather your baggage, get your car, and drive away.

If, however, you decide to go with a rental-car agency operating outside the airport, don't worry. Many such places offer free airport shuttles, and if they don't have a shuttle service, simply grab a cab and they can deliver you to the agency's front door. Once you've collected your bags at the airport terminal in the lower level of the airport, simply walk out the swinging doors behind you. Cross the general pickup area and proceed to the line of cabs, 90 feet straight ahead. Cab drivers here know when every flight is arriving from the Lower Forty-Eight, and there will be no problem getting quick service.

Though it's not often advertised, many RV rental agencies will also pick you up at the airport and take you back at the end of your journey. Be sure to ask about this service when inquiring about your RV rental package. If for some reason your RV agency doesn't offer airport shuttle service, they will provide you with complete directions to give the cab driver. Upon your return, the RV agency will arrange a cab to take you back to the airport and may even pick up the tab.

For a realistic look at what to expect when renting an RV or car, I contacted several agencies and determined an average cost. Keep in mind that exact figures will vary from agency to agency and with the season. However, for the most part, the figures listed below should put you in the ballpark.

When reserving any vehicle, be sure to confirm that taxes are included, as these can add up over extended periods. If you're traveling on a budget, this can be a rude awakening. Some agencies include the tax rates in their quotes, others don't, so be certain to ask, especially if the deal sounds too good to be true.

The cost of renting a Class C, 24-foot RV averages roughly $200 a day, including tax. If you wish to reserve an RV for one week—7 days on the road—the cost will be about $1,400. For a month's rental of the same vehicle, expect to pay somewhere in the neighborhood of $5,500.

Before you dismiss these figures as being outrageously high, stop and think a moment. These rates may indeed be high if you're traveling with a spouse or a small family. But if you're going with a group of anglers, splitting the costs between a half-dozen folks is not as painful.

If you're interested in renting a mid-sized car, you're looking at a ballpark rate of $80 a day. For a week's rental, expect a bit of a discount, about $500. If you need this car for four weeks, $1,650 would be an average cost. Again, make sure the rates you are quoted include Alaskan state tax.

Another point to consider when renting a vehicle is where you'll be taking it. If your journey leads off pavement, on unimproved gravel roads, expect to pay a bit more. Many of Alaska's gravel roads are rough and, when wet from rain, can be a mess. This takes a toll on any vehicle, especially a car. In fact, some agencies won't rent cars to customers going off road, so do your homework.

There are additional costs to consider no matter what vehicle you rent. Fuel rates largely depend on where you're going, how many miles you plan on covering, and what type of mileage your rental vehicle gets. Factor all of this in when budgeting your trip. For example, if you're planning to drive down to Homer, exploring many of the off-road waters, then swing over to Seward for a few days, then head north of Anchorage for more fishing, your gas bill will add up. If you're heading straight to Soldotna and plan on sticking close to area waters, fuel costs will be minimal.

Food is another cost that must be taken into consideration. If you've never been to Alaska, the first thing you'll notice is the high cost of everything. Through all my years of living in Alaska I never got used to the exorbitant cost of basic items, and each time I return I'm always caught off guard again.

When I fish Alaska, I typically plan on bringing one cooler of fish home. (Keep in mind that each airline passenger is allowed two checked pieces of luggage, not to exceed 70 pounds per bag, though this may change. Also, since 9-11, a rod case now counts as a bag on most airlines, so if traveling by plane try taking your fishing rods as carryon baggage.) For the trip in, I fill the cooler with food from home. These items will usually last me two weeks, with a savings of a couple hundred dollars before it's all over. Of course, I do hit a few of the local restaurants while moving from town to town, but taking my own food along helps ease the overall bill.

Another way to cut food costs is to carry a compact barbecue or propane stove along in your rig. Cooking your daily catch can provide you with great meals and even leftovers, greatly reducing food costs.

If, on the other hand, you don't want to worry about hauling around your own food, plan on spending at least $30 per person, per day on average. Of course, this figure may fluctuate depending on what you eat and where you eat it.

Fuel and food aside, if traveling in an RV, you'll usually find hookups everywhere you wish to go. On average, daily hookup fees are about $20. Weekly rates are around $125, while monthly charges average $450.

If traveling by car, you'll need a place to sleep each night. You can carry your own tent and gear and pay only a minimal fee of $5 to $10 a night at roadside campgrounds. But if you don't want to camp, there are several other options available.

Bed and breakfasts will average about $100 a night, and typically include one meal. Cabin rentals vary upon guest count, running in the neighborhood of $75 to $100 for the first person, and $15 for each additional occupant. Motels will average around $80 for double occupancy. During peak summer months, expect to spend an average of $80 a night for a place to crash, though this can vary.

So, for the RV traveler wishing to spend seven days on the road, you're looking at $1,525. Split this among five anglers and you're at $305 each, plus gas and food bills. With incidental costs like a fishing license and perhaps some gear, this isn't bad. And if you each bring home 70 pounds of salmon fillets, going the RV route can be cost efficient.

For the traveler going by car, a seven-day rental with overnight costs will set you back about $1,050, not including fuel. Divide this among four anglers and it comes out to about $260 each, with gas and food to be settled.

Again, when planning a road trip, it's important to figure in your mileage. Also, keep in mind that costs can vary greatly depending on your personal taste. An evening of fine dining and a few drinks can easily set each person back $75. On the other hand, a hefty burger and fries may run only $10 at the local diner.

Below is a chart showing how many miles it is from Anchorage to the towns you'll most likely drive to on your fishing adventure. Once you've determined the mileage your rental vehicle gets, and the price of fuel per gallon in the area at the time of your trip, you can determine an accurate fuel rate.

Driving Distance from Anchorage

FROM ANCHORAGE TO:	MILES
Cooper Landing	100
Eagle River	13
Eklutna	26
Fairbanks	360
Girdwood	39
Homer	226
Hope	88
Kenai	159
Moose Pass	98
Palmer	42
Seward	127
Soldotna	148
Talkeetna	113
Wasilla	42

ANCHORAGE SERVICES

Alaska Area Code: 907
Population: 260,283
Elevation: 38 feet

TOURIST INFORMATION

Alaska Convention and Visitors Bureau, Current Events Recording 276-3200; www.anchorage.net

Alaska Department of Fish & Game, 333 Raspberry Road, Anchorage; 267-2218; www.sf.adfg.state. ak.us/region2/html/r2home.stm

Alaska Public Lands Information Center, 605 W. 4th, Anchorage; 271-2737; information on outdoor recreation lands throughout the state

Alaska Statewide Road Conditions Information Line; 1-800-478-7675

Alaska Travel Industry Association Information; 929-2200

Anchorage Chamber of Commerce, 441 W. 5th Ave., Anchorage; 272-2401; www.anchoragechamber.org

Anchorage Visitors Center Information, 4619 Spenard Road; 257-2363; offers complete assortment of brochures, books, and maps relating to the area

Bureau of Land Management Public Information Center, located on the 1st floor of the new federal building at 8th Avenue and A Street, Anchorage; 271-5960

Log Cabin Visitor Information Center (Alaska Convention and Visitors Bureau), 4th Avenue and F Street, Anchorage; 274-3531; find a wide variety of brochures and maps

FISHING GUIDE SERVICES

Acord Guide Service, P.O. Box 870790, Wasilla, 99687; 376-0692; www.acordguideservice.com

Alaska Outdoor Adventures, P.O. Box 241125, Anchorage, 99524; 1-888-414-7669; www.akadventures.com

Alaska Skyways/Regal Air, P.O. Box 190702, Anchorage, 99519; 243-8535; regalair@alaska.net

Bush Air Tours, 2400 E. 5th Avenue, Anchorage; 279-9600; email: flybai@alaska.net

Fisherman's Choice Charters, P.O. Box 940276, Houston, AK 99694; 1-800-989-8707; voted Mat-Su areas best fishing charter in 2000 and 2001; www. akfishermanschoice.com

Fish Tale River Guides, P.O. Box 155, Palmer, AK 99645; 1-800-376-3625

Fly Guys Urban Angler, 1210 Nelchina St., Anchorage; 274-1923; local fishing guides for Anchorage-area rivers and Southcentral region; www.alaskanflyguy. com

Gardner's Sport Fishing Adventure, 1900 Meander Circle, Anchorage; 344-3690; acgardner@gci.net

Great Northern Airlines, 4151 Floatplane Drive, Anchorage; 1-800-243-1968; email: gnag@alaska.net

Ketchum Air Service, Inc., P.O. Box 190588, Anchorage, 99519; 1-800-433-9114; offering fly-in fishing, guided and unguided, cabins available; www.ketchumair.com

Rust's Flying Service, Inc., P.O. Box 190325, Anchorage, 99519; 1-800-544-2299; offering fly-in fishing, guided and unguided, cabins available; www.flyrusts.com

Women's Flyfishing, P.O. Box 243963, Anchorage, 99524; 274-7113; float tubing and guided fishing trips; www.halcyon.com/wffn/

TACKLE SHOPS

Worldwide Angler, Inc., 510 West Tudor #3, Anchorage; 1-907-561-0662

6th Avenue Outfitters, 520 W. 6th Ave., Anchorage; 1-800-276-0233

Alaska Raft and Kayak, 401 W. Tudor Rd., Anchorage; 1-800-606-5950; raft, canoe, and camping gear rental

Boondocks Sporting Goods, Eagle River Loop Road, Eagle River; 694-2229

MacAfee's Fly Shop, 750 West Dimond Blvd., Anchorage; 344-1617; fully outfitted shop, a must-see for any fly angler traveling through Anchorage

Mountain View Sports, 3838 Old Seward Hwy., Anchorage; 563-8600; the most comprehensive collection of fishing tackle in town, source of fishing reports and other valued information

FISHING LICENSE VENDORS

Note: While several sporting good stores around the city distribute fishing licenses, they may not be open 24/7. The following stores are open for long hours.

Carrs Quality Center, offering grocery, bakery, deli and pharmacy supplies, in addition to fishing license and salmon tags; open 24 hours a day, 7 days a week; 6 locations in Anchorage:
    1501 Huffman Road, 348-1300
    900 Dimond Boulevard, 341-1000
    4000 West Dimond Boulevard, 342-1200
    1650 West Northern Lights Boulevard, 297-0500
    600 East Northern Lights Boulevard, 297-0600
    1340 Gambell Street, 339-0200

Fred Meyer, offering complete grocery, deli, bakery, sporting goods; open 7 days a week from 7:00 a.m. to 11:00 p.m.; 4 locations in Anchorage: 7701 Debarr Road, 269-1700

    2300 Abbot Road, 365-2000

    1000 East Northern Lights Boulevard, 264-9600

    2000 West Dimond Boulevard, 267-6700

Wal-Mart, 3101 A Street, Anchorage; 1-800-833-BUSH; in addition to fishing licenses, has fishing tackle to meet your basic needs; open 24 hours a day, 7 days a week

GEAR RENTAL

Alaska Raft and Kayak, 401 West Tudor Road, Anchorage; 1-800-606-5950; www.alaskaraftandkayak.com

ACCOMMODATIONS

Anchorage Alaska Bed & Breakfast Association, P.O. Box 242423, Anchorage, 99524; 1-888-584-5147; www.anchorage-bnb.com

Chelsea Inn Hotel, 3836 Spenard Road, Anchorage; 1-800-770-5002; close to airport, 24-hour shuttle

Dimond House Bed & Breakfast, 2201 W. 48th Avenue, Anchorage; 245-8080; www.dimondhousebnb.com; midtown location, 5 minutes from airport

Econo Lodge, 642 E. 5th, Avenue, Anchorage; 1-800-55-ECONO

Hotel Captain Cook, 939 W. 5th Avenue, Anchorage; 1-800-843-1950; www.captaincook.com; a personal favorite, plush hotel with 3 restaurants and classy gift shops. (Author's Note: This is where my teams would stay every year when we flew down from the Arctic for the state basketball tournament.)

Inlet Tower Suites, 1200 L Street, Anchorage; 276-0110; www.inlettowersuites.com

Puffin Inn, 4400 Spenard Road, Anchorage; 1-800-4PUFFIN; www.puffininn.net; offers a wide range of rooms from economy to deluxe

Salmon Run Guest House, 3801 W. 67th Avenue, Anchorage; 99502; www.salmonrun.com; private cabins, jacuzzi, freezers, fishing advice, 5 minutes from airport

Sheraton Anchorage Hotel, 401 E. 6th Avenue, Anchorage; 276-8700

WestCoast International Inn, 3333 W. International Airport Road, Anchorage; 1-800-544-0986; www.westcoasthotels.com; close to airport, minutes from town

CAMPGROUNDS AND RV PARKS

Alaska Campground Owner's Association, P.O. Box 101500, Anchorage, AK, 99510; 277-4603; acoa@pobox.alaska.net; www.alaskacampgrounds.net

Anchorage RV Park, 1200 N. Muldoon Road, Anchorage; 1-800-400-7275; www.anchrvpark.com; 10 minutes from downtown Anchorage, 195 full hookups, pull-through, cable TV, main lodge, dump station, BBQ pavilion, groceries, gift shop, modem access, laundry, showers, reservations recommended

Bird Creek Campground and Overflow, Chugach State Park, 101.2 Seward Hwy.; 47 campsites, camping fee, picnic sites, toilets, water, trails, fishing

Eagle River Campground, Chugach State Park, 12.6 Glenn Hwy., Eagle River; 57 campsites, camping and parking fee, picnic sites and shelter, toilets, water, trails, dump station, fishing

Eklutna Lake Campground, Chugach State Park, 26.5 Glenn Hwy.; 50 campsites, camping fee, picnic sites and shelter, toilets, water, trails, cabins, fishing

Electronic Solutions Midtown Camper Park, 545 E. Northern Lights Blvd., Anchorage; 277-2407; 42 spaces, full hookups, on-site lounge, tailor, dog grooming, hair salon, close to Sears Mall, Safeway, Fred Meyer, Midas, movie theater

Golden Nugget Camper Park, 4100 DeBarr Road, Anchorage; 1-800-449-2012; email: gnugget@alaska.net; 215 spaces, full hookups, free showers, laundromat, tours and guided fishing trips, picnic tables at all sites, souvenir shop, close to shopping centers, restaurants, service stations, beauty salon

Hillside on Gambell Motel & RV Park, 2150 Gambell Street, Anchorage; 1-800-478-6008; 71 spaces, 59 full hookups, central location, free showers, fish freezer available, laundry, propane, close to Sullivan Arena, shopping and groceries; www.hillside-alaska.com

John's Motel & RV Park, 3543 Mountain View Drive, Anchorage; 1-800-478-4332; www.johnsmotel.com; full hookups available year-round, adults only, pets allowed, tour information, free cable TV, gift shop, level concrete pads, laundromat, clean free showers, no reservations accepted in RV Park

Portage RV Park, Mile 1.5, Portage (south of Anchorage, on Turnagain Arm); 1-877-477-8243; email: autoamerica@yahoo.com; located near good fishing stream and hiking trails

Ship Creek Landings RV Park, 150 N. Ingra Street, Anchorage; 1-888-778-7700; www.alaskarv.com; full hookups, pull-through and dry sites, showers, toilets, handicap access, laundry, modem access, RV/car wash, tour information, gift shop, caravan rates available, close to downtown

RESTAURANTS

Double Musky Inn, Crow Creek Road, Girdwood; 783-2822; need reservations for this high-end restaurant during the summer months; great meat selection, specializing in Cajun cuisine, most famous for pepper steak dish; insider secret for the best value is to fill up on appetizers in the bar

Gwennie's Old Alaskan Restaurant, 4333 Spenard Road, Anchorage; 243-2090; vintage Alaskan atmosphere and food to match

La Mex Restaurants, 900 W. 6th Avenue, Anchorage; 274-7678; serving both Mexican and American cuisine; also have restaurants in midtown and south Anchorage serving Mexican cuisine only; La Mex Spenard, 274-7511; La Mex Dimond, 344-6399; voted best Mexican restaurant by Anchorage press

Moose's Tooth Pub & Pizzeria, 3300 Old Seward Hwy., Anchorage; 258-2537; outstanding hand-crafted pizza with a fun family atmosphere

Phyllis's Cafe & Salmon Bake, 436 D Street, Anchorage; 274-6576; steaks, seafood, burgers and salads, good family find

Ristorante Orso, 737 W. Fifth Avenue, Suite 110, Anchorage; 222-3232; inspired by flavors and traditions of Italy, serving grilled meats, pastas, and seafood specialty desserts

Sea Galley Restaurant, 4101 Credit Union Drive, Anchorage; 563-3520; voted best seafood restaurant in Anchorage, fresh daily seafood, ribs, steaks, burgers, lounges

Snow City Cafe, 1034 W. 4th Avenue, Anchorage; 272-2489; all day breakfast, omelets, homemade soups, sandwich, salads

Sorrento's Restaurant, 601 Fireweed Lane, Anchorage; 278-3439; 1011 E. Dimond Boulevard, Anchorage; 344-9986; excellent family place with great Italian foods

Villa Nova Restaurant, 5121 Arctic Blvd., Anchorage; 561-1660; very good and affordable European cuisine, Italian a specialty with good seafood specials

RV RENTALS

ABC Motor home Rentals, 3875 Old International Airport Rd., Anchorage 99502; 1-800-421-7456; email: rvalaska@alaska.net

Alaska Economy RV's, 4517 Old Seward Hwy., Anchorage 99503; 1-800-764-4625; www.goalaska.com

Alaska Frontier RV Rental, 1850 Viking Drive, Anchorage 99501; 1-866-802-2900; email: akrvrental@alaska.com; www.akrvrental.com

Alaska Panorama RV Rentals, Inc., 712 Potter Drive, Anchorage 99518; 1-800-478-1401; email: akpanorama@cs.com

Alaska Truck and Camper, 502 West Northern Lights Blvd., Anchorage 99503; 1-877-562-0897; email: alaskacamper@gci.net; www.alaskacamper.com

Alexander's RV Rental, 6617 Arctic Blvd., Anchorage; 1-888-660-5115

Alaska Vacation Motorhome Rentals, P.O. Box 222112, Anchorage 99522;1-800-648-1448

Clippership Motorhome Rentals, 5401 Old Seward Hwy., Anchorage; 1-800-421-3456; email: clippership@customcpu.com; www.clippershiprv.com

RV Barn, 5400 Old Seward Hwy., Anchorage 99518; 563-9099

RENTAL CARS

Affordable New Car Rental, 4707 Spenard Road, Anchorage; 1-800-248-3765; free airport shuttle

Avis Rent-A-Car, Anchorage International Airport; 1-800-331-1212

Budget, 5011 Spenard Road, Anchorage; 1-800-248-0150

Denali Car Rental, 1209 Gambell Street, Anchorage; 276-1230

Frontier Rent-A-Car, 321 E. 5th, Anchorage; 1-877-677-9959

Hertz, Anchorage International Airport; 1-800-654-3131

High Country Car & Truck Rental, 3609 Spenard Road, Anchorage; 1-888-685-1155

National Car Rental, Anchorage International Airport; 1-800-CAR-RENT

Thrifty Car Rental, Spenard Road and Minnesota Drive, Anchorage; 1-800-THRIFTY

U-Save Auto Rental, 400 W. International Airport Road; 1-800-254-8728; free airport shuttle

AIR SERVICE

Alaska Airlines, 1-800-426-0333
American Airlines, 1-800-433-7300
America West, 1-800-235-9292
Continental Airlines, 1-800-525-0280
Delta Air Lines, 1-800-221-1212
ERA Aviation, 1-800-866-8394
Northwest Airlines, 1-800-225-2525
PenAir, 1-800-448-4226
TWA, 1-800-221-2000
United Airlines, 1-800-241-6522

AUTO TOWING & REPAIR

American Tire & Auto, 832 East 4th Ave., Anchorage; 276-7878; brakes, shocks, alignment and motor home servicing
American Tire & Auto, 7835 Old Seward Hwy., Anchorage; 336-7878; brakes, shocks, alignment and motor home servicing
Area Wide Towing, 1005 E. 5th Avenue, Anchorage; 1-888-306-0444; 24-hour towing and repair
Dean's Automotive & RV Service Center, 1131 E. 7th Ave., Anchorage; 276-5731; electric tune ups, starters, shocks, brakes, alternators, engines, electrical, transmissions, AC, alignments
Mobile Trailer Supply, Inc., 300 La Touche Street, Anchorage; 277-1811; complete parts, service, accessories and installations for campers, motor homes 5th wheels and travel trailers

MEDICAL

Alaska Native Medical Center, 4315 Diplomacy Drive, Anchorage; 563-2662
Alaska Regional Hospital, 2801 DeBarr Road, Anchorage; 276-1131
Providence Hospital, 3200 Providence Drive, Anchorage; 562-221124-Hour Dental Emergencies; 279-9144 or 279-2000

VETERINARY CLINICS

Diamond Animal Hospital, 2545 E. Tudor Rd., Anchorage; 562-8384
Pet Emergency Treatment, 3315 Fairbanks Road, Anchorage; 274-5636
VCA East Anchorage Animal Hospital, 2639 Boniface Pkwy., Anchorage; 337-1561

TOURIST ATTRACTIONS

Alaska Museum of Natural History, 11723 Old Glenn Hwy., Eagle River; 694-0819; www.alaskamuseum.org
Alaska Native Heritage Center, Inc., 8800 Heritage Center Drive, Anchorage; 1-800-315-6608; www.alaskanative.net
Alaska Zoo, 4731 O'Malley Road, Anchorage; 346-3242; Open 9 a.m.-6 p.m. daily; be sure to check out the polar bear, Apun, in the bear exhibit; a former of student of mine in Point Lay shot Apun's mother in self defense as she charged him. He dropped the bear a few feet from him. He then discovered the cub and the Anchorage Zoo immediately adopted her.
Anchorage Museum of History & Art, 121 W. 7th Ave., Anchorage; 343-4326; www.anchoragemuseum.org
Big Game Alaska - Drive Thru Wildlife Park, Portage Glacier Turnoff, P.O. Box 949,
Portage, 99587; 783-2025; www.biggamealaska.com; 42 miles south of Anchorage, park and wildlife center are open all year
Eagle River Nature Center, 32750 Eagle River Road, Eagle River, 99577; 694-2108; www.emc.org; 40 minutes from downtown Anchorage, hiking trails, natural history, interpretive walks
Fort Richardson Wildlife Museum, check in at the gate located north of the Arctic Valley Road exit off the Glenn Highway; 384-0431; this museum houses the world- record Dall sheep and several other mounted animals indigenous to Alaska
Imaginarium, 737 W. 5th Ave., Suite G; 276-3179; award-winning science discovery center offers hands-on experiences and fun exhibits for kids and adults

Surprisingly good fishing exists within and around the Anchorage area.

Anchorage Area Water

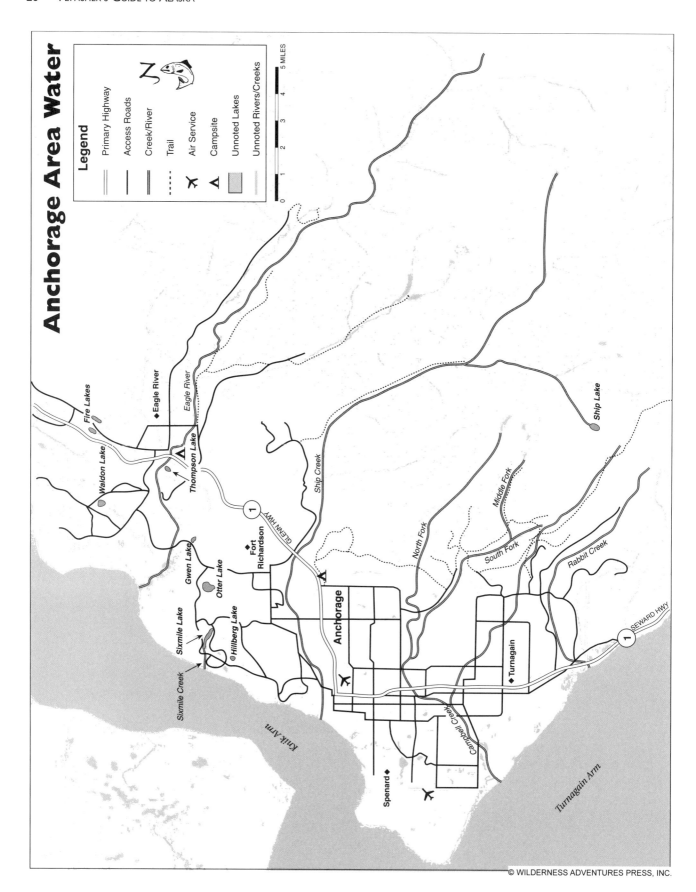

Legend

Primary Highway
Access Roads
Creek/River
Trail
Air Service
Campsite
Unnoted Lakes
Unnoted Rivers/Creeks

0 1 2 3 4 5 MILES

Fire Lakes
Eagle River
Eagle River
Waldon Lake
Thompson Lake
Ship Lake
Ship Creek
Middle Fork
North Fork
South Fork
Rabbit Creek
GLENN HWY
Gwen Lake
Fort Richardson
Otter Lake
Sixmile Lake
Hillberg Lake
Sixmile Creek
Anchorage
Turnagain
SEWARD HWY
Knik Arm
Campbell Creek
Spenard
Turnagain Arm

FLYFISHING
AROUND ANCHORAGE

For anglers who don't have time to see much of Alaska outside of Anchorage—whether because of health considerations or accommodating other family members on vacation—there is still a wealth of fishing at hand. Within an hour of landing at the Anchorage airport, you can have a rental car secured, fishing license purchased, and line in the water—it's that easy. You can literally go in any direction from Anchorage and find reasonably good fishing. True, the banks may be crowded, but some of the rivers in and around Anchorage receive solid runs of salmon, which makes this city a top-notch seasonal fishery.

Anchorage can be reached by way of daily jet service from cities throughout the Lower Forty-Eight. It can also be reached by driving on the Glenn, Parks, and Seward Highways. With more than 75 hotels and motels in the city, along with many bed and breakfasts, hostels, RV parks, and campgrounds, finding a place to stay is usually not a problem. However, if you're traveling during the height of the tourist season (from June through mid-August) it's a good idea to make reservations in advance. More than 600 restaurants, numerous local shops, and some impressive shopping malls make Alaska's largest city a fun place to explore if you can't get farther afield.

Anchorage accounts for roughly half of the state's 627,000 people and is the primary hub for travel to the rest of the state. Fly-out fishing opportunities abound from this metropolis, and accessing remote fishing by road is a cinch. But if you're spending time in and around the Anchorage area, you won't be disappointed in the local fishing if you've done your homework.

While fishing in this area is largely an urban experience, that in itself is unique. Where else in the United States can you battle rush-hour traffic, then minutes later be fighting a 25-pound king salmon in the shadows of a city skyline? If you're willing to wade a little, even the urban crowds can be left behind, and fishing can be surprisingly productive in many area streams. From big rivers to small streams to lakes and ponds, the Anchorage bowl has it all.

As for fishing Anchorage-area rivers and creeks for salmon, rainbow trout, and Dolly Varden, it's almost entirely a wade-fishing show, with the exception of the Twentymile River to the south on Turnagain arm. The fact that all the fishing you'd ever want to do here can be done on foot is a real advantage for the traveling angler with limited time or a limited budget.

The Anchorage-area fisheries include the lakes and streams from the Eklutna River to the north to Twentymile River to the south. And there's no dearth of species to target: rainbow and lake trout, Dolly Varden, northern pike, arctic grayling, and all five species of Pacific salmon.

Anchorage has nearly 30 lakes that are stocked twice each year, providing very good year-round sport fishing. Though many of the streams within the Anchorage area support wild runs of multiple salmon species, most of the native runs are too small in number to support an active sport fishery. Consequently, Anchorage-area sport fishing is a result of hatchery stocking programs that have created a successful put-and-take system. Salmon fishing regulations vary widely among streams around Anchorage. It is up to every angler to read the fishing regulations book very carefully before wetting a line in any Anchorage waters. Many local waters are closed to salmon fishing, and others are constantly being monitored.

Estuaries are popular fisheries in the Anchorage areas, but pay close attention to extreme tide changes.

Major Fisheries Run Times Around Anchorage

T Bird Creek

Species	Jan	Feb	Mar	Apr	May	Jun	Jul	Aug	Sep	Oct	Nov	Dec
Silver Salmon	-	-	-	-	-	-	+/++	+++	-	-	-	-
Pink Salmon	-	-	-	-	-	-	++/+++	+++	-	-	-	-
Chum Salmon	-	-	-	-	-	-	-/++	+++	++	-	-	-

Campbell Creek

Species	Jan	Feb	Mar	Apr	May	Jun	Jul	Aug	Sep	Oct	Nov	Dec
Silver Salmon	-	-	-	-	-	-	++	+++	+++	-	-	-
Rainbow Trout	+	+	+	+	++	+++	+++	+++	+++	++	++	+
Dolly Varden	+	+	+	+	++	+++	+++	+++	+++	++	++	+

Ship Creek

Species	Jan	Feb	Mar	Apr	May	Jun	Jul	Aug	Sep	Oct	Nov	Dec
King Salmon	-	-	-	-	-/++	+++	+++	-	-	-	-	-
Silver Salmon	-	-	-	-	-	-	-/++	+++	+++	-	-	-

Twentymile Creek

Species	Jan	Feb	Mar	Apr	May	Jun	Jul	Aug	Sep	Oct	Nov	Dec
Silver Salmon	-	-	-	-	-	-	++	+++	+++	-	-	-

Area Stocked Lakes

Species	Jan	Feb	Mar	Apr	May	Jun	Jul	Aug	Sep	Oct	Nov	Dec
Rainbow Trout	+	+	+	+	++	+++	+++	+++	+++	++	+	+
Arctic Char	+	+	+	+	++	+++	+++	+++	+++	++	+	+
Lake Trout	+	+	+	+	++	+++	+++	+++	+++	++	+	+
Grayling	+	+	+	+	++	+++	+++	+++	+++	++	+	+
Landlocked Salmon	+	+	+	+	++	+++	+++	+++	+++	++	+	+

GENERAL FISH RUN TIMES AROUND ANCHORAGE

Species	Jan	Feb	Mar	Apr	May	Jun	Jul	Aug	Sep	Oct	Nov	Dec
King Salmon	-	-	-	-	++	+++	+++/++	-	-	-	-	-
Sockeye Salmon	-	-	-	-	-	++	+++	+++/++	++	-	-	-
Coho Salmon	-	-	-	-	-	-	++	+++/+	+/-	-	-	-
Pink Salmon	-	-	-	-	-	-/+	+++	+++/11	1/	-	-	-
Chum Salmon	-	-	-	-	-	-	++	+++/+	+/-	-	-	-
Dolly Varden	+	+	+	+	+	+	+	++	+++	++	+	+
Rainbow Trout	+	+	+	+	+	+	+	++	+++	++	+	+
Lake Trout	+	+	+	+	+++	+++	+	+	+++	++	+	+
Pike	+	+	+	+	+++	+++	+	+	+++	+++	+	+

+++ Excellent   ++ Good   + Fair   - Nonexistent/Closed Season

Bird Creek is your best bet for chum salmon near Anchorage.

From May through August, a fisheries hotline is updated weekly by the Anchorage office of the Alaska Department of Fish & Game. For current reports and up-to-date information regarding regulatory changes, call 907-267-2510. Additional, year-round updates can be had on weekdays by phoning the Division of Sport Fish at 907-267-2218. For free informational brochures or personal assistance stop in at the ADF&G office at 333 Raspberry Road in Anchorage.

Because some of the Anchorage-area streams are heavily silted, fishing bait is often the only reliable way to catch salmon. It can be a long, expensive journey to reach Alaska, and having the flexibility to alter your fishing technique is wise. While die-hard flyfishers may not be interested in adapting their style of fishing to the waters at hand, it can be the only way to catch fish in some heavily silted Anchorage waters. Rest assured, though, that there are many other opportunities available for flyfishers traveling from Anchorage to the rest of Alaska.

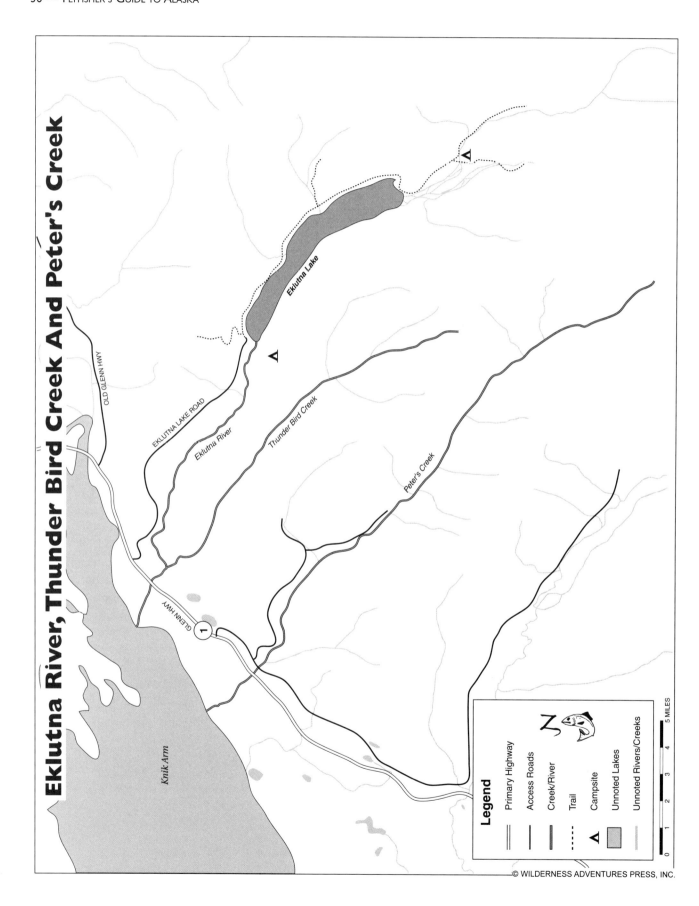

Eklutna River, Thunder Bird Creek And Peter's Creek

OLD GLENN HWY

EKLUTNA LAKE ROAD

Eklutna Lake

Eklutna River

Thunder Bird Creek

Peter's Creek

GLENN HWY

1

Knik Arm

Legend

Primary Highway
Access Roads
Creek/River
Trail
Campsite
Unnoted Lakes
Unnoted Rivers/Creeks

0 1 2 3 4 5 MILES

Fishing North of Anchorage

Eklutna River

Although the Eklutna River serves as the northern boundary of municipal fishing opportunities, the actual catching of fish can be spotty at best. This river is fed by several glaciers, and their silt is carried through large Eklutna Lake and then transported into the river. This heavy siltation reduces visibility and makes flies, and even lures, very unproductive here.

However, there are opportunities for those eager to fish this river. Traveling approximately 20 miles north of Anchorage along the Glenn Highway puts you at the Eklutna tailrace. At times, local anglers have good luck fishing bait in the tailrace, where silvers and the occasional dog salmon may congregate. Again, the silting can make flyfishing a tough proposition at this site, but if you're willing to toss heavily scented, well-cured roe on a spinning outfit, the fish should be able to sniff out your bait.

Down at the mouth of the Eklutna, bank fishing is the rule, and it's a good idea to have a pair of waders handy.

If you don't want to try any angling but fly casting, it might be a good idea to skip the Eklutna completely. There are other streams in the area that offer better chances at catching fish the way you want to. If you're interested in how the Eklutna River is producing during your time in Anchorage, employees at local tackle shops will be able to keep you informed. The bite can still be good if you know where to go when the fish are in.

In the same area as the Eklutna River, you'll find Thunder Bird Creek and Peter's Creek. For the same reason I wouldn't spend much time on the Eklutna, I'd also forego these creeks. The silting is simply too heavy for dependable, productive fishing.

Many flowing streams in the Anchorage area are closed to salmon fishing, but opportunities do exist for king salmon. Eagle River and Ship Creek are best during May and June.

Stream Facts: Eklutna River

Seasons

- From its mouth upstream to the Glenn Highway bridge, the Eklutna River drainage is open year-round to fishing for salmon 16 inches or longer (except king salmon 20 inches or longer).

- Upstream from the Glenn Highway bridge, fishing is open from January 1 to September 30 for salmon 16 inches or longer (except king salmon 20 inches or longer).

Special Regulations

- For salmon 16 inches or longer (except king salmon 20 inches or longer), the daily limits are three fish per day, three in possession, of which only two per day or two in possession may be silver salmon.

Fish Species

- Silver and chum salmon

River Characteristics

- Heavy silting makes for difficult fishing conditions in the Eklutna River, especially for fly anglers. Bait, such as cured roe, fished in the tailrace is the most common method of taking salmon here.

Fishing Access

- Travel approximately 20 miles north of Anchorage on the Glenn Highway to the Eklutna tailrace. Bank fishing at the mouth.

Maps

- *Alaska Atlas and Gazetteer*, page 83

Eagle River

Moving to the south, mile 12.9 on the Glenn Highway puts you on the Eagle River. This is a restrictive fishery due to its locale within Chugach State Park and Fort Richardson U.S. Army Base, but there are a variety of fish species to pursue here. Eagle River is open to salmon fishing, with a 16-inch minimum length on those being kept. Fishing here is from Bailey Bridge on the Army base upstream to markers located in the Chugach State Park Eagle River Campground at mile 12 on the Glenn Highway, off the Hiland Road exit.

What makes the Eagle River so enticing to many anglers is that it's one of only two Anchorage-area streams currently open to the taking of adult king salmon. Unfortunately, a hatchery-release program failed on the Eagle, but a small number of kings still return to the river. As a result, king salmon fishing is restricted to four consecutive three-day weekends—Saturday, Sunday, and Monday—beginning Memorial Day weekend.

The Eagle River also has a small run of chum salmon, with 150 fish or so taken annually. Silver salmon are perhaps the most popular of the salmon species anglers target here, especially upstream of the Route Bravo bridge.

Rainbow trout and Dolly Varden fishing can also be excellent in the Eagle, particularly during the salmon spawn and die-off. Glo-Bugs, beads, and flesh flies are effective patterns during the salmon spawn, with nymphs being a good choice earlier in the season.

The area from Bailey Bridge upstream to the ADF&G markers in the campground is accessible only by passing through the Fort Richardson guard station. Call the Fort Richardson Wildlife Center at 907-384-0431 and the Chugach State Park at 907-345-5014 for details before fishing here. Don't let these obstacles stand in your way, though, as the fishing can be very good at times. The folks who answer your call will be happy to point you in the right direction.

To reach the Fort Richardson guard station, take the Arctic Valley Road exit off the Glenn Highway, then turn left. Anglers fishing on the base need to have a current sport-fishing license and are required to sit through a 10-minute orientation course. After the brief course, you'll be issued a free season-long fishing pass for the base.

The expansive Eagle Glacier and a handful of surrounding, smaller glaciers within the Chugach Mountains combine to create the Eagle River. As a result, glacial silting can be heavy at times, but not as intense as many other glacial-fed rivers in the region. The Eagle typically runs opaque and is a swift-moving body of water. For this reason, attention-getting flies like large, flashy streamers are the norm when targeting salmon.

A word of caution when wading the Eagle River. First and foremost, pay close attention to each step, especially when navigating across the stream or in areas of swift water. The silting can greatly impede visibility, and you don't want to take unnecessary risks, especially in quick, deep stretches of water. If traveling blind, make certain of your footing before each step. Also, beware of brown bears. I know some Anchorage-area residents who won't take to the river unless they have their bear pepper spray strapped to their belts.

Not long ago a husband and wife were taken by surprise along the river when a brown bear attacked their five-year-old child. With no other option, they shot and killed the bear as it stood over their son.

Stream Facts: Eagle River

Seasons

- From the mouth upstream to the Route Bravo bridge on Fort Richardson, fishing is closed year-round.

- For king salmon 20 inches or longer, the Eagle River is open to fishing only from Bailey Bridge on Fort Richardson upstream to the ADF&G markers situated in the Chugach State Park Eagle River Campground and is restricted to four consecutive three-day weekends—Saturday, Sunday and Monday—beginning Memorial Day weekend. The remainder of the Eagle River drainage is closed year-round to king salmon fishing.

- For other salmon species, the Eagle River drainage from the Route Bravo bridge upstream to the ADF&G markers situated at mile 7.4 of the Eagle River Road, including the waters within 100 yards of its confluence with the South Fork (but not including the South Fork) is open year-round to fishing for all species (except king salmon 20 inches or longer).

- For salmon species other than king salmon, the remainder of the Eagle River drainage, including waters upstream from the ADF&G markers at mile 7.4 of the Eagle River Road and the North Fork and its tributaries (but not including the South Fork) is open from September 16 to May 31.

- The South Fork Eagle River, from its confluence with Eagle River upstream to the falls, is open from August 15 to May 31 for salmon less than 16 inches and for other species. This area is closed for all salmon 16 inches or longer.

Special Regulations

- King salmon 20 inches or longer daily limits, one per day, one in possession.

- For all other salmon 16 inches or longer, three per day, three in possession, of which only two per day, two in possession may be silver salmon.

Fish

- King, silver, and chum salmon, rainbow trout, Dolly Varden

River Characteristics

- The Eagle River is fed by glaciers, which leaves the water silted. Due to limited visibility, wading across the stream can be challenging in places.

Fishing Access

- To access the Eagle River, head to the Fort Richardson guard station. Take the Arctic Valley Road exit off the Glenn Highway, 12.9 miles north of Anchorage, then turn left.

Maps

- *Alaska Atlas and Gazetteer*, page 83

Fort Richardson Area Lakes

There are also a series of lakes around Fort Richardson that offer good flyfishing. These lakes are stocked from the hatchery on the base, a site worth seeing in itself. Check in at the guard station and request a map of these lakes, you may even get some pointers on where the current hotspots are. **Waldon**, **Thompson**, **Gwen**, **Sixmile**, **Hillberg**, and **Otter Lakes** all offer good fishing for a mix of rainbows, grayling, and even landlocked king salmon. A friend of mine has had good success on most of these lakes by launching a small boat and roll casting flies beneath overhanging branches.

The **Fire Lakes** sit at mile 17 on the east side of the Glenn Highway. Lower Fire Lake used to have good rainbow trout fishing and is still stocked, but the trout are being devoured by northern pike. If the trout fishing wanes, look for some large pike. Keep in mind that management goals for this lake may change in the future.

The best chance of catching a sockeye salmon in the Anchorage area is at the mouth of Sixmile Creek on Elmendorf Air Force Base.

Sixmile Creek (mouth)

Sixmile Creek itself is closed to fishing, but it's open at the mouth. Sixmile offers the best opportunity for anglers looking to catching a red salmon in the Anchorage area. Sixmile is located on Elmendorf Air Force Base. Before fishing here, call the Elmendorf Natural Resources office

at 907-552-2436. You'll need to check in at the North Boniface Parkway gate. The area open to sport fishing is seaward of a steel cable that stretches across the mouth of the creek.

Mid-July through the middle of August is the best time to fish the mouth of Sixmile for returning sockeye salmon. Streamers stripped through the saltwater will take red salmon. At the time of this writing, a three-fish daily limit of reds is in place for Sixmile Creek.

Ship Creek

Ship Creek, located on the northern fringe of Anchorage, is the main salmon fishery in the metro-area and provides the best opportunity for catching a king salmon, which are the first salmon species to enter Ship Creek (beginning in mid-May). Along with the Eagle River, Ship Creek is the only Anchorage-area stream open to king salmon fishing.

The Ship Creek king run is a result of a hatchery program maintained by the ADF&G on Elmendorf Air Force Base. Each spring 200,000 to 300,000 smolt are released into Ship Creek, with a small percentage returning one to five years later. Around 3,000 king salmon are harvested here annually by sport anglers, with a record harvest of 5,200 kings occurring in 1999.

Silver salmon are also a big draw for Ship Creek anglers. In 1998 a record harvest of 14,000 silvers was taken from Ship Creek. Silver salmon enter the creek from mid-July through October, with the peak of the run coming in late August and early September. Chum salmon are also in the stream at this time, with some 150 being taken annually. The chum runs coincide with the coho, and most chum are caught by anglers targeting silver salmon.

When the salmon are in Ship Creek, things can get a little crowded. This is combat fishing in the truest sense, but don't let the crowds drive you away. This is an interesting experience. If nothing else, it will make a great story after you return home.

Ship Creek drains Ship Lake in the Chugach Mountain Range to the east before emptying into Knik Arm of Cook Inlet. On its way to the ocean, several other mountainous streams join the flow. Because it's not glacial fed, Ship Creek runs clear, making it ideal for fly anglers.

This is a fast-moving stream with plenty of prime riffles in which to work flies. Wading and casting is the best way fish this creek, not only to reach more fish, but also to break away from other anglers. Some of the best flyfishing opportunities lie off Post Road, as the creek bottom in this area is composed of small gravel. With a host of riffles, this stretch just plain looks "fishy." Post Road parallels the northern shore of the creek, and it can be accessed by several connecting roads leading through the city.

Dolly Varden are native to many Anchorage area waters.

From its mouth upstream approximately a half-mile to 100 feet below the Chugach dam fishing is open for salmon 16 inches or longer. The ADF&G cable marker stretches across the creek at this point, delineating where fishable water ends.

This stretch of Ship Creek lies in an industrial part of town and is actually owned by the Alaska Railroad. When fishing this area, proceed with great caution and abide by all "no trespassing" signs. Stay clear of all railroad tracks and bridges.

In addition to scattered roadside pulloffs along the creek, there are three public daily-fee parking areas. Two parking facilities are located along Whitney Road, with another on Western Avenue. The best way to access the river is to head north on E Street, going through the light on West 4th Avenue. Turn right at the three-way stop sign and head down the hill on North C Street to Whitney Avenue, which sits on the right side of the road. Western Avenue is farther up the road on the left side. There are excellent foot trails along the north and south sides of Ship Creek.

A word of caution when fishing near the creek mouth: The glacial silt that accumulates here is firm and convenient to stand on, but as the tide goes out, the silt acts like quicksand. Every season several anglers have to be pulled free before the tide returns. So be careful not to venture too far into the mud. Observe other anglers and if in doubt don't chance it; there are plenty of other fishing opportunities around.

There are a number of places where Ship Creek can be fished from shore, but because the timing of salmon runs can vary, check with local tackle shops and the ADF&G for up-to-date information. One of the best ways to locate fishing hotspots is to drive along looking for cars parked at pullouts. If the fish are in, you can bet that the anglers will be there. There are no secrets on Ship Creek, and the only way to catch fish here is to join the crowd.

At the dam, a fish ladder allows you to watch king, silver, and pink salmon moving upstream. Fishing above the dam—more specifically, upriver from the upstream side of the Reeve Boulevard bridge to Fish and Game markers 300 feet above the Elmendorf power plant dam—is prohibited. From here upriver, though, the fishing for Dolly Varden and rainbow trout can be good.

When fishing near the mouth of Ship Creek, coho patterns on a falling tide early in the morning can be dynamite on silver salmon. On the north side of the creek, just down from the marker below the dam, silver fishing can be excellent. On the south side of the creek, there's a run of holes that are seriously overfished, so you may want to check other options before settling on one of these spots. Trout fishing for fish of average size is good all the way to the headwaters.

Be sure to observe all posted Alaska Railroad regulations regarding access to Ship Creek. Park only in the designated areas. For more information, call 907-265-2463. It is also worth noting that a handful of downtown businesses cater to anglers here, renting rods, boots, and providing valuable advice. For more information on which businesses can assist you with this fishery—as they can change with time—contact the Anchorage Visitor Information Center at 907-276-4118.

Stream Facts: Ship Creek

Seasons

- Ship Creek is closed to all fishing May 15 to July 13 between 11:00 p.m. and 6:00 a.m.

- King salmon 20 inches or longer is open from January 1 to July 31.

- Open season for salmon (except king salmon 20 inches or longer) is year-round.

- Ship Creek is closed year-round to all fishing in the following locations: the area between 100 feet upstream and 100 feet downstream of the Chugach power plant dam, on the downstream edge marked by a cable crossing Ship Creek; upstream from the upstream side of the Reeve Boulevard bridge to markers 300 feet above Elmendorf power plant dam.

Special Regulations

- Daily bag and possession limit on king salmon 20 inches or longer is one fish.

- Daily bag and possession limits on salmon (except king salmon 20 inches or longer) is three fish, including silver salmon.

- After taking a king salmon 20 inches or longer, a person may not fish for any species that same day in waters open to king salmon sport fishing.
- Upstream of a point 100 feet upstream of the Chugach power plant dam to the upstream side of the Reeve Boulevard bridge, rainbows/steelhead must be released.

Fish

- King, silver, and chum salmon, rainbow trout, Dolly Varden

River Characteristics

- Ship Creek is a clear-running stream with many good riffles to fish. Near the Post Road area, Ship Creek has a small gravel bottom with stretches of ideal fly water. Wade fishing is the rule here.

Fishing Access

- Two public parking facilities are on Whitney Road, with another on Western Avenue. There are excellent foot trails along both the north and south side of Ship Creek.

Maps

- Alaska Road & Recreation Maps, Anchorage and Vicinity; *Alaska Atlas and Gazetteer*, page 83

Silver salmon inhabit some Anchorage-area streams and offer excellent angling opportunities. Bird, Ship, and Campbell Creek offer the best coho fishing.

Ship Lake

For dry-fly fishermen looking to escape the urban crowds, there's an easy option. The Ship Creek Valley trailhead will take you on an easy to moderate 12-mile hike up a breathtaking valley filled with small brooks and a network of beaver ponds, ending at Ship Lake. The trailhead can be accessed via the Glenn Highway, then the Arctic Valley exit on the northeastern edge of Anchorage. Stay on Arctic Valley Road for 4.5 miles until you reach the trailhead. Count on an 8-hour walk to reach the lake, longer if you fish on the way.

The real attraction here is the excellent Dolly Varden fishing in Ship Lake. These fish aren't big, just 8 to 10 inches, but the lake is loaded. The beauty of the fish themselves, coupled with the stunning views of the Chugach Mountains, make for a special angling experience within easy range of the city.

For anglers eager to see new territory, skip returning the way you came in and just continue south through Indian Creek Pass and down the Indian Valley Trail. From January 1 through June 30, fishing is open on this stretch of Indian Creek. The 8-mile hike down this trail will bring you to the Powerline Pass trailhead, which is about one mile from the Seward Highway. You can arrange to have a car meet you here or hitch a ride back to your vehicle.

Indian Creek

If you're interested in fishing for salmon on Indian Creek, stay west of the Seward Highway. Anglers typically drive directly to the stream, rather than hike down the Indian Valley Trail. Indian Creek Rest Area, at mile 102.9 on the Seward Highway, is the best place to park. From here, it's an easy walk to the creek mouth.

Indian Creek is a very small stream, easily seen from the highway. East of the Seward Highway, the water runs so low in places that you can cross in tennis shoes without getting the laces wet. Because it lacks water volume, many people dismiss this stream as void of fish. But fishing opportunities do exist here.

West of the Seward Highway, the fishing pressure on Indian Creek can be intense. This is especially true when the pink salmon are running on even-numbered years. But if you don't mind the tight action, the catching can be good. If things are really crowded, just wait your turn until anglers in front of you have caught their limits or a hole has opened up.

A small number of silver salmon make their way into Indian Creek, with the best fishing right at the mouth. Because the returning numbers of silver salmon are low here, it's not the best place to concentrate your efforts, but on the other hand, it only takes a few minutes to pull off the shoulder of the road, walk down the trail, and wet a line. If the fish are in, and by some odd chance you have the hole to yourself, you might come away thinking it's the best fishing in the area.

Indian Creek is home to good sea-run Dolly Varden action from June through September. And rainbow trout are present in Indian Creek, too. Both rainbows and Dollys can be found upstream in tiny, isolated pockets. If you like the idea of fishing in holes the size of phone booths, then you may want to spend some time exploring these waters.

East of the Seward Highway, Indian Creek is closed to salmon fishing year-round, but other fish can be taken from January 1 through June 30.

Stream Facts: Indian Creek

Seasons

- Indian Creek is open year-round downstream from the Seward Highway for all species except king salmon 20 inches or longer.

- Indian Creek is closed year-round upstream of the Seward Highway for king salmon 20 inches or longer and other salmon 16 inches or longer.

- Upstream of the Seward Highway, Indian Creek is open to fishing for species other than salmon from January 1 to June 30.

Special Regulations

- Daily limits on the downstream side of the Seward Highway are three per day, three in possession, of which only two per day, two in possession may be silver salmon.

Fish

- Silver and pink salmon, rainbow trout, Dolly Varden

River Characteristics

- Indian Creek is a very small stream, best known for its pink salmon fishing. Small, restricted holes are what you're hitting here. So small are these holes, in fact, that surprisingly few people spend time fishing Indian Creek.

Fishing Access

- Located at mile 102.9 on the Seward Highway, Indian Creek Rest Area provides plenty of parking space for anglers.

Maps

- Alaska Road & Recreation Maps, Anchorage and Vicinity; *Alaska Atlas and Gazetteer*, pages 83 and 71

Campbell Creek

Campbell Creek is the second most popular fishing stream in the city of Anchorage (after Ship Creek). Campbell Creek flows from the Chugach Range east of Anchorage and then winds its way right through the middle of town south of Northern Lights Boulevard. As a result, many private residential and business properties border this stream. Take extra precautions here to be sure you're not unintentionally trespassing.

If you're a flyfisher who likes to spot individual fish before casting, Campbell will be perfect for you. Because it's fed by so many mountain streams, the stream runs gin clear a large percentage of the time. Sight fishing fans will love spending time on this river, and you'll be surprised how easy it is to get into good fishing all on your own.

Getting yourself in position to locate fish and then make well-placed casts is critical, so bring your waders. Brush-choked banks mean anglers need to give themselves room by wading before attempting to cast. The clear water in this stream makes it easy to see where to step as you wade—as opposed to some of the area's heavily silted waters.

Once you break through the brushline, a wide-open stream awaits. If other anglers are where you want to be, simply follow them or move on. Covering several hundred yards up and downstream is common, and if you can position yourself to fish both banks from midstream, the opportunities double.

And casting to the banks is important here because that's where the silvers hold in this system. Due to the water clarity and the shallow midsection, migrating salmon tend to hug the banks where deep, sweeping holes protect them. This is where anglers will want to focus their fishing energy.

Search for fish directly beneath overhanging branches and trees. And look for fish holding tight to grass-covered banks and undercut banks, and I mean tight. Careful searching will reveal fish holding mere inches from shore. When you see other anglers fishing this stream, don't be turned off; instead, closely observe where they are casting, and more importantly, look to see if they're spotting fish.

If these anglers aren't casting tight against the bank, especially in areas heavy with vegetation or where banks create prime holding water, you can often move right behind them and whack fish. Anywhere foliage hangs in the water, you can find suspended silvers.

If you find yourself on Campbell Creek during the prime silver salmon months of mid-August through September, but you're not catching fish, just wait until the next rain. Campbell Lake sits near the ocean on the southwestern fringe of Anchorage, and because the lake is so close to the sea, incoming silvers are known to hold over here for extended periods, acclimating to their new environment. If there's not a lot of fresh water flowing into Campbell Lake, silvers may hold here longer than normal. This makes it tough for anglers, as the fishing opportunities fall above the lake.

But when the rain comes, waste no time getting to the open fishing zones of Campbell Creek. A new freshet making its way downstream will lure silvers out of the lake and create outstanding fishing conditions. Even if the water is a bit high or off-color from recent rains, don't be discouraged. Large, pink bunny-hair patterns and Flash Flies can still entice a bite in turbid waters. As water levels drop, reducing the size of the fly will pay off.

Because these silvers have held in Campbell Lake, some are a bit darker in color when they continue their journey upstream. If you're looking for good-eating meat, don't let the darker skin coloration turn you off. Once you slice through the skin, you'll find rich, healthy red meat.

With an average of 2,000 coho harvested annually, it's definitely the silver salmon that attract anglers to Campbell Creek. In fact, silvers are the only salmon species sport anglers are currently allowed to fish for in Campbell Creek, and the season opening can vary.

Three easily accessible access points along the creek are available to the public. One parking area sits on the north side of Dimond Boulevard, just west of Victor Road. Here, anglers can walk down a small slope and fish from a boardwalk structure. You can also hike upstream on the foot trail and get into good fishing. This section of Campbell Creek is open for silver salmon from July 25 through October 1. A second access point is at the boardwalk at Folker Street, just east of Lake Otis and south of Tudor Road. Portions of this trail are paved and ideal for wheelchair access. This section of Campbell Creek is open from August 5 through October 1 for the taking of silver salmon.

The third access point is located in the upstream section of both the North and South Forks of Campbell Creek. This area can be reached by turning south on the Campbell Airstrip Road off Tudor Road, about a half-mile east of the Boniface Parkway. Foot trails along the bank and a footbridge across the South Fork lead to good trout fishing. This section is closed to all salmon fishing, but open for catch-and-release fishing for rainbows, which run in the 10- to 12-inch class. The flyfishing can be good in these two forks with nymphs and streamers. When it's not raining, this is a very clear, rather small creek.

It should be noted that the section of Campbell Creek downstream of Lake Otis Parkway to the markers at Shelikof Street is closed. Though Campbell Creek has both red and king salmon, it is closed for these species. However, it is open year-round for the taking of king salmon less than 20 inches long, and other salmon less than 16 inches long. (Note: undersized salmon are referred to as jack salmon, or simply jacks, a term you may hear in your fishing ventures around the city. These are salmon that spend only one year in the ocean before returning to their natal streams.) Consult the South-Central fishing regulations for current laws applying to Campbell Creek.

There is one additional access point for Campbell Creek, one used often by locals. To find it, get on Old Seward Highway and head to Dowling Road. Head west a quarter-mile until you reach the creek. There's a roadside pullout here, and excellent wade fishing opportunities exist in both directions. When the silvers are in, and you find yourself tied to the city, a few hours on this creek will make you realize you are indeed fishing in Alaska.

Stream Facts: Campbell Creek

Seasons

- From its mouth upstream to ADF&G markers under the Dimond Boulevard bridge, the Campbell River (including Campbell Lake) is closed year-round to all fishing.

- From ADF&G markers near Shelikof Street upstream to ADF&G markers on the upstream side of the Lake Otis Parkway bridge, Campbell Creek is closed year-round to all fishing.

- Upstream of the forks near Piper Street, only one unbaited, single-hook, artificial lure is allowed year-round.

- Campbell Creek is open to fishing for silver salmon 16 inches or longer and king salmon 20 inches or less from July 25 to October 1 between ADF&G markers under the Dimond Boulevard bridge upstream to ADF&G markers at the downstream side of the C Street bridge.

- Campbell Creek is open to fishing for silver salmon 16 inches or longer and king salmon 20 inches or less from August 5 to October 1 between the ADF&G markers at the downstream side of C Street bridge upstream to the ADF&G markers near Shelikof Street and between the ADF&G markers on the upstream side of the Lake Otis Parkway bridge upstream to the ADF&G markers near Piper Street.

Special Regulations

- In water open to silver salmon fishing, anglers are allowed three silvers per day, three in possession.

- Rainbow/steelhead trout catch-and-release only upstream of the forks near Piper Street.

- In all waters of Campbell Creek open to rainbow/steelhead trout fishing, daily limits are five per day, five in possession, only one of which can exceed 20 inches.

- For arctic char/Dolly Varden, there is a limit of five per day, five in possession, only one of which can be over 12 inches.

Fish

- Silver salmon, rainbow trout, Dolly Varden

River Characteristics

- The Campbell River is a very clear stream that provides excellent spot-and-stalk fishing opportunities. A gravel bottom dominates, with sand and mud present in a few spots. Wade fishing is the rule, and given the shallow, wide nature of the river, anglers can cover a great deal of water. Look for silver salmon holding near brushlines and tight against cutbanks. Watch your backcast on this brush-lined river.

Fishing Access

- Parking area on the north side of Dimond Boulevard, just west of Victor Road.

- Just east of Lake Otis and south off Tudor Road look for the boardwalk at Folker Street. In the upstream section of both the North and South Forks of Campbell Creek, turn south on the Campbell Airstrip Road off Tudor Road, go a half-mile east of the Boniface Parkway and look for the trails.

- Dowling Road, off the Old Seward Highway.

Maps

- Alaska Road & Recreation Maps, Anchorage and Vicinity; *Alaska Atlas and Gazetteer*, page 83

Rabbit Creek

Rabbit Creek flows south of the South Fork of the Campbell Creek. Fishing is closed year-round on Rabbit Creek downstream of the Old Seward Highway, but upstream of the highway general seasons apply. Consult current sport-fishing regulations prior to heading up this creek.

Fishing South of Anchorage

Bird Creek

Bird Creek, one of the more popular and productive streams in the area, is located 25 miles south of Anchorage, right on the Seward Highway. Two paved parking lots and an improved overlook make this fishery easy to access. To top it off, a paved trail leads right down to the creek. Bird Creek is open to fishing for salmon (other than kings) 16 inches or longer from its mouth upstream 500 yards to the Fish and Game markers.

Approximately 350 yards upstream from the Seward Highway bridge, a cable across the creek marks the beginning of private property. All land upstream is private, and anglers must obtain landowner permission before fishing there. There is a land-swap proposal on the table between private landowners and Chugach State Park that, if approved, would move the marker upstream an additional 150 yards.

When you see cars parked along the highway at Bird Creek, it's hard to pass by without wetting a line. If fishing east of the highway, work flies behind small boulders for

Just south of Anchorage, Bird Creek offers excellent angling for multiple fish species.

Fishing Water South of Anchorage

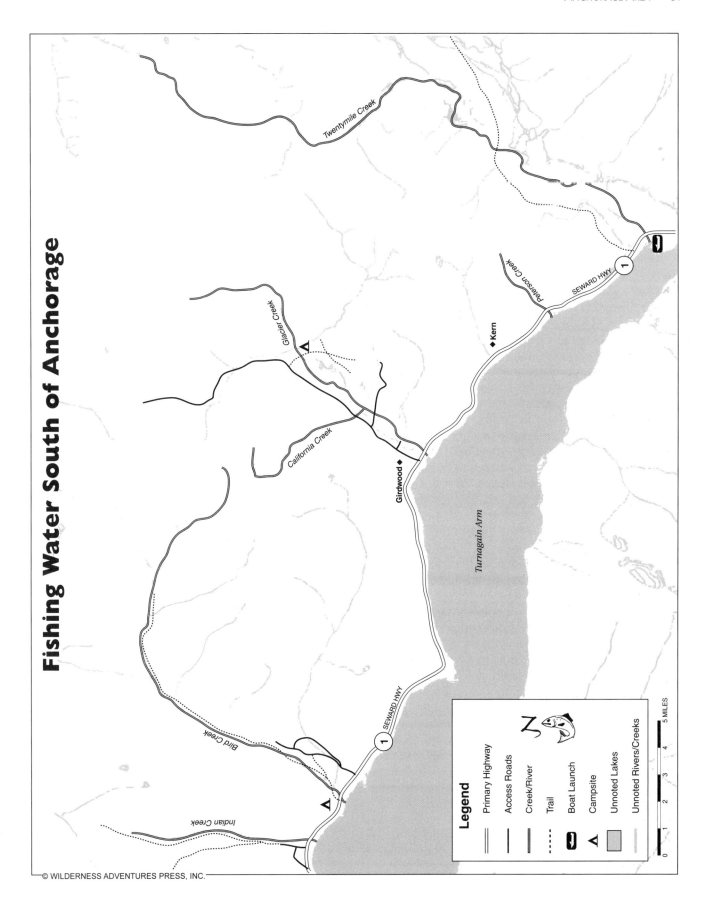

Twentymile Creek

Peterson Creek

SEWARD HWY

♦ Kern

Glacier Creek

California Creek

Girdwood ♦

Turnagain Arm

Bird Creek

1 SEWARD HWY

Indian Creek

Legend

	Primary Highway
	Access Roads
	Creek/River
	Trail
	Boat Launch
	Campsite
	Unnoted Lakes
	Unnoted Rivers/Creeks

0 1 2 3 4 5 MILES

resting salmon. The problem with Bird Creek is that there is very little holding water. It's a shallow, fast stream, and competition among anglers trying to hit the limited number of holes can be stiff. If you've found one of these places, don't be surprised when someone moves in right next to you—or even behind you—and starts hitting the same exact water.

If you can't make your way to one of the few prime holding spots, try dropping a fly behind single rocks and small boulder patches where fish might temporarily pause on their way to more optimal holding waters. Due to it's shallow nature, salmon will travel anywhere in the creek, but they prefer to stick to broken waters and deeper, boiling slicks.

A word of caution: If there is a large number of anglers around you, wear protective eyewear, a jacket, and perhaps even hip or chest waders. Although this stream could be fished in sneakers, it helps to have this gear for simple protection. Because of the gravel and rocks that make up the bottom of Bird Creek, drift-fishing anglers hang up a lot. One of the more common types of sinker used by drift fishermen are pencil sinkers. When breaking free from a shallow-water hangup, these sinkers can come rocketing back your way, frequently striking any of a number of people along the bank.

I was fishing Bird Creek one time when the guy next to me got a pencil sinker buried in his thigh. There are stories of lost eyes, broken noses, and serious injuries resulting from such unfortunate mishaps. With this in mind, pick your fishing spot with care. And pay close attention to how those around you are fishing. But this is a very productive fishery, so don't let the number of anglers deter you from giving it a shot.

If fishing west of the bridge, at the mouth of Bird Creek, avoid walking too far out on the mud flats. Anglers are routinely cut off from land when doing this, and with some of the world's strongest tides in Turnagain Arm, the situation can quickly turn life-threatening. Observe other anglers and don't get greedy.

If you time it right, fishing the incoming tides near the mouth of Bird Creek can be red hot. This is what many locals try to hit. A few red salmon swim up Bird Creek, and the highest concentration of dog salmon in the Anchorage area can be found here. On even-numbered years, a considerable number of pinks work their way into Bird Creek, making it the premier stream in the area for this species. In good years, more than 2,000 pinks are harvested from Bird Creek, with the peak of the run coming in mid-July and extending through August.

But it's the enhanced run of silvers that really attracts anglers to this stream. In 1998 a record number of silvers were taken from Bird Creek by sport anglers, totaling 22,000 fish. The stocking of smolt has since been reduced, and the average harvest now holds at around 5,000 silvers per season.

Due to the low, clear water flowing through Bird Creek, sight fishing for salmon can be highly effective. Search for salmon as they work upstream, cruising from one holding spot to another. Due to the fast water, you'll want to get your fly down fast and hold on. Because there are no deep holes for fish to run to once hooked they move up and down the creek at breakneck speed. As soon as you hook a fish, let neighboring anglers know so you can avoid a massive tangle.

Try to hit the creek on a low, outgoing tide or just prior to an incoming tide. High tides affect fishing all the way to the legal boundary 500 yards upstream from the mouth. During a high tide, there is no way to reach the gravel bars on either side of the stream. At such times, Bird Creek is unfishable.

I've had some great fishing on Bird Creek when I least expected it. I usually fish it when I'm heading to or returning from the Kenai Peninsula and not in a hurry. I often stop to take a look at the water and then spot a few fish being caught, which always gives me the twinge to wet a line. But if I spot fat silvers on the move or tucked behind rocks I know the action can be spectacular. At those times, I'm lucky if I get to camp or the airport with even minutes to spare, still wishing I'd devoted more time to fishing this stream.

A campground a half-mile south of the mouth of Bird Creek makes this a popular tourist fishery.

Stream Facts: Bird Creek

Seasons

- Open year-round to fishing for salmon (other than king salmon) 16 inches or longer from its mouth upstream 500 yards. The remainder of the drainage is closed to salmon fishing year-round.

Special Regulations

- Upstream of the ADF&G cable above the Seward Highway, all land is private.

Fish

- Silver, chum, pink, and red salmon

River Characteristics

- Bird Creek is very fast and clear. Limited holding water makes this a competitive stream to fish. The angling will be shoulder to shoulder during the peak of the silver run. On high tides, the creek is unfishable.

Fishing Access

- Twenty-five miles south of Anchorage, right on the Seward Highway.

Maps

- Alaska Road & Recreation Maps, Anchorage and Vicinity; *Alaska Atlas and Gazetteer*, pages 71 and 83

Glacier Creek

The aptly named Glacier Creek is the next fishable water as you continue south on the Seward Highway. Fed by a labyrinth of glaciers hung high in the mountains of Chugach State Park, the creek crosses beneath the Seward Highway at mile 89.7, at the town of Girdwood. An access road between the Girdwood turnoff and the creek itself—on the east side of the highway—makes reaching Glacier Creek simple. Park on this access road and simply walk upstream to reach good fishing. (You'll be on an improved private road where the landowners have allowed access in past years.)

The first big hole that silver salmon gravitate to lies just upstream of the railroad bridge, about a quarter-mile from the Seward Highway bridge. This honeyhole can be packed with silvers, humpies, and even reds. Dolly Varden in the 20-inch class are also very common here, providing fly anglers with plenty of action. When the silver salmon are in, this creek can yield outstanding fishing and the pressure by nonresidents is often surprisingly light.

From this first hole, continue wading upstream to access even more fishing opportunities. Concentrate your efforts where clear-flowing feeder creeks enter this heavily glaciated stream. Due to the lack of visibility and the number of deep holes present throughout the creek, wade fishing can be a challenge. To put it more bluntly, flyfishing can be tough. If you're not against working eggs with a drift or spinning outfit, this would be a good place to give them a try.

The deep, silted holes are perfect holding water for salmon, but with visibility so restricted, it's tough to elicit a bite on artificial gear. But salmon, being the chemical junkies they are, thrive on scents, and anglers can use this to their advantage. Cured eggs with a dab of artificial scent placed on them can be just the ticket in these spots.

But if you're a flyfishing purist, there are specific conditions you can look for in Glacier Creek that will still lead to successful hookups. In addition to feeder streams entering the creek, don't overlook grassy bogs growing along the shorelines. Natural seeps of fresh water often trickle into the main creek, nourishing streamside vegetation in these areas. And this fresh water will bring salmon tight to the bank. Such sites are often passed over by anglers and can yield some great flyfishing opportunities.

Glacier Creek maintains a uniform character throughout its length. Deep holes, a streambed of rocks and large boulders, and heavy silting are the norm. New rainfall can boost the bite on this creek, though, as long as the rain doesn't add too much to the siltation and water level. When a freshet does come, hitting the mouths of clear-flowing tributaries will be particularly productive.

California Creek

California Creek, one of the main tributaries of Glacier Creek, offers good salmon fishing near its mouth, which is located just east of the railroad bridge. A Fish and Game marker sits 25 yards above the confluence where California Creek feeds into Glacier. Up to these markers, fishing is currently open year-round for salmon 16 inches or longer, except king salmon 20 inches or longer. Above the markers, fishing is open from January 1 through September 30.

California Creek itself also offers very good angling. This beautiful shallow little creek is barely ankle deep near the mouth, but it gains a bit of depth upstream. It winds its way beneath overhanging alders, and the good gravel bottom makes it a fun place to sight fish for silvers. Make sure your reel has a good drag system on it, though, because with no deep holes the salmon will rip you up and down the stream as they attempt to escape.

On even-numbered years, the humpy salmon fishing can be phenomenal in California Creek, to the point that they make reaching any silvers nearly impossible. But if you're looking to target humpies close to the city, this a prime spot unknown to even some of the locals in the area.

Glo-Bugs are good Dolly flies all season long.

Stream Facts: Glacier Creek

Seasons

- From its mouth upstream to the ADF&G markers 25 yards above the confluence of California Creek, Glacier Creek drainage is open year-round to salmon fishing (16 inches or longer), except king salmon 20 inches or longer. Upstream of these ADF&G markers, the salmon season is open from January 1 to September 30.

- In the California Creek drainage, from its confluence with Glacier Creek upstream 25 yards to the ADF&G markers above the confluence, the season is open year-round for salmon 16 inches or longer, except for king salmon 20 inches or longer. Above these ADF&G markers, the salmon season is open from January 1 to September 30.

Special Regulations

- Daily limits of salmon 16 inches or longer, except king salmon 20 inches or longer, are three per day, three in possession, of which only two per day, two in possession may be silver salmon.

Fish

- Silver, pink, and red salmon and Dolly Varden

River Characteristics

- Heavy silting makes for tough flyfishing on Glacier Creek. Deep holes and fast runs are the norm. Try clear-water tributaries. Dolly Varden fishing is good throughout.

Fishing and Access

- Glacier Creek sits at mile 89.7 on the Seward Highway, at the town of Girdwood. Park along the access road between the Girdwood turnoff and the creek itself, east of the highway. Walk upstream to reach good fishing.

Maps

- Alaska Road & Recreation Maps, Anchorage and Vicinity; *Alaska Atlas and Gazetteer*, page 71

Peterson Creek (mouth)

Located approximately five miles south of Glacier Creek, Peterson Creek can be seen running beneath the Seward Highway. This is a clear-flowing stream that empties into a graveled delta in Turnagain Arm. While the creek doesn't get a run of silvers, if your timing is right the fishing can be exceptional in the delta. On a low tide, big and flashy saltwater streamers can be worked over the gravel far out into the mouth. It helps to have a shooting head attached to your fly line because the objective is to reach the edge where fresh water meets silt. Great numbers of silver salmon gather on this edge at low tide.

You can often spot silvers holding here in big, dark schools. If you do, waste no time slipping on the waders and making your way onto the gravel, where the fish are. You want to hit these fish on the low tide, before the raging waters start closing in. And those incoming tides move quickly. Fishing here is a short-term proposition, but it can be fantastic. This is a secret spot known mostly to locals, so don't tell people you heard about this one from me...

Twentymile River

Although we're starting to get farther from Anchorage, Twentymile River is another fishery within easy reach of the city. This is the only area river where fishing opportunities can only be accessed by boat, and only by experienced boaters at that. And it's the last river directly off the Seward Highway that we'll look at in this chapter—the remainder of the Seward Highway fisheries are covered in detail with the Kenai Peninsula.

Twentymile River, or Twentymile Creek as it's often referred to, can be found at mile 80.7 on the Seward Highway. The lush setting of the Twentymile is a sight to behold. The green grass seems to glow in the sunlight, and moose can frequently be seen feeding in the area.

An unimproved boat launch is located directly off the highway in plain view. Motorized boats are the only way to go here, and unless you're out with someone who knows the river, I'd even recommend avoiding it with a prop setup. Jet sleds are ideal, and more and more airboats are making their way onto Twentymile River these days. If a prop motor is your only option, be sure to bring a spare, or two.

Proceed with utmost caution if you launch at the roadside ramp on low tide, as there's a severe drop-off that can swallow your trailer, not to mention your rig, if you're not paying attention. The water near the launch is often too laden with silt to consistently produce fish, so head quickly upstream where the water runs a little cleaner.

If you're heading up on a low tide, be alert for the remnants of pilings from an old railroad bridge that was removed years ago. These hidden pilings claim boats every season, so go slow. Once clear of the pilings, stay to the outside edge of the bends in the river; this is a good idea when traveling both up and downstream. Even the middle of this fast-flowing river can be heavily silted and extremely shallow, so take extra care to stick to the deep slots, even if running a jet sled. Due to the lack of visibility in most sections of the river, you won't be able to see bottom.

But the great thing about the Twentymile is that you need not go far to find fish. There's a small slough about 2 miles upstream from the launch that you'll want to hit. If you can locate fish moving here, you'll be well rewarded. It's best to hit this spot on a rising tide, as the water will turn murky later in the tide change.

As with many silt-infested streams in the area, the key to finding fish in the Twentymile is to concentrate your angling in areas where clear tributaries make their way into the river. Salmon will congregate here to hold in cleaner waters that are ideal for aiding in their transition from salt to fresh water. You can often sight fish for suspended fish during times of good water clarity near these tributaries. Simply casting streamers in front of holding fish can be productive, and it's always a thrill to actually see fish take your fly.

If you run into water with low visibility, try increasing the size of the fly and experiment with retrieves of different depths. Sink-tip lines can make the difference here, as they allow you to cover more water. And while I always try to flyfish first, it's not a bad idea to bring along a spinning rod with some lures or bait. When you're in an exotic locale like Alaska it pays to be fully prepared. If that means setting the fly rod down and tossing some bait or a coho lure into silted waters, so be it.

In the fall, a small number of fishable red and chum salmon make their way up Twentymile, and the silver salmon fishing can be outstanding here, as well. In fact, the Twentymile supports the largest wild stock of Anchorage-area silvers, with some 2,000 native fish harvested each year. If you've ever aspired to do battle with Alaska's notorious silver salmon, this can be as good as it gets.

Pink salmon also make their way into the Twentymile, and they can be well worth the effort if multiple hookups are what you're after. For big Dollys, early spring is the time to be on the water.

For traveling anglers based in Anchorage, the Twentymile is a great, often overlooked, fishery. It's far enough out of Anchorage to remove you from the bustling activities of the big city, yet you can still be back in town to meet the Mrs. for a fine dinner. The only drawback is that you need a good boat and the know-how to navigate these tricky waters.

Stream Facts: Twentymile River

Seasons

- The Twentymile River drainage is open year-round to fishing for all species but king salmon 20 inches or longer, with the following two exceptions: Upstream from ADF&G markers 10 miles upstream of the Seward Highway, fishing the Twentymile drainage is open for all species except king salmon 20 inches or longer from January 1 to July 13; In the Upper Carmen and Glacier River drainages, upstream from the ADF&G markers at their confluence, the fishing season is open for all species except king salmon 20 inches or longer from January 1 to July 13.

Special Regulations

- The Twentymile River is closed year-round to fishing for king salmon 20 inches or longer.

- The daily limit for other salmon 16 inches or longer is three per day, three in possession, of which only two per day, two in possession may be silver salmon.

Fish

- Silver, red, chum, and pink salmon, and Dolly Varden

River Characteristics

- The Twentymile River is a heavily silted glacier-fed stream. Anglers can access good fishing by boat only. When navigating, stick to the wide, outside corners of the river, so as to avoid sand bars that build up just under the surface on the inside corners and well into midstream.

Fishing and Boating Access

- First timers to the river will want to have an experienced local along for guidance. Concentrate fishing efforts on areas around the mouths of clear tributaries. Fish anywhere you find clear water. This is a wide river, but it's surprisingly shallow in spots. There's a boat ramp at mile 80.7 on the Seward Highway. Motorized boats are the only way to go, jet sleds being the best choice.

Maps

- *Alaska Atlas and Gazetteer*, page 71

TAGGING ALL FIVE SALMON SPECIES AROUND ANCHORAGE

The many streams and rivers flowing through or near Anchorage provide anglers with a unique opportunity to take all five species of Pacific salmon. Though not every stream is open to all salmon fishing, anglers can conceivably catch all five species in one trip—if their timing is right on a few select waters.

The toughest of the five to catch is the king salmon. This is because their run starts early in the Anchorage area and ends right about the time the other four species are making their way into the rivers. And because Eagle River king salmon fishing closes in June, the only option for anglers to score on a king in Anchorage later in the summer lies in Ship Creek. The king season on the Ship ends in mid-July, and many anglers focus their efforts on kings at this time.

Once you've landed an Anchorage-area king, nailing the other four species is mostly a combination of luck and timing. The pink salmon would be next in line, and as they primarily run on even-numbered years, you have to make sure your trip falls in the right year. If you are in town on an even-numbered year, head to Bird Creek, which has the best pink fishing in the area. The peak of the pink run is around mid-July, and pulling one from the creek should be no problem.

Since you're already on the banks of Bird Creek, this is also the best opportunity to tag a chum, or dog, salmon. Twice as many chums are taken from Bird Creek than any other Anchorage-area stream, with an average of 300 coming to net each season. These fish can be hit or miss, but I've seen plenty of the mottled-bodied salmon taken from this creek.

Sockeye, or red, salmon are next on the list. While Bird Creek holds a small run, your best bet at landing an Anchorage-area red is at the mouth of Sixmile Creek on Elmendorf Air Force Base. This fishery peaks in mid-July, and casting flies into the saltwater is one of the best ways to tie into these hard-fighting, excellent-eating fish.

The fifth and final species, the silver salmon, is the easiest to come by. Like the chum salmon, silvers begin arriving in Anchorage in mid- to late July, peaking in August and early September. A few streams carry silvers well into October, but if you're looking to score on all five species, you must target the early fish.

Your best crack at silver salmon will come in Ship Creek, thanks to a highly successful hatchery-release program. Bird and Campbell Creeks also receive good silver runs. The Twentymile and Placer Rivers offer good silver fishing, as does Placer Creek to the south.

Spawning sockeye salmon can be observed in a few Anchorage-area streams.

Anchorage-Area Stocked Lakes

The many stocked lakes in and around Anchorage are worth mentioning along with the better rivers and streams in the area. The ADF&G goes to great effort to consistently keep fish numbers up in these waters. Most Anchorage-area lakes do not support a wild, natural population of fish, but all area lakes, with the exception of Campbell Lake, are open year-round to sport fishing.

Due to their success with raising arctic char—and due to the success of anglers catching them—the ADF&G is shifting their focus to this fish species rather than rainbow trout. Rainbow trout are, however, the first fish to be stocked in Anchorage lakes, usually prior to Memorial Day and again around the Fourth of July. The size of these planter trout range from 8 to 10 inches, with some 20-inch fish in the mix, as well. Small nymph patterns are very effective for taking char and trout in these waters.

Landlocked king salmon are also planted in many area lakes. These fish typically range from 7 to 10 inches long, and they are usually added by November to enhance ice fishing throughout the winter months. Holdover fish are routinely taken by summer and fall anglers.

Unfortunately, the illegal introduction of northern pike into many area lakes has affected the stocking program of trout, char, and salmon. Because pike are such voracious feeders, it's not wise for the ADF&G to invest money and effort into raising additional fish for stocking programs when they know the pike will quickly wipe them out. But as a result of the illegal plantings, there are some exceptionally good pike lakes to be fished. Large, flashy streamers stripped across the surface can be deadly when pike are in the shallows.

Anchorage-Area Lakes

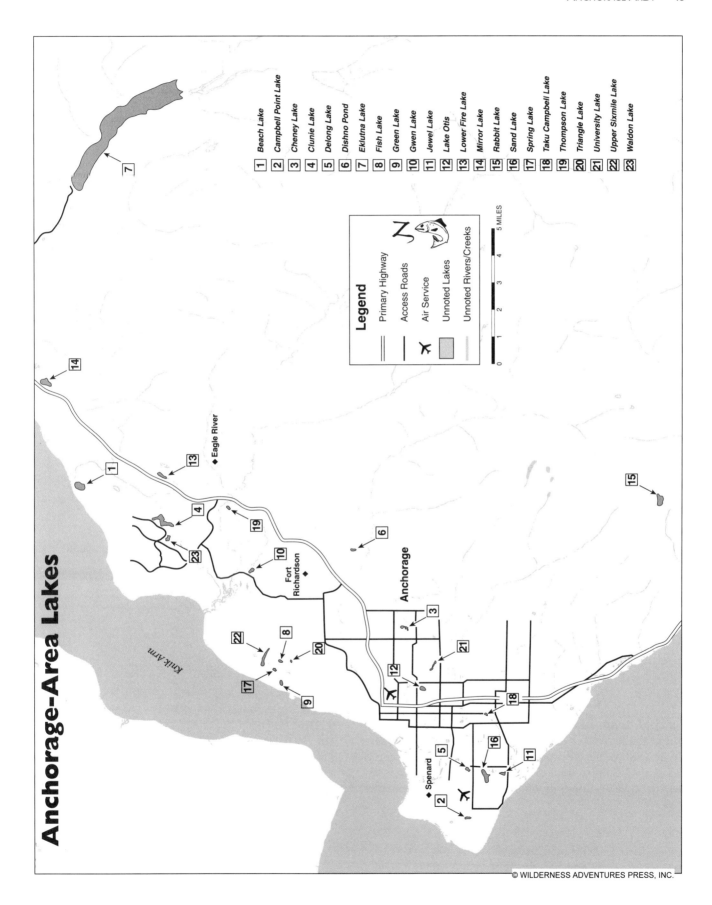

Legend

‖	Primary Highway
	Access Roads
✈	Air Service
▨	Unnoted Lakes
	Unnoted Rivers/Creeks

0 1 2 3 4 5 MILES

1 Beach Lake
2 Campbell Point Lake
3 Cheney Lake
4 Clunie Lake
5 Delong Lake
6 Dishno Pond
7 Eklutna Lake
8 Fish Lake
9 Green Lake
10 Gwen Lake
11 Jewel Lake
12 Lake Otis
13 Lower Fire Lake
14 Mirror Lake
15 Rabbit Lake
16 Sand Lake
17 Spring Lake
18 Taku Campbell Lake
19 Thompson Lake
20 Triangle Lake
21 University Lake
22 Upper Sixmile Lake
23 Waldon Lake

Knik Arm

◆ Eagle River

◆ Fort Richardson

Anchorage

◆ Spenard

For lakes on Fort Richardson Army Base, anglers must check in at the gate located north of the Arctic Valley Road exit off Glenn Highway. A short orientation course is required prior to fishing the lakes on this property, and at the completion, anglers will receive a free seasonal fishing pass for the base. Maps of base-area lakes are also provided. Call 907-384-0431 for more information.

For anglers looking to fish the lakes situated on Elmendorf Air Force Base, check in at the gate off North Boniface Parkway. You can gain permission to fish the base lakes here, and maps are also provided. Call 907-552-2436 for more information.

Bank fishing can be effective on most Anchorage lakes. Getting that fly tight to the bank, near overhanging foliage, is often the key. If you have a small raft, belly boat, canoe or jonboat, though, you'll improve your chances of getting into fish. If you'd like to rent a craft for use on the area ponds, Alaska Raft and Kayak at 401 West Tudor Road in Anchorage can set you up.

What follows is an alphabetical listing of the stocked lakes in the Anchorage-bowl area, along with the species present and directions for how to access each lake.

Alder Pond

Rainbow trout are available in this pond, which sits 48 miles south of Anchorage. Travel south on the Seward Highway, then turn east on Portage Valley Road and continue 1.4 miles to a dirt road leading off the south side of the road. Go 0.1 mile on the dirt road to reach Alder Pond.

Beach Lake

Rainbow trout, arctic grayling, and landlocked king salmon are available in this lake. Beach Lake is located 21 miles north of Anchorage. Travel north on the Glenn Highway, then take the South Birchwood exit. Go north past Chugiak High School, 0.9 mile to Beach Lake Road. Stay on Beach Lake Road for approximately 2 miles, where the road ends at Beach Lake. Arctic grayling, which love dry flies, are stocked in this lake every odd-numbered year.

Campbell Point Lake

Rainbow trout, arctic char, and landlocked king salmon are available in this lake, which is situated on the east-central side of the city, within Kincaid Park. On Raspberry Road, go 1.5 miles west of the intersection of Raspberry and Sand Lakes Roads and follow the signs directly to the lake.

Cheney Lake

Rainbow trout, northern pike, and landlocked king salmon are available in this lake in the heart of Anchorage. Go 1 mile west of Muldoon Road, between East Northern Lights Boulevard and DeBarr Road. Turn on Beaver Place, which leads to the city park and the western shores of the lake. To access the eastern shore by way of 16th Avenue, turn off Beaver Place and head south on Otter Street. Go one block, turn west on Foothill Drive, and continue to the end of the street. Foot trails lead to the lake. In the past, this lake has been overrun with pike; thus trout stocking efforts were put on hold.

Clunie Lake

Located on Fort Richardson Army Base, Clunie hosts rainbow trout, lake trout, arctic char, and landlocked salmon.

Delong Lake

Rainbow trout and landlocked king salmon are available in Delong, which is close to the airport. Delong Lake Park can be found on the west side of Jewel Lake Road, two blocks north of the corner of Jewel Lake and Raspberry Roads, on 63rd Avenue.

Many Anchorage-area lakes are planted with rainbows, creating a dependable fishery.

Dishno Lake

Dishno holds rainbow trout and can be reached by heading north on the Glenn Highway. Cross over Ship Creek, turning right on Ski Bowl Road. Go approximately 2 miles and you'll find the lake on the left side of the road.

Eklutna Lake

Rainbow trout are available on this large lake. Travel north on the Glenn Highway to the town of Eklutna. Turn right on Eklutna Lake Road and follow it approximately 8 miles to the west edge of Eklutna Lake. Lakeside Hiking Trail borders the northern shore of the lake and leads to a campsite situated approximately 9 miles from the trailhead.

Fish Lake

Rainbow trout are available in Fish Lake, which is located on Elmendorf Air Force Base.

Green Lake

Green lake hosts rainbow trout and landlocked king salmon and is located on Elmendorf Air Force Base.

Gwen Lake

Rainbow trout are available on this lake, which is located on Fort Richardson Army Base.

Hillberg Lake

Rainbow trout and landlocked king salmon are available on this Elmendorf Air Force Base lake.

Jewel Lake

Rainbow trout and landlocked king salmon are available on this central city lake. Go west on Dimond Boulevard, about 3.25 miles west of New Seward Highway. Turn north on Jewel Lake Road and go 0.25 mile. Turn west on 88th Avenue. You can also find parking on the southern lakeshore off Dimond Boulevard, just west of Jewel Lake Road.

Lake Otis

Lake Otis holds rainbow trout. It's situated between Northern Lights Boulevard and 36th Avenue, off Stanford Drive by way of Carlson Park.

Lower Fire Lake

Rainbow trout and northern pike are available here. This lake is located 14 miles north on the Glenn Highway. Take North Eagle River exit and go south 0.1 mile to Old Glenn Highway. Go northeast 0.5 mile to West Lake Ridge Road, then go another 0.1 mile to the lake.

Mirror Lake

Rainbow trout, arctic char, and landlocked king salmon are found in this easily reached lake. Travel north to mile 23.6 on the Glenn Highway. Mirror Lake sits on the east side of the road.

Starr Lake

Located on Fort Richardson Army Base, Starr holds rainbow trout.

Rabbit Lake

Rainbow trout are available in this hike-in lake. Travel south on the Seward Highway for 15 miles to the trailhead at McHugh Creek State Recreation Area. Rabbit Lake sits 7 miles up the Chugach State Park hiking trail.

Sand Lake

Rainbow trout, lake trout, northern pike, and landlocked salmon are available in this urban lake. Sand Lake is located west of Jewel Lake Road, between Dimond Boulevard and Raspberry Road. A foot trail on Caravelle Drive, west of Jewel Lake Road, leads to the northeast shore of the lake. The eastern shoreline can be accessed behind Sand Lake Elementary School. A small boat launch is situated on the canal on the south end of the lake, which can be reached by way of 80th Avenue, east off Sand Lake Road. Small canoes and boats can be carried over a berm to the canal. The shores surrounding this lake are private, so park only along the public roadway.

Spring Lake

Rainbow trout and landlocked king salmon are available in this lake, which is located on Elmendorf Air Force Base.

Taku Campbell Lake

Rainbow trout, northern pike, and landlocked king salmon occupy this lake, which sits on the southeast edge of Anchorage. Head west on Dimond Boulevard, traveling approximately 0.75 mile to King Street. Go north on King Street, then west on 76th Avenue to the city park. This is another lake that received an illegal introduction of northern pike, so stockings of trout and salmon have been put on hold in recent years.

Tangle Pond

Tangle Pond is located 48 miles south of Anchorage and holds rainbow trout. Head out of town on the Seward Highway, then turn on Portage Valley Road. About 3.2 miles up Portage Valley Road you'll find a pullout on the north side of the road that sits beside Tangle Pond.

Thompson Lake

Rainbow trout are available in this lake, which is located on Fort Richardson Army Base.

Triangle Lake

Rainbow trout are available here. Triangle is located on Elmendorf Air Force Base.

University Lake

Rainbow trout are available in this APU lake. You'll find it by heading east on University Lake Drive, off Bragaw between University Drive and Tudor Road.

Upper Sixmile Lake

Rainbow trout are available here. The lake is located on Elmendorf Air Force Base.

Waldon Lake

Rainbow trout are available on this lake, which is located on Fort Richardson Army Base.

Willow Pond

A 48-mile drive south of Anchorage on the Seward Highway will bring you to Willow Pond. Turn east on Portage Valley Road, continuing 0.8 mile to a dirt road on the north side of the road. Go 0.2 mile north on the dirt road, which leads to Willow Pond. Rainbow trout are found here.

Scott Haugen shows off a pink salmon.

SALMON VIEWING AREAS AROUND ANCHORAGE

One unique aspect of many locations in and around Anchorage is the opportunity to view all five species of salmon on their spawning beds. This is something many anglers read about and see on TV, but rarely get the chance to observe in person. The fact that so many easy-to-access streams flow through the Anchorage bowl makes it an ideal location for travelers to observe one of nature's most magnificent rituals. Beginning in early June and running through the month of October, there are five primary sites that allow observers to witness spawning salmon.

One of the more popular viewing destinations is located approximately ½ mile upstream from the mouth of Ship Creek at the Chugach Dam. To get there, follow E Street north of 4th Avenue. King salmon can be seen on their spawning beds at the dam.

On Elmendorf Air Force Base, king salmon spawning activity can also be viewed at the ADF&G hatchery, which is approximately 2.5 miles from the mouth of Ship Creek. Go to the corner of Reeve Boulevard and Post Road to access the hatchery.

Just south of Anchorage on the Seward Highway you'll find Potter Marsh. In addition to being a popular site for birders, silver salmon can be seen spawning in the calm, shallow waters along the edge of the marsh. A boardwalk allows observers to walk over the water and watch fish spawn directly underfoot.

Campbell Creek is another salmon spawning stream that's easily accessed. Turn south off Tudor Road onto Folker Street and follow it to the creek. Here, salmon can be observed spawning in the shallows. They can also be seen on the North Fork of Campbell Creek above Bicentennial Park.

In the South Fork of Eagle Creek, between the falls and its confluence with the Eagle River, is another great spot. Salmon can be followed at the Williwaw Creek viewing area in Portage Valley, which is located approximately 46 miles south of Anchorage on the Seward Highway.

Fly-In Fishing Trips from Anchorage

Floatplanes, commonly referred to as air taxis, access Anchorage-area lakes, waters on the Kenai Peninsula and Kodiak Island, and rivers and lakes across Cook Inlet, as well as areas farther afield such as Bristol Bay, King Salmon, Lake Iliamna, and Lake Clark.

On average, air taxi rates run about $50 per hour, per person. Parties of four are the norm. These trips usually depart the Anchorage area early in the morning, returning in late afternoon or early evening. If you want to camp on such trips and have meals provided for you, tack on another $100 per day, per person, which includes all camping gear.

When driving is not an option, an air taxi can deliver you to myriad lakes and streams, from Seward to Dutch Harbor to the Talkeetna River. For a listing of floatplane fishing operators, refer to "Fishing Guide Services" in the Anchorage hub city information.

Flyfishing Techniques

The rivers and small streams around the Anchorage area can be ideal for fly anglers when conditions are right—and when there's enough elbowroom to fish. Nymphing is the favorite method of many anglers, and it's one of the most productive means of flyfishing these streams. Drifting and stripping wet flies is also effective for the salmon, trout, and char you'll find in the area.

Because many area streams are shallow, floating lines are usually all you'll need to work nymphs and wet flies below the surface. This is particularly true for streams in which silver, red, and pink salmon are traveling close to shore or when wade fishing for rainbows and Dollys in pocket water.

One of the most important things anglers need to remember is to let the fly drift downstream on a "relaxed" line. A floating line or 5-foot sink-tip line is an excellent choice in these waters. When bank fishing, cast the fly out to the desired distance and allow it to float naturally downstream. The objective is to keep the fly moving at the same rate as the stream. To do this, you'll need to mend your line constantly.

Basic flick-of-the-wrist mends are all that are needed. Simply roll your wrist over, which should generate rod-tip movement to lift the line and gently lay it back down on the surface. You should try to create a serpentine, slack effect in the line that will allow it to be carried downstream in front of you without drag. In many of the smaller rivers you'll be fishing in the Anchorage area, a good mend is considered more important than a long cast. Making a picture-perfect cast 30 yards out to midstream may look impressive, but isn't necessary if fish are holding and traveling close to shore.

Bring a pair of good hip or chest waders, as one of the best fishing approaches is to cover as much water as you can. Don't waste too much time standing in one spot, unless of course you're fishing near the mouth of a river and waiting on the arrival of fresh fish on a high incoming tide.

Being mobile is often to your advantage. If the fishing action is fast, move slow; if the action is slow, move fast.

Bushplane operations around Anchorage offer fly-in fishing excursions to much of the surrounding region.

Salmon Drift-Fishing Tactics

Because many Anchorage-area rivers run a bit turbid and may be crowded with drift fishermen, having such gear handy and knowing how to use it properly may make the difference between catching fish or going home empty-handed. While we'd all prefer to cast flies, conditions sometimes make rolling bait and/or drift bobbers along the bottom the only effective choice. If you're only able to fish for salmon close to Anchorage, you may not have the luxury of time to head farther afield in search of flyfishable waters.

Rigging for drift fishing is easy. It can be done in several ways, but the two methods that follow are the most basic and effective. The first method involves the use of hollow pencil lead. Simply tie your mainline to a size 7 barrel swivel, leaving a 4- to 6-inch tag on the end. Then pinch the appropriate amount of hollow core pencil lead on this tag. (Spools of lead can be purchased at local sporting good stores and tackle shops.) If you get hung up on the rocks, the lead often pulls free, releasing the rest of your terminal gear.

The second method requires the use of a bank sinker. What size bank sinker you use will depend on the water conditions being fished. You may be hitting a 12-foot-

Working flashy colored flies in stream mouths is a good approach for targeting salmon around Anchorage.

deep swirling hole that requires 3 ounces of lead. Minutes later you may be in 3 feet of fast-moving water that requires nothing more than a ½ ounce of lead. In other words, if using bank sinkers, be sure to bring along a wide variety to meet your fishing needs. If you skimp on the lead when drift fishing you might as well not be fishing, as you won't draw many strikes if you're not getting down to the bottom where salmon lay up.

When rigging to fish a bank sinker, tie the mainline to one end of a size 2 or 4 three-way swivel. The leader attaches to the opposite end of the mainline. On the third eye, tie a 4- to 8-inch piece of line, to which the bank sinker will be attached.

With both rigging styles, the idea is to bounce or roll the bait along the bottom. It may take a few casts to determine the right amount of lead to use, and this is an important, often overlooked, step. If the sinker is hanging up, switch to lighter lead. If it drifts too fast, without touching bottom, add more lead. You want the lead to occasionally tic the bottom, staying down where the salmon are.

The rest of the terminal tackle is the same for both sinker systems. A leader extending 18 to 36 inches is most common. For the salmon you'll find in these waters, a 3/0 hook is a good all-around choice. Tie the hook to the leader using a knot that will create an egg loop. An Egg Loop Knot and a Fly Knot are the two most common knots used for this type of fishing, creating the perfect loop to hold bait-sized pieces of roe in place. (Stop in at local tackle shops for help if these knots are unfamiliar.)

Tie a piece of yarn to the leader above the eye of the hook. Yarn serves two primary purposes: to provide color that attracts fish and to hang in the teeth of fish once they bite. The color yarn can vary, but reds and oranges are most popular for salmon. Observing what color other anglers are using can pay off, too. Yarn alone can catch salmon, so don't go without this item.

Above the yarn, slide a drift bobber onto the leader. The drift bobber also serves two purposes: to visually appeal to fish and to keep the bait and hook floating off the bottom. Drift bobbers are made of foam or cork that floats. This is what makes them so effective for presenting baits while drift fishing. Drift bobbers have become so advanced that many anglers now use them alone, without any bait.

Corkies, Spin-N-Glos, and Cheaters are among the most popular salmon drift bobbers used in Alaska. If using a 3/0 hook, a size 2 or 4 Spin-N-Glo is a good choice. For Corkies on this hook, a size 4 is the way to go.

Cheaters have no wings while Flashing and Spinning Cheaters have wings in an assortment of colors. Size 4 and size 6 Cheaters are a good choice when fishing a 3/0 hook. The metallic prism wings are popular in Alaska, especially in silted rivers. In fact, I caught my biggest Alaska king, a 70-pounder, on a silver metallic-winged Flashing and Spinning Cheater with a pink body.

When using a spinning drift bobber such as the Spin-N-Glo or Flashing and Spinning Cheater, it's a good idea to first thread one or two 4mm beads onto your leader, followed by the drift bobber. The beads keep the drift bobber spinning by providing a hard surface for it to spin against. If the drift bobber is threaded directly onto the leader without the beads, it will ball up and stop spinning if it comes in contact with the yarn. The more action you can impart, the greater the likelihood of attracting a bite.

When changing hook sizes, be certain to match the drift bobber accordingly. You want the gap of the hook exposed, so when the fish attacks you can bury the hook. A drift bobber that's too large will obscure the point of the hook, meaning the fish will not be hooked.

Drift fishing is probably the most popular fishing technique for Anchorage-area streams. It's an easy method to learn, and allows anglers to fish shoulder-to-shoulder with minimal hangups. When everyone works together, casting upstream in sequence and letting the drift move downstream, a high number of anglers can fit into a small area. It may not seem ideal to flyfishers, but sometimes it's the only viable option.

Once you get the hang of it, this presentation is easy, but until that time, multiple hangups are the rule. When "combat" fishing, constant hangups can greatly impede the fishing action for you and for neighboring anglers. The more proficient you are at this technique, the better for everyone.

Another bait-fishing technique that's popular in Anchorage-area rivers is floating cured salmon roe beneath a bobber. The advantage of this technique is that it allows bait to be fished just off the bottom, without the worry of hanging up. Because the depth of the bobber you're fishing can be regulated, you're in control of how deep you're fishing. The result is fewer hangups and more time with gear in the water. Of all the drift-fishing techniques, this is the easiest to learn and master, and the number of fish it yields can be amazing.

By this point, you're probably starting to question why I'm elaborating so much on drift-fishing techniques in a flyfishing book. The reason is simple. Because salmon entering Anchorage-area streams often congregate in small areas, so too do anglers. When the riverbanks are lined with drift fishermen, there's no way a fly angler can get in and cast without tying up several other driftcasters.

The only options are to relocate to another section of the stream or join the crowd and start casting bait. If you choose to move, the chances are low that you'll find a section of water teeming with salmon but not anglers. However, on some small streams, serious fly anglers will line the banks, which makes it easier for you to work into the line. Then again, if you don't find such a place, there's nothing more frustrating than helplessly watching thousands of salmon swim by as anglers yank them from the stream while you can't get into the action with a fly rod. If you've traveled a great distance to fish for Alaskan salmon and are restricted to these streams by time constraints, being prepared to try a variety of angling tactics will net the best results.

Bobber/bait-fishing is one of the more widely used ploys by local anglers and is effective on all five salmon species, especially silvers. The setup is easy and inexpensive. On an 8½- to 9½-foot, medium-to-heavy-action spinning rod spooled with adequate weight line, a bobber stop is threaded onto the mainline. Below the bobber stop, add a 3mm bead, and below that, the bobber. Choose a low-profile bobber that will ride high in the water and offer little resistance as it's carried downstream.

Tie a size 7 barrel swivel on the mainline, and attach your leader to the other end of the swivel. Leaders range anywhere from 15 to 24 inches in length and are rigged with an Egg Loop on the hook. It's a good idea to pre-tie a few dozen hooks prior to heading to the river. I even have my colored yarn tied onto the leader before hitting the river. Then, when I break off a rigging, I simply retie the prepared leader, bait the hook, and I'm fishing in less than a minute.

Long downstream drifts are possible when fishing with bobber and egg, and this works great when everyone around you is fishing the same way. If anglers below you are dragging bottom, their drift rates will be slower than yours, so be sure to keep your bobber from floating over their fishing hole or over the top of their lines. Courtesy is a must when fishing with bobber and jig in crowded conditions, as it's easy to let the rig get away from you.

Simply cast the bobber and eggs out, keeping the bail open so line can freely spool off. Using a floating mainline, such as Berkley's Fireline, is best for this technique. But don't go to sleep on the job. Keep a sharp eye on the bobber at all times and one hand on the reel. As soon as that bobber goes down, reel quickly and set the hook. It's that simple.

Before drift fishing any Anchorage-area stream, check regulations regarding the use of such gear, especially bait. Artificial scents are also considered bait, so make sure there are no emergency closures to bait-fishing on any stream you intend to fish. The ADF&G may change regulations at any time of the year through emergency orders. These orders are publicized through the ADF&G website, radio, TV, and newspapers. Tackle shops are also another great resource for regulatory changes, and it's the angler's responsibility to know all current regulations.

A variety of bunny-hair streamers have proven effective on all salmon species.

Kenai Peninsula

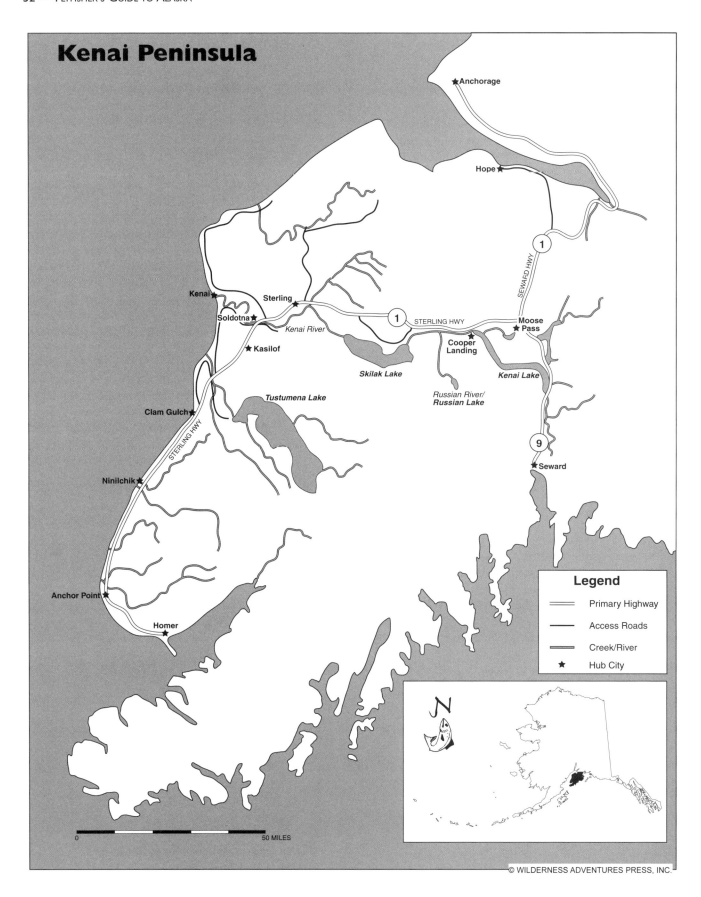

★ Anchorage

Hope ★

1 SEWARD HWY

Kenai ★

Sterling

1 STERLING HWY

Moose Pass ★

Soldotna ★

Kenai River

Cooper Landing

★ Kasilof

Skilak Lake

Kenai Lake

Tustumena Lake

Russian River/ Russian Lake

Clam Gulch ★

9

STERLING HWY

★ Seward

Ninilchik ★

Anchor Point ★

Homer ★

Legend

	Primary Highway
	Access Roads
	Creek/River
★	Hub City

N

0   50 MILES

© WILDERNESS ADVENTURES PRESS, INC.

Fishing the Kenai Peninsula

By Scott Haugen

Some of the lakes on the Kenai Peninsula are simply too large to accommodate flyfishers.

The Kenai Peninsula would have to be considered one of the world's most popular sport-fishing areas. It yields astounding numbers of fish each year to astounding crowds of anglers. If you're searching for the ultimate fish-catching experience, and don't mind summer crowds, the Kenai Peninsula is the place to be.

What is it that makes the Kenai so special? It's home to some of the most prolific salmon and trout streams on earth. Home to the world-record king salmon and various other state records, the streams and rivers of the Kenai Peninsula flow into the rich waters of Cook Inlet. And all of these wonderful fishing streams are easily accessible by road. For the traveling angler, there's no other place in the state that is so user-friendly.

With Anchorage and the town of Kenai so close and easy to fly into, anglers from around the globe can rent a vehicle and spend weeks fishing and traveling in comfort. As the road system crosses many of the best rivers and streams on its way from town to town, it's easy to plan a trip on your own or take advantage of the many resorts in the area. And depending on the time of year you choose, you can chase fish with hordes of other anglers or find complete seclusion.

On one July day, I stood on the banks of the Kasilof River, surrounded by anglers. Everyone was catching salmon, so the mood was relaxed and happy. The anglers wading within earshot of me represented seven different countries. While some may complain at having to fish so closely with other anglers, none of us could have been more pleased with the experience that day. We all chose to fish the same section of water for the simple reason that this was where the bulk of the salmon were congregating. We shared fishing secrets unique to our respective home waters, swapped tales, and truly enjoyed one another's company. If approached with an open mindset, fishing among crowds can be quite gratifying.

On some rivers, such as the Kenai during the peak of the king salmon run, escaping crowds is unrealistic. If beating that world-record king is your goal, the only way it's likely to happen is by battling boats on the lower river. But when fishing in this way, nearly every nonresident angler will hire a guide. And it's the guide who does the battling, not the angler. This is part of what you pay a guide to do.

By the same token, if it's seclusion you desire that too can be had on the Kenai Peninsula. I've spent my fair share of early September days fishing rivers and streams along the peninsula where I never saw a single angler. Not only did I have these waters to myself, I caught all the steelhead, silver salmon, and Dolly Varden I could handle.

Don't let the size of the Kenai Peninsula intimidate you; much of its central interior is covered by the Harding Ice Field. From Homer northeast to Seward, roads are nonexistent. Along the southern and southwestern

RUN TIMING FOR KENAI PENINSULA FRESHWATER FISHERIES

Kenai River

Species	Jan	Feb	Mar	Apr	May	Jun	Jul	Aug	Sep	Oct	Nov	Dec
King Salmon	-	-	-	-	++	+++	+++	-	-	-	-	-
Sockeye Salmon	-	-	-	-	-	-/+	+++	+++	-	-	-	-
Pink Salmon	-	-	-	-	-	-	+++	+++	++	-	-	-
Rainbow Trout	-	-	-	-	+	++	+++	+++	+++	++	+	-
Dolly Varden	-	-	-	-	+	++	+++	+++	+++	++	+	-

Russian River

Species	Jan	Feb	Mar	Apr	May	Jun	Jul	Aug	Sep	Oct	Nov	Dec
Sockeye Salmon	-	-	-	-	-	+/+++	+++	+++	-	-	-	-
Rainbow Trout	-	-	-	-	-	-	+++	+++	+++	++	-	-
Dolly Varden	-	-	-	-	-	-	+++	+++	+++	++	-	-

Kasilof River

Species	Jan	Feb	Mar	Apr	May	Jun	Jul	Aug	Sep	Oct	Nov	Dec
King Salmon	-	-	-	-	++	+++	+++	-	-	-	-	-

Anchor River, Deep Creek, Ninilchik River

Species	Jan	Feb	Mar	Apr	May	Jun	Jul	Aug	Sep	Oct	Nov	Dec
King Salmon	-	-	-	-	++	+++	+++	-	-	-	-	-
Coho Salmon	-	-	-	-	-	-	-	+++	++/+	+/-	-	-
Rainbow Trout	-	-	-	-	-/+	+	+++	+++	+++	++	+/-	-
Dolly Varden	-	-	-	-	-/+	+	+++	+++	+++	++	+/-	-
Steelhead	-	-	-	-	-	-	-	-/++	+++	+++	++/+	-

+++ Excellent   ++ Good   + Fair   - Nonexistent/Closed Season

GENERAL RUN TIMING FOR KENAI PENINSULA FRESHWATER FISHERIES

Species	Jan	Feb	Mar	Apr	May	Jun	Jul	Aug	Sep	Oct	Nov	Dec
King Salmon	-	-	-	-	++	+++	+++	-	-	-	-	-
Sockeye Salmon	-	-	-	-	++	+++	+++	++/+	-	-	-	-
Coho Salmon	-	-	-	-	-	++	+++	+++	++	+	+/-
Pink Salmon	-	-	-	-	-	-	++	+++	++	-	-	-
Steelhead Trout	-	-	-	-	-	-	+	++	+++	+++	++	+/-
Rainbow Trout	+	+	+	+	++	++	+++	+++	+++	+++	++	+
Dolly Varden	+	+	+	+	++	++	+++	+++	+++	+++	++	+
Lake Trout	+	+	+	+	+++	++	++	++	+++	+++	+++	++
Northern Pike	+	+	+	+	+++	++	++	++	+++	+++	+++	++
Grayling	+	+	+	+	+	+	++	+++	+++	++	+	+

fringes, access to fishing is by boat or floatplane, and that's only if you can get to areas not tied up in private native land settlements or if weather permits traveling. In other words, while the peninsula covers a lot of territory only a portion of it is fishable.

Still, a person could spend an entire lifetime fishing here and not see it all. With such vast opportunities available, some waters will be neglected in this book; there's just too many. But that's the beauty of fishing in this great land, for an angler can still explore on his or her own, finding that one special body of water no one else seems to know about.

It should be noted that rivers and streams throughout the Kenai Peninsula can undergo emergency closures at any time. Or sections along a body of water may be closed. And regulations within any body of water may change from one year to the next. Anglers are responsible for keeping abreast of any change in the regulations. This can be done by tuning in to local radio stations, reading daily newspapers, inquiring at tackle shops, or contacting local fish and game officials. Signs noting regulation changes are often posted within campgrounds, along streams, and at access points. Always take the time to read bulletins posted on billboards when you pull into streamside parking lots.

And keep in mind that highway mileage within Alaska is calculated from the city in which the highway originates. For example, the Seward Highway originates in Seward, which sits at milepost 0 and terminates in Anchorage at milepost 127. As we'll be looking at fishing access along the Seward Highway coming from Anchorage, the mileage numbers will actually go down as we make our way toward Seward.

So let's start our journey by following the Seward and Sterling Highways and taking in the streams and rivers associated with these roads. Then we'll look at the lakes throughout the peninsula, including ones accessed by road and those to which you must hike. We'll also break down the famous Kenai canoe trails, where traveling anglers can find all the seclusion—and fishing—they've ever dreamed of.

Rainbow trout attract many anglers to the Kenai Peninsula in the fall.

There are several small streams right on the highway near Seward that offer good fishing.

SEWARD HIGHWAY: PORTAGE CREEK TO TERN LAKE

There's only one road leaving Anchorage for the Kenai Peninsula, the Seward Highway. This scenic drive takes you along the shores of Turnagain Arm where beluga whales can often be seen. When making the drive along the eastern shores of Turnagain Arm, be sure to keep an eye out for white Dall sheep feeding along cliff ledges or basking in the sun. Chances are, if you see cars pulled off the road and people craning their necks skyward, there are sheep about. If you pull off to observe these Alaskan beauties, though, be sure to get your vehicle well off the road. This is a dangerous stretch of highway.

At the end of Turnagain Arm, the Seward Highway curves back to the west, leading into the heart of the Kenai Peninsula. Along its southerly route, moose can often be seen wading in lush swamps, feasting on the rich vegetation just off the highway.

In this section, we'll look at the waters accessible by road from the town of Portage south to where the Seward Highway meets the Sterling Highway. The remainder of the Seward Highway and the Sterling Highway will be detailed in subsequent sections.

Before you even wet a line, however, you may want to stop at the world famous Portage Glacier. This massive block of ice sits just off Portage Glacier Road, south of the town of Portage. A newly constructed road now connects the Seward Highway to the town of Whittier, another place worth seeing if you're not in a rush.

But prime fishing awaits in the opposite direction. Rounding the corner of Turnagain Arm, it's hard keeping an eye on the road. Flooded fields and glacial-fed streams will keep you wondering what fish are out there. Keep in mind, however, that the farther you get into the Kenai Peninsula, the better the fishing typically gets. But if it's easy access to small-stream fishing you're after, start right at Portage Creek.

Portage Creek

Portage Creek lies at mile 79 on the Seward Highway and flows from Portage Lake before draining under the highway and into Turnagain Arm. A boat launch is located at the mouth of the creek, and Portage Glacier Road will take you to Willow Creek, a tributary to Portage Creek.

Focus your efforts in the deeper holes where fish tend to congregate in this stream. Fishing for Dolly Varden and silver and red salmon can be good here, though heavy restrictions are in place for king salmon. Camping facilities are also available on this stream.

Placer River

The Placer River sits right at the switchback of Turnagain Arm. This braided river actually crosses beneath the Seward Highway in two places, and the fishing can be good if your timing is right. Locals like to work below either bridge on a strong incoming tide. Getting that fly in the heart of the surf is imperative if you want to see fast-paced silver action. Cast directly into the rolling tide and strip Flash Flies or pink streamers. Silver salmon travel inside these rolling wakes, and fishing at either of the braided mouths can be dynamite.

If you choose to fish any of the stream mouths in Turnagain Arm, be sure you have a small can of WD-40 along. (This can be picked up in Anchorage at a Fred Meyer or Carrs store when you get your fishing license.) Dousing your reel in WD-40 immediately after fishing in salt water is very important, especially if this is going to be an early stop in your trip. The salt water in these bays—even at river mouths—can quickly eat up a reel, ruining drags overnight. Don't let this keep you from fishing these unique locations, though, just take care of your gear. Many fly anglers drive right by these streams, with little idea of how good the fishing can be.

When fishing anywhere around Turnagain Arm avoid wading in muddy places and keep a watchful eye on the extremely fast tidal changes. Many lives have been lost by

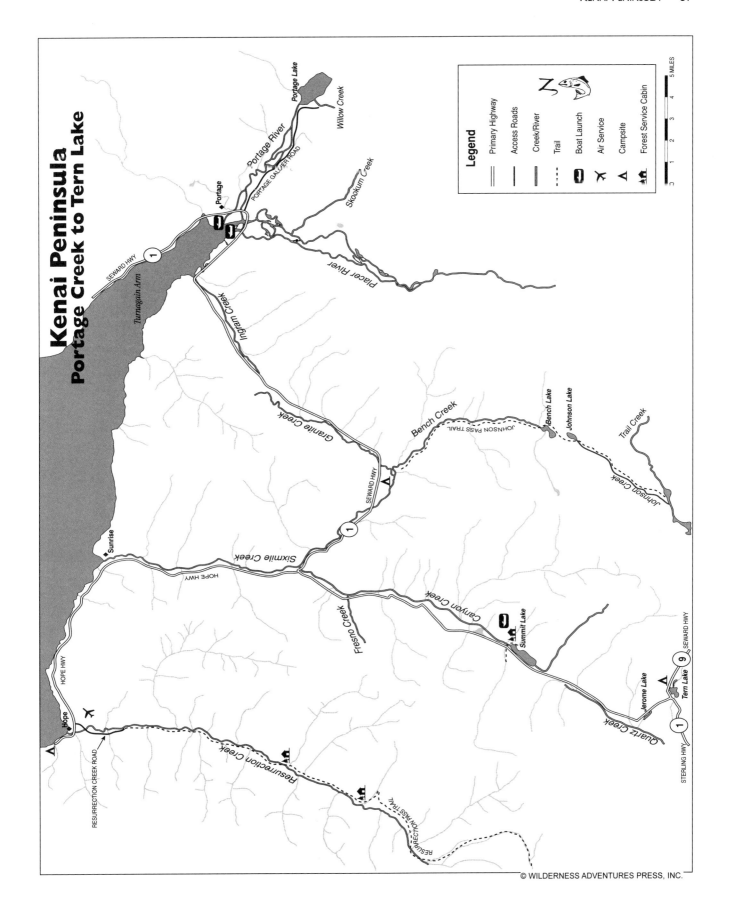

Kenai Peninsula
Portage Creek to Tern Lake

Portage Lake

Willow Creek

Portage River

PORTAGE GALOER ROAD

Portage

Skookum Creek

SEWARD HWY

Placer River

Turnagain Arm

Ingram Creek

Granite Creek

Bench Creek

Bench Lake

Johnson Lake

JOHNSON PASS TRAIL

Trail Creek

Johnson Creek

SEWARD HWY

Sunrise

Sixmile Creek

HOPE HWY

Canyon Creek

Fresno Creek

Summit Lake

Jerome Lake

Tern Lake

SEWARD HWY

Quartz Creek

Hope

HOPE HWY

RESURRECTION CREEK ROAD

Resurrection Creek

RESURRECTION PASS TRAIL

STERLING HWY

Legend

Primary Highway	
Access Roads	
Creek/River	
Trail	
Boat Launch	
Air Service	
Campsite	
Forest Service Cabin	

0 1 2 3 4 5 MILES

anglers stuck in the mud, unable to free themselves on the face of incoming tides. Remember, these are the second highest tide changes in the world, so even if you're used to fishing along the sea, unless you've been around 20-foot tidal fluctuations, be very cautious and pay close attention to the water and what it's doing.

Back to the fishing. It's possible to travel up the Placer River, but it takes some effort and the river is heavily silted. Being a glacial-born stream, the river is not ideal for flyfishing. Bait angler do well here, though, so if you're serious about bringing meat home from this river, use a spinning rod and cured roe. Some folks take it upon themselves to access the Placer by walking up the railroad tracks on the eastern side of the river, but be careful. This is not a commonly accepted practice, and if caught by railroad personnel, you'll get a tongue lashing at the least.

Your best bet would be to run a boat upstream to reach those prime fishing spots. Shallow-draft crafts are a must, as there are some very shallow sections and a few touchy spots to negotiate. Frankly, I wouldn't boat on this river unless I was with a local who knew the water and every obstacle. If you do decide to launch your own boat here, make certain you have a spare prop on board, and wear your life jacket at all times.

If you're into hiking, I have heard of anglers who walk to Skookum Creek, off Portage Glacier Road, then travel to where the creek dumps into the Placer River. No doubt the fishing can be exceptional here, but this is an arduous hike of some 6 to 8 miles. It should be noted that Skookum Creek upstream of the Alaska Railroad bridge is open to all salmon fishing except king salmon 20 inches or longer from January 1 through July 13. If you're planning to hike in to reach the Placer anytime after July 14—when many of the salmon start making their journey into this stream—remember it's closed through the end of the year.

But it is creeks like Skookum that lead to good fishing on the Placer River, particularly for fly anglers. Any of the clear streams emptying into the river provide especially good silver fishing. The Placer also offers solid chum salmon fishing, and the Dolly Varden action is usually good.

For the silvers, pink bunny hair streamers are your best bet. Chums, on the other hand, love anything that's bright green. In fact, many spin-fishermen prefer plain green yarn on a bare hook when fishing for chum salmon. Green and white Russian River Coho flies can be good choices for chum salmon, as can streamers in the same color. Red also works well on chums.

Time will likely be the deciding factor for whether or not you stop to fish the Placer River. If you're in no hurry and wish to explore a productive river, then it's worth stopping to check it out. If you've gone to the effort of bringing a boat along, with the intent of fishing as many Alaskan rivers as possible, then go for it. For the rest of us, it might be wise to move farther along the Kenai Peninsula.

Stream Facts: Placer River

Seasons

- With two exceptions, the Placer River drainage is open year-round to fishing for all species of salmon (except king salmon 20 inches or longer). The two exceptions are as follows: In Lower Explorer Creek, upstream from ADF&G markers near its confluence with Lower Explorer Pond, the season is open to salmon fishing from January 1 through July 13; in Skookum Creek, upstream of the Alaska Railroad bridge, the season is open to salmon fishing January 1 through July 13.

Special Regulations

- Daily limits for salmon (except king salmon) 16 inches or longer are 3 per day, 3 in possession, of which only 2 per day, 2 in possession may be silver salmon.

- The Placer River is closed to the taking of king salmon 20 inches or longer.

Fish

- Silver, chum, and pink salmon and Dolly Varden

River Characteristics

- The Placer River is a fast-flowing, heavily silted river, not ideal for flyfishers. Running a boat upstream is the best way to find good water, but only experienced boaters should attempt this. Silver salmon often gather in large numbers where the mouth enters Turnagain Arm, and flyfishers have a shot here.Fishing and Boating Access

- Boat access is right along the highway, where the Placer flows under the Seward Highway. Bank-fishing opportunities are limited.

Maps

- *Alaska Atlas and Gazetteer*, page 71

Salmon anglers in the Seward Harbor.

Ingram Creek

Ingram Creek sits at mile 75 as you make your way around Turnagain Arm. It's a popular Dolly Varden and pink salmon stream. This is primarily a summertime fishery, with the pinks making their way into the river in even-numbered years. When the pink spawn is on, Dolly action can heat up on egg patterns and flesh flies.

Ingram Creek parallels the highway for approximately 6 miles, providing many good wade-fishing opportunities. As there are no big salmon in these waters, a 4-weight rod and lightweight gear is all you need to have a blast.

Granite Creek

The next creek you'll find along the highway is Granite Creek, which offers even more roadside pullouts than Ingram. Dolly Varden are the main course here, with egg patterns proving effective throughout the summer. Nymphing can also be productive at times. There's a campground on Granite Creek near the guard station.

Johnson Pass Trail Lakes

At mile 63.8 on the Seward Highway, a short hike up the road—or a quick drive if the road is open—from Granite Creek Campground will get you to **Bench Creek**. Dolly Varden exist throughout this creek, and the trail is fairly flat and easy to follow. This is also one of the first places on the road system where a family of anglers can hike in to a lake.

You can also follow the Johnson Pass Trail a little over 9 miles to **Bench Lake**, which is nestled in the Kenai Mountains. The Johnson Lake Trail is part of the original Iditarod Trail, and old cabins can still be seen along this route.

Bench Lake runs about a mile in length and sits above tree line. Don't overlook the first mile or two of Bench Creek below the lake, as this section is a good locale for grayling. Grayling and rainbow trout are also abundant in the lake. While traditional Dolly patterns will prove useful, you should also bring a variety of small, dark patterns, both wet and dry, for grayling. Leech patterns and Woolly Buggers are good choices for Bench Lake rainbows. If targeting grayling, the Black Gnat, Adams, and Mosquito are tough dry flies to beat.

Continuing along the Johnson Pass Trail for a half-mile will bring you to **Johnson Lake**. Less than a mile in length, Johnson is home to rainbow trout. The best fishing typically is found at the lake's southern outlet.

Johnson and Bench Lakes are best fished from June through September. It's also not a bad idea to pack a selection of small spinners and an ultralight spinning rod if you're making the effort to reach these lakes.

If you'd rather hike a loop than backtrack, you can continue hiking down the Johnson Pass Trail, which borders Johnson Creek. The trail then follows the west bank of Upper Trail Lake before terminating at mile 32.5 on the Seward Highway, near the Trail Lakes Fish Hatchery. Dropping a car at the other end before starting out is a good idea. If you're intent on covering ground quickly, a mountain bike can greatly reduce the travel time.

Hope Area Fishing

The Hope Highway heads north at milepost 56.5, near the Canyon Creek bridge. Even if you don't have plans to fish this area, the historic town of Hope is worth spending time in. Hope sits 17 miles off the Seward Highway and is the peninsula's northernmost community, settled during gold rush days.

More than 3,000 people passed through the Hope area searching of gold in the mid- to late 1800s. Some of the original homesteads are still standing, either occupied or owned by private parties. Many of the historic buildings were pushed into the waters of Turnagain Arm during the 1964 earthquake. Today, just 200 residents make Hope their home, and gold mining and logging operations keep the community alive.

The paved 17.8-mile-long Hope Highway takes you through dense forests, along roadside beaver ponds, and offers sweeping views of both the mountains and the sea. When I first visited this quaint town, I found it hard to leave.

The Hope Highway ends at Porcupine Campground, and there's a sweeping view of the area from the nearby cliffs. From this point, several well-marked trails are easily accessed for hikers. You can even get on the famous Resurrection Pass Trail, which leads 38 miles and

Scott Haugen with a nice rainbow taken on a stream in the heart of the Kenai Peninsula.

ascends to more than 2,600 feet in elevation before ending on the Sterling Highway near Cooper Landing. There is good fishing on this trail, but because it lies closer to the opposite end of the journey, we'll cover it in detail later in the chapter.

For the first 8 miles after turning onto the Hope Highway, you'll be traveling along **Sixmile Creek**. This small creek eventually drains into Turnagain Arm. There are several small, good-looking tributaries dumping into Sixmile Creek, but none are worth spending time in. Instead, focus your efforts closer to the outlet of the main creek, where fishing for Dollys is better than it is in the steep, fast water above.

At the town of Hope, you will also find **Resurrection Creek**, home to pink salmon and Dolly Varden. The first few miles upstream from the mouth of this turquoise stream is where you should spend the majority of your time. Beyond this point, several turbid tributaries feed Resurrection Creek, making for tough fishing. You can follow the creek on foot or move along Resurrection Creek Road, which borders the creek.

In early July on even-numbered years pink salmon begin entering Resurrection Creek in astounding numbers, making bank and wade fishing highly productive. The key to having a positive angling experience with pink salmon lies in meeting them as soon as they begin to arrive in freshwater streams. At that time the silver-bullet speedsters are fresh, full of life, and a blast to catch, especially on a 5-weight rod.

Due to the steepness of the terrain, Resurrection Creek quickly turns into a fast, rumbling stream. But there are several prime pockets dispersed throughout the fast water that harbor pinks, and surprisingly, anglers often overlook these areas. In fact, this creek doesn't get hammered even close to what you'd expect. If you're looking for a tranquil experience in a gorgeous setting where you can catch loads of salmon, it's worth spending time on this stream.

Pink salmon will chase and attack any bright pattern. I like $1/32$- and $1/16$-ounce Stuart Steelhead Bullet Jigs in pink and pink/white colors in turbulent waters such as Resurrection Creek, as they quickly get down to where the fish are. Weighted flies are also a good idea if venturing upstream. Flash Flies and pink bunny hair streamers are very productive patterns for humpy salmon, as are the Red Rascal, Comet, and most of the vivid, attention-getting egg patterns.

Underrated and often passed over by anglers, the pink salmon has a lot to offer in terms of high catch numbers and scrappy fights. They've earned a bad reputation because they often frequent streams occupied by silver salmon, which are the primary target of many traveling anglers. Because the silvers arrive later than the pinks, the pink salmon are nearing the end of their life cycle when most fishermen see them. They've metamorphosed into hook-jawed, off-colored salmon sporting teeth like a crocodile and a distinct hump on the back.

They still attack anything in their path, but this can make getting to the silver salmon difficult and frustrating. But give the pinks a try as soon as they hit fresh water, a good month and a half before any silvers show up, and you'll discover how much sport they can really provide. And Resurrection Creek is just the place to do it.

Canyon Creek

Back on the Seward Highway at mile 55, Canyon Creek borders the road all the way to its headwaters at Summit Lake. There are plenty of roadside turnouts on this stretch, and the fishing for Dollys can be pretty good. Heavy silting is the main obstacle here. Poor visibility, combined with only average-sized fish, usually means anglers pass right on by. But if you're eager to explore off-road creek fishing, this isn't a bad place as long as the water is not too far out of shape.

Fresno Creek

Fresno Creek crosses the Seward Highway at mile 48. Only a small number of Dolly Varden call this little stream home, meaning catches can be few and far between. The main factors inhibiting angling here are the steep gradient of the creek and the rugged terrain through which it passes.

Summit Lakes

Lower Summit Lake, situated at mile 46 on the Seward Highway, is an excellent family fishery with plenty of parking, though it receives a great deal of pressure. This lake offers very good bank fishing opportunities with just a short walk down the trail on the north end of the lake. The Dollys in Lower Summit Lake tend to hang in deeper waters later in the summer, and bait-fishermen have an advantage at this time. Despite its 50-foot depth, this lake is more fly-friendly in the spring and early summer.

Summit Lake is located 2 miles farther down the highway and is another great family destination. With its ideal Forest Service campground and boat ramp, many angling families target this lake for one- or two-day trips. This is one of the few bodies of water with lake trout that is easy to reach, although the can be tough to catch.

The primary attraction on the upper lake is Dolly Varden. With a 15-inch being a good catch, these Dollys run a bit on the small side. Nonetheless, they are worth the effort of catching just to admire their beauty. There are plenty of bank-fishing options around Summit Lake, or a boat can be launched to more effectively cast or troll flies around the shoreline. Float tubes can also get anglers into good water on both the upper and lower lakes. For winter travelers interested in ice fishing, Summit Lake can be good early in the year.

Quartz Creek

Another mile south will bring you to where Quartz Creek flows beneath the Seward Highway. Though the fishing in this creek is good, I prefer spending time on the Sterling Highway side of the creek, closer to where it empties into Kenai Lake. Thus, Quartz Creek will be addressed with the Sterling Highway waters later in this chapter.

Jerome Lake

At mile 38.5 on the Seward Highway, just prior to reaching the junction of the Sterling and Seward Highways, you'll find Jerome Lake. Jerome is a year-round fishery, holding good numbers of rainbow trout and Dolly Varden. Bank fishing can be very productive, with plenty of access for fly anglers. A small boat can also be launched here, providing even more casting and trolling options in this shallow lake. If you're targeting rainbows, spend time near the south end of the lake, near its outlet. Nymphs and streamers are good choices here, with dry flies often producing in the evening.

Tern Lake

Next, we come to a fork in the road; turn right and you're on the Sterling Highway heading toward Homer, stay left and you're still on the Seward Highway, on your way to the end of the road and the town of Seward. At the junction of these two highways sits one of the most striking roadside views on the Kenai Peninsula.

At mile 38, Tern Lake, named after the arctic terns that nest here, is surrounded by towering peaks and laced with lush vegetation—just the scene you envision when closing your eyes and thinking about Alaska. I've gone through more roles of film on this lake than perhaps any other on the peninsula, for every time I drive by it seems to reveal another hidden characteristic of its beauty.

On the Sterling Highway side of the lake, Tern Lake Campground provides you with the option of spending more time in this setting. If you have a good set of binoculars with you, or better yet a spotting scope, spend time glassing the hills north of the Seward Highway. In spring and early summer, there's a good chance you'll spot a few black bears. Mountain goats can be seen here at any time.

Rainbows like this can be taken in many streams around the Kenai Peninsula during the fall salmon spawn.

When it comes to fishing Tern Lake, the marsh-like habitat makes bank angling a challenge. A canoe is perhaps the best way to spend time on this lake. Dolly Varden are the main attraction, with a few rainbow trout to be had. This is a very shallow lake, teeming with weeds, and the Dollys run below average size. Abundant migratory bird life keeps the fish at bay here, too. Though it's beautiful, there's a reason why few people fish Tern Lake.

HOPE

Population: 140
Alaska Area Code: 907
Zip Code: 99605

TOURIST INFORMATION

Hope Chamber of Commerce, P.O. Box 89; 566-5656; www.advenalaska.com/hope

ACCOMMODATIONS

Angle 45 Adventures, Mile 8.1 Hope Hwy.; 782-3175; www.angle45.com
Bear Creek Lodge & Cafe, Mile 15.9 Hope Hwy.; 782-3141; www.bearcreeklodgencafe.com
Discovery Cabins, P.O. Box 64; 1-800-365-7057; www.AdvenAlaska.com/cabins.htm

CAMPGROUNDS AND RV PARKS

Coeur d'Alene USFS Campground, take Palmer Creek Road 0.6 miles south of Hope and go 6.5 miles to the campground; 6 tentsites, tables, toilets, firepits
Henry's One Stop, P.O. Box 50, Mile 15.8 Hope Hwy.; 782-3222; full-service hookups, dump station, water, showers, toilets, laundry, groceries, tent camping; onestop@alaska.net
Porcupine USFS Campground, located at mile 17.8 at the end of Hope Highway; 24 sites, tables, tent spaces, outhouses, firepits, drinking water, trash disposal, campground host, provides access to two overlooks of Turnagain Arm; fee
Seaview Cafe & Bar (RV park, campground, cabins), P.O. Box 110; 782-3300, on-site fishing, snack bar; aussiealaska@hotmail.com

RESTAURANTS

Bear Creek Lodge Cafe, Mile 15.9 on Hope Hwy.; serves breakfast, lunch and dinner; 782-3141/ www.bearcreeklodgencafe.com
Tito's Discovery Cafe, Mile 16.5 Hope Hwy.; 782-3274

TOURIST ATTRACTIONS

Hope/Sunrise Historical and Mining Museum, Box 88; 782-3740

SEWARD HIGHWAY: STERLING HIGHWAY JUNCTION TO SEWARD

This section focuses on the fishing to be had by continuing on the Seward Highway from the Sterling Highway junction to the town of Seward. It should first be noted that all fresh waters of Resurrection Bay and the Seward Lagoon are closed to salmon fishing year-round. Your main target here is the Dolly Varden, and if you're into exploring small streams you'll love this stretch. There are also plenty of lakes in the area that will test your hiking legs and fishing skills.

Carter Lake Trailhead

If catching big grayling has always been your dream, this is the trail for you. In one of the lakes on this trail, Crescent Lake, these fish stretch 20 inches or more, the largest grayling on the entire Kenai Peninsula.

At mile 33 Carter Creek flows under the Seward Highway before dumping into Upper Trail Lake. The Carter Lake Trail takes off from the south side of the highway at this point, and it's a good place to take the family on a hike for some lake fishing. The first couple miles of trail are a bit steep, but nothing too daunting for youngsters to tackle. The beauty of the hemlock forest and willow and alder thickets eventually gives way to open subalpine terrain. Beautiful wildflowers grace this area, where even the dainty chocolate lily can be seen.

A hike of just over 3 miles will put you on **Carter Lake**. Rainbow trout have been stocked in Carter, and arctic grayling can be had here, as well. Plenty of bank fishing opportunities exist around the shores of this lake, but hauling a float tube into Carter is easy, and good campsites make this a comfortable place to stay for those wishing to pitch a tent.

Continuing up the Carter Lake Trail another mile will bring you to **Crescent Lake**. This is the shortest route to this large lake and the best way to access the northeast corner. A very rugged trail connects the northeast corner with the northwest corner of the lake, which can be more easily accessed off the Sterling Highway at mile 45 on the Crescent Creek Trail. The Crescent Creek Trail is about 6.5 miles long, though the walk is very easy. With a gradual elevation gain, the walk through birch and subalpine terrain is a tranquil one.

As with Carter Lake, Crescent has good camping available. There are also two U.S. Forest Service cabins, and boats are provided for anglers making advanced reservations. Crescent Lake is home to Dolly Varden, but it's the arctic grayling that attract flyfishing fanatics. Bring an assortment of wet and dry flies for the grayling, and if you intend to keep some of these fish for the pot, be sure

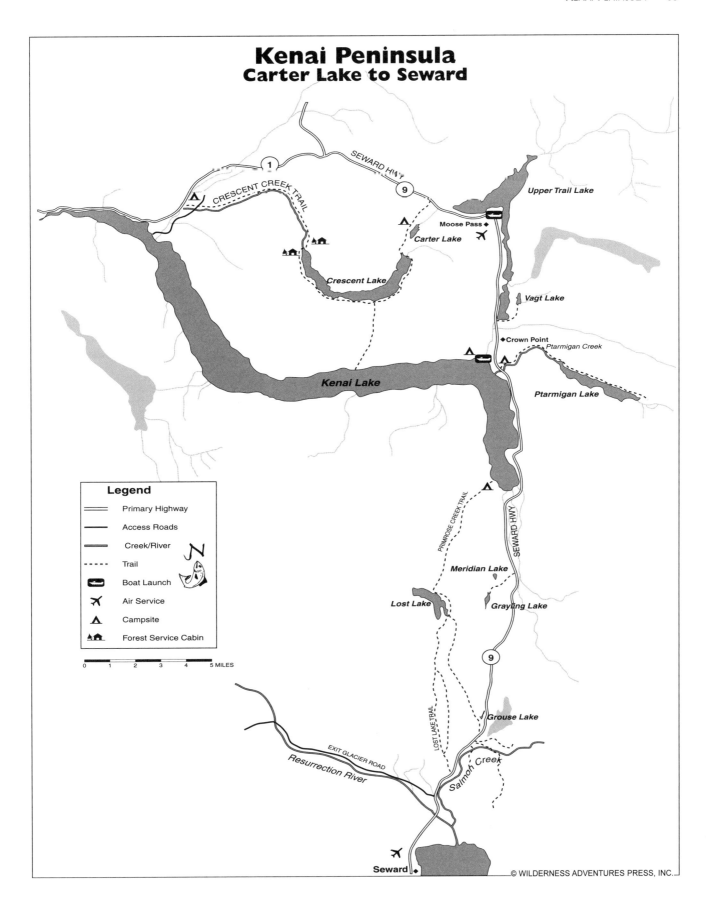

Kenai Peninsula
Carter Lake to Seward

Upper Trail Lake

SEWARD HWY

CRESCENT CREEK TRAIL

Moose Pass ◆

Carter Lake

Crescent Lake

Vagt Lake

◆ Crown Point

Ptarmigan Creek

Kenai Lake

Ptarmigan Lake

Legend

═══	Primary Highway
───	Access Roads
───	Creek/River
----	Trail
🛥	Boat Launch
✈	Air Service
⛺	Campsite
🏚	Forest Service Cabin

0   1   2   3   4   5 MILES

N

PRIMROSE CREEK TRAIL

SEWARD HWY

Meridian Lake

Lost Lake

Grayling Lake

LOST LAKE TRAIL

Grouse Lake

EXIT GLACIER ROAD

Resurrection River

Salmon Creek

Seward ◆

to check current regulations regarding possession limits and open seasons.

One word of caution: The Crescent Creek Trail can be very dangerous in winter and early spring due to avalanche activity, so time your hike accordingly. In addition, if you'd like to fish **Crescent Creek** but are unable to cover the distance on foot, there are fly-in opportunities out of Moose Pass.

If you're accessing Crescent Lake from the Sterling Highway, go to mile 45 and turn south on Quartz Creek Road. Continue 3.5 miles up the road and you'll hit the Crescent Creek Trailhead. Much of the trail parallels Crescent Creek, where Dolly Varden and a few grayling hold in deeper holes. Dry flies are often the ticket for coaxing grayling from this creek, with the best fishing near the Crescent Lake outlet, above where the trail bisects the creek.

Grayling will routinely hit patterns such as the Mosquito, Adams, Royal Wulff, and Black Gnat. When searching for these distinctively dorsal-finned beauties subsurface, Muddler Minnows, Woolly Buggers, and streamers are effective on a sink-tip or full sinking line.

Back on the Seward Highway, across from the Carter Lake Trailhead, you'll come to Trail Lakes Fish Hatchery. If it's open when you're passing through, this salmon rearing facility is worth seeing. You may even get a mini-tour of the complex if they're not too busy.

Upper Trail Lake and Moose Pass

At mile 31, the Seward Highway takes a big bend at Upper Trail Lake. There's a boat ramp here, and Dolly Varden, rainbow, and lake trout inhabit this immense body of water. However, this lake is often very silty and off-color, which is why few people fish it, electing instead to spend some time in the quaint little roadside town of Moose Pass.

In the late 1800s, the original Iditarod Trail passed through Moose Pass, transporting supplies and gold into the interior. The construction of the railroad line also played a major part in shaping the community. Today the town, which was named for the surplus of moose observed in the area at the turn of the century, has about 150 year-round residents.

Though small, Moose Pass offers one of the best opportunities for fly-in fishing on the entire Kenai Peninsula. From here, you're close to several high lakes that can be accessed in minutes with a floatplane. Scenic Mountain Air (1-800-478-1449) charges about $200 per person for fly-in fishing to local lakes. They can get you on to the best grayling lakes on the entire peninsula, as well as any other lake you may be interested in.

If you choose a fly-in trip, it's a good idea to bring your own float tube to access waters that can't be reached from the bank. Fly-in trips can range anywhere from one hour to several days. If you want to camp on a lake and be picked up a week later, no problem. If you want to reserve a Forest Service cabin (907-271-2500), Scenic Mountain Air can drop you on the lake and even rent you a little motor and tank of gas to use with the rowboat that often accompanies such cabins.

All of the lakes covered in this chapter are fair game for fly-ins out of Moose Pass, so read on, find what appeals to you, and consider a floatplane fishing adventure.

If you're heading through the town of Moose Pass on the weekend nearest the summer solstice (June 21), you may want to be a part of the annual Moose Pass Summer Festival. Main Street is the site of this event, which features barbecues, an auction, arts and crafts booths, and even a triathlon.

Vagt Lake

Continuing south on the Seward Highway, Vagt Lake Trailhead can be accessed from the south end of Lower Trail Lake at mile 25.2, at the Trail River outlet. A short 1-mile jaunt up this trail is easy going for all ages. Though Vagt Lake is small, its beauty is worth seeing and the fishing for stocked rainbow trout can be very good, especially if you hook into some of those monster fish that have held over a season or two. Check regulations before fishing this lake, as it's seasonally regulated for the protection of spawning fish.

Upper Kenai Lake

Past Crown Point, there's a public boat launch on Kenai Lake at mile 24. While rainbows, lake trout, and Dolly Varden are the target species here during the summer and fall months, king, silver, pink, and red salmon also thrive in Kenai Lake. Given the vastness of this lake, however, it can be a challenging one for fly anglers. We'll take a closer look at Kenai Lake on its lower end, where the fishing is more productive, in the Sterling Highway segment.

Ptarmigan Creek

At mile 23.2 on the Seward Highway, picturesque little Ptarmigan Creek flows beneath the road. During the red salmon spawn, the crimson color of this stream is a sight to behold, and with newly constructed viewing platforms, getting vivid photos is simple.

From mid-July into early September, egg patterns are

ideal for taking Dolly Varden that follow the spawning salmon into the creek. When the salmon spawn tails off and corpses litter the bottom, switch to flesh patterns. If you're fishing prior to the salmon run, be sure to cover lots of water, nymphing your way along while searching for Dollys in pockets and tucked behind rocks.

Ptarmigan Creek Campground is off the east side of the highway, and there's plenty of parking. This campground makes a good base of operations if you're looking to fish area lakes and streams.

From the campground, Ptarmigan Creek Trailhead winds through the Chugach National Forest for nearly 4 miles before meeting **Ptarmigan Lake**. This trail can be moderately steep in places, but there's a good possibility of seeing both mountain goats and Dall sheep on the mountains surrounding the lake. The trail continues along the north shore of Ptarmigan Lake for another 4 miles, with good camping facilities available at both ends of the lake. Dolly Varden are the primary target for bank anglers whipping flies on Ptarmigan Lake.

Grayling Lake

Moving 10 miles down the road, you'll find the Grayling Lake Trailhead at mile 13. A 1-mile hike from the highway will bring you to this lake, where grayling up to 12 inches can be taken on small flies. Because this is the shortest hike to reach a body of water containing grayling, it receives a good amount of angling pressure. However, packing a belly boat into the lake is easy and will help you get some space for yourself and let you reach better fishing.

Continuing another ¾ mile along the trail will bring you to Meridian Lake, another good grayling fishery. Dry flies like Gnats, Ants, and Mosquitoes will produce rises on both lakes, though an assortment of subsurface patterns like Muddlers and Woolly Buggers will prove useful.

Golden Fin, Troop, and Grouse Lakes

At mile 11 on the Seward Highway, a short half-mile hike ends at Golden Fin Lake. Be warned, this trail is steep and unmarked, so despite the fact that it's short, it can take some time to reach. Golden Fin Lake hosts a self-sustaining population of landlocked Dolly Varden. Though the fish average only about 8 inches, the action can be fast-paced for these little beauties.

Troop Lake can be found off the east side of the Seward Highway at mile 10. Again, an unmarked trail leads 1 mile to the lake. (Continue hiking until you pass the railroad tracks.) This lake is stocked with rainbows on odd-numbered years, and bank fishing can be good.

Grouse Lake provides another road-accessible fishing

opportunity at mile 7.4 along the west side of the Seward Highway. Beginning in August and continuing through September, Dolly Varden enter this lake in large schools. From mid-May through early June, the Dollys are on the out-migration. Fishing for these migratory char during the height of their travels can be exciting. Because salmon spawn in this small, slender lake, egg and flesh patterns can produce high-volume catches of good-sized Dollys. Salmon fishing is closed at all times in this lake.

Lost Lake

Lost Lake Trailhead can be found on the west side of the Seward Highway at approximately mile 5.5. The hike into Lost Lake is about 8 miles long and the going moderately challenging. There is another access point to Lost Lake along the Primrose Creek Trail, which takes off back at mile 17 on the Seward Highway. The moderately difficult Primrose Trail is about 6 miles long, with a campground at its entrance. A large die-off of self-sustaining rainbow trout prompted ADF&G authorities to launch an extensive stocking program here in 1999. Before hiking in to this lake, check with the ADF&G to get an update on the status of the rainbows here.

Salmon Creek

One of my favorite little streams to fish along the Seward Highway is Salmon Creek. The highway crosses the creek at mile 5.9, and there is a small pullout on the west side of the road just before the bridge. One time, good friend and Kenai-area guide Brett Gesh (www.bitefinders.com) and I fished this creek in early September. The water level was lower than we'd hoped, but the number of dead and decaying pink salmon got our hopes up.

Directly beneath the bridge, Brett spotted a nice Dolly feeding on a dead pink salmon. The white-fined char would dart from the shadow cast by the bridge, grab a morsel of food, then retreat back into the safety of the shadow. Brett stayed put while I grabbed my camera and crossed the river in a shallow spot well downstream. With the sun at my back, I snuck through the willows, gaining a perfect angle where I could see the Dolly, the salmon on which it was feasting, and Brett.

A flesh fly that was dropped in the perfect spot began its pulsating downstream journey like it had done a half-dozen times previously. But this time Gesh set the hook and the Dolly went berserk, running up and downstream trying to shake free. Guiding the 16-inch prize to his net, Gesh admired its beauty for a moment and then bid it farewell, and we caught the whole sequence on film.

With spotting glasses on, we waded along the shores of the creek, observing more Dollys as they picked pieces of floating flesh making their way to sea. Targeting these ravenous fish with flesh flies was the perfect way to spend the afternoon.

The Dollys in Salmon Creek are anadromous, entering the stream with the salmon and feasting on their favorite food—roe. When the river runs low, concentrate on pools, where Dollys often congregate. But don't overlook the occasional char working the shallows in August, picking up loose roe, and feasting on flesh through September.

The key to success in this small stream is obtaining the best pair of polarized glasses you can afford and letting them do the work. Do to the narrow sections of this creek, you'll also want to move slowly, sneaking quietly into good fishing position. Sight fishing for Dollys is good all along this creek, but make sure you see them before they see you.

No Name Creek

Another favorite creek is one that, despite all my efforts, I cannot find a name for. Surprisingly, this creek is easy to find and choked with monster Dollys from late August through September. Given its proximity to civilization and the number of big Dollys present, I'm sure there's a name for it somewhere, but I couldn't find it on any of the maps I poured over or through any of the people I spoke with. In a way, I don't want to learn its true name, for the mystique surrounding the find of such a great little stream is the stuff flyfishing dreams are made of. I'm sure I'll drive over it one day and see a sign with a name on it, but I hope not.

At mile 3.7 on the Seward Highway, you'll come to the Exit Glacier Road, which turns west. Continue up Exit Glacier Road for about 1 mile and turn right on the road marked Old E.G. Road. Old E.G. Road splits off at the foot of a bridge that crosses my No Name Creek. Just after the turn onto Old E.G. Road, there's a turnout on the left side of the road with a small, primitive campsite. Park or camp here and get ready for some of the best wade fishing on this stretch of the Seward Highway.

My friend Gesh and I worked this mysterious stream one fall day and I honestly could not believe the size of the Dollys we landed and released. The pinks were spawning everywhere, and we couldn't keep the Dollys off our bead setups. The key here is hitting every bit of water, no matter how shallow.

Unlike Salmon Creek, where the Dollys can be sight fished, the flow on our anonymous little stream is too turbulent for spotting fish. But the broken, shallow water provides ideal cover for the char. On a short leader, float the bead below a strike indicator. Pegging the bead 2 inches above a small, low-profile hook is a good idea.

Take the time to match your bead to the size and color of the roe being released by the pink salmon. Pinks lay surprisingly large eggs, and matching the size is crucial for consistently fooling these Dollys. We caught many in excess of 20 inches.

When you're done fishing here, an 8-mile drive will take you to the end of Exit Glacier Road, where hiking trails lead to the massive Exit Glacier.

The Town of Seward

The fishing to be had around the town of Seward is almost all in salt water. One of the world's premier silver salmon, halibut, and lingcod fisheries exists offshore out of Resurrection Bay. If spending time in this quaint little town is on your agenda, you might want to look into an ocean fishing expedition. The world-renowned Seward Silver Salmon Derby runs in the middle of August, and the town is typically packed with anglers from around the globe trying their luck at catching high-dollar silvers. For information on Salmon Derby dates, prizes, and rules go to the Seward Chamber of Commerce website (www.seward.net/chamber). And if you hire a guide, your skipper can arrange for your catch to be frozen, processed, and shipped wherever you desire.

For overnight visitors, Seward has plenty of options. Along the Seward beach, undeveloped camping and parking areas are abundant, as are RV hookup sites. Pay showers are available for public use at the Harbormaster's Office, as well as at several Seward businesses. Across Resurrection Bay, on the eastern shore, more undeveloped camping and parking is available around Fourth of July Creek.

Just outside the Seward city limits, there are other privately owned and operated commercial campgrounds. In addition, Seward offers many motels, hotels, and bed and breakfasts, along with several cafes, restaurants, and convenient stores. (Please refer to the Seward hub city information at the end of this chapter.)

Seward has plenty to offer visitors looking to spend a few days in the area. Founded in 1903, Seward was established during the construction of the railroad and now boasts a year-round population of some 3,000 people. The many shops in the town make it fun and easy to take to the streets and see it all, but if you don't want to go by foot, hop on the trolley. The Alaska SeaLife Center and the Seward Museum are just a sampling of the sites worth seeing in this quaint town.

SEWARD

Population: 3,010
Alaska Area Code: 907
Zip Code: 99664

TOURIST INFORMATION

Seward Chamber of Commerce, P.O. Box 749;
224-8051; www.seward.net/chamber

GUIDE SERVICES

Bear Lake Air & Guide Service; 1-800-224-5985

Scenic Mountain Air, P.O. Box 4; 1-800-478-1449;
288-3646; offers very good fly-in fishing to any lake
in the area where they can land a plane; also rents
motors for use on boats that come with Forest
Service cabins on many lakes

ACCOMMODATIONS

Box Canyon Cabins, 31515 Lois Way; 224-5046;
www.boxcanyoncabin.com

Cabin on the Cliff, P.O. Box 670-SG; 1-800-942-0255

Clear Creek Cottage, P.O. Box 241; 1-888-586-8420;
www.auroracharters.com

Harborview Inn, 804 Third Ave.; 1-888-324-3217;
www.sewardhotel.com

Ho Hum Lodge Bed & Breakfast, P.O. Box 1123;
224-7798; www.hohumlodge.com

Kenai Fjords Wilderness Lodge, P.O. Box 1889,
Dept. SVG; 1-800-478-8068

Seward Waterfront Lodging, 550 Railway Ave., 224-
5563; www.alaskas-sewardwaterfrontlodging.com

The Beach House Rentals, Lowell Point; 224-7000;
www.beachhousealaska.com

The Farm Bed & Breakfast Inn, Box 305; 224-5691;
www.alaska.com/thefarm

CAMPGROUNDS AND RV PARKS

Bear Creek RV Park, P.O. Box 2209, Mile 6.6 Seward
Hwy.; 1-877-924-5725; largest park in Seward; full
and partial hookups, dumping, private restrooms,
showers, store, propane, modems, TV, videos, liquor
store, laundry, courtesy van; www.bearcreekrv.com

Creekside RV Park, P.O. Box 375, Milepost 6.6 Seward
Hwy.; 224-3647; on-site fishing; full-service
hookups, dump station, water, showers

Fjords RV Park, Mile 1.0 New Exit Glacier Road;
224-9134; www.fjordsrv.com

Miller's Landing RV Parking & Camping, P.O. Box 81;
224-5739; on-site fishing, water, showers, toilets

RESTAURANTS

Chinooks Waterfront Grill, 4th Ave.; 224-2207

Exit Glacier Salmon Bake, ¼ mile up Exit Glacier
Road; 224-4752

Peking, 338 4th Avenue; 224-5444

Railway Cantina, Small Boat Harbor; 224-8226

Ray's Waterfront Restaurant, Seward Boat Harbor;
224-5606

Terry's Fish & Chips, Small Boat Harbor; 224-8807

The Crab Pot, 303 Adams Street; 224-2200

RENTAL CARS

Hertz Car Rental Seward; 224-4378 or 1-800-654-3131

AUTO REPAIR

Auto Tech, Mile 5.5 Seward Hwy.; 224-8667

Performance Auto Body & Paint, Mile 5.5 Seward
Hwy.; 224-7999

MEDICAL

Harbor Medical Clinic, Seaview Plaza, 302 Railway
Ave.; 224-8901

VETERINARY CLINICS

Seward Animal Clinic, 99664 Seward Highway at mile
3.5; 224-5500

TOURIST ATTRACTIONS

Alaska SeaLife Center, 301 Railway Ave.;
1-800-224-2525; www.alaskasealife.org

Kenai Fjords National Park, 1212 4th Ave.; 224-3175;
www.nps.gov/kefj

Seward Museum, 336 3rd Ave.; 224-3902

U.S. Forest Service, Chugach National Forest,
P.O. Box 390, Seward; 224-3374

MOOSE PASS

Population: 118
Alaska Area Code: 907
Zip Code: 99631

TOURIST INFORMATION

Moose Pass Chamber of Commerce, P.O. Box 558;
www.seward.net/moosepass

GUIDE SERVICES

Scenic Mountain Air (fly-out fishing), P.O. Box 4;
1-800-478-1449; 288-3646

ACCOMMODATIONS

Alaska Nellie's Inn, Mile 23, P.O. Box 88; 288-3124
Alpenglow Cottage, Mile 30; 288-3142
Crown Point Lodge, Mile 24, P.O. Box 28; 288-3136
J & J Bed & Breakfast, Mile 23; 288-5677
Jewel of the North Bed & Breakfast, Mile 25; 288-3166
Lake Lodge & Restaurant, Mile 29.5 Seward Hwy.;
288-3101;www.traillakelodge.com
Midnight Sun Log Cabins, Mile 28.9 Seward Hwy.;
288-3627
Moose Pass Inn, Mile 30; 288-3110
Trail Lake Lodge, Mile 29.5; 288-3103

CAMPGROUNDS AND RV PARKS

Moose Pass RV Park and Campground, Mile 29.1
Seward Hwy.

RESTAURANTS

Crown Point Restaurant, Mile 24; 288-3136
Estes Brothers Groceries & Water Wheel; 288-3151;
www.moosepass.net
Moose Pass Inn, Mile 30; 288-3110; open-pit roasted
pig on a spit Saturdays and Sundays
Trail Lake Lodge Restaurant, Mile 29.5; 288-3101

TOURIST ATTRACTIONS

Trail Lake Hatchery, Mile 32; has viewing area and
offers tours; 288-2688

*Salmon carcasses litter the banks of many streams in the fall.
They are a good source of protein for Dolly Varden and
rainbows, and anglers will do well with flesh flies.*

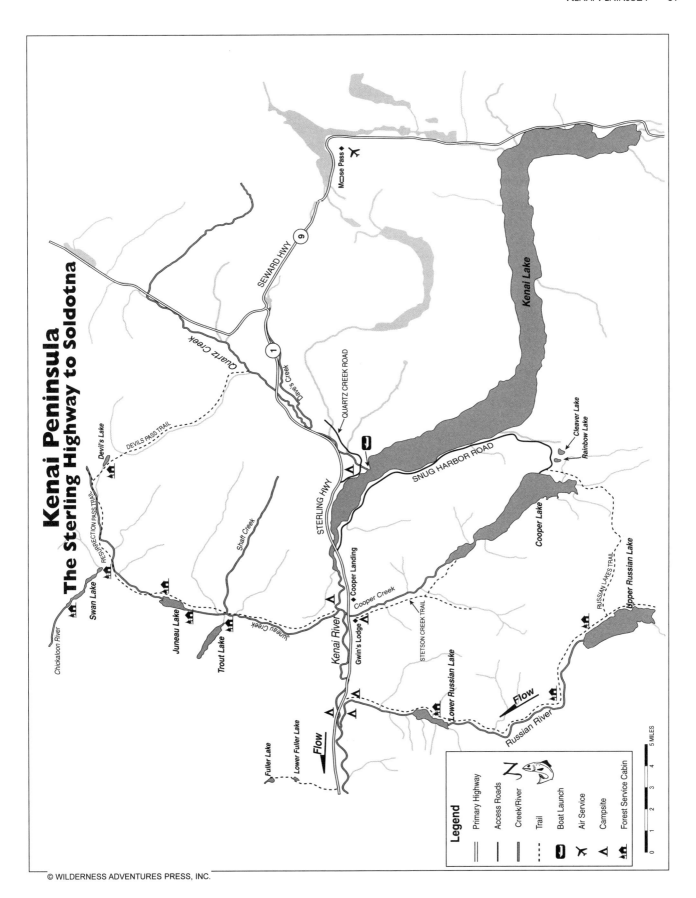

Kenai Peninsula
The Sterling Highway to Soldotna

Moose Pass

SEWARD HWY

9

1

Quartz Creek

Dave's Creek

QUARTZ CREEK ROAD

Kenai Lake

Cleaver Lake

Rainbow Lake

SNUG HARBOR ROAD

Devil's Lake

DEVILS PASS TRAIL

RESURRECTION PASS TRAIL

STERLING HWY

Shaft Creek

Cooper Lake

RUSSIAN LAKES TRAIL

Upper Russian Lake

Swan Lake

Chickaloon River

Juneau Lake

Cooper Landing

Cooper Creek

STETSON CREEK TRAIL

Trout Lake

Juneau Creek

Kenai River

Gwin's Lodge

Lower Russian Lake

Flow

Russian River

Fuller Lake

Lower Fuller Lake

Flow

Legend

N

▤▤▤	Primary Highway
│	Access Roads
▱	Creek/River
┈┈	Trail
🛏	Boat Launch
✈	Air Service
⛺	Campsite
🏚	Forest Service Cabin

0 1 2 3 4 5 MILES

THE STERLING HIGHWAY: SEWARD HIGHWAY JUNCTION TO SOLDOTNA
Quartz Creek

If you're searching for a tranquil stream in which to wet a line, Quartz Creek is it. Rainbows and Dollys can be taken here with regularity, especially once the salmon make their way into the stream. Though a few smaller trout and Dolly Varden take up residence in this creek early in the summer, from mid-July on is when you want to devote some serious time to fishing Quartz Creek. The more your timing coincides with the salmon spawn, the better the fishing will be for hungry trout and char. The trout fishing usually peaks from late July to mid-August, when spawning red salmon blanket the bottom, turning it a crimson hue.

When the salmon arrive in Quartz Creek, they are mature and ready to spawn. As with many Kenai Lake drainages, salmon fishing is prohibited in Quartz Creek. Not so for the ravenous predators on their tails. Catching Dollys and rainbow in the 4- to 6-pound class is not rare here. But it's when one of those 25-inch hogs takes you into your backing that you truly experience the best of small-stream fishing.

Although the water runs as clear as glass, it can be tough to spot rainbow trout holding in pools and hanging behind spawning salmon. A quality pair of polarized glasses are the key to finding fish before they see you.

Dolly Varden are another story. At this time of year their ivory-edged fins are dead giveaways to their presence. When closing in on schools or spawning pairs of red salmon, do so with stealth. Not only does spooking salmon off their beds disrupt the spawning process, it can sour a good opportunity for trout.

Cover as much water as you can in order to take full advantage of the fishing opportunities. Limiting yourself to a few confined spots can lead to frustration.

Though Quartz Creek borders a good section of the Sterling Highway and can be accessed virtually anywhere between miles 41 and 44, some of my favorite spots are near mile 42. Here, anglers can pull off the highway and easily reach prime stretches of the creek. The fish in this section may not be huge, nor their numbers overwhelming, but it provides a quick fix when you feel the need to stand in a beautiful little stream surrounded by spawning salmon.

Heading west, another access point that leads to good fishing can be found just before crossing the Sterling Highway bridge at mile 40.9. A power station is situated on the north side of the highway, and generous parking is available nearby. Pull in to the power station and you'll see where cars have previously parked. There is good bank access both up and down the creek from this spot. If the water is low enough, which it will be in the prime months, you can freely wade fish your way up or downstream. I've spent the better part of an afternoon at this spot, catching fish without seeing another angler.

Another popular access Quartz Creek, but one that receives a lot of pressure, is at mile 45 on the Sterling Highway. Here, Quartz Creek Road turns south, leading to Quartz Creek Campground and the mouth of the creek. Walk a quarter-mile or so past the campground to a wooden bridge on Quartz Creek Road that crosses the creek. Fishing your way from the bridge down to the mouth can be very productive. Due to some deep holes— and to avoid spooking spawning red salmon—it will be necessary to forge through some brush along the banks. Typically, the closer you can fish to the outlet of Quartz Creek, the better the catching will be for rainbows, Dolly Varden, and even an occasional lake trout coming out of Kenai Lake.

When the salmon are spawning, drifting egg patterns behind them is the ticket. Once the salmon begin to die, switch to flesh flies. If you find yourself on this creek in late August and early September, when thousands of salmon carcasses litter the banks and bottom of the creek, the stench can be gut wrenching. But the fishing for Dollys can be good at this time.

On a number of occasions, I've observed Dollys ascending from deep holes here to nab bits of flesh floating by. I've also seen them cruise tight to the shore, stripping meat from rotting salmon like piranhas. This is the ideal time to get that flesh fly in the water.

On the upstream and downstream side of the Sterling Highway bridge (at mile 40.9), split fishing openings usually apply. Traditionally, fishing above the bridge is open June 15 through September 14 and again from November

Flesh flies are great patterns for taking rainbow trout and Dolly Varden in the fall.

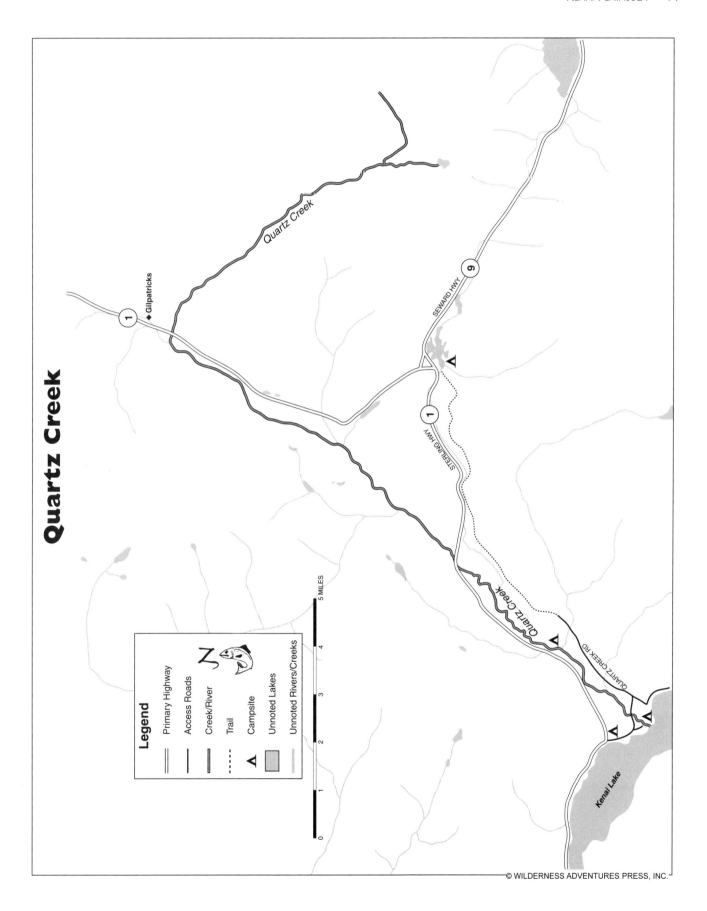

Quartz Creek

Legend

Primary Highway
Access Roads
Creek/River
Trail
Campsite
Unnoted Lakes
Unnoted Rivers/Creeks

0 1 2 3 4 5 MILES

Quartz Creek

Gilpatricks

SEWARD HWY

STERLING HWY

Quartz Creek

QUARTZ CREEK RD

Kenai Lake

1 through April 14. Downstream of the bridge, the open season is June 15 through April 14. Be sure to consult current regulations and pay close attention to posted signs on this creek. In early to mid-August, it's worth standing on the Sterling Highway bridge to watch the spawning rituals of red salmon in the creek, even if you have no intention of wetting a line.

You're getting into serious grizzly territory along Quartz Creek, so be prepared and proceed with caution.

Dave's Creek, flowing from Tern Lake at the Seward and Sterling junction, eventually joins Quartz Creek at mile 42.5. From miles 38 to 40 and near the end of Dave's Creek, the fishing for rainbows and Dollys can be good. Generous roadside parking and easy walking access make the area where the two creeks join a popular spot to wet a line. As with Quartz Creek, you'll be wade fishing in very clear water.

Where Quartz Creek runs into **Kenai Lake**, the Quartz Creek Campground is a popular destination for tourists and locals alike. Camping facilities, RV hookups, and motels are available here. A boat launch allows easy access, but be careful on this big water. High winds carving their way through the mountains can make the lake look more like an ocean at times. Fly anglers who pull minnow imitations stand a good chance of latching onto one of the many predatory fish species in this lake.

High glacial silt content gives this lake a striking hue, but the limited visibility means bait-fishermen have an advantage here. With so many other prime fly waters nearby, I'd advise flyfishers to quickly move on from this lake.

Cooper Landing

Continuing down the Sterling Highway, through the upper portion of the Kenai River (which is covered in its entirety later in this chapter), you'll pass through Cooper Landing, the first major fishing hub on the Sterling Highway that offers access to famous rivers, lakes, and trailheads in the region.

Cooper Landing was named after Joseph Cooper, a miner who struck gold here in the mid-1880s. Today, some 300 residents live here. Because this roadside community spreads itself along 6 miles of the Sterling Highway, and lacks a community center, it's hard to get a handle on what this small town really has to offer. But don't blow through with tunnel vision, for you're only minutes away from some of Alaska's best known fishing grounds.

Whether it's a fly-in adventure to a high lake, a shoulder-to-shoulder combat fishing experience, or a hike to remote lakes you're after, Cooper Landing is the place for

Alaska Troutfitters, located on the highway at Cooper Landing, is the premier fly shop in the area. In addition to guided trips, they have a comprehensive fly selection worth seeing.

you. The famous Russian River, noted for its world-class run of red salmon, is only minutes away. Trophy rainbows and Dollys can be pursued in the upper stretch of the Kenai River, the turquoise waters of which can be seen from town. A number of trailheads in and around Cooper Landing lead to secluded lakes, where anglers can spend days or weeks hiking, fishing, camping, and living the good life.

Located at mile 52 on the Sterling Highway, Gwin's Lodge is a good place to start your search for up-to-the-minute information. In addition to the latest fishing news, Gwin's can supply you with area-specific fishing tackle and a license and even has a restaurant and cabins available. Gwin's can also arrange fly-in fishing trips for you out of Cooper Landing.

In the nearby hills, **Upper Russian Lake** and its tributaries offer great rainbow action from mid-June through September. And if you're traveling through during the months of July and August you might want to take a quick floatplane flight out to famous Crescent Lake for grayling. As soon as you know when you'll be passing through Cooper Landing, be sure to call well in advance to make reservations (907-595-1266), these trips book up fast.

Whenever you pass through Cooper Landing, it pays to stop at Alaska Troutfitters (907-595-1212), which is situated right on the highway. With its huge, colorful sign on the south side of the road, you can't miss this place. Alaska Troutfitters is one of the best flyfishing resources in the area, and they can set you up with the hottest selection of flies for local rivers and lakes. They also have rooms available in their adjacent motel.

The guides at Troutfitters are young, energetic, die-hard anglers who live for one thing: catching trophy rainbows. They take their jobs very seriously, yet offer fun and adventure you'll never forget. In addition to first-class guiding services on the Kenai, they provide an outstanding flyfishing school that can turn the novice into an accomplished angler in a matter of days. For fly fanatics looking to expand their collection of unique patterns, Alaska Troutfitters always has something interesting in the fly bins.

Snug Harbor Road Fisheries

At mile 50.7 you'll find Cooper Creek Campground. The fishing has been spotty in Cooper Creek in recent years due to hydroelectric projects. Before spending too much time here, check with the folks at Troutfitters. The safer bet is to perhaps head to Cooper Lake, which can be accessed by hiking some 4 miles up the Stetson Lake Trail from the campground.

If driving to Cooper Lake sounds more appealing, turn south on Snug Harbor Road at mile 47.9, just after crossing the bridge at Kenai Lake. Continue along the road as it borders the shores of Kenai Lake and after 11 miles you'll end up at Cooper Lake. Cooper is very large body of water, and predominantly home to Dolly Varden. Because this lake runs deep, trolling hardware is common. However, fly anglers with sinking lines and weighted leeches or Woolly Buggers can do well working the shoreline and any structure.

From the point where Snug Harbor peaks between Kenai and Cooper Lakes, the Rainbow Lake Trailhead goes a quarter-mile before hitting **Rainbow Lake**. Rainbow trout averaging in the mid-teens are common here, and bank fishing can be quite productive, as can fishing from a belly boat.

Just to the east of Rainbow Lake, **Cleaver Lake** also holds rainbow trout. Work around the island or concentrate your efforts around broken shorelines and near cover that holds baitfish and provides cover. Trolling sinking lines with streamer patterns can work well in these clear lakes.

Russian Lakes Trail

Approximately a half-mile west of the Rainbow Lake Trail and east of Cooper Lake, you'll find the Russian Lakes Trailhead. The rugged, meandering trail winds some 9 miles before hitting **Upper Russian Lake**. The 12-mile-long Russian Lakes Trail, which starts at the Russian River Campground, is another way to reach both the lower and upper lakes. The trail leading from the Russian River Campground is very well maintained, even handicap-accessible to the lower lake, and is the best choice for reaching Lower Russian Lake.

Hiking in to Upper Russian Lake, however, is best done from the Russian Lakes Trail at the end of Snug Harbor Road. The hike will be worth the effort, as the fishing can be excellent here. The trail is good enough for experienced mountain bikers or you can go by foot. Another option would be to hire a floatplane out of Cooper Landing to drop you on the lake for a day or two.

No matter how you go about getting there, taking a float tube or inflatable raft along will increase your fishing success, as the Upper Russian is a large lake. Concentrate your efforts around both the inlet and outlet of the lake, as well as around points of land.

One of the best ways to fish the Upper Russian is by reserving the Forest Service cabin located on the south end of the lake. Though reservations must be made well in advance, you'll have access to a rustic cabin and a boat. And having a boat on this large lake can mean the difference between success and failure.

Though closed to salmon fishing, Upper Russian Lake routinely kicks out rainbows in the upper-teens and occasionally over 20 inches. There are also some very nice Dolly Varden here.

To reach **Lower Russian Lake**, continue down the trail leading from Snug Harbor Road, which allows you to fish your way down the upper stretch of the Russian River, or hike 2.6 miles up the Russian Lakes Trailhead that takes off from the Russian River Campground off the Sterling Highway. The second choice is the most popular.

To get to the Russian River Campground, turn south at mile 52.7 on the Sterling Highway. This is one of the most heavily used campgrounds in the area, but also one of the best gateways to a high number of prime fishing locales. From the campground, follow the trailhead signs to Lower Russian Lake. The trail is suitable for handicap travel and in excellent condition. Due to the ease of access, this is a super place to take the family on a fishing/picnic combo outing.

A Forest Service cabin is located on the eastern shore of the lake, and it's also wheelchair accessible. You can camp off-trail in the area, but be on the lookout for bears. There is a high concentration of brown and black bears in the area around both Lower and Upper Russian Lakes. Heavy brush makes a perfect setting for chance bear encounters. When walking such trails, make plenty of noise to alert the bears to your presence.

Bank anglers at Lower Russian Lake should focus their efforts at the lake's outlet. A hike of a bit more than a mile will lead you to the lake's headwaters, where the Russian River flows in at the south end.

In the upper and lower lakes, leeches, Woolly Buggers, and nymphs are good all-around choices. When the red and silver salmon are spawning in the lakes, black, brown, or purple Egg-Sucking Leeches are dynamite, as are a variety of egg patterns.

Anglers should note that the Upper and Lower Russian Lakes are closed year-round to fishing for king salmon 20 inches or longer and other salmon 16 inches or longer. They are open to rainbow trout from June 15 through April 14 and anglers are allowed two fish per day, two in possession, of which only one may be 20 inches or longer. Dolly Varden fishing in the lakes is open year-round, with a one per day, one in possession that must be 18 inches or less.

Upper Russian River

For anglers who want to escape the crowds but still fish the Russian River, there is another option. The stretch of river between the Upper and Lower Russian Lakes, along the Russian Lakes Trail, will offer you fair fishing in beautiful scenery away from the combat zone. This section of the Russian River, affectionately referred to as the Upper Russian River, is closed to salmon fishing. So it's rainbow trout and Dolly Varden you'll be chasing.

During the sockeye salmon spawn, bead patterns are usually deadly on trout and char.

There is approximately 8.5 miles of trail between the two lakes. The forest in this area consists of beautiful spruce and hemlock surrounded by subalpine terrain that is infested with bears. Only experienced outdoorsmen who know what they're getting into should venture into this land, especially if planning to camp along the river. Don't even think about going into this area without pepper spray. There is a Forest Service cabin 9 miles above the trailhead at the Russian River Campground, which does offer an added level of comfort.

The rainbow and Dolly Varden that inhabit this stretch of the river don't run as large as those in the lower stretch, but 20-inchers are taken with regularity. The average fish would be more in the neighborhood of 15 inches. The most productive places are just where you'd expect, at both the head and tail ends of the river. This is especially true when the salmon make their way into the drainage, pulling trout and char out of both lakes to feast on the loose roe tumbling downstream.

Hitting this upper stretch of the Russian River during the salmon spawn means fishing with egg imitations and beads. As the salmon die, flesh flies become more useful. This is slower water than what you'll see in the lower river, with more pools to be fished. As long as you keep a watchful eye out for bears, the experience in this pristine valley can be one of the most memorable of your entire trip.

Russian River

Backtracking to the Russian River Campground, let's take a look at the lower section of the Russian River from Lower Russian Lake to the river's confluence with the Kenai River. One of Alaska's most pressured, yet most productive, rivers the Russian River is easily accessed from the campground. This primarily flyfishing-only stream is tailor-made for the wading angler.

An abundance of camping slots makes the Russian River a good place to stop for a day, and if the red salmon run is at its zenith, you may want to stay longer. Modern trails complete with sturdy steps and hand railings wind their way from the campground to the banks of the river. Hip boots or waders help here, as river flows can vary depending on the time of year.

Two runs of sockeye salmon make their way into the Russian River. In mid-June some 25,000 salmon arrive in the river, followed a month later by twice that number. This makes for good fishing for red salmon from mid-June through mid-August. Silver salmon can also be taken at the Russian/Kenai confluence from mid-August through September. From where the Russian meets the Kenai River on up to the falls, the fishing can be world-class. In fact, there are more red salmon caught on rod and reel here than any other place on earth.

Russian River

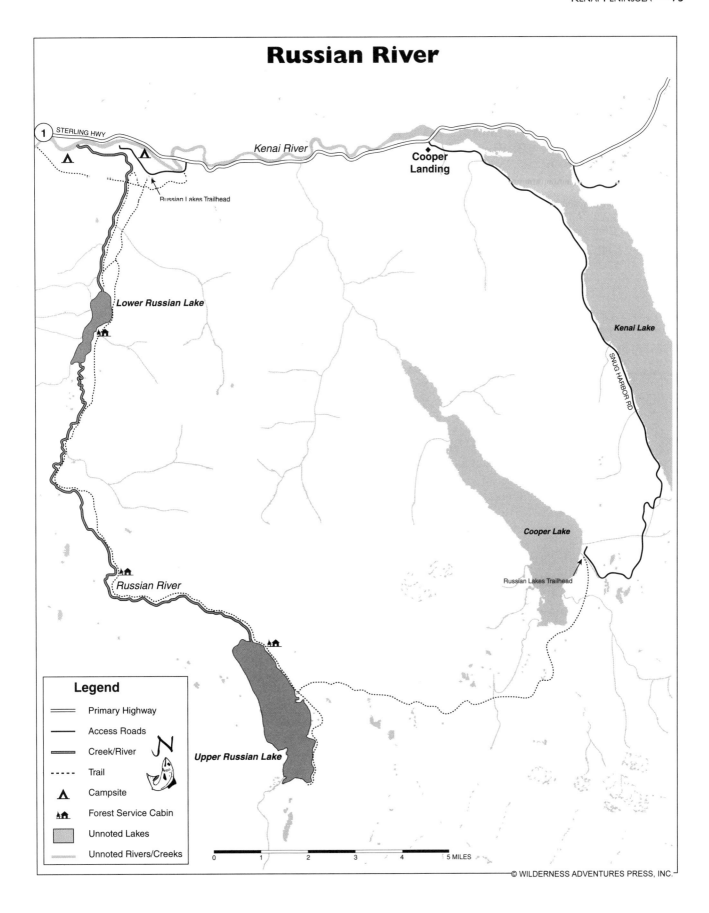

Legend
- Primary Highway
- Access Roads
- Creek/River
- Trail
- Campsite
- Forest Service Cabin
- Unnoted Lakes
- Unnoted Rivers/Creeks

© WILDERNESS ADVENTURES PRESS, INC.

But there's a trick to catching red salmon that is unique to the Russian and Kenai Rivers. It's called the "Kenai Flip," and done properly it's a very efficient way to seek out traveling salmon. Red salmon rarely bite a fly, so many ardent anglers dismiss fly color as a true indicator of red fishing success. Rather, these fish swim close to shore in astounding schools, mouths agape. The key to this method is getting your leader into the mouth of a fish, dragging it across its jaw, and irritating it into striking.

Locals call this technique "lining," and once you get the hang of it, you'll find it surprisingly successful. Keep a short line, often less than 10 feet long. Rather than casting long distances into the fast midsection of the river where reds rarely travel, try getting your fly down to the bottom as quickly as possible, right near your feet. Steep cutbanks are prime areas for red salmon.

Eighteen inches above the fly, attach a split shot to ensure the fly gets down quickly. Flip the terminal gear upstream, letting it drift by your feet until the fly rides just off the bottom. Now repeat the flip. The idea is to stay in one place, letting the sockeyes swim to you. When they travel past your feet, pick a fish and try to slide your fly into its mouth.

This method is the one of choice—as well as necessity—at the Russian/Kenai confluence and throughout much of the Kenai River. However, up the Russian River, the water shallows and slows considerably, making casting throughout the entire width of the stream productive from late July on. It's in this section of the Russian that fly

The famous Russian River Ferry hauls thousands of anglers across the river each summer in search of red salmon.

color will have its biggest impact on success. Don't be afraid to try dark Coho Streamers on bright days or brightly colored flies on overcast days.

To access the Russian River Falls follow the Fisherman's Trail along the river or take the Russian Lakes Trail 2.5 miles from the campground's Pink Salmon or Grayling parking lots. The Fisherman's Trail allows you to fish all the way to Lower Russian Lake, and it can take you all day to get there and back, even though it's just over two miles each way. The Russian Lakes Trail is gravel, and the 45-minute walk is a breeze.

While fishing the trail with my friend and Alaskan resident Art Peck late one July day, we put together a good stringer of bright sockeyes. Stopping to try our luck on a monster rainbow Art had spotted, we laid the salmon down and waded out to cast our flies. When we turned around, our stringer of salmon was gone. Just that fast, a bear had moved in, nabbed our fish, and melted back into the brush. Beware of both black and grizzly bears in this area. Due to the dense brush, encounters can be close, and the last thing you want to do is catch a bear by surprise.

No matter which way you go about getting there, the Russian River Falls are worth seeing, especially when the river is crammed with red salmon. The falls are large and fast, which is why the ADF&G has installed a fish ladder to help migrating salmon reach their spawning grounds. Nonetheless, it takes a good while for thousands of fish to filter through this bypass, creating the perfect salmon viewing area in the process. Numerous fish can be seen jumping in the fast water as well as staging in the shallows.

An elevated viewing platform rises some 30 feet above the water, giving visitors a great look at these magnificent fish. Remember, the immediate area is closed to all fishing, but it's worth seeing just the same.

For trout aficionados, the clear waters of the Russian River are hard to resist, especially when the salmon spawn is in full swing. When the red salmon spawn commences in August, the Dolly Varden and rainbow trout action can be incredible. My friend Art regularly nabs rainbows up to 10 pounds from this stream in the fall. In early September one season, Brett Gesh and I hit the river and got into astounding numbers of Dollys as we worked egg patterns and flesh flies. During the spring and summer months, prior to the salmon spawn, Muddlers, sculpin patterns, and caddis imitations work well for rainbows.

Due to its low level and high clarity, you can even take fish with dry flies on the Russian River. A small Black Gnat or an Adams is a good choice. These are most effective when sight fishing or when working beneath cut-

Boondoggling from a boat creates a natural presentation when fishing egg patterns.

banks where you know fat rainbows are holding. Though not nearly as productive as nymphing or dead drifting egg imitations, those who are patient and persistent with a dry fly will likely be rewarded.

Another sometimes overlooked trout and char opportunity lies tight to shore, where everyone who wades into the river must pass on their way in and out. It's the fish cleaning tables I'm referring to, put in place for anglers to clean their red salmon before hiking up the trail to the campground or parking lot. Trout and char will congregate downstream from these cleaning tables, nibbling flesh from the carcasses and entrails tossed into the stream. Such remains play an integral part in the food chain of streams like this, and anglers with flesh flies on hand can often pull a good redside or char from these places.

If you don't mind fishing with a crowd, head to the mouth of the Russian River downstream from the campground or drive down the Sterling Highway to mile 55, the site of the famous ferry launch. The cost of parking in the U.S. Forest Service's Russian River Campground parking lots is $5 for 12 hours. And a round-trip fee of $6 is all it takes to get you across the river on the U.S. Fish and Wildlife Service's Russian River Ferry. The term "combat fishing" has deep roots here, as hundreds of anglers annually gather shoulder to shoulder to try their luck at the mind-boggling numbers of red salmon moving up the Kenai and turning into the Russian River. Upwards of 50,000 sport-caught reds may be taken from this region in a single season by more than 5,000 anglers.

But don't let the number of anglers discourage you, I've never had a negative experience on this river, even when wedged between flying arms and flailing rods. In fact, it can be quite comical when two or three salmon are simultaneously hooked, as anglers are kept guessing as to who has what fish.

Because everyone employs the same fishing style, the "Kenai Flip," the riverbanks will accommodate anglers standing elbow to elbow. As long as the lines are kept close and each person pays attention to his own line, the fishing is usually tangle-free. If you just sit and watch for a few minutes you'll see an amazing number of fish caught.

Be certain to keep abreast of any emergency orders when fishing the Russian River; these are usually posted in and around the campground.

Stream Facts: Russian River

Seasons

- Upstream of an ADF&G marker 600 yards downstream of the Russian River Falls, the river is closed year-round to salmon fishing.

- In the Upper Russian River/Goat Creek, upstream from the ADF&G markers 300 yards from its confluence with Upper Russian Lake, the river is closed to all fishing August 1 to 31.

- From 100 yards upstream of its mouth to an ADF&G marker 600 yards downstream of the falls, the Russian River is open to all fishing, except king salmon 20 inches or longer, from June 15 to April 14. The same water is designated flyfishing only from June 15 to August 20.

- From its mouth upstream 100 yards to ADF&G markers, the Russian River is open from July 15 to May 1. The same water is designated flyfishing only from July 15 to August 20.

- Except in flyfishing-only waters, only one unbaited single-hook artificial lure is allowed in the Russian River drainage.

Special Regulations

- The Russian River, from its mouth upstream 100 yards to ADF&G markers, is open to red salmon fishing from July 15 to August 20 and for silver salmon July 15 to 31 and August 4 to September 30. During these open seasons, a 3 salmon per day, 3 in possession limit is in effect, but only 1 per day, 1 in possession may be a silver salmon.

- The Russian River, from 100 yards upstream of its mouth to ADF&G markers 600 yards downstream of the falls, is open to red salmon fishing from June 15 to August 20 and for silver salmon July 1 to 31 and August 4 to September 30. During these open seasons, a 3 salmon per day, 3 in possession limit is in effect for, but only 1 per day, 1 in possession may be a silver salmon.

- Rainbow trout must be released downstream of the outlet of Lower Russian Lake.

- Upstream of the outlet of Lower Russian Lake, anglers are allowed 2 rainbow trout per day, 2 in possession, only 1 of which may be 20 inches or longer

Fish

- Red salmon, silver salmon, rainbow trout, Dolly Varden

River Characteristics

- The Russian River is a very clear, shallow river that's perfect for flyfishing. Wading and sight fishing are the name of the game for salmon, trout, and char. Rainbows in the 12-pound class inhabit the lower river during the peak of the salmon spawn. Combat fishing for red salmon at the mouth of the river is something that must be at least observed, if not participated in.

Fishing Access

- Bank access can be had at the Russian River Campground or by way of the ferry at the Kenai/Russian River Campground.

Maps

- Alaska Road & Recreation Map, Kenai Lake & Vicinity; Alaska *Atlas and Gazetteer*, page 70

Resurrection Pass Trailhead

Across the Sterling Highway from the Russian River Campground, you'll find the Resurrection Pass Trailhead (at mile 53.2). This trail leads to Trout, Juneau, Swan, and Devil's Pass Lakes and is the most popular trail in the Chugach National Forest. Utilized in the 1890s by gold miners traveling from Seward to Hope, this particular trailhead actually marks the midway point between the two towns. Today this beautiful and historic trail combines good hiking and fishing. The trail itself is rated moderate to strenuous in places, with a variety of grades, long gradual climbs, and steep switchbacks. Many people use this trail all the way through September.

Designated campsites are located along the trail, as well as eight Forest Service cabins. You can also arrange fly-in trips to these lakes from Cooper Landing.

Because the lakes in this area are deep, anglers should bring sinking lines and weighted flies. Leeches and Woolly Buggers in a variety of colors are good bets.

Throwing in some Krystal Flash or Flashabou is a good way to bring these patterns to life, and may be just the ticket for convincing fish to travel from the depths to attack your fly. If you can secure one of the Forest Service cabins, and the boat that goes with it, be sure to give trolling a shot. Rowboats are perfect for trolling flies. Strip all 90 feet of your sinking line out as you row around the lake. Vary your speed and direction and you should get into fish.

Two miles up the trailhead, the path approaches **Juneau Creek**, and periodically meets the stream all the way to Swan Lake. Juneau Creek offers fair Dolly Varden fishing, with June and July the peak times.

Nearly a half-mile before you reach Trout Lake you find the Shaft Creek tentsite on the eastern side of Resurrection Trail. If you get caught up in the beauty of the hike or explore fishing opportunities in Juneau Creek, don't feel pressured to make it to Trout Lake. You can simply make camp at the Shaft Creek site and continue on the next day.

Approximately 5 miles into the hike up Resurrection Pass Trail, you'll see **Trout Lake** about a quarter-mile to the west. This lake exceeds 100 feet in depth and is over 1.5 miles long, and there's some good lake trout fishing here. There are also good numbers of stocked rainbow trout.

Anglers who reserve the Trout Lake Forest Service cabin in advance will gain access to the rowboat that comes with it. This is a huge advantage on water this big. Fishing bait off the bottom of the lake or jigging Buzz Bombs offers the best chance at hooking into a laker. Flyfishing is tougher here because the lake trout are typically found in deeper water. You can also pack a small inflatable rubber raft or float tube in with you. The spring and fall months are best for lake trout, while stocked rainbows can be caught all spring, summer, and fall.

Two more miles up the trail will put you on the southern shores of **Juneau Lake**. The unique draw at this lake is the burbot fishery. To this day, biologists are stumped as to why this is the only lake on the Kenai Peninsula that supports a burbot population. Lake trout also inhabit this lake. If targeting burbot or lake trout, jigs or bait-fished right on the bottom will yield the best results. For rainbow trout, flies are productive. Whitefish ranging upwards of 17 inches can also be had in Juneau Lake, and small egg patterns are probably the best choice.

There are two Forest Service cabins at Juneau Lake, both with rowboats. If you're serious about nailing burbot, you might want to consider a fly-in trip, which will allow you to bring in a small motor to better cover the water. Romig Cabin sits on the southeast shores of the lake, while Juneau Lake Cabin occupies the central-eastern lakeshore. When reserving these cabins through the Forest Service, be sure to inquire about the availability of boats on the lake. If the cabins are unavailable, you can also use the Juneau Creek tentsite on the west side of the trail.

Juneau Lake is as far as most people hiking into the area choose to go. But if time is on your side and you just can't seem to get enough of the fresh mountain air, the trail doesn't end here.

Nine miles from the trailhead, and approximately 2.5 miles from the northern shore of Juneau Lake, you'll find **Swan Lake**. This long, slender lake holds very good numbers of rainbow, lake trout, and Dolly Varden. In the fall, when migrating red salmon make their way into Swan Lake by way of the Chickaloon River, the fishing can be great. As would be expected, egg patterns and Egg-Sucking Leeches are tough to beat at this time.

Forest Service cabins sit at the east and west ends of the lake, but the west side cabin can only be reached by floatplane. Campsites are also readily available on the eastern end of the lake. For anglers serious about catching fish in a high mountain lake, this one is worth spending some time on.

If you really want to test your hiking legs, **Devil's Pass Lake** is a 13-mile hike from the Resurrection Pass Trailhead. This lake is miniscule compared to the others encountered along the way, but it does offer good bank fishing. The narrow nature of this lake and the many points of land protruding into the water make this lake good for fly anglers. Flyfishing from shore will no doubt get you into Dollys, though they'll run considerably smaller than what you'll find in surrounding waters. If you do make it this far, though, I'd be willing to bet you'll have the pond all to yourself.

Another access point leads directly to Devil's Pass Lake, but you'll have to work at this one. At mile 39.5 on the Seward Highway, Devil's Pass Trailhead climbs to the top of Devil's Pass at an elevation of 2,400 feet. With an uphill climb of 7 miles through some moderate to rugged country, this journey is best left to serious anglers who are in good shape and know how to travel light.

Fuller Lakes Trailhead

Fuller Lakes Trailhead is located north of the Sterling Highway at mile 57. A hike just shy of 2 miles will put you at **Lower Fuller Lake**, which is noted for its grayling fishing. Due to the demanding uphill hike, the only watercraft you can realistically get into this lake is a float tube, but it will be worth every bit of effort. The deeper the water you can fish in, the larger the grayling tend to run, especially on the northern end. Expect these little beauties to reach up to 15 inches and hit on a variety of dry flies. Mosquitoes, Adams, and Black Gnats are all good grayling standbys.

One more mile up the trail puts you at **Fuller Lake**, where you'll find good Dolly Varden angling. Again, those who go to the effort to pack a float tube into this little lake will be rewarded. Sinking lines are useful if you're fishing from a tube, as are weighted Woolly Buggers and leech patterns.

Skilak Road Lakes and Streams

Skilak Lake Road turns south off the Sterling Highway at mile 58, rejoining it at mile 75.3. There are numerous lakes and streams off both sides of the road. While some of these bodies of water are barren of fish, there are plenty of angling opportunities available on this scenic route. The improved gravel road also runs by several trailheads and campgrounds.

Hidden Lake

The turnoff to Hidden Lake is 3.5 miles up Skilak Lake Road. This large lake offers tent and RV camping and a boat ramp at its eastern entrance. Hidden Lake is one of the most popular lake fisheries on the peninsula and is one of only three lakes on the Kenai holding kokanee, or landlocked red salmon. Rainbow and Dolly Varden are also abundant here, and the best fishing is usually at the west end of the lake, around the islands, and inside the many shallow bays.

Lake trout also thrive here. The best time for fly anglers to tie into these hefty mackinaw is in early spring, as soon as the ice recedes from the banks. Lakers move in tight to shore at this time, cruising for food. Leech patterns cast into the shallows will take some nice fish.

During the summer months, lake trout retreat to deeper waters, and fishing bait or jigs and trolling plugs is your best bet for pulling lakers from this water. As the lake has a depth of 150 feet, finding lake trout this time of year can be a challenge.

Mid-August through September is the best time for rainbow trout and Dollys, while kokanee can be caught throughout the summer. For kokanee, Red-Butted Woolly Buggers tied with black or green bodies can be effective when stripped behind a fast-sinking line. If you're boating, remember that high winds can develop very quickly here.

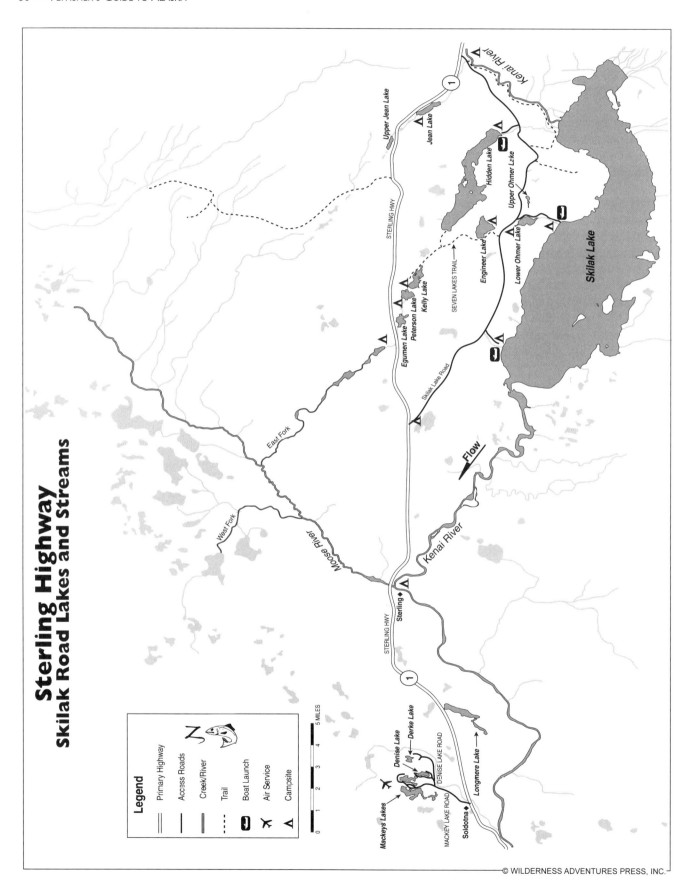

Sterling Highway
Skilak Road Lakes and Streams

Legend

Primary Highway	
Access Roads	
Creek/River	
Trail	
Boat Launch	
Air Service	
Campsite	

0 1 2 3 4 5 MILES

© WILDERNESS ADVENTURES PRESS, INC.

Skilak Lake is fun to fish on a calm day like this, but on windy days be careful not to get caught out on the lake.

Ohmer Lakes

Upper and Lower Ohmer Lakes sit just south of Skilak Lake Road at miles 7.5 and 8.5 respectively. These lakes have good numbers of Dollys and rainbows, but due to their proximity to the road, they can receive a great deal of fishing pressure. If you get here just as the ice is melting off these lakes the fishing can be good and the crowds dramatically less than what you'll find a few weeks later. Plenty of bank access gives fly anglers a shot at a lot of water. There's a campground on the north end of Lower Ohmer Lake.

Skilak Lake

Three-quarters of a mile south of Lower Ohmer Lake there's another campground on the shores of one of the peninsula's largest bodies of water, Skilak Lake. The Upper Skilak Lake Campground and boat launch offer big-lake fans a chance to camp and fish to their hearts content. Remember to use caution when launching a boat on this lake due to the extreme winds that kick up off the Kenai Mountains.

At mile 13.7, there's a more popular boat launch and campground. Lower Skilak Lake Campground puts anglers in a better place to target the world-famous trophy rainbows found lurking at the lake's outlet on the upper Kenai River. Because Skilak Lake is so silt infested, fishing with just about anything but bait is unproductive. This is why most anglers concentrate at the mouth of the lake.

To the west of Skilak Lake, several attractive lakes tempt the angler, but waste no time wetting a line in them. Frisbee, Olson, Fire, Kaknu, Hunter, and Sahot Lakes, just to name a few, are barren of fish.

Engineer Lake

At mile 9.5 on the Skilak Lake Road you'll come to Engineer Lake, which has a campground on its south shore. This is a special little lake for the simple reason that it is home to landlocked silver salmon as well as rainbow trout and Dolly Varden. The success rate for the little 14- to 16-inch salmon on a fly is surprisingly high, and the easy access makes Engineer Lake popular among locals and tourists alike.

If you're willing to launch a small craft, you can get away from the high-pressure areas and into some good fishing. Try trolling sinking lines for the salmon. Red-Butted Woolly Buggers and Beadhead Crystal Buggers will convince the mini-salmon to strike.

Seven Lakes Trailhead

Engineer Lake is also the starting point for the Seven Lakes Trailhead. This trail runs into the Sterling Highway at mile 70.8, where Egumen Lake Wayside is located. Unless you're looking to stretch your legs with a 5-mile hike, I recommend accessing the trail off the Sterling Highway. From here, the three main lakes that hold fish can be reached with less time and trouble.

Egumen Lake, **Peterson Lake**, and **Kelly Lake** are all connected by the Seven Lakes Trail and offer very good bank fishing for rainbows. While Egumen Lake requires a quarter-mile hike, both Peterson and Kelly can be reached by car off the Sterling Highway at mile 68.3. There are campgrounds on the north shores of both of these lakes.

You'll find **Watson Lake** and its campground on the north side of the Sterling Highway at mile 71.2. There's a boat launch here, and the fishing is best early and late in the season. Small boats are useful for tracking down the rainbows in this water. The fishing can be very productive at the lake's outlet. If the weather is calm, fishing dry flies in the evening can be a blast. Don't be afraid to cover the water by trolling sinking lines and weighted flies, either.

Jean Lake and Upper Jean Lake

Backtracking east on the Sterling Highway, the only fisheries we missed by taking the Skilak Lake Road were Jean Lake and Upper Jean Lake. The Jean Lake Campground sits right along the highway at mile 60. Despite its location, this lake receives relatively little pressure, but this could be due to the fact the fish run small. Beginning in August, the rainbow fishing can be very good, though, especially on egg patterns. Boats can be launched on this lake, and trolling flies and casting along shorelines is productive for both rainbows and Dollys.

Upper Jean Lake is just a little farther down the road at mile 62 on the Sterling Highway. This lake also has plenty of nice rainbow trout, with silver salmon in abundance. Flyfishing from the bank is possible here and is especially productive for rainbows from the second half of July through August.

Moose River

Moving west from where Skilak Lake Road meets the Sterling Highway, there's little fishing opportunity until you pass through the town of Sterling, home of the Moose River.

The town of Sterling boasts more than 6,000 residents and is most noted for it's location at the confluence of the Kenai and Moose Rivers, as well as for being the gateway for the Swanson River Canoe System within Kenai National Wildlife Refuge. This attraction alone draws a large number of anglers during the summer and fall months.

Northern pike were illegally introduced to the waters around Anchorage. Here, Tanner Hanes shows just how big the pike in the area are getting, and why many anglers are now intentionally targeting them. (Photo Cameron Hanes)

The Moose River is best accessed from the Izaak Walton Campground on the south side of the road at mile 82.1. The most popular spot on this river is where it flows into the Kenai. Red and silver salmon are the main quarry, with kings, pinks, rainbows, and Dollys also present.

In June, the first run of red salmon makes its way into the Moose River, with an even greater run arriving in August. The silver salmon fishing is best in September and October, while king fishing is most productive from June through the annual July 31 closure. Fishing from the bank is the main approach on the Moose River. Though drifting the river in canoes and small skiffs is also popular and effective, this activity is restricted to the section of water above the Sterling Highway bridge.

Due to excessive fishing pressure on the Moose River, the ADF&G has been obligated to enforce specific regulations applying to this fishery. Be certain you're up to date on current regulations before wetting a line here.

Longmere, Mackey, Denise, and Derik Lakes

Longmere Lake is located at mile 89 on the Sterling Highway and is home to good stocked rainbow trout.

At mile 92.8, Mackey Lake Road turns north off the Sterling. Follow this road for 2 miles and you'll see both West and East Mackey Lakes. Denise Lake can be reached by turning right on Denise Lake Road 1.5 miles up East Mackey Road. Derik Lake can also be found off Denise Lake Road. All four of these lakes are famous for their northern pike fishing. Northern pike are not indigenous to these lakes; they were illegally planted there around the mid-20th century. It's no surprise that these fierce predators have all but destroyed the rainbow populations in these lakes. Boats can be launched at both Mackey Lakes. While most pike are taken on big spoons, spinners, and plugs, big flashy flies can also be productive.

COOPER LANDING

Population: 285
Alaska Area Code: 907
Zip Code: 99572

FISHING GUIDES/LODGING

Alaska River Adventures, P.O. Box 725; 595-2000; www.AlaskaRiverAdventures.com

Alaska Troutfitters, P.O. Box 570; 595-1212; www.aktroutfitters.com; offers a flyfishing school program complete with lessons on the river

Alaska Wildland Adventures, 16520 Sterling Hwy.; 1-800-478-4100; www.alaskasportfish.com

Bruce Nelson's Float Fishing Service, P.O. Box 545; 595-1313

Gwin's Lodge, 14865 Sterling Highway; 595-1266; www.gwinslodge.com; will arrange fly-in fishing to remote lakes

Ingram's Sport Fishing Cabins, milepost 48.1 on Sterling Hwy.; 1-866-595-1213; www.kenairiverlodging.com

Kenai Cache Tackle & Guiding, P.O. Box 533; 595-1401; www.kenaicache.com

Kenai Princess Wilderness Lodge & RV Park, Cooper Landing; 1-800-426-0500; mile 3 Bean Creek Road, off Milepost 47.7 Sterling Hwy.; on-site fishing, full-service hookups, dump station, water, showers, toilets, laundry, groceries, snack bar, pets allowed; www.PrincessAlaskaLodge.com

Upper Kenai River Inn, P.O. Box 838; 595-3333; www.upperkenairiverinn.com

TACKLE SHOPS

Alaska Troutfitters, mile 48.2 on Sterling Hwy., P.O. Box 570; 595-1212; www.aktroutfitters.com

Cooper Landing Grocery & Hardware, Cooper Landing; 595-1677

Gwin's Lodge, 14865 Sterling Highway; 595-1266; www.ool.com/gwins

ACCOMMODATIONS

Hamilton's Place, P.O. Box 569; 595-1260; 24-hour emergency towing, locksmith, minor car repair service and parts; Information center for Russian River and surrounding area; hamspl@arctic.net

Kenai Princess Wilderness Lodge, mile 47.7 on Sterling Road, mile 3 Bean Creek Road; 1-800-426-0500, 595-1425

The Hutch B&B, P.O. Box 823; 595-1270

The Shrew's Nest, P.O. Box 762; 595-1257

CAMPGROUNDS AND RV PARKS

Cooper Creek Campground, Mile 50.7 on both sides of the Sterling Hwy.; 29 campsites, 17 of which are suited for RV use, firepits, water, tables, toilets; fees

Crescent Creek Campground, Mile 45 on Sterling Hwy., 1+ miles of Quartz Creek Road; 9 campsites, toilets, water; fees

Kenai Princess RV Park, Mile 2 on Bean Creek Rd.; 595-1425

Kenai-Russian River Campground, Mile 55 on the Sterling Hwy.; 180 campsites if which175 are suited for RV use, toilet, water, boat launch, wheelchair access observation area; fees

Miller's Homestead, P.O. Box 574; 595-1406; on-site fishing, dump station, water, showers, toilets

Russian River Campground, Mile 52.7 Sterling Hwy.; 83 RV suitable campsites, toilets,water, firepits, tables, dump station, fish cleaning station; fee; this is the site of theferry that transports anglers across the Kenai River to access bank fishing opportunities along both the Kenai and Russian Rivers

Sunrise Inn & RV Park, Mile 45 Sterling Hwy.; 595-1222; drinking water, toilets, snack bar

Quartz Creek Campground, Mile 45 Sterling Hwy., on Quartz Creek Road; 45 campsites, 5 picnic sites, tables, firepits, water, flush toilets, dump station, boat ramp, paved; fees

STERLING

Population: 6,138
Alaska Area Code: 907
Zip Code: 99672

GUIDE SERVICES

Flipp & Finn Charters, P.O. Box 731; 1-800-759-6679; www.flipnfincharters.com

Big Sky Charter & Fishcamp; 1-877-536-2425; www.kenaiguide.com

Bill White's Alaska Sports Lodge, Mile 82.5, Sterling Hwy.; 1-800-662-9672;www.kenai-river.com

Silver Bullet Guide Service/Bed & Breakfast, P.O. Box 444; 262-0887;www.alaska.net/~silverb

ACCOMMODATIONS

Alaska Cozy Cabins, P.O. Box 604; 262-2401

Alaska Mountain View Cabins, P.O. Box 423; 1-888-388-4827; www.alaskacanoetrips.com

Angler's Lodge & Fish Camp, P.O. Box 508; 1-888-262-1747; www.alaska.net/~anglers/

Blue Moose Lodge, 35555 Kenai Spur Hwy., Suite 275; 1-877-256-6673; though located in Soldotna, the Blue Moose offers guided trips on the Kenai Canoe Trails; www.blue-moose.com

Vacation Cabins, Mile 81.7, Sterling Hwy.; 1-800-759-6679

CAMPGROUNDS AND RV PARKS

Alaska Canoe & Campground, 35292 Sterling Hwy.; 262-2331

Bing Brown's Sportsman's RV Park & Motel, P.O. Box 235, Mile 81 Sterling Hwy.; 262-4780; full hookups, drinking water, showers, toilets, laundry, tent camping

Cast Away Riverside RV Park & Cabins, P.O. Box 189; 1-800-478-6446; on-site fishing; dump station, water, showers, toilets, laundry, snack bar, tent camping, pets allowed, each site has a private yard, social and sport activities are available

Fish On Inn & RV Park, P.O. Box 25, Mile 79.2 Sterling Hwy.; 262-5297; on-site fishing, full-service hookups

Hamilton's Place, P.O. Box 569, Mile 48.5 Sterling Hwy.; 782-3222; on-site fishing; full-service hookups, water, showers, toilets, laundry, groceries, snack bar, tent camping

Izaak Walton Campground, Mile 81 Sterling Hwy.; 8 acres, 26 campsites, camping fee, picnic sites, toilets, water, boat launch

Morgan's Landing Campground, 85 Sterling Hwy.; 279 acres, 42 campsites, camping fee, picnic sites, toilets, water, trails

Polar Campground, P.O. Box 571; 262-7877

Sterling Gifts & Campground, P.O. Box 211, Mile 83,. 1 Sterling Hwy.; 262-2331; dump station, water, groceries

Real Alaskan Cabins, RV Park & Boat Rentals, P.O. Box 69; 262-6077; www.realalaskan.com

RESTAURANTS

Cook's Corner Gas & Deli, Mile 81.7 Sterling Hwy.; 262-6021

CANOE RENTALS

Alaska Canoe & Campground, 35292 Sterling Hwy., at milepost 84 in Sterling; 262-2331;rentals and guided trips on Swanson River Trails, showers, laundromat, shuttle service, camping and fishing gear; alaskacanoe@yahoo.com

Alaska Raft and Kayak, 401 West Tudor Road, Anchorage; 1-800-606-5950; www.alaskaraftandkayak.com

Weigner's Backcountry Guiding, on Otter Trail Road in Sterling; 262-7840; must make reservations in March or April to secure summer activities

AUTO REPAIR

Moose River Auto & RV Parts, P.O. Box 689; 262-5333; 1-800-760-5333

TOURIST ATTRACTIONS

Scout Lake State Recreation Area, 85 Sterling Hwy.; 164 acres, 10 picnic sites, picnic shelter, toilets, water, trails, fishing

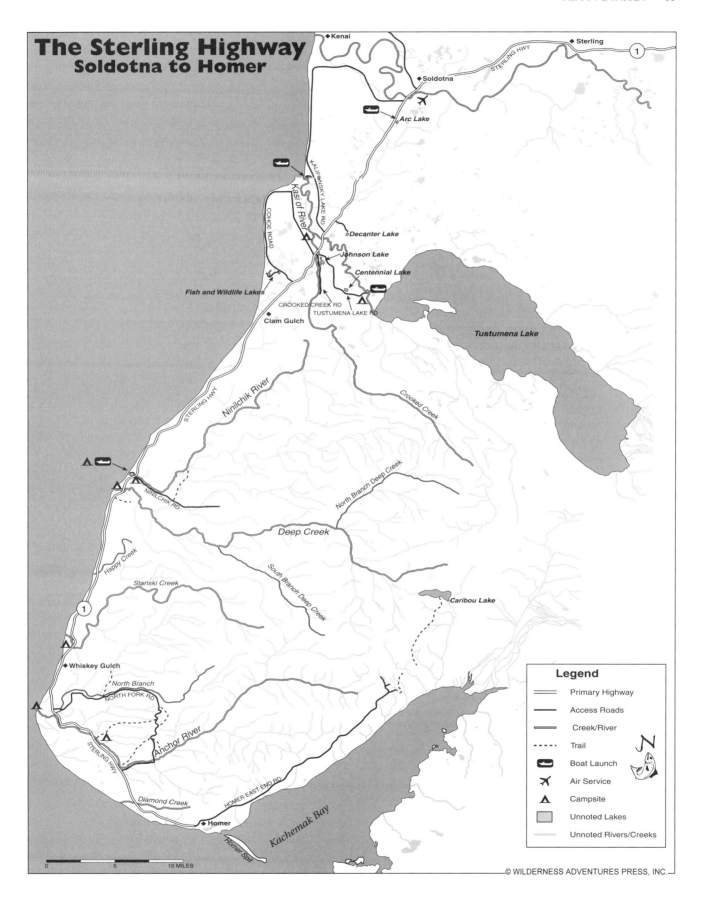

The Sterling Highway
Soldotna to Homer

Kenai

Sterling

1

STERLING HWY

Soldotna

Arc Lake

KALIFONSKY LAKE RD

Kasilof River

COHOE ROAD

Decanter Lake

Johnson Lake

Centennial Lake

Fish and Wildlife Lakes

CROOKED CREEK RD

TUSTUMENA LAKE RD

Clam Gulch

Tustumena Lake

STERLING HWY

Ninilchik River

Crooked Creek

North Branch Deep Creek

NINILCHIK RD

Deep Creek

Happy Creek

Stariski Creek

South Branch Deep Creek

Caribou Lake

1

Whiskey Gulch

North Branch

NORTH FORK RD

STERLING HWY

Anchor River

HOMER EAST END RD

Diamond Creek

Homer

Homer Spit

Kachemak Bay

Legend

═══	Primary Highway
───	Access Roads
───	Creek/River
----	Trail
🚤	Boat Launch
✈	Air Service
⛺	Campsite
▢	Unnoted Lakes
	Unnoted Rivers/Creeks

N

0   5   10 MILES

© WILDERNESS ADVENTURES PRESS, INC.

THE STERLING HIGHWAY: SOLDOTNA TO HOMER

When you reach Soldotna on the Sterling Highway, you have three options: continue along the highway to Homer, stop and fish the Kenai River, or head north into the lake-rich country via the extensive canoe trails.

It may feel like you're leaving civilization when you continue south on the Sterling Highway after Soldotna, but don't be fooled. Some of the Kenai Peninsula's finest fishing awaits you on this stretch of road, and there are plenty of small towns to cater to your every need. Be it small lakes or mid-sized streams, the next several miles of road will lead you to angling paradise. Many tourists base themselves in Soldotna and make day trips to the surrounding fisheries.

Following the July 31 king salmon closure, tourist traffic in the Soldotna area declines considerably. Wait another month and you won't even recognize the place. This means that the wonderful rivers and streams in the area are wide open just as the silver salmon and steelhead are arriving. I've spent many days fishing some of the most popular waters along this stretch of road without seeing another angler from daylight to dark. The chance to land more than two-dozen hard-fighting fish ranging upwards of 15 pounds on a fly rod only sweetens the deal.

The World-Famous Kenai River

The city of Soldotna serves as the primary hub on the Kenai Peninsula, including traffic around the mighty Kenai River. Though a main attraction to the peninsula now, Soldotna was not so popular in the early days.

Anglers travel from all over the world to experience what the Kenai River has to offer.

Because there was no access into the current town site, settlers had to cover many miles of rugged terrain on foot.

While some settlers flew or took a barge to the town of Kenai then hiked 11 miles to Soldotna, others boarded a train to Moose Pass then trod 70 miles through flooded bogs and high mountains to reach their final destination. The incentive was the chance to homestead new land, which was opened for the first time in 1947 when WWII veterans were granted a 90-day preference in filing claims over nonveterans.

There are two stories of how Soldotna got its name, although which one is the truth may forever remain a mystery. One version claims the city of Soldotna derived its name from an Athabascan word that means "the forked stream," while the other claims it came from the Russian word for "soldier." Whatever the case, Soldotna it is.

Today more than 3,750 permanent residents call Soldotna home. Many people work outside the city in the gas, oil, mining, or commercial fishing industries. But banks, stores, malls, restaurants, and offices abound in Soldotna, meaning there's more than you'd ever need to live comfortably here. But it's the summer months, during the height of the sport-fishing season, when Soldotna bustles with activity—and for good reason.

Not only is the Kenai River, which flows right through Soldotna, Alaska's most renowned salmon fishery, it's likely the best-known salmon stream on earth. It's also home to the current world-record king salmon (97 pounds, 4 ounces). No doubt there have been fish hooked that have eclipsed this coveted record, which was set on May 17, 1985, but none have been landed. Many experts predict the next world-record salmon will come from the Kenai, a river that holds the largest strain of king, or chinook, salmon on earth.

Besides the superlative king fishing—pursued almost exclusively by drift fishermen—the fly angling for rainbows, Dolly Varden, and red, silver, and pink salmon can be world class. The key to success is timing your arrival with fish runs and tourist traffic, then deciding which of the three sections of the Kenai you want to fish.

If you want to flyfish for king salmon on the lower Kenai, few guides will be eager to assist you. It's not that they don't like flyfishing, it's just that in order to get you onto big kings, they have to go in the same area where they would normally bait-fish, which means all the other guides will be there as well. As the other guides won't be flyfishing, it'll be tough for one boat to work into prime water and expect to tease a king into biting. However, that's not to say it can't or doesn't happen.

If and when a monster king is hooked on a fly rod, you may have to spend hours following it up and down the

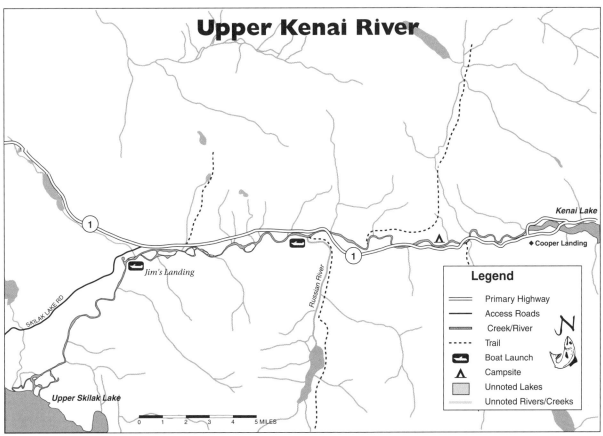

Upper Kenai River

Kenai Lake

Cooper Landing

Jim's Landing

Russian River

SKILAK LAKE RD

Upper Skilak Lake

Legend
- Primary Highway
- Access Roads
- Creek/River
- Trail
- Boat Launch
- Campsite
- Unnoted Lakes
- Unnoted Rivers/Creeks

N

0 1 2 3 4 5 MILES

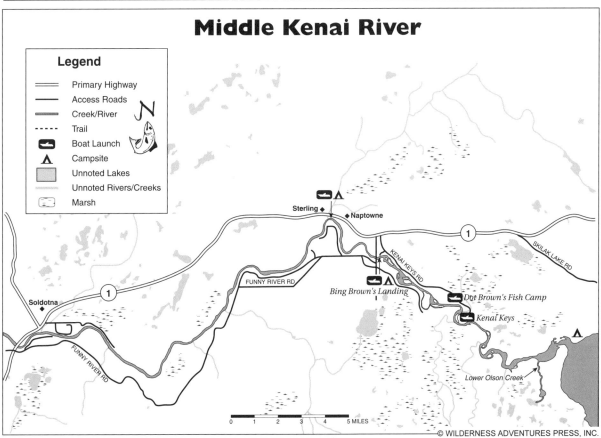

Middle Kenai River

Legend
- Primary Highway
- Access Roads
- Creek/River
- Trail
- Boat Launch
- Campsite
- Unnoted Lakes
- Unnoted Rivers/Creeks
- Marsh

N

Sterling ◆
◆ Naptowne

SKILAK LAKE RD

FUNNY RIVER RD

KENAI KEYS RD

Bing Brown's Landing

Dot Brown's Fish Camp

Soldotna ◆

Kenai Keys

FUNNY RIVER RD

Lower Olson Creek

0 1 2 3 4 5 MILES

© WILDERNESS ADVENTURES PRESS, INC.

Scott Haugen is happy with an exceptional humpy, or pink, salmon taken on the Kenai River.

river. Not only is this hard on the fish if you're planning to release it, but chasing your quarry amid the phalanx of boats can rub other anglers the wrong way. If you're targeting kings with a fly rod, the middle and upper sections of the Kenai are where you want to be. These areas are further removed from the crowds and have plenty of open water to roam when you do hook that king of a lifetime.

The Upper Kenai River

The upper Kenai River runs from Kenai Lake to where the river meets massive Skilak Lake. This stretch has good boat access and some of the best trophy-trout fishing in Alaska. Rainbows and Dolly Varden up to 15 pounds are taken with surprising regularity from the upper river. When the salmon spawn commences, big trout are rou-

tinely nabbed on egg patterns nymphed below a floating line on a 9-foot tapered leader. Adding a split shot 2 feet above the fly helps achieve a natural presentation. And a large strike indicator is critical. I've had the best luck with a West Coast Floats strike indicator, as the bright foam body rides high in the water and is easy to keep track of even when your line is 30 yards downstream.

Experienced driftboaters can put in at Cooper Landing boat launch at the base of the Sterling Highway bridge, where it crosses the river at mile 82. From here, the river varies in width and depth, with holes, slots, and runs changing with the seasons—and sometimes with each new storm. Toward the end of the run, there is excellent red salmon fishing at the mouth of the Russian River, with the peak occurring from mid- to late July. The take-out for this scenic float is at the Russian River Ferry and boat launch at mile 73.5 on the Sterling Highway. If you want to repeat this run over the course of a few days, camping is available at Cooper Creek Campground, on the south bank of the river at mile 79.

Another very popular and productive drift takes boaters from the Ferry Launch to Jim's Landing. This 4-mile drift has some spectacular flyfishing opportunities, be it from the bank, wading amid gravel bars, or from the boat.

The third and final run on the upper Kenai is also one of the most pristine in all of Alaska. The beauty of this float is enough to make the trip worthwhile; throw in some trophy rainbows and it will be the angling journey of a lifetime. But this is a run only experienced oarsmen should attempt. This 5-mile float from Jim's Landing to the headwaters of Skilak Lake takes you through Class II and III rapids in the famous Kenai River Canyon. Bringing along a little kicker motor is a wise choice, for once you reach Skilak Lake 5 miles of dead water still lie ahead. Though rowing through the lake to reach the Upper Skilak Lake ramp is not grueling, it does take some time. But the most sensible reason for including a motor is in case high winds kick up from the glaciers surrounding this lake. Every year boats are claimed by treacherous winds, so proceed with caution.

Hire a guide to take you through if you're unfamiliar with the Upper Kenai. Not only will this decision make the journey a safer one, the guides who routinely work this water know how it's constantly changing and where the big trout are.

When the salmon make their way into the upper river, the pattern of choice to fool trophy trout is undoubtedly the single egg. Prior to this time, however, trout can be taken on large, dark streamers such as leeches, sculpins, and Woolly Buggers. Switch to flesh flies after the spawn and then to smolt patterns from November on.

Because the majority of the upper river remains free of ice throughout the winter, you can have exceptional Dolly fishing right through the month of January. In addition, the silver action can be red-hot during January and into February, despite the chilly weather.

The opening for trout fishing on the upper river is usually on or around June 11, but, as with all waters on the peninsula, regulations are forever changing and it is up to each angler to keep informed about current notices.

The Middle Kenai River

While the ADF&G designates the remainder of the Kenai River—below Skilak Lake all the way to the mouth—as the lower Kenai, local anglers and guides commonly split it into two sections, based largely on the extent to which fish are actively pursued in each. In what we will refer to as the middle section of the Kenai River—from the mouth of Skilak Lake to the Soldotna bridge—the fishing can be exceptional for rainbow trout, Dolly Varden, and king, red, and silver salmon.

For trophy rainbows and Dollys, the upper portion of the middle section is where you'll want to spend time. Driftboaters can launch at the state campground at the bottom end of Skilak Lake. After floating through 3 miles of slack water, you'll come to Lower Olson Creek. The fishing begins around the next bend. Segments of river dubbed the Super Hole, Secret Hole, and Renfro's Hole delineate areas on the river known for consistently producing big rainbows. The rainbow and Dolly fishing is good all the way down to Bing's Landing. There is also a private launch within the Kenai Keys known as Dot's, or Dot's Fish Camp, which can be accessed off Kenai Keys Road on the south side of the Sterling Highway.

Perhaps the best bank-fishing opportunities in this section come at the Upper and Lower Torpedo Hole. Turn south on Kenai Keys Road at mile 79.3 on the Sterling Highway. Follow the road to its terminus near Torpedo Lake. From here, you can follow trails to some of the best red salmon fishing anywhere on the Kenai River.

It was at this exact spot that I had my first Kenai River fishing experience. The red salmon were running and everyone was catching fish. It was great. We even had a black bear pay us a visit, although nothing serious came of it. Shoulder to shoulder we stood, using the Kenai Flip to slip our Coho flies into the mouths of red salmon on the move. No more than a dozen anglers lined the bank at that time, but since then I've seen three times that many folks trying their luck at the Torpedo Hole.

The fishing is relatively easy here, with shallow water in which you can see the schools of fish swimming by. And there are more than enough fish to go around.

Multiple hookups are the norm when the reds are in thick during the last couple weeks of July and the first week of August.

Silvers, pinks, rainbows, and Dollys can also be taken from shore at the Torpedo Hole. In fact, while filming a trout fishing show for the Outdoor Channel's "Outdoor America," guide Brett Gesh got our crew onto a whopping 14-pound rainbow right at the point of the Lower Torpedo Hole, and we even managed to land it. We were operating from a boat on this occasion, but were within easy casting distance of shore.

Near Dow Island on this same drift, Gesh got me into the biggest rainbow of my life on a fly rod, a 13-pound trophy. The crazy thing is, I'd lost a 12-pounder only minutes earlier. Gesh has an incredible success rate on this stretch of river for landing trophy rainbows and Dollys from mid-August through October on fly rods. He credits much of his success to keeping tabs on the king spawn. If the kings die out in one stretch, he'll move to find active redds, as it's behind these nests that you'll find ravenous trout and char.

In addition to the king spawn, Gesh concentrates on the red salmon spawn, and in even-numbered years, the pink spawn cycle. When all the salmon spawning is complete, he'll switch to flesh flies. Surprisingly few guides operate in this stretch at this time of year. If you're after big trout and wish to escape the crowds in the upper river, try the upper portion of the middle section of the Kenai; you'll soon see why this is one of my favorite areas on the entire river.

The author's father, Jerry Haugen, admires a dandy mid-summer rainbow taken on the middle section of the Kenai.

Fishing bead patterns behind schools of spawning sockeye salmon is a great method for taking Dollys and rainbows.

There's good fishing throughout the river from Naptowne Rapids down to Sterling. If you want to take a crack at landing a king from the bank, hit Morgan's Hole at river mile 31. In addition, there's a public boat landing and state recreation area at Morgan's Hole, which can be reached by turning south on Scout Lake Loop Road at mile 84.7 off the Sterling Highway. This turns into Lou Morgan Road, which leads to the river. From May 15 through the end of the king season, fishing in this area is prohibited from a boat, meaning bank anglers have the river to themselves.

The next 7 miles are best left to experienced boaters. If you're determined to go it alone, consult local authorities for current river conditions and places to watch out for. Ken Lacy of Ken's Tackle in Soldotna (907-262-6870) has been around for years. He knows this river as well as anyone and is willing to share valuable advice and words of wisdom.

As you near the town of Soldotna, you can stop at Swift Water Campground by turning east on East Redoubt Avenue at mile 94.1. After a half-mile, take the first right and follow the signs to the camp and boat launch. Though this is not a prime king stretch, some trophy salmon are taken from this run every summer.

Right beneath the Soldotna bridge, on the downriver side, platforms have been put in place for red salmon anglers. In fact, various sites along the banks of the Kenai have been blessed with such structures, offering safe and easy bank access. More and more such sites are being added, so inquire at local tackle shops or visitors centers for updated information on platform fishing access.

Please resist the urge to pull kings off their spawning beds in this stretch, though. A large percentage of these fish are at their spawning grounds, and they should not be harassed. Toward the end of the king season I referred to above, Gesh and I spent some time chasing big rainbows in the upper half of the middle section of river. I was dumfounded to see a licensed guide pull king after king off spawning beds at this time. Though he wasn't technically doing anything illegal, he was certainly violating the unwritten law of ethical fishing. To preserve the wild runs of the world's largest salmon, all anglers must exercise common sense.

To maximize your fishing efficiency on the middle and lower runs of the Kenai, a jet boat is ideal. If you're launching at Bing's Landing, which is located off the Sterling Highway at mile 80.3, be aware that there's a big, heavy set of rapids just below. The navigation of Naptowne Rapids should be left to trained professionals. And from the middle of June on, negotiating these rapids is best done in a jet boat.

A Kenai River double—a Dolly Varden and rainbow trout, both over six pounds, taken on beads.

FISHING THE BEAD

Another form of flyfishing common to the Kenai Peninsula—and one you'll want to be sure to have in your arsenal if you visit during the salmon spawn—is working the bead. Beads are made to represent eggs deposited on the river bottom by spawning salmon, be they kings, reds, silvers, pinks, or chums. In the Kenai River drainage, it's king salmon eggs that are most closely matched by trophy-trout anglers.

Alaska Troutfitters in Cooper Landing is well versed in bead fishing techniques and has the best selection of beads I've ever seen. They specialize in hand painting and crafting beads to perfectly mimic what's found in the river at any given time, and this plays a huge role in their success. Because salmon eggs vary in size and color among different species, matching the bead to the egg is important.

Having personally tried every possible tactic for big rainbows and trophy Dollys during August and September on the Kenai, I have no doubt that the bead draws the most success. Beads are effective everywhere in Alaska that there are salmon spawning and trout and char following. In fact, my largest trout taken on a fly rod, a 31-inch, 13-pound beauty, fell to a bead.

Whether you're fishing beads on the Kenai or Russian Rivers, or anywhere else in the state, hitting the salmon spawn is critical. Too early, and the trout aren't yet targeting eggs; too late, and not enough salmon eggs remain to keep trout interested. Two weeks before catching my 13-pound rainbow you could have fished beads all day and not gotten a nibble, as the salmon spawn had not yet begun.

To select the right bead color, first observe loose eggs in the stream. One of the biggest errors anglers make is to hold an egg in the palm of the hand (and out of the water). The hand becomes nothing more than a reflective surface that masks the true color of the egg. If you're unable to assess egg color in the water, hold it up in natural light, between thumb and forefinger. This way, light can freely pass through the egg, revealing its true colors.

Anglers should note that egg coloration can vary among a single species. For example, infertile eggs are red to orange in color and are transparent, carrying a whitish film; trout love these. Fertilized eggs turn milky white moments after being fertilized, while eggs that are further developed will carry a visible embryo.

The setup for bead fishing is very simple. Peg the bead no more than 2 inches above a size 8 or 10 scud hook. The "2-inch rule" is Alaska state law, meant to prevent fish from getting snagged and injured by a dangling hook. Pegging a bead above the hook allows it to move naturally, while ensuring the gap of the hook is not covered. The design of scud hooks makes them ideal for bead fishing.

Place a small split shot on the leader 18 inches above the bead. This will keep the bead near the bottom, where salmon eggs naturally roll along. If you're not occasionally nicking bottom, increase the size or number of split shot.

A 9-foot tapered leader and a floating line are ideal for fishing moving water with a bead. Match the tippet to the size of the trout you're targeting as well as the prevailing water conditions. For trophy Dollys and trout of 10 pounds or more, 0X tippet is a solid choice. For small trout in small streams, 5X tippet may suffice. If the water is gin clear, I'll use a fluorocarbon leader, as the refraction index ensures low visibility while maintaining impressive strength and abrasion resistance.

As for the strike indicators when fishing beads, I like one that stays on top and is highly visible. West Coast Float's new strike indicator is perfect for nymphing beads on the Kenai and other big rivers, especially when you have 30 feet of floating line out in a turbulent stretch of water. These foam floats can be pegged to the leader with a toothpick and are easy to adjust for proper depth. Let the bead drift naturally along the bottom and focus on the strike indicator.

If you're fishing from a boat, dead drifting is the best way to achieve the perfect speed of presentation. Let the boat drift with the natural current flow, and then feed line out from the side and even behind the boat, depending on how many anglers are present. In murky waters like the Kenai, drifting over fish with the boat doesn't stop them from striking your rolling bead. When fishing this way, the strike indicator can be anywhere from directly off your rod tip to 30 feet away from the boat. It's not critical to make long casts when floating, as you can just adjust the position of the boat.

REGULATION UPDATE: As of 2004, it is now illegal to use the bead technique in fly fishing only waters in Alaska. This includes the Russian River and a section of the Kenai.

Lower Kenai River

Most anglers consider the run from the Soldotna bridge to where the Kenai River flows into Cook Inlet as the lower river. This stretch of water extends more than 21 miles and offers what is perhaps the best king salmon angling in the world. But don't go here thinking you'll be fighting monster kings every minute of the day; you won't. It takes an average of 25 hours per angler to take a single king on the Kenai River. For the record, it took me more than 60 hours of fishing this river before I took my first king. The fact that it tipped the scales to 70 pounds helped me forget about those long, slow days when I didn't get so much as a bite.

Of course, I was fishing the river on my schedule, not that of the kings. Although there are fish to be had from May through July—barring emergency closures—the odds of success skyrocket when bait is allowed. On the trip I got my 70-pounder, my friend Gesh, my father, and I went on to hook 20 kings in 3 days, landing 15. While these numbers are above average, they are not unrealistic when you hook up with the right guide—or if you know what you're doing.

The lower stretch of river is the most user-friendly for do-it-yourself boaters. But prior to launching, check current regulations pertaining to the use of motorized boats: what days they can be run and what closures might be in force. On the days when guides are restricted from fishing, the amount of open water can leave a sport-fishing angler drooling—and catching fish.

Below the Soldotna bridge, there's a boat launch and good bank fishing at Centennial Campground. Turn north on Kalifornsky Beach Road at the four-way stoplight just west of the Soldotna bridge. Hang a right and follow the signs to the campground. Bank anglers take an astounding number of red salmon here each season, with good numbers of silvers and pinks in the catch, too. There are also some nice kings taken from shore, with plenty of bank to chase the fish once hooked.

The Visitor Information Center located on the northwest side of the Soldotna bridge is worth a visit when you're in the area. There's plenty of information for traveling around the peninsula, and you'll see the world-record king salmon mounted under glass. But beware, the sight of this glorious fish will bring on a case of salmon fever, the likes of which you've never known.

You'll also want to spend some time in the area's most

complete tackle shop, Ken's Alaskan Tackle, on the southeast side of the Soldotna bridge. Ken has all the gear an angler needs for fishing the peninsula. Fred Meyer, situated on the east end of town, also has a good tackle supply, including fly gear.

From the Centennial boat launch downriver to Stewart's Landing, The Pillars, and the Eagle Rock ramp, it's a boating show for king salmon. While jet boats are the most popular choice, driftboats can also provide good angling, especially on the section that begins at the Centennial ramp.

From the Centennial launch, you can concentrate your efforts for kings on holes dubbed the College Hole, Sunken Island, and Big Eddy. Reds and silvers can be had near the banks throughout much of this run, with some bank-fishing opportunities available, mostly for boaters wishing to park and stretch their legs a bit.

From Stewart's Landing, you can access a private launch site 2 miles up the Kenai Spur Road. The Falling-In Hole and Honeymoon Cove are prime king holes, with outstanding silver fishing in these spots in September. Don't overlook the water tight to the bank when fishing silvers here. They hold right on the banks and can often be sight fished. On several occasions, Gesh and I pulled double-digit silvers from these banks using big pink bunny hair flies with a quick strip.

At mile 3.9 on the Kenai Spur Highway, Golden Eagle Avenue takes you down to The Pillars State Park and a public boat ramp. If you're using a jet boat, this launch site will allow you to reach the best holes both above and below the park.

Eagle Rock Campground and boat launch can be reached by turning on Eagle Rock Drive, at mile 5.1 on the Kenai Spur Highway. A big rock sits directly across from the ramp, smack in the middle of the river. The eagles that frequent this rock give the area its name. From here down to Beaver Creek, the king salmon action can be blue-ribbon.

Down to The Bluffs, the technique most commonly used to take kings is backtrolling diver and bait or working a K-16 Kwikfish. At The Bluffs, "boondogging" is popular and very effective. Cast your terminal gear upstream with ample weight to keep the bait on the bottom. Bounce it along the gravel bottom behind the boat as the craft drifts freely with the current. While it's not flyfishing, it's an efficient way to cover water and catch fish.

The Pasture is typically the final king hole on the Kenai. You'll know this hole when you see it, as it's flanked by lush green grass on either side, with the occasional caribou wandering about. Anchoring and letting the kings come to your diver and bait is popular in this hole. This is where—and how—I took my 70-pound king.

Make no mistake, if you want to score on a trophy-class Kenai king, using bait is virtually the only way to go. If you've come this far and if you've ever dreamed of battling a giant king, possibly the next world record, don't pass up the opportunity to fish this thrilling river. To further increase your odds, hire a reputable guide. I've had the pleasure of spending time on the river with several, and Brett Gesh (907-223-8704), Jason Dunkin (907-252-2296), and Jeff Webster (907-262-5038) are among those I can personally recommend.

The same holds true if trophy rainbows are your target. Unless you have time to devote to learning a section of water, your odds of success dramatically increase when you employ the services of a guide. Working with Alaskan Troutfitters out of Cooper Landing will be one of your best investments when it comes to nailing big 'bows on the fly.

If you're an experienced boater and towing your own sled or driftboat from home, you're all set to run the Kenai. But if you're visiting without a boat and feel proficient enough to go it alone, without the aid of a guide, consider renting a boat. If you're an experienced salmon

There are many improved platforms along the Kenai River that allow anglers easy access to fish for red, pink and silver salmon.

angler and have all the right gear and know-how, then give it a shot. Both motorized boats and driftboats can be rented through the Alaska Fishing Club in Soldotna (907-262-2226), but be sure to call ahead for reservations and price quotes. The last sled we rented during the peak of the king season in 2001 ran $200 a day, which included a 6-gallon can of gas. If you're planning to spend all day on the water, pick up an extra tank of gas.

Once you experience all the Kenai River has to offer, you'll understand why it is such a special place to so many people around the globe. If I had one day left in my life to spend fishing, it would be on the Kenai River, where I've taken large kings, silvers, reds, pinks, Dollys, and rainbows.

Because Kenai River king salmon are such a difficult species to manage, seasons and special regulations can change overnight. It's up to visiting anglers to keep abreast of current rules by observing the ADF&G fishing regulations for these waters. You can learn about emergency orders by tuning into local radio stations, reading the daily paper, or inquiring at area tackle shops.

Stream Facts: Kenai River

Seasons

- King salmon season is open on the mainstem Kenai River from the mouth up to and including Skilak from January 1 to July 31.

- For king salmon 20 inches or longer in the above waters from January 1 to June 10, anglers are allowed 1 king per day, 1 in possession, and it must be less than 40 inches or greater than 55 inches. From June 11 to 30, the one salmon must be 55 inches or longer. From July 1 to July 31, there is no size limit to the 1 salmon daily limit.

- Silver salmon season for fish measuring 16 inches or more runs from July 1 to 31 and August 4 to September 30.

- For red, pink, and king salmon under 20 inches and other salmon under 16 inches, the season is open year-round.

- From the mouth of the Kenai River upstream to the Moose River, the rainbow trout season runs from June 15 to April 14, with a 1 fish daily limit, 1 fish in possession of any size.

- From the mouth of the Kenai River upstream to Skilak Lake, the rainbow trout season runs from June 15 to April 14, with a 1 fish daily limit, 1 fish in possession limit that must be 18 inches or less.

- From the mouth of the Kenai River upstream to the Upper Killey River, the season for Dolly Varden is open year-round, with a 2 per day, 2 in possession limit.

- From the Upper Killey River upstream to Skilak Lake, the Dolly Varden season runs from June 15 to December 31, with a 1 per day, 1 in possession limit that must be 18 inches or less.

- In Skilak Lake, Dolly Varden season is open year-round, with a 1 per day, 1 in possession limit that must be 18 inches or less.

Special Regulations

- January 1 to June 30, from its mouth upstream to the outlet of Skilak Lake, only 1 unbaited single-hook artificial lure is allowed in the Kenai River.

- July 1 to July 31, from its mouth upstream to the outlet of Skilak Lake, only one single-hook artificial lure is allowed in the Kenai River.

- August 1 to December 31, from the Upper Killey River upstream to the outlet of Skilak Lake, only one unbaited single-hook artificial lure is allowed.

- October 1 to December 31, from its mouth upstream to the outlet of Skilak Lake, only unbaited artificial lures are allowed in the Kenai River.

- August 1 to 3, only unbaited artificial lures are allowed in the Kenai River from its mouth upstream to the Sterling Highway bridge at Soldotna.

- All king salmon 55 inches or longer must be sealed by ADF&G staff in Soldotna within 3 days of being caught.

- The season limit on king salmon taken from the Kenai River is 2 fish per year.

- For salmon other than kings, the daily limit is 3 fish, 3 in possession, of which only 2 per day, 2 in possession may be silver salmon.

- After taking a bag limit of 2 silver salmon 16 inches or longer from the Kenai River, a person may not fish on that same day downstream from the Upper Killey River.

- From January 1 to June 30, within a 100-yard radius of the mouth of the Moose River, the Kenai River is flyfishing only.

- Between ADF&G markers placed 100 yards upstream and 300 yards downstream from the mouth of Slikok Creek, the area is designated flyfishing-only water from January 1 to July 14 and is closed to king salmon fishing and fishing from boats during these dates.

Fish

- King, silver, red, and pink salmon, rainbow trout, Dolly Varden

River Characteristics

- The Kenai is a large, fast-flowing glacial river with a plethora of fishing opportunities. In many areas its banks can be waded for red, silver, and pink salmon, as well as Dolly Varden and rainbow trout. King salmon, trout, and char are best pursued from a boat, be it a sled or driftboat.

Fishing and Boating Access

- From its mouth all the way to Skilak Lake, there are numerous bank and boating access points along the Kenai River. Some of the best bank fishing is from campground areas, boat launches, and platforms constructed specifically for anglers. Though it's a big, fast river, the Kenai can be run in a boat by experienced hands.

Maps

- Alaska Road & Recreation Map, Kenai River (Skilak Lake to Cook Inlet); *Alaska Atlas and Gazetteer*, pages 69, 70

Arc and Decanter Lakes

Prior to heading off to the famous Kasilof River, there are two small lakes worth a look. Arc Lake is the first, sitting at mile 98.3 with camping and day-use areas available. In addition to being a popular lake for summer swimmers, it's home to stocked silver salmon. Arc also has a boat ramp, which gives fly anglers a few more options. The presence of northern pike here means that silver salmon stocking has been discontinued at present.

On the east side of the Sterling Highway at mile 107, you'll find Decanter Lake and its rainbow fishery. A short gravel road leads to this small pond, where bank fishing is the norm.

Scott Haugen relied on bait to take this 70-pound Kenai River king salmon. Landing a fish like this on a fly rod is nearly impossible on the crowded Kenai.

But if you're lucky enough to battle a hefty king on the fly, you'll never forget the thrill.

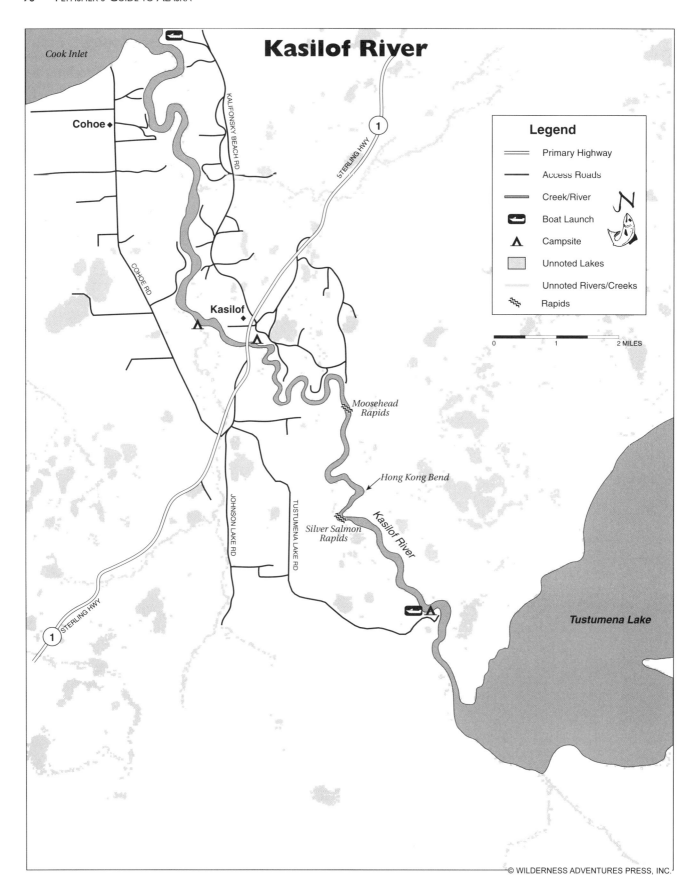

Kasilof River

Cook Inlet

Cohoe ♦

Kasilof ♦

KALIFONSKY BEACH RD

COHOE RD

STERLING HWY

1

JOHNSON LAKE RD

TUSTUMENA LAKE RD

STERLING HWY

1

Moosehead Rapids

Hong Kong Bend

Silver Salmon Rapids

Kasilof River

Tustumena Lake

Legend

Primary Highway	
Access Roads	
Creek/River	
Boat Launch	
Campsite	
Unnoted Lakes	
Unnoted Rivers/Creeks	
Rapids	

N

0   1   2 MILES

Kasilof River

At mile 109.5 the Sterling Highway crosses over the Kasilof River. The nearby settlement of Kasilof was established by the Russians back in 1786, who dubbed it St. George. Today the population of Kasilof is 550, and its residents derive their income from commercial fishing and fish processing.

The Kasilof River flows north for 12.5 miles from its headwaters at Tustumena Lake to Cook Inlet. This glacial-silted river is home to some of the best river fishing in all of Alaska. Rainbows, Dollys, and pink salmon are present here, but the real draw is king and silver salmon. The fall steelhead run is also excellent, beginning in late August and peaking in November. Though the steelhead fishing on the Kasilof is catch and release, and early winter temperatures can be brutally cold, the action is often downright sizzling. Be sure to check the current regulations if you're targeting steelhead.

Due to the heavy silting flyfishers can have a tough time on the Kasilof. Flash Flies and large, gaudy streamers will definitely help capture the attention of fish here. Many diehard fly anglers simply choose not to wet a line here, while others are willing to give it a shot. Flies worked tight to the banks are productive for red salmon, and to some extent, for silver salmon later in the fall. But for trout, char, kings, and most silver salmon, this river is difficult to fish well with traditional fly gear.

Trout and char anglers in particular are better off seeking other waters to fish. The best way to experience the true salmon fishing potential of the Kasilof River is to use bait. It's an easy river to float in a driftboat, if you are pulling your own. If not, there are plenty of guides who operate on this river. There are also ample bank-fishing options, where fishing with bait will allow you to reach fish that are traveling in the turbid waters at midstream.

Many anglers looking for relief from the heavily fished Kenai River will seek solace on the Kasilof. But the Kasilof doesn't really get pressured until emergency closures hit the Kenai River. During such times, the Kasilof is the only show in town for salmon anglers. This means that literally overnight the Kasilof can go from a quiet little river to the most crowded river on the entire peninsula.

However, it's not as intense as one might imagine because the Kasilof is only open to non-motorized boats from the first of the year through July 31. So while the river may be crowded, it's still void of gas fumes.

A large majority of the king salmon on the Kasilof River are the products of enhancement programs. For this reason, fish here don't grow nearly as big as those found on the Kenai River. A king on the Kasilof may average around 25 pounds, with a 40-pounder being exceptional.

Driftboaters have the best access to salmon on the Kasilof. Though the river flows wide and fast, it's safe water for experienced oarsman to navigate. Due to the low clarity, working flies, even from a boat, is difficult. Drifting cured salmon roe is the most popular method of tagging silvers and kings. Saturating a large, bright bait with scents is the way to go if you're serious about catching salmon from a driftboat here. Running diver and bait and backbouncing are the methods of choice here for conventional anglers. It's critical to keep that bait on the bottom where the salmon are, and these approaches allow you to do just that.

There are two good driftboat runs on this river. The upper launch site can be reached by turning onto Tustumena Lake Road at mile 110.4 on the Sterling Highway. Follow the road to the end, where you'll also find a campground. This drift meanders over 4.5 miles before hitting the boat ramp 100 yards above the Sterling Highway bridge. If you launch at the bridge you can run approximately 6 miles to the take-out at the mouth of the river, where the Kasilof empties into Cook Inlet.

Scott Haugen took this chrome-bright steelhead on Deep Creek. Steelhead like this can be had from the Kasilof River down to the Anchor River.

To reach the lower take-out leave the Sterling Highway at mile 108.9 and head north on Kalifornsky Beach Road. After traveling approximately 4 miles on Kalifornsky Beach Road, turn left on Kasilof Beach Road and follow the signs to the Kasilof Harbor boat ramp.

Not only is the Kasilof Harbor ramp ideal for pulling out a driftboat, it's perfect for launching a sled in the fall when the silver salmon are in the river. Though motorized boats are only allowed on the Kasilof River after August 1, they're very useful when the silvers are in. This is an often-overlooked site at which to launch, with incredible silver salmon fishing nearby.

Another special feature I like about the Kasilof Harbor ramp is that Ed's Kasilof Seafoods, Inc. is located here. Countless times I've been thankful to drop off my fish for complete processing at the end of a long day of fishing. They can clean, smoke, fillet, and freeze your salmon, and ship it wherever you like or have it ready for pickup on your return trip home. For the traveling angler, this is a great service.

As far as bank access on the Kasilof, Crooked Creek Campground is the best bet. Crooked Creek flows into the Kasilof here, and with the developed campground it would be easy to spend a week bank fishing for silvers, reds, and kings as they migrate upriver. The campground can be reached by turning north off the Sterling Highway at mile 111 onto Cohoe Loop Road. Go 1.3 miles up the road, following the signs to the campground. Ample parking is available for day use.

What makes this area such a great fishery is the presence of a state fish hatchery, which is located upstream on Crooked Creek. For all salmon entering the Kasilof, Crooked Creek is the first influx of fresh water. As a result of the hatchery scent carried down by Crooked Creek, the fish hug the bank as they move up the Kasilof. "Look for the tea-colored waterline flowing from Crooked Creek as it runs into the darker-colored Kasilof," offers guide Brett Gesh. "Bank anglers should concentrate on fishing this line of water 10 feet off the bank in front of them."

I've fished this stretch of the Kasilof many times, from both the bank and a driftboat. If you're fishing from the bank, make your casts close to shore—using the Kenai Flip technique discussed earlier—for the best success. Though riverboats may be pulling fish from the opposite shore, observe the locals fishing from the bank. They know the best fishing is right at their feet.

More than half the bank fishing done in this area is with a fly rod. But just like on the Kenai and Russian Rivers, most of the fish are caught by lining. By this I mean getting the fly on the bottom and dragging the leader through the mouth of a salmon until he's irritated enough to bite the fly. This is the classic technique for red salmon, but silvers and kings are more apt to attack on their own. Drift anglers tossing spinners or roe also pick up many salmon around Crooked Creek.

Brett Gesh and I once spent an incredible afternoon chasing silvers on the Kasilof while filming an installment for "Outdoor America." It was the final day of August, and we'd already had a heck of a morning on the Kenai filming a flyfishing segment on rainbow trout. Feeling that we couldn't top the 14-pound redside that stole the show, the producer of the series suggested we spend the afternoon searching for silvers.

Launching the driftboat at the Sterling Highway bridge, we were soon backbouncing eggs for silver salmon on the Kasilof. Over the course of the next two hours, four of us would each land our limit of bright, fat fish. They ranged from 10 to 15 pounds and all were captured on film. The perfect ending to a perfect day. But that's typical of the silver fishing on the Kasilof if you hit it right.

Due to the run timing of salmon on the Kasilof, anglers often spend several weeks camping here. The first run of kings appears in mid-May, tapering off in late June. Often, it's hard to recognize the end of the first run before the second run makes its way into the river. The second run of kings typically arrives in early July, and the fish may stick around until the last day of the season, traditionally July 31.

By the time the second run of kings arrived, the red salmon have also made their presence known. Late June is usually when red salmon start showing up in the catch on the Kasilof, and the action tapers off early in August.

Silver salmon begin trickling into the Kasilof toward the end of July, and by the end of August they are here in full-force. By the middle of September, the silver fishing is nearly complete; but don't despair. From mid-August through the month of November, steelhead migrate up this river, rounding out several consecutive months of world-class angling. If you happen to arrive here any time between late April and the end of May, try your luck with the steelhead that hold over for the winter.

Because the Kasilof is such a delicate system—at the time of this writing its enhanced king salmon program was undergoing reevaluation—rules and regulations can change from season to season. Emergency orders can even cause changes with as little as a day's notice. It's your responsibility to keep abreast of any changes and all rules and regulations before fishing here.

Stream Facts: Kasilof River

Seasons

- From its mouth upstream to the Sterling Highway bridge, the Kasilof River is open to king salmon fishing from January 10 to July 31.

- Upstream of the Sterling Highway bridge, the Kasilof River is open to king salmon fishing from January 1 to June 30.

- Year-round from its mouth upstream to the Sterling Highway bridge, retention of rainbow/steelhead trout is not allowed.

- Year-round above the Sterling Highway bridge, rainbow/steelhead trout can be fished and retained.

Special Regulations

- From the mouth of the Kasilof River upstream to the Sterling Highway bridge only one unbaited single-hook artificial lure is allowed from September 1 to May 15 in all flowing waters of the river.

- From January 1 to July 31, sport fishing from a motorized boat is prohibited.

- From its mouth upstream to the Sterling Highway bridge, the Kasilof River is open to king salmon fishing, 20 inches or longer, from January 10 to July 31, with a limit of 1 fish per day, 1 fish in possession.

- Upstream of the Sterling Highway bridge, the Kasilof River is open to king salmon fishing, 20 inches or longer, from January 1 to June 30, with a limit of 1 fish per day, 1 fish in possession.

- No more than 3 king salmon, 20 inches or longer, may be taken in the Kasilof each year.

- Year-round above the Sterling Highway bridge, the daily limit of rainbow/steelhead trout is 2, with a possession limit of 2, only one of which may be over 20 inches long.

- There are special regulations that apply for guided fishing trips on the Kasilof, refer to the ADF&G's "Southcentral Alaska Sport Fishing Regulations" for details.

Fish

- King, silver, red, and pink salmon, steelhead, rainbow trout, Dolly Varden

River Characteristics

- The Kasilof is a large, fast-flowing, shallow, and very turbid river. Its lack of visibility due to heavy silt makes it difficult for fly anglers to be successful when fishing for anything other than red salmon. Bait anglers have the advantage for latching into salmon and steelhead on this glacial-fed river. There is good boat access here with some bank/wade fishing available.

Fishing and Boating Access

- The best bank fishing is at Crooked Creek Campground. Driftboaters have two runs. The upper run is more for experienced oarsmen and can be reached by turning off the Sterling Highway at mile 110.4, onto Tustumena Lake Road. Follow the road to the end, where a campground and the boat launch await. It's a 4.5-mile drift to the take-out at the Sterling Highway bridge. The second run takes you six river miles from the Sterling Highway bridge to the mouth of the river at Kasilof Beach Road, off Kalifornsky Beach Road.

Maps

- Alaska Road & Recreation Map, Kenai Peninsula; *Alaska Atlas and Gazetteer*, page 69

Scott Haugen and guide Brett Gesh with a Kenai rainbow that tipped the scales at over 10 pounds.

Why Bring Spin-Fishing Gear?

While most flyfishers prefer to stick to their traditional tackle, due to the murky waters you'll find throughout the Kenai Peninsula, this may not always be the best option. Since you're taking the time and investing the money to make such a unique fishing journey, equipping yourself accordingly is essential. So it's a good idea to bring a spinning rod along with all the tackle to bobber and jig fish or backbounce for salmon.

Sudden storms and warm spells that cause rapid snowmelt can turn a clear stream ugly in a hurry. Such waters may be totally unfishable for a day or two, but when they do come back into shape, they may still be murky or moving too fast for flyfishing to be effective. Casting large, bright lures may be the only way to pick up fish.

There are also times you may need to try a variety of techniques before you hit on one the fish like at that particular moment. Once, while filming a TV show on a popular river on the peninsula, we thought it was a sure bet that the newly arriving silvers were going to thrash our pink bunny leeches. We'd been picking up bright fish the past two days this way, and we were sure we'd be able to capture it all on film.

I stripped a fly past the nose of fat chromer, and he didn't even flinch. Repeated casts into the school of more than two-dozen salmon failed to elicit even the slightest interest. Grabbing a spinning rod, I tossed a bobber and jig into the school. Nothing. Even a variety of failsafe lures let me down. Then I tied on a cluster of roe and the fish went berserk. We started pulling in coho after coho using eggs. Had we banked on any one method, we would have left frustrated and fishless.

Tustumena Lake

Six-mile-wide, 25-mile-long Tustumena Lake forms the headwaters of the Kasilof River and is the largest lake on the entire Kenai Peninsula. Though it's an impressive body of water, the fishing here is less than stellar. Because of heavy silting, anything but bait-fishing is virtually useless. The immense size of the lake, and its location amid the mountains, means that high winds can transform the lake into an ocean of whitecaps in a matter of minutes. So proceed with caution when boating on Tustumena Lake and constantly monitor the wind conditions.

Tustumena Lake Campground, though closed to king salmon fishing, does have some rainbow and Dolly fishing opportunities for bank anglers. If you hike close to the shores of the lake, be on the lookout for bears—grizzly and black—as well as pockets of quicksand scattered throughout some of the bogs.

Centennial Lake

Centennial Lake sits 3 miles up Tustumena Lake Road on the north side. A picnic and camping area make this a fun place to fish from the bank for landlocked silver salmon. These fish are planted by the ADF&G and range from 12 to 14 inches. On light gear, they can provide good action and lots of fun for the family.

Crooked Creek

If you find yourself at the Crooked Creek Campground, or anywhere along the Kasilof after August 1, there is an excellent option now available to flyfishers. Rather than spend time soaking flies in the silty waters of the Kasilof River, you can hit the first tributary that feeds into it. Crooked Creek is open from August 1 to December 31 and offers great fishing opportunities in a clear environment.

Turn off the Sterling Highway at mile 110.5 and follow Crooked Creek Road, which parallels the creek. There are numerous spots along the 3 miles of creek here where fly anglers can pull off to the side of the road and wet a line.

Wade fishing is the rule here, with excellent opportunities for Dollys, rainbows, steelhead, and red, pink, and silver salmon. Red and pink salmon are not typically sought after much on this creek, as they are at the end of their runs and have either expired or are near the end of their spawning cycle. It's the silvers, steelhead, rainbows, and in particular, Dolly Varden that bring anglers to Crooked Creek.

Given the low, clear water this time of year, Crooked Creek is also a good stream in which to sight fish for all of the species listed above, especially silvers and steelhead. There are some brush-choked sections along the creek, however, so you'll need to use abbreviated roll casts with plenty of mending. Nymphing and dead drifting are good approaches for this little stream. Anglers should note, though, that the retention of rainbow/steelhead trout is prohibited year-round.

The lack of fishing pressure makes Crooked Creek a good locale for traveling anglers. Abide by any special regulations that are posted along the banks of this stream and be considerate of privately owned properties.

From late August through the middle of September, I've spent a lot of quality time along Crooked Creek. Pristine waters, plenty of fish, and believe it or not, no people and great weather made for unforgettable memories.

For anglers looking to combine creek fishing with some lake fishing, Johnson Lake Wayside is a good spot to spend some time. **Johnson Lake** holds a good number of stocked rainbow trout, with plenty of bank fishing and boating water available. Off Crooked Creek Road, turn south on Pollard Loop Road, which leads directly to Johnson. From here, you can easily fish Crooked Creek and Johnson Lake.

Stream Facts: Crooked Creek

Seasons

- Crooked Creek is open to fishing from August 1 to December 31.

Special Regulations

- No retention of rainbow/steelhead trout year-round.

- Closed year-round to the taking of king salmon 20 inches or longer.

- Except for king salmon, there is a limit of 3 salmon per day, 3 in possession, of which only 2 per day, 2 in possession may be silver salmon.

- For Dolly Varden, there is a limit of 2 per day, 2 in possession.

Fish

- Silver, red, and pink salmon, steelhead, rainbow trout, Dolly Varden

River Characteristics

- A small, clear stream, Crooked Creek is ideal for fly anglers looking to escape the silt-laden Kasilof. Wade fishing with stealth and delicate presentations is the best way to take fish in the low, clear water.

Fishing Access

- There are several places to park along Crooked Creek Road, just off the Sterling Highway at mile 110.5.

Maps

- Alaska Road & Recreation Map, Kenai Peninsula; *Alaska Atlas and Gazetteer*, page 69

Fish and Wildlife Lakes

To reach the Fish and Wildlife Lakes, take Cohoe Loop Road at mile 111 on the opposite side of the Sterling Highway; go 1 mile and turn south. Dolly Varden thrive in both of these lakes, and bank fishermen can take some fish. These are also good lakes on which to launch a small craft or belly boat.

Floatplanes can get you to many remote lakes on the Kenai Peninsula.

Clam Gulch is the world's most popular razor-clamming beach. If you like clams, you must experience this incredible place.

THE BEST CLAMS IN THE WORLD

If you're searching for a break from the fishing on the Kenai Peninsula, or just looking for some of the best-eating shellfish in the world to dine on, you're almost there. Continuing south on the Sterling Highway will bring you to what is perhaps the best clamming destination on earth. Clam Gulch is home to world-class razor clamming, and you can expect to dig a limit on any minus tide.

Turn off at the marked wayside campground at mile 117.3, just prior to entering the tiny town of Clam Gulch. From here, it's just a short hike to the beach. A shovel and bucket are all you need, although a fishing license is also required for digging clams in the state of Alaska.

The thrill of clamming can be experienced for more than 50 miles along the coast, stretching all the way from Kasilof to Anchor Point, but Clam Gulch offers the highest continuous density of delectable razor clams. With upward of one million clams being harvested annually from this region, it's something you won't want to miss.

At the time of this writing, the limit on razor clams from the Kenai River south to the tip of the Homer Spit is the first 45 clams dug per day. This means that the first 45 clams you come across when digging must be kept, regardless of their size. This rule is necessary to ensure that clammers don't discard small clams they've damaged when digging with the shovel. Once broken, the shells of clams are incapable of repairing themselves, and these clams will die. To make sure this area of Alaska remains the best clamming site on the planet, every clammer must do his/her part and abide by the "first 45" rule. Many people prefer the taste and tenderness of the younger, smaller clams anyway.

The possession limit for each person is twice the daily bag limit, or 90 clams. Once you've gone out with a few buddies or the family and dug your limit of clams, the real work begins. Unless you're well practiced in clam cleaning and preparation, I'd suggest you take your catch to Clam Gulch just down the road, where you can have your clams cooked and cleaned for a reasonable fee.

On one two-day trip to Clam Gulch that still stands out in my memory, my dad, myself, and three friends made the mistake of digging a possession limit each, then cleaning them all ourselves. We easily dug our limits on the early morning minus tides, then spent the rest of the day boiling, cutting, cleaning, and packaging the clams. We were crazy enough to do this two days in a row, and that was back when the limit was 60 clams per person, per day. We all seemed to forget about the painstaking efforts, though, when winter rolled around and we sunk our teeth into fried clam strips and enjoyed superb homemade chowder from what most people consider to be the world's most tasty clam.

Ninety minutes before and after a minus tide is the best time to be on the beach digging razor clams. Bring knee-high rubber boots, or better yet, hip boots. I usually don't bother wearing a long-sleeved shirt, no matter what the weather conditions. You'll be up to your elbows in mud and muck from the moment you start digging. Trying to stay clean will only put a damper on the experience.

So hop into your boots, throw on a grubby shirt, and go play in the mud on a low tide. Just be careful when you're blindly reaching into a freshly dug hole, as the broken shells of these clams are indeed "razor" sharp. If clamming is new to you, Clam Gulch Lodge (1-800-700-9555) offers guided clamming trips.

Ninilchik River

The next fisheries along the highway are two of my favorite fall flyfishing streams in all of Alaska. Once the crowds have left this area in August, you'll likely be alone on the banks of both the Ninilchik River and Deep Creek from late August through September. Because the fall fishing is so good here, this is often as far as I'll go when traveling south down the peninsula.

The village of Ninilchik is a favorite of both anglers and photographers. This warm little community nestled into the coastal shores and rolling hills is worth seeing. Originally a Russian settlement, Ninilchik is rich in history and a very active place during the summer months, despite having a population of just 800 or so people.

There are a few weekend dates travelers should keep in mind when passing through Ninilchik. On Memorial Day weekend, when the river first opens to spring king fishing, Ninilchik is said to be the third largest city in Alaska. At this time, thousands of anglers descend on the river, trying their hands at strong-fighting kings. And on the third weekend of August, Ninilchik hosts a large fair and the Peninsula Rodeo. The May-to-June king salmon derby and a summertime halibut derby also attract large numbers of people. Though these events are a lot of fun, if you're looking for some quiet fishing wait until the end of August or early September to come here. The crowds will be gone and the silvers and steelhead will be in.

Due to the ruggedness of the land surrounding the Ninilchik River, it is one of the most untrammeled rivers on the peninsula. Near the village of Ninilchik, the best fishing is for kings arriving in early spring and silvers in early fall. Here, fishing in tidewater is the rule, right up to where the river dumps into Cook Inlet. But it's what lies upstream that makes this river so attractive.

In the upper river, you can find rainbows up to 8 pounds, with some nice Dollys also falling to flies. But it's the fall steelhead fishing that can be world class, and this is no doubt the best-kept secret on the river. Silver salmon are also in abundance from late August through October and will leave an angler's arm throbbing at the end of a day.

Start by heading north on Mission Avenue at mile 135.1, just west of where the Sterling Highway bridge crosses the Ninilchik River. From here, there's easy access for bank anglers all the way to the mouth of the river, where a state-run campground lets you camp right on the beach. For spring king fishing, this is exactly where you want to be. You'll be parked alongside everyone else, but if you want to catch a king from the bank, this is the place to do it.

King salmon season on the Ninilchik River historically begins on Memorial Day weekend. It runs three consec-utive weekends, Saturdays through Mondays, and receives a great deal of local pressure. You'll see anglers pursuing kings by doing everything from floating bait beneath a bobber to casting K-16 Kwikfish to drift fishing and tossing clusters of cured eggs on a fly rod. The occasional fly angler will take these fresh-from-the-ocean kings on large Flash Flies and big egg patterns.

Despite the excitement generated by the kings, I like to fish this river after mid-August. When turning off on Mission Avenue, look for little pulloffs on the gravel road. Then hike down to the river and start casting. These holes are more suited for holding silvers and steelhead than king salmon.

The Ninilchik River is open to all salmon fishing, except for king salmon, from July 1 through the end of the year. And in August and September the silver salmon and steelhead action can be phenomenal.

If you're interested in hiking up and down the river in

Brett Gesh with a Ninilchik River silver salmon.

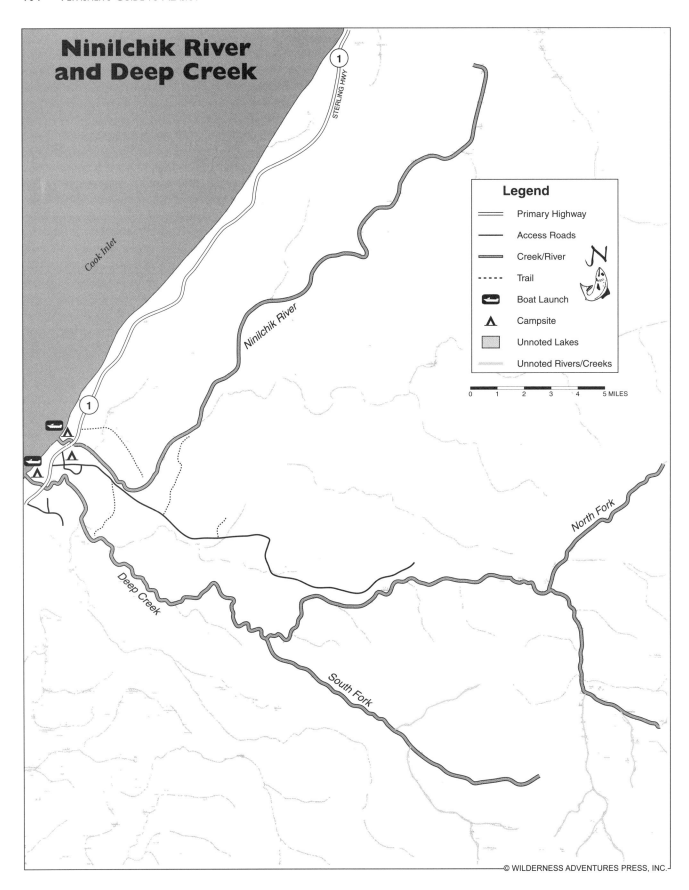

Ninilchik River and Deep Creek

Legend

Primary Highway
Access Roads
Creek/River
Trail
Boat Launch
Campsite
Unnoted Lakes
Unnoted Rivers/Creeks

N

0 1 2 3 4 5 MILES

Cook Inlet

STERLING HWY

1

1

Ninilchik River

Deep Creek

North Fork

South Fork

© WILDERNESS ADVENTURES PRESS, INC.

pursuit of silvers and steelhead, it might be wise to drive down to the park near the beach. Leave the car here for the day and work upstream and back. When you park here you'll observe locals casting spoons for incoming silvers a few hundred yards downriver, near the mouth. I don't like fishing that low for the simple reason that it's not good fly water, and there are too many people employing methods that make it tough to work a fly. Instead, hit the first bend in the river. You'll be wading along the north bank, which overlooks the river and the village of Ninilchik.

On low tides, it can be extremely muddy and slippery around this big bend. In fact, it can be so frustrating to work out of this mud that people often avoid fishing it. But don't pass it up if you've come this far. Simply slip into your waders and ease your way through the mud, wading into the river up to or just above your knees. The water is tea-colored here, but you can still see the bottom with ease. Keep to the gravel that is present in patches along the bottom and you can fish this entire big bend. The unmistakable silhouette of the Russian Orthodox church perched atop the hill above where you're fishing tells you you're in the right place to fish this hole. A friend and I once hit this corner and had it all to ourselves. We hooked over a dozen silvers on the fly and were soon surrounded by eager anglers. As there was plenty of other water to fish, we headed out.

This corner can be very shallow at times, and the wakes made by silvers milling around are often prime indicators that fish are in the area. I've pulled salmon from no more than a foot of water here as they stage, waiting for a rise in the tide to push them upriver. Because there are so few fly anglers on the water at this time, and a constant supply of fresh fish moving into the river, these holes don't get much pressure.

You can walk from this corner of the river all the way up to the bridge, hitting every pocket and riffle. The water is so low in the fall that fish will be searching for any holding water they can get. Large groups of salmon will often crowd into an area from which you'd normally be pleased to pull a single Dolly. When you see 20 silvers packed tightly into a pool that would barely fill a garbage can, you can't help but feel the surge of what's about to happen. Hooking big, hard-fighting salmon in this small, shallow water is the ultimate Alaskan flyfishing experience.

If you don't feel like hiking up to the bridge from the beach, cover only the spots that appeal to you, then drive up to the bridge and work from there. On the south side of the bridge at mile 134.5 (just prior to crossing over if coming from Clam Gulch), turn left into the Ninilchik River Scenic Overlook. You can spend an entire day here, fishing up and down the river. From the mouth of the Ninilchik River upstream 2 miles to ADF&G markers situ-ated on the banks of the river the fishing for silver and pink salmon is open from July 1 through December 31.

To access this water, strap on the waders and hit the well-worn trails that lead down a steep bank to the narrow river. The Ninilchik looks more like a creek here, especially in the fall. In fact, it's the low water levels that allow you to cover so much water and get into steelhead and silvers all day long. You'll nail both silvers and steelhead by nymphing through fast sections of water, tailouts, and holes tight against the bank.

Casting and stripping is tough here—as is getting a fly down quickly—due to the small water in the upper section and the size of the little pockets that hold fish. Using a $1/16$- or $1/32$-ounce Stuart Steelhead Bullet Jig on a 9-foot leader, dangled beneath a strike indicator on a floating line, has proven to be the ticket for me on many occasions.

One morning Brett Gesh and I each hit double-digit silvers and steelhead using this setup, right at the base of the hill at the scenic overlook. The largest steelhead went 13 pounds, the largest silver 14 pounds. We tried pink bunny hair streamers, along with a few other proven salmon and steelhead patterns, but the micro jigs blew everything else away.

In tight holes and behind swirling boulders, the jig drops quickly—even more so than a weighted fly—allowing you to reach fish the second the jig touches water. Peg the strike indicator to the leader so you can fish at various depths. We literally pulled fish from water as shallow as a foot on down to 4 feet in the holes. But hang on tight because there's nowhere for these hot fish to run but up and downstream. The battles are as aggressive as any fly angler could wish for.

At mile 135 on the Sterling Highway, Ninilchik Road leads 18 miles to the upper river and even more hardcore fishing opportunities. If you're into climbing up and down steep ridges and busting through heavy brush to access secluded fishing, this spot is for you. Though you can spend more time walking than fishing in this stretch, the results may keep you wanting more. Double-digit days will be the norm here. Look for trails already carved by the locals as indications of where the good fishing will be. Once on the river, you may be able to navigate by wading, although you should be on the lookout for deep holes as well as bears. The tall grass and brush-choked banks are good bear haunts, so it would be wise to have a can of pepper spray attached to your belt.

Bring egg patterns for the trout and Dolly Varden. Egg-Sucking Leeches are also effective. Flesh flies work well when the pinks are in the river. For steelhead and silvers, anything pink or pink and white will work wonders. I've tried lots of other color combinations here, but the pinks definitely outperformed everything else.

Stream Facts: Ninilchik River

Seasons

- The Ninilchik River is closed to all fishing January 10 through the Friday prior to Memorial Day weekend.

- From the mouth of the Ninilchik River upstream 2 miles to the ADF&G markers, the open season for king salmon 20 inches or longer traditionally runs for 3 consecutive weekends beginning on Memorial Day weekend (open to fishing on Saturdays, Sundays, and Mondays).

- From the mouth of the Ninilchik River upstream 2 miles to the ADF&G markers, the open season for all other species traditionally runs for 3 consecutive weekends beginning on Memorial Day Weekend (open to fishing on Saturday, Sunday, and Monday). The season opens again from July 1 to December 31.

- Upstream from the ADF&G markers placed 2 miles upstream from the mouth of the Ninilchik River, the area is closed year-round to king salmon fishing 20 inches or longer and other salmon 16 inches or longer.

- Upstream from the ADF&G markers placed 2 miles upstream from the mouth of the Ninilchik River, the area is open to fishing for rainbow/steelhead trout and Dolly Varden from August 1 to December 31.

Special Regulations

- Only one unbaited single-hook artificial lure is allowed September 1 to December 31.

- The retention of rainbow/steelhead trout is prohibited on the entire river.

- Once a king salmon 20 inches or longer is taken, a person may not continue fishing for other species in that river on the same day.

- Anglers are allowed to keep 1 king salmon per day that is 20 inches or longer and have 1 in possession.

- For salmon other than king salmon, anglers are allowed 3 per day, 3 in possession, of which only 2 per day, 2 in possession may be silver salmon.

- For Dolly Varden, anglers are allowed 2 per day, 2 in possession.

Fish

- King, silver, and pink salmon, rainbow trout, Dolly Varden

River Characteristics

- The Ninilchik is a small stream, easily waded by fly anglers. Fall is the best time for anglers to hit this river for multiple species of fish and some of the best steelheading around. The steelhead fishing is good until ice-up, usually around mid-November.

Fishing Access

- The Ninilchik River is a bank-fishing show, as it's too small for any boats to run. Two popular access areas are near the village of Ninilchik (reached by way of Mission Avenue, which leads to the beach and the river) and at the Ninilchik River Scenic Overlook.

Maps

- *Alaska Atlas and Gazetteer*, page 69

Deep Creek offers excellent fishing for several salmon species and fall steelhead.

Deep Creek

Deep Creek is another fall favorite of mine, especially when it comes to silver salmon and fresh steelhead. It's a twin to the Ninilchik River, and their close proximity to each other makes fishing both easy, even in a single morning, with the same tackle and techniques. But while the streams are close, they don't share the same headwaters. This means that one can be fishable when the other is blown out. If you find yourself on one of these streams when it's out of shape, head to the other before moving on; there's a good chance it will be fishable.

You'll find Deep Creek at mile 136.5 on the Sterling Highway, a two-minute drive from the Ninilchik. Just before crossing the bridge on the Sterling Highway, there's a pullout on the north side of the road that offers easy parking. This is a great place for fall anglers to begin their journey.

Most people head to the other side of the bridge or to the popular recreation area nearby, but if you're looking to escape the crowds, stop before you cross the bridge. It will require a bit more work to reach the river, and the wading will be challenging at times, but it's nothing anyone in fair condition can't handle. The number of fish and the seclusion make it very appealing.

The Creekside Inn, located right in front of the bridge, offers walk-in guided fishing, and if you're unsure of the terrain, this may be the way to go. On the other hand, if you're confident in your small-stream navigational and fishing skills, the do-it-yourself route is relatively straightforward.

The trail down to the water is short, no more than 100 yards, but can be laden with mud, especially where it veers off to the left side of the river. If it has been raining or the trail is wet from dew, use the large rope secured to the bank to ease your descent.

The trail ends on the north side of the river, but you should be able to find a shallow place and cross over. You should hit this spot, which I call the Rope Hole, from the south bank. Nymphing is an excellent way to slam both silvers and steelhead where the water swings against the high cutbank. Brett Gesh and I have fished this hole a number of times and taken both of these species. Once, on two consecutive casts I latched into a 12-pound chrome steelhead still covered with sea lice and then a 12-pound silver. As this is one of the deeper holes in the area, the fish can really keg up here. Once you've played a few fish in this spot, move on; but return for more action later on when things have settled down again.

From the Rope Hole, you can work your way up or downstream. I prefer working upstream, as there seems to be better holding water and deeper pockets for the fish to hold in. But given the surge of water making its way down the valley during the spring melt, new holes can be created virtually anywhere. Hit everything that looks like it should hold fish. There are typically many logs across the creek and casting behind their rootwads where large washes have developed can be productive, especially for Dolly Varden. When the water is particularly low, concentrate most of your efforts on the bends in the river, where deeper waters hold more fish.

Crossing the bridge on the Sterling Highway will put you at Deep Creek South Park, where you can wade fish all the way down to Cook Inlet. This area gets hammered by anglers due to the ease of access and ample parking. But such is the case anywhere in Alaska; the more willing you are to walk, the fewer people you'll see.

While many anglers fish right at the bridge or drop downstream a couple hundred yards, you can find relative isolation and good fishing by going a bit farther. When you break through the brush and hit the grassy valley through which Deep Creek meanders before meeting Cook Inlet you're into great holding water. There are few trees and limited structure this low in the creek, so work the cutbanks and outside edges of sweeping holes where the water runs deeper.

Just down the highway at mile 137.3, Deep Creek State Recreation Area is a popular locale. This is the best place to tie into a king salmon from the bank in the spring. You can also wade fish or hike upstream and cover all the fishable water you'd ever want to. The same methods apply here as on the Ninilchik, with seriously patient fly anglers having the best success.

Fishing can be outstanding in Deep Creek, especially within the tidal zones. The Dolly Varden fishing is especially good above the bridge. Like the Ninilchik, the upper stretches of Deep Creek, including the north and south forks, are virtually unexplored yet provide phenomenal flyfishing for monster rainbows and steelhead for anyone willing to do the legwork.

Because it's easy to get off the beaten path at Deep Creek and still catch big fish, this is an appealing place, particularly in the fall.

Stream Facts: Deep Creek

Seasons

- Deep Creek is closed to all fishing January 10 through the Friday prior to Memorial Day weekend.

- From the mouth of Deep Creek upstream 2 miles to the ADF&G markers, the open season for king salmon 20 inches or longer traditionally runs for 3 consecutive weekends beginning on Memorial Day weekend (open to fishing on Saturdays, Sundays, and Mondays).

- From the mouth of Deep Creek upstream 2 miles to the ADF&G markers, the open season for all other species traditionally runs for 3 consecutive weekends beginning on Memorial Day weekend (open to fishing on Saturday, Sunday, and Monday). The season opens again from July 1 to December 31.

- Upstream from the ADF&G markers placed 2 miles upstream from the mouth of Deep Creek, the area is closed year-round to king salmon fishing 20 inches or longer and other salmon 16 inches or longer.

- Upstream from the ADF&G markers placed 2 miles upstream from the mouth of Deep Creek, the area is open to fishing for rainbow/steelhead trout and Dolly Varden from August 1 to December 31.

Special Regulations

- Only one unbaited single-hook artificial lure is allowed September 1 to December 31.

- The retention of rainbow/steelhead trout is prohibited on the entire river.

- Once a king salmon 20 inches or longer is taken, a person may not continue fishing for other species in that river on the same day.

- Anglers are allowed to keep 1 king salmon per day that is 20 inches or longer, and have 1 in possession.

- For salmon other than king salmon, anglers are allowed 3 per day, 3 in possession of which only 2 per day, 2 in possession may be silver salmon.

- For Dolly Varden, anglers are allowed 2 per day, 2 in possession.

Fish

- King, silver, and pink salmon, rainbow trout, Dolly Varden

River Characteristics

- Deep Creek is a small stream, easily waded by fly anglers during the height of the silver salmon and steelhead runs in the fall. The first quarter-mile or so from the mouth, Deep Creek winds through tall grass. The higher you go upstream, the more blowdowns you must negotiate. Getting around and over these fallen trees is usually routine, but they can clog the creek, so be carefully when crossing such areas. The tannic acids from decaying leaves can turn this stream a tea color, but don't let that keep you from fishing.

Fishing Access

- Too small for launching a boat, Deep Creek is a bank-fishing stream. The most popular access point is Deep Creek State Recreation Area lies at mile 137.3. At the Sterling Highway bridge, Deep Creek South Park is easy to find and offers several good trails to the creek's edge. At mile 136.5 on the Sterling Highway, a roadside pulloff offers rudimentary parking, but leads to good fishing.

Maps

- *Alaska Atlas and Gazetteer*, pages 62 and 69

Happy Creek

Happy Creek is the next stream on the Sterling Highway, but it pales in comparison to the last two fisheries. Located at mile 144, the creek can be reached right from the highway. Though there are a good number of Dollys ranging up to 10 inches in this small stream, it receives little pressure, most because bigger fish can easily be had nearby.

But if you want lots of action on a lightweight rod and a dry fly, you'll probably enjoy a few hours on this stream. The higher up you go, the brushier it gets, so proceed with caution and patience. While you'll likely find the creek void of other anglers, you stand a good chance of meeting a bear or two.

Stariski Creek

Many anglers zip past Happy Creek on their way to Stariski Creek. The Sterling Highway crosses this creek at mile 151, and it's a nice little stream. With a good number of steelhead and large rainbows available, anglers willing to blaze their own trail on the upper section of water can expect very good results. The retention of rainbow/steelhead trout is prohibited year-round on Stariski Creek, but the catch-and-release fishing can be excellent early in the fall.

Three to four miles upstream from the mouth, rainbows in the 6-pound class are caught with regularity, though the banks are quite brushy. For steelhead and silver salmon, stick closer to the mouth of the stream. Stariski Creek used to be open for kings, but at present the entire creek is closed year-round to fishing for king salmon 20 inches or longer. Check the regulations if you're passing through in the spring. This is a good site for kings if the season ever reopens.

From the mouth of Stariski Creek upstream to the Sterling Highway bridge, fishing is usually open from July 1 through the end of the year. Upstream from the bridge, fishing usually opens August 1 and runs to the end of December.

Stariski Creek Campground sits at mile 151.3 and offers some bank fishing access. Anglers should be aware that a good deal of private property borders this creek, so ask permission before setting foot on private land. Also, bear densities run high in this area. Make plenty of noise when on the move through the brush and don't forget your pepper spray.

CLAMMING AT WHISKEY GULCH

Less than 2 miles south of Stariski Creek, more shellfishing opportunities lie in wait. For clam lovers seeking relief from the crowds at Clam Gulch, Whiskey Gulch is the place to go. Exceptional razor clamming can be had on this wonderful beach.

The same clamming strategies apply as in Clam Gulch. Look to hit a minus tide, and be prepared to get covered in muck. For tourists based in Homer, Whiskey Gulch is a great place to break away for a morning of quick clam digging.

Anchor River

The stretch of highway extending from Whiskey Gulch on the Sterling Highway to Homer is revered as one of the most breathtaking on the entire peninsula. It also takes you by the westernmost point on the U.S. highway system and the town of Anchor Point. Anchor Point was first named Laida by Captain James Cook in 1778 while he was searching for the Northwest Passage. The town was eventually renamed by homesteaders to pay homage to an anchor lost off the point by Captain Cook.

Anchor Point is home to one of the best flyfishing streams in the area, the Anchor River. Like Deep Creek and the Ninilchik River, the Anchor receives a run of fall steelhead, which adds to the smorgasbord of fish already available in this river.

With several camping facilities nearby, serious salmon, trout, and steelhead anglers will want to spend some time getting to know the Anchor River. With clamming and deep-sea fishing nearby as well, many anglers set up camp here for quite a while.

At mile 157, the Anchor River approaches the Sterling Highway. The turnoff here eventually leads to the Anchor River State Recreation Area, and with five large camping areas and plenty of roadside pullouts along this stretch, finding a place to camp is usually not too difficult.

Beginning in late May and continuing through mid-June, the king salmon run draws many anglers. As with the Ninilchik River and Deep Creek, fishing for king salmon on the Anchor River historically gets its start on Memorial Day weekend. The season runs four consecutive weekends, Saturdays through Mondays, and has a limit of one fish per day, one in possession, with only two kings allowed for the year.

In the fall, the run of steelhead is superb, with silvers, rainbows, and Dollys also in abundance throughout the river into October. The highest percentage of angling pressure on the Anchor River comes at the mouth and continues for the first mile or so upstream. Beyond that, few anglers are willing to work for what lies in wait, despite the fact that there's 15 more miles fishable river. The Anchor has a greater human population around it than the Ninilchik or Deep Creek, but there's still plenty of freedom left for anglers willing to work for it.

In the lower river, Grass Hole extends about a half-mile from the mouth of the river and is one of the more popular sites. Several good holes exist along both banks for the next mile upstream, but again, check with landowners to gain permission to private land. Right after the turnoff from the highway, the fishing can be dynamite. Due to its easy access and the number of fish available, this section of river receives the greatest amount of pressure. Chum and red salmon can also be taken on occasion from these lower holes.

The **North Fork Anchor River** is excellent for sea-run Dolly Varden and good- sized rainbow trout. From where the Chakok River joins the North Fork Anchor River upstream about 4 miles, the rainbow trout fishing can be astounding. For those willing to put on the hiking boots, the size and number of rainbows upstream make the effort worthwhile.

The **South Fork Anchor River** runs beneath the Sterling Highway in three different places between miles 161 and 165. At mile 164.3, turn onto North Fork Road, which leads to even more secluded fishing for Dollys and steelies.

One of the most productive holes on the South Fork is near its mouth, where the power lines are located. For another 10 miles upstream, the Dolly fishing can be very good. Most of the steelhead entering the South Fork spend their time in the first few miles of river, though the occasional fish does continue moving upriver. From mid-August through September, fresh steelhead are continuously making their way into the South Fork. Rainbow trout fishing can be excellent throughout this river, with 5-pound fish routinely taken. However, be certain to check regulations for current retention laws on rainbows, as well as regulations regarding salmon angling.

Stream Facts: Anchor River

Seasons

- From January 1 through the Friday prior to Memorial Day, the entire Anchor River drainage is closed to all fishing.

- From its mouth upstream to the confluence of the North and South Forks, the open season for king salmon 20 inches or longer traditionally runs for 4 consecutive weekends beginning on Memorial Day weekend (open to fishing on Saturdays, Sundays, and Mondays).

- From its mouth upstream to the confluence of the North and South Forks, the open season for all other species traditionally runs for four consecutive weekends beginning on Memorial Day weekend (open to fishing on Saturday, Sunday, and Monday). The season opens again from July 1 through December 31.

- Upstream from the confluence of the North and South Forks, the Anchor River is closed year-round to fishing for king salmon 20 inches or longer and other salmon species 16 inches or longer. The open season for small salmon in this stretch runs from August 1 to December 31.

- Upstream from the confluence of the North and South Forks, the Anchor River is open to fishing for rainbow/steelhead trout from August 1 to December 31, but retention of rainbow trout and steelhead is not allowed.

- Upstream from the confluence of the North and South Forks, the Anchor River is open to fishing for all other species not listed above, from August 1 to December 31.

Special Regulations

- One unbaited single-hook artificial lure is allowed on the Anchor River from September 1 to December 31.

- The retention of rainbow/steelhead trout is prohibited on the entire river.

- Once a king salmon 20 inches or longer is taken, a person may not continue fishing for other species in that river on the same day.

- Anglers are allowed to keep 1 king salmon per day that is 20 inches or longer and have 1 in possession.

- For salmon other than king salmon, anglers are allowed 3 per day, 3 in possession, of which only 2 per day, 2 in possession may be silver salmon.

- For Dolly Varden, anglers are allowed 2 per day, 2 in possession.

Fish

- King, silver, pink, chum, and red salmon, steelhead, rainbow trout, Dolly Varden

River Characteristics

- The Anchor River is a small stream, not large enough to run with a boat, but bigger than Deep Creek. It's a wade-fishing stream, and waders are essential for crossing from bank to bank. The river runs clear most of the time, making it ideal for sight fishing with a fly rod.

Fishing Access

- Bank access is available at mile 157 on the Sterling Highway. Turn off here and follow the signs to the Anchor River State Recreation Area. Roadside park-and-walk opportunities exist. At mile 164.3, North Fork Road provides further river access.

Maps

- Alaska Road & Recreation Map, Kachemak Bay; *Alaska Atlas and Gazetteer*, page 62

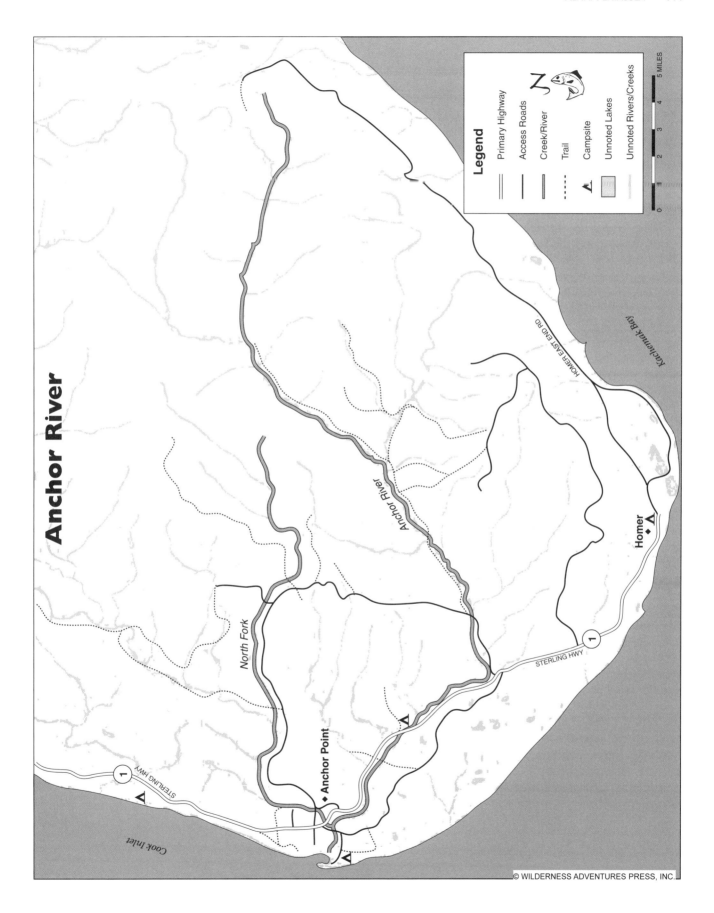

Anchor River

Legend

Primary Highway
Access Roads
Creek/River
Trail
Campsite
Unnoted Lakes
Unnoted Rivers/Creeks

0 1 2 3 4 5 MILES

Kachemak Bay

HOMER EAST END RD

Anchor River

North Fork

STERLING HWY

1

Homer

♦ Anchor Point

Cook Inlet

STERLING HWY

1

© WILDERNESS ADVENTURES PRESS, INC.

Kachemak Bay near Homer, Alaska.

The Homestretch to Homer

Just 5 miles north of Homer, **Diamond Creek** slips beneath the Sterling Highway. If you're spending time in Homer and looking for some quick and easy Dolly fishing, simply pull off the side of the road, walk to this creek, and start fishing.

From Homer to the end of the Sterling Highway, the terrain is steep and the rivers move fast. While some fishing opportunities exist for a variety of salmon species, their presence can be spotty, with fishing limited to the mouths of the streams. For those desiring another crack at kokanee, as well as more Dolly Varden, a hike from the end of the road up to **Caribou Lake** is a possibility. You can also fly in to this lake.

Many of the bays, coves, and streams across **Kachemak Bay** offer very good fishing for silvers, reds, pinks, and Dollys. These bodies of water are best accessed by boat and are within easy reach of the Homer Spit. Flyfishing for salmon in the many estuaries of Kachemak Bay is also an option. One summer day my dad, good friend Don Kassube, and I spent a day catching countless pink salmon up **Tutka Bay**.

In Tutka Bay—directly south and across Kachemak Bay from the Homer Spit—pink salmon are drawn to the lagoon by the presence of an ADF&G hatchery. In even-numbered years, thousands of pink salmon will spend several weeks staging here before entering a small stream in which they spawn. Some of the best fishing comes off the grassy banks in the lagoon. Seeing thousands of pinks swim at your feet while you're surrounded by vertical cliffs makes this a unique experience that fly anglers will never forget. During the first two weeks of July, when the peak of the run is in, catching in excess of 100 pinks a day on the fly is not uncommon. It's a good idea to enter Tutka Bay on a high tide, as the entrance is very narrow.

Another special bay fishery lies directly across from the Homer Spit in **China Poot Bay**. China Poot is known for its world-class sea duck hunting in the winter, but in July and early August it offers some of the Kenai Peninsula's most generous red salmon fishing. The ADF&G annually stocks China Poot Lake with red salmon fry. During their return to their natal waters as adults, the salmon stage for several days in China Poot Bay. Fishing in the bay can be very productive, but for a really great experience wait until the salmon begin making their way into the creek.

There's a large falls 200 yards up the creek, and this is as far as the salmon can go. Because of this natural barrier, every fish will eventually die at the foot of the falls. For this reason, the ADF&G has, in the past, allowed and even encouraged the taking of as many of these red salmon as sport fishermen care to take. If you're a fan of red salmon meat and looking to stock your freezer for the winter this is the place to do it. But before heading out for a boatload of sockeyes, contact the Homer ADF&G office for current regulations on China Poot Creek. Because much of China Poot Bay dries up at low tide, accessing the area is best done at high tide.

While in the Homer area, you might want to try what is perhaps the world's best halibut fishing. Offshore trips can be arranged on the spot when you get to town. If you're after a 300-pound barn door, a 3- to 4-hour run may be required to get you to big halibut waters. If it's small, 40-pound, good-eating halibut you desire, they can be had closer to the marina. With several commercial charters available, booking a trip for Homer halibut is easy.

Homer's comfortable climate, array of small cozy shops, and beautiful setting make it a great place to stay for a day or two. Late in the 1800s coal mining attracted people to Homer. And gold seekers in the Hope region disembarked in the Homer harbor. Around WWI coal mining came to a halt in Homer, though settlers continued moving into the area to work at the local canneries. Today, commercial fishing, tourism, and trade keep the "Halibut Capital of the World" afloat.

ANCHOR POINT

Population: 1,800
Alaska Area Code: 907
Zip Code: 99556

TOURIST INFORMATION

Anchor Point Chamber of Commerce, P.O. Box 610; 235-2600

TACKLE SHOPS

Anchor Angler, 235-8351; excellent local source for fishing reports and where-to information for fly anglers and campers

ACCOMMODATIONS

Anchor River Inn, P.O. Box 154; 1-800-435-8531; www.anchorriverinn.com
Northwood Cabins, P.O. Box 201; 1-888-972-2246

CAMPGROUNDS AND RV PARKS

Anchor River State Recreation Area, Anchor River Road; 228 acres, 5 campgrounds available, 161 total campsites, camping fee, toilets, fishing, water available at Halibut and Sidehole Campgrounds
Eagle Crest RV Park & Cabins, P.O. Box 249; 1-888-235-2905; full-service hookups, water, showers, toilets, laundry
Kyllonen RV Park; 1-888-848-2589; on-site fishing, full-service hookups, water, showers, toilets, laundry, pets allowed; www.kyllonenrvpark.com
Short Stop Storage & Camping, P.O. Box 596; 235-5327; Mile 153.2 Sterling Hwy., Anchor Point; dump station, drinking water, showers, toilets, laundry

TOURIST ATTRACTIONS

Anchor Point Wildlife Museum, 34030 Sterling Hwy.; 226-2269

CLAM GULCH

Alaska Area Code: 907
Zip Code: 99568

ACCOMMODATIONS

Clam Gulch Lodge & RV Park, Box 499; large rooms, private and shared baths, 3 RV sites with full hookups; offer guided razor clamming trips; 1-800-700-9555; www.clamgulch.com

Clam Gulch State Recreation Area, 117 Sterling Hwy.; 495 acres, 116 campsites, camping fee, toilets, water, picnic shelter, fishing

AUTO REPAIR

Clam Gulch Storage & RV Repair Services, P.O. Box 377; 262-3786

HOMER

Population: 4,154
Alaska Area Code: 907
Zip Code: 99603

TOURIST INFORMATION

Alaska Department of Fish & Game; 235-8191
Alaska Department of Fish & Game Fishery Hotline; 235-6930
Homer Chamber of Commerce, P.O. Box 541; 235-7740; www.homeralaska.org; extremely nice folks willing to assist with any questions you have

FISHING GUIDE SERVICES

Alaska Salmon Connection, P.O. Box 1947; 235-2504; www.alaskasalmonconnection.com
Homer Floatplane Lodge; 1-877-235-9600; www.floatplanelodge.com
Silverfin Guide Service, P.O. Box 1657; 235-7352; www.silverfinguides.com
The Bookie, P.O. Box 195, Homer; 1-888-335-1581; www.alaskabookie.com

TACKLE SHOPS

Kachemak Gear Shed, Kachemak Drive; 235-8612
Slim's Alaska Fishing Lures, P.O. Box 2012; 235-1961
Sportsman's Supply & Rental, Boat Launch Road, under the big Alaska flag across from the boat ramp at Homer harbor; 235-2617
The Sport Shed, 3815 Homer Spit Road, Suite A; 235-5562

ACCOMMODATIONS

Alaska Adventure Cabins, 2525 Sterling Hwy.; 223-6681; www.AlaskaAdventureCabins.com
Almost Home Accommodations, 1269 Upland Court; 235-2553;www.alaskaexcursion.com
Bay View Inn Lodging, P.O. Box 804; 1-877-235-8485; www.bayviewalaska.com

Best Western-Bidarka Inn, 575 Sterling Hwy.;
1-866-685-5000

Chocolate Drop Inn, P.O. Box 70; 1-800-530-6015;
www.ChocolateDropInn.com

Forest Light Cottage, P.O. Box 2613; 235-2313;
forlight@xyz.net

Holland Days Cabins, P.O. Box 2449; 1-888-308-7604;
www.bbhost.com/hollanddays

Homer Bed & Breakfast Association; 1-800-473-3092;
www.HomerBedBreakfastcom

Homer's Finest Bed & Breakfast Network, P.O. Box
1909; 235-4983; finest@eagle.ptialaska.net

Homer Floatplane Lodge, 1244 Lakeshore Drive;
1-877-235-9600; www.floatplanelodge.com

Homer Seaside Cottages, 58901 East End Road;
1-877-374-2716; www.homerseasidecottages.com

Lighthouse Village, P.O. Box 819; 235-7007;
www.lighthousecabins.com

Magic Canyon Ranch, 40015 Waterman Road;
235-6077;www.magiccanyonranch.com

Ocean Shores Motel, 451 Sterling Hwy.;
1-800-770-7775; www.oceanshoresalakska.com

Seaside Farm Hostel, 5 miles East End Road;
235-7850; seaside@xyz.net

Woodside Private Condos, P.O. Box 1445;
235-8389;www.alaskawoodsidelodging.com

CAMPGROUNDS AND RV PARKS

Driftwood Inn & RV Park, 135 West Bunnell Ave.;
1-800-478-8019; on-site fishing; full-service
hookups, dump station, water, showers, toilets,
laundry, tent camping, pets allowed;
www.thedriftwoodinn.com

Homer Spit Campground, P.O. Box 1196; 235-8206;
oceanfront camping, on-site trailer rentals, electric
hookups, dump station, water, showers, toilets,
laundry, gift shop, will book local activities

Land's End RV Park, 4786 Homer Spit Road; 235-
0404; on-site fishing, dump station, water, showers,
toilets, laundry

Oceanview RV Park, mile 172.7 on Sterling Hwy.;
235-3951; full-service hookups, dump station,
water, showers, toilets, laundry, tent camping;
www.oceanview-rv.com

RESTAURANTS

Captain Patties Fish House, Homer Spit Road;
235-5135

Don Jose's, 127 Pioneer Ave.; 235-7963

El Pescador Bar & Grill, Homer Spit Road; 235-9333

Sourdough Express Bakery & Cafe, Ocean Drive;
235-7571

Starvin Marvin's Pizza, 1663 Homer Spit Road #7;
235-0544

The Homestead Restaurant, mile 8 East End Road;
235-8723

The Rookery Restaurant, Kachemak Bay; 235-7770

The Saltry, Halibut Cove; 296-2223

Young's Oriental Restaurant, 565 East Pioneer Ave.;
235-4002

RENTAL CARS

Adventure Alaska Car Rentals, 1368 Ocean Drive;
1-800-882-2808; www.adventurealaskacars.com

Jeep's 4 You Car Rentals, P.O. Box 70; 235-8640;
www.homercarrental.com

Pioneer Car Rental-Hertz, 3720 FAA Road #123;
235-0734

Polar Car Rental, 3720 FAA Road #125; 1-800-876-
6417; polarcar@xyz.net

AIR SERVICES

Bald Mountain Air Service; 1-800-478-7969;
www.baldmountainair.com

Emerald Air Service; 235-6993;
www.emeraldairservice.com

ERA Aviation, Inc.; 1-800-866-8394;
www.eraaviation.com

Homer Air; 1-800-478-8591; www.homerair.com

Kachemak Bay Flying Service; 235-8924;
www.alaskaseaplanes.com

Maritime Helicopters; 235-7771;
www.maritimehelicopters.com

Smokey Bay Air; 235-1511

AUTO REPAIR

Scruggs Automotive, 1180 Ocean Drive; 235-1999

MEDICAL

Homer Medical Clinic, 4136 Bartlett Street; 235-8586

South Peninsula Hospital, 4300 Bartlett Street;
235-8101

ER/Acute Care; 235-0247; www.sphosp.com

Kachemak Bay Sportsmedicine, 4285 Hohe Street;
235-2261; www.kbaybones.com

VETERINARY CLINICS

Homer Veterinary Clinic, P.O. Box 1445; 235-8660

TOURIST ATTRACTIONS

**Alaska Maritime National Wildlife Refuge Visitor
Center**, 451 Sterling Hwy.; 235-6961; R7_home-
rvc@fws.gov

Center for Alaskan Coastal Studies, Inc.; 235-6667;
cacs@xyz.net

Pratt Natural History Museum, 3779 Bartlett St.;
www.prattmuseum.org

KASILOF

Population: 548
Alaska Area Code: 907
Zip Code: 99610

ACCOMMODATIONS

Alaska's Inn Between, P.O. Box 1209; 335-2769;
www.AlaskaInnBetween.com
Cohoe Lodge, P.O. Box 147; 262-2993
Crooked Creek Cabin Rentals, P.O. Box 295; 262-2729;
www.ak-cabins.com
Ingrid's Inn Bed & Breakfast, 51810 Ariel's Lane;
1-888-422-1510; www.AlaskaOne.com/ingrids
Kasilof River Cabins, P.O. Box 1972; 262-6348
Kasilof Sunset Cabins; 1-866-286-6946;
www.alaskansunset.com

CAMPGROUNDS AND RV PARKS

Crooked Creek RV Park & Guide Services, P.O. Box
601; 262-1299; on-site fishing, full-service hookups,
dump station, water, showers toilets, laundry, tent
camping
Crooked Creek State Recreation Site, Coho Loop
Road; 83 campsites, 36 day-use sites, toilets, water,
camping fee; trails lead to banks of Kasilof River and
some of the best fishing on the entire Kenai
Peninsula
Johnson Lake State Recreation Area, 110 Sterling
Hwy.; 332 acres, 50 campsites, camping fee, picnic
sites, toilets, water, boat launch, fishing
Kasilof River State Recreation Site, 109.5 Sterling
Hwy.; 30 acres, 10 campsites, nightly camping fee,
toilets, water, trails, boat launch, fishing
Kasilof RV Park, P.O. Box 1008, Mile 111 Sterling Hwy.;
262-0418; www.kasilofrvpark.com

KENAI

Population: 7,058
Alaska Area Code: 907
Zip Code: 99611

TOURIST INFORMATION

Kenai Chamber of Commerce, 402 Overland;
283-7989; www.kenaichamber.org
Kenai Peninsula Tourism Marketing Council, Inc.,
14896 Kenai Spur Hwy., Suite 106A; 283-3850;
www.KenaiPeninsula.org

Kenai Convention & Visitors Bureau, Inc., 11471
Kenai Spur Hwy.-KP; 283-1991; www.visitkenai.com
Kenai Visitor's Center, 11471 Kenai Spur Hwy.;
283-1991

GUIDE SERVICES

Blue Moose Lodge, 35555 Kenai Spur Hwy., Suite 275,
Soldotna; 1-877-256-6673; Offers guided trips on the
Kenai Canoe Trails; www.blue-moose.com
Family Charters, 1345 Angler Drive; 398-3066
Fish On with Gary Kernan, P.O. Box 642;
1-888-283-4002; www.alaskafishon.com
Hi-Lo Charters, 1105 Angler Drive; 1-800-757-9333;
www.hilofishing.com
Hook-y Charters, 2915 Clipper Circle; 283-9026

FLY-OUT FISHING

Mavrik Aire Transport, P.O. Box 2157; 1-888-628-7457;
www.mavrikaire.com

ACCOMMODATIONS

Best Ball Bed & Breakfast, 101 Highbush Lane &
Lawton; 283-2265
Daniels Lake Lodge Bed & Breakfast, P.O. Box 1444;
1-800-774-5578; www.DanielsLakeLodge.com
Harborside Cottages, Box 942; 1-888-283-6162
Kenai Airport Lodge, Kenai Airport; 283-1577
Kenai Merit Inn, 260 South Willow; 1-800-227-6131;
www.kenaimeritinn.com
Kenai Peninsula Bed & Breakfast Association,
P.O. Box 2992; www.kenaipeninsulabba.com
Tanglewood Bed & Breakfast, 2528 Beaver Loop;
283-6771
The Fish Hut Lodging & Guided Fishing, 1125 Angler
Drive; 283-2675
The Log Cabin Inn, P.O. Box 2886; 283-3653

CAMPGROUNDS AND RV PARKS

Beluga Lookout Lodge & RV Park, 979 Mission
Avenue; 283-5999; on-site fishing, full-service
hookups, water, showers, toilets, laundry, snack bar,
tent camping, pets allowed
Kenai RV Park, P.O. Box 2027; 398-3382; full-service
hookups, water, showers, toilets,laundry, tent camping
Stedi RV Park, 3410 Kalifornsky Beach Road;
283-2056; full-service hookups, dump station, water,
showers, toilets, laundry, tent camping, pets allowed

RESTAURANTS

Charlotte's, 115 South Willow, Suite 102; 283-2777
Nero's Restaurant & Cafe, Spur Hwy.; 776-7696

New Peking, 145 South Willow; 283-4662
Old Town Village Restaurant, 1000 Mission Ave.;
  283-4515
Ruben's International, Spur Hwy.; 283-6670

RENTAL CARS

AVIS Rent A Car, Kenai Airport; 1-800-331-1212
Budget Rent A Car, P.O. Box 267; 1-877-673-4506
Great Alaska Car Company, 10288 Kenai Spur Hwy.;
  283-3469
Hertz Rental Car, Kenai Airport; 1-800-478-7980
Payless Car Rental, P.O. Box 1510; 283-6428

AIR TAXI

ERA Aviation, 1-800-866-8394; www.eraaviation.com

AUTO REPAIR

Kenai Chrysler Center, 10288 Kenai Spur Hwy.;
  283-3949
Alyeska Sales & Service, P.O. Box 1331; 283-4821

MEDICAL

Kenai Health Center, 630 Barnacle Way; 283-4495
Central Peninsula General Hospital, 250 Hospital
  Place, Soldotna; 1-888-565-4404

VETERINARY CLINICS

Kenai Veterinary Hospital, 10976 Kenai Spur Hwy.;
  283-4148

TOURIST ATTRACTIONS

Kenai National Moose Range, P.O. Box 2139, Soldotna,
  AK 99669

NINILCHIK

Population: 687
Alaska Area Code: 907
Zip Code: 99639

TOURIST INFORMATION

Ninilchik Chamber of Commerce, P.O. Box 39164;
  567-3571;www.ninilchikchamber.com

GUIDE SERVICES

Ninilchik Charters, P.O. Box 39638; 1-888-290-3507
Chihuly's Anglers Retreat, P.O. Box 39294; 567-3374

TACKLE SHOPS

Ninilchik General Store, P.O. Box 39434; 567-3378

ACCOMMODATIONS

Alaska Caribou Creek Cabins, Mile 131 Sterling Hwy.;
  567-7330; www.cariboucreek.com
Bluff House, P.O. Box 39327; 567-3605
Inlet View Lodge, Mile 135.5 Sterling Hwy.; 567-3330;
  www.inletviewlodge.com
Ninilchik Cabins and Fishcamp, P.O. Box 98; 567-3635
Ninilchik Point Overnighter, Mile 130.5 Sterling Hwy.;
  567-3423
The Eagle Watch Hostel, P.O. Box 39083; 567-3905

CAMPGROUNDS AND RV PARKS

Alaskan Angler RV Resort & Cabins, 15640 Kingsley
  Rd.; 1-800-347-4114; 70 units, 50 units with full-service hookups including electricity and cable TV, laundry, vacuum packing available, tent camping, pets
  allowed; www.afishunt.com
Country Boy Campground, P.O. Box 39697; 567-3396;
  full-service hookups, dump station, water, showers
  toilets, laundry, tent camping
Creekside Inn & RV Park, P.O. Box 39236; 567-7333;
  water, showers, toilets
**Deep Creek State Recreation Area-Deep Creek
  Campground** (138 Sterling Hwy.) and
Deep Creek North Campground (137.3 Sterling Hwy.);
  172 acres, 189 total campsites, camping fee, toilets,
  water, fishing, boat launch at Deep Creek
Deep Creek View Campground, P.O. Box 23;
  1-888-425-4822
Hylen's Camper Park, P.O. Box 39388; 1-800-347-4114;
  full-service hookups, dump station, water, showers,
  toilets, laundry, tent camping
Ninilchik Corners, P.O. Box 39076, Mile 172.7 Seward
  Hwy.; 567-3929; water, showers, toilets, laundry
Ninilchik State Recreation Area (93 acres, 4 camp-
  grounds, 117 total campsites, camping fee, toilets,
  water, picnic shelter at Ninilchik River Campground,
  boat launch at Ninilchik Beach Campground, sani-
  tary dump station at Ninilchik View Campground
  Ninilchik Beach Campground, 135.5 Sterling Hwy.;
  Ninilchik River Campground, 135.2 Sterling Hwy.;
  Ninilchik Overlook Campground, 135.3 Sterling
  Hwy.;
  Ninilchik View Campground, 135.9 Sterling Hwy. -
Reel Em Inn, Inc., Cook Inlet Charters RV Park, P.O.
  Box 39292, Mile 135.4 Sterling Hwy., Ninilchik; 1-
  800-447-7335; 12 full hookups, BBQ and firepit to
  cook the catch of the day, small, clean and friendly,
  fish cleaning, freezing and storage available, water,
  showers, toilets,
  laundry;www.cookinletcharters.com

Scenic View RV Park, P.O. Box 39253, Mile 127 Sterling Hwy.; 567-3909; full hookups, daily, weekly, monthly rates, dump station, water, showers, toilets, laundry, snack bar, tentsites; www.scenicviewrv.com

RESTAURANTS

Boardwalk Cafe, on Ninilchik Beach; 567-3388
Happy Valley Bar & Cafe, Mile 145 Sterling Hwy.; 567-3357
The Happy Wok, P.O. Box 39556; 567-1060
The Whaler, P.O. Box 39430; 567-3555

FISH PROCESSING

Deep Creek Custom Packaging, Inc., P.O. Box 229; 1-800-764-0078; www.deepcreekcustompacking.com

SOLDOTNA

Population: 3,759
Alaska Area Code: 907
Zip Code: 99669

TOURIST INFORMATION

Soldotna Chamber of Commerce, 44790 Sterling Hwy.; 262-9814; www.SoldotnaChamber.com
Alaska Department of Fish & Game, 43961 Kalifornsky Beach Road; 262-9368; www.ak.gov/adfg/sportf/sf_home.htm
Alaska Department of Fish & Game Fishery Hotline; 262-2737
Alaska State Parks, P.O. Box 1247; 262-5581

Ken's Alaskan Tackle in Soldotna is the best-stocked shop in the area, and is a valued source of the latest fishing information.

Kenai River Sport-Fishing Association, P.O. Box 1228; 262-8588; www.kenairiversportfishing.org
Visitor Information Center, 44790 Sterling Hwy.; 262-9814

GUIDE SERVICES

Alaska Bite Finders, Guide Brett Gesh, P.O. Box 3093; 223-8704; bitefinders@yahoo.com
EZ Limit Guide Service, P.O. Box 4278; 262-6169
Harry Gaines Kenai River Fishing Guide; 1-888-262-5097; www.harrygaines.com
Johnson Brothers, P.O. Box 3774; 1-800-918-7233
Kenai River King Guide Service, 45964 Paulk Drive; 1-888-865-3474
Slam Dunkin Guide Service, Guide Jason Dunkin; 907-252-2296 or 503-623-6965; Dunkin@slamdunkin.com
Webster's Outdoor Adventures, Guides Jeff & Shella Webster; 93.2 Sterling Hwy., Soldotna; 262-5038; jweb@ptialaska.net

FLY-IN CHARTERS

Alaska Kenai fishing Cub Driver Inc., P.O. Box 8215, Nikiski; 776-8220; www.alaskakenaifishing.com or www.cubdriverinc.com
High Adventure Air Charter, P.O. Box 486, Soldotna; 262-5237; offers fly-in fishing, both guided and nonguided, to remote lakes throughout the Kenai Peninsula as well as across Cook Inlet for silver and red salmon; www.highadventureair.com
Natron Air, 619 Funny River Road; 262-8440; www.natronair.com
RW's Fishing Guide Service, P.O. Box 3824; 1-800-478-6900; www.rw-s-alaskafishing.com
Talon Air Service, P.O. Box 1109; 262-8899; offers fly-in fishing, both guided and nonguided, to remote lakes throughout the Kenai Peninsula as well as across Cook Inlet for silver and red salmon; www.talonair.com

TACKLE SHOPS

Fred Meyer, 43843 Sterling Hwy.; 260-2220; well stocked to meet all general fishing needs
Ken's Alaskan Tackle, P.O. Box 1168, Sterling Hwy.; 262-6870; one of the most complete tackle shops in the state, knowledgeable employees will put you on the fish and can recommend guides
The Fishin Hole, 139 B Warehouse St.; 262-2290; www.thefishinholealaska.com

ACCOMMODATIONS

A Fisherman's Bed & Breakfast, 154 Marydale Ave.; 262-3570; 1-866-255-6343; www.alaskalegends.com

April's Cozy Cabins, 37623 Mackey Lake Road; 262-4168; www.aprilscozycabins.com

Aspen Hotels, 326 Binkley Circle; 1-866-483-7848; www.aspenhotelsak.com; 63 rooms,breakfast, business center, fitness, pool, laundry, 500 AK air miles per stay

Beaver Creek Lodge, P.O. Box 4300; 1-888-480-7919; www.captainblighs.com

Holly House, 220 Small Circle Street; 262-4762; www.ptialaska.net/-hollyhse

Jana House Hostel, Swanson River Road; 260-4151

Kenai Peninsula Condos, P.O. Box 3416; 262-1383; www.kpcondos.com

Kenai River Inn, 339 Porcupine Ct.; 262-7835; www.kenairiverinn.com

Kenai River Raven Dinner House & Lodge, P.O. Box 1670; 1-888-262-5818; www.KenaiRiverRaven.com

King's Kitchen Bed & Breakfast, 309 Vine Ave.; 262-2973; www.alaskakingskitchen.com

Marydale Manor Apartment Suites, 122 W. Marydale; 1-888-261-9238; www.KenaiPeninsulaLodging.com

Moose Creek Lodge, P.O. Box 2247; 260-3380; www.moosecreek.com

Moose Hollow Bed & Breakfast, 35645 Brians Street; 1-800-262-7548; www.AlaskaOne.com/moosehollow

Orca Lodge, P.O. Box 4653; 262-5649

Silvertip Lodge Guest Cabins, P.O. Box 425; 262-4450

Soldotna Bed & Breakfast Lodge & Fishing Charters, 399 Lovers Lane, Soldotna; 1-877-262-4779; www.SoldotnaLodge.com

Sprucewood Lodge, P.O. Box 3956; 1-888-844-9737; www.sprucewoodlodge.com

CAMPGROUNDS AND RV PARKS

Across the River RV Park, Mile 13.8 Funny River Rd.; 1-800-276-2434; on-site fishing, launch, dump station, electricity, showers, restaurant, phone, laundry, tent camping

Best Western King Salmon Motel & RV Park; 35546 A, Kenai Spur Hwy.; 262-5857

Centennial Campground, at the corner of Sterling Hwy. and Kalifornsky Beach Road; 262-3151

Diamond M Ranch B&B, Cabins, RV Park, P.O. Box 1776; 283-9424; full-service hookups, dump station, water, showers, toilets, laundry, tent camping, pets allowed; www.diamondranch.com

Edgewater RV Park, 44770 Funny River Road; 262-7733; on-site fishing; full-service hookups, water, showers, toilets, laundry

Kenai Riverbend Campground & Resort, P.O. Box 1270; 283-9489; on-site fishing; full-service hookups, dump station, water, showers, toilets, laundry, tent camping

Kenai River Family Campground, Box 8616; 262-2444; on-site fishing, water, tent camping

King Salmon Motel & RV Park, P.O. Box 430; 262-5857; full-service hookups, dump station, water, showers, toilets, laundry, tent camping, pets allowed

River Quest RV Park, P.O. Box 3475; 283-4991; www.riverquestalaska.com

Riverside Hotel & RV Park, 4611 Sterling Hwy.; 262-0500; on-site fishing, full-service hookups, water, snack bar, pets allowed

River Terrace RV Campground, P.O. Box 322, Mile 95.7 Sterling Hwy.; 262-5593; on-site fishing, full-service hookups, dump station, water, toilets, laundry

RESTAURANTS

Acapulco Mexican Restaurant, 44758 Sterling Hwy., Suite A; 260-4999

Buckets Sports Grill, 43960 Sterling Hwy.; 262-7220

Don Jose's, 44109 Sterling Hwy.; 262-5700; authentic Mexican food

Jersey Subs Inc., mile 111.5 on Sterling Hwy.; 260-3343

Mykel's Restaurant, 35041 Kenai Spur Hwy. (in the Soldotna Inn); 262-4305; mykels@ptialaska.net

Pizza Petes, 35433 Kenai Spur Road; 262-7797; excellent menu to choose from, great ambiance, orders to go, free delivery.

Sal's Klondike Diner, 44619 Sterling Hwy.; 262-2220; the most popular restaurant in town, known for their giant cinnamon rolls and burgers; arrive well in advance but the wait is worth it no matter what your menu selection

The Riverside House, 44611 Sterling Hwy.; 1-877-262-0500; specializes in Alaskan seafood

Tides Inn, 44789 Sterling Hwy.; 262-1906

FISH PROCESSING

Echo Lake Superior Meat & Processing, P.O. Box 346; 283-9456

Ed's Kasilof Seafoods, Inc., at the bridge in Soldotna; 1-800-982-2377; this is the outfit the author has used for years and has been extremely pleased

Peninsula Processing, 720 Kalifornsky Beach Road; 262-8846

CANOE RENTALS

The Fishin Hole, 139 B Warehouse St.; 262-2290; www.thefishinholealaska.com

BOAT RENTALS

Alaska Fishing Club, 262-2226; with a main office located in Soldotna, they have sled and driftboats docked along various places in the Kenai River

MOTOR HOME RENTALS

Alaska Recreational Rentals, 50755 Sterling Hwy.; 262-2700; www.akrecrentals.com

AUTO REPAIR

Dan's Mobile RV Service, P.O. Box 2705; 283-5976
Hutchings GM, Inc., P.O. Box 950; 262-5891
Kenai Auto, Inc., P.O. Box 587; 262-5885
Soldotna "Y" Chevron, 44024 Sterling Hwy.; 262-4513; complete car & RV repairs, 24-hour towing, propane, dump station, diesel

LOCKSMITHS

Arkeys Locksmith, P.O. Box 3504; 262-1801
Iliamna Lock & Key Mobile Locksmith, P.O. Box 1602; 262-5012

MEDICAL

Central Peninsula General Hospital, 250 Hospital Place; 1-888-565-4404
Family Medical Clinic, 206 Rockwell Ave.; 262-7566
Peninsula Eye Clinic, N. 161 Binkley; 262-4462
Soldotna Medical Clinic, 315 S. Kobuk; 262-6454; soldotnamedical@gci.net
Soldotna Professional Pharmacy, 245 Binkley; 262-3800

VETERINARY CLINICS

Richards Veterinary Clinic, 44539 Sterling Hwy., at Blazy Mall; 262-9385; rvcsoldotna@gci.net
Soldotna Animal Hospital, 42479 Sterling Hwy.; 260-7851; drbowser@alaska.net

TOURIST ATTRACTIONS

Soldotna Historical Society & Museum, located behind the Visitors Center; 283-7437

Between Soldotna and Homer, there are some good king salmon opportunities. Here, area guide Brett Gesh of Alaskan Bitefinders releases a 55-pound chrome king.

Scott Haugen with a nice Kenai area silver salmon.

KENAI PENINSULA CANOE TRAILS

The Kenai canoe trails add a dimension to the Alaskan fishing adventure that few roadside anglers even know about. If you've ever taken a shuttle flight from Anchorage to the town of Kenai, you've likely gazed out the window, wondering what fish those countless lakes harbored and how to get to them. What you were probably looking at was the canoe trail lakes. If you're looking for solitude, good fishing, and a peek at beaver, moose, bear, waterfowl, and an array of other Alaskan wildlife, the canoe trails are for you. If you're not hauling your own canoe, you can rent one in Anchorage or Sterling, at locations listed under "Canoe Rentals" in the hub city information at the end of this chapter.

These lakes are located on the peninsula's plateau—north of the Sterling Highway and west from the northern shores of Gull Rocks all the way to Cook Inlet. There are two unique canoe trails on this plateau: the Swanson

River Canoe Trail and the Swan Lake Canoe Trail. Both canoe trails are accessible from the Sterling Highway, and both require that you portage/paddle through a loosely connected series of lakes. Portages are typically short and easy, depending on how heavy your load is. A portage of approximately 1 mile is the longest on the Swanson River Trail, while on the Swan Lake Trail the longest haul is about a half-mile.

Because the lakes are typically locked in ice from late October to May, the canoe trails are only usable from late May through September. Weed growth can slow portage progress in July and August, so if you're traveling during these times be prepared for a bit more pushing and pulling. Striking out on these trails in September, when the birch and aspen leaves have turned golden, will saturate your senses like nothing else can.

To ensure your feet remain dry, wear knee boots. Many travelers prefer hip boots, or at least carry them along, as there are boggy areas and wet waterways that must be forded. It's also recommended that you wear a life jacket at all times when on these lakes, especially when crossing some of the large bodies of water. Though you may be an adept swimmer, the waters up here are cold, and only a few minutes in the water can leave you without muscle control. Some of these lakes are very remote, meaning help and medical assistance are all but nonexistent. In other words, there's no room for mistakes out here.

The use of motors on the canoe trails is prohibited, and because all the lakes are similar in depth and fish content, the same gear and fly patterns can be used throughout. Rainbows and Dolly Varden are the most abundant species, with the feisty Swanson River rainbow being perhaps the most prized. There are also runs of red and silver salmon present in some streams, and many lakes are stocked with trout and silver salmon.

Egg patterns, general streamers, leeches, and Woolly Buggers are popular trout and char flies in these lakes, while the Coho and pink bunny hair streamers are preferred for red and silver salmon. Many anglers bring along a small spinning rod with a variety of spinners and Rooster Tails for waters where flyfishing is more difficult. Being able to cast or troll lures in deeper waters, where fish often retreat during the height of summer, may mean the difference between having fresh fish for dinner or resorting to the granola bars in your pack.

It should also be noted that no matter how enticing a stream or lake may appear in these areas, a good number are barren of fish. Don't be afraid to move along to the next fishery if you can't get a strike. The descriptions of each canoe trail below include information on which lakes hold fish and which do not.

Time of the year can make a difference in your fishing success on many of the canoe-trail lakes, and may even influence the portages you use. Because many of the lakes and waterways on which you'll be traveling are full of aquatic grasses and vegetation, some anglers prefer to hit the lakes prior to midsummer, before the foliage starts to thicken. Heavy grass, lily, and reed beds impede travel and can make for frustrating fishing in some areas. This vegetation isn't such a big problem that you should avoid the trails in late summer, but traveling will require more effort. Also, you might not be able to hit some of the smaller, more remote lakes. Still, you'll see plenty of striking panoramas and get into good fishing regardless of when you come.

Both the Swanson River and Swan Lake Canoe Trails are located within the Kenai National Moose Range, and camping is permitted along lakeshores. There are no established campsites along the way, only signs of where earlier travelers have camped. Setting up camp at previously used sites will likely be easier and reduce further impact on the land.

Due to the dry peat beds common along the trails, it's a good idea to pack a cookstove, as this will prevent underground fires. If you're building a fire, do so only on rocky ground or bare soil. Dead and downed trees provide plenty of firewood, and the cutting of live trees is prohibited. What trash cannot be burned needs to be packed out, not buried. Use common sense and leave each area as you would like to find it.

Kenai Peninsula canoe trails present excellent wildlife-viewing opportunities.

Swanson River Canoe Trail

The Swanson River Canoe Trail links more than 40 lakes in its 46-mile system. If you're pushing it, the entire 80 miles of this trail—including a float down the Swanson River—can be covered in less than a week. But there are a number of lakes located off the main path that are just waiting to be explored. Of course, the more you deviate from the primary travel routes, the more time will be required to reach your final destination.

To reach the starting point, turn north on Swanson River Road at mile 83.7 on the Sterling Highway. Just past mile 16 on Swanson River Road, turn east onto Swan Lake Road. After traveling 3.9 miles on Swan Lake Road, you'll come to the west entrance of the Swan Lake Canoe Route, where the road meets Canoe Lake. Continuing east along Swan Lake Road takes you to the east entrance at Portage Lake. The Swanson River Canoe Trail's entrance is at Paddle Lake, at the end of the Swan Lake Road.

Getting to the headwaters of the Swanson is relatively easy, as the portage trails are easy to find and the lakes simple to navigate. With many lakes awaiting exploration along the way, you can travel at your own pace. Many people elect to set up camp along snaky and long **Paddle Lake**, making day trips from there.

If you're short on time but want to see what the canoe trails have to offer, spend a day at Paddle Lake. The scenery is great and the fishing for rainbows isn't bad, either. At the end of the eastern arm of the lake, a portage of a few hundred yards puts you on **Channel Lake**. Though Channel Lake is pretty to see, and reportedly holds rainbows and char, there are other lakes nearby that offer better fishing.

At the northern end of Paddle Lake, two options await. First, a short portage to the east connects you with two often overlooked lakes, both of which offer good rainbow trout fishing and reportedly have char, as well. **Dog Lake** appears small at first glance, but the short portage is worthwhile. Chances are, you'll encounter few, if any, people here. The same holds true for **Chum Lake**, which is connected to Dog Lake by a portage of only a few hundred yards. Your second option at the north end of Paddle Lake is to continue along the main route, which goes through the west-side portage.

The west portage is roughly a half-mile in length and joins up with **Lure Lake**, the first in a small string of lakes, all of which offer good trout fishing. From Lure Lake you can paddle your way to **Pot Lake**, on through a nameless little pond and into **Pond Lake**. From Pond Lake, a short hike leads to another small pond, one that goes by the name **Balloon Lake**. The only real obstacles in this little

Swanson River Canoe Trail

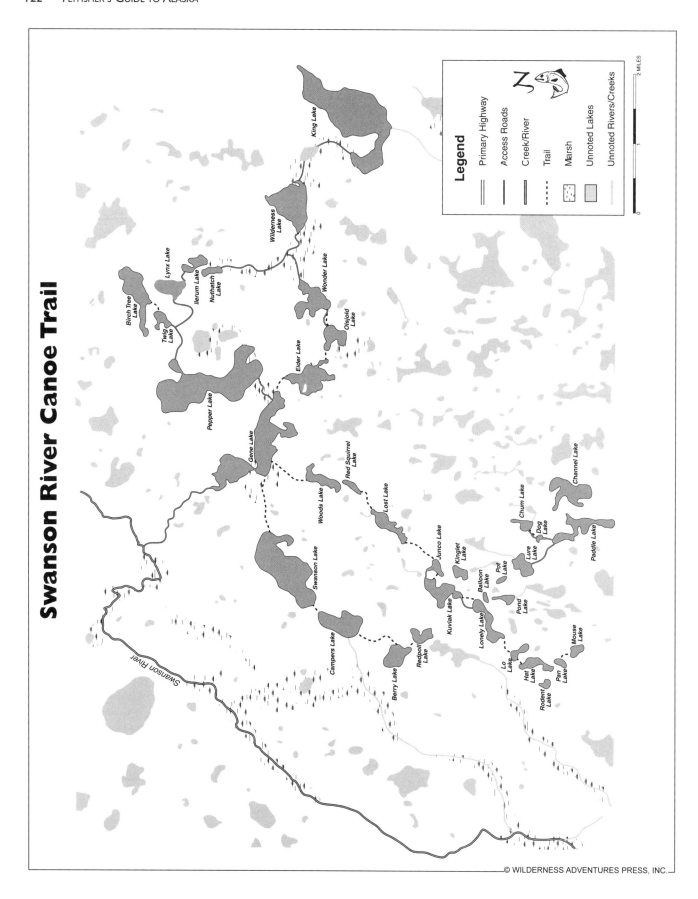

Legend

Primary Highway
Access Roads
Creek/River
Trail
Marsh
Unnoted Lakes
Unnoted Rivers/Creeks

2 MILES

King Lake

Wilderness Lake

Lynx Lake

Birch Tree Lake

Ilerum Lake

Nuthatch Lake

Twig Lake

Wonder Lake

Olsjold Lake

Eider Lake

Pepper Lake

Gene Lake

Red Squirrel Lake

Woods Lake

Lost Lake

Swanson Lake

Junco Lake

Kinglet Lake

Chum Lake

Dog Lake

Lure Lake

Channel Lake

Paddle Lake

Balloon Lake

Pot Lake

Kuvlak Lake

Lonely Lake

Pond Lake

Campers Lake

Berry Lake

Redpoll Lake

Lo Lake

Mouse Lake

Hat Lake

Pan Lake

Rodent Lake

Swanson River

chain of lakes are the beaver dams, which may require a bit of grunt work to get by.

A quick paddle out the north end of Balloon Lake brings you to **Lonely Lake**, one of the most popular waters in the system. Not only does Lonely Lake serve as a great central location from which to reach several other lakes along the trail, it also has very good trout and char fishing. If you want to slow down and do a bit of exploring rather than push on to the Swanson River, paddle your way to the southwest corner of Lonely Lake.

From here, a series of five lakes lie off the beaten path, and few people take the time to venture into this beautiful southerly chain of waters. Be prepared for a bit of legwork, though. These trails are seldom traveled so the pathways are not nearly as beaten down as more popular portages.

Following a hike of no more than 400 yards, you'll find yourself at **Lo Lake**. This 20-acre lake runs 30 feet deep in places, and is home to rainbow trout measuring in the 17- to 18-inch class. Though the lake isn't loaded with fish, it's worth spending a day here.

Moving out from the northwest end of Lo Lake, a very short trail takes you to **Hat Lake**. Hat is the largest of the five lakes in this side trip, but it runs about half the depth of Lo. The rainbows are similar in size to those found in Lo, but the catch rate appears to be a bit higher here. This may be due to its shallower depth, which makes the fish more accessible to flyfishers.

To the west of Hat Lake, **Rodent Lake** is connected by a portage of approximately ⅛ mile. Just shy of 10 acres in size, Rodent Lake has an outlet on its north end that eventually flows into the Swanson River. Due to this connecting waterway, reports of silver salmon in the creek and in Rodent Lake itself have been reported in past years. So few people fish this area, however, that accurate reports of the true status of silvers in these waters is unknown. The rainbow action in Rodent Lake is average in comparison to other lakes in the system.

At the southern tip of Hat Lake, a stream flows in from **Pan Lake**. Because Pan Lake feeds into Hat Lake, the fishing action is similar.

Since you've come this far on the little side route, you'll want to hit the last lake in the chain, **Mouse Lake**, home to perhaps the best fishing of all. After leaving the southeastern shores of Pan Lake, another trek of a bit more than ⅛ mile will bring you to the northern edge of Mouse Lake. This 18-acre lake is framed by stunning scenery and home to rainbows up to 20 inches. Its 15-foot average depth makes it ideal for flyfishing. Mouse Lake is at the end of the trail, and the only way out is to backtrack to Lonely Lake.

Once you're back at Lonely Lake, it's easy to continue on to the Swanson River. First, though, you need to get to **Kuviak Lake**, which you can do via the portage on the northeast corner of Lonely Lake. Kuviak is not noted for its fishery, so most anglers push on through.

From Kuviak Lake, two different routes will eventually lead you to the Swanson River. If you take the western route, **Redpoll Lake** will be the first water you come to. Redpoll is void of fish, as is **Berry Lake**, the next in line. Due to the lack of fishing opportunities, few people camp along either body of water. A good trail connects Redpoll to Berry, so it's easy to cover some territory.

A portage on the northeast shore of Berry Lake leads three-quarters of a mile to **Campers Lake**. Though it's a long haul, planked areas and solid trails make for good travel along this portage. Over 100 acres in size, Campers Lake is the largest lake on the trail to this point. And the fishing here can be very good. In addition to a good number of rainbow trout, fish to 20 inches can be found in Campers Lake. Work flies along the shorelines and around the island in the southeast quadrant of the lake.

An even larger lake waits down the trail, but the walk is short and easy. From the north end of Campers Lake you can portage over to **Swanson Lake**. Well over 300 acres in size, Swanson Lake is one of the largest lakes in this entire system. Due to its unbroken shoreline, anglers usually prefer the northern side when crossing this lake. The south shoreline is jagged, but this can be a good fishing route if you're not in a hurry. The rainbow trout and char fishing can be very good here, with some above average fish available. Avoid getting caught too far out in this lake, as strong winds can turn calm water into whitecaps in a matter of minutes. As in all lakes, be sure to wear a life vest here; the cold waters can take a person by surprise.

Gene Lake is the next stop, and if you're heading to the Swanson River this will be your entry point. The hike from Swanson Lake across to Gene Lake is a long one, nearly a mile, and is ranked as moderate. (Gene Lake is covered below on the eastern route from Kuviak Lake.)

Back at Kuviak Lake, you can also take the eastern route, which is the most direct way to reach Gene Lake and the Swanson River. There are many lakes and remote regions to explore on this route. From the eastern shores of Kuviak Lake, you can take a brief side trip to two lakes, but if fishing tops your agenda, you'd be better off pushing north. However, a short portage does join **Junco Lake**. Junco offers spotty fishing, at best, and most people who choose this route do so for the aesthetics of the area, not the fishing. Junco Lake adjoins **Kinglet Lake**, but this water is barren of fish.

Instead of spending time in lakes that are tough to fish, push through Junco Lake until you reach the eastern

Spawning red salmon often grab a fly when you're targeting other fish species.

shoreline, where a portage of about a half-mile brings you to **Lost Lake**. The southern shoreline of Lost Lake has many bays and arms, creating good habitat for char. This is also a great area in which to camp, although there are two improved campsites at the north end of the lake, too. Lost Lake is nearly 50 acres in size and fairly deep in places.

Red Squirrel Lake is next along this eastern pathway and can be easily reached by portaging about 1/3 mile from Lost Lake through a dense spruce forest. Red Squirrel is a small lake that connects to **Woods Lake** through a creek on its north end. Nearly 50 acres in size, Woods Lake is home to rainbow, char, and undersized silver salmon. Because Woods and Red Squirrel are connected, their fisheries are thought to be similar, though reports of silver salmon are more common in Woods.

Woods Lake, in particular, can offer consistent fishing action, with char exceeding 20 inches in length and rain-

bows reaching into the mid-teens. The silvers taken here typically run about trout size. And if the fishing doesn't keep you at this lake for an extended period, the wondrous setting might. You may want to plan an extra day just to hang out here.

A portage of about a half-mile, beginning on the northern end of Woods Lake, leads to **Gene Lake**, the central hub of the Swanson River Canoe Trail. Gene Lake covers more than 300 surface acres and is no doubt one of the most beautiful settings on the entire Kenai Peninsula. Gene offers excellent fishing too, and many anglers choose to make this their base camp for a few days. You can either fish Gene Lake itself or branch out and explore neighboring waters.

Silver salmon up to 12 inches or more are often taken from Gene Lake, as these fish move freely among many of the area lakes connected by running water. But it's the rainbow and char fishing that attracts people to this lake and keeps them here. Both trout and char populations are abundant, with trout running into the high teens and the char into the low teens. Due to the size of this lake, you shouldn't be surprised if you happen upon trout exceeding 20 inches or more.

For a large percentage of travelers, Gene Lake marks the last lake in the trail. From here, you can simply head to the northern end of Gene Lake and begin your journey on the Swanson River. But if you feel the urge to continue investigating remote lakes, get ready for even more action.

There are two portages at the eastern arm of Gene Lake. If you're looking for a good day trip from your base camp on Gene, take the northern trail to **Pepper Lake**. You can paddle all the way to Pepper through the water passage here. Not only does this half-mile connection make traveling easy, but it's a picturesque setting, as well. Pepper Lake offers fine rainbow and char fishing, and the creek connecting Pepper and Gene is worth fishing, too. The fish here are about average, with some in the 17- to 18-inch class.

If you want to push forward, head to the northeast end of Pepper Lake. Approximately halfway through, a trail off to the left leads to **Twig Lake**, and through that to **Birch Tree Lake**. Both of these lakes are void of fish, though I have heard reports of small trout and char in Twig. I'd recommend pushing past these lakes.

You can also head all the way to **Lynx Lake** through the waterway on the northeast corner of Pepper Lake. Roll up your sleeves and slap on the hip boots, as this leg will no doubt require some intense paddling, pushing, and pulling. But the level of isolation at the lakes you'll reach on this route is unmatched by any lake on either of the canoe trails.

Lynx Lake offers good char and rainbow opportunities, as does **Ilerun Lake** and **Nuthatch Lake**. The water route connecting Lynx and Ilerun is easy to negotiate, while the route from Ilerun to Nuthatch, though short, can be a challenge. The fish in these three lakes are not huge, but you'll catch a lot of fat, scrappy fighters in the 10- to 14-inch range.

Nuthatch Lake is linked to Wonder and Wilderness Lakes by Wilderness Nuthatch Passage, a formidable challenge for the less-than-fit. In fact, this entire loop east of the main trail requires dedication and perseverance. You should be in good physical condition and capable of surviving on your own in the wilds if you take this route. Go light on the gear when making this loop, as there are some serious portages. Remember, this section is off the beaten path and is by far the least visited area of the canoe trails. And this is for a reason.

Wilderness Lake and **King Lake** lie on the extreme eastern boundary of the Swanson River Canoe Trail. Though they are both beautiful bodies of water, they are also open to aircraft usage, which will dampen your enthusiasm after all the work you put in to reach them. Guides are now operating in the area, and if you don't have floatplanes buzzing around you're still likely to see motorboats. For me, it's not worth the energy to travel to these lakes given the amount of human activity and the fair-sized char and rainbows you're competing for.

If you're intent on completing this northern loop, though, head for **Wonder Lake**. A rough portage from Wilderness Nuthatch Passage leads you to the eastern shore of this lake, so be prepared for more physical labor. The saddest part is that Wonder Lake is barren of fish. So push right on through to **Olsjold Lake**.

A water route connects Wonder to Olsjold Lake, so make your way through this passage and keep moving, for the fishing is poor here, as well. There are some char in Olsjold, but better fishing lies ahead.

A short, easy trail connects Olsjold Lake to **Eider Lake**, the last lake in the loop. Eider is rated one of the most beautiful lakes on the Kenai Peninsula and is worth seeing. However, unless you're making the entire northern loop, it may be in your best interest to see and fish this lake by way of Gene Lake. As the fishing leaves something to be desired the farther you get on the northern loop, you'll want to stick close to the main trail if catching fish is your primary goal.

Eider Lake has a good number of bays, points, and islands and is home to fair char fishing. You will catch fish here, just not in high numbers. But this lake is worth laying eyes on anyway. Spend an evening here watching the sun go down and you'll carry the image with you for a lifetime.

A 500-yard portage on the north end of Eider Lake connects you with Gene Lake. Again, it may be wise to just pop down to Eider Lake on a day trip from Gene and avoid the weak fishing on the rugged northern loop.

Gene Lake's outlet is on the extreme northwest corner of the lower section of the lake. Search for the reed beds that mask the northern expanses of water and push through them to the outlet.

Continue north through Gene Lake to the **Swanson River**. But be warned, this is one of the most physically challenging sections of the trip. Some travelers elect, upon hitting Gene Lake, to simply backtrack to the trailhead at Paddle Lake or continue making the central loop before heading back to the trail entrance.

Gene Lake is only a tributary to the Swanson, and the going can be rough until you reach the main stem, which actually flows out of Wild Lake. You'll be traversing beaver dams and gravel bars, paddling through brush-choked water, and pushing, pulling, and dragging your canoe for several hundred yards, but once you finally make it to the river, things begin to look up. From this point, you can float 19 miles down the Swanson River, ending your trip at the Swanson River Campground, or continue an additional 24 miles to Cook Inlet, taking out where the river meets a spur off North Kenai Road just south of the Captain Cook Recreation Area. Depending on your approach, there are up to 48 miles of river to be navigated, and there is solid fishing for rainbows, Dolly Varden, char, red salmon, and silver salmon.

As there are so many fishing options along the Swanson River Canoe Trail, the following list should help you keep straight which lakes contain fish and which don't.

A proud fisherman with an arctic char.

Swanson River Canoe Trail Fisheries

- Pad Lake and Odd Lake *(beside the main entrance)—rainbow trout*
- Paddle Lake—*rainbow and char*
- Channel Lake—*rainbow and char*
- Dog Lake—*rainbow and char*
- Chum Lake—*rainbow and char*
- Lure Lake—*rainbow and char*
- Pot Lake—*rainbow*
- Pond Lake—*rainbow*
- Balloon Lake—*rainbow*
- Lonely Lake—*rainbow and char*
- Lo Lake—*rainbow*
- Hat Lake—*rainbow*
- Rodent Lake—*rainbow and silver salmon*
- Pan Lake—*rainbow*
- Mouse Lake—*rainbow*
- Kuviak Lake—*rainbow and char and possibly silver salmon*
- Junco Lake—*rainbow and char*
- Kinglet Lake—*barren*
- Lost Lake—*rainbow and char*
- Red Squirrel Lake—*rainbow, char, reports of silver salmon*
- Woods Lake—*rainbow, char, silver salmon*
- Gene Lake—*rainbow, char, silver salmon*
- Redpoll Lake—*barren*
- Berry Lake—*barren*
- Campers Lake—*rainbow*
- Swanson Lake—*rainbow and char*
- Eider Lake—*char*
- Olsjold Lake—*char*
- Wonder Lake—*barren, past reports of char*
- Nuthatch Lake—*rainbow, char, silver salmon*
- Ilerun Lake—*rainbow and char*
- Lynx Lake—*rainbow and char*
- Twig Lake—*barren, past reports of rainbow and char*
- Birch Lake—*barren, past reports of rainbow and char*
- Pepper Lake—*rainbow, char, silver salmon*
- Swanson River—*rainbow, Dolly Varden, char, red salmon, silver salmon*

SWAN LAKE CANOE TRAIL

To reach the Swan Lake Canoe Trail, follow the same general directions as you did for the Swanson River Canoe Trail. Turn north on Swanson River Road at mile 83.7 on the Sterling Highway. Just past mile 16 on Swanson River Road, turn east onto Swan Lake Road. After traveling 3.9 miles on Swan Lake Road, you'll come to the west entrance of the Swan Lake Canoe Route. Continuing east along Swan Lake Road takes you to the east entrance at Portage Lake.

The west entrance at **Canoe Lake #1** is perhaps the most popular entry point on the entire system. If you want to stay close to the west entrance trailhead, you can reach **Sucker Lake** from a trail off the east side of Canoe Lake #1. The going here can be challenging, as fallen trees impede progress. However, if you find yourself here in September, be sure to check out Sucker Creek for spawning silvers and feeding trout.

On the west shore of Canoe Lake #1, a wooded pathway leads to **Waterfowl Lake**. Rainbow trout, char, and silver salmon can be found in this lake, though population densities aren't high for any of these species.

Continuing on the west trail, you'll be paddling and portaging through **Canoe Lake #2** and **Canoe Lake #3**. The portage between Canoe #2 and #3 could be dubbed the "stumbling trail," due to the labyrinth of tree roots protruding above ground. Watch your step, especially in low-light conditions. Because the three Canoe lakes are situated so close to the trailhead, they often receive light pressure, as people pass by en route to more secluded waters. Don't overlook the fishing and camping opportunities on these lakes, though. If you only have a little time to spend on the canoe trails, these are great lakes to visit.

An easy portage out of Canoe #3 leads to **Contact Lake**, the fishing can be good for rainbow and char. This narrow 20-acre lake offers plenty of shoreline to explore and has a fabulous campsite available. The beautiful setting here will likely cause you to move slowly on your way through.

Moving from Contact to **Marten Lake** means walking a planked pathway that meanders through the woods. An easy-going creek flows from the south end of Marten and directly into **Spruce Lake**. Marten and Spruce are each about 75 acres in size and offer pretty good rainbow and char fishing. Landlocked silver salmon are also present in both lakes. Marten offers a bit more shoreline and points to work than Spruce.

Once you reach Spruce Lake, you have a choice to make. For solitude, head to the portage at the southwest end of Spruce Lake. This is perhaps the most unexplored portion of the Swan Lake Trail. Accessing the remote

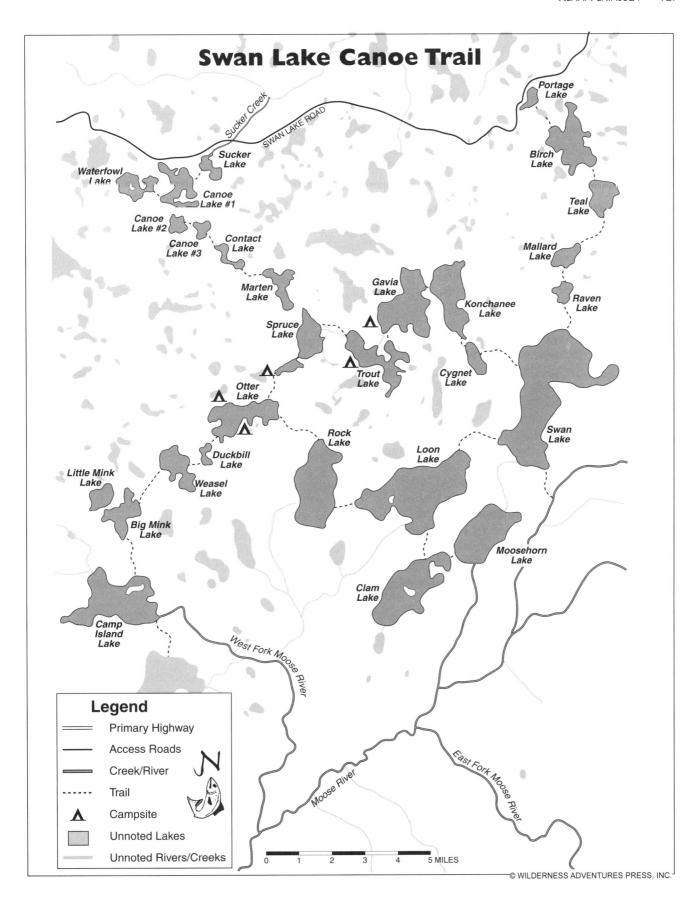

Swan Lake Canoe Trail

Portage Lake

Birch Lake

Teal Lake

Sucker Creek

SWAN LAKE ROAD

Sucker Lake

Waterfowl Lake

Canoe Lake #1

Mallard Lake

Canoe Lake #2

Canoe Lake #3

Contact Lake

Raven Lake

Marten Lake

Gavia Lake

Konchanee Lake

Spruce Lake

Trout Lake

Cygnet Lake

Swan Lake

Otter Lake

Rock Lake

Loon Lake

Duckbill Lake

Little Mink Lake

Weasel Lake

Big Mink Lake

Moosehorn Lake

Clam Lake

Camp Island Lake

West Fork Moose River

Legend

═══	Primary Highway
───	Access Roads
───	Creek/River
·····	Trail
Λ	Campsite
▒	Unnoted Lakes
───	Unnoted Rivers/Creeks

N

Moose River

East Fork Moose River

0 1 2 3 4 5 MILES

© WILDERNESS ADVENTURES PRESS, INC.

lakes that this trail leads to can be challenging, yet rewarding. **Otter Lake** is the first lake you'll find on this trail. Campsites are situated at the end of the portage from Spruce Lake, as well as along the north and south shores of Otter Lake. Otter is a big lake, known more for its beauty than its fishing.

Leaving the southwest corner of Otter, a short portage puts you on the shores of **Duckbill Lake**, the smallest lake in this string of waters. You're now entering the most remote sector of all the canoe trails. The likelihood of seeing other humans here is small, and while these lakes are noted for their beauty, they're not revered as fisheries. But if you're after seclusion on the canoe trails, it doesn't get any more isolated than this. If you're seeking big fish, though, don't waste your time here; there are richer waters elsewhere. As you'd expect, these remote portages may not be maintained like ones that see consistent use, so be prepared to tackle windfalls, overgrown trails, and rough walking conditions.

If you want to forge even deeper into the unknown, proceed to the southwest end of Duckbill Lake and head directly west to **Weasel Lake**. A short but treacherous portage links Duckbill to Weasel, so be careful, this is not a good place to get injured. Weasel Lake holds few if any fish, so pass right on through.

On the west shore of Weasel Lake, there's a half-mile portage—often covered in reeds at the starting point and difficult to find—will lead to **Big Mink Lake**. Because Big Mink has no fish, few people venture this far. The south shore of Big Mink has yet another half-mile or so long portage that leads to **Camp Island Lake**. You can also take a portage on the west side of Big Mink to reach **Little Mink Lake**. Little Mink has a population of rainbow trout, but if you've made it this far, I'd pass on Little Mink and head instead for Camp Island Lake.

For those willing to make the effort, Camp Island Lake is one of the most breathtaking places on the Swan Lake Canoe Trail, and it does offer good fishing for rainbow trout and char. The only drawback is that you have to go through so much fishless water to reach Camp Lake. With more than 400 acres of surface area, there is plenty of shoreline to fish on this big pond. The northern shore, with its islands and structure, is also the shallowest portion of the lake. Here rainbows and char can be fished in 10 to 15 feet of water, which is ideal for casting and stripping leech patterns. The island in the northeast corner of the lake offers good camping and explains how this lake got its name.

If exploring the outer reaches of the canoe trail is not of interest to you or doesn't fit your time schedule, there are two other options back at Spruce Lake. Head out the south portage of Spruce Lake and continue through Otter

Lake, but take the east portage this time. An easy ¾-mile-long trail leads you to **Rock Lake**, which holds some kokanee, although few people spend much time here.

A portage of less than a half-mile leads from Rock Lake to **Loon Lake**, the second largest lake in the system at more than 600 acres. Loon also has a population of kokanee, though neither Loon nor Rock Lake receive much fishing pressure. You'll have to paddle all the way across Loon Lake to reach the next portage on the northeast corner. Another ¾-mile portage brings you to Swan Lake. The southeast corner of Swan Lake connects to the Moose River, which completes the southern part of this central loop trail.

The final option back at Spruce Lake is to take the northern portion of the central loop of the trail, which will lead to Trout, Gavia, Konchanee, and Cygnet Lakes before hitting Swan Lake. A half-mile portage from Spruce to **Trout Lake** is planked in the boggy sections, with easy walking the rest of the way. Trout Lake is aptly named, and serious rainbow anglers may wish to spend some time here. There are some nice campsites on this lake. While most of the trout in Trout Lake average around 10 inches, I've heard rumors of the occasional 18- to 20-incher being landed here.

To reach **Gavia Lake**, you'll have to cover the entire north shore of Trout Lake, then take the portage on the northeast corner. The portage from Trout to Gavia Lake is short, no more than a few hundred yards, and is a straight shot that's easy to negotiate. Upwards of 20 campsites surround 300-acre Gavia Lake, which is also home to a good rainbow trout population.

The short portage on the northeast corner of Gavia leads to **Konchanee Lake**. Trout in excess of 20 inches have been taken from this lake, making it a fairly popular destination among anglers. But for flyfishers, this 225-acre body of water, which is nearly 100 feet deep in places, is a tough place to present a fly.

Along the southern shores Konchanee Lake you'll find a very short "deluxe" portage connecting to **Cygnet Lake**, which covers about 50 surface acres and offers good fishing for rainbow trout and char. The northern and southern shores of Cygnet are fairly shallow, with an abundance of lily pads. Working flies around the edges of these aquatic plants can pay off. Dry flies fished on the fringes of the lilies right at dusk can also yield good results. A ¾-mile-long portage on the eastern shore of Cygnet Lake connects you to Swan Lake, terminating one of the most traveled loops in the maze that is the Swan Lake Canoe Trail. We'll look more closely at what Swan Lake has to offer below, but first let's see how to reach this giant lake from the east entrance of the canoe trail.

You'll be launching at **Portage Lake** if you begin your

journey from the east entrance of the Swan Lake Canoe Trail. Don't spend too much time at Portage if fishing is on your mind. There are no fish on this route until you reach Swan Lake. Though the trail leads south through **Birch**, **Teal**, **Mallard,** and **Raven Lakes** before meeting up with Swan Lake, all four bodies of water are barren of fish.

When you get to Swan Lake you can connect with the northern loop trail to Cygnet Lake from the northwest corner. Or you can head to the southwest corner of Swan Lake where the southern loop trail leads to Loon Lake. At the southern edge of Loon Lake, you can take a side trip to two lakes that are often passed by. These lakes mark the southern boundary of the Swan Lake Canoe Trail and are not all that difficult to reach.

An easy half-mile portage from the south end of Loon leads to **Clam Lake**. Both rainbow trout and silvers are found in Clam Lake, and those who stop here bring back positive reports on the fishing, and especially the fact that few anglers fish it.

Out the northeast corner of Clam Lake, a portage of about 200 yards connects to **Moosehorn Lake**. Moosehorn holds a few coho but is mostly noted for its good rainbow fishing, with redsides measuring in the high teens showing up with surprising regularity.

As you could probably figure out through the discussion above, the centerpiece of all the lakes in this web is **Swan Lake**, which is the largest lake on both the Swan Lake and Swanson River Canoe Trails. And Swan offers one of the best shots at finding big trout. But because it's such a big, deep lake, you may have to resort to trolling hardware to pull these big trout from the depths. Rainbows of 23 inches have been taken from Swan Lake, and anglers can expect some high-number days. Char and red and silver salmon also occupy Swan Lake, offering even more variety for anglers.

Throughout the Swan Lake Trail, portages are easy to find and well marked, with boardwalks and lodgepole walkways in place along various routes. The Swan Lake Trails connect 30 lakes and over 60 miles of canoe routes with the Moose River. The beauty of this trail system is the number of options you have. If you don't wish to head all the way to the Moose River, excellent fishing can be had in several of the lakes. Furthermore, you can take several routes amid the numerous lakes, all the while seeing new water and eventually ending up at a place different from where you started. But if the Moose River, the Kenai River's largest tributary, is your final destination, it's best accessed through Swan Lake.

From the southernmost point of Swan Lake, a half-mile portage leads to the **Moose River**. This trail is very smooth, much more appealing than the portage neces-sary to reach the Swanson River at the end of the Swanson River Canoe Trail. Once on the **Moose River**, the floating is easy and the fishing superb throughout the entire drift. The Moose is slow flowing, with no rough waters to worry about. Your biggest concern here will be which rod to grab in order to target the three species of salmon, rainbow trout, and char that frequent its waters. Pike have also been reported in the Moose River.

Floating down to the Moose River bridge at Sterling is the choice of many who travel the Swan Lake Trail. From the mouth of Swan Lake, there are approximately 11 miles of river ahead, with ideal campsites along the way. Sit back, relax, and let the current carry you downstream as you take in the beauty of this part of the world. And don't forget to fish!

From either the west or east entrance to the Swan Lake Trail, the Moose River bridge can be reached in as short as four days, although that doesn't leave much time to take in the sights and relax while fishing.

As for fishing along the Swan Lake Canoe Trail, the following is a list of lakes and the fish species they hold.

With bountiful runs and liberal bag limits, silver salmon are one of the best choices for putting meat in the freezer.

Swan Lake Canoe Trail Fisheries

- Canoe Lake #1—*rainbow, char, silver salmon*
- Canoe Lake #2—r*ainbow*
- Canoe Lake #3—*rainbow, char*
- Sucker Lake—r*ainbow, char, silver salmon*
- Waterfowl Lake—r*ainbow, char, reports of silver salmon*
- Contact Lake—*rainbow, char*
- Marten Lake—*rainbow, char, silver salmon*
- Spruce Lake—*rainbow, char, silver salmon*
- Otter Lake—ba*rren*
- Duckbill Lake—*barren*
- Weasel Lake—*reports of silver salmon*
- Big and Little Mink Lakes—rainbow
- Camp Island Lake—*rainbow, char, silver salmon*
- Rock Lake—k*okanee*
- Loon Lake—s*ilver salmon, red salmon*
- Clam Lake—*rainbow, silver salmon*
- Moosehorn Lake—*rainbow, silver salmon*
- Trout Lake—*rainbow, char, silver salmon*
- Gavia Lake—rainbow
- Konchanee Lake—*rainbow, char, silver salmon*
- Cygnet Lake—r*ainbow, char, silver salmon*
- Portage Lake—r*eports of silver salmon*
- Birch Lake—*barren*
- Teal Lake—*barren*
- Mallard Lake—*barren*
- Raven Lake—*barren*
- Swan Lake—r*ainbow, char, silver salmon, red salmon, reports of pink salmon*
- Moose River—*rainbow trout, Dolly Varden char, salmon, silver salmon*

Kenai Peninsula General Information

Cabin Reservation & Information: U.S. Forest Service, Chugach National Forest, 3301 C Street, Anchorage, 99501; 271-2500

National Recreation Reservation Center (for cabins & campgrounds), 1-877-444-6777; www.reserveusa.com

USGS Topographical Maps, U.S. Geologic Survey, Earth Science Information Center, 4230 University Drive, Anchorage, 99508-4664; 786-7011; located on APU campus

TIPS FOR LAKE FISHING DURING ALGAE BLOOMS

If you're traveling the Kenai Canoe Trails—or fishing any other shallow lakes around the peninsula—from midsummer on, you may encounter an algae bloom. Depending on what lake you hit, its depth, ability to hold heat, and potential for fostering algae growth, the severity of an algae bloom can greatly vary.

But if you go to great efforts to put yourself on a body of water only to discover it's experiencing an algae bloom, don't despair. If you know you're going to be on the lakes during July or August, come prepared.

As water temperatures warm in lakes, the fishing action can slow down. The water has been absorbing ultraviolet radiation for months, and the trapped heat begins to take a toll. Oxygen-deprived fish get lethargic and line-tangling weeds flourish. But since you've come this far, be aggressive, battle through algae and weeds and do what you have to in order to find fish.

Though it may appear thick on the surface—which sends most fishermen back to camp once they see the water—algae develops in stages and may actually be only a foot or two deep. Before you get frustrated, check out the situation beneath the water's surface.

In mid- to late summer water temperatures can run a tad above normal, so stick your hand in a little deeper to see what it actually feels like 2 feet down. Better yet, tape a thermometer to a 6-foot-long stick or tie it to a section of fishing line with a weight attached and see what the temperature is where you'll be fishing.

If the water is warm on top but cools 8 to 12 inches below, you are in luck despite the amount of algae floating around. The deeper you probe, the cooler the water will become. This means fishing can be good, despite the warm water on top that is laden with algae.

Standing weeds that reach for sunlight from lake bottoms often corral algae, holding it in easy-to-locate pockets. As the algae collects among the weeds, fish often congregate here to find shade and food, especially in shallow lakes. These are the areas you should seek out. Lily pads are present in many of the Kenai canoe lakes and offer the same appealing habitat, so don't pass them by if you're in a lake that holds good fish.

A sinking line is a must, for you need that added density to cut through the algae bloom, which is buoyant and gathers near the surface. A reliable sinking line will slice right through it and get you down to where the fish are.

At the very least, you'll need an intermediate type II line. You'll find the most success with uniform sinking lines of type II, III, and IV and experience even better luck with hi-speed high-density lines of the same type. I've found these to be perfect on a 6- to 8-weight rod. Aggressively stripping or trolling works well for fishing the algae bloom. Keep the rod tip low when casting and stripping, even partially submerging it. Holding the rod tip low prevents tangling the heavy line around the guides and leaves you in a better position to give an occasional jerk, either to vary the velocity of your retrieve or to power through weeds.

Trolling offers a fun change of pace to line whipping. Paddling allows you to regulate your speed, thus controlling the depth at which you are fishing. It also adds sporadic line movement. In other words, don't be obsessed with paddling in straight line. The fish love irregular fly action, as it mimics fleeing or injured prey.

Paddle-powered trolling also gives you the flexibility to alter your route and quickly change direction, which will cause your line to go slack and your fly to drop quickly, often enticing a fish to strike. When that monster fish finally strikes, he'll yank your rod right out of the boat if you're not paying attention.

The first time I trolled through an algae-choked weed bed, I stopped a half-dozen times to clean my fly. Flustered by the slow progress, I decided to plow right through the weeds on my next pass. My fly latched onto every weed in its path, but I kept right on going. My momentum generated enough force to yank the fly free, and the trout didn't hesitate to attack.

Likewise, retrieve with vigor when casting into submerged greenery. Keep the fly moving; the fish seem to be attracted to the sporadic movement and are not bothered by the toppling weeds.

Hot summer days can make fish finicky and lethargic, so it's important to choose the right pattern. Leech and Woolly Bugger patterns are consistent fish-producing flies in Kenai lakes. Investigate for yourself too by wading in shallow sections and turning over logs and rocks to discover what baitfish are present. Better yet, slice open the stomach of the first fat fish you catch for the frying pan to see what it's been eating.

Pay close attention to factors such as wind, rain, and even clouds. On sunny summer days, natural weather changes can impact the temperature or conditions of a lake, turning the fish on. Wind puts a chop on the water, and moving water creates convection currents, often cooling sections of a lake. Winds also move algae blooms around, forming clear, productive pockets to fish through.

Rainy and overcast days can have a positive effect on your fishing success, too. If the algae bloom isn't too thick rain and clouds can suppress its development. Rain also helps cool the water, as does cloud cover if heavy enough.

However, if it's been overly hot or it's a bit late in the season and the algae is almost too thick to fish through, rain and clouds can be detrimental to your success. On rainy or overcast days, much of the algae on a lake dies. In an effort to stay alive the algae eats up great quantities of oxygen, often shutting down fish activity. Fortunately, temperatures rarely, if ever, reach this level on the Kenai Peninsula, but if you're working shallow sections tight to shore, you may see what I'm talking about.

If you want to wade fish in the presence of algae, don't worry. Since algae moves with the wind and is carried by currents, you can often find good fishing. Where weeds grow near shore, algae often hangs up. Within this microenvironment tiny chubs, minnows, leeches, and other foods gather. Big rainbows and even char will seek out these areas.

Belly boaters also have great success, as they're able to move around to reach prime fishing locations. Many anglers bring their float tubes along on the Kenai Canoe Trails, opting to fish from these rather than the canoe.

A good leader is a must when you're fishing in heavy weeds. For some of the big rainbow up here, it's not overkill to go with 15-pound monofilament tapering down to 8-pound test. Given the fact that you're pulling patterns through algae, line visibility is of little concern. I'm comfortable using 10- and 12-pound tippet in this scenario. I believe it's better to go heavy on the gear when hooking and landing fish than it is to hook a big one and risk breaking it off on light line.

Flyfishing these lakes late in the season can be fruitful no matter what the water conditions. It may be that you won't encounter any algae at all—and if you stick to the big lakes, you'll be safe—but it's nice to be prepared just in case.

FLY-IN FISHING ON THE
KENAI PENINSULA

Y ou're planning a trip to Alaska's Kenai Peninsula and are fired up about the prospects of wetting a line in its remote high mountain lakes. But maybe the group you're traveling with is suddenly on a tight schedule. Or it could be that you've come to experience high lake fishing but are physically unable to conquer the rugged trails. Whatever the case, it may be time to consider hiring an air taxi to get you into beautiful territory and superlative fishing.

Two options await anglers who choose air taxis: guided and unguided trips. When you utilize the services of a guide your costs increase, but so do the fishing opportunities. And if bad weather strikes or high winds make for tough fishing, having a pilot at your disposal is a huge benefit. If the bite is slow on one lake, the guide can have you fishing on another in a matter of minutes. Maybe you want to experience the best grayling, Dolly, and rainbow action on the peninsula. This may require moving to three different lakes, something that's easy to do if you have your own guide and pilot. Finally, many fully guided fly-in operations will outfit you with premium gear, from rods to flies and waders.

Prices for fly-in fishing adventures can fluctuate with the cost of aircraft fuel and ever-changing insurance rates. But for a ballpark figure, let's consider the average costs you can expect for a trip into a high lake fishery.

The air taxi business is a tough, competitive market. Take Scenic Mountain Air in Moose Pass, for example. At the time of this writing no other air taxi service exists in this little community, but that hasn't always been the case, and it may not be in the future. In other words, air taxi services are constantly coming and going, so it's not a bad idea when planning your trip to check with the

local chamber of commerce to inquire about a complete listing of companies offering such services.

If you're in Moose Pass or the Seward area, you're in prime fly-in country. High mountain lakes are only minutes away, but if you wish to fly across the entire peninsula to access a lake closer to Homer, that too can be done. As this book went to print, Scenic Mountain Air (1-800-478-1449) could get you into any lake you yearn to fish for $199 per person. They specialize in accessing waters where grayling up to 22 inches and rainbows up to 24 inches can be caught.

In Cooper Landing, booking flights through Gwin's Lodge (907-595-1266) is an easy way to go. The lodge can point you in the direction of the hottest action at the time of your visit, be it Crescent Lake for outstanding grayling or some remote body of water for giant rainbow trout, Dollys, or even silver salmon. If you have the flexibility to follow the best action, it's best to call the lodge and tell them what you want and then get a price quote.

The air charters in Soldotna are another story. The market is competitive, but the demand is definitely there. As a result, there are several air taxi services to choose from. Their prices are similar, averaging about $350 per person for a guided fly-in trip to area lakes. If you're hitting a lake close to town, the price may drop to $250 per person. If you're traveling to a faraway lake or plan on fishing a couple different lakes in one day, the rate may climb to $450 per person.

While some air taxi services provide fishing gear, I'd recommend bringing your own fly equipment and even a float tube. Float tubes can get you into water not accessible from the bank, and in these remote lakes that can prove invaluable. Be sure to inquire as to what gear is provided and even what brand names are supplied. I know one company who offers top-of-the-line Loomis fly rods, and you may not feel the need to risk your own cherished rod if a quality stick is available.

If costs are a concern, there are still options you can explore. Air services are often able to combine smaller groups for one fishing trip, resulting in lower rates for everyone. Rather than book an entire plane for you and a friend, ask about combining with another small group and sharing the costs.

Another option might be a package deal, booking four or five days with the same air service. The best bet for a bargain here is to book the largest group allowed by the air taxi service. This way, not only are there more of you to share the costs, but the air service is then operating with no voids. You can camp in the field with your party and the guide or return to town each night to be with the family. Though these trips appear costly at first, they can actually turn into good deals when you consider that they usually include lodging, food, guides, and access to the most remote waters on the peninsula.

No matter how you go about it, fly-in trips to the Kenai Peninsula's secluded lakes are one of the purest, most enriching fishing experiences an angler can have. Just seeing this incredible land from the air is worth the investment, but to touch down on one of the many lakes dotting the mountainscape, then step out and hook an electrifying trout or grayling—well, life just doesn't get any better.

Guide Brett Gesh prepares to release a 31-inch, 14-pound Kenai Peninsula rainbow.

Bristol Bay

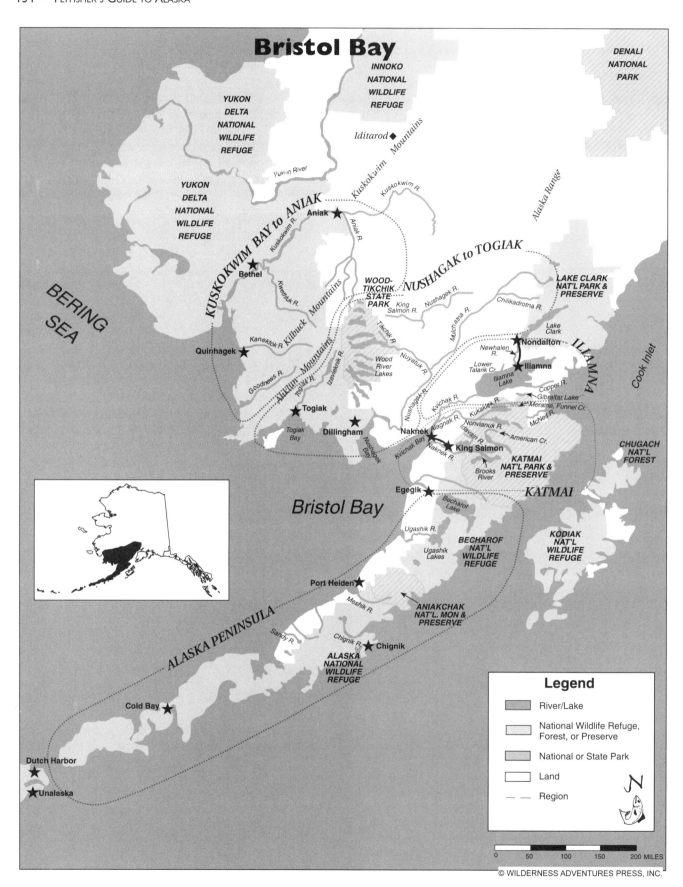

DENALI
NATIONAL
PARK

INNOKO
NATIONAL
WILDLIFE
REFUGE

YUKON
DELTA
NATIONAL
WILDLIFE
REFUGE

Iditarod ◆

Kuskokwim Mountains

Yukon River

YUKON
DELTA
NATIONAL
WILDLIFE
REFUGE

Kuskokwim R.

Kuskokwim R.

Alaska Range

KUSKOKWIM BAY to ANIAK

Aniak ★

Aniak R.

Kuskokwim R.

Bethel ★

Kwethluk R.

LAKE CLARK
NAT'L PARK &
PRESERVE

WOOD-
TIKCHIK
STATE
PARK

NUSHAGAK to TOGIAK

King Salmon R.

Nushagak R.

Mulchatna R.

Chilikadrotna R.

BERING
SEA

Kilbuck Mountains

Kanektok R.

Tikchik R.

Nuyakuk R.

Lake
Clark

Newhalen R.

Nondalton ★

ILIAMNA

Quinhagek ★

Goodnews R.

Izaviekni k R.

Wood
River
Lakes

Lower
Talarik Cr.

Iliamna ★

Ahklun Mountains

Togiak R.

Nushagak R.

Iliamna
Lake

Copper R.

Gibraltar Lake

Togiak ★

Dillingham ★

Kvichak R.

Kukaklek R.

Moraine, Funnel Cr.

McNeil R.

Magnak R.

Nonvianuk R.

Naknek ★

Nushagak R.

Bay

Togiak
Bay

Kvichak
Bay

Naknek R.

King Salmon ★

Alagnak R.

American Cr.

CHUGACH
NAT'L
FOREST

Cook Inlet

KATMAI
NAT'L PARK &
PRESERVE

Brooks
River

KATMAI

Egegik ★

*Becharof
Lake*

Bristol Bay

Ugashik R.

KODIAK
NAT'L
WILDLIFE
REFUGE

BECHAROF
NAT'L
WILDLIFE
REFUGE

Ugashik
Lakes

Port Heiden ★

Meshik R.

ANIAKCHAK
NAT'L. MON &
PRESERVE

ALASKA PENINSULA

Sandy R.

Chignik R.

Chignik ★

ALASKA
NATIONAL
WILDLIFE
REFUGE

Cold Bay ★

Dutch Harbor ★

Unalaska ★

Legend

	River/Lake
	National Wildlife Refuge, Forest, or Preserve
	National or State Park
	Land
---	Region

N

0   50   100   150   200 MILES

© WILDERNESS ADVENTURES PRESS, INC.

Bristol Bay and Surrounding Areas

By Will Rice

When fishermen fantasize about visiting Alaska, Bristol Bay often comes to mind. Floatplanes, grizzly bears, and sparkling water are the backdrop to visions of a 2-foot arctic char gobbling a deer-hair mouse. Remote and expensive to reach, its rivers have for years remained only a dream for those without the money or experience necessary to crack its secrets. Now, though, a myriad of guides, lodges, outfitters, and air taxis provide access for thousands of anglers every summer. The Bay will never be cheap, familiar, or easy—but it experiencing its splendor can now be a reality.

For the purposes of this guidebook, I have used an expansive definition of Bristol Bay, including everything from the tip of the Alaska Peninsula north and west to the Kuskokwim River. This encompasses an area roughly the size of Idaho and it is all wilderness, except for a few tiny pockets of population. Roads are essentially nonexistent and travel outside (and sometimes inside) the towns and villages is by river or air.

This area has an amazing ecosystem, fueled by the millions of salmon that return to its streams and rivers every year. Bears and eagles, trout and grayling, everything depends on the salmon. In August, the rivers are red with spawning sockeye, interspersed with the dark-olive backs of rainbows the size of salmon. And although thousands of people fly in to fish its waters, it's still not unusual to find yourself outnumbered by the four-legged fishermen.

In spite of its wildness, humans have inhabitant Bristol Bay for thousands of years. The Yu'pik (an Eskimo culture) have villages along the lower sections of almost every major river. Like everything else, their survival depended on the salmon. This is still true today, and the subsistence use of salmon by the local residents is the first priority for ADF&G's management of the salmon runs. Visitors will see traditional drying racks hung with the winter's food supply smoking over a slow fire. They represent a vibrant and enduring culture—not some museum re-creation of the past. Those of us who travel in the Bay must remember that we are guests of the local residents and act accordingly.

As you might expect in an area this size, there are significant differences in the terrain and type of fishing. The Alaskan Peninsula, stretching towards the Aleutians, is a windswept country with short rivers that fill with anadromous fish—big silvers and kings, sea-run Dolly Varden, and in a few streams, that most elusive of Pacific salmonids, steelhead. There are few guides or lodges and few rivers that get fished regularly. This is the place for anglers who enjoy fishing the outer fringes.

Great fishing and beautiful scenery bring thousands of people to this part of the state every year, but you can still find an afternoon of solitude and feeding rainbows.

General Fish Run Times For Bristol Bay

Species	Jan	Feb	Mar	Apr	May	Jun	Jul	Aug	Sep	Oct	Nov	Dec
King Salmon	-	-	-	-	-	+/+++	+++	-	-	-	-	-
Sockeye Salmon	-	-	-	-	-	-/+++	+++	+	-	-	-	-
Coho Salmon	-	-	-	-	-	-	-/+	+++	++/-	-	-	-
Pink Salmon	-	-	-	-	-	-	++/+++	+++	+/-	-	-	-
Chum Salmon	-	-	-	-	-	-/+++	+++	++	++/-	-	-	-
Rainbow Trout	-	-	-	-	-	++	+	++/+++	+++	+++	-	-
Dolly Varden	-	-	-	-	-	+++	++	++/+++	+++	+++	-	-
Grayling	-	-	-	-	-	+++	+++	+++	+++/++	++	-	-
Pike	-	-	-	-	-	+++	+++/++	++	+++	++/+	-	-

+++ Excellent   ++ Good   + Fair   - Nonexistent/Closed Season

The primary means of transportation throughout Bristol Bay are boats and floatplanes, like this elegant old Otter.

To the north lies the Katmai country, with a broad mix of water to be fished. Several big lakes fill with sockeye salmon in July, providing food for the biggest rainbows in the state. The tributaries to these lakes provide some of the best flyfishing water imaginable, and some of the heaviest bear populations. The bigger rivers that flow out of the lakes hold very large fish and are popular float trips.

Butting against Katmai, and very similar, is Lake Iliamna and its rivers. This is the realm of the floatplane, with small, clear streams flowing into a lake that is 65 miles long and 12 miles across. Its streams, particularly its outlet, the Kvichak, hold huge trout. Much of the Iliamna area is private property, and access is difficult on some rivers.

West of Iliamna is the huge Nushagak drainage. This area has some of the heaviest runs of silver and king salmon in the state. The upper stretches of the rivers are remote rainbow and char streams best accessed with a raft or riverboat. Tucked into the middle is the Wood River system of interconnected lakes.

Beyond the western edge of Bristol Bay is an area of renowned float rivers, like the Kanektok. These are medium-sized streams, with good salmon runs and a strain of beautifully spotted rainbows known as leopard 'bows. Although there are some camps along the rivers that use riverboats, these streams seem designed for weeklong raft trips.

Fishing Bristol Bay is a far cry from dropping into the local fly shop to hire a guide for the day. With a couple of exceptions, just getting to the fishing water requires a plane or boat, and often both. Nevertheless, there are several options, with varying costs. None are cheap, but for the trip of a lifetime, there are some that can be considered reasonable. There is a lot of overlap between the alternatives that I have discussed here, so don't assume that every lodge, guide, or outfitter works the same way.

Let's start with the top end, the fly-out lodge. You will get gourmet food in spectacular settings, and an expensive floatplane will whisk you to a different river every day. Some of these lodges have access to private water (typically owned by a local native corporation), which gets very little pressure. Because they can cover such large distances, they can put you on reliable fishing under most conditions. Many are located right on good fishing water and, therefore, are less dependent on good flying weather. Fly-out lodges are typically located in the Katmai, Iliamna, and, to a lesser extent, Nushagak areas. Figure about $6000 a week.

Not every area requires, or is conducive to, the use of airplanes. Many lodges operate on a single river (although some have spike camps in more remote locations). They use riverboats, often with jet units, to access the fishing.

The facilities run the gamut from elegant lodge to a weatherport camp (the space age version of the wall tent). Regardless of the level of luxury, there is still a hot shower and good food at the end of the day. Prices range from $3500 to $5400 per week.

Some rivers deserve to be floated in a weeklong exploration. The only way to experience how special they are is to float the entire length, camping on gravel bars. A number of rafting operations will take you into some of the finest waters in Bristol Bay, but you will have to do without the pampering that you'd get from a lodge. Some guides operate only a single raft; others may run several boats. Many guides run a small selection of streams and schedule the various rivers for specific weeks. They charge about $2500 per person.

There are also independent guides available. They often use riverboats, rafts, or a chartered plane to give you a custom trip. Most are flexible about the number of days they will book. Some of them are very good and can take you to streams that are little known and rarely fished. Plan on spending about $300 a day, plus the cost of any aircraft charter.

There are a few operations that cater to the self-guided fisherman. They will provide a room and kitchen and rent you a boat. They generally operate on the larger rivers and near a town or village. They can be an excellent choice for the angler whose budget is tight, but who prefers a comfortable bed and a hot shower at the end of the day. Rooms are about $150 per day, with boat rentals running about $100 per day.

For those who prefer to be totally self-reliant, it is certainly possible to go on your own. However, this is not like spending a week camping in Yellowstone and fishing the Madison River. Virtually all trips require a floatplane drop-off, and there are very few places where you can simply go and camp.

The best way to fish Bristol Bay on your own is to float one of its spectacular rivers. The most popular areas for do-it-yourself floats are the Alagnak River, the Nushagak drainages, and western Bristol Bay. Rafts and gear can be rented and there are air taxis in every hub town. The outfitters and air taxis have lots of options. The cost is a function of the air taxi flight time, but $1000 per person is typical for most rivers.

However you choose to go, timing is everything. There are steelhead, sea-run Dolly Varden, and five species of salmon, and each species enters the various rivers at a specific time. Fishing for rainbows and arctic char also depends on the salmon runs. Whether you schedule your trip to target a specific fish or are trying to figure out what will be available when you are there, always check the run charts to determine the type of fishing that will be at its peak. You don't want to show up in the middle of the king salmon season carrying your 5-weight fly rod.

Regardless of when, or where, you go, you'll need the appropriate attitude to truly appreciate the Bay. The weather is unpredictable, and occasionally harsh, even in midsummer. The mosquitoes have a well-deserved reputation, but they are the least annoying of the biting insects that you will encounter. Accommodations may be a bit more primitive than those to which you are accustomed. Good gear and the right frame of mind will minimize these problems. The biggest issue is often a sense of territoriality toward other fishermen on the stream.

Sport fishing in Bristol Bay has changed dramatically over the years. Rivers that were once closely held secrets, with euphemistic names like the Chosen River or Bear Creek, now see dozens of fishermen a day, most of whom come from a world in which success is measured by numbers and competition. Unfortunately, too many people carry that attitude onto the river, and their enjoyment of the trip is dependent on the size and number of fish caught.

Given that many of these rivers host large numbers of big fish, it's an easy trap to fall into—and let's face it, we all want to catch a lot of big fish. When that becomes the sole reason for the trip, though, it creates a subtle poison that affects everyone. It can be seen in the pressure on the lodges and guides to produce not just good fishing, but more fish than the group just downstream is catching. Techniques are developed that push or exceed the boundaries of what can legitimately be called flyfishing, to the detriment of the resource and the sport. A few guides and unguided fishermen alike become aggressive, and occasionally rude, trying to stake out a particular run. The result can be a trip that is as tense and competitive as work.

If you plan to travel to the Bay, whether with a guide or on your own, do it with an attitude that respects the special character of the area and the enjoyment of your fellow fishermen. We all want to have the river to ourselves, but don't blame the other guy for showing up. Courtesy and basic flyfishing ethics go a long way to improve everyone's experience. Accept the fact that it's raining and the bugs are biting, give other anglers room and time to fish a hole, and take the time to appreciate your surroundings. Remember, you could be back in the office.

ON YOUR OWN IN BRISTOL BAY

Bristol Bay has long had a reputation as a retreat for the rich. And with fly-out lodges running about six grand a week, the reputation is well earned. It is possible to enjoy the fishing for a more reasonable amount of money, but it is not like traveling in the Lower Forty-Eight. For the most part there are no motels and no rental cars (well, there are rental cars, there just aren't any roads on which to drive them). There are not even a lot of places where you can pitch a tent and fish from camp. The only access is by air, usually by floatplane, and in most cases, the only suitable landing sites are far removed from the best fishing.

What Bristol Bay does have is some of the finest floating rivers in the world, and fishing doesn't get much better than floating a salmon stream in western Alaska. These rivers are typically crystal-clear and gravel-bottomed, with good runs of salmon and big rainbows. Although some require extensive whitewater experience, many rivers, like the Alagnak and the Kanektok, are relatively easy to float.

Doing an Alaskan river trip without the benefit of a guide or lodge is certainly feasible for anyone with some wilderness experience and a strong measure of good sense. They are not trips to be taken lightly, however. Underestimating the conditions, or overestimating your abilities, will at best prove uncomfortable, and at worst, fatal. I have tried to provide an accurate assessment of the difficulties with each individual river discussed in this chapter. Remember, though, that these are general day-to-day conditions. The unexpected happens. Heavy rains can turn a quiet river into a maelstrom; a bear can tear up your camp, or worse, your raft; one of your party can slip and break an ankle.

Perhaps the best way to fish western Alaska on your own is to float one of its spectacular rivers.

If any of those things happen in the Lower Forty-Eight, there is always someone there to help and you can just pull the plug and go home. That is not the case on these rivers. You need to have the ability to deal with these problems safely and on your own. And while you can rent high-tech communication gear like EPIRBs or sat-phones (obviously, cell phones are useless here), they should never be considered a substitute for skill and preparation. Do not rely solely on the river descriptions that I have provided. They are the combination of personal experience and information garnered from others, but you should always do additional research to confirm current details on the river you choose.

If you have the necessary background, high-quality gear, and a willingness to stay within your limits, you can have a dream trip for about a fourth the cost of a full-service lodge. There are few other trips as satisfying and enjoyable as floating a remote wilderness on your own. It is a once in a lifetime experience no matter how often you do it.

Picking a river. Selecting a river is the first order of business—a function of your interests, skills, and budget. Timing is everything in Alaska. Read the river descriptions carefully. They will help you determine the rivers and the dates most suited to your interests.

There are advantages and disadvantages to every part of the summer. Early season gives you a shot at kings and the first of the sockeyes. Trout fishing is generally good for about a week after the season opens. But this time of year also means high water and a lack of good gravel bars for camping. The weather and water conditions are usually ideal in July, but fishing is limited to sockeyes and the latter part of the king run. The trout fishing improves as summer progresses, but the weather deteriorates, with August considered the start of the monsoons.

Be conservative in assessing your whitewater skills. These rivers are very cold and help may be days away. The rule of thumb is to drop down one class from your usual skill level. I am comfortable running Class IV whitewater in warmer climes, but I try to stick with Class III in Alaska. Keep in mind that the real danger is rarely the whitewater, which can usually be portaged if necessary. It's the sweepers that kill people. A high-quality raft may get you through the rapids, but it won't help if you suddenly find that the entire river pours under a fallen spruce tree.

Logistics. Once you pick a river, you need to figure out logistics. You will be traveling through one of the Bay's hub towns—King Salmon, Dillingham, Iliamna, or Bethel. Air taxi operators are listed for each town. Call them to discuss their experience and costs. Remember, even though you are only flying one way, you pay for the roundtrip for the plane. Make sure you know the type of airplane being used and its weight limitations. Weight limits are strictly enforced, and using a bathroom scale at home is easier than figuring out what can be left behind when you're at the airstrip. Always leave a float plan with someone in addition to the air taxi operator.

Unless you are using a raft rental place that handles logistics, you will need to air freight your gear to the selected hub town. Allow a few extra days. It is very discouraging to spend the first day of your vacation camped at the side of an airport, waiting for your raft to arrive. Air freight operations are available near the Anchorage airport and will palletize your gear when you arrive. It is best to plan on buying your stove fuel in the destination hub town, rather than attempting to ship it with your gear. Ammo and bear spray need to be declared as hazardous material.

If you do not have your own gear, there are places from which rafts and other equipment can be rented. (These outfitters are listed with the hub city information.) For many trips it is easiest to use an Anchorage outfitter, who will often handle the expediting of gear to your destination. Make sure you and the outfitter are absolutely clear on what you are renting, where it is to be delivered, and the date you intend to pick it up. Always use a detailed email or letter to confirm. Some air taxi operators have rafts for rent, but you should be very careful about the quality. You really don't want to float a river in some leaky paddle raft that has been sitting in the back of the hangar for a couple of years.

You should also determine the route your pilot will be flying. Some rivers require that you fly through mountain passes that are frequently socked in. If that is the case, you may want to pick a backup river that is easier to access. If a low ceiling keeps you from your first choice, you may still be able to fly up a river valley to an alternate float. You should carry USGS topo maps for both rivers, carefully folded and slipped into large Ziploc bags.

Gear. There is a simple standard for selecting camping gear. It has to be able to keep you reasonably warm and dry if you catch a full week of cold driving Bristol Bay rain, always a possibility in August. The biggest difference between an Alaskan float trip and other fishing expeditions is that there will be no dry room or hot shower at the end of the day. If your gear gets wet, it will remain wet for the rest of the trip. Summer-weight tents and plastic raingear have no place in Alaska, regardless of the season.

Clothing should be pile, polypropylene, and Gore-Tex. There are occasions when a T-shirt is comfortable, but there a lot more times when long underwear, a pile coat, and serious raingear are necessary. If you cannot afford top-quality breathable raingear, buy a set of the rubberized Helly Hansens used by commercial fishermen. They are heavy, uncomfortable, and have no ventilation, but they will keep you dry. Cheap raingear won't.

Take a stove. There is little fuel for fires in many places, and it is no fun trying to build a cook fire in pouring rain when you are cold and hungry. You will also need a water filter (I always take a spare). *Giardia* is very common in Bristol Bay, and it is an unpleasant condition.

Mosquitoes, black flies, and no-see-ums can be a major annoyance. I don't usually bother with a head net, but there are a few occasions when the bugs are thick enough to warrant one. Bug dope is essential, but remember that it eats fly lines. Mosquito coils help, but just camping on gravel bars is the best way to minimize the bugs.

I use a 13-foot raft with a rowing frame. I've floated rivers in collapsible kayaks, inflatable canoes, and paddle rafts, but in most rivers they are no match for a rowed raft. Gear should be packed in waterproof bags and stacked into cargo nets suspended above the floor of the raft. Drape a tarp over the top of the gear and secure the load with nylon cinch straps.

As mentioned above, you will find that gravel bars are the best campsites. They provide level tentsites and have fewer bugs. Freestanding dome tents work best under these conditions, but carry extra nylon cord in case you need to tie your tents to some willows or stake them down with deadmen (driftwood logs buried in the gravel). I always afford myself the luxury of a private tent.

The first camp chore is usually the erection of a cook shelter, using the boats and oars to support a tarp. When there are two boats, we prop one halfway up on the other, the upper one upside down, allowing us to sit on one tube, with the second boat at our back. The upper boat forms the back of the shelter, with the tarp tied to the far D-rings. The front corners of the tarp are tied to the oars, which are then guyed out with nylon parachute cord. A third oar holds up the center of the tarp, minimizing the low spots that catch the rain.

At night, we simply drop the tarp over our gear and lay the oars over it to prevent the wind from catching it. Setting it back up in the morning is a quick one-person job. It is a simple arrangement and bulletproof in a high wind. You can set up a similar arrangement with a single raft, although you won't have the headroom. If it is a one-raft trip, I usually take along a collapsible tent pole as an extra support.

Try to avoid setting up your tent in the rain and don't bring wet bags into the tent with you. Once gear gets wet in this climate, it will not dry out without a sunny day, and you can never count on those. By being careful, you can go for three or four days of steady rain before things begin to get uncomfortably damp.

Wilderness Ethics. Several years ago, I stopped at the prettiest campsite on my favorite river, a remote and rarely floated stream. We found a ring of fire-blackened stones, complete with half-burned garbage, and a hatchet-scarred spruce tree. Our predecessors were no more considerate in disposing of their own waste. There was toilet paper, unburned and unburied, behind every bush. A hundred miles from the nearest settlement, we found a camp reminiscent of the debris in an urban vacant lot.

Pollution by fishermen is a major issue in Alaska, and one that threatens access to the rivers we all want to fish. Several years ago, my usual fishing partner called the village that served as a take-out point for a trip we were planning. When he said he was rafting the river, the man at the other end said, "Oh, you're one of those people who crap in our drinking water." Despite thirty years as a lawyer, he could think of nothing to say in our defense.

Actually, it's not just the downstream villages that are affected. We all take our water from the river. In most places, the willows and alders make it impossible to get far enough away from the river to safely dig a cat hole. So take a portable toilet system. They cost about $50. At least one outfitter I know supplies one with his rental gear if you request it. If you don't have toilet system, then move as far from the stream as possible. Dig a hole, burn your toilet paper, and bury everything. Women should carry a Ziploc bag for used feminine-protection products.

With long hours of daylight and little good firewood available, campfires just do unnecessary damage. If you must have a fire, build it in a shallow pit and skip the bizarre concept of building a little ring of rocks around it.

Weather is always a consideration. Go prepared, both physically and mentally, for a week of hard rain and wind. It will usually appease the weather gods.

When the fire is completely out, bury the embers and scatter the logs. Needless to say, carry out all your garbage and police your campsite when you leave.

This is some of the last pristine country we have left, and there is no excuse for leaving any sign that you have been there. Unfortunately, there are still some people (including, with all due respect, many Europeans), who do not understand the concept of leave-no-trace camping. If you are the type of person who feels compelled to chop down saplings, throw your beer cans into the firepit, or leave toilet paper scattered in the willows, do us all a favor—stay home.

Protecting the fisheries resource is also important. Bristol Bay may have some of the finest rainbow trout fishing in the world, but the fish are at the extreme end of their range. It takes far longer to grow one of those 20-inch Kanektok 'bows than its Montana counterpart. It is illegal to keep rainbows in most Bristol Bay drainages—more important, it is unethical. Grayling and char are better adapted to Alaskan waters, but are still vulnerable and should also be released.

That is not to say you can't take fish. The sport-fish take on salmon is almost always an insignificant impact, and if you find bright fish, there is no better meal than a fresh sockeye or coho grilled over an alder fire. However, "bright" is the operative word. Salmon fresh from the ocean are chrome silver and firm fleshed. As they get farther upstream, the colors darken, the body changes shape, and the flesh begins to disintegrate. Once they have reached the spawning beds, the color has changed to red and the fish are essentially inedible. On many rivers, it is a mistake to plan on a fish dinner at the start of the trip, where the fish are already near the end of their upstream journey. But on low-elevation rivers, like the Alagnak, you can often find prime fish throughout the river.

There is competition for salmon from subsistence and commercial users. The people who live in this country rely on salmon for much of their year's food supply, and in years with low returns, sport-fish take must give way to the need for food. Salmon are managed on a day-by-day basis and you should always check the emergency regulations before you take a trip. Keep in mind that salmon are the lifeblood of the entire ecosystem, and escapement is critical to survival of all the species in the river. If you want to take home a couple of fish for the barbecue, it's rarely a problem, but filling the fish box probably isn't appropriate. Besides, unless you have a commercial-grade freezer (minus 40 degrees), salmon have such a high fat content that they deteriorate within a month or two.

Finding fish. Many visitors to Alaska are surprised to find themselves fishing what appears to be a perfect trout stream that is barren of fish. There is an idea that because the fishing is so good in Alaska, it must be good in *all* of Alaska. In fact, the fish are concentrated, both in terms of geography and timing. Even the resident rainbows migrate long distances from their wintering-over areas to their summer feeding grounds.

The salmon runs are date specific and usually predictable within a few days. A week early, and you won't see a fish. If you are late in the run, most of the fish in the river will be colored up and ready to spawn, but there will still be some bright fish among them. Generally speaking, kings enter the rivers in early June and the fishing lasts until late July. Sockeyes come in about the third week in June, and peak about the Fourth of July. Cohos are a mid- to late-August fish. Sea-run Dolly Varden come in with the sockeyes, usually about the first of July. Trout fishing has a brief window at the beginning of the season, and then slacks off until the salmon begin to pair up for spawning. On most rivers in the Bay this means prime trout fishing is from August until freeze-up. The specific times vary a bit by river, but the type of fishing available will always be determined by the dates you are fishing.

Location on the river is also critical, particularly if you are doing a headwaters-to-the-mouth float. Salmon may be spread throughout the system, but as you get higher up, their status changes from a prime game fish to a food source for the rainbows and char. Once they are on the spawning beds, they should not be harassed. The fight is sluggish and the flesh is soft and mushy. Alaskans always laugh at those magazine photos of a fisherman proudly holding a hook-jawed, scarlet-colored sockeye. Limit your salmon fishing to the lower stretches of the river, where you can find those sleek, tough chromers.

Freshwater fish also have areas of preferred habitat. Arctic char, or Dolly Varden, can survive higher up in the river than rainbows, but their ranges overlap. Both spend the late summer feeding behind spawning salmon and may occupy only a relatively short stretch of river. If you're not catching fish, or seeing spawning salmon, just keep drifting. The best trout fishing is usually found in that stretch where the river emerges from the mountains onto the foothills and plains. Logjams and snags provide cover, but they will lie in the open areas behind the salmon as long as there are eggs in the water. Keep in mind the old adage, "never leave fish to find fish." The lower reaches of the rivers, where they become deep, slow pools, may hold silver salmon, but the best trout fishing is usually over.

Problems. Many visitors tend to look at the whitewater ratings of a river and judge its suitability on that basis alone. That is a mistake. Rapids, ledge drops, and big hydraulics are a problem on a few rivers, but they can usually be portaged or lined. The real risk from most whitewater is getting separated from your boat and gear. I am not much of a Boy Scout, but I always keep a match case, bug dope, and a pocketknife on my person.

The most dangerous aspect of most rivers is actually encountering a sweeper. Spring floods will wash out the root systems of bankside trees, dropping them into the water at right angles to the current. The same current that creates a sweeper will carry your raft right into the worst part of it. Sweepers are most prevalent in sections where the river cuts new channels every year. These braids can be swift, winding, and narrow. On more than one occasion, I have had to use a bow saw to cut my way through a dangerous spot, while my raftmate desperately held onto the streamside vegetation.

Any place you find sweepers, you will find logjams. The same spring floods that create a new crop of sweepers wash the previous year's victims into massive piles of logs and branches. Like the sweepers, they are creatures of the current, and the river will try to take your raft into the worst of them.

Sweepers and logjams are a problem at normal water levels, but if the river is susceptible to blowing out in the rain, they can be deadly. Once every two or three years, Bristol Bay gets hit with the remnants of a tropical storm, usually in August or September. Rivers that drain large areas, as opposed to being lake fed, will blow out of their banks and run directly through the trees and alders. It is an ugly situation. All float trips should be weather contingent. I have pulled the plug on a number of trips because of weather and rarely regretted the decision. It is an easier choice if you have a backup spot in mind.

There is a second, and less important, problem with the braided sections of the rivers. There is no way to tell where you are. You can't see any landmarks, the channels are always different than what you see on the maps, and you can't judge your speed. Before the invention of the GPS, I was usually lost for a couple of days on nearly every trip. We always floated out at the bottom, but sometimes mistimed our pickup. Take a GPS and make sure that you check your location on the maps several times a day. That way, if your GPS goes out, you will have a good starting point for identifying the sometimes-confusing landmarks. Marking the lines of latitude and longitude at home on a flat surface will make your GPS readings easier to correlate with the map.

Of course, everyone's favorite Alaskan danger is the bears. They are a constant, but some rivers have more than others. I usually assume that we will run into two or three, but on one adrenaline-soaked trip we saw 127 of them. Generally speaking, the highest concentrations are found in the Katmai drainages and down the Alaskan Peninsula, but all fishing rivers have significant populations. Grizzlies, or brown bears (they are the same ani-

mal), are the most common, but spruce forests and other wooded areas often have large numbers of black bears, which can often be more troublesome than their larger brethren.

Carrying a gun is a personal decision. If you are not completely familiar with it, leave it at home. I carry a shotgun and rifled slugs for camp, and although I have never had to use it, there have been times that it was a comfort to me. I carry bear spray when fishing. We ship it air freight and transport it in the pontoon of the floatplane. If you do carry a gun, be considerate and do your target practice at home. Out-of-season gunshots often mean that someone is in trouble and needs help, and you don't want your neighbors mounting an armed rescue just because you decided you wanted to touch off a few rounds.

Most campsites have no bear-proof trees, so we simply store the food, cooking equipment, and garbage at the far end of the gravel bar on which we are camping. Meals are precooked, frozen, sealed, and stored in a cooler. Bear-proof canisters are a better option, and you can now buy portable electric-fence systems that are reasonably effective at deterring a curious or hungry bear. We are careful to minimize any food odors and we keep a scrupulously clean camp. I have never had a camp torn up by bears, but it is not an uncommon occurrence. An emergency supply of food in a bear-proof canister is good insurance. There is no way to avoid camping on the bear trails, but peeing on the trail will at least alert a bear walking downwind to your presence.

In areas with a lot of pressure, the bears are acclimated to people and will generally treat you as they treat other bears. Subordinate bears will run from you and dominant bears expect you to get out of their way. Problems on

Silver salmon can be frustratingly close-mouthed at times, but when they are aggressive, they will wear your arms out.

salmon streams usually come from surprising a bear in the willows, running into an adolescent bear, or keeping a dirty camp. Nothing alerts a bear to your presence faster than the sound of a human voice, so forget your inhibitions and talk or sing loudly. Don't forget to make noise if you are floating through narrow, winding sections of river. They are one of the most likely spots to surprise a bear.

In spite of all these warnings, most trips to Bristol Bay are pleasant and trouble free. The only problem that you will certainly encounter is the bugs. You can minimize the risk and discomfort of the less likely problems with good gear, careful planning and river selection, a willingness to change plans if conditions are inappropriate, and an ability to be self-reliant if the unfortunate happens.

Alaska holds a special place in the hearts and imagination of flyfishers throughout the world—and rightly so. It reaches its peak, though, when you are camped on a gravel bar next to a run full of fat rainbows, knowing that your neighbors include more wolves, bears, and caribou than people.

Services for Do-It-Yourselfers

RAFT RENTALS

Alaska Raft & Kayak, www.alaskaraftandkayak.com; 401 W. Tudor Rd., Anchorage, AK, 99503; 561-7238

Alaska Downstream, www.alaskadownstream.com; P.O. Box 113143, Anchorage, AK , 99511; 1-800-608-7238, 868-3704

Alaska Raft Rentals, www.alaskaraftrentals@alaska.com; Palmer, AK; 745-2447

AIR FREIGHT

Northern Air Cargo, www.nac.aero; 3900 W. Intl. Airport Rd., Anchorage, AK; 1-800-727-2141, 243-3331

Lynden Air Freight: www.las.lynden.com; 6441 S. Airpark Place, Anchorage, AK 99502 1-800-926-5703, 243-6150

FLIES FOR BRISTOL BAY

The waters around Bristol Bay are remarkable not only for the number of fish, but also the variety. There are five kinds of salmon, rainbow trout, arctic char/Dolly Varden, grayling, and northern pike. Many of the river systems hold all of these species. And each of these species has its preferred fly patterns. Although there is a bit of overlap with flies used in other parts of the Lower Forty-Eight, most of the patterns discussed here are unique to Alaska. If you're making your first trip north, plan on spending some time at the tying bench.

The first step in filling those Alaskan fly boxes is to establish the time of year that you will be in Bristol Bay. Timing is more important than location in determining the species for which you will be fishing. Salmon runs have a schedule that varies little from year to year. Trout and char move around in the river systems, following the food sources. Whether you pick your quarry and plan your trip around it or choose your travel dates and take what's available, those dates will determine your fly selection.

With some exceptions, Alaskan fish are not highly selective and rivers do not contain an abundance of insect life, so resident fish species are by necessity opportunistic feeders. The primary exception is at the height of sockeye spawning season, when trout and char go on an all-egg diet, and size and color can be critical.

Salmon do not feed in fresh water, and will hit a fly only out of some poorly understood primal aggressiveness. For the most part, presentation is more important than pattern. This is true whether you are bouncing some fluorescent and tinsel monstrosity across the bottom for kings or swimming a smolt pattern for rainbows. Still, some patterns work better than others and having confidence in the fly that you are using goes a long way toward getting a fish to hit.

Trout and Char

Many people still come to Alaska expecting to find big, unsophisticated trout that are willing to hit anything that resembles a food source. The trout are still big, but they are no longer stupid. Most have seen, and been stuck by, a lot of flies, and they learn just as fast as those 20-inchers living in your home waters. Using the right flies for each season is the first critical step. Because trout and char (arctic char/Dolly Varden) utilize the same food sources, the same flies generally work for both.

Trout flies fall into three categories. Some patterns imitate a natural food source so closely that the fish cannot distinguish the fly from the real thing. The best egg patterns fit this description. Others

Will Rice enjoying an autumn day in Bristol Bay.

trigger a feeding response by creating the illusion of a familiar food. Using a white bunny fly during the smolt out-migration is a good example. Finally, there are flies that don't resemble any living thing, but prompt some visceral reaction that causes a trout to hit it. The Egg-Sucking Leech immediately comes to mind. Most successful fishermen understand and use all three types.

The design and selection of trout flies for the Lower Forty-Eight is generally grounded in entomology—imitating the life cycles of the insects on which trout feed. Not so in Alaska, where the primary food source for rainbows and char is actually their larger cousins, Pacific salmon. The match-the-hatch patterns used here hold little resemblance to the delicate wisps of fur and feather used in most places. The first step in filling your trout fly box is to determine which stage of the salmon's life cycle will be in the water at the time you will be fishing it. Once you have an appropriate selection of those imitations, you can begin to fill it out with flies to match the sculpins, leeches, and insects that trout take opportunistically. Like all trout streams, the patterns change over the course of the year.

Early season. An analysis of trout behavior in Alaska always starts with salmon, and in the early season that means alevins (just-hatched salmon still carrying the yolk sac), fry (first-year fish), and smolt (juveniles ready to migrate to sea). Alevins emerge from the gravel before the season opens in most areas, and are usually of limited interest. Fry and smolt, though, can provide heart-attack fishing.

The two most important salmon for trout streams

are kings and sockeyes. With some exceptions, both species spend the first year in fresh water as fry and then migrate seaward in their second summer as smolt. King salmon fry rear in the rivers, but sockeyes migrate downstream to a lake. In June, clouds of sockeye fry haunt the edges and backwaters of their natal streams, making their dash for the safety of the lake under cloudy or twilight skies. The fry move in the upper inches of the water column, and those slashing rises you see aren't trout chasing caddis.

Fry are about an inch long, largely silver with dark backs, have prominent eyes, and exhibit a lot of movement when they swim. There are a number of patterns that imitate them well, but all are measured against the effectiveness of a sparsely tied Thunder Creek, usually size 10. Fish fry patterns almost dead drift, then let them swing across the current below you. Resist the urge to pick up and cast immediately. Many fish are unable to resist a fry pattern just hanging in the current.

Sockeye fry are found in the spawning streams above the lake in which they spend their first winter. The following year, as smolt, they head downstream to the ocean. The choice of patterns, fry or smolt, is largely a function of whether you are fishing above or below the lake in which the fish rear. Both fry and, to a lesser extent, smolt migrate in a quick surge, and timing the runs can be tricky.

In larger rivers below the lakes, an out-migration of hefty, 3-inch smolt will really bring the big fish up. The first notice of their arrival is often a flock of screaming terns and gulls moving downstream. As the birds get closer, you can see a frenzy of smashing strikes as the trout chase the fleeing smolt. Throw a size 2 or 4 white streamer into the middle of the frenzy and hold on. I like white Zonkers, gray over white Double Bunnies, and white Woolly Buggers tied with a few strands of peacock over the back. A little weight will keep the fly a few inches deep. Fish smolt patterns like a more vigorous version of the fry.

Fry and smolt patterns are fun, but for truly big fish, try working big, dark streamers along the bottom. One of my cold-weather favorites is a heavily weighted black Bunny Bugger with a twinkle of red or green Flashabou and a matching glitter head (mix the appropriate color of fine glitter with epoxy and coat the head). Fill out the rest of your fly box with sculpin imitations, black and purple Bunny Leeches, Egg-Sucking Leeches, Conehead Muddlers, and dark Double Bunnies. Don't be afraid to go large for these fish. Big Articulated Leeches with a little flash and large lead eyes can be incredibly effective all season long.

Midseason. Trout fishing generally slows during mid-June through July because the sockeye runs push the rainbows into marginal water. Fish the side channels and the pocket water. This is dry fly and nymph time. You don't often see fish feeding steadily on the surface, but they will still come up for a dry.

My selection is simple. Yellow Humpies, Elk Hair Caddis, Black Gnats, and Parachute Adams in sizes 12 through 16 will cover 90 percent of the imitative patterns that you need. I also carry a few big attractors like a Katmai Slider or Madam X in sizes 8 and 10, and some small emergers for those occasions (and they happen) when the fish go Henry's Fork on you. Those deer-hair mice can also be a lot of fun on the right water. If you aren't getting strikes on a dead drift, try skating the flies. This is particularly effective on char, which seem to prefer a fly with action.

As in most places, nymphs are generally more effective than dries. Beadheads are the order of the day for fishing pocket water. My favorite searching pattern is a Beadhead Prince Nymph, in sizes 8 to 16. I also carry Beadhead Hare's Ears, and some simple beadhead fur nymphs in green, brown, and black. If you aren't getting strikes in the pockets, try moving your indicator closer to the fly—18 to 24 inches. The swirling currents of the pockets create slack in the tippet, and the trout can often spit out an imitation before the leader tightens. For tough fish, it is hard to beat a small Pheasant Tail, but you may have to drift the fly right down the fish's throat to get him to take.

Streamers, both dark sculpin patterns and bright smolt imitations, are also good in midsummer. If you are floating a riffle-and-pool stream, try them in faster water. The trout will often move in there to feed and to escape the sockeyes resting in the slower water.

Spawning season. This is the time everyone waits for. In late July, the kings begin to spawn. Look for those rust-red logs lying in midstream. By early August you will find wide, knee-deep runs measled with scarlet-colored sockeye. It's not hard to locate trout. Just look about 3 feet behind every pair of spawners. There is no question that the trout are keyed on eggs, and egg patterns are the first choice.

Before any spawning actually takes place, the salmon pair up and begin digging their redds. This nest-building activity flushes out insects from the gravel, and the trout are looking for nymphs and caddis larvae. My favorite fly for this period is a Flashback Pheasant Tail, size 14. Hare's Ears and caddis emergers are also effective.

Once the eggs are ripe and the trout can smell them in the water, they will key on them, and although they will still hit other flies occasionally, they can be quite selective to egg patterns. The days when Alaskan trout were so unsophisticated that they would gobble anything that was red and round are long gone. They can be very selective to size and color. King salmon eggs are larger and more orange than sockeye eggs, and both begin to change color when the water hits them, becoming paler and more opaque. As the season progresses, many fishermen move to more cream-colored flies.

Glo-Bugs and Iliamna Pinkies have been the traditional egg patterns, but in recent years people have developed more realistic imitations. MOE Eggs (made from epoxy), Hot Glue Balls, and Pettis Unreal Eggs are all good. Many guides just string a bead on their client's leader, sometimes pegging it with a toothpick. This is a controversial practice essentially designed to prevent the fish from being able to reject the fly. When the trout spits out the bead, the trailing leader drags through its mouth, snagging the fish. The guides that use them argue, with some merit, that this system eliminates the risk of a fish taking the fly deep and results in less damage to the fish. Opponents simply say it is indistinguishable from using a Spin-N-Glo rig, and a far cry from flyfishing.

Beads are defined as attractors, not flies, and are closely regulated. If you decide to use them, be sure you know the regulations in the area you're fishing. A bead fished above a bare hook is illegal in flyfishing-only waters, and it is illegal to peg a bead more than 2 inches above the hook anywhere in Bristol Bay.

There is no question that beads are an accurate imitation of an egg. Fastening a bead to a hook will create an equally compelling fly, without the ethical questions entailed in pegging. My favorite egg pattern is to tie a small wisp of Glo-Bug yarn to a size 12 Tiemco 2312 hook. Slip a bead over the eye of this hook, pull the yarn over the bead, creating a translucent veil (which imitates the change in color that the egg undergoes), and tie off. You can use other hooks, but you may have to drill out the hole in the bead or heat the hook and let it melt its way through the bead.

End of the Season. As the sockeyes begin to die, flesh flies become effective. White, white and pink, and ginger Bunny Bugs are the standard patterns. The smaller size provides a more realistic imitation of the scraps of flesh that drift loose. My favorite is a mix of dirty white and salmon pink marabou roughly dubbed on a size 8 or 10 hook.

There are still eggs in the water, but at this point most are dead and have been attacked by fungus. Use cream or dull yellow patterns to imitate them. If the river has risen, it will have washed old salmon carcasses into the water. A maggot imitation (forgive me, Theodore Gordon) can be deadly, particularly along the stream edges. A curved-shank, size 14 hook wrapped with white yarn or tight dubbing is all you need.

With the salmon gone, those big leech and streamer patterns work well again. Sculpins are rooting through the redds for eggs, and rabbit-strip imitations fished slowly along the bottom catch a lot of big trout. Try crawling a black Articulated Leech through the deep holes. By this time, though, the trout are beginning to drop back down to their wintering grounds, and the upper parts of smaller streams will suddenly go blank. Be prepared to fish bigger water and go deeper.

King (Chinook) Salmon

If fly-tying reaches its zenith in the elegant and complicated flies tied for Atlantic salmon, then king salmon flies are on the other end of the artistic spectrum. King salmon like them big, bright, and gaudy, as if designed by someone with the artistic sense of a three-year-old. The quintessential king salmon fly, known as the Fat Freddie, is simply a ball of bright pink yarn lashed to the hook with a bit of Flashabou and some marabou added as an afterthought.

King salmon enter Bristol Bay rivers in late May and early June. Fishing for them extends to the end of July (when their season closes), and they should not be harassed on the spawning beds. A hooked king will usually choose to just slug it out with you, only expending the energy necessary to avoid being caught. That means that you need tackle heavy enough to take the fight to the fish.

Kings are big fish (Bristol Bay fish usually run from 20 to 40 lbs.), they hug the bottom of the rivers, and they will not move to take the fly. They do not feed in fresh water, which means that they are only biting something that annoys them (actually, no one know why they bite, but annoyance is a good starting point). If you are going to hook kings on a fly, you need to be down at their level and show them something that is dramatic enough to prompt a reaction.

Kings do not usually hit a fly hard, so you need needle-sharp hooks. Sizes 2 to 4/0 will cover most situations. Flies with lots of inherent movement seem more productive, so bunny fur and marabou are the most popular materials. Start with colors as bright as you can find them, and then tie some that are a bit smaller and more somber for those shallow, clearwater sections. The most popular colors are fluores-

cent reds, yellows, oranges, and chartreuse. Purple holds its color in deep water and can be effective. Add substantial amounts of tinsel, Mylar, or other flash materials. Everglows in chartreuse, orange, and red are good in the late evening (but watch for bears at that time of day). Whatever you come up with out of these combinations will probably catch a fish as long as you bounce the fly in front of its nose. There are some specific patterns, though, that have proven productive.

The aforementioned Fat Freddie is essentially a supersized Glo-Bug with a tail of tinsel and white marabou. Wiggletails are brightly colored Woolly Buggers with unraveled Mylar tubing tied in at the head. Alaskabous are tied with a marabou and tinsel tail and a contrasting color of marabou wound as a hackle. The fly is tied near the back of the hook, a la tarpon flies, to avoid fouling the marabou. Popular color combinations include white/pink, orange/purple, and white/chartreuse.

Flash Flies consist of a tail and wing of silver Flashabou, a woven Mylar body, and a wrapped hackle of red, orange, pink, or purple. Perhaps the simplest pattern is an over-sized bunny fly tied in the brightest colors available. Tie a bundle of Flashabou under the tail to give it some flash. All of these flies should be weighted, with the amount of weight dependent upon the type of water that you will be fishing.

Having said that, the biggest king that I have taken on a fly rod hit a size 8 Crazy Charlie that I was experimenting with for rainbows. You never know.

Kings prefer the deep water of the main channel, and in larger rivers that may put them out of range of a fly rod. Most fishermen backtroll with large plugs in this situation. Big Tadpollys, Wiggle Warts, and Flatfish account for a lot of fish. Spin-N-Glos, rigged behind a pencil sinker and bottom bounced, work well. They can be cast from shore or backtrolled. The other classic Alaskan lure is the Tee-spoon, actually a large spin-

An Egg-Sucking Leech will take almost every species of fish in Alaska.

ner with a fluorescent plastic body. Mepps and Vibrax spinners also work well, and are much easier to cast. Replace the treble hooks with super-sharp single hooks.

Chum Salmon

Few flyfishermen actually target chum salmon. This is a mistake. Pound-for-pound, they are as strong a fish as you will find in fresh water. They can be aggressive and willing to take a fly, particularly when found in large schools. The fight is often aerial and always long.

Chums enter most rivers in July. Look for fish that are holding rather than moving through. They will lie in the soft water along the edges of sloughs and backwaters. Chums that are scattered in shallow, clear water can be very difficult. The best fishing comes from large groups of fish stacked up in slightly turbid, slow-moving water. The brightest fish are usually found in the lower end of the rivers, near salt water, but some chums migrate well upstream.

Flies for chum salmon are often just smaller versions of king salmon flies and are fished in the same manner. Cerise and chartreuse are favorite colors. Comets and Bosses also catch fish, probably because they get deep. Egg-Sucking Leeches work well on chums, just like every other species in the state.

Chums have also been known to take the same skating dry flies sometimes used for cohos. Fish a pink or cerise skater, tied with a riffle hitch, quartering below you. Let the fly simply swing across the current without stripping. The big males are particularly susceptible to a waking fly.

Spin-fishermen should use the same spoons and spinners recommended for silver salmon.

Silver (Coho) Salmon

Cohos have everything that a flyrodder could want in a salmon. They are aggressive and will take a fly readily. And they are explosive fighters and wear themselves out, even when hooked on light tackle. They prefer slower water and deep pools and are usually found in medium-sized schools, where they are accessible without the need for arm-wrenching distance casts. They are also great on the grill, and in these days of catch and release, there is an additional pleasure in taking a fish for the table without feeling guilty about it.

Silvers enter the rivers in mid-August, which makes them available at the peak of the rainbow fishing. Silvers like slower water than other salmon species, so look for them in the backwaters, eddies, deeper pools, and confluences with feeder creeks. Fishing in the tidal stretches of the rivers can be particularly effective. Silvers are aggressive when they first hit the rivers, often willing to chase skated dry flies. Typically, they then go off the bite while their body acclimates to fresh water.

This is an effective survival mechanism for them, because they have a very high mortality rate from catch and release during this period. Once they have moved upriver, they will continue to hit a fly, but are less willing to chase them. Silvers also develop group lockjaw, sometimes going for several hours when not a single fish will look at a fly. When that happens, keep changing flies. It may not draw any strikes, but it helps with the boredom.

A fisherman targeting cohos should carry a wider selection of flies than is necessary for other species. The basic selection should include Flash Flies, Crystal Bullets, and other brightly colored, flashy creations. Most coho fishing, particularly in the lower rivers, will be done with this type of fly. Egg-Sucking Leeches, green and black Woolly Buggers, egg patterns (often oversize), and Comets also work well and will often tempt fish that have been in fresh water for a while. Dennis McAfee, of McAfee's Fly Shop in Anchorage, has some large Articulated Leeches in fuchsia and chartreuse, as well as some brightly colored Super Prawns that will take fish that want something big and bright.

Don't fall in love with a single pattern or one type of retrieve. Start with a flashy fly and a fast strip. Keep varying the retrieve until you find one that the fish want. If that doesn't work, go to a darker, smaller fly and fish it slowly, even dead drifting or letting the fly hang in the current. Silvers can be notoriously fickle.

If you are fishing smooth water near tide line, and there are aggressive fish around, try a skated dry fly. The classic coho skater is a hot pink deer-hair fly called the Pink Pollywog (usually just called the 'wog). It is such a standard that the technique is often referred to as 'wogging the fish. A number of other patterns have now proven successful and are often more durable. In any case, riffle hitch the fly and let it skate across the surface, quartering below you.

Cohos are great fly-rod fish, but if you are using spinning tackle, Pixies and Vibrax spinners are the Alaskan standards. Other large spinners or spoons will also work. Like flies, flash and bright colors are usually the essential ingredient. Remember that on many rivers in Bristol Bay you will need to replace those treble hooks with singles.

Sockeye (Red) Salmon

Sockeyes are the building blocks of the entire food chain in Bristol Bay. Arriving by the tens of millions, they feed not only the trout, but also the bears, eagles, gulls, and local residents. They pour into the rivers in mid-June, running a gauntlet of commercial nets, seals, and hooks, and bringing with them the stored nutrients of their years at sea. Without the sockeyes, Bristol Bay would be a barren place.

Those who have fished for trout behind spawning sockeyes may think of these salmon as aggressive in taking a fly, sluggish fighters, and if an angler is foolish enough to try them, poor eating. They would be wrong on all counts. A sockeye, fresh from the ocean, is the most obstinate of the salmon to hook, explosive at the end of a line, and perhaps the best tasting of all. Never confuse those grotesque, harlequin-colored spawners with a dime-bright, tear-your-arm-off chromer hooked in early July.

No Pacific salmon eats after entering fresh water, but at least the other species have lived on smaller fish and have the search image imprinted in their brain. Sockeyes feed on krill and plankton. There are many who insist that sockeyes will never hit a fly in fresh water, and they are almost right. Sockeyes will not move up, down, or sideways to take a fly. If the right fly bumps them in the nose they may open their mouth long enough to take it in and spit it back out. Frankly, most sockeyes are caught because they move in such abundance that the leader drags through a fish's mouth and the fly snags on the outside of the jaw as it pulls tight. It is possible to catch them legitimately, though.

Sporting goods stores in Anchorage will usually try to sell you a large crudely-tied bucktail called a Coho Fly for reds (as Alaskans invariably call sockeyes). Resist. The best flies for sockeye are small and sparse. McAfee's Fly Shop in Anchorage sells a small but effective selection of flies, including Krystal Shrimp, Montana Brassies, and Sockeye Oranges (also tied with green). McAfee also likes green Crazy Charlies. Each of these flies is tied on a size 6 hook and consists of a slim, simple body, a sparse wing, and a touch of color. They are far more effective on sockeyes than the big, bright creations used for other salmon species.

Grayling

As a kid growing up in the Rockies, grayling were our most exotic fish. Not so in Alaska, where they fall in the same category as panfish—small, easy to catch, and fun for the kids. They will come up from the bottom of a deep clear hole to smack a dry fly or hit a drifting egg pattern. Many streams hold 18-inchers and fish over 4 pounds have been taken in places like Ugashik. Grayling are ubiquitous in Bristol Bay, and they have saved the day on a lot of trips.

Unfortunately, grayling suffer from the same level of disrespect common to all panfish, particularly when they are grabbing flies intended for big 'bows. Much of the problem stems from the fact that the type of equipment necessary to land Alaskan-sized trout overpowers grayling. When that happens, they simply go rigid, putting up very little fight. On light tackle, though, they are as feisty as you could hope for. A day casting dry flies to grayling with a 3-weight will remind you why you enjoy fishing.

The fly selection for grayling is pretty basic. The larger fish will hit fry patterns and other small streamers, and all grayling love eggs. Basically, however, grayling are insectivores and not particularly discriminating ones. A selection of size 12 to 14 Adams, Humpies, Black Gnats, Light Cahills, and Elk Hair Caddis will suffice for dries.

Nymph selection is equally basic. I prefer Beadhead Prince Nymphs, Hare's Ears, and caddis imitations. Glo-Bugs and Iliamna Pinkies will almost always fool them during the salmon season. If you are targeting grayling, you may want to expand your fly box a bit, both in size and color range.

Northern Pike

Northerns are found in parts of Bristol Bay, primarily in the Nushagak and Wood River systems and in some of the lakes in the Naknek system. Look for them in backwater sloughs, weedy shallows, and around the mouths of slow-flowing streams. Pike are ambush hunters, so they prefer areas with cover ranging from weeds or glacially-turbid water.

Few people target pike in Bristol Bay, but it is always worthwhile to take along a few wire leaders and some cheap deer-hair bugs or streamers. A 6- or 8-inch bite tippet of wire is essential. Pike will go through nylon like a pair of sharp scissors. Those teeth are equally destructive to flies, so you don't want to use those fancy, hard-to-tie patterns.

The simplest set-up for top water is bit of bucktail tied to a hook (size 2 to 1/0) and a homemade popper head strung on the leader. I use ¾-inch foam garage door insulation. Cut it into 1-inch lengths and insert a piece of plastic tubing to keep the leader from cutting into the foam. The fish will tear them up, but you can make a couple of dozen for the cost of a single popper. Red and white or red and yellow bucktails will work as surface trailers or deep-running flies.

One last tip: Look for sloughs and backwaters without any baby ducks—a sure sign that large pike are in the area.

Alaskan flies are more specialized than those used in the rest of the country. They are generally bigger, uglier, and more difficult to cast. This is not to say that Bristol Bay trout or salmon won't hit the more genteel flies used elsewhere. But if you want to improve your chances of success, forget aesthetics and go with what the locals recommend.

KATMAI PARK AND PRESERVE

Katmai is the heart of Bristol Bay. It is a land of short rivers, big trout, and lots of bears. If your vision of fishing Alaska is a floatplane flight into some salmon-choked river shared by bears, and catching football-shaped trout before returning to an elegant lodge with meals of king crab and chardonnay, then you have been visiting the websites of too many Katmai-area lodges. Not to say that this is an inaccurate view, it's just a bit limited. Those lodges and those rivers exist, and for those fortunate enough to visit them, they are the peak of North American flyfishing. But there are other, less expensive, alternatives available, too.

The major river systems of Katmai, together with the Iliamna drainages just to the north, have the biggest rainbows in the state. Most are found in streams that appear to have been designed by a flyfisher. Brown bears are common, wandering the stream with their two-legged competitors. The fuel for this incredible ecosystem is the tens of millions of sockeye salmon that flood the rivers every summer.

Katmai is a magnificent place that may ultimately be loved to death. Thousands and thousands of dollars worth of fly rods go through the King Salmon airport every Saturday. Rivers that were once solitary sanctuaries for bears and a few intrepid fishermen now host a fleet of floatplanes every morning. But in spite of the crowds, every visitor leaves with a spot of magic—an interaction with a bear, one particular fish, or perhaps an hour in the sunshine when the caddis were coming off and big trout took every good drift.

Alagnak River

The Alagnak (often called the Branch River) is Bristol Bay's most popular river for float trips, both guided and unguided, and for good reason. It has massive runs of sockeye salmon, good fishing for king and coho salmon, and big rainbows. It also has char, grayling, chum salmon, and in a few back sloughs, northern pike. It is easily accessible from the town of King Salmon, which has jet service to Anchorage. It is a relatively large river, and the float, at least using the Nonvianuk Branch (discussed here) is essentially trouble free. Several lodges fish the salmon runs in the lower river and run upstream to look for trout.

The Alagnak is formed by the outlets of two large lakes, the Kukaklek to the north and the Nonvianuk to the south. It flows out of the west side of the Alaska Range to empty into the Kvichak River and Bristol Bay. The lakes lie between the fabled Iliamna and the Naknek drainages, and in terms of productivity, the Alagnak can easily hold its own with its much larger neighbors. The upper river is located in Katmai National Preserve, and most of it has been designated as a Wild and Scenic River. Like all of the rivers in this area, it supports a large bear population.

Although the Kukaklek is considered the main branch of the river, for our purposes, we will treat the Alagnak as originating in Nonvianuk Lake, where most fishermen start their float. The Kukaklek is not only a more expensive flight, but the upper river has some rapids that can be difficult even for experienced oarsmen, at least during high water. The Nonvianuk, on the other hand, is a trouble-free float, with an easy put-in at the outlet of the lake.

The Alagnak is a full-sized river as it flows from Nonvianuk. Floatplanes line up along its banks and guides move their clients into the best positions. This is one of the best fishing sections on the river, with big rainbows, arctic char, and lake trout working the edge of the moving water. There are some big fish in here. More than one angler has released a foot-long char only to have a huge lake trout grab it as it swam away. The lake's heavy-bodied rainbows patrol the shoreline in the almost imperceptible current, looking for smolt moving out of the lake. There is good fishing as far down as you can comfortably walk, so don't feel like you need to join the crowd at the outlet. There is camping available on both sides of the river.

This is prime water for streamers. Big black bunny flies, sculpins, Woolly Buggers, and Egg-Sucking Leeches are all deadly. Work them slowly on the swing, crawling them across the bottom. Zonkers, White Crystal Buggers, and other smolt imitations will bring smashing strikes, particularly in June, when tens of thousands of migrating baby salmon have passed this way. Use a wet-fly swing, and let the fly drift downstream in short spurts, just slower than the current. When the fly swings below you, let it

The confluence of the Nonvianuk and Kukaklek branches of the Alagnak provides great fishing.

hang in the current to see if anything has been following it.

In July, thousands of sockeye salmon power into the lake. Occasionally one will deliberately take a fly, but most simply move out of its path as it swings past. That is not to say the fishing is poor. With this many fish, there is still plenty of action. Use a sink-tip line with a weighted fly and you will wear your arm out. Smaller flies like a Boss or Comet work best. Sight fishing is always preferable to blind casting. Just remember, these fish will not move to take a fly. You need to drift the fly right into their mouth to have any hope of a take.

Frankly, most of the fish are caught by accident. They are hooked when the leader drags through one of the open mouths, pulling the fly into the outside of the jaw. Either way, once you set the hook, you will have your hands full. Sockeyes are powerful fish, willing to go airborne to throw the fly. With the current and size of the Alagnak, you will need stout tackle to turn a salmon that decides to head downstream. An 8-weight with a sink-tip line is a good choice for these fish.

Understandably, rafters are often in a hurry to get going. But you should first stop to contact the National Park Service rangers stationed on the south side of the river. They can explain the regulations and provide advice on camping and dealing with bears.

At low water, there may be several sets of Class II rapids in the upper 5 miles of the river. There are also several islands below the outlet. They can provide good fishing, but you will also discover one of the downsides of the Alagnak. The very size of Nonvianuk Lake means that water fluctuations are kept to a minimum, eliminating the gravel bars that make beaching a raft so easy. The current is fairly fast and stopping to fish is often a process of setting up well ahead of time and having someone ready to grab at willows and alder to pull the raft ashore. Too often, you cannot see the best lies until you are right on top of them and it is too late to pull over. And the banks are brushy, with pockets of thick spruce, so it is difficult to move far on foot. Be sure to have a pair of strong painters (lines tied to the front and back) securely attached to the boat. Use both of them if the boat is afloat in the current—it is easy insurance.

The confluence of the Nonvianuk and Kukaklek branches is one of the best fishing areas on the river, with access to a lengthy stretch of good water. The seam

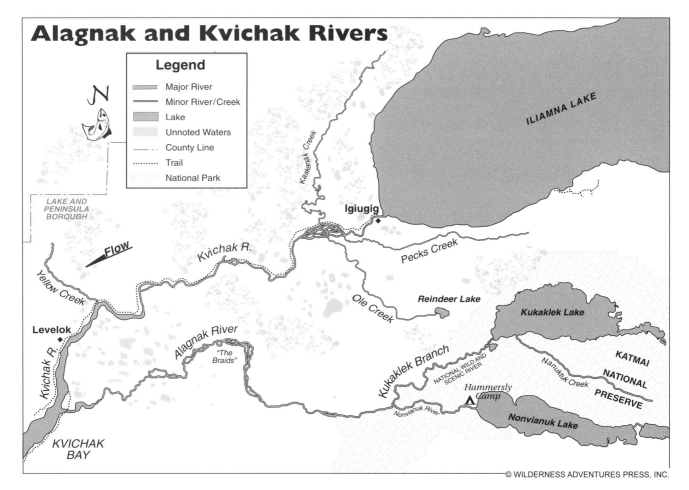

© WILDERNESS ADVENTURES PRESS, INC.

between the two branches is obvious, but don't limit your fishing to that area. Both branches hold big fish as far up as you can get. Be aware that the size of these streams has a tendency to funnel bears down to the confluence. Keep an eye out.

The river changes below the confluence, spreading out into a maze of intersecting channels called "the braids." The size of the individual channels becomes manageable and there are more places to pull over. At low water, much of the river can be waded, and it is possible to find a day's fishing without covering a lot of distance in the boat. At high water, which you can expect in early June (but may also get later in the summer), the river is less accessible. Try the smaller braids, where the wading may be easier. This is flat tundra and spruce forest, and campsites are at a premium, especially at high water when the low-lying flat ground may be waterlogged.

The braids provide the best trout fishing on the river. And early season is the time to fish smolt patterns. Huge schools of sockeye smolt are moving from the lake down to the ocean and the trout have been keying on them for several weeks. Look for trout along drop-offs, in the riffles, and behind any rocks or other structure; rootwads and brushy banks will hold fish. A size 4 Blue Smolt, White Zonker, or gray-over-white Double Bunny works well. Fish them high in the water column. The opposite tactics will also catch fish. Try Black Bunny Buggers, Egg-Sucking Leeches and Olive Sculpins fished slowly right on the bottom. Both techniques will fool some big trout.

Trout fishing slows down by late June, when the sockeye are moving through in force. The large schools of salmon push the rainbows out of their favored lies and into the back channels or faster water. Streamers are the most productive flies for trout at this time. I like sculpin patterns, Woolly Buggers, and bunny flies. At times dry flies will work well. A day of big 'bows on the surface will be remembered for a long time. Katmai Sliders and other attractors work particularly well on the Alagnak. And if the trout aren't looking up, the river has a large population of grayling eager to hit an Elk Hair Caddis or Adams.

Most of the early-July fishing is targeted on those migrating sockeyes. Your best bet is to find a shallow bar on an inside bend of the main stem of the river. The sockeyes will come up into water a couple of feet deep to cross the bar. Again, you need to have the fly right at the fish's depth in order to be successful, and small flies are usually more productive than large ones.

During August, when the sockeyes and kings are spawning, it is easy to find the trout. If the salmon are big and dark-brick red, you are looking at a pair of kings. Those big schools of scarlet fish are spawning sockeyes. The rainbows hold from 2 to 10 feet below both species of

salmon and will be tight to the bottom. Occasionally you will see one dash forward to steal an egg right from under the spawners, but usually they simply wait for the loose ones to wash down to them. Just drift an egg pattern behind each pair of salmon. Salmon eggs discolor quickly when they hit the water, going from translucent reddish-orange to solid creamy-white. Carry several different colors.

By early September, the sockeyes have started to die and wash downstream. The trout are now desperately trying to put on as much weight as possible before winter hits, and those salmon carcasses are a prime source of protein. Flesh flies can be deadly. They come in several variations, including white or pink and ginger Bunny Buggers. Don't rely just on sizes 2 and 4. Some of those fish seem to prefer a smaller bite, say size 8.

The braids continue for about 15 miles, and if you are targeting rainbows, you want to dawdle as long as possible. If you are after salmon, however, the best is yet to come. Once you have moved below the braids, the river becomes deeper and slower. The Alagnak is renowned for its runs of king, chum, and silver salmon, and this is the place to find them. I camped on an island in this stretch once and watched a parade of sockeyes, four abreast and swimming nose to tail, pass over a bar in front of camp. They swam by without pause or gaps 24 hours a day, and had been doing so for several weeks. We chased five grizzly bears off the island during the course of the night, until we finally just moved our tents away from the beach and decided to ignore them.

The river here ranges from 2 to 8 feet in depth, which means that some of it is wadeable and some must be fished from the boat. Carry an anchor if you plan to fish this stretch for salmon. You will be spending a fair amount of time casting over the same stretch of water. The lower reaches are tidal influenced and the salmon here are dime-bright and covered with sea lice.

The kings enter the river in early June and the first are beginning to show by the time the season opens. Fishing for kings remains strong until late July. Kings are best fished deep using brightly colored flies slowly stripped along the bottom.

The most overlooked fish in the Alagnak are chum salmon. They are a powerful, aggressive fish that under the right circumstances will eagerly take a fly. The Alagnak supports two runs of chums—the first in early July and the second a month later.

Although chums typically spawn close to the ocean (like pinks, chum fry go directly out to sea, without wintering over in fresh water), there are ocean-bright fish in the lower river. Look for their distinctive twisting leaps, with the fish falling back on their sides. Chums are most likely to take a fly when they are holding along the edges of sloughs and backwaters. Angling author Trey Combs, who at one time guided the Alagnak, swears that they will hit any fly as long as it is cerise (a moderate red)—and that includes waking dry flies.

For flyrodders, though, the real prize is silver salmon, and the Alagnak supports a healthy run. They enter the river in early August and continue into September. Unlike the kings and chums, which may jump a time or two but prefer to slug it out on the bottom, a fresh coho will put on an aerial display worthy of a rainbow. They are aggressive fish and will move to a stripped fly. The Alagnak is also one of the rivers in which it is possible to take silvers on the surface. Flies like Hotlips and Pink Pollywogs are stripped and waked across the surface. The churning and splashing is at times more than the fish are willing to tolerate.

Most float trips end about 10 miles upstream from the mouth. Below this stretch, the river flows slowly and much of the land is private property. The usual take-out is about an hour's float below Agnes Estrada's easily spotted cabin. A small, corrugated metal cabin on the south side of the river acts as a marker.

Whether you float it alone, take a guided raft trip, or stay in a lodge, the Alagnak is a fine way to learn about Alaska's rivers. The fishing is excellent, and depending on the season you will have shots at rainbow, grayling, char, and any of five species of salmon. You will almost certainly see a bear or two, and other wildlife is plentiful. If it is your first trip to Alaska, the Alagnak is a good place to start.

Kukaklek River

If you are looking for more adventure on your Alagnak float, and you would prefer to avoid the crowds, consider starting on the Kukaklek branch. It flows out of Kukaklek Lake and runs 17 miles to its confluence with the Nonvianuk. Calling it the Kukaklek River is a bit of a misnomer. It is actually the main branch of the Alagnak and is often so named on the maps.

The Kukaklek gets less boat traffic for a simple reason. About 5 miles downstream from the lake, the river valley narrows until it becomes a sheer-walled canyon impassable on foot. In the heart of the canyon is a set of rapids that cannot be lined or portaged. At high water, they will test the skills of the best oarsman. Even at low water, you should scout the river from the air before floating it, with your pilot flying low enough to get a feel for the size of rapids. The Kukaklek is not a river to be taken lightly.

The lake and upper river lie in rolling tundra. The land surrounding the outlet is private property, owned by the local native corporation. Its use is prehistoric, as evi-

denced by a number of housepits, or barabas, overlooking the lake. There is a small easement available to beach a plane and launch boats. The outlet of Kukaklek Lake is one of the state's prime spots for true trophy rainbows. A number of fly-out lodges bring guests here to try their luck on trout that may run over 30 inches.

The upper river is broad and featureless. This is prime spawning habitat for king salmon, with their attendant rainbows and char. Once the kings are paired up, they should not be disturbed. However, an egg pattern drifted just below them will often fool one of those big 'bows. Lake trout also drop well down into the river, feeding on salmon smolt and other baitfish. In late June and early July, massive schools of sockeyes stage here before moving into, and in some cases through, the lake to spawn. Grayling are numerous and there are plenty of char.

The first stretch of the river is fast, and at low water it's little more than a shallow rock garden. The river begins to pick up speed as its banks close in, and by about 7 miles in, the valley begins to narrow. It gradually becomes an incised canyon, with steep, spruce-covered walls. Approximately 13 miles from the mouth, the river makes a sharp right turn, and the first of the rapids is directly in front of you. And there may not be an opportunity to pull over and scout the upcoming excitement.

The rapids begin with a short ledge drop (waterfall). At low water, it is usually considered a Class III rapid and can be safely negotiated in most rafts. At high water, however, it has a keeper, or back-curling wave, that will easily flip a 13-foot raft. For most amateur rafters, this section should be considered impassable in June or at any other period of high water. The ledge drop cannot be lined, and although a long, steep, brush-choked portage is theoretically possible, it would difficult in the extreme.

The rapids in the canyon of the Kukaklek cannot be portaged and are dangerous at high water levels. Scout them from the air on the flight in.

Below the ledge drop is another 100 yards or so of Class II rapids. From this stretch to the confluence with the Nonvianuk, the canyon begins to widen out. The river remains rocky, with several sets of Class II rapids. This area can hold spawning kings and sockeye, and the fishing for trout and grayling can be very good.

The Kukaklek provides an exciting float with great fishing. It is best run in mid- to late summer, however, when the spring water levels have dropped. If you intend to fish it in June, make sure you have a large raft, well-secured gear, and a lot of experience in big whitewater.

Stream Facts: Alagnak River

Seasons

- June 8 to April 10; no retention of rainbow trout June 8 to August 31.

Special Regulations

- Only unbaited single hook artificial lures may be used year-round.

- No retention of rainbow trout from June 8 to Oct. 31. From Nov. 1 to April 9 daily limits for rainbow trout are 5 per day, 5 in possession, must be less than 18 inches.

- The daily limit for salmon, except king salmon, in the Alagnak River drainage is 5 per day, 5 in possession; only 3 per day, 3 in possession may be coho salmon.

- Open season for king salmon is May 1 to July 31. The limit for king salmon is 3 per day, 3 in possession, only one fish over 28 inches. The season limit on king salmon is 5. The limit on king salmon less than 20 inches (jacks) is 10 per day, 10 in possession. Any king salmon removed from the water must be retained and become part of the bag limit of the person originally hooking it. A person who intends to release a king salmon may not remove it from the water before releasing it.

- Beads: In all flowing waters of Bristol Bay, attractors (beads) fished ahead of flies or lures must be fixed within 2 inches of the fly or lure, or be free to move (slide) on the line or leader. This applies to both fly and spin-fishing. A bead not attached to the hook is defined as an attractor, not a fly. A bead fished on the line above a bare hook is not legal gear in waters where only flies may be used.

Species

- King (chinook) salmon average 25 to 35 lbs. Enter river in early June, season closes July 31.

- Chum salmon average 8 to 15 lbs. Best fishing is in lower river. First run begins in early July, with a second run in early August. The second run fish are larger.

- Pink salmon run strongest in even-numbered years. Average 4 to 6 lbs.; fish enter river in July.

- Sockeye (red) salmon average 5 to 7 lbs. Enter river in late June.

- Silver (coho) salmon average 9 to 12 lbs. Enter river in early August, with run peaking by late August.

- Rainbow trout average 18 to 22 inches; with some much larger fish available near the lakes. They are present year-round, but best fishing is early and late in the season.

- Arctic char/Dolly Varden average 16 to 22 inches; present year-round. Best fishing is behind spawning salmon.

- Arctic grayling average 14 to 18 inches. Present year-round.

River Characteristics

- The Nonvianuk (south branch of the Alagnak) flows from Nonvianuk Lake 11 miles to its confluence with the Kukaklek. It is not as fast as the Kukaklek, but still moves at about 3 or 4 miles per hour. It has a couple of minor rapids at low water, but no significant navigational problems.

- The Kukaklek (north branch of the Alagnak) is 17 miles long, flowing from Kukaklek Lake to its confluence with the Nonvianuk to form the main branch of the Alagnak. The river is fast with significant rapids located about 13 miles downstream from the lake outlet. Most of the river is in an enclosed valley/canyon, heavily forested with white spruce. The river runs clear with few gravel bars suitable for camping.

- Below the confluence of its two branches, the Alagnak becomes Class I flat water and goes through a long braided section. This is a large river and becomes even more spread out as it slows below the braids. There are few gravel bars suitable for camping and most camps must be pitched in the tundra. The last section is sluggish and tidal influenced.

- The total length of the river is about 66 miles from Nonvianuk Lake, or 72 miles from Kukaklek. Most rafters take out about 10 miles above the mouth.

Alagnak River Lodges and Guides

- Alagnak Lodge, www.alagnaklodge.com; lodge near tidewater; (winter) P.O. Box 144, Warrenton, VA 20188, 808-877-9903; summer: P.O. Box 351, King Salmon, AK, 907-246-1505

- Angler's Alibi, www.anglersalibi.com; weatherports near tidewater; (winter) 6105 Poplart Beach, Romulus NY, 607-869-9397; (summer) P.O. Box 271, King Salmon, AK, 907-246 1510

- Ouzel Expeditions, www.ouzel.com; float trips; P.O. Box 935, Girdwood, AK 99587, 1-800-825-8196

- Adventures on the Fly, float trips; P.O. Box 180446, Boston, MA 02118, 1-888-857-6700 ed_blank@msn.com

- Alaska River Adventures, www.alaskariveradv.com; float trips; 1-888-836-9027, 907-235-2647, P.O. Box 725, Cooper Landing, AK

- Alaska Rainbow Adventures, www.akrainbow.com; float trips; 1-877-235-2647; P.O. Box 456 Anchor Point, AK 99556

- Alaska Trophy Adventure, www.alaskatrophyadventure.com; lodge; 315-761-0941; P.O. Box 31, King Salmon, AK

- Katmai Lodge, www.katmai.com; lodge; 1-800-330-0326

- Northern Rim Adventures (Brian Richardson), raft trips on Mulchatna, Chilikodratna; www.northernrim.com; 1120 East Huffman Rd., Anchorage, AK 99515; 1-800-616-7238

Maps

- *Alaska Atlas and Gazetteer,* pages 58 and 59

Preparing for a day of flyfishing.

Naknek River

The term "big trout" is relative, varying dramatically from the fish of a small West Virginia creek to those of famous western rivers like the Green. But there is nothing relative about the size of the fish from the Naknek. A big trout here usually refers to a 30-inch fish. The Naknek and its sister river the Kvichak are probably an angler's best opportunity to take a 20-plus-inch rainbow on a fly. The Naknek also hosts a major sockeye run, good fishing for king salmon, and a short but intense silver fishery.

The Naknek begins in Naknek Lake, a turquoise-colored expanse that stretches well back into the Katmai Wilderness Area. The floating lumps of pumice that make up its beaches betray the volcanic nature of the surrounding mountains. A maze of rivers and smaller lakes drain into Naknek Lake and provide the spawning grounds for salmon and habitat for rainbows. Anglers trolling through the intricacies of the Bay of Islands regularly take cover-photo rainbows, and although there is little flyfishing available in the lake, many of those fish move into the rivers that flow into the lake. The largest of them, though, drop down into the Naknek River to feed and spawn.

The Naknek is a big, blue-tinted river that flows some 25 miles past the town of King Salmon to Bristol Bay. King Salmon survives on fishing. Much of the commercial fleet winters in its boatyards—chunky 32-foot gillnetters lined up gunwale to gunwale. The river also acts as the landing strip for floatplanes carrying Orvis-clad anglers to distant lodges, dodging other fishermen motoring upstream in their ubiquitous red Lund skiffs. The Naknek is as close to an urban river as you will find in Bristol Bay, but I have still seen wolves walking its banks.

The Naknek is a popular and very productive river. Kings spawn throughout much of it, and sockeyes move up to the headwater streams and lakes. Its tributaries get good runs of silvers and chums. The rainbows grow fat on all of the smolt, eggs, and flesh. Although the lower tidal sections of the river are fished heavily for kings (primarily by backtrolling or drifting), most of the flyfishing action takes place in the upper 8 miles of the river, from the lake outlet to Rapids Camp.

A gravel road leads from King Salmon to the outlet of the lake, and the scattering of cabins and boat launches is referred to as Lake Camp. There is good fishing for about a mile above Lake Camp, up to what is known as Trefon's cabin. The lake is shallow and the fish are lying in the slightly deeper slots. The current is almost nonexistent here, but everything moving between the lake and the river has to go through this section.

The opening of the season in early June finds hundreds of thousands of 3-inch salmon smolt heading out to sea. They run a gauntlet of terns, gulls, and some incredi-

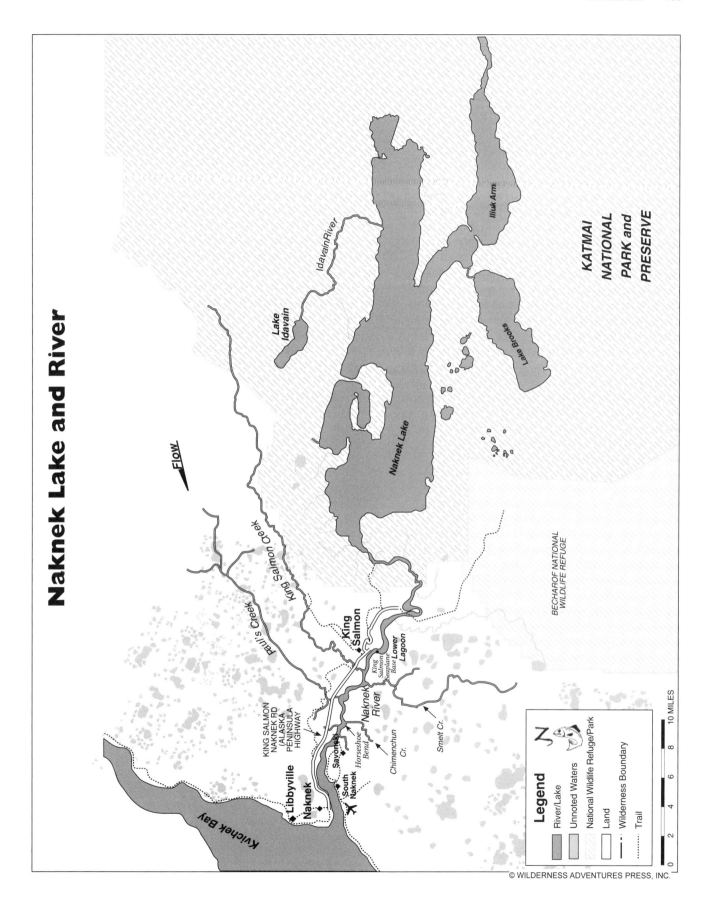

Naknek Lake and River

FLOW

KATMAI
NATIONAL
PARK and
PRESERVE

Illuk Arm

Lake
Idavain

Idavain River

Lake Brooks

Naknek Lake

BECHAROF NATIONAL
WILDLIFE REFUGE

King Salmon Creek

Paul's Creek

King Salmon

King Salmon
Seaplane
Base

Lower
Lagoon

Smelt Cr.

KING SALMON
NAKNEK RD
(ALASKA
PENINSULA
HIGHWAY)

Naknek
River

Chimenchun
Cr.

Horseshoe
Bend

Savonski

South
Naknek

Libbyville

Naknek

Kvichek Bay

Legend

�--	River/Lake
	Unnoted Waters
	National Wildlife Refuge/Park
	Land
---	Wilderness Boundary
⋯⋯	Trail

N

0   2   4   6   8   10 MILES

© WILDERNESS ADVENTURES PRESS, INC.

bly large rainbows. When a school moves through, the diving birds and slashing trout make it look more like you're fishing tuna or bluefish. The holding slots may not be easy to find, but in the early season, locating the trout is not a problem.

There is excellent spring fishing all the way down to Rapids Camp, some 7 miles below Lake Camp, but the fish are not as easy to find in the broad deep water of the main river. Look for deeper runs, boulders, and other traditional holding water. Like all large rivers, the Naknek is somewhat featureless and difficult to read. It is best fished with a guide, at least for the first couple of days.

Rapids Camp marks the point at which the river begins to broaden out after coursing between a set of low 50-foot ridges. There is little in the way of trout fishing below this point, but some of the best early-season fishing is found here. Rapids Camp can be accessed directly by a dirt road that leads down to the river.

Smolt migrate in the top of the water column, and the trout are looking up. Nanci Morris, one of the Katmai area's most respected guides, suggests trying topwater bugs and small poppers for them. Dahlberg Divers, deer-hair sliders, and even small bass bugs can be effective. A lot of smolt are wounded by birds and other fish and make easy pickings for the rainbows, so the closer you can make your fly resemble an injured minnow, the more successful you will be. More traditional patterns include subsurface flies like Zonkers, Clousers, and Woolly Buggers. Nanci says that color can be important, and she likes to carry a selection of white, blue, black, and olive. As the season progresses, the topwater action slows and you will do better working the bottom of the river. To be prepared, you should carry both floating and sink-tip lines.

The sockeye begin to arrive about June 20. The run peaks about the Fourth of July, and the Naknek is host to a steady stream of migrating fish. The best area to target sockeye is from Rapids Camp up through the canyon to a landmark known as Preacher's Rock, about 4 miles upstream. There are plenty of fish above that, but because of the water conditions, it's difficult to avoid snagging them. Sockeye tend to run upstream along the banks (unlike kings) and the best way to find them is visually. Look for rolling fish or spot them holding in the edges. Small, sparsely tied flies with a bit of flash are the most effective, but it is essential to get the fly to the right depth. Sockeyes will not move to take a fly.

The Naknek is a premier king salmon river, but most of the fishing is done by backtrolling in the lower river. There is some flyfishing available for a few miles above Rapids Camp, where the river is no longer tidally influenced. The kings begin to arrive in late May, but there are rarely catchable numbers of fish available until the third week of June. Nanci Morris likes to use large shrimp patterns in peachy-orange and hot pink for kings. She also does well with her version of a bushy purple Woolly Bugger, size large. Because the Naknek is somewhat glacial, you want a fly with color. And it needs to be weighted and fished with a sink-tip.

The kings tend to spawn a bit later in the Naknek, but the trout fishing behind them can be very good. It starts to pick up about mid-August at Rapids Camp and quickly moves upstream. Like all fall rainbow fisheries, egg patterns are the ticket. King eggs are slightly larger and more orange than sockeye eggs, and both tend to become opaque after they have been in the water for a while. By early September, the trout will start hitting flesh flies. Sockeyes, like the kings, tend to spawn late in the Naknek drainages, so egg patterns remain the fly of choice for a longer period than in many rivers.

Unlike the kings, the sockeyes spawn all the way up to Lake Camp, making the entire upper river productive. The fall fishing for rainbows is the best of the year, and gets better as the season progresses. The best shot at those 30-inchers comes after the end of September, and for those willing to brave the October weather, there are big fish available.

The Naknek also has a number of char. Most are sea-run Dolly Varden that move into the river in June, but there are also resident fish in the river year-round. Egg and smolt patterns are productive, and the most consistent spot to target them is the flats just above Rapids Camp.

The Naknek also gets a run of silvers, and the fishing can be hot. However, it is a short season for flyrodders. The fish are available throughout the river, and in the fishable water above Rapids Camp by the third week of August, but the fishing drops off after about September 10. Try traditional Popsicles and Flash Flies in purple, pink, orange, and red. Chartreuse can be good, and Nanci Morris says that she occasionally does well on a black and white combination. The contrast seems to draw their attention.

For some people, the convenience of the Naknek is offset by its size and popularity. Big Creek, a tributary flowing into the south side of the Naknek just below Rapids Camp is a good alternative. It is closed to the taking of king salmon, but it also has good runs of chums and silvers. The trout are not as large here as in the main river, but there is some nice flyfishing water. A combo trip for rainbows and silvers in late August is a good way to explore Big Creek. There is some fishing in the other tributary creeks, but check the regulations. The mouths of most streams are closed to all fishing and the upper stretches are seriously restricted in order to protect spawning kings.

Unlike most of the rivers discussed in this chapter, the Naknek is easily accessible. There is a range of accommodations and restaurants available in King Salmon, and boats can be rented from several dealers. There are independent guides who don't require a full week's booking (and they are recommended for anglers who want to unravel the mysteries of this sometimes difficult river).

The Naknek's abundant sockeyes, great king salmon fishing, and huge rainbows make for a combination that is difficult to beat. If you like big water and big fish, this is a good destination.

Nanci Morris with a happy client and big Naknek rainbow. Late season may be cold, but the fishing is hot.

Stream Facts: Naknek River

Seasons

- From an ADF&G marker located ½ mile above Rapids Camp upstream to ADF&G markers at Trefon's cabin at the outlet of Naknek Lake sport-fish season is June 8 to April 10; unbaited single-hook artificial lures only.

Special Regulations

- From June 8 to Oct. 31, daily limit for rainbow trout is 1 per day, 1 in possession, must be less than 18 inches. From Nov. 1 to April 9, daily limits for rainbow trout are 5 per day, 5 in possession, must be less than 18 inches.

- Big Creek: Upstream of an ADF&G marker located approximately ½ mile upstream from the confluence with the Naknek River, all king salmon angling is catch-and-release only.

- Beads: In all flowing waters of Bristol Bay, attractors (beads) fished ahead of flies or lures must be fixed within 2 inches of the fly or lure, or be free to move (slide) on the line or leader. This applies to both fly and spin-fishing. A bead not attached to the hook is defined as an attractor, not a fly. A bead fished on the line above a bare hook is not legal gear in waters where only flies may be used.

Species

- Rainbow trout average 18 to 30 inches, with an occasional fish to 32 inches.

- Arctic char (Dolly Varden) average 16 to 20 inches; present all season.

- Arctic grayling average 14 to 18 inches. Present all season.

- King salmon begin entering river in late May, but are in fishable numbers by the third week in June.

- Sockeye (red) salmon average 5 to 7 lbs. Begin entering river about June 13. Run peaks around July 4.

- Silver (coho) salmon average 7 to 9 lbs. Begin entering river about August 15.

River Characteristics

- A big, deep river that holds some huge rainbows, good silvers, and lots of king salmon. Easily accessible, with local facilities for food and lodging.

Guides and Lodges

- (See the hub city King Salmon for a listing of guides and lodges.)

Maps

- *Alaska Atlas and Gazetteer*, page 50

Brooks River

In many ways, Brooks is the Alaska experience condensed—lots of bears, big trout, and huge schools of salmon, all in a setting of spectacular beauty. Relatively easy access, photogenic bears, and a fish-rich, wadeable river have made it Bristol Bay's most popular fishery. Its beauty comes at a cost, however. Brooks also has crowds of tourists, harried park rangers, and too many fishermen, all crammed onto a river that barely exceeds a mile in length.

The river flows out of Brooks Lake through a thick spruce and cottonwood forest to Brooks Falls, a 20-foot waterfall that provides one of the best bear viewing opportunities in the world. Below the falls, the character of the river changes. It loses its turbulence, and offers long shallow runs through grassy meadows. At the lower end, it empties into the aquamarine waters of Naknek Lake, a vast nursery for the millions of salmon smolt that hatch every year. The river itself is crystal-clear, however, and offers a number of opportunities to sight fish for salmon and trout.

Archeological evidence indicates that humans have been fishing here for thousands of years. Brooks appeared on the modern fishing radar screen back in the fifties, when a few early fishermen brought back photos of the 30-inch trout they caught with regularity. Ray Petersen built a lodge at the mouth of the river in 1960, and in 1971, Brooks Camp, as it was known, was incorporated into the newly formed Katmai National Park. The lodge, and its surrounding grounds, provides a focal point for the numerous day visitors that come to fish or to see and photograph the bears.

As good as the fishing is, Brooks real claim to fame is its bears. Coastal grizzlies (brown bears) weighing up to a thousand pounds congregate on the stream to feed on its accessible salmon. During July and again in late August and September, an average of 30 bears fish the river on a daily basis. The number goes up as winter approaches. Most visitors use the bear-proof viewing platforms to safely watch the boars, sows, and cubs feed and interact. Fishermen, however, are down on the river among those same bears. Fortunately, Brooks grizzlies are well habituated to people—not tame, but habituated. They still rule the river and they understand that it is your responsibility to get out of their way. There have been occasional frightening confrontations, but thus far, no injuries.

Brooks provides a wide spectrum of fish. It is best known for its healthy rainbow population, but it also has char and some very large grayling. Huge schools of sockeye salmon migrate up the river, most of them spawning in Brooks Lake and its tributaries. But enough stay in the river to provide a superb fall rainbow fishery. Brooks is one of the few rivers where the normally closed-mouth sockeyes can be caught on a fly, making for an exciting July experience (exciting because the number of four-legged fishermen often exceeds the two-legged variety). In late August, schools of silver salmon move into the river.

The region's fly-out lodges bring groups in on a daily basis. They usually start at Brooks Lake and fish downstream to the mouth. It's a good way to experience the entire river. The water drops over a small ledge at the outlet of Brooks Lake, creating a chute that is black with salmon by August. The first hundred yards or so can be difficult to wade at high water, but there are often some nice trout lying under the trees on the far side. The first prime water comes at the bend. A large number of trout hold over the flat rock bottom, and if the salmon haven't filled the river with eggs, flyfishing with nymphs and dry flies can be productive.

The character of the river changes at the bend. A long stretch of pocket water provides some of the best nymphing on the river. The fish average a bit smaller here, but there are still plenty of 'bows over 20 inches. Unless the trout are locked into egg patterns, beadheads usually prove the most effective. Use a strike indictor, but keep it closer to the fly than you normally would. These fish are experts at spitting out an imitation before there is any clue that they have eaten the fly.

Below the pocket water, the river becomes a long smooth run. This is prime spawning habitat for the sockeyes and provides some of the best fishing on the river in August and September. This is a good place to drop an egg pattern behind a couple of scarlet sockeyes and hold on. There are often some real hawgs that hang out in here, usually tucked up under some impossible-to-cast-to logjam.

This stretch of the river ends in a deep, fast run bordering a slow back eddy—an area known as Gomer's Hole. Sockeyes hold on the edge of the eddy, hanging in the still pool. It is also prime rainbow water, and fishermen tend to stack up in it the way the trout do. It is considered the worst of form to park yourself on the hole, regardless of how tempting it may be. Work your way through it and give the group behind you a shot at it. The biggest fish from Gomer's seem to come on large sculpin or bunny patterns fished deep, but fry, egg, and nymph patterns can all be effective.

There is one last stretch of water to be fished before you hit the closed area surrounding the falls. A small island sits in the middle of the next bend, and, at times, there are some nice fish on either side of it. Just below the island is the beginning of the closed area, marked by a sign. From here you have to walk around the falls to the

Brooks River

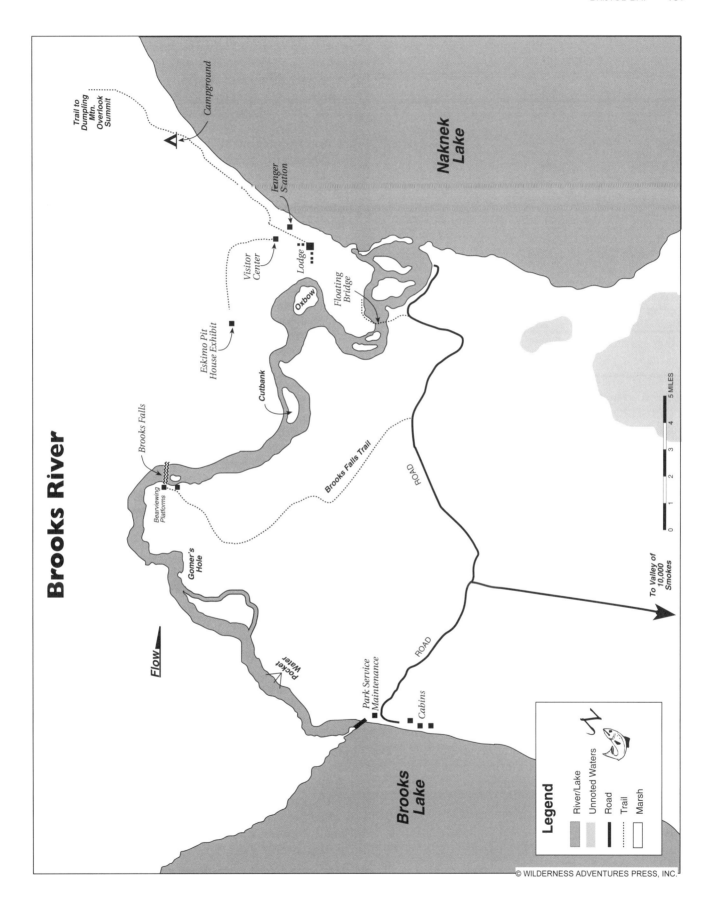

Naknek Lake

Trail to Dumpling Mtn. Overlook Summit

Campground

Ranger Station

Visitor Center

Lodge

Floating Bridge

Eskimo Pit House Exhibit

Oxbow

Cutbank

Brooks Falls

Brooks Falls Trail

ROAD

Bearviewing Platforms

Gomer's Hole

Flow

Pocket Water

To Valley of 10,000 Smokes

ROAD

Park Service Maintenance

Cabins

Brooks Lake

5 MILES

0 1 2 3 4

Legend

River/Lake

Unnoted Waters

Road

Trail

Marsh

© WILDERNESS ADVENTURES PRESS, INC.

By August, when the fishing is at its best, it is not unusual to have 20 bear encounters a day.

point where the fishing reopens. The walk can be an amusing proposition if the grass is high and there are a lot of bears around. Talk loudly and stay in a group.

The fishing begins again in a stretch of difficult-to-wade rapids. The lower end of this fast water can provide good dry-fly fishing. Throw a Royal Wulff or Parachute Adams up into the pockets for trout and grayling.

The character of the next stretch of river has changed over the last 15 years, and it no longer is as consistent as it once was. Most fishermen now move quickly through it to the cutbank, a spectacular long run in which the fish are easily spotted and very difficult to catch. This is one of the better places to fish for sockeyes during June and early July. The fish are moving, which is an important criterion for sockeye fishing (unlike some other species, which are more likely to hit when they are resting).

There are often some arrestingly large trout lying in plain sight under the cutbank, but every fisherman on the river has seen them and cast to them. They quickly become as educated as any Henry's Fork rainbow. A small nymph, drifted carefully right onto their nose will occasionally fool them.

The corner at the bottom of the cutbank can be almost as frustrating. You can see some large and difficult fish holding in a line, and there is always a big fish or two against the far bank. The fish you see on the inside of the bend are mostly grayling, and they are susceptible to a dry fly or a well-drifted nymph. The classic run below the bend is worth fishing. It is not a place where you can see fish, but you can catch them.

The next sweeping curve holds a lot of trout, primarily in the deep water along the far bank. Sculpins fished on the swing can be effective here. There is usually a school of large grayling holding at the mouth of the tiny channel that enters on the left. During early summer, the salmon move along the edge of the deep water and cut the edge of the corners. Drift a small and subtle fly through the school. There can be good sockeye fishing all the way to the oxbow, but most people are in too big a hurry to get to the prime corner on the river.

The oxbow is probably the quintessential hole on Brooks. The river sweeps past the large slough left when the river changed course many decades ago. The backwater is prime rearing habitat for salmon fry, and the seam that forms along its edge always holds trout. The best trout I've taken from Brooks came from the middle of the run, hitting a small dead-drifted streamer. Small dry flies fished along the edge of the dead water can hook some surprisingly large trout. This is one of the best salmon holding areas, and when the sockeyes have moved in, the hole gets fished heavily.

The oxbow is within sight of the floating bridge and the wonderful stretches of water above and below it. Rainbows, sockeyes, and silvers all stack up in the gin-clear water, eliciting gasps of surprise and anticipation from every fisherman who gazes downward as he crosses the bridge. The salmon school up below the bridge, waiting for the cover of darkness before they'll venture under it. At times the broad flat ripples with the wakes of hundreds of nervous salmon, trapped for the first time in skinny water.

The last stretch of river includes the run alongside the path from the lodge and the outlet to the lake. You will occasionally find fish sipping dries in this stretch, and they can be as selective as any spring creek trout. The actual mouth of the river changes year to year, but it can be worth exploring. The fishing can also be good in the lake itself, just outside the mouth.

There is often a short window of trout fishing at the beginning of the season. The quality of the fishing varies from year to year depending on weather conditions, and the fish tend to be concentrated near the two lakes. Small fry patterns like Thunder Creeks are the best flies to use.

The trout fishing drops off dramatically once the sockeyes hit the river in mid-June, but the salmon fishing comes into its own. Sockeyes are among the most acrobatic and hard fighting of all salmonids, and the large numbers that pour into the river make this an experience not to be missed. To top it off, Brooks River sockeyes, unlike those in most streams, will actually hit a fly.

A 7- or 8-weight rod is about right for these fish. Contrary to most fishing, where a strong tippet is preferred to avoid exhausting the fish, you should not use anything heavier than about 8-pound test here. You need to be able to deliberately break off a fish any time a bear appears. Many fishermen make the mistake of using large, bright streamers. Smaller, sparser flies such as Montana Brassies and Comets are generally more productive.

The most fundamental aspect of successful sockeye fishing is to keep the fly at the right depth. They will not move up or down for a fly and you must drift it right past their nose. Use a floating line with split shot on the leader or a sink-tip with a short leader (3 or 4 feet). Make your cast quartering upstream, so the fly has a chance to sink to the fish's depth as it comes even with you. Keep your line taut and your casts short. Sockeye strikes are extremely subtle. Any hesitation in the line warrants a hookset.

Sockeyes are also among the tastiest of fish. Brooks, however, is not the place to go for dinner. The regulations are designed not to protect the salmon run, but to avoid conflicts between bears and fishermen. All fish caught above the bridge must be released. Only one fish may be kept below the bridge, and it must be removed from the water, placed in a plastic bag (available at the lodge), and taken to the lodge freezer immediately. Hooked fish must be broken off if a bear approaches.

By early August, the trout have reestablished themselves, and the fishing picks up. Dry-fly fishing is at its peak, nymphs are effective, and the trout will hit streamers if you can fish them without snagging the omnipresent sockeyes. Try nymphs in the upper river. Beadhead Prince Nymphs and Hare's Ears (size 14) take a lot of fish. If the weather is hot and sunny, dry flies can be productive. Adams, Elk Hair Caddis, Royal Wulffs and a couple of large attractors, such as a Katmai Slider, will cover most situations. I have had only limited luck with mouse patterns on Brooks and prefer more traditional dead-drifted attractors.

The peak of the trout fishing for Brooks, like most rivers, comes in late August. The trout are fattening up for winter and feasting on an orgy of salmon eggs. Brooks River sockeyes spawn in early September, but the trout begin to key on egg patterns well before the redd building begins. The flies should be dead drifted just above the bottom. Use a strike indicator.

The guides like to have their clients use beads, and there is no denying their effectiveness. However, a bead not attached to the hook is defined as an attractor, not a fly, and this type of rig is both controversial and tightly regulated. Beads must either be free-sliding or affixed to the leader not more than 2 inches above a fly. A bare hook may not be used. The river is frequently patrolled, and the regulations are strictly enforced. The growth in the use of pegged beads at Brooks has been marked by the number of rainbows that are missing their upper lips.

It is perfectly possible to catch as many fish as a person would reasonably want by using just an egg pattern without a bead. You do have to be able to detect subtle strikes, though. Even if you find it necessary to start with a bead in order to get the feel of a proper drift, once you have caught some fish, switch to a fly or move the bead down adjacent to the hook.

For those who venture to Brooks in September—it closes in early September—try flesh flies and streamers. Some very large trout have moved up out of the lake by this time. However, there is increased bear activity, and not all of these newly arrived bears are used to sharing their fishing holes with flyrodders.

As good as the fishing is, the bears add a special *frisson* to the mix. The rangers will explain the rules for dealing with them at your mandatory orientation. However, there are a few points that fishermen need to keep in mind.

If a bear comes down the river (and in August this will happen 20 times a day), it is your responsibility to get out of the way. Those are the requirements of the park, but remember also that the bear is trying to earn a living, while you are just there to have fun. On the meadow stretches of the lower river, it is often possible to simply back off the river and still keep the bear in sight. On the

Bears aren't the only draw at Brooks, one of the most popular rivers in Bristol Bay.

upper river, however, you will need to wade the stream—not always an easy proposition at high water. If there is any question, carry a wading staff. You might not always have a choice as to where you need to cross the river.

Bears that have learned to steal fish from fishermen cause some of the most difficult problems. Several years ago, we were plagued by a young bear that would slip unseen through the woods alongside fishermen and come charging out full-tilt whenever he heard the scream of a reel. We all referred to him as Psycho-bear. Don't teach a bear this trick. If a bear approaches and shows any interest in your fish, break it off immediately—even if it's the fish of a lifetime. Again, this means using relatively light tippet, even for salmon. Quit fishing whenever a bear is so close that you cannot hook and land a fish before you have to move off the river. It will save you flies—and that sinking feeling that comes from deliberately popping off a really big fish.

These are habituated bears that are used to having people around. The non-threatening attitude of most of them can easily create a sense of overconfidence about all of them. That is a mistake. The most dangerous bear that I have had to deal with anywhere in Alaska was a young Brooks River boar that aggressively approached to within a fly rod's length.

Brooks may not provide the wilderness experience that you can find on some of the area's more remote rivers, but it is a very special place nonetheless. It's easy to access, forgiving of mistakes, and provides fishing that would be the pride of any other state. It should be on every flyfisher's list of must-see rivers.

Idavain Creek

Idavain Creek is a small stream flowing into the north arm of Naknek Lake. About 12 miles long, it originates in Idavain Lake. It is a pretty little clear-water stream with very good fishing for rainbows, grayling, and sockeye salmon. Nanci Morris, who has guided this area for years, describes Idavain as a "really fun taste of Alaska. It is a small stream with easily visible fish that don't get over-fished."

Although many of the fly-out lodges take their guests here, it sees only limited use by unguided fishermen. Access to Idavain is by floatplane or by boat from King Salmon. A few people combine a trip to Idavain with a stay at Brooks Camp, although it is a long boat ride.

The approach to Idavain requires a certain amount of boating caution. There are a number of large boulders that lie just submerged outside the mouth. Coming in too fast can cost you a prop or worse. The first quarter-mile of the stream runs through a sandy beach. The water here is fast with a slippery rock bottom. Wading can be tricky. Behind the beach, the stream flows through a flat and boggy area with little current. About a mile upstream, Idavain bends west and becomes a clear creek with good current. This is an ideal river for sight fishing, with the trout and salmon clearly visible. From here up to the lake, the river meanders with lots of tight turns. The banks are brushy and roll casting is often required.

In the spring (early June), there is good trout fishing in both the upper and lower sections of the river. The trout are focusing on fry moving downstream. Thunder Creeks and other fry patterns are productive. There can also be good dry-fly fishing on warm days. Nanci says that early in the season, the stream can be fished by hiking down from Idavain Lake to Naknek Lake. But this is a long hike and only for the physically fit.

In the fall, the river must be fished up from Naknek Lake. You can fish as high as you can find trout, which may be for several miles. Look for sockeyes in the gravel riffles, and drift a Glo-Bug or Iliamna Pinkie below them for the trout. By mid-September, earlier than in other nearby streams, the salmon have died and been washed out into the lake.

Be forewarned—you will not be the only fisherman on the river, particularly from July through September. Idavain has a large population of bears, and for some reason, it is prime habitat for sows with cubs. Brushy streams and grizzly cubs are a bad combination. There are also a lot of juvenile bears around. They are still learning their place in the world and can be ill-mannered. These are not Brooks Camp bears—habituated to people and used to sharing their river. They can be territorial, and the sows may see people as a threat to their cubs. Because of the number of bears, camping is not recommended near Idavain.

Margot Creek

In many ways, Margot Creek is similar to Idavain. Both are small clear tributaries of Naknek Lake. Margot is actually a bit larger than Idavin and flows into Iliuk Arm about 8 miles southeast of Brooks River. It meanders its way well back into the low-lying hills south of Naknek Lake.

The mouth if Margot is all sand, but from there up it is lined with alder and spruce. Like Idavin, it is tight and brushy without a lot of room for a backcast. A good roll cast is helpful here. The stream has a number of spots that are too deep to wade, and bushwhacking may be required.

For reasons known only to the fish gods and biologists, Margot is a char fishery, with very few rainbows moving up with the salmon. In June, try fishing fry patterns at the

Brooks River Area: Idavain and Margot Creeks

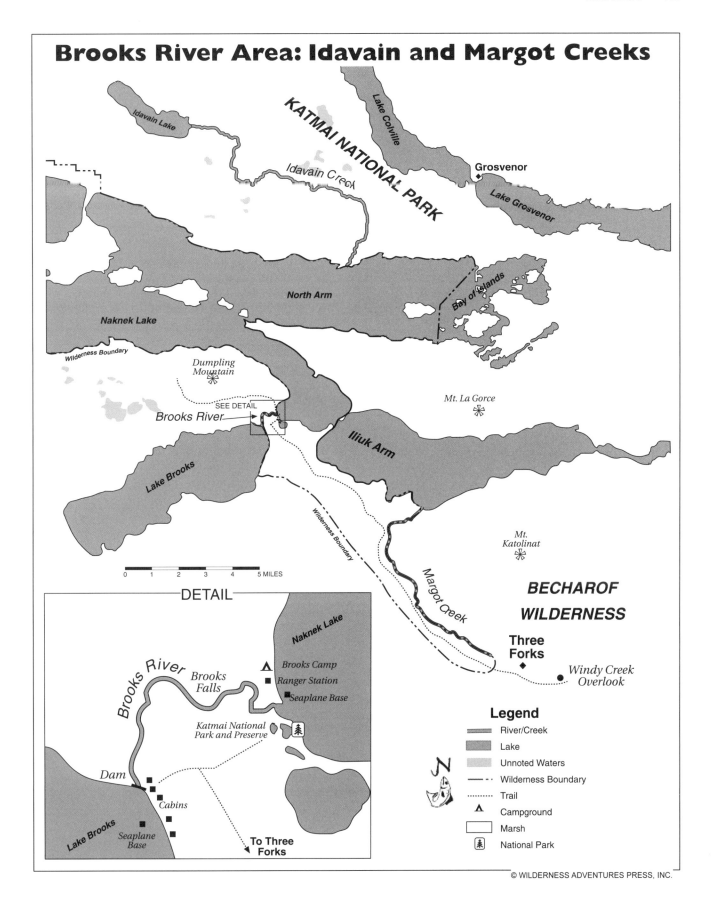

KATMAI NATIONAL PARK

Idavain Lake

Lake Colville

Idavain Creek

Grosvenor

Lake Grosvenor

North Arm

Bay of Islands

Naknek Lake

Wilderness Boundary

Dumpling Mountain

SEE DETAIL

Brooks River

Mt. La Gorce

Iliuk Arm

Lake Brooks

Wilderness Boundary

Mt. Katolinat

Margot Creek

BECHAROF

WILDERNESS

0 1 2 3 4 5 MILES

Three Forks

Windy Creek Overlook

DETAIL

Naknek Lake

Brooks River

Brooks Falls

⚑ Brooks Camp
■ Ranger Station
■ Seaplane Base

Katmai National Park and Preserve

Dam

■ Cabins ■
■
■

Lake Brooks

Seaplane Base

To Three Forks ◀

Legend

▬▬▬	River/Creek
▬	Lake
▬	Unnoted Waters
–·–	Wilderness Boundary
····	Trail
▲	Campground
▭	Marsh
🌲	National Park

N

mouth, right along the edge of the gray glacial water. Char are famous for ambushing young smolt and fry. By August, the sockeyes have moved into the stream and the char will have established themselves well up the river.

Not surprisingly, Margot has a large population of bears. Given the proximity to Brooks, many of them are more habituated to people than the Idavain bears. Nevertheless, they can be territorial, and may woof a bit at intruders. You are also more likely to run into the big boars at Margot. Friends who have visited Margot have said that there are so many bears that it is difficult to fish. They were constantly looking over their shoulders or being pushed from their holes. If you plan on camping, it is probably best to stay at Research Bay, a couple of miles to the west.

Iliuk Arm is a notorious wind tunnel, and it is not always possible to land a plane (or boat) here. Many experienced guides want the plane with them, so if the wind comes up they can get out before it becomes overwhelming. More than one person has had the wind prevent a pickup and spent a cold and frightening night on the beach with the bears at Margot.

Stream Facts: Brooks River

Seasons

- June 8 to April 10; no retention of rainbow trout June 8 to August 31. Area 60 yards above and below Brooks Falls (within markers) closed to all fishing.

Special Regulations

- No retention of rainbow trout from June 8 to Oct. 31. From Nov. 1 to April 9 daily limits for rainbow trout are 5 per day, 5 in possession, only 1 over 20 inches.

- In Brooks River, from the outlet of Brooks Lake downstream to the bridge at Brooks Camp, fish of all species must be released immediately year-round.

- In Brooks River, from the outlet of Brooks Lake to the bridge at Brooks Camp, only unbaited single-hook artificial flies may be used June 8 to Oct. 31. In Brooks Lake, Naknek Lake, and Brooks River below the bridge at Brooks Camp, only unbaited, single-hook artificial lures year-round.

- Beads: In all flowing waters of Bristol Bay, attractors (beads) fished ahead of flies or lures must be fixed within 2 inches of the fly or lure, or be free to move

(slide) on the line or leader. This applies to both fly and spin-fishing. A bead not attached to the hook is defined as an attractor, not a fly. A bead fished on the line above a bare hook is not legal gear in waters where only flies may be used.

Species

- Rainbow trout average 16 to 22 inches with an occasional fish to 30 inches.

- Arctic char (Dolly Varden) average 16 to 20 inches; present all season.

- Arctic grayling average 14 to 18 inches. Present all season.

- Sockeye (red) salmon average 5 to 7 lbs. Begin entering river about June 13, peak around July 4.

- Silver (coho) salmon average 7 to 9 lbs. Begin entering river about August 15.

River Characteristics

- Less than a mile long, Brooks River is easily wadeable except at high water levels. The section 60 yards above and below Brooks Falls is closed to fishing.

Guides, Lodges, and Outfitters

(Brooks is fished by most of the fly-out lodges in the King Salmon and Iliamna areas. The Park Service, Katmai Air, and Katmailand are the only resident outfitters at Brooks.)

- Katmai National Park and Preserve, Field Head - quarters, P.O. Box 7, #1 King Salmon Mall, King Salmon, AK 99613-0007 , 907-271-3751 (Headquarters), 907-246-3305 (Visitor Information), Fax: 907-246-4286

- Katmai Air and Katmailand, Inc., (Brooks Lodge) 4125 Aircraft Drive, Anchorage, AK 99502; 246-3079 (May 15 to Oct. 1); 1-800-544-0551 (year-round); www.bear-viewing.com

- Wet Waders, Mark Emery; P.O. Box 526, King Salmon, AK 99613 (May to Oct.); 246 NE 59th St., Ocala, FL 34479, 352-622-3412 (Oct. to May); email:memerym@aol.com

Maps

- *Alaska Atlas and Gazetteer,* page 50

Kulik River

Although far less famous than its neighbor, Brooks River, the Kulik River shares many of the same attributes. Like Brooks, it is a short stream connecting two large lakes. It has the same concentration of salmon, trout, and bears that have made Brooks a destination for fishermen, photographers and tourists, and it has a historic lodge operated by the same concessionaire that runs Brooks. In spite of that, it is relatively little known.

The Kulik is a 1½-mile-long stream that connects Nonvianuk Lake with its upstream counterpart, Kulik Lake. Nonvianuk Lake is one of the great trout factories of Bristol Bay. Every year huge numbers of sockeyes move up through Nonvianuk Lake into Kulik. Thousands of those salmon spawn in the Kulik, and the trout follow them in to feast on the eggs.

Kulik lies at the edge of the Walatka Mountains about 65 miles northeast of King Salmon, inside Katmai National Park. Angler's Paradise Lodge hosts a large number of guests here. Those Nonvianuk rainbows also bring Kulik a lot of pressure from other area lodges.

In June, spring snowmelt raises the level of the river enough to make wading difficult. For those with boats, including the guests at Angler's Paradise, fishing with both smolt and fry patterns can be very good. Hatching salmon eggs in the river produce thousands of inch-long fry that move down the river to grow in Nonvianuk Lake. At about the same time, the smolt, which spent their first winter growing larger in Kulik Lake, begin their migration to the sea. You can see slashing rises throughout the river as the rainbows gorge on their first good meal of the summer. Thunder Creeks and other small, light-colored streamers work well as fry imitations. White or ginger bunny flies are best for fish looking for a larger meal. Black leeches, in their various manifestations, are also productive.

As summer progresses, the sockeyes arrive in big numbers. Although many of them will spawn in the river, the best fishing is for salmon moving through into the upper lake and its tributaries. A 7- or 8-weight rod will be needed to handle these fish. The best flies tend to be small (size 6) and weighted with lead eyes or bead chain. Sockeye Johns, Brassies, and Comets work well. Use a light sink-tip or a mini-head with about a 5-foot level leader. Stick with 8- or 10-pound test tippet material. The salmon don't mind the heavier stuff, but you need to be able to intentionally break off a fish if a bear approaches.

And make no mistake—there are a lot of bears at Kulik. The backside of Kulik Lake is within a few miles of the McNeil River Game Sanctuary, the world's premier bear viewing location. The banks surrounding the river are covered with high grass, making it impossible to keep track of bears movement. Although most of these bears

High grass and a lot of bears means that camping on the Kulik is not feasible, regardless of the quality of the fishing.

are habituated to people, they must be treated with the respect that any 400-pound, top-of-the-food-chain predator deserves. The large number of bears makes it essentially impossible to camp here, particularly given that the camp would be deserted during the day while you are fishing.

The best trout fishing takes place in the fall, when the sockeyes have started to spawn. These fish, like their cousins in Brooks River, spawn late, sometimes continuing until early October. That doesn't mean that the trout fishing can't be good before the spawning begins. The rainbows can smell the ripening salmon and are eager to hit an egg pattern. In addition, the redd digging by the females stirs up the river bottom, flushing insect life out of the gravel. If you have spotted a big fish too smart to eat another fake egg, try a Pheasant Tail or a caddis nymph.

Once the spawning begins in earnest, the fish will generally become selective not just to eggs, but to size and color. Carry flies ranging from traditional salmon pink to pale cream. As the season progresses, there is a higher percentage of old eggs washing through the water column, and they tend to be pale and opaque.

Fall is the time to find big rainbows in the Kulik, with a few fish reaching the fabled 30-inch mark. Having said that, most of the Kulik's fish run a bit smaller than in other area streams—generally between 16 and 20 inches. There are a lot of them, however, and they stay in the river until things begin to freeze up in October. The water is lower than in the spring and becomes more easily wadeable. If the light cooperates, there can be some exciting sight fishing.

Although there are trout all through the river, the better fishing is generally found in the bottom half. The river makes a 90-degree bend about halfway down, with a large island just below the bend. This is a stretch of good water, with lots of fish. Some pockets, like Laker Hole, get taken early by the lodge boats, but there is plenty of water. Thick brush makes walking the banks very difficult in many places.

There are several islands in the river, and the tail end of each provides good holding water, particularly in the spring. The fall trout hold below the salmon, but if there are a lot of eggs in the water, they will drop back a bit into easier holding lies. Look for drop-offs, subtle ledges, or hollows in the gravel. There are a couple of back channels, one on each side of the river, that can be worth a try.

The fishing on Kulik can be world class, but it suffers from two almost contradictory problems—it is heavily fished and access is difficult. The fishing pressure comes from the adjoining lodge, which accommodates up to 40 guests (many lodges host as few as eight rods at a time). It is also within flying distance of a number of other facilities, which bring in fishermen on day trips. For most anglers, these are the only alternatives. Although the river is located in a national park, and camping is allowed, the tall grass and number of bears make overnight stays very risky. The risk is not personal danger (although that is a consideration), but the likelihood of a bear tearing up a camp while it is deserted during the day. One of the portable electric fence set-ups used by field biologists would be a minimal requirement for camping at Kulik.

KULIK RIVER LODGES

Kulik is fished by many of the fly-out lodges in the King Salmon and Iliamna areas.

Katmailand, Inc. (Kulik Lodge), 4125 Aircraft Drive, Anchorage, AK 99502; 1-800-544-0551; www.bear-viewing.com

The middle section of American Creek is almost continuous whitewater. Expect excellent fishing, great scenery, and lots of bears.

American Creek

In a state blessed with wild rivers, there are few wilder than American Creek. It rises in a spectacular setting, cuts through two deeply incised canyons, and hosts good populations of sockeye salmon, rainbow trout, and char. A large section of the river is continuous whitewater, and fallen logs and sweepers occasionally block the entire stream. Wildlife is abundant, and none more so than the bears. Raptors, including eagles, rough-legged hawks, and osprey, hunt this area. Jaegers soar overhead, like some arctic version of a frigate bird. Except for the extreme upper and lower end, it is a stream largely untouched by man.

American Creek begins at Hammersley Lake, 1,600 feet high in the Walatka Mountains. It tumbles down out of the hills as if heading toward Nonvianuk Lake before reversing course and turning south to Lake Coville, some 40 miles from its beginnings. Hammersley and Coville can both be reached by air from King Salmon, about 50 miles to the west.

Hammersley Lake is nestled in a small bowl of alpine tundra surrounded by gently rising mountains. Ridges are flecked with wildflowers. Wild iris, rhododendron, geraniums, monk's hood, cinquefoil, and mountain avens are all abundant in season. Low ridges, dry ground, and spectacular scenery beckon hikers and photographers.

The lake is almost shockingly transparent, with 75 to 100 feet of visibility. Hammersley is subject to frequent high Bristol Bay fog, though, and getting in and out can be frustrating.

There is some fishing in Hammersley itself, primarily for lake trout, but most people fish the upper stretch of American Creek. The first 4 miles of the river are shallow and rocky. There are game (bear) trails along the river that make access easy. And the low-lying tundra allows you to spot wildlife at a distance. Fishing has historically been good in this section, and it gets some traffic from the nearby lodges at Kulik and Nonvianuk. The fish, mostly rainbows and char, run from 16 to 20 inches—not large for this country. At this altitude, arctic ecosystems are fragile, and the fishing has declined over the past several years.

About 4 miles below the outlet, the river enters a narrow canyon characterized by steep bluffs. The speed of the river picks up substantially here, and there's a Class IV rapid in the middle of the canyon. The river drops about 12 feet over a 50-foot span, including one 4-foot plunge. A second ledge drop occurs about a quarter-mile downstream. The canyon lasts about 2 miles and beyond that is about 5 miles of very shallow continuous rapids and rock gardens. The fishing can be good in here, with healthy populations of rainbows and even a few lake trout. This

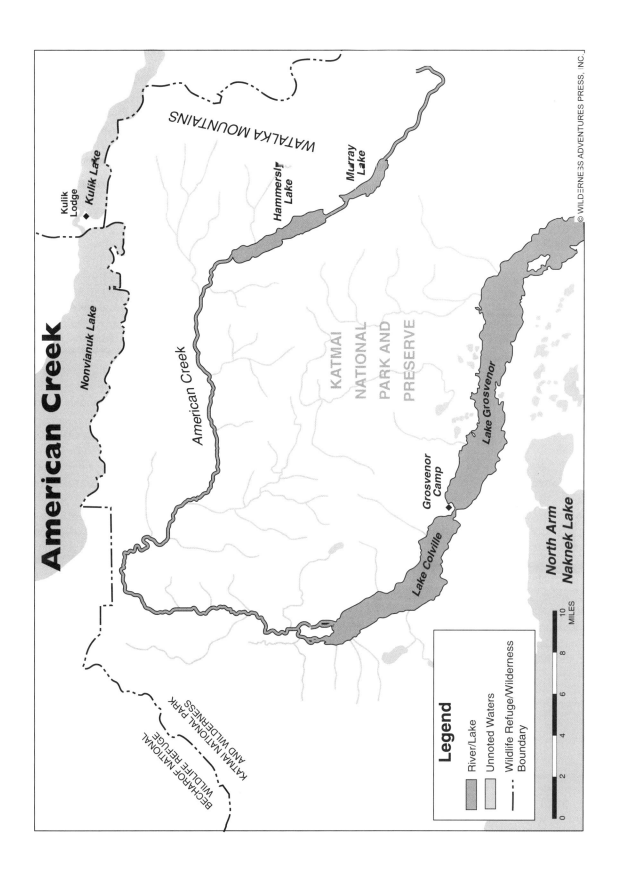

American Creek

WATALKA MOUNTAINS

Kulik Lake

Kulik Lodge

Nonvianuk Lake

American Creek

Hammersly Lake

Murray Lake

KATMAI NATIONAL PARK AND PRESERVE

Lake Grosvenor

Grosvenor Camp

Lake Colville

North Arm Naknek Lake

BECHAROF NATIONAL WILDLIFE REFUGE

KATMAI NATIONAL PARK AND WILDERNESS

Legend

River/Lake

Unnoted Waters

Wildlife Refuge/Wilderness Boundary

MILES

0 2 4 6 8 10

stretch has a lot of bears, though, and the speed of the river sometimes puts you on top of them with little warning to you or the bear. The river hits the beginning of the spruce forest in this stretch, and with it the most significant danger on the trip—sweepers.

About 9 miles from the lake the river narrows a bit, making it possible to float, albeit by continually scraping rocks. For about 10 miles the river is a series of rapids and chutes, with short, fast 50-foot runs between them. There are a few deep pools that hold rainbows. This is spruce and polar forest and the banks are brushy.

At this point the river enters the lower canyon, with lots of tight bends and steep gradient. The entire river is Class II whitewater, with five to eight Class III rapids (2- to 4-foot drops with rocks and 2- to 3-foot standing waves). The river here is 2 or 3 feet deep and 50 to 60 feet wide. Sight distances are very short.

The canyon walls are about 200 feet high, a mix of rocky outcropping and forested gullies. The river covers the canyon floor in many places. When you get a break from watching for rocks or worrying about bears and sweepers, the scenery is spectacular.

Below the canyon, the river continues as a mix of Class II and III whitewater for several miles as it winds through the last of the mountains. It then begins to flatten out and braid into a number of smaller channels. There are a lot of sweepers and logjams in this section of the river, often blocking the entire channel. The river is still swift in the upper section (5 to 7 mph), and the sweepers can pose a danger to the unwary. The shore is lined with heavy brush and trees. The smaller channels often divide so frequently, and have so many sweepers, that rafts must be walked through or, in some cases, lined back upstream in order to find a passable route.

This is a primary sockeye spawning area, which means that it has large trout and lots of bears. As the river approaches Lake Coville, it slows dramatically, with the last mile very sluggish. The spruce and polar forest gives way to willows and then to marsh and grasslands. The river remains small, but there are deep runs along the cutbanks. The mouth of the river is very shallow, often less than a foot deep. There is a dearth of campsites near the mouth, but a small hill holds an old National Marine Fisheries site and there is room for tents. There are a lot of bears in this area, so unattended camps are at risk.

The lower stretch of the river has good fishing and several lodges keep boats near here in order to run clients up the first few miles of the river. There are a number of large (6- to 10-lb.) pike cruising the shoreline of the lake and ambushing small trout, whitefish, suckers, and salmon smolt. If you see a large swirl, go to a wire leader. Like the upper river, fishing near the mouth has declined over the past few years, in spite of healthy sockeye runs. Hopefully, this is a cyclical pattern that will reverse itself.

Fishing in American Creek is focused on rainbow trout and char (Dolly Varden). The primary salmon species is sockeye, which arrive in late June. Mark Emery, a local guide who has fished American Creek for years, reports that the river has some fry and a small smolt run out of Hammersley Lake. The early-season fishing is largely focused on those two prey items. Fry are about an inch long and are moving down into Lake Coville, where they will spend their first year. They are best imitated with Thunder Creeks or other small streamers. Smolt are year-old salmon that are migrating out to sea and are from 2 to 4 inches long. Zonkers, white Woolly Buggers, and other bright streamers are good imitations.

By midsummer, the sockeyes have moved into the river and the trout and char fishing slows. However, there can be some excellent dry-fly action in some of the long slicks and in the stretches near the lakes. Try Elk Hair Caddis, Yellow Humpies, and large attractors. The best fishing begins about the first of August and improves into September. The sockeye have spread throughout the system and are beginning to spawn. Egg patterns are the most effective flies, although in the clear water at the upper end you can often induce a stubborn trout to take a small nymph.

Floating American Creek is a serious proposition that should be undertaken only with a guide or by skilled whitewater rafters with extensive Alaskan experience. The rapids are intimidating, but are the least of the problems. Mark Emery talks about once dropping through a chute into a pool being fished by several bears, knowing that he just had to trust that they would get out of his way. These bears do not see a lot of fishermen and are not habituated.

The lower stretch of American Creek is heavily braided with sweepers and logjams, making passage difficult at times.

They are unpredictable and some of them require a lot of personal space. They are also numerous. I had a friend tell me he counted over 40 bears during a float.

Emery points out that the real risk is the sweepers and logs that may cover the entire river. Even guided trips have had fatalities caused by the sweepers. The river is fast, dropping 30 to 60 feet per mile, with short sight distances.

For most fishermen, there are three options for fishing American Creek. You can fly into Hammersley Lake, camp, and fish the several miles of river above the first canyon. The second option is to fly into a pothole lake located about 5 miles below the outlet and hike to the river. You can also go with a guide and a boat from a lodge or one of the park concessionaires. They will run you a few miles upstream from Coville.

The American is a beautiful and exciting river, and a great fit for the fisherman with a sense of adventure. Most of the guides who run it have extensive experience and a good feel for the country.

Stream Facts: American Creek

Seasons

- June 8 to April 10; no retention of rainbow trout June 8 to August 31.

Special Regulations

- No retention of rainbow trout from June 8 to Oct. 31. From Nov. 1 to April 9 daily limits for rainbow trout are 5 per day, 5 in possession, only 1 over 20 inches.

- Beads: In all flowing waters of Bristol Bay, attractors (beads) fished ahead of flies or lures must be fixed within 2 inches of the fly or lure, or be free to move (slide) on the line or leader. This applies to both fly and spin-fishing. A bead not attached to the hook is defined as an attractor, not a fly. A bead fished on the line above a bare hook is not legal gear in waters where only flies may be used.

Fish Species

- Rainbow trout average 16 to 22 inches.

- Arctic char (Dolly Varden) average 16 to 20 inches; present all season.

- Arctic grayling average 14 to 18 inches. Present all season.

- Sockeye (red) salmon average 5 to 7 lbs. Begin entering river about June 20. Run peaks around July 4.

River Characteristics

- American Creek can be accessed at the upper end by floatplane, either landing on Hammersley Lake or on a small pothole lake a few miles downstream. The latter approach requires hiking to the river. The lower river can be accessed by boat from Coville Lake. The middle section of the river is raftable only by persons with extensive wilderness whitewater experience.

American Creek Guides and Lodges

- **Northern Rim Adventures** (Brian Richardson), raft trips on Mulchatna, Chilikodratna; 1120 East Huffman Rd., Anchorage, AK 99515; 1-800-616-7238; www.northernrim.com

- **Wet Waders**, Mark Emery, independent guide; email memerym@aol.com; (winter) 246 NE 59th St., Ocala, FL 34479, 352-622-3412; (summer) 907-246-6330, P.O. Box 526, King Salmon, AK 99613

- **Adventures on the Fly, float trips**; P.O. Box 180446, Boston, MA 02118, 1-888-857-6700; ed_blank@msn.com

Maps

- *Alaska Atlas and Gazetteer*, page 51

Moraine Creek

My journal entry for a recent trip to Moraine Creek reads, "Monday, August 14: 6:30 p.m.—Have seen 64 bears since landing on Sat. Oops, just got up to look around—Make that 68, 69 bears and three more caribou."

It is hard to say which aspect of Moraine Creek is more impressive—the size of the trout or the number of bears. We saw 127 bears on that weeklong float trip and caught some very nice rainbows. Although the fly-out lodges hit Moraine hard, we were the only fishermen dumb enough to camp on it. We survived with our gear intact, but other campers have been left with nothing but shreds of rubber and nylon.

Moraine and its primary tributary, Funnel Creek, flow out of the west side of the Aleutian Range into Kukaklek Lake. It is most easily reached from Iliamna, about 35 miles away. It's a short stream, with most of the fishing taking place on about 7 miles of river.

Most lodges fly into a small tundra pothole, often called Crosswind Lake. It is near the mouth of Funnel Creek and about 8 miles above Kukaklek Lake. This approach allows fishermen to move up Funnel Creek or fish Moraine. Fishing Funnel Creek entails a fair amount of walking over rough terrain, and you need to be reasonably fit.

It takes a high tolerance for bears to fish for Moraine Creek's big 'bows.

A second, and less strenuous, alternative used by some lodges is to land on a small pond located about 4 miles upstream from Kukaklek Lake. The guides then take their guests down to the mouth in rubber rafts. The landing pond is so small that although planes can land on it with a full load, they can only take off empty. It is also possible to land at the mouth and hike upstream, although there are some long and deep sloughs that need to be negotiated.

Moraine Creek was a closely held secret for many years. Most of us just referred to it as Bear Creek, even to our friends. Its small size and big fish have since been discovered, and it is at the top of everybody's list of prime trout water. As an indication of its value, the ADF&G has designated it flyfishing only for all species, and catch and release for rainbow trout. Now it is one of the most heavily fished waters in Bristol Bay, and unfortunately, the trout are showing the effects.

The trout winter in Kukaklek Lake, growing fat on sockeye smolt that rear in the lake. In early July, thousands of sockeyes begin running up Moraine, and the trout fol-

low them. By spawning season, the rainbows are distributed throughout the system. As you would expect, they can be found behind the paired-up salmon. In a good year, though, the system is so rich that the trout can hold in traditional lies and still reap the rewards of a stream of eggs drifting downstream.

The lodges get their guests moving early for a trip to Moraine, and Crosswind Lake is a busy place by 7:00. The lake sits on a bluff on the south side of the stream, opposite the mouth of Funnel Creek. The stretch of Moraine Creek above the confluence is little fished, although there is an alternative landing lake about a mile upstream, sometimes used by people rafting the river. Most fishermen go up Funnel Creek or move downstream on Moraine.

The elevation here is about 900 feet, well above timberline in this country. This is spectacularly beautiful high alpine tundra, with rolling hills and long vistas. Stream banks and other low places are a maze of chest-high willows, tall enough to hide a sleeping bear. To the east, the peaks of the Aleutian Range light up in the evening's alpenglow. Caribou can be common (although with caribou even day-to-day predictions are difficult). The weather is problematic, and winds can be fierce. (I have been hunkered down here in gusts reported at over 80 mph.)

Directly below Crosswind Lake is an island large enough to camp on. Although at first glance the island would seem to be free of bears working the stream banks, it is in fact the primary path by which they cross the river to fish Funnel Creek. Both sides of the island hold trout. For a mile or so below the island, the river winds through willow-lined banks and alongside long gravel bars. It is about 30 yards wide, but can be waded at the riffles. Look for fish in the long gravel-bottomed runs or wherever you see spawning salmon. If the light is right, you can see the fish, but Moraine is too deep and full of riffles to be a true sight-fishing river.

A couple of miles below Funnel Creek, the river makes a sharp bend and enters a shallow canyon. This is Class II whitewater, with lots of rocks and some maneuvering required. It is within hiking distance of Crosswind Lake, and there are a few good runs in here for fishermen who want to wander downstream. Most of the boulder pockets hold trout, and the current is fast enough that they don't get a good look at the fly. You can fish from a moving boat in the upper stretch, but the river soon becomes so fast that you either pop everything off or risk injuring the fish by jerking it from a slow-water pocket.

About halfway through the canyon, the river makes a hard left against a wall. Just before the turn you'll find a ledge drop that runs the width of the river. At the right water level, you can run the slot in the middle. In any case, the drop can be lined easily on the left side.

Below the canyon, the valley spreads out and the river slows. At about 5 miles below the Crosswind Lake, a large bluff looms on the south side of the river. The gravel bar provides a good campsite with fine fishing, but it is directly across from the small lake from which the lower river is rafted. As a consequence, it is busy in the morning, as the lodges' guests line up to fish the bar while the guides inflate the rafts.

The next stretch of river contains some long gravel spawning grounds, and although the fish are not evenly distributed, there are some excellent stretches of water. The terrain here is much flatter than the upper stretch, with sloughs and backwaters that hold spawning salmon and attract bears. The willow banks give way to high grass and swamp.

A couple of miles up from Kukaklek Lake there's a tall cutbank on the south side of the stream, and some pilots will land just below that. It can be a difficult take-off with a full load, however, and unless you are in a Beaver, the lake may be a better pull-out spot. The lower stretch of the river is flat tundra and grass. Long deep sloughs wind back away from the river, making it difficult to hike very far upstream from the lake. If you plan on hiking up from the mouth, you are better off walking up on the higher ground and then cutting back to the river.

Moraine and Funnel Creeks are quintessential Alaskan rainbow streams. A few people may cast for sockeyes, and there is the occasional char, but these rivers were designed for trout. The lower stretches have some large trout early in the spring, but the fishing is unreliable. The spawners have dropped back down into Kukaklek Lake, but there are a few fish holding there to ambush the fry.

By July, the sockeyes have begun pouring into the river. Look down at those moving schools of salmon and you will realize that scattered in among them are dark-colored fish the same size as the salmon—big 'bows. It is too early for the fish to be turned on to eggs, so try stripping streamers. A tippet of 3X is the minimum for these fish. Big attractor dry flies will also work on occasion.

Moraine Creek hits its prime in mid-August, when the sockeye have begun to spawn. Egg patterns are the order of the day, but these are not easy fish. Much of their food is gained by rooting in the fine gravel of the redds (you can see the wear on their noses). They quickly learn to distinguish the difference between a real egg and whatever else may end up in their mouths. The result is a river full of fish that are adept at spitting out a fly before you can detect a strike.

Unfortunately, many of the lodges decided that the remedy for difficult fish was pegged beads. Some guides had their clients peg the bead 5 or 6 inches above a bare hook. When a fish would attempt to spit out the imitation, the tippet would simply drag through the fish's mouth and the trout would be snagged. Too often the fish were hooked in the gills or pectoral fins. The result was excessively high catch rates, killed and injured fish, and a major controversy over whether this was an ethical technique in an area ostensibly limited to flyfishing.

The ADF&G attempted to restrict the use of beads, but the guides argued that too many clients were unable to catch fish by any other method. Ultimately, a compromise was reached. A bead that is not attached to the hook is now defined as an attractor, not a fly. A bead may fixed not more than 2 inches, or allowed to slide freely, above a fly. On Moraine Creek (and other flyfishing-only streams) bare hooks may not be used.

Personal aesthetics aside, there is no problem with the beads themselves. A properly colored bead is an almost perfect visual imitation of a salmon egg. It is a simple matter to slip a bead over the eye of some hooks (a size 12 Tiemco 2312, for instance) and tie it in place. This not only constitutes a legal fly, but it eliminates the issue of snagging fish. Strikes are subtle and rejections swift, but in a river with as many big trout as Moraine, a decent nymph fisherman will land many fish. Use a strike indicator (yarn is the most sensitive) and adjust the depth as needed to keep the fly on the bottom and ensure a tight line between the indicator and the fly. Set the hook at every hesitation in the indicator.

Once the salmon start to die, flesh flies become effective. I prefer smaller ties with a hint of salmon pink in them, but the traditional ginger bunny flies are also good. Maggot patterns will sometimes work on stubborn fish, but I reserve those for fish that I've spotted. Sculpin patterns and leeches come into their own again at the end of the season.

Oh, yes, all those bears. Well, the number I saw on my last trip to Moraine was an aberration, but the area always has a high concentration. It is, after all, only 20 miles from McNeil River, the most famous bear viewing area in the world. Even with a mountain range to cross, this is an easy day hike for a grizzly. There are enough fishermen on Moraine these days that the bears are somewhat habituated. However, these are not Brooks River bears. They have their own hierarchies and rules and expect you to live by them. Try wading through some boar's fishing hole, and you will get a quick lesson in bear etiquette.

This is one of the riskiest places to camp in Alaska, in part because you will be leaving your food and gear unattended during the day. We were there at the peak of the salmon run, when food was plentiful and even the unskilled juveniles were adequately fed. The adrenaline ran high, but in the end we had very few problems. It is a different place when the bears are hungry. Some of them can get a little testy, and while being attacked is unlikely, having your camp destroyed is a real possibility. That is not just a problem for you, but for everyone who comes after you.

A bear that associates humans with food will continue to do so until someone finally shoots it. Frankly, unless you are experienced in dealing with bears at close range, know how to properly store food, gear, and garbage, and are scrupulous about keeping a clean camp, you should limit yourself to day trips to this area. At a minimum, use a portable electric fence system and camp away from the river corridor.

This is a special place with spectacular scenery, lots of wildlife, and a healthy population of big rainbows. Those who are lucky enough to fish here should treat it with the respect it deserves.

The spectacular rainbows are no longer a secret on Moraine Creek, but it still has some of the best wade fishing available.

Funnel Creek

Funnel Creek is the primary tributary of Moraine, and although it is less than half the size of the main branch of the river, it is more heavily fished. Funnel begins at Mirror Lake, about 8 miles from its confluence with Moraine. Set in rolling hills covered with dry alpine tundra, Funnel is a spectacular example of the richness of Bristol Bay. Only about 30 feet wide and easily waded, it is used by thousands of sockeye salmon and holds innumerable large trout.

There are two ways to approach Funnel Creek. A few people fly into Mirror Lake and fish down, but most land at Crosswind Lake and move upstream. Fishing right at the point where Funnel enters Moraine can yield some big trout, and many people start here and work their way up. This lower stretch is braided and thick with willows,

and although it is easy to move back and forth across the stream, it is not always easy to see what may be around the corner. There are some channels in this lower section, and all are worth exploring. Work the slots and cutbanks as well as the salmon spawning runs. Because the stream is so small, the trout tend to lay up in sheltered spots, but they will still hit a drifting egg pattern.

Many fishermen head directly for the midsection of the river, a mile or two upstream. The ridgeline that runs along the west side of the valley gives a good view of the stream and provides easy access to the upper stretches of the river. The runs in this area are somewhat easier to read, and there is a good amount of sight fishing. Don't neglect any of the deeper pools or any place you find a pod of salmon. The trout will often hang right with the sockeyes, usually lying just on the outside of the school. At any disturbance, including a poorly cast fly, they will simply drift into the center of the sockeyes for protection.

In spite of the remoteness, these are not unsophisticated fish. Not only have they seen a lot of flies, but also they are very wary of bears, and with good cause. In a stream this small, even trout are vulnerable. This means that any trout that has spotted you is more worried about being eaten than about missing a meal. If you want to catch trout on Funnel Creek, particularly the old wise ones, stealth is essential.

There are times when the stream is so crowded with fishermen, both two-legged and four-legged, that it is difficult to find a good run to fish. If it happens, don't let your fish lust prevent you from appreciating the fact that you are in one of the wildest and most beautiful places left on earth.

Stream Facts: Moraine and Funnel Creeks

Seasons
- June 8 to April 10; no retention of rainbow trout June 8 to August 31.

Special Regulations
- No retention of rainbow trout from June 8 to Oct. 31. From Nov. 1 to April 9 daily limits for rainbow trout are 5 per day, 5 in possession, only 1 over 20 inches.

- Only unbaited single-hook artificial flies may be used June 8 to Oct. 31.

- Beads: In all flowing waters of Bristol Bay, attractors (beads) fished ahead of flies or lures must be fixed within 2 inches of the fly or lure, or be free to move (slide) on the line or leader. This applies to both fly and spin-fishing. A bead not attached to the hook is defined as an attractor, not a fly. A bead fished on the line above a bare hook is not legal gear in waters where only flies may be used.

Fish Species

- Rainbow trout average 16 to 22 inches, with an occasional fish to 30 inches.
- Arctic char (Dolly Varden) average 16 to 20 inches; present all season.
- Sockeye (red) salmon average 5 to 7 lbs. Begin entering river about June 25. Run peaks around July 4

River Characteristics

- Moraine and Funnel Creeks are small streams that are accessible to wading anglers. Access is by floatplane only. These are flyfishing-only streams managed for their populations of large rainbows, which enter the river in conjunction with the sockeye salmon run.

  Moraine Creek is fished by most of the fly-out lodges in the King Salmon and Iliamna areas.

Maps

- *Alaska Atlas and Gazetteer*, page 59

KING SALMON AND KATMAI PARK
Population: 696
Alaska Area Code: 907
Zip Code: 99613

LODGES AND GUIDES

Katmai Fishing Adventures, www.katmaifishing.com; Nanci Morris, independent guide; P.O. Box 221, King Salmon, AK; 246-8322

Wet Waders, Mark Emery, independent guide; email memerym@aol.com; (winter) 246 NE 59th St., Ocala, FL 34479, 352-622-3412; (summer) 246-6330, P.O. Box 526, King Salmon, AK 99613

Royal Wolf Lodge, www.royalwolf.com; fly-out lodge; (winter) P.O. Box 190207, Anchorage, AK 99519, 248-3256; (summer) P.O. Box 299, King Salmon, AK, 1-877-587-7509

Enchanted Lake Lodge, www.enchantedlakelodge.com; remote fly-out lodge; (winter) P.O. Box 111249, Anchorage, AK 99511; (summer) P.O. Box 97, King Salmon AK, 246-6878

Fox Bay Lodge, www.foxbaylodge.com; Naknek River lodge, with fly-outs; (winter) Box 13, King Salmon, AK 99613, 1-800-555-744, Email Us fox_bay@hotmail.com, Winter Contact: P.O. Box 1023 Shady Cove, OR 97539

Rapids Camp Lodge, www.rapidscamplodge.com; P.O. Box 501 5800 Maple Avenue, King Salmon, AK 99613 Dallas, TX 75235, 907-246-8345; 214-654-0682

Open: May - October Open: Year Round mail us fishing@rapidscamplodge.com

Alaska's Naknek Anglers, www.naknekanglers.com; fly-out lodge on Naknek; 1-800-677-2701; (winter) P.O. Box 210542, Anchorage, AK 99521; (summer) P.O. Box 513, King Salmon, AK

Katmailand, Inc., www.katmailand.com; operates lodges at Brooks Camp, Kulik, and Grosvenor; 4125 Aircraft Dr., Anchorage, AK 99502; 1-800-544-0551, 243-5448

ACCOMMODATIONS

Antler's Inn, King Salmon; 246-8525; self-service kitchens. auto/boat rental; www.antlersinnkingsalmon.com.

King Ko Inn, King Salmon; 246-3377

Quinnat Landing Hotel, King Salmon; 246-3000

Eagle Bluff Lodge, Naknek River; 246-4464

Antler's Inn, Naknek River; 246-8525

Rainbow Bend Cabin and Boat Rentals, www.bristolbayfishing.com; cabins and boats on the Naknek; (winter) P.O. Box 4281, Soldotna, AK, 262-2750; (summer) P.O. Box 185, King Salmon, AK, 246-1500

RESTAURANTS

Eddies Fireplace Inn, King Salmon; 246-3403

King Ko Inn, King Salmon; 246-3307

Mel's Diner and Espresso, King Salmon; 246-7629

AIRCRAFT CHARTERS

Alaska Katmai Express, King Salmon; 246-8850

Branch River Air Service, King Salmon; 246-3437

C-Air, King Salmon; 246-6318; www.gtesupersite/c_air

Egli Air Haul, Inc., King Salmon; 246-3554

Katmai Air, King Salmon; 246-3079 (May 15 to Oct. 1); 1-800-544-0551 (winter)

Pen Air, King Salmon; 246-4264; Anchorage 1-800-448-4226

AIRLINES AND AIR CARGO SERVICES

Alaska Airlines Passenger Info, 1-800-252-7522; cargo info 1-800-225-2752

Pen Air, Passenger Anchorage, 1-800-448-4226; cargo King Salmon 246-3461

Northern Air Cargo, Anchorage, 1-800-478-3330; King Salmon 246-3461

GROCERIES, BEER, LIQUOR, AND SUPPLIES

Alaska Commercial Company King Salmon, 246-6109

BOAT RENTAL

Antler's Inn, King Salmon; 246-8525; auto/boat rental; www.antlersinnkingsalmon.com

R & G Boat Rental, King Salmon; 246-3353

Rainbow Bend Cabin & Boat Rental, King Salmon; 246-1500

Naknek Marina, 246-3491

ALASKA PENINSULA

The southern edge of Bristol Bay is delineated by a volcanic spine that tails off into the Aleutian Islands, separating the cold waters of the Bering Sea from the warm flow of the Japanese Current. The Alaska Peninsula is a land known for its weather. Barren, beautiful, and windswept, the peninsula is one of the last frontiers of fishing in North America. Its crystal-clear rivers host char, king salmon, silver salmon, and, in a few, our westernmost strain of steelhead.

The peninsula, for our purposes, begins with the Becharof drainages on the edge of Katmai National Park. Char, silvers, and kings provide good fishing in the right streams. Moving down the peninsula, we come to the Ugashik Lakes, home of Alaska's biggest grayling. The country below Ugashik includes dozens of clear streams and rivers formed by the constant flow of moisture off the Bering Sea. Some of these rivers are actually artesian springs, bursting full-blown from the volcanic rubble and creating perfect spawning conditions for sea-run fish.

Few anglers ever see these waters. Less than a dozen guides or lodges fish the myriad of rivers that flow off the west side of the Aleutian Mountains. It is a land owned by its bears, caribou, geese, and walrus. And for those who like to fish the edges, the Alaska Peninsula is as edgy as it gets on this continent.

Becharof Lake and the Ugashik Lakes Area

Becharof is a huge lake, some 300 square miles, surrounded by largely unexplored country. Although it has no rainbows (well, there are rumors of some in particular creeks), it has one of the largest sockeye runs in Bristol Bay, and the char and grayling ably fill the niche left vacant by trout. For those intrepid and experienced souls

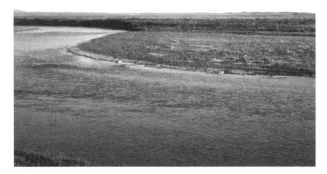

The Alaska Peninsula is a windswept land of volcanoes and crystal-clear salmon streams.

who want to see Alaska as it once was, there are few places better than Becharof.

Needless to say, there are good reasons why Becharof has not succumbed to the industrial tourism that covers most of the fishing rivers. The lack of rainbows is obviously a major factor, but weather plays a large part, too. Becharof, and for that matter the entire peninsula, lies between Bristol Bay and the Gulf of Alaska, two of the stormiest places on earth. When you separate two dramatically different pressure gradients with a range of mountains, every pass becomes a wind tunnel. And the east end of Becharof lies at the base of a pass that is only 600 feet high. It howls.

Becharof also has the state's highest concentration of grizzly bears. These are not the laconic, habituated bears that you run into on heavily fished streams in the national parks. They are hunted here, and their fight-or-flight switch has a hair trigger.

If you are prepared to deal with the bears and the weather, though, there is some fine fishing in the feeder streams that run into the lake. Places like **Featherly Creek** get good runs of sockeye, with lots of char and grayling following them upstream. Simply walk up the first mile or so and you will find some of the wildest, most remote fishing left in the state. Most visitors fish the Becharof area on day trips flown out of King Salmon. Some lodges fish these streams, and there are a few independent guides, like Mark Emery, who will show you places few other people ever fish.

For anglers who want to catch sockeyes till their arms give out, the **Egegik River**, right at the outlet of the lake, is a prime spot. Every salmon that goes into the lake has to pass right in front of you in water that is only a couple of feet deep—perfect for taking sockeyes on a fly. The run typically peaks on the Fourth of July. You can land on wheels or floats, making access relatively easy. There are also char and grayling in this stretch.

Below Becharof you'll find the two smaller **Ugashik Lakes** that have long been famous for their trophy grayling. Eight of the 10 biggest grayling recorded (all 4 pounds or over) came from the Ugashik system. Unfortunately, grayling are very susceptible to overharvest, and the cooler loads of trophies that a few people took decimated the population. Special regulations have been instituted, and hopefully they will help restore these watersheds to their former status.

The **Ugashik River** is now completely closed to fishing for grayling and **Ugashik Narrows** (from the outlet of Upper Ugashik Lake to the inlet of Lower Ugashik Lake) is catch-and-release only. Nevertheless, if you want a shot at a 4-pound grayling, the Narrows is still one of the best spots in the state. All the streams flowing into the lakes have big grayling and char.

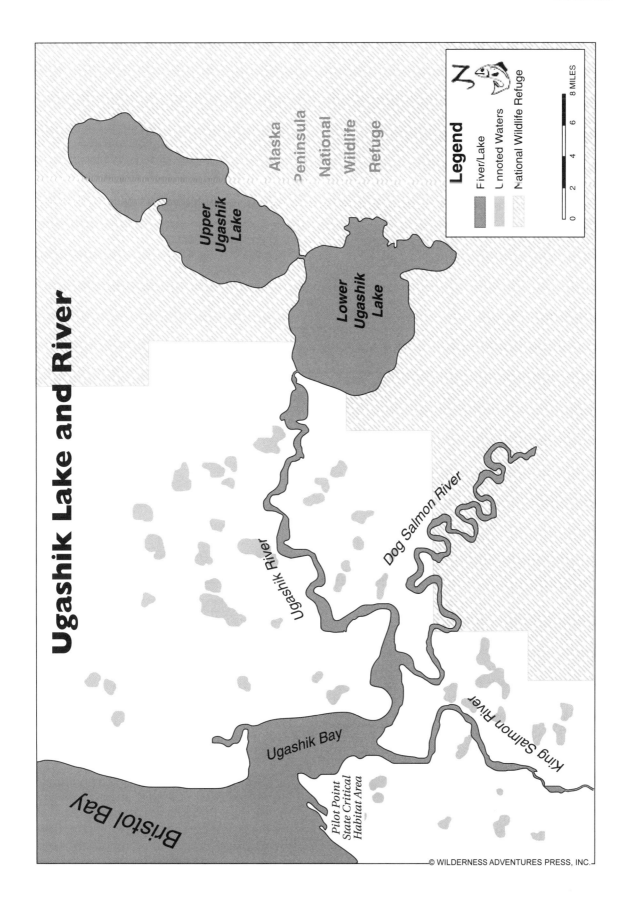

Ugashik Lake and River

Upper Ugashik Lake

Lower Ugashik Lake

Alaska Peninsula National Wildlife Refuge

Ugashik River

Dog Salmon River

Ugashik Bay

Bristol Bay

Pilot Point State Critical Habitat Area

King Salmon River

Legend

Fiver/Lake

Unnoted Waters

National Wildlife Refuge

0 2 4 6 8 MILES

© WILDERNESS ADVENTURES PRESS, INC.

Becharof Lake is largely untapped and little explored, but has great potential for char and sockeye fishing.

Grayling are primarily insectivores and eagerly take dry flies and nymphs. However, they supplement their diet with fry and other small fish and can be taken on streamers and Woolly Buggers (sizes 6 to 10). When the salmon are spawning, the grayling feed voraciously on the eggs. Grayling will often hold in schools, with the larger fish at the bottom. The biggest difficulty is drawing a strike from the best fish before the little ones get to it. You may have to start at the head of the run and work a fly deep underneath the smaller fish to get to the real trophies. Grayling fight much harder on light tackle. If they are overpowered, they seem to simply go rigid and quit, but on a 3- or 4-weight they are a lot of fun, particularly on dries.

The rivers below Ugashik host some excellent runs of king and silver salmon and sea-run char. There are chum salmon in many drainages, and sockeyes in most streams with a lake at the head. These streams have lots of fish and see very few fishermen.

The kings typically peak about the third week in June and continue until late July, by which time they are on the spawning beds and should not be harassed. Look for them in the lower 10 miles of the rivers and you will find them still bright. The chums come in at about the same time as the kings. Big char follow the kings in. Many of these rivers host char that average about 3 pounds and may go up to 15. The best fishing is from late July until freeze up. Silvers begin to come into the rivers in mid-August, and the best fishing lasts about three weeks.

Painter Creek Lodge is one of the very few operations that fish this remote area. Jon Kent, the owner, has had over 20 years to work out some of its secrets. Kings are a staple of the lodge, and Jon recommends that his clients bring a 10-weight rod with 200- to 250-grain shooting heads. A good reel with lots of backing is mandatory. He

likes big Bunny Leeches (size 2/0) in purple and pink combinations, orange, and chartreuse.

Catching silvers on the surface has become increasingly popular as people figure out how to do it successfully. Jon says that you need to find fish holding in water about 2 feet deep with a moderate current. Although Pink Pollywogs are the usual fly, Jon has had equally good luck with bass poppers. Paint 'em pink and add pink marabou and Flashabou. If you are fishing in deeper water a 200-grain sinking head or a high-density sink-tip will get your fly down to the fish.

There are no rainbows to speak of in this part of the state, but there is great char fishing (think big brook trout). Char will also take a fly on the surface, but it usually has to be waking. They seem to show little interest in dead-drifted dries. Size 6 or 8 skaters or heavily hackled flies will create the right amount of surface disturbance. Jon says he has the best luck with a fly tied with heavily palmered orange hackle.

Sandy River

The Sandy is a 15-mile-long, clear-water stream far down the Alaska Peninsula—an hour-and-twenty-minute flight from King Salmon. It is wild country, with great fishing for kings and silvers. It has volcanoes, walrus hauling out on the beach, and Boone & Crockett–sized bears. But beyond all that, it has the holy grail of coldwater fishing—big steelhead.

The mountains of the Aleutian Range rise sharply behind Sandy Lake, their origins evident in the steaming cone of Mt. Veniaminof a few miles to the north. The river flows through a short coastal plain of tundra and muskeg. It is a medium-fast stream with a gravel bottom and easy wading. The upper half of the river is riffle and pool, with classic tailouts. The lower section contains longer runs. Both sections hold lots of fish.

Fishing begins in late April, when the first spring steelhead show. This is a smaller run than occurs in the fall. About a third of the fish in the river are fresh, while the rest are holdovers that entered the river the previous October and spent the winter waiting to spawn. Like spring-run steelhead everywhere, the fish move into the river, spawn, and drop back out to sea again. Fishing is always a short affair and timing is essential. The spring season on the Sandy lasts two weeks, from about April 24 to May 8.

The king salmon enter the river around June 10. The Sandy is a good river for fly-rod kings. It is small enough that you can get a fly down into the deeper runs that kings prefer. The fish average about 25 pounds, although they can go as high as 50. There are plenty of fish to go around.

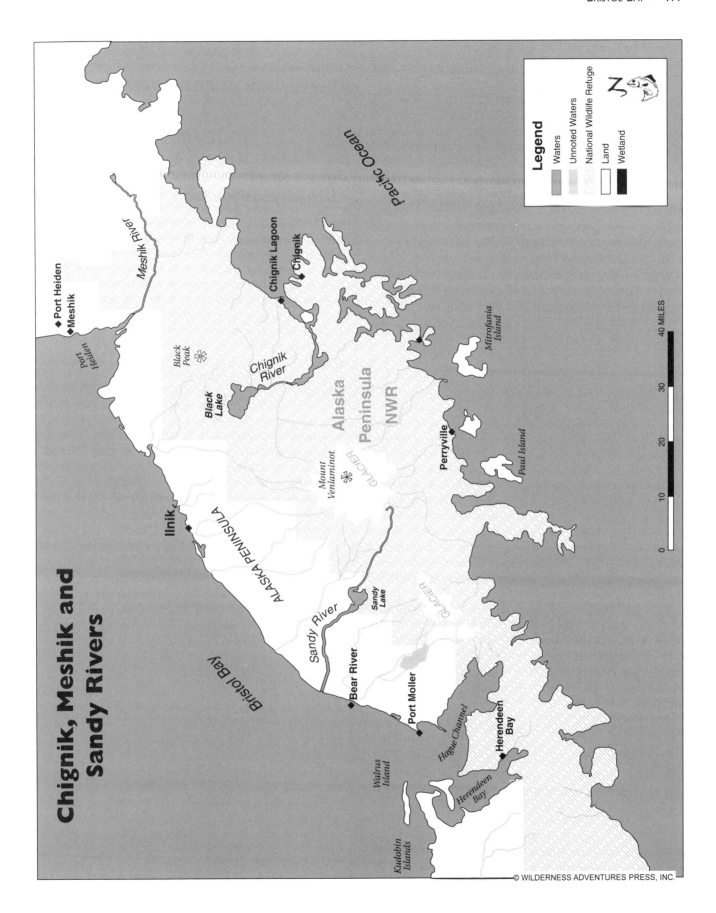

Chignik, Meshik and Sandy Rivers

Legend

Waters
Unnoted Waters
National Wildlife Refuge
Land
Wetland

Pacific Ocean

Port Heiden
Meshik
Port Heiden

Meshik River

Black Peak

Black Lake

Chignik River

Chignik Lagoon
Chignik

Alaska Peninsula NWR

Mitrofania Island

Paul Island

Mount Venlaminot

GLACIER

Perryville

ALASKA PENINSULA

Ilnik

Sandy River

Sandy Lake

GLACIER

Bristol Bay

Bear River

Port Moller

Hague Channel

Herendeen Bay

Walrus Island

Herendeen Bay

Kudobin Islands

0   10   20   30   40 MILES

© WILDERNESS ADVENTURES PRESS, INC.

The kings are on their redds and have started to color up by mid-July. Although the season doesn't close until July 25, those who push it to the end are fishing for poor-quality fish that have started to spawn.

Silvers make their appearance during the last week in August, and the fishing continues through September. This is one of the best areas in the state for silvers, and although the Sandy does not have the run strength of the nearby Ocean River, there are enough aggressive, acrobatic fish to keep everyone happy.

The fish average between 12 and 15 pounds, but there are some that go as high as 18 to 22. Mel Gillis, who runs the only lodge on the river, the Sandy River Lodge, recommends the usual Egg-Sucking Leeches and Flash Flies, but says his clients also do well on Fat Freddies, a fly usually reserved for kings. There is not much dry-fly fishing ('wogging) for silvers because of the speed of the river.

October is the time for fall steelhead. The days are short and the weather is lousy, but the river is full of big heavy fish, with an average length of about 32 inches. Fish up to 43 inches have been taken in the past. Unlike the steelhead rivers of Southeast Alaska, the Sandy supports a large run of fish, and a good steelheader can expect multiple-fish days.

Gillis says that the most effective flies are usually dark, either black or purple, and include some particularly long String Leeches. Double Bunnies (with some in pink) and the ubiquitous Egg-Sucking Leeches are also good. There is limited dry-fly fishing when the weather cooperates.

This is also the time for cast-and-blast trips. It is possible to see hundreds of ptarmigan in a day, and this is a primary migration route for geese and ducks, with lots of pintail and widgeon moving through. Bear, moose, and caribou roam the area, and dozens of walrus haul out on the beach at Cape Seniavin, a few miles up the coast.

Ocean River

The Sandy is not the only river in this area that draws fishermen. The Ocean River provides a great opportunity for anglers hoping to land a silver on a skating dry fly. It is a slow frogwater stream that flows about 12 miles from Wildman Lake to the Bering Sea. Deep near the mouth, the river becomes wadeable about 4 or 5 miles upstream.

The Ocean is a great coho river, and its sluggish current provides perfect conditions for 'wogging up an aggressive fish. Pink Pollywogs or Waller Wakers should be fished slowly, with short strips. If the fish and the weather don't cooperate, try Egg-Sucking Leeches or String Leeches fished deep. The river has a few small resident rainbows, but no kings or steelhead.

Three outfitters work the Ocean River. Sandy River Lodge and Rainbow Lodge operate spike camps here, and Wildman Lodge is situated near the headwater lake. It is possible to land a plane on the beach, but the sand is a bit soft and local knowledge is required. Winds through Black Lake Pass can be ferocious at times.

Other Rivers

Most visitors to this area fish the Sandy or Ocean Rivers. The locals, however, understand that there is tremendous fishing in many of the streams. Access and weather are the primary inhibiting factors. The Ilnik River has some very good sea-run char fishing, as well as a decent silver run. The same outfitters that fish Ocean River will often put their guests on the Ilnik for a change of pace.

There are good runs of king and silver salmon, as well as big char, in the **Meshik River**, which flows out of Aniakchak National Preserve and empties into Port Heiden. The Meshik is shallow and easily wadeable. It can be floated from a lake about 40 miles upstream or accessed by boat or plane from Port Heiden, a commercial fishing town (so don't expect to be greeted with open arms when you roll in with your fly rods). Count on a lot of bears and lousy weather if you decide to explore this spectacular area.

The **Chignik River** has a huge run of sockeyes, but there are also kings, cohos, char, and even a few steelhead. The river can be accessed by boat from the towns of Chignik Lake or Chignik Lagoon. Steelhead have also been reported in the **Bear River**, and in some of the streams around Cold Bay. **Cinder River** has good fishing for silvers and kings.

The lower edge of the Alaska Peninsula is truly one of the last frontiers left in North America. Its fishing resources are untouched and sometimes even undiscovered. It is expensive to get there, the weather is remarkably bad, and there are a lot of unhabituated bears. But if you are looking for wild country and amazing fishing, it's a good place to start.

The windswept grasslands of the Sandy provide a classic backdrop for a speycasting steelheader.

ALASKA PENINSULA LODGES, GUIDES, AND OUTFITTERS

Sandy River Lodge, www.sandyriverlodge.com; steelhead and salmon lodge located on Sandy River; P.O. Box 220247, Anchorage, AK 99522; 907-344-8589

Painter Creek Lodge, www.paintercreeklodge.com; salmon, char, and grayling lodge near Ugashik Lakes; P.O. Box 190105, Anchorage, AK 99519; 907-248-1303

Wildman Lake Lodge, www.wildmanlodge.com; lodge on Ocean River; 2024 Stonegate Circle, Anchorage AK 99515; 907-522-1164

Alaska Trophy Adventure, www.alaskatrophyadventure.com; lodge; 315-761-0941; P.O. Box 31, King Salmon, AK

Wind River Lodge, www.alaskareel.com; remote weatherport camp with silver salmon fishing; 1-800-877-2661

Blue Mountain Lodge, www.bluemountainlodge.com; salmon, grayling, and char lodge near Becharof Lake; P.O. Box 670130, Chugiak, AK 99567; 907-688-2419

LAKE ILIAMNA REGION

Tucked up in the corner of Bristol Bay, right at the hip of the Alaska Peninsula, Lake Iliamna covers hundreds of square miles. It is home to freshwater seals, Alaska's version of the Loch Ness monster, and some monstrous trout. Millions of sockeye salmon return to this system every summer. They move up through the Kvichak, a huge crystal-clear river, into the lake, and then into spawning streams that drain the surrounding mountains and hills. With them travel some of the largest rainbow trout in North America. Only one large river, the Newhalen, feeds into the lake. The rest are small, intimate streams that provide an opportunity to wade and sight fish.

Iliamna has some of the best dry-fly fishing in Alaska, and a few of its streams, particularly the Kvichak and Lower Talarik Creek, are home to an astonishing number of rainbows that will push, or exceed, 10 pounds. Its big rivers, the Kvichak and Newhalen, are easily accessed by the traveling fisherman, with B&Bs and small do-it-yourself lodges available. But much of the area's charm lies in its smaller streams, and for the most part they yield their secrets only to those who can afford the cost of a high-end lodge.

Although there is some salmon fishing on the Kvichak and the Newhalen, Iliamna's reputation as a world-class fishery is based on its rainbows. They are large, numerous, and often eager. The area's major drawback is that much of the land is privately owned by the local native corporations, and access to much of the best fishing is very limited. What is available, however, is tough to beat.

Kvichak River

Iliamna's outlet, the Kvichak (pronounced kwee-jack) River, is as astounding as the lake it drains. It pours out a hundred yards wide and crystal-clear at the tiny village of Igiugig. Millions of sockeye salmon return to this system every summer. Most move up into the lake and its justly famous tributaries, but thousands remain to spawn in the Kvichak. Those salmon draw Iliamna's rainbows downstream into the spawning beds, where they grow fat on eggs and salmon flesh. In doing so they create what may be North America's best big trout (30-plus-inch) fishery, although fans of the Naknek would probably argue that point.

The Kvichak is about 50 miles long, emptying into Bristol Bay about 10 miles north of the mouth of the Naknek River. It flows through low hills and a broad featureless flood plain, primarily wet muskeg, but people don't come to the Kvichak for the scenery. They come to fish the upper 12 miles or so, from the outlet of the lake down to the end of a section known as the braids.

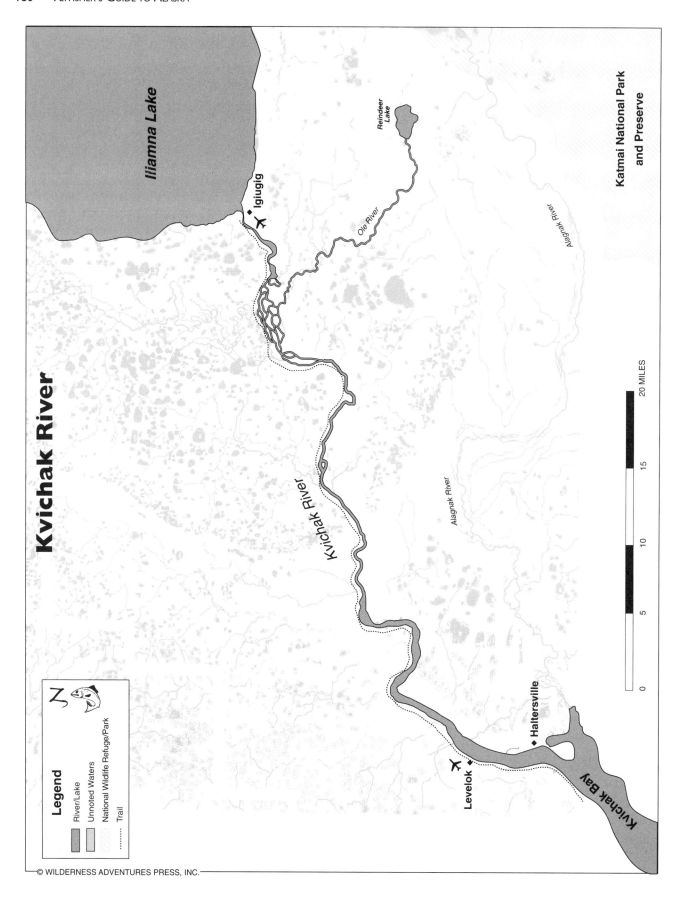

Kvichak River

Iliamna Lake

Igiugig

Reindeer Lake

Ole River

Kvichak River

Alagnak River

Alagnak River

Katmai National Park
and Preserve

Haltersville

Levelok

Kvichak Bay

Legend

N

River/Lake
Unnoted Waters
National Wildlife Refuge/Park
Trail

0   5   10   15   20 MILES

© WILDERNESS ADVENTURES PRESS, INC.

The Kvichak can be reached from either King Salmon or Iliamna. There are a number of lodges on the river that maintain fleets of jet boats. There are also a couple of do-it-yourself outfitters in Igiugig that will provide you a place to stay and rent you a boat to explore downstream. There is good fishing right at the mouth of the lake and at several spots within walking distance of greater downtown Igiugig. Be forewarned—Igiugig is one of the buggiest places in Alaska, with hordes of mosquitoes, black flies, deer flies, no-see-ums, white sox, and other unidentified bloodsuckers. Take a head net for those few times that the wind isn't blowing.

The upper 5 miles of river, down to Pecks Creek, are open and broad, broken by about a dozen islands. Several of these islands have large flats where the trout lie in June, waiting to ambush migrating smolt. There are also gravel beds where the sockeye spawn in August, and they attract some of the large rainbows that move down from the lake.

The braids begin just below Pecks Creek. The river splits into innumerable channels—creating a maze of interconnected waterways a mile and a half wide. Kaskanak Creek flows in from the north, draining a vast expanse of pothole lakes and swamp. From the south, Ole Creek, a much smaller stream than Kaskanak, joins the river. Fishing is good at the mouth of both of these creeks.

Navigating a boat through the braids is not an easy chore. The river opens up and then closes down, and there are numerous shallow shelves that can take out a prop (which is why most boats are equipped with jet units) or ground the hull. Running aground in a lightweight jonboat is one thing. It is another matter entirely in a big jet boat that is too heavy to move. Treat the braids with respect. If you are not experienced in running power boats through this kind of water, and you want to get out

There are a number of lodges in all price ranges along the banks of Kvichak, and there are plenty of big rainbows to go around as well.

of the main channel, get a guide before you venture past Pecks Creek.

Below the braids, the river reforms into a single channel. There are some large trout in here, but there is very little fishing to be done. The river is simply too deep, wide, and featureless to find the fish. A few kings spawn in the lower river, particularly around Yellow Creek, although the Kvichak is not considered a prime king salmon river.

Sockeyes are the primary salmon species in the Iliamna drainage, with an average run of several million fish. The escapement goal for the Iliamna drainage is two million fish. If projections fall below that number, harvest restrictions are imposed by emergency order. The regulations may change daily, so never fish for sockeyes without checking the current status.

The sockeyes move into the river in late June, with the run peaking about the Fourth of July. They pass by in a never-ending line of fish four or five abreast, moving steadily upstream. The best place to fish for them is in the lower braids. Look for an island with a gradually sloping bottom to the river. Sockeye prefer to travel near shore and you can usually find a spot where they will come up over a bar or shallow spot. If you find the right spot and get the fly down into the passing school you will catch fish till your arms give out.

Sockeyes are strong, acrobatic fish. John Holman, of No-See-Um Lodge, recommends that his guests use a 7- or 8-weight rod. Unlike guides in many areas who prefer sink-tips, John recommends a floating line and a 7- to 9-foot leader. An experienced sockeye fisherman will almost always opt for small bright flies, heavily weighted, and with needle-sharp hooks. Holman agrees, but says that classic shad patterns meet all those criteria and can be particularly effective. Comets, Brassies, and Sockeye Oranges are also effective.

The Kvichak gets a pretty good run of silver salmon in August. They can be found around the outlet of Ole Creek and occasionally near the mouth of Kaskanak. Look for them on the backside of the islands, along the edge of the tailout. You can also find the fish in deeper holes, where, with the Kvichak's typically clear water, they can be spotted lying on the bottom. Having said that, the Kvichak is not a silver salmon destination. They are tough to find and should be considered a bonus if you stumble into them. Carry a few bright bunny flies just in case.

The real draw on the Kvichak, of course, is its big rainbows. Some anglers claim they are the strongest trout in Alaska, which is high praise indeed. They are certainly capable of reel-burning runs, aerial cartwheels, and dogged stubbornness. It is not unusual for an 8- or 10-pound 'bow to bust out of the water in a frantic display more typical of a 14-incher. These are tough, broad-shouldered fish, which most of the year make their living chasing down salmon smolt. Don't expect gentle strikes on streamers.

There are several large pods of fish that overwinter in the river itself, hunkering down in the deeper holes. Most, however, move up into the lake, dropping back down into the braids in early May to spawn. There are still a few of these fish around when the season opens on June 8. The sockeye smolt, about 3 inches long, begin to move downstream in late May, and there are still enough in the river throughout June to keep the trout looking for them. At times there will be a flood of smolt racing downstream, marked by diving terns and gulls, and the slashes of big rainbows chasing them to the surface. Throw a white Woolly Bugger or Double Bunny into the maelstrom and hold on. Poppers and surface patterns can be even more fun.

Most of the June fishing is done with big dark leeches, though. Black or purple bunny flies, Woolly Buggers, and Articulated Leeches are often irresistible to an early season trout. Fry patterns will also work in the Kvichak, at least in odd-numbered years. In even-numbered years, a large run of pink salmon spawn in the river. Those eggs hatch the following spring, and the fry out-migrate to the ocean immediately. The trout love these little inch-long snacks.

On a hot day, you might also get in some dry-fly fishing, primarily with large attractor patterns. The Kvichak also has a healthy population of big grayling, so a light rod and a box of dries will make for an evening's entertainment.

Don't go undergunned. These are big fish in a large river and the wind is a factor. Throwing a sink-tip line and a weighted fly under these conditions takes a heavy outfit. A spey rod can be a definite asset, particularly in the early season. For single-handers, an 8-weight is not too much rod, and 1X or 0X tippet is not too heavy. A few years ago, I watched a fellow fisherman, who had already caught a couple of fish that were pushing 10 pounds, lose one that was much larger. His buddy just said, "I told you that you have to be prepared for some *big* fish here."

Many people confuse these trout with steelhead, and there are a lot of similarities. However, these are not anadromous fish. There is a noticeable difference between the lake fish and those that reside in the river year-round. The lake fish maintain their silvery sheen even after they have been in the river for a while. Resident fish have more color and are better camouflaged against the dark gravel bottom. Lake fish are also often heavier for their size than their river-dwelling cousins.

In July, when the salmon are moving through, the rainbows disappear. This is true in almost all of Alaska, with the trout fishing dropping off dramatically after the first few days of the season. However, as the chums and sockeyes spread out on their spawning beds and pair up, the 'bows return in force. Once the salmon start to color up, and the males develop their distinctive kype, it is time to forgo the streamers and switch to egg patterns. Even though there may not yet be any eggs in the water, the trout can smell the ripening salmon and are looking for the beginning of the spawning season. More importantly, the male sockeyes become very aggressive, and it becomes almost impossible to swing a streamer through them without drawing a strike from a salmon.

This is the time to go headhunting—looking for that trophy lying behind the salmon. The same size as the salmon (or larger), the trout will be moving back and forth looking for drifting eggs. The distinctive scarlet bodies and green heads of the sockeye easily distinguish them from the rainbows.

As the female salmon dig their redds, they often dislodge the eggs laid by earlier arrivals. The result, particularly just after the spawning peaks, is a constant flow of eggs drifting along the bottom and collecting in the dead spots behind drop-offs and ledges. When this happens, the trout will often drop back into more traditional lies, where they can feed in relative safety. Don't ignore the edges and current seams when you are looking for fish.

There are a number of egg patterns available, and the standard Glo-Bug will take fish as long as it matches the sockeye egg in color and size. Most commercial Glo-Bugs are too large. Many people prefer beads, and there is no question that they can be exact matches for eggs. A bead slid onto the leader is legal, but is not considered a fly under Alaskan law. Remember that it's illegal to peg a bead more than 2 inches above the hook.

Whatever fly you choose, you need to fish it dead drift and close to the bottom. Real eggs are slightly heavier than water and bounce slowly along the gravel or flow with the current a few inches up. Use a floating line and a 9- or 10-foot leader. In order to avoid stressing the fish by playing them too long, you should use the heaviest tippet that the fish will accept. A 3X leader is about as light as you can get away with and even at that you had better have room to chase your fish. You cannot drag a big Kvichak 'bow upstream with 7-pound test. A split shot just above the fly will get it down and allow it to drift naturally.

Most experienced fishermen prefer yarn indicators because they are so much more sensitive to that brief hesitation that marks a trout closing its mouth around your drifting fly. Don't use brightly colored indicators of any type, particularly red. They may not spook the fish, but they will definitely draw the trout's attention away from the fly. The golf ball–sized hunk of yarn used by some people is unnecessary. It's a strike indicator, not a bobber. Use just enough to mark the drift of your fly. The smaller amount of yarn will also make it easier to determine if your fly is dragging, and it's easier to cast in the wind.

All of this makes an unwieldy setup to throw, particularly if you have a stiff Bristol Bay headwind. Open up your casting loop and slow down your stroke. It will feel like you are lobbing the fly out there instead of casting, but you will cut down on the number of tangles. Mend immediately or use a reach cast to avoid drag. Holman says that the guides at No-See-Um prefer to fish from the boat by drifting down the channels between the eslands, which ensures a long drag-free float.

Trout normally quit feeding if they sense danger. There is sometimes a brief period, however, when the rainbows are so constantly harassed by the male sockeyes that they will continue to feed even when they feel threatened. When this occurs, you can get remarkably close to the fish, guaranteeing a good drift. Once the sockeyes begin to focus on spawning and ignore the trout, the rainbows will revert to their usual spookiness.

Late in the season, when the salmon have started to die, flesh flies and streamers come back into their own. The trout will drop out of the shallow spawning areas into more protected lies. Look for places where salmon carcasses have hung up, and drift a bunny or marabou flesh fly below it. Sculpin patterns will get hammered if you crawl them along the bottom or hang them over the lip of a drop-off.

The Kvichak is a big river, not easy to read, with trophy trout and lots of sockeyes. The scenery is mediocre, the wildlife is scarce, and there are other boats moving up and down the channels. But if you have a single-minded desire to catch a double-digit rainbow, the Kvichak has to be one of the top destinations in the state.

The Kvichak is a big river. Here, a commercial gillnetter heads down to Bristol Bay for the opening of the salmon season.

Stream Facts: Kvichak River

Seasons

- June 8 to April 10; no retention of rainbow trout June 8 to August 31.

Special Regulations

- Only unbaited single hook artificial lures may be used year-round.

- Above the confluence of the Kvichak and Yellow Creek, no retention of rainbow trout from June 8 to Oct. 1. The daily limit Oct. 1 to Oct. 31 is 1 per day, 1 in possession, no size limit. From Nov. 1 to April 9 daily limits for rainbow trout are 5 per day, 5 in possession, only one over 20 inches.

- The daily limit for salmon, except king salmon, in the Kvichak River is 5 per day, 5 in possession; only 2 per day, 2 in possession may be coho salmon. The Kvichak is managed for sockeye escapement, and regulations regarding bag limits and waters open to sport fishing may be changed by emergency order at any time. Never fish for sockeyes in the Kvichak without checking the current status of the regulations. The Bristol Bay emergency order hotline is 907-842-7347.

- Open season for king salmon is May 1 to July 31. The limit for king salmon is 3 per day, 3 in possession, only one fish over 28 inches. The season limit on king salmon is 5. The limit on king salmon less than 20 inches (jacks) is 10 per day, 10 in possession. Any king salmon removed from the water must be retained and become part of the bag limit of the person originally hooking it. A person who intends to release a king salmon may not remove it from the water before releasing it.

- Beads: In all flowing waters of Bristol Bay, attractors (beads) fished ahead of flies or lures must be fixed within 2 inches of the fly or lure, or be free to move (slide) on the line or leader. This applies to both fly and spin-fishing. A bead not attached to the hook is defined as an attractor, not a fly. A bead fished on the line above a bare hook is not legal gear in waters where only flies may be used.

Species

- Rainbow trout average 18 to 24 inches with an occasional fish to 32 inches.

- Arctic char (Dolly Varden) average 16 to 20 inches; present all season.

- Arctic grayling average 14 to 18 inches. Present all season.

- Sockeye (red) salmon average 5 to 7 lbs. Begin entering river about June 18. Run peaks around July 4.

- Silver (coho) salmon average 7 to 9 lbs. Begin entering river about August 15.

- King salmon average 18 to 30 lbs. Begin entering river in late May.

Maps

- *Alaska Atlas and Gazetteer*, page 58

Copper River

The Copper is perhaps the most famous of the Iliamna tributaries. In many ways it epitomizes most flyfishers' vision of an Alaskan river. It's a superb stream for a fly rod, easily waded, and flush with nice rainbows. Public access is essentially nonexistent, but several fly-out lodges have usage permits from the landowner, and there are several outfits that travel up from the bottom by boat. In spite of the difficulties in getting onto the river, it is a fishery that deserves its reputation.

The Copper begins well up in the Chigmit Mountains, about 20 river miles above Intricate Bay on Lake Iliamna. A chain of lakes—Meadow, Upper Copper, and Lower Copper—are connected by a millrace of whitewater, including a set of Class IV rapids between Upper and Lower Copper Lakes. It is beautiful wooded country, but the fishing in this stretch is mediocre and travel down the river difficult.

From a fishing standpoint, the Copper begins at a set of waterfalls about 12 miles upstream from the mouth. The upper drop is only a few feet high, but the lower, horseshoe-shaped falls are about 15 feet high and impassable to salmon, concentrating the fish in the lower stretch of the river.

The land below the falls is private property (native village corporation), and although the river is navigable, and therefore open to the public, the only upriver access is across native lands. As a practical matter, this means that in order to fish the Copper, you need to go with a lodge that has a trespass permit or one that fishes the lower section of the river by jet boat.

The lodges that fish the upper river usually fly into Fog Lake, about a third of the way down from the falls. One group will travel upstream by jet boat while the second group floats down, ensuring that the Copper is one of the few remaining streams that consistently provide a solitary experience for the visiting angler. Other lodges fish the lower part of the river, where solitude is a rarity.

The Copper is a small stream, only 10 to 20 yards across, ideal for a fly rod. It is fast, clear water with lots of rocks and pocket water, making a navigational challenge for jet boats. The upper stretch, below the falls, flows between high banks that are heavily forested with spruce and cottonwood. There are few gravel bars from which to fish, but it has some beautiful deep runs that beg for a fly.

As the river proceeds into the middle section, it becomes shallower, with grass banks, a few streamside bluffs, and more sand bars. There is a fair amount of whitewater, particularly on the sharp bends, and a small ledge drop about halfway down to Lower Pike Lake. Undercut banks provide classic holding water. At the bottom, the river widens out, with a more even flow. All in all, it is a very pretty stream, with an intimacy lacking in its willow and tundra counterparts.

Fishing on the Copper begins in the early summer, with the fry from the previous year's salmon run migrating downstream to Lake Iliamna. They are about an inch long, and tend to move in low-light conditions. The trout are keyed to them, though, and will take a fly opportunistically, even at midday. Small, bright streamers, particularly Thunder Creeks, work well, although no fly seems to work in all conditions. Although the fry are moving downstream, they do so by holding in the current, and then slipping down a foot or so. Try working the flies around the rocks and pocket water, walking them downstream in spurts.

A bushy dry fly will bring up some surprisingly large trout during the late June hatches.

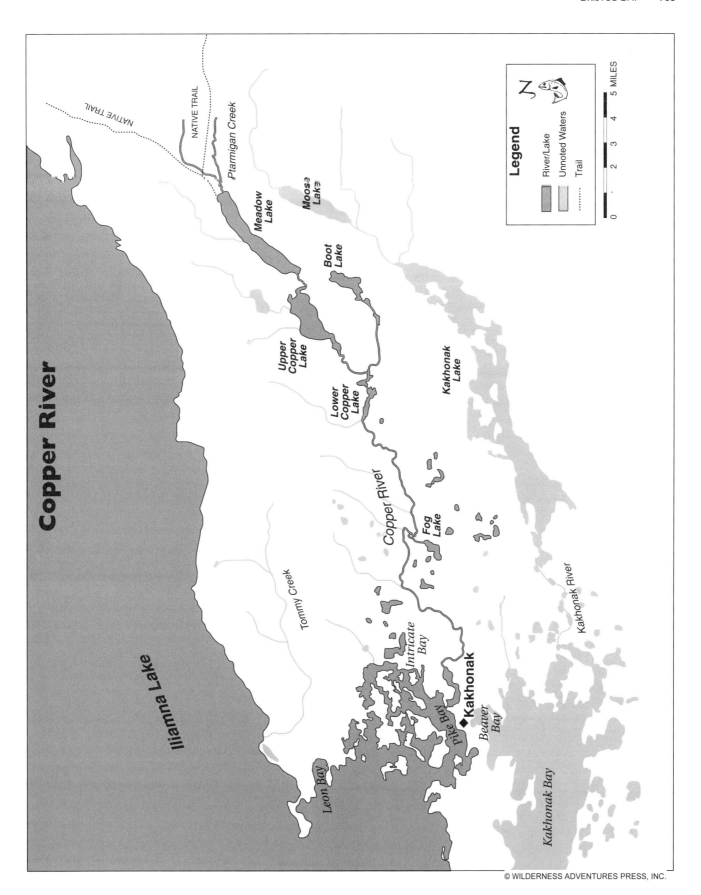

Copper River

Iliamna Lake

NATIVE TRAIL

NATIVE TRAIL

Ptarmigan Creek

Meadow Lake

Moose Lake

Boot Lake

Upper Copper Lake

Lower Copper Lake

Kakhonak Lake

Copper River

Fog Lake

Tommy Creek

Kakhonak River

Intricate Bay

Kakhonak

Pike Bay

Beaver Bay

Leon Bay

Kakhonak Bay

Legend

River/Lake
Unnoted Waters
Trail

N

0 1 2 3 4 5 MILES

© WILDERNESS ADVENTURES PRESS, INC.

The Copper is perhaps best known for its dry-fly fishing, though. In a state where dry flies are only occasionally effective, the Copper stands out as providing relatively consistent surface fishing. The topwater action lasts well into July, providing opportunities for trout fishing that are missing in most of the state, where the sockeyes drive the rainbows out of good holding water and back into the lakes.

Bill Sims, of Newhalen Lodge, has been fishing the Copper since he opened the lodge many years ago. He says that the Copper hosts good populations of caddis and black and brown stoneflies, with the best action coming in the evening. He and his well-experienced guides like Stimulators, Elk Hair Caddis, Parachute Adams, and similar western-style dries. Royal Wulffs and other attractors account for a lot of their clients' fish. The rainbows are more likely to hit a dead-drifted, drag-free presentation. The river has a lot of char, though, and they will take a skated fly, usually preferring it to a free-floating one.

As in most rivers, nymphs will catch more and larger fish than dry flies. Beadhead Prince Nymphs, Pheasant Tails (particularly with a flashback), Zug Bugs, and caddis emergers are all good flies for the Copper. This is a flyfishing-only river, and unfortunately, that means you cannot use a dropper. Only a single fly is allowed.

Nymphs can be effective when "high-sticked" on a tight line through pocket water or fished with a strike indicator. I avoid red indicators like the plague. The fish are so keyed to eating eggs that anything round and red attracts their attention. They don't necessarily spook, but they won't pay any attention to your fly if they spot the indicator. White yarn is the best in most situations. If the day is bright overcast and you can't see the white indicator against the glare, switch to black yarn. It will stand out better than fluorescent colors under those conditions.

Although insect life is important to Copper River rainbows, there are also sculpins and sticklebacks present. Bunny Muddlers and Zonkers are worth a try. Leeches also work well. In fact, Lake Iliamna has a large population of lampreys, and big String Leeches can be effective in all its rivers.

Because the Copper River fish are primarily residents, as opposed to fish migrating in from the lake, the fishing remains good throughout the summer. When the sockeyes pair up and begin to spawn, though, the fishing heats up. As usual, egg patterns are the most productive, but leeches and flesh flies also work as the season progresses.

The rainbows on the Copper are not particularly large, at least compared to their cousins in Lower Talarik and Kvichak. Sims says that the size range often varies from year to year, as different age classes mature, die out, and are replaced by a group of smaller fish. Sizes may run from 17 inches one year to 20 inches or more a year or two later. These are only the averages, though, and there are always a few larger fish around. Bigger fish will move upstream when the salmon are spawning. Char are plentiful and usually run a bit smaller than the rainbows. Although grayling are infrequent (an anomaly, considering the abundant bug life), they tend to be large.

The Gibraltar has some of Alaska's finest dry fly fishing, particularly during the sunny days of June and early July.

Gibraltar River

Gibraltar Lake lies cupped in a valley on the south side of Lake Iliamna. Fed by smaller streams like Dream Creek, it is the headwaters of a river that is a favorite with anglers lucky enough to fish it. The Gibraltar River runs for about 6 miles to its outlet on Lake Iliamna. It is a small stream, about 50 feet across, but it holds numerous fish throughout its length. The fishing is almost exclusively for rainbows and sockeyes. There are some Dolly Varden present, but for some reason there are almost no grayling in any of the streams flowing into the south side of Lake Iliamna. Like the Copper and Lower Talarik, the Gibraltar is flyfishing only and catch and release for rainbows.

Gibraltar's charm is in large part a function of the fact that it sees less pressure than many of the other nearby rivers, and there is a reason for that. The land surrounding the lake and river is private property, belonging to the people of the nearby village of Kakhonak. Although the waters are navigable, and therefore public, it is not possible to inflate your raft or get picked up at the bottom without trespassing. And the local villagers are very sensitive about strangers entering their land without permission. Several of the local lodges have negotiated trespass fees that allow them to use the river, but the cost is high enough to keep casual anglers off the water. Some lodges run boats upstream from the bottom, taking advantage of the public access, so most of the fishing here takes place in the lower stretches of the river.

The best way to appreciate the Gibraltar is to float it. The mouth of Gibraltar Lake is surrounded by native allotments (a form of homestead) and the use of that land for landing a plane and inflating a raft is part of the trespass-fee system. The river itself is moderately fast, flowing about 3 to 5 miles per hour. It is crystal-clear and for the most part flows over gravel bottom, ideal spawning habitat for the run of sockeyes that moves in during early July. There is a stretch near the middle with a bit of whitewater and a few rocks to be avoided, but it is not a difficult float. The river is tucked between alder-covered banks, which makes a backcast problematic at times.

Unlike many Alaskan rivers, there is an even distribution of rainbows in the Gibraltar. That is not to say that some portions of the river don't fish better than others. Don't neglect the first half-mile as the river flows out of Gibraltar Lake. The rainbows will hold there in the spring waiting for smolt that wintered over in Gibraltar Lake to make their run to the sea. In the fall, many of the trout that follow the sockeyes upstream will hold just before the salmon enter the lake. About a mile and half downstream, just where the riverbanks open up a bit, there's a stretch

that should be worked hard.

Early-season fishing on the Gibraltar is some of the best in the area. The smolt that reared the prior winter in Gibraltar Lake have begun to migrate to the ocean. At the same time, the eggs laid in the river itself the previous fall have hatched and the fry, about an inch long, are dropping down into Lake Iliamna, where they will spend their first year. Thunder Creeks and other small streamers (size 10) will work as fry imitations, and Zonkers, Alaska Mary Anns, and Double Bunnies (tied about 2½ inches long) are good imitations of smolt. These tiny salmon are facing into the current but dropping downstream, so fish them accordingly. By July, the smolt have moved out of the river, but there are still plenty of fry hiding in the slower edges. Try hanging a Thunder Creek along the cutbanks and next to any back eddies.

Sculpins are plentiful in the river, and the trout have seen enough leeches and lamprey eels over the course of the winter to attack anything long, black, and slinky. Work a weighted leech or bunny fly around the rocks and structure.

All that sunken stuff is fine, but if you hit a warm sunny day when the caddis and stoneflies are coming off and the trout are looking up you will know why people love the Gibraltar. It's one of the few streams in Bristol Bay

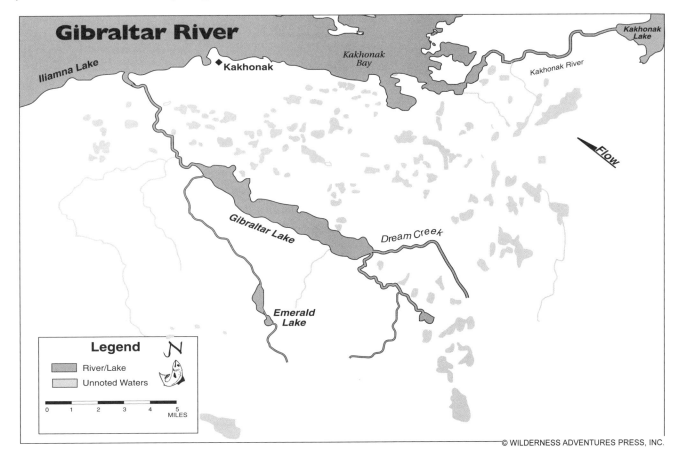

Gibraltar River

Iliamna Lake
◆ Kakhonak
Kakhonak Bay
Kakhonak Lake
Kakhonak River
Flow
Gibraltar Lake
Dream Creek
Emerald Lake

Legend
N
River/Lake
Unnoted Waters

0 1 2 3 4 5 MILES

with reliable dry-fly fishing during late June and early July. Small dark stoneflies and caddis are the predominant insect species, and trout feed not only on the adults, but also the nymphs. Caddis hatches peak in July, lengthening the period of good fishing beyond that available in most rivers.

This is a freestone river, and you'll need buoyant flies that ride high and can be easily seen. An Elk Hair Caddis in sizes 12 to 16 will cover most caddis hatches. If the fish aren't hitting a dead drift, try skating the fly. For stoneflies, I like attractors like the Stimulator and Madam X, usually tied with a peacock herl body. Again try both dead drifts and twitching the fly to give it some action. Renegades, Parachute Adams, Royal Wulffs, Black Wulffs, Double Humpies, and Katmai Sliders are good flies to have in the box. I usually carry a few very small dark patterns for the occasional trout that you find keying on midges. There is rarely a hatch prolific enough to cause the fish to become selective, but like trout anywhere, they become more careful if they have been fished over.

Nymphing during the early season can also be very productive, particularly in the middle of the day when the fry are not moving. I like Beadhead Prince Nymphs (sizes 10 to 16), Gold-Ribbed Hare's Ears, and Flashback Pheasant Tails. Sight fishing to large rainbows with a high-stick nymphing technique, or dead drift with an indicator, will definitely keep you focused.

Although most people fish the Gibraltar for rainbows, there can be good fishing for sockeyes when they move into the river. Most of them are headed up into the lake and beyond, so they are still pretty bright when they hit the lower river. Sockeyes are an anomaly among Pacific salmon, feeding not on baitfish, but on krill and plankton (hence their bright red flesh).

They don't have the instinctive trigger that prompts other species to chase a fly and can be notoriously difficult to tempt. Once they are hooked, though, they make it all worthwhile, with an aerial fight and head-shaking runs. Look for fish that are on the move, rather than holding. Get the fly right at their level—they won't move for it. Although there are a few patterns that are effective in sizes as big as a 2, most successful fishermen use a small (size 4 to 6) sparsely tied fly. Sockeye Johns, Comets, and Brassies are all good.

The real action starts in August, when the sockeyes are paired up and the rainbows are looking to put on enough fat to survive another winter. The entire length of the Gibraltar will hold spawning salmon, and the 'bows will be lying behind them. There is still some dry-fly fishing available in the early part of August (try deer-hair mice), but once the eggs hit the water, the trout become fixated.

The eggs have a specific gravity just slightly heavier than water, which means that loose eggs that escape the redds swirl and tumble just above the bottom. I like to fish a strike indicator and just enough weight to get the fly down to the fish's level. Trout will move for an egg, so you have a large feeding lane to work with. Even on rivers like the Gibraltar, the fish have become selective. It is no longer good enough to drift anything round and red in front of them. Carry some variations in color and make sure you have the size right. Many commercial patterns are too large.

By September, the trout are fattening up, and some bigger fish begin to move in. Eggs become scarcer and the trout become more opportunistic. Flesh flies are the standard answer, but they are by no means the only patterns the fish will hit. Try those dark sculpins and leeches again. And although I am quite sure that no trout has ever seen a purple leech sucking a salmon egg, it makes a pretty good fly.

The Gibraltar is a wonderful little stream much appreciated by those lucky enough to fish it. Its exclusivity can be a bit galling, but it preserves a sense of privacy that most other Bristol Bay rivers lost long ago. If you get a chance, and can afford the ticket, it is a gem.

Lower Talarik Creek

Lower Talarik Creek has long had a reputation for big rainbows. Most of the fish stories that originate here begin with fish in the 8- to 12-pound range. And most of the people who have heard those stories are stunned when they see Lower Talarik for the first time. It is indeed a creek—small, easily waded, and because of its small size, very crowded. The floatplanes arrive at first light, the guides jockeying to get their clients onto the good runs before the next plane can unload. Three planes tied up on the beach means that the best water will already be taken, and most lodges will opt to take their clients elsewhere.

Lower Talarik is an unassuming stream, flowing through low scrub willow and wet muskeg as it wends its way across a featureless plain on the way to Iliamna Lake. It looks no different than half a dozen other tundra streams, and expectations normally would be for rainbows in the 18- to 21-inch range. But Talarik has a unique strain of fish that grow even larger than those in other Iliamna rivers. That, combined with ideal feeding conditions, produces a remarkable number of 30-inch fish.

There are anecdotal stories of fish arriving in the river in October, already full of eggs, and wintering over under the ice in order to spawn in the spring. In fact, ADF&G's extensive tagging program has shown that most of the spring spawners spend the winter near the outlet of the lake, returning to the creek in early April. Although trout

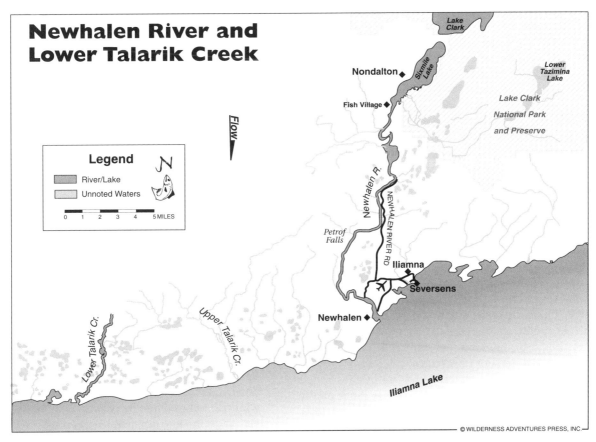

Newhalen River and Lower Talarik Creek

Legend
River/Lake
Unnoted Waters

0 1 2 3 4 5 MILES

Flow

N

Lake Clark

Nondalton

Fish Village

Skumlie Lake

Lower Tazimina Lake

Lake Clark National Park and Preserve

Newhalen R.

Petrof Falls

NEWHALEN RIVER RD

Iliamna

Seversens

Newhalen

Upper Talarik Cr.

Lower Talarik Cr.

Iliamna Lake

© WILDERNESS ADVENTURES PRESS, INC.

do not have the same homing instincts as spawning salmon, most of these fish were probably born in the river and make up a unique genetic stock. Like the fabled Lahontan cutthroats, they simply are capable of growing larger than their near kin.

The spawners are actually one of two overlapping stocks that utilize Lower Talarik. The spawners drop back into the lake in late June after feeding on the outgoing salmon fry. In August a second surge of fish appears, following the spawning sockeyes. These fish include not only the native Talarik fish, but also opportunistic fish from other watersheds. Regardless of their source, the late-fall fishing, into October, yields an inordinate number of monsters.

The last quarter-mile of Lower Talarik, known as "the ditch," flows behind a low grassy berm that parallels the lake in a fashion reminiscent of a barrier island. Depending on the wind direction, planes will land on the ditch and tie up in the small pond. If winds are not favorable, they may land on a nearby pothole and walk to the creek. Only on rare days of no wind will pilots put down on the lake itself. A few experienced bush pilots will put down on wheels on a spot on the tundra near the adjoining ADF&G cabin.

Some of the best fishing in Lower Talarik is in the ditch, particularly at the upper and lower ends. It is an

unappealing stretch of water, but amazingly productive. At the upper end, the river makes a right-angle turn towards the mountains. About a quarter-mile upstream from the bend is a run known as "the rock." A large pyramid-shaped rock juts from the river, marking one of the most amazing fishing holes in Alaska. Lodges have been known to travel by boat in the darkness to get to the rock before rival planes have enough light to land.

For those who don't beat the crowds to those three prime spots, there is still good fishing upstream, particularly later in the season when the salmon have moved up and are starting to spawn. The fish run a bit smaller than those in the lower stretches (everything is relative—you may still get a 25-incher). There are two forks to the river and both hold fish. Most people fish the western fork. A few anglers will land on the headwater lakes of either fork and work downstream.

As on most Alaskan streams, the trout fishing on Lower Talarik comes during two periods. Some of the spring spawners hang around until mid-June (the season opens June 8) feeding on thousands of newly hatched fry that are migrating downstream to the lake. The fishing is far less productive than during the fall, but there is the chance of tagging a big fish. Small (size 10) streamers are the most productive flies. Try a Thunder Creek fished high in the water column. Sculpin imitations, bunny flies, and leeches are also effective, particularly in black and dark olive. Fish them right on the bottom.

But Talarik's reputation is built on the fall fishery. The sockeyes arrive a bit later here than in some other area streams, usually about mid-July. By early August, the rainbows have begun to follow them in. The trout, excited by the smell of the ripening salmon, will hit an egg pattern well before any spawning has begun to take place.

Another alternative is to fish a nymph behind the salmon. The female sockeyes, in building the redds, stir up the insect life in the substrate, and the trout will hit Pheasant Tails and a variety of beadheads. Fishing a streamer is almost impossible early on. The male sockeyes are very aggressive toward other fish, and you will spend all your time battling some over-the-hill spawner. At this stage, the males will also grab any eggs that drift by. The secret is to drop your egg so it sinks just behind the paired-up salmon, which is where the trout will be lying.

As the season progresses, the number and size of the fish grow. Once the spawning begins, the trout will lock onto the eggs and become selective as to size and color. As sockeyes begin to die, flesh flies can be productive, and because the salmon no longer have the strength to be aggressive, you can fish sculpins and bunny flies. Brian Kraft, of Alaska's Sportsman's Lodge, a fly-out lodge on the Kvichak, loves big Articulated Leeches in black and olive. His clients do well on flies that are sometimes 4 inches long (remember, these are *big* trout).

The bottom stretch of the river has such a low gradient that its depth is affected by the water height in the lake. Bill Sims, of Newhalen Lodge, has been fishing Lower Talarik for over 20 years, and he compares it to tidal streams where the lake water slows the outflow of the creek, effectively deepening the ditch. In low-water years, that effect disappears and fewer trout move into the creek to feed in the fall.

Lower Talarik has a well-deserved reputation for producing large rainbows from a small stream. This fish is only average.

Stream Facts: Copper River, Gibraltar River, Lower Talarik Creek

Seasons
- June 8 to April 10; no retention of rainbow trout June 8 to August 31.

Special Regulations
- Only unbaited single hook artificial lures may be used year-round, except in lake waters more than ½ mile from inlet or outlet streams.

- No retention of rainbow trout is allowed June 8 to Oct. 31 in Lower Talarik Creek, Upper Talarik Creek, Gibraltar River drainage, and the Copper River drainage downstream from Lower Copper Lake, and in the waters within ½ mile of these streams outlet into Lake Iliamna.

- Only single-hook artificial flies (one fly only, no dropper) may be used June 8 to Oct. 31 in Lower Talarik Creek, Gibraltar River drainage and Copper River drainage, and within ½ mile of these streams outlet into Lake Iliamna.

- Beads: In all flowing waters of Bristol Bay, attractors (beads) fished ahead of flies or lures must be fixed within 2 inches of the fly or lure, or be free to move (slide) on the line or leader. This applies to both fly and spin-fishing. A bead not attached to the hook is defined as an attractor, not a fly. A bead fished on the line above a bare hook is not legal gear in waters where only flies may be used.

Species
- Rainbow trout in Copper and Gibraltar Rivers average 16 to 22 inches with an occasional fish to 28 inches. Lower Talarik Creek fish average 20 to 26 inches with a significant number of larger fish.

- Arctic char (Dolly Varden) average 16 to 20 inches; present all season.

- Sockeye (red) salmon average 5 to 7 lbs. Begin entering river about June 18. Run peaks around July 4.

River Characteristics
- These are all small clear streams with excellent rainbow fishing. The Copper and Gibraltar have smaller resident fish, but provide good dry-fly fishing well into July. Lower Talarik fish move in from the lake, and are present only during portions of the summer. They are much larger than you would expect from a river this size, however.

Maps
- *Alaska Atlas and Gazetteer*, pages 59, 60

Newhalen River

The Newhalen is big, brawling river that drains the Lake Clark and Tazimina Lakes systems. It flows past the town of Iliamna, within a short walk of the airport, making it one of the most accessible rivers in Bristol Bay. Most of the fishing takes place near the end of the runway, just below a set of very large rapids (Class V) usually referred to as simply "the falls."

The Newhalen is known primarily for its sometimes-spectacular sockeye salmon fishing. During a good season, the fish stack up in huge numbers below the falls, providing an opportunity for anglers to fill the fishbox. The sockeyes arrive a little later than they do in many area streams, showing up around July 10. Unfortunately, the runs have suffered badly over the last few years. The reasons are unknown, but probably are environmental rather than man-caused, although overfishing by the commercial fleet may contribute to the problem. Hopefully, the problem is cyclical, and once we return to the historic levels the Newhalen will again be a river of easy opportunity.

Although it is primarily fished as a salmon river, the trout fishing is as good as you would expect in a major Lake Iliamna drainage. A number of very large trout patrol the lower stretches of the river. However, as the salmon runs have dwindled, so has the quality of the trout fishing.

The Newhalen is not an easy river to fish for trout or salmon with a fly rod. It is big, deep, and fast. There are some places that you can cast from the bank to good water, but the best way to fish here is with a boat. There are local guides who will take you out into the flatter water near the mouth or into some fishable stretches above the falls. This can be particularly effective for rainbows, including some of those large ones. The best rainbow fishing is in the early season, when they wait at the mouth for the outgoing smolt and fry, or in the fall when the flesh and eggs of spawners are drifting down.

Smolt patterns and leeches are the flies of choice in the spring. The lake has a large population of lampreys, which are often a dirty white color and about 2½ inches long. Try a big String Leech tied with a strip of rabbit fur. Black and purple are also good colors. In the fall, egg and flesh patterns work best, but Bunny Leeches can still be effective. For sockeyes, big Brassies or Teeny nymphs work well.

When the Newhalen salmon are in full swing, the competition can be fierce, and not only from the two-legged anglers. Fish waste, poor camping practices, and too many salmon stored in coolers has led to some significant wildlife problems, usually resulting in an unfortunate number of dead bears. Much of the problem has been caused by people who see the sport fishery as an opportunity to take home semi-commercial quantities of smoked salmon. The aroma of slowly-cooked salmon is irresistible to the local bears, who find stealing fish much easier than catching them.

The Newhalen will never be a prime fly-rod stream, but it does provide the option of good salmon fishing with easy access. A cheap flight from Anchorage to Iliamna and some camping equipment will put you into some true Bristol Bay fishing.

ILIAMNA AND IGIUGIG

Population: 94
Alaska Area Code: 907

LODGES AND GUIDES

No-See-Um Lodge, www.noseeumlodge.com; fly-out lodge on banks of Kvichak; (winter) 6218 Beechcraft Circle, Wasilla, AK 99654, 746-5395; (summer) P.O. Box 382, King Salmon, AK, 439-3070

Newhalen Lodge, www.newhalenlodge.com, newhalenlodge@gci.net; 3851 Chiniak Dr., Anchorage, AK 99515; 522-3355 (winter); 294-2233, (summer)

Iliaska Lodge, www.iliaska.com; flyfishing-only, fly-out lodge with exclusive access fishing; (winter) 6160 Fairpoint Dr., Anchorage, AK 99507, 337-9844; (summer) P.O. Box 228, Iliamna, AK, 571-1221

Ole Creek Lodge, www.olecreeklodge.com; Kvichak River; (winter) 506 Ketchikan Ave., Fairbanks, AK, 452-2421; (summer) Igiugig, AK, 533-3474

Big Mountain Lodge, www.bigmountainlodge.com; Kvichak River; 3000 McCollie, Anchorage, AK, 99517; 1-800-247-0601

Kvichak Lodge, www.kvichaklodge.com; Kvichak River; 403 E 24th, Anchorage, AK 99503, 272-0209

Rainbow River Lodge, flyfishing-only, fly-out lodge with exclusive access fishing; www.alaskarainbowriverlodge.com; (winter) P.O. Box 1070, Silver City, NM 88062, 505-388-2259; (summer) P.O. Box 330, Iliamna AK, 570-1210

Alaska's Legends Lodge, 4 guests max; (winter) 13389 Birchview Dr. NE Bemidji, MN, 218-586-3313; (summer) P.O. Box PVY, Iliamna AK, 571-1740

Copper River Lodge, info@sweetwatertravel.com; 215 E. Lewis, Suite 305, Livingston, MT 59047; 1-888-294-0624

Alaska Rainbow Lodge, www.alaskarainbowlodge.com; fly-out lodge, P.O. Box 39, King Salmon, AK 99613; 246-1506 (summer); P.O. Box 10459, Fort Worth, TX 76114, 817-236-1024 (winter)

Rainbow King Lodge, fly-out lodge; www.rainbowking.com; (winter) 333 S. State St. V PMB 126, Lake Oswego, OR, 503-697-4415; (summer) P.O. Box 106, Iliamna, AK, 571-1277

Alaska Sportsmans Lodge, www.alaskasportsmanslodge.com; P.O. Box 231985, Anchorage, AK 99523-1985; 907-276-7605 (Oct-May); 907-533-2121

Bristol Bay Sportfishing, www.bristol-bay.com; (winter) 212 N. 4th Ave. #139, Sandpoint, ID, 208-263-8954; (summer) P.O. Box 164, Iliamna, 571-1325

Rainbow Point Lodge, www.akrpl.com; (winter) 1441 S. Pennsylvania Ave. Apt. 2, Casper, WY 1-877-850-5858 or 1-617-899-2326; (summer) P.O. Box 390, Iliamna, AK, 570-1757

Fishing Unlimited, www.alaskalodge.com; Fly-out lodge; P.O. Box 190301, Anchorage, AK, 99519, 243-5899

Valhalla Lodge, www.valhallalodge.com; 243-6096, P.O. Box 190583, Anchorage AK, 99519

Chilaska, www.chilaska.com; custom float trips, P.O. Box 47039, Pedro Bay, AK, 99647, 571-1502

ACCOMMODATIONS IN ILIAMNA (MAY ALSO HAVE GUIDES, BOAT RENTALS, ETC. AVAILABLE)

Iliamna Lake Lodge, P.O. Box 110, Iliamna, 571-1525

Red Quill Lodge, P.O. Box 49, Iliamna, AK, 571-1215

Airport Hotel, PO Box 157, Iliamna, AK 99606, 571-1276

Beaver B Resort, Iliamna, AK, 99606, 282-2230

Grams Café B&B, P.O. Box 248, Iliamna, AK, 571-1463

Kokhanok Falls Lodge, Kokhanok, 571-1300

Lake Crest B&B, Iliamna, 99606, 282-2262

Point Adventure Lodge, P.O. Box 141, Iliamna, 571-1251

ACCOMMODATIONS IN IGUIGIG (MAY ALSO HAVE GUIDES, BOAT RENTALS, ETC. AVAILABLE)

Blueberry Island Lodge, ww.blueberryislandlodge.com; on banks of Kvichak, provides rooms kitchen and boat for self-guided fishing; P.O. Box 16, Naknek, AK 99633, 246-8228

Igiugig Boarding House, 907-533-3216

Kvichak Cabin, 907-533-3216

Andrews Cabins, 907-571-1648

NUSHAGAK AND WOOD/TIKCHIK AREA

The Nushagak River, with its tributaries the Mulchatna and Wood/Tikchik drainages, and its sister river, the Togiak, drains thousands of square miles reaching deep into the interior of Alaska. Unlike the Katmai and Iliamna areas, this is not predominantly a sockeye-based ecosystem. Although there is a tremendous run of reds (as Alaskans invariably call sockeyes) in the Wood River Lakes, the primary species in most systems are kings, chums, and cohos. As a result of the vast size of the system, and the migration and spawning patterns of the salmon, the trout and char fishing is more scattered than in the shorter, sockeye-rich streams to the east.

These rivers are best fished by boat rather than plane. Even the fly-out lodges use their floatplanes to commute to jet boats tied up along the rivers. For the fisherman interested in an unguided trip, there are lakes and rivers that will provide miles and days of relative solitude and pockets of truly great fishing. Rafts, kayaks, and riverboats will all get you to fish.

For those who like big game, the Nushagak has the largest run of king salmon in the state, with 50,000 to 65,000 fish moving upstream. There is also some excellent coho fishing on some rivers. Much of this takes place amid some of the best scenery in the state.

Nushagak River

The Nushagak is an immense river system that drains over 10,000 square miles of western Alaska. The main stem of the river is 275 miles long. It also picks up two large tributaries, the Mulchatna and the Nuyakuk, so that by the time it reaches its lower stretches it is over a mile wide. Along its length, a fisherman can find everything from small-stream dry-fly fishing for grayling to some of the state's best fishing for king salmon.

In order to make sense of a river this size, it is necessary to divide it into sections, and the Nushagak readily lends itself to such a division. The upper river is a single channel stream with pockets of excellent fishing for rainbow, char, and grayling. In the center, the river braids up into an area that received the state's first designation as a catch-and-release fishery. The lower stretch is broad and deep, and between 40,000 and 75,000 king salmon pass through it in a four-week period every summer.

Nushagak River and Tributaries

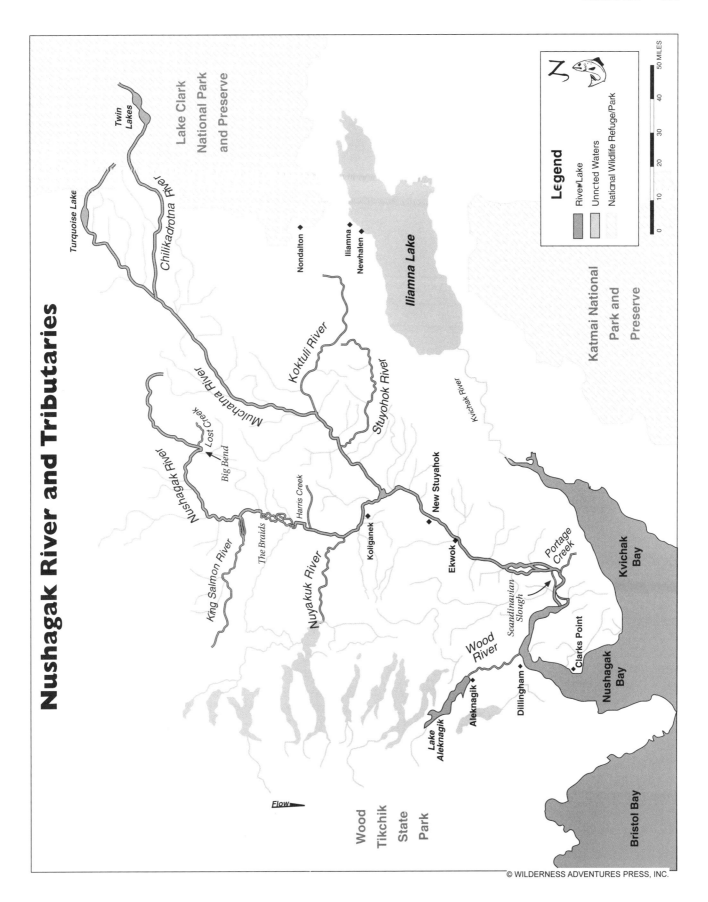

© WILDERNESS ADVENTURES PRESS, INC.

The upper Nushagak has a healthy population of big rainbows, to go with its salmon char and grayling.

Upper Nushagak

From an angler's standpoint, the Nushagak begins at Big Bend, 110 air miles north of Dillingham and about 75 miles east of Iliamna. The name comes from a stretch of the river that winds around a steep-sided mountain, almost doubling back on itself. This is the highest point on the river that can accommodate a floatplane. The Nushagak does not flow out of a lake, so access requires a stretch of river deep and straight enough for landing and takeoff. At high water, a Beaver can put down a few miles above Big Bend. At lower water levels, it may be necessary to put in a few miles downstream. This is not a difficult float, but it is a long (read expensive) flight, and the upper river receives little pressure.

If you are lucky enough to get access above the bend, you will find some large king spawning beds, and the fishing for rainbows and Dollys can be spectacular (kings are protected in the upper river). Lost Creek enters the river directly opposite the bend. It is a tiny stream, but has good fishing. Access is limited without a jet boat, but the

lower stretches are worth exploring. Just below Lost Creek, look for spawning kings and sockeyes. Much of the river can be waded, and this is a very productive stretch.

Western Alaska Fly Fishing operates a tent camp about a mile and a half below Big Bend and they run riverboats upstream into waters that are otherwise untouched. There are no good campsites for several miles below Western Alaska's operation, so you need to allow an extra hour or so to reach an appropriate gravel bar.

The fish are not equally distributed anywhere in the Nushagak system, but this part of the river has enough spawning beds that the fishing is fairly consistent. Look for straight stretches with an even flow where kings or sockeyes are paired up.

The surrounding hills are covered with spruce forest, with enough fallen trees to create snags and some large logjams. The river is big enough that these are not a navigational problem, but they provide cover for trout and should be fished carefully. This is particularly true later in the summer, when the salmon have begun to die and the carcasses are trapped.

There is good grayling fishing throughout the upper river. I even came across a hatch of size 10 pale yellow mayflies one afternoon that had big grayling, and a few rainbows, feeding steadily. We were a little short on oversized Light Cahills, though.

The 20 or so miles of river below Big Bend hold a number of scattered pockets stacked with Dolly Varden and rainbows. Both species are brightly colored and run from 2 to 4 pounds. There aren't a lot of sockeyes in the Nushagak (at least compared to other major rivers), but the trout seem to prefer them to most other salmon. Always fish any area in which you see sockeyes holding, even if they have not started to spawn.

King salmon can be equally good. Their distinctive brick-red color can be seen at a distance. King eggs are slightly larger and more orange than sockeye eggs, but these trout haven't seen enough artificials to become overly selective. Chums will also attract trout, but they tend to spawn in the tiny feeder sloughs and creeks and are more common downstream in the braids.

I often rig two rods for this stretch of river, one with a strike indicator and egg pattern and a second with a leech or Woolly Bugger. Much of the fishing from the boat is done with the leech, particularly in the riffles and tailouts between pools. Any time we spot salmon, though, I can quickly switch to an egg and drift it behind them. There are a lot of nice grayling in the Nushagak, and they will readily take the egg pattern. The back sloughs have pike that will attack any kind of topwater fly.

There are also coho in the deeper, slower stretches. It is usually not productive to cast blindly for them, but if you spot them rolling on the surface or see them lying in pools, you can sight fish to them. Brightly colored bunny flies, Flash Flies, and Egg-Sucking Leeches all work well.

The character of the river changes dramatically just above the Chichitnok River. From there down to the confluence with King Salmon River, the Nushagak becomes a long slow-moving pool. Fishing is mediocre, and if there is an upstream wind (and Murphy's law is always in effect) it is a hard row with a fully-loaded raft. This is also an easy place to lose track of your location. A GPS is not essential, but you should keep track of your movement on the map. The penalty can be a hard row to reach your take-out point on time or spending far too much time in a stretch of river with little fishing.

King Salmon River is the major tributary on the upper Nushagak, and it recaptures the feel of the Big Bend area. It's small enough to be manageable, is surrounded by spruce forest, and its riffles and runs are full of spawning salmon, which rainbows and Dollys follow upriver. It is accessible only by jet boat, but Western Alaska Fly Fishing has a camp on it, and several other outfitters run boats up from its confluence with the Nushagak. Most rafters floating down from Big Bend will pull out at the mouth of the King Salmon.

The Braids

Below King Salmon River, the Nushagak separates into a maze of smaller channels. Like the upper river, this stretch is a rainbow and char fishery. The banks and islands are covered with cottonwood and spruce, and although they shift and move through the years, the channels are large enough that sweepers are not a significant problem. There are a lot of gravel bars, and camping is good through this stretch. This is fairly slow water, and during periods of heavy rain, it will silt up.

The braids are most efficiently fished from a powerboat, which allows exploration of the various channels. It is also possible to fish here with a raft, though. The smaller channels and those with riffles are more easily waded and you have a better chance of pulling over and fishing a spot before you blow by it. About half a dozen fly-out lodges fish this stretch, as well as a several river-based outfits. But there is enough water that it doesn't feel crowded.

This section of the river is most productive during June, July, and August. The trout are not particularly large by Alaskan standards, with most running 16 to 20 inches. A 25-inch fish is big for this river, although there are a few that will go even larger. In July and August, sea-run Dolly Varden arrive in numbers, and there are some nice fish

among them.

In July, the kings and chums arrive. The chums are the first to spawn, and they prefer the slower and shallower channels. The kings will look for somewhat heavier water, but don't forget that it is illegal to fish for them above Harris Creek. Some sockeyes spawn in the braids. Look for them in channels with finer gravel than that chosen by the kings.

Regardless of the species, the trout and char will be lining up behind them. Chum and king eggs are a size larger than sockeye eggs, but the trout are not highly selective. The egg patterns should be fished dead drift, usually with a strike indicator. However, at the end of the drift, allow the fly to hang momentarily in the current. It is totally unnatural, but frequently a char that has ignored a free-drifting egg will hammer it as soon as it swings to a stop.

The fishing in August is essentially the same as July, with more emphasis on fishing behind sockeyes and the few silvers that move in. Flesh flies become more effective, particularly in the snags and sweepers. Dan Michels of Crystal Creek Lodge fishes the braids regularly and recommends that you look for cover in the side channels and work a ginger Bunny Bugger or marabou flesh pattern back into the branches.

The salmon will be spawning in the riffles. But August rains can silt the river up badly, and if that occurs, the fishing will deteriorate dramatically. By early September, the first good rain will raise the river and wash the salmon carcasses out. Once that happens, the trout will move out, and the fishing declines.

There are a lot of small grayling in the braids, and although there is little dry-fly fishing for trout in the Nushagak, the grayling are always looking up. The back sloughs hold pike, and they can provide a few hours distraction from the fast-water fish. Look for weeds and cover, and a lack of baby ducks. Use a short length of wire leader or they will snip off your flies as fast as you can re-rig.

The most effective flies are probably streamers, particularly red and white or red and yellow. However, it is much more fun to take them on the surface. They will tear up your flies, so you don't want to waste those elegant eyes-and-whiskers mouse patterns on them. Tie up some rough spun-deer-hair bugs in red and yellow or use a cheap popper. Throw the fly back into the weeds and chug it out in foot-long strips. Just be sure you have needle-nosed pliers or long forceps for removing the hook without the pike removing your finger.

Lower River

The braids end around Harris Creek, and the character of the river changes to a broad even flow through low-lying muskeg. The river swells with the inflow from its major tributaries. The Nuyakuk, which drains the Tikchik system, comes in from the west. The fishing is poor from that confluence down to the next major tributary, the Mulchatna. There are a few silvers, but it is not good holding water for king salmon and there are essentially no rainbows.

The lower river, from the Mulchatna down to Scandinavian Slough, is a major king fishery. Between 50,000 and 100,000 king salmon move through every year in June and July. Most years there are 60,000 to 70,000 fish in the river. The season for kings runs from May 1 to late July (the closing date varies) with the peak of the run coming in late June and early July.

The Nushagak probably provides the best king salmon fishing in the state (but the Kanektok, because it is much smaller, provides better flyfishing for kings). The fish are smaller than the monsters of the Kenai, running about 30 pounds, but the success ratio is much higher, with several fish per day rather than several days per fish being the norm.

The lower river is essentially a boat-fishing area. Kings prefer the deeper channels, which are often impossible to reach from the bank. Except for a few places near Portage Creek, the fish are constantly moving. Salmon do not enter the river in a steady stream. Instead, they come in surges. Although it begins as a function of the tides, the separation between concentrations of fish continues well upstream.

Fishing for kings is a matter of finding them, and that search must be done on a daily basis. The guides are following the fish regularly and know the spots in a broad expanse of water where they are likely to hold or cross a shallow bar or otherwise be vulnerable to an angler. Fly-out lodges have the added advantage of spotting the fish from the air.

Although the success rate is far below that of a guided trip, it is possible to look for fish on your own. Some outfitters have established spike camps and will provide a boat and motor to unguided fishermen. Don't bother blind fishing—it's rarely successful. Look for V-shaped wakes and nervous water. The secret is to find fish that are holding on the edge of a slough or backwater within casting distance or find a corner where the fish are crossing a shallow bar and can be intercepted.

There are sand bars and sand flats both above and below Portage Creek that border a slot of deeper water. They can provide a good opportunity to ambush fish within casting range. Check the back sloughs and side channels for rolling fish. If you see a single salmon roll, it is probably indicative of many more fish holding deep. At times the fish will stack up in slack water.

The lower river is so big that it's difficult to fish with a fly rod. Long casts are the order of the day, a tiring experience with the 10- or 12-weight rods needed to hold these fish in the current. Ty Johnson, of Bear Bay Lodge, sees a lot more clients interested in using spey rods and says that the lower 'Nush provides ideal water for spey casts. They help get the distance needed and can throw the heavy sinking heads needed get the fly deep.

Fat Freddies, bright bunny flies, and other big gaudy creations are the most effective. Ty says that tube flies work great, particularly in combinations of chartreuse and black, red and black, and purple and pink. He fishes them very slowly and right on the bottom. The best fishing is in dim light, which at these latitudes means midnight or 4 a.m. Fishing at these times has the added advantage of avoiding the crowds of boats pulling gear through the few section in which you can effectively swing a fly.

Kings are difficult fish for a fly rod. It is not only hard to get a fly to them, but a hooked king usually won't fight any harder than is necessary to keep from being caught. You have to take the fight to a king salmon, and many anglers feel that is easier to do with spinning or baitcasting gear, particularly in a river the size of the Nushagak.

Most anglers fish this water by backtrolling plugs—moving the boat very slowly downstream while working a big, deep-diving plug along the bottom. A large Spin-N-Glo, rigged about 18 inches behind a pencil weight, is probably the most effective rig for fishing from the bank. The weight, held in a piece of surgical tubing, bounces along the bottom while the buoyant lure spins a few inches above the gravel. Big spinners also work. Tackle needs to be heavy enough to handle a 40-pound fish in the current.

The Nushagak, with its attendant tributaries and lake systems is an amazing fishery. It hosts a variety of lodges, outfitters, and do-it-yourselfers ranging from high-end fly-out operations to blue-collar spike camps. Although it has perhaps less of the mystique attributed to the Iliamna drainages to the east and the Kanektok/Goodnews Rivers to the west, it can certainly hold its own as a destination.

Stream Facts: Nushagak River

Seasons

- General season: June 8 to April 10 (but see special regulations for king salmon).

Special Regulations

- The entire Nushagak/Mulchatna drainage is a special chinook and coho salmon management area, which may require in-season adjustments to regulations for seasons, bag limits, gear, and open waters, dependent upon escapement levels. Always check the current status of the regulations before fishing for king or coho salmon.

- King salmon: The Nushagak River downstream from the confluence with the Iowithla River, excluding the Wood River drainage, is open to the harvest of king salon from May 1 to July 31, with a daily limit of 2 per day, 2 in possession, only 1 over 28 inches. There is a yearly limit of 4 king salmon of any size taken from the entire Nushagak/Mulchatna drainage.

- The Iowithla River upstream to Harris Creek, and including the Iowithla River, is open May 1 to July 24 to the harvest of king salmon, with a daily limit of 2 per day, 2 in possession, only 1 over 28 inches.

- The Kokwok River drainage and all waters of the Nushagak within ¼ mile of its confluence, is closed to king salmon fishing year-round.

- Upstream from the confluence of the Nushagak and Harris Creek, the drainage is closed to the taking of king salmon year-round.

- Other species: From its confluence with Harris Creek, upstream to its confluence with Chichitnok Creek only unbaited single hook artificial lures may be used year-round. No retention of rainbow trout is allowed in this area. In the remaining river, from June 8 to Oct. 31, the daily limits for rainbow trout is 2 per day, 2 in possession, only 1 fish over 20 inches. From Nov. 1 to June 7, daily limits for rainbow trout are 5 per day, 5 in possession, only one fish over 20 inches.

- The daily limit for salmon, except king salmon, in the Nushagak/Mulchatna drainage is 5 per day, 5 in possession.

- Any king salmon removed from the water must be retained and become part of the bag limit of the person originally hooking it. A person who intends to release a king salmon may not remove it from the water before releasing it.

- Beads: In all flowing waters of Bristol Bay, attractors (beads) fished ahead of flies or lures must be fixed within 2 inches of the fly or lure, or be free to move (slide) on the line or leader. This applies to both fly and spin-fishing. A bead not attached to the hook is defined as an attractor, not a fly. A bead fished on the line above a bare hook is not legal gear in waters where only flies may be used.

Species

- Rainbow trout average 16 to 20 inches with an occasional fish to 26 inches.

- Arctic char (Dolly Varden) average 16 to 20 inches; present all season.

- Arctic grayling average 14 to 18 inches. Present all season.

- Sockeye (red) salmon average 5 to 7 lbs. Begin entering river about June 20. Run peaks around July 4.

- Silver (coho) salmon average 7 to 9 lbs. Begin entering river about August 15.

- King salmon average 18 to 30 lbs. Begin entering river in late May.

- Chum Salmon average 8 to 12 lbs. Begin entering the river in early July.

River Characteristics

- The Nushagak is a huge complex system. The upper stretch of the river is a small remote wilderness stream with good trout and char fishing—an excellent float destination. The central part of the river consists of a braided series of channels that was Bristol Bay's first area designated as catch and release for rainbows. The lower stretch of the river is Alaska's most productive king salmon fishery. Along the way, the Nushagak is joined by tributaries that themselves can rival its fecundity. It is a river that can be enjoyed in a week, but can't be learned in a lifetime.

Maps

- *Alaska Atlas and Gazetteer*, page 131, 57

The upper Nushagak is one of Bristol Bay's premier float trips.

Chilikadrotna and Mulchatna Rivers

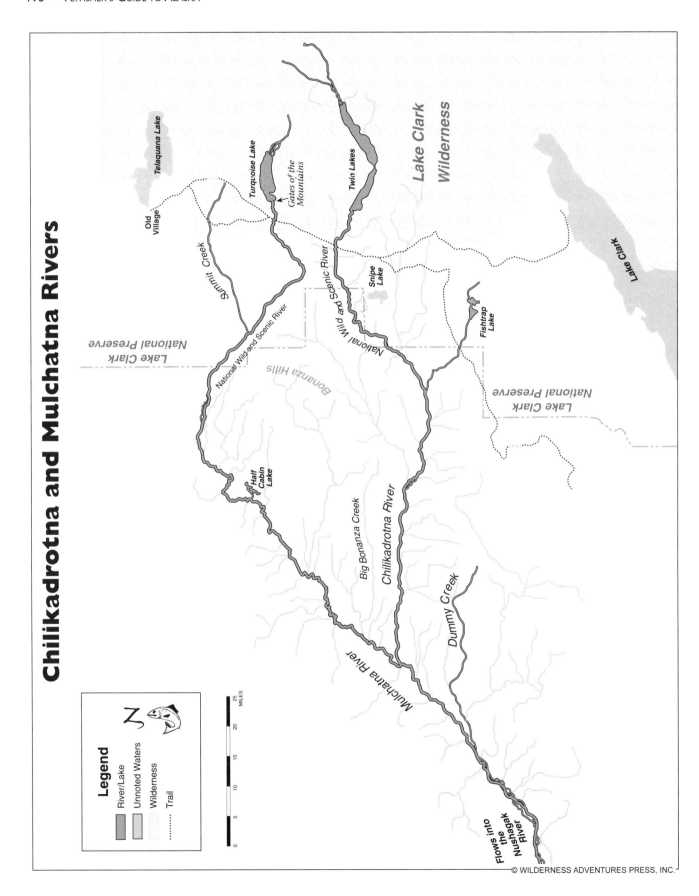

Legend
River/Lake
Unnoted Waters
Wilderness
Trail

N

0   5   10   15   20   25
                          MILES

Telaquana Lake

Turquoise Lake

Gates of the Mountains

Twin Lakes

Lake Clark Wilderness

Lake Clark

Old Village

Summit Creek

Snipe Lake

National Wild and Scenic River

Fishtrap Lake

Lake Clark National Preserve

Bonanza Hills

Lake Clark National Preserve

National Wild and Scenic River

Half Cabin Lake

Big Bonanza Creek

Chilikadrotna River

Dummy Creek

Mulchatna River

Flows into the Nushagak River

Chilikadrotna River

Lake Clark National Park, just north of Iliamna, was created to protect an expanse of sheer, snowcapped peaks, forested hills, and deep, glacial-carved lakes. Twin Lakes, which have long epitomized Alaska's wilderness, lie nestled in a valley on the west side of the range. The Chilikadrotna, one of Bristol Bay's most rewarding float trips, begins at the outlet of those lakes. Designated as a Wild and Scenic River, it lives up to both appellations. It is an exciting whitewater river that races through wild country with good fishing and lots of wildlife.

Because it has few tributaries and most of its water is filtered through the lakes, the Chilikadrotna remains clear even after the August monsoons hit. There are no lodges on the river and only a few outfitters float it. It receives a fair amount of do-it-yourself trips, but it is a demanding river and not a trip for someone who intends to lie back in the boat and let the world flow by.

The Chili, as it usually called, can be accessed from Iliamna or directly from Anchorage, which is about 100 miles away. Leaving from Anchorage is a bit more expensive, but it avoids the risk inherent in air freighting gear to Iliamna. There are few things more discouraging than pitching a tent next to the airfield for a day while waiting for some vital piece of equipment to show up. On the other hand, Iliamna Air Taxi has one of the best reputations in the state, and their pilots know the country intimately.

Like many Alaskan rivers, the most scenic section is right at the put-in. Twin Lakes are superb. Mountains sweep up from the classic glacial-carved, U-shaped valleys. The lower slopes are covered with spruce forest, which opens up to rolling tundra ridges and patches of waist-high willow and dwarf birch. Wildflowers and berries abound. Dall sheep graze on the upper slopes and caribou wander the hills.

Upper Twin Lake is a turquoise-blue gem. A small lodge operation allows hikers and boaters to enjoy this corner of the park. The upper lake acts as a settling pond, and by the time the water has reached the lower lake and river, it has shed its distinctive color. There is good fishing for big grayling and lake trout in the junction between the two lakes. The upper lake was memorialized by Richard Proenneke's journals and photographs, published as *One Man's Wilderness* in 1973. The book exemplifies the level of respect due to places of this beauty.

Most rafters land near the outlet of the lower lake. There is a small park service cabin on the southern edge, and the staff is a good source of advice about river conditions. Be aware that the rangers will turn back any commercial operations that do not have the required concessionaire's permit, which are not required for unguided operations.

There is very good hiking in this area, with dry ridgelines and beautiful views. Although caribou are not as prevalent as they were several years ago, there are still racks scattered across the tundra. There are some large grayling near the outlet.

The Chili begins as a stream about 25 yards wide, 2 or 3 feet deep, and running about 5 or 6 mph. It is sprinkled with large rocks, both above and below the surface. The river continues as a fast, rocky Class II stretch for about 4 miles as it cuts through the ancient moraines left by receding glaciers.

Brian Richardson, who guides float trips down the Chili as North Rim Adventures, says that most people are in too much of a hurry to get moving and consequently miss one of the best parts of the trip. It takes a day or so to adapt to river time, and this is a great place to let life slow down. The scenery is great, hiking is pleasant, and the campsites comfortable. More importantly, the fishing is good in this stretch, largely for grayling, although the salmon get this high and a few rainbow and char follow them.

Brian says there are some big sailfins in the deeper pools here, and with the clear water you can usually see them lying on the bottom. Egg patterns and nymphs work well, but grayling are always at their best on dry flies. You should have some buoyant, high floaters like Elk Hair Caddis or big Royal Wulffs.

At the end of this 4-mile stretch, the river dramatically transforms itself into a sluggish, mud-bottomed marsh. You'll need to row the 4 miles it takes to cross this area, and with the headwinds that often prevail here, it may take three hours to do so. Plan accordingly and pay attention to your route—this is a soft bottom, and you do not want to have to drag the boat back out of some shallow side channel. There is no fishing in this stretch and no place to camp.

Below the swamp, the river again becomes a swift Class II stream running between spruce-covered hills. The river's course is pretty straightforward for the next 8 miles, with few braids or meanders. There are lots of rocks and small standing waves, but maneuvering is not difficult. Campsites are plentiful.

There is a lot of wildlife in this area, with tracks of moose, caribou, wolves, and bears common. However, the thick spruce woods that line the river make spotting animals difficult. Try howling late at night. There are a lot of wolves and you may prompt a serenade. This stretch of the river, with its high banks, is one of the prettiest sections and worth spending time on.

Fishing is good for rainbows, char, and grayling. Try egg patterns or streamers such as an Egg-Sucking Leech. There are nice fish holding in the shelter provided by numerous rocks. Some of the best fish, particularly rainbows, will hold in the pillow of water that builds up against the upstream side of the boulders. They get first crack at any food and they can see it coming. Much of the fishing will be done from the boat. Drop your fly just far enough upstream to give it a chance to sink and avoid letting a belly in your line produce drag. Mend or recast so you can fish the eddy behind the rock. The strikes will be hard. In August, a Glo-Bug fished in this manner will keep you busy with grayling and trout. Flesh flies are another good choice. If you have people in your party who are not flyfishers, they can pick up some fish with small Mepps spinners fished in the same manner.

Surprisingly, there is also good fishing for sockeye, which are notoriously close-mouthed. The Chili is one of the few river systems in which sockeyes are aggressive and will take a fly. Brian Richardson recommends using smaller, brightly colored flies fished right on the bottom.

From here down to the confluence with the Little Mulchatna, the river runs very swift, 6 to 7 mph. There is very little meandering and the river stays pretty much in a single channel. This is continuous whitewater, with large barely submerged rocks scattered throughout and lots of 1- to 2-foot standing waves. Some maneuvering is required, but nothing particularly difficult. About 5 miles above the Little Mulchatna there is a ¼-mile stretch of high Class II water, the most difficult stretch of whitewater on the river. Keep an eye out for the occasional sweeper or large logjam. The current will want to take you right into them.

The Little Mulchatna is about 15 yards wide, a foot deep, and usually very clear. It is probably worth exploring a bit if the salmon have started to spawn. The fishing on the main river is very good through this stretch and continues all the way to the Mulchatna.

The Chili hosts a good run of silver salmon, and they are aggressive. Look for them behind the boulders and logjams, where they have some protection from the current. Eddies and the edges of sloughs will also hold silvers. Work the mouths of any tributary streams, particularly just inside the current seam. Because the river runs clear, you can often spot salmon holding, allowing you to work the fly right in front of their noses. Try chartreuse and black Woolly Buggers, Crystal Bullets, and bunny flies.

The whitewater begins to diminish as you pass the Little Mulchatna, and ends about 3 miles farther downstream. However, the river continues to run swiftly, and more sweepers, snags, and logjams appear. As you approach Ptarmigan Creek, the river begins to braid up a bit, with new channels being cut by spring runoff. As with all rivers in this country, the new channels can be problematic. You may find serious sweepers and logjams, large

standing waves, or radically sharp changes of direction.

There are adequate, but not plentiful, campsites in this section. The gravel bars have little sand and the woods are brushy. Ptarmigan Creek and its confluence hold rainbows and grayling. Rainbows particularly like the cover provided by fallen trees, which have the added advantage of trapping spawned-out salmon. Bears know this too, though, and often work those same snags and sweepers.

From Ptarmigan Creek to the confluence with the Mulchatna, the river is easy traveling. There is very little whitewater, and although it remains swift, the only challenges are a few chutes with some standing waves. There is a lot of brush and snags on the bends, however, so whoever is on the oars needs to remain vigilant. There are some side channels, but the main river is easy to follow. It is about 30 yards wide and 2 to 4 feet deep here, with reasonably good visibility. The scenery does not match the upper river, but there is an occasional view of the surrounding hills.

There will be no question when you have reached the confluence. The color of the Mulchatna is distinctly different from that of the Chili. If it is running clear, it will have that glacial blue tinge. Usually, though, there will have been enough rain to color it up a bit—or more than just a bit.

The only camping at the confluence is directly across the river from where the Chili flows into the Mulchatna. The fishing in the Mulchatna can be fairly good if it hasn't blown out. It is limited, however, and you do not want to arrive at the take-out spot with days to spare. The take-out is usually a straight stretch of river near Dummy Creek. Be sure to have your pilot mark it clearly on your maps.

For someone with wilderness experience who wants a scenic and challenging trip, the Chili is a fine choice. It is demanding but not dangerous; it has good fishing,

The Chili is a beautiful float with abundant wildlife.

although not the size or numbers of some more popular streams; and it is reasonably accessible without being overused. For those without the necessary experience to do it themselves, a guided float trip here will open up one of Alaska's most beautiful areas.

Mulchatna River

The Mulchatna River begins at Turquoise Lake, tucked up against the Chigmit Mountains in Lake Clark National Park. It flows for 250 miles to its confluence with the Nushagak about 75 miles northeast of Dillingham. The upper river has fine fishing for salmon, trout, char, and grayling, but it is a difficult and potentially dangerous river. Most, but not all, of those problems can be avoided by beginning the trip about 30 miles below the headwaters. As the Mulchatna drops toward the Nushagak, its size swells with the inflow from large tributaries such as the Chilikadrotna, the Koktuli, and the Stuyahok. The lower river is a major source of salmon and moose for the local residents and receives a lot of boat traffic from the villages that line the Nushagak.

The Mulchatna below the Bonanza Hills is a popular float trip, but very few people start at the outflow from Turquoise Lake. The upper stretch, however, is the most scenic part of the river, with 6,000-foot peaks rising from the shores of the lake and hills of rolling tundra with large herds of caribou. Dall sheep are abundant.

There are a lot of grayling at the outlet and in the creek flowing into the lake. The hiking near Turquoise Lake is delightful, with dry tundra-covered ridgelines and spectacular views. The charms of this country are considerable, but they carry a price.

Because the Mulchatna and the Chilikadrotna originate close together, flow through similar country, and merge some 60 miles downstream, many people think of them as interchangeable. That can be an unfortunate mistake. For the average floater, the Chili is a safer and more productive trip. It has fewer sweepers and better fishing. Unlike the Mulchatna, the Chili is not subject to blowing out when the August rains hit. Still, the upper Mulchatna provides an exciting and remote float trip for the experienced wilderness rafter, and the lower section of the river is a prime salmon fishing area.

For those beginning at the top, the first obstacle to be negotiated is the Gates of the Mulchatna, just below the outlet of the lake. A large boulder blocks the river, but it can be negotiated on either side. The left side is narrower, barely wide enough for a raft, but it is deep enough to shoot through without bottoming out. The right side has more room, but the boulder garden is more difficult and it may be impassable at some water levels. There is good grayling fishing in this area and a pleasant campsite about 100 yards downstream. The river has a blue-green glacial cast to it and lacks the clarity found in many Bristol Bay rivers.

From here to the Bonanza Hills, the river runs steep and fast. Logjams and sweepers may block the entire river. Because of the speed of the river it may be impossible to stop before you hit something—a very dangerous proposition. Most of the trees in this area are spruce, which means that there are a lot of sharp, raft-ripping branches among the snags.

Just to add to the excitement, the area's numerous bears know that dead salmon get caught up in these logjams, which represent one of their favorite feeding areas. Brian Richardson, who takes clients down the Mulchatna on a regular basis, tells of standing on one end of a stream-blocking sweeper, trying to saw open a channel, while a grizzly bear rooted for a trapped salmon carcass on the other end of the log.

The fishing in this area is only moderate by Alaskan standards. There are big grayling and some silvers, but the rainbow fishing is poor to fair, a function of the relatively poor clarity of the water. Much of the country is wide open, however, and begs for exploration. Caribou racks dot the tundra, and the views back toward the mountains are stunning. As you descend, the valley floor turns to spruce and birch forest.

About 22 miles from the outlet of the lake, the river begins to wind through the Bonanza Hills. It picks up pace, and at Summit Creek enters a narrow incised canyon. Constricted by the walls of the canyon, the river becomes a rocky 2-mile-long chute of Class II and III whitewater. There are some abrupt turns and slot rapids.

The river slows below the canyon as it enters a thick spruce forest, but the difficulties simply change from whitewater to the much more dangerous sweepers, which are more prevalent here than above the canyon. The river meanders through the next 15 miles or so, with lots of gravel bars and easy camping.

Because the upper river is so shallow, fast, and rocky, most floaters put in at Half Cabin Lake, about 20 miles below the Bonanza Hill Canyon. Two of the river's most experienced guides—Brian Richardson of Northern Rim Adventures and Chuck Ash of Brightwater Adventures— are emphatic that this is the best choice for most rafters. The upper stretch is unrunnable at low water, and at normal levels the current speed and sweepers make it dangerous.

The river near Half Cabin Lake is about 60 feet wide and 2 to 4 feet deep, with some deeper holes. It is slow and peaceful in this stretch, with a speed of about 3 mph. There are a lot of gravel bars, and campsites are plentiful.

The upper Mulchatna is a beautiful, but difficult and potentially dangerous float. Whitewater and sweepers abound.

The kings and silvers do get this high and there are good populations of char, grayling, and trout in the river. The fish tend to be concentrated in specific spots, however, and are not always easy to find in the jade-green water. This problem is exacerbated if there has been significant rain because the Mulchatna drains a large area and muddies up quickly in bad weather.

About 5 miles below Half Cabin Lake, small bluffs begin to constrict the channel. After about a mile of Class I whitewater the river swings south following a large bend and cuts through a ridge (section 13, Twnshp. 8N. R. 33 W). A series of rocky ledge drops stretch across most of the river, leading to a Class III chute. The chute is blocked on one side by a large boulder, leaving only a single, and narrow, 3-foot drop as the channel. There are some very large haystacks on the edge of the drop, and a miscalculation here could easily flip a raft. If you get separated from your boat and gear in this stretch, you are a long way from help.

Below this is about a mile of whitewater that's easy to run. Keep an eye out in this area for examples of a rare white race of great horned owls, a subspecies known as the Wapacuthu. This is good wildlife country, with moose, bears, and wolves common, though not easily seen. There are more salmon in the river at this point, particularly kings, chums, and silvers.

It is about 25 miles from the end of this whitewater to the confluence with the Chilikadrotna. The river here is a series of long pools broken by shorter faster riffles—easy floating. The pools can be 5 or 6 feet deep, and chum, kings, and silvers can be found. Look for trout where the riffles break into the deeper pools and along the back channels.

Below the Chilikadrotna, the river again changes char-acter, picking up size and speed. It braids up into numerous channels and there are lots of sweepers, logjams, and snags, although the size of the river allows maneuvering room around them. Most people end their float a few miles below Dummy Creek, but it is possible to float all the way to the Nushagak. This lower stretch of the river is heavily braided, flowing through forested lowlands, with its inevitable sweepers.

It receives a lot of powerboat traffic from residents of the Nushagak villages, who come upriver to fish for kings and silvers and hunt the resident moose population. The mouths of the three main tributaries—the Chili, the Koktuli, and the Stuyahok—receive a lot of usage, with long-term camps frequent. In June and early July, there is good fishing for king salmon throughout this lower stretch of river.

The Koktuli and the Stuyahok Rivers

Although the Chili is the most popular tributary to the Mulchatna, it is also possible to float both the Koktuli and Stuyahok. These are smaller streams with abundant sweepers, but no whitewater. They can be accessed by floatplane from Iliamna, but short portages from the put-in lakes may be necessary. Both streams are short floats with few people in the upper stretches.

The Koktuli runs clear and consequently has more consistent fishing than the Mulchatna. It has grayling, rainbows, char, and salmon. The most popular time to float is the latter half of August, when the silver salmon begin to ascend the river. This is also prime time to find rainbows feeding behind the sockeyes and kings that moved in earlier in the summer.

The Stuyahok begins in the hills above Iliamna Lake, close to the headwaters of the Koktuli, and flows west for about 50 miles. It has good runs of kings, chums, and silvers, and the fishing for rainbows, grayling, and Dollys can be good. The local residents, and a few guided anglers, heavily fish the last few miles of the Stuyahok down to its confluence with the Mulchatna. This stretch is particularly good for kings and silvers. Because of its popularity, ADF&G has declared the confluence a special-use area and restricts camping to seven consecutive days.

Stream Facts: Mulchatna River

Seasons

- General season: June 8 to April 10 (but see special regulations for king salmon).

Special Regulations

- The entire Nushagak/Mulchatna drainage is a special chinook and coho salmon management area, which may require in-season adjustments to regulations for seasons, bag limits, gear, and open waters, dependent upon escapement levels. Always check the current status of the regulations before fishing for king or coho salmon.

- King salmon: The Mulchatna is open May 1 to July 24 to the harvest of king salmon, with a daily limit of 2 per day, 2 in possession, only 1 over 28 inches. There is a yearly limit of 4 king salmon of any size taken from the entire Nushagak/Mulchatna drainage. Any king salmon removed from the water must be retained and become part of the bag limit of the person originally hooking it. A person who intends to release a king salmon may not remove it from the water before releasing it.

- Other species: From June 8 to Oct. 31, the daily limits for rainbow trout is 2 per day, 2 in possession, only 1 fish over 20 inches. From Nov. 1 to June 7, daily limits for rainbow trout are 5 per day, 5 in possession, only one fish over 20 inches.

- The daily limit for salmon, except king salmon, in the Nushagak/Mulchatna drainage is 5 per day, 5 in possession.

- Beads: In all flowing waters of Bristol Bay, attractors (beads) fished ahead of flies or lures must be fixed within 2 inches of the fly or lure, or be free to move (slide) on the line or leader. This applies to both fly and spin-fishing. A bead not attached to the hook is defined as an attractor, not a fly. A bead fished on the line above a bare hook is not legal gear in waters where only flies may be used.

Species

- Rainbow trout average 16 to 20 inches with an occasional fish to 26 inches.

- Arctic char (Dolly Varden) average 16 to 20 inches; present all season.

- Arctic grayling average 14 to 18 inches. Present all season.

- Sockeye (red) salmon average 5 to 7 lbs. Begin entering river about June 20. Run peaks around July 4.

- Silver (coho) salmon average 7 to 9 lbs. Begin entering river about August 15.

- King salmon average 18 to 30 lbs. Begin entering river in late May.

- Chum salmon average 8 to 12 lbs. Begin entering the river in early July.

River Characteristics

- The upper 30 miles of the Mulchatna is a remote, difficult, and sometimes dangerous float. It has spectacular scenery and good grayling fishing. There are also trout, char, and silver salmon. Below Half Cabin Lake the river is easier, but prone to muddying up after heavy rains. The lower stretches of the river offer good king and silver salmon fishing.

Maps

- *Alaska Atlas and Gazetteer*, pages 66, 67, 131, 58

THE WOOD-TICHIKS

Even in a state known for spectacular scenery, the Wood-Tikchik area is a true gem. Twelve lakes, all long, thin, and deep, lie like steppingstones along the east side of the Wood River Mountains. The lakes, which range from 15 to 45 miles long and are hundreds of feet deep, mark the path of ancient glaciers that once ran from deep in the mountains. The lakes lie parallel to each other, cutting fjord-like into an alpine setting of granite peaks. The entire region is protected as a state park, and the waters eventually flow into the sea at Dillingham, which sits at the southernmost end of the system.

There are actually two drainage systems in the Wood-Tikchiks. The northernmost lakes drain through Tikchik Lake into the Nuyakuk and eventually flow into the Nushagak just above Koliganek. The southern lakes (the Wood River system) connect with each other and ultimately empty into the mouth of the Nushagak right at Dillingham. Although the Tikchik system provides a spectacular wilderness float trip, the best fishing is found in the rivers connecting the Wood River Lakes. These include two of Bristol Bay's better-known (and most difficult to keep straight) trout streams, the Agulowak and the Agulukpak.

The Wood River System

The Wood River system is composed of six interconnected lakes, ranging in size from tiny Mikchalk Lake to the multi-armed expanse of Lake Nerka. Most of the fishing is done in the streams that run between the lakes. Typically, these are short, fast rivers with boulders and rapids. The outlets are usually large alluvial fans that host schools of hungry char waiting for the salmon smolt to make their run to the sea.

The northernmost lake, **Grant Lake**, sits in rolling hills east of the mountains about 50 miles north of Dillingham. It is cold at this altitude and ice often does not leave the lake until late June. The **Grant River**, a tiny stream, drops over a waterfall near the outlet and then runs through a narrow canyon before flowing out onto a broad plain. About 7 miles long, it contains grayling and, during June and July, lots of Dolly Varden. By the time the sockeyes have come this far they are well past their prime.

Lake Kulik is next, a long narrow expanse of water that winds back up into the mountains. It too can have late ice, but by the second week in July it has filled with sockeyes and the hordes of Dolly Varden that follow the salmon through the lakes. Its outlet, the **Wind River** flows into **Mikchalk Lake**. The Wind has a set of boulder-pocked rapids near the top, but then braids up in the middle. It has a resident population of big grayling (16 to 20 inches), Dolly Varden at the bottom of the river, and a few rainbows.

Golden Horn Lodge, one of the original Bristol Bay fly-out lodges, sits on Mikchalk Lake. It says something of the beauty of this area that it was one of the first sites chosen for bringing guests to this part of the country. From Mikchalk Lake, the **Peace River** drains into **Lake Beverly**. Slower than the other rivers in the system, the Peace has grayling and the usual collection of char waiting at the bottom for the outgoing smolt run.

West of the mouth of the Peace, Lake Beverly divides into two narrow arms, Golden Horn and Silver Horn. It is perhaps the prettiest area in the entire park. The spruce forest that follows the shoreline gives way to sheer granite peaks rising 3,000 feet above the lake's surface. Several of the smaller streams that feed into Lake Beverly host a run of spawning sockeyes, with their attendant rainbows and char. However, it is the outlet of the lake that helps give rise to the system's reputation as a great fishery.

The **Agulukpak River** is about a mile and half long. It is a large, fast river that is difficult to wade, but it has a lot of big rainbows. The top of the river is a set of classic shelves and drops, with good cover for big fish and a current that will supercharge their fight. The middle section of the river is a flat gravel pan, with paired-up sockeyes keeping the trout holding in place. The bottom of the river is large cobble that turns to a gravel delta as it enters the lake. The gravel fan drops off rapidly, and the number of char hanging just on the edge of the lip can be astonishing.

In order to fish the 'Pak effectively, a boat is essential. Guides will often walk the boat downstream or anchor at productive spots. Dan Michels, of Crystal Creek Lodge, has put his clients into some great dry-fly action in June and July. He reports that some big caddis come off early and can be imitated with a high-floating Goddard Caddis. Smaller caddis, size 12 to 16 and olive-slate in color, are good as the season progresses. There is also a good hatch of Lime Sallies, a small lime-green stonefly. Sparkle pupa and beadheads work in the pockets, where the trout feed opportunistically between the smolt run and the spawning season.

The smolt run in June gives trout and char a chance to recover from the hunger of winter. They prefer to hunt where the young salmon are funneled into a frantic mass. Look for large concentrations of char and some 'bows at the upper and lower ends of the river. Work a smolt pattern deep through here, and there will be few unrewarded casts.

The trout in the 'Pak tend to move in and out, but by July, there are a lot of them moving through with the salmon. Try swinging streamers—smolt patterns, sculpins, and Woolly Buggers are all effective. Look for fish above and behind the larger rocks, along the drop-offs and shelves, and lying over flat rock surfaces. There are spawning sockeyes in the upper third of the river, and the trout will key on them. The lower section, with its cobble bottom, has few 'bows, but lots of char and big grayling.

The 'Pak empties into **Lake Nerka**, the largest lake in the system. It's a 35-mile boat trip from the 'Pak to the lake's outlet at the Agulowak, but there are a few spots to

Huge schools of sockeyes pour through the lakes and rivers of the Wood River system in July.

Wood River Lakes

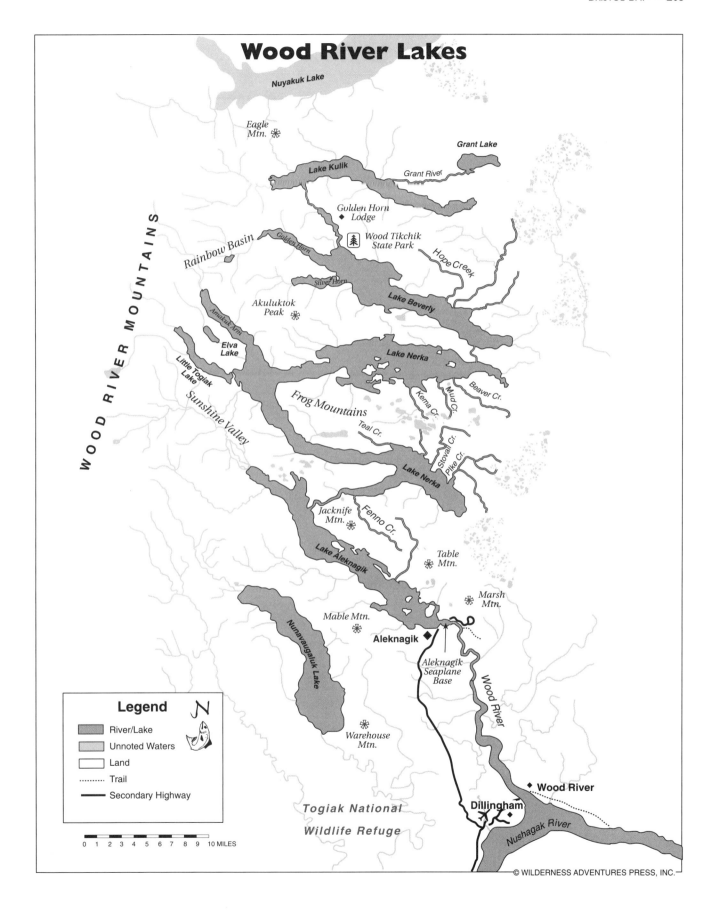

Nuyakuk Lake

Eagle
Mtn. ✳

Grant Lake

Lake Kulik

Grant River

WOOD RIVER MOUNTAINS

Golden Horn
◆ Lodge

Rainbow Basin

Golden Horn

Wood Tikchik
State Park

Hope Creek

Silver Horn

Akuluktok
Peak ✳

Lake Beverly

Amakuk Arm

Elva
Lake

Lake Nerka

Little Togiak
Lake

Beaver Cr.

Sunshine Valley

Frog Mountains

Kema Cr.

Mud Cr.

Teal Cr.

Stovall Cr.

Pike Cr.

Lake Nerka

Jacknife
Mtn. ✳

Fenno Cr.

Table
✳ Mtn.

Lake Aleknagik

Marsh
✳ Mtn.

Mable Mtn.
✳

Nunavaugaluk Lake

Aleknagik ◆

Aleknagik
Seaplane
Base

Wood River

Legend

N

▨	River/Lake
▨	Unnoted Waters
☐	Land
⋯⋯	Trail
▬▬	Secondary Highway

✳
Warehouse
Mtn.

◆ **Wood River**

Togiak National

Dillingham

Wildlife Refuge

Nushagak River

0 1 2 3 4 5 6 7 8 9 10 MILES

The Agulapak has become one of Alaska's premier rainbow destinations.

fish along the way. There is good pike fishing in the warm shallows near Kema Creek, Mud Creek, and the aptly named Pike Creek. The outlet of Little Togiak Lake has trout and char. Look for fish near the outlets of creeks that flow into the northeastern side of the lower arm of Nerka. Any stream in this system that has a lake at the top will probably host a run of sockeyes, and that means trout and char.

The **Agulowak River** is one of those Alaskan gems— short, fast, and full of trout. It stretches about 4 miles from the head of River Bay on Lake Nerka to its outlet on **Lake Aleknagik**. It starts with a big slow trench as the accumulation of the upstream lakes moves toward the river proper. There is a series of rubble riffles and cuts near the upper end. The middle of the river has several flat areas, flanked above and below by a pair of large (2- or 3-foot) rollers capable of swamping the unwary. In the high water flows of June, this is a big swift river that is almost impossible to wade. The lower section of the river has a bottom of gravel and smaller cobbles, which gives way to a large gravel delta that shelves off into the lake.

Much of what has been said about fishing the Agulukpak holds true for the Agulowak. The smolt run of early June brings in large numbers of char, particularly at the upper and lower ends of the river where they can easily ambush the bait. If you see the gulls and terns working the water, the char will be lying underneath them. The 'Wak will continue to smolt into late July, providing exciting streamer fishing even as the adult salmon are moving upstream. There are a number of archaeological sites on both rivers, testaments to the wealth of salmon that have moved up them for thousands of years.

Like its upper counterpart, the 'Wak is very difficult to fish without a boat, and preferably, a guide. It's just long enough that the trout are concentrated in certain spots, and although unguided anglers can find the fish, it is

essential to hold the boat in a position from which you can cast to them. There are, however, a lot of big rainbows holding at the top of the river. The guests at Wood River Lodge take fish right near the dock.

There is good sockeye fishing for bright, fresh fish heading into the upper reaches of the system. Dan Michels prefers to forgo the usual large bucktail patterns often sold for sockeyes. His guests do far better with bright Teeny nymphs, tiny Comets (size 10 or so), and other small, sparse, brightly colored patterns. Small white bunny flies fished dead drift also take a lot of fish.

Stream Facts: Wood River System

Seasons

- General season: June 8 to April 10 (but see special regulations for king salmon).

Special Regulations

- King salmon: The Wood River drainage is open May 1 to July 31 to the harvest of king salmon 20 inches or longer, with a daily limit of 1 per day, 1 in possession. There is a yearly limit of 2 king salmon of 20 inches or longer taken from the Wood River drainage. Any king salmon removed from the water must be retained and become part of the bag limit of the person originally hooking it. A person who intends to release a king salmon may not remove it from the water before releasing it. The daily limit for king salmon less than 20 inches (jacks) is 10 per day, 10 in possession, year-round.

- Other species: From June 8 to Oct. 31, the daily limits for rainbow trout is 2 per day, 2 in possession, only 1 fish over 20 inches. From Nov. 1 to June 7, daily limits for rainbow trout are 5 per day, 5 in possession, only one fish over 20 inches.

- Agulowak River: Only unbaited single-hook artificial lures may be used in the Agulowak River from the outlet of Lake Nerka, downstream to Lake Aleknagik, including waters of Lake Aleknagik within ½ mile of the Agulowak River outlet. The daily limit for rainbow trout is 1 per day, 1 in possession, no size limit, year-round. The daily limit for arctic char and Dolly Varden is 2 per day, 2 in possession, no size limit, year-round.

- Agulupak River: From the outlet of Lake Beverly to the island located 1.2 miles downstream, only unbaited single-hook flies may be used June 8 to Aug. 31. Only unbaited single hook lures may be used Sept. 1 to June 7. From the outlet of Lake Beverly to the island located 1.2 miles downstream, no retention of rainbow trout is allowed from June 8 to Oct. 31.

- Beads: In all flowing waters of Bristol Bay, attractors (beads) fished ahead of flies or lures must be fixed within 2 inches of the fly or lure, or be free to move (slide) on the line or leader. This applies to both fly and spin-fishing. A bead not attached to the hook is defined as an attractor, not a fly. A bead fished on the line above a bare hook is not legal gear in waters where only flies may be used.

Species

- Rainbow trout average 16 to 22 inches with an occasional fish to 30 inches.

- Dolly Varden average 16 to 22 inches and begin entering the system in mid-June with the sockeyes.

- Arctic grayling average 14 to 18 inches. Present all season.

- Sockeye (red) salmon average 5 to 7 lbs. Begin entering river about June 20. Run peaks during July.

- King salmon average 18 to 30 lbs. Begin entering Wood River in late May.

River Characteristics

- This is a series of large, deep lakes connected by fast, rocky streams. Most of the fishing occurs in the two lower rivers, the Agulukpak and Agulowak. The lakes get immense runs of sockeye salmon, which bring in large numbers of sea-run Dolly Varden. The rivers contain some of the best trout fishing in the state, but a boat is almost essential to fish them properly.

Maps

- *Alaska Atlas and Gazetteer*, page 56

Tikchik River

The Tikchik system is lovely, with a relatively easy float trip through the upper reaches of Wood-Tikchik State Park. The fishing is only fair, but if that is not your primary goal, there are few floats that provide a better example of Bristol Bay wilderness. It is more affordable than most trips, and the hazards involved are limited and manageable. The river is managed to maintain its wild character, including a permit system that ensures that you are unlikely to encounter another party while on the float. (The permit system is primarily in place to control the number of sport hunters that float the river in early fall.)

The Tikchik system actually provides several options. There are two alternative put-in points, a couple of take-outs that provide trips of different length, and for those who are not interested in floating a river, a couple of lakes that you can explore with sea kayaks. For an introduction to the beauty of the area, check out Robert Glenn Ketchum's photos in *The Wood-Tikchiks*.

Those who want to float the river can either fly in with an air taxi service out of Dillingham or charter in with Bud Hodson, who has run Tikchik Narrows Lodge for the last 20 years. Bud holds an air taxi certificate, but more importantly, he has an airstrip at the lodge. This allows you to fly in on wheels, transfer to a floatplane for the flight up to the lake, and then fly back on wheels. Since wheelplanes are a much cheaper charter than a plane on floats, it cuts the cost of the trip substantially.

Most floaters start at Nishlik Lake, a lovely high tundra lake surrounded by the spectacular peaks of the Kilbuck Mountains. Visitors should consider spending an extra day at the lake, which has the best hiking available on the trip. At an elevation of a thousand feet, the lake is typically not ice-free until early July, and the river itself runs too high and muddy to be enjoyable before that date. There are lake trout and char in the lake, but little worth fishing for in the upper stretches of the river.

The river begins as a small riffle-and-pool stream that flows through a broad valley. The streamside brush prevents good views of the mountains, but there are opportunities to climb out of the river bottom. The current is fast, but there are no rapids or obstacles.

The second starting point for floaters is Upnuk Lake, a much larger lake a few miles south of the outlet of Nishlik. The upper end of Upnuk is constrained by steep granite slopes, providing a dramatic backdrop to the first night's camp. It, too, presents an opportunity to hike the rolling hills that surround the lower half of the lake. The float down from Upnuk to the confluence with the Tikchik is about 10 miles shorter than the trip from Nishlik.

Regardless of the starting point, the fishing begins at the confluence of the two streams with the appearance of grayling. A few miles below the confluence, the river enters a stretch known as "the gorge." With walls a few hundred feet high, it is one of the prettiest parts of the trip. The water moves pretty fast through here, and although a few sockeyes get this high, there is not enough good holding water to provide good fishing.

Below Grayling Creek, however, the river enters a long braided section. The back channels provide good spawning beds and the sockeyes arrive here about mid-July. The char show up just before the time the salmon begin to spawn—about July 25. Egg patterns are the fly of choice. There is a smattering of rainbows in here, but you are unlikely to catch more than a couple in the course of a float.

Be forewarned, the Tikchik area has a healthy popula-

Tikchik and Nuyakuk Rivers

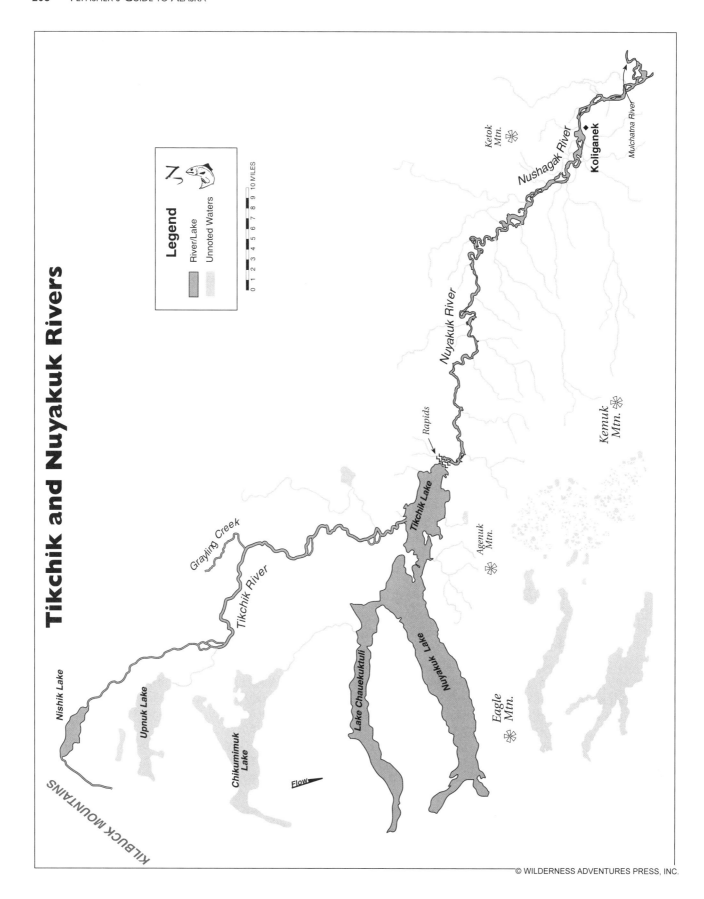

Legend

River/Lake

Unnoted Waters

0 1 2 3 4 5 6 7 8 9 10 MILES

Ketok Mtn.

Nushagak River

Koliganek

Mulchatna River

Nuyakuk River

Kemuk Mtn.

Rapids

Tikchik Lake

Agenuk Mtn.

Grayling Creek

Tikchik River

Nishik Lake

Upnuk Lake

Chikumimuk Lake

Lake Chauekuktuli

Nuyakuk Lake

Eagle Mtn.

Flow

KILBUCK MOUNTAINS

tion of bears that congregate on this river when the salmon arrive. If you are exploring the back channels, you will almost certainly have a few encounters. There are also some sweepers, and if you take the wrong channel, you might run into some problems. This is particularly true if you attempt to run the river in a collapsible kayak, which most people can maneuver only by going faster than the current.

Below the braids, the river forms into pretty much a single channel, but there are still some back channels available for fishing. There is also good fishing at the outlet of the river as it runs into Tikchik Lake.

Tikchik Lake is the first opportunity for take-out. Most air taxi services pick up floaters at the small island just off the mouth of the river. For those floaters who came in with Bud Hodson, the lodge is located a few miles west of the river. Many floaters prefer a longer trip, and float on out the Nuyakuk to the Nushagak and take out at the small village of Koliganek.

There are two other alternative trips in this area. Lakes Chauekuktuli and Chikuminuk are tucked back into the spectacular landscape of the Taylor Mountains. Very few people ever get back to this area, and while you probably won't have the entire lake to yourself, you are unlikely to see more than the pinprick light of a distant campfire. These are large lakes that have good fishing for char along the stream outlets. They also hold some monstrous lake trout. Chikuminuk is a non-motorized lake, so your only disruption will be the occasional floatplane going over and the sound of wolves.

Bud Hodson keeps a couple of kayaks for rent on these lakes, providing a great opportunity for people who want a magnificent solitary experience. The Allen River, which flows between the two lakes and looks very tempting on

Nestled in one of the most spectacular places in Alaska, Tikchik Lake is the jumping-off point for exploring the surrounding lakes and rivers.

the map, cannot be floated due to some very large rapids that can't be portaged.

Kuskokwim Wilderness Adventures (in Bethel) runs a small camp on Chauekuktuli Lake. This is spruce forest, and the moose population draws hunters once the season opens. Go early and you will have the lake to yourself.

The Tikchik system is one of Alaska's undiscovered gems. It is beautiful country with lots of wildlife and few people. Anyone wanting to discover the pleasures of a wilderness float trip should put this area near the top of their list.

Nuyakuk River

The Nuyakuk is a deep, fast river that covers some 35 miles from Tikchik Lake to the Nushagak River. It has some spots with good fishing, primarily near the upper end, but in general it is too large to be easily fished with a fly rod. But for those who want to extend their Tikchik trip and see some different country, including a Yu'pik village, it provides an additional experience.

The Nuyakuk flows out of Tikchik Lake about 7 miles from the outlet of the Tikchik River—a long row in a raft if the wind is blowing the wrong direction. There is long set of Class II+ rapids just below the outlet of the lake. They should be scouted, but are runnable in rafts or collapsible kayaks at most water levels. If you are not comfortable with them, they can be portaged along the right side. Don't be in a hurry to move through them, though. The best fishing on the river is in this stretch, with some decent rainbows, char, and lake trout.

About 5 miles downstream from the lake, the river pours over Nuyakuk Falls, a Class V waterfall. There is an obvious portage on the right side. The sockeye and char stack up below the falls and there is good fishing for them, together with some rainbows and lots of grayling. The falls prevent many salmon from making it upstream, which is why the Tikchik is not the trout fishery you can find in other area rivers.

There is a nice campsite right at the falls. If I were to float this river again, I would concentrate as much time as possible in the area from the lower falls upstream to the lake. This stretch provides good camping and fishing, unlike the remainder of the river.

The Nuyakuk flows through white spruce forest, and because of the stabilizing influence of the lake there are few exposed gravel bars. The result is a river that is somewhat featureless below the falls. It is difficult to fish the Nuyakuk, due in part to the lack of obvious holding water. More importantly, the banks are brushy and forested, and the river itself is too deep to wade. There are some nice trout in the river, but fishing from the boat is hit and miss.

The lack of gravel bars also makes camping problem-

The falls on the Nuyakuk require a portage, but have some of the best fishing on the river.

atic. There are sites available in the upper three-quarters of the river, but you will be camping back in the woods, as opposed to on an open bar. As you come out of the forest onto the coastal plain, there is little but wet muskeg and tall grass. Camping on wet tundra will make you believe the stories of caribou being sucked dry by the mosquitoes.

The lower 10 miles of the river, just above the confluence with the Nushagak, is a medusa-like tangle of oxbows and old sloughs. Try to avoid camping in this stretch. Once you reach the Nushagak, there are good gravel bars, and the chance of catching a silver or king salmon. You can easily float down to Koliganek in a few hours and get picked by a wheelplane there.

Stream Facts: Tikchik and Nuyakuk Rivers

Seasons
- General season: June 8 to April 10 (but see special regulations for king salmon).

Special Regulations
- The entire Nushagak/Mulchatna drainage is a special chinook and coho salmon management area, which may require in-season adjustments to regulations for seasons, bag limits, gear, and open waters, dependent upon escapement levels. Always check the current status of the regulations before fishing for king or coho salmon.

- King salmon: The Nuyakuk is open May 1 to July 24 to the harvest of king salmon, with a daily limit of 2 per day, 2 in possession, only 1 over 28 inches. There is a yearly limit of 4 king salmon of any size taken from the entire Nushagak/Mulchatna drainage. Any king salmon removed from the water must be

retained and become part of the bag limit of the person originally hooking it. A person who intends to release a king salmon may not remove it from the water before releasing it.

- Other species: From June 8 to Oct. 31, the daily limits for rainbow trout is 2 per day, 2 in possession, only 1 fish over 20 inches. From Nov. 1 to June 7, daily limits for rainbow trout are 5 per day, 5 in possession, only one fish over 20 inches.

- The daily limit for salmon, except king salmon, in the Tikchik/Nuyakuk drainage is 5 per day, 5 in possession.

- The Tikchik River drainage and in the Nuyakuk River from the outlet of Tikchik Lake to an island located about 2 miles downstream from Nuyakuk Falls, only unbaited single-hook artificial lures may be used.

- Beads: In all flowing waters of Bristol Bay, attractors (beads) fished ahead of flies or lures must be fixed within 2 inches of the fly or lure, or be free to move (slide) on the line or leader. This applies to both fly and spin-fishing. A bead not attached to the hook is defined as an attractor, not a fly. A bead fished on the line above a bare hook is not legal gear in waters where only flies may be used.

Species
- Rainbow trout average 16 to 20 inches.
- Arctic char (Dolly Varden) average 16 to 20 inches; present all season.
- Arctic grayling average 14 to 18 inches. Present all season.
- Sockeye (red) salmon average 5 to 7 lbs. Begin entering river about June 20. Run peaks around July 4.
- Silver (coho) salmon average 7 to 9 lbs. Begin entering river about August 15.
- King salmon average 18 to 30 lbs. Begin entering river in late May.

River Characteristics
- The Tikchik River is a small scenic stream that is easily floated. It has a limited population of rainbows, but good fishing for char and grayling. The Nuyakuk is much larger, and has two sets of rapids (one of which is unrunnable and must be portaged). The only good flyfishing is in the upper river from the outlet of the lake to a section below the falls. Camping is limited.

Maps
- *Alaska Atlas and Gazetteer*, pages 131, 56, 57

DILLINGHAM AND ALEKNAGIK AREA
INCLUDES NUSHAGAK AND WOOD-TIKCHIK OPERATIONS

Population Dillingham: 2,200
Alaska Area Code: 907
Zip Code: 99576

LODGES AND OUTFITTERS

Crystal Creek Lodge, www.crystalcreeklodge.com; fly-out lodge, numerous other activities, has access to private water; 1-800-525-3153 or 357-3153; P.O. Box 872729, Wasilla, AK 99687

Tikchik Narrows Lodge, www.tikchiklodge.com; fly-out lodge located on Tikchik Lake; P.O. Box 220248, Anchorage AK 99522; 243-8450

Bear Bay Lodge, www.bearbaylodge.com; fly-out and other options, tent camp on the upper Nushagak; (winter) 22708 SE Naomi Dr., Boring OR, 1-866-232-7229 Fax: (503) 907-6010; (summer) P.O. Box 3051, Dillingham AK, 842-5060

Bristol Bay Lodge, www.bristolbaylodge.com; fly-out; (winter) 2422 Hunter Rd.,Ellensburg, WA, 509-964-2094; (summer) P.O. Box 1509 Dillingham, AK, 842 2500

Royal Coachman Lodge, ww.royalcoachmanlodge.com; located on the Nuyakuk, fly-out lodge with options; (winter) 1062 W Ridge Rd., Cornville, ME, 1-800-457-6191 or 1-207-474-8691 Fax 1-207-474-3231; (summer) P.O. Box 450, Dillingham, AK, 868-6033

Reel Wilderness Adventures, www.reelwild.com; 6 guests, fishes Wood River lake system; (winter) P.O. Box 329, Mountain View, HI,; (summer) P.O. Box 922, Dillingham, AK, 842-3807

Nushagak Paradise Lodge, www.nushagakparadiselodge.com; primarily lower river salmon fishing; 2906 Peppertree Pl., Plano, TX, 1-888-395-3474; (summer) P.O. Box 1351,Dillingham, AK, 1-888-395-3474

Nushagak Salmon Camp, P.O. Box 104179, Anchorage, AK, 99510; 522-113; fax 344-5648

Alaska Bush Guides, www.akbushguides.com; Portage Creek Store and lodge, primarily salmon fishing on lower Nushagak, boat rentals; P.O. Box PCA, Dillingham, AK, 842-7191

Wood River Lodge, www.woodriverlodge.com; Agulowak River; 1-800-842-5205 (winter) P.O. Box 17107, Missoula, MT 59808; (summer) P.O. Box 1369 Dillingham AK

Ultimate Rivers, www.ultimaterivers.com; tent camp on lower Nushagak, float trips on Upper Nushagak; P.O. Box 670534, Chugiak, AK 99567; 688-6535

Northern Rim Adventures (Brian Richardson), raft trips on Mulchatna, Chilikodratna; www.northernrim.com; 1120 East Huffman Rd., Anchorage, AK 99515; 1-800-616-7238

Brightwater Alaska (Chuck Ash), raft trips on Mulchatna; www.brightwateralaska.com; P.O. Box 110796, Anchorage, AK 99511; 344-1340

Mission Creek Lodge, www.missionlodge.com; fly-out lodge on Lake Aleknagik; 5409 Overseas Highway, Marathon, FL, 33050; 1-800-819-0750

AIR TAXIS

Freshwater Adventures, Inc., www.fresh-h2o.com; seasonal air taxi, rents rafts and gear; P.O. Box 62, Dillingham, AK 99576; 842-5060

A Ball Air, P.O. Box 745, Dillingham, AK 99576; 842-4180 Bristol Bay Air Service, P.O. Box 1135, Dillingham; 842-2227

Shannon's Air Taxi, P.O. Box 131, Dillingham; 842-2735

Tucker Aviation, P.O. Box 1109, Dillingham; 842-1023

Yute Air, P.O. Box 890, Dillingham; 842-5333

RAFT AND GEAR RENTALS

Freshwater Adventures, Inc., www.fresh-h2o.com; seasonal air taxi, rents rafts and gear P.O. Box 62, Dillingham, AK 99576; 842-5060

Dan's Rental Equipment, P.O. Box 162, Dillingham, AK 99576; 1-877-423-3400

ACCOMMODATIONS

Alaska Cabins B&B, Aleknagik; www.alaskancabin.com; 3801 Lupine Drive, Dillingham, AK, 842-5022

Beaver Creek B&B, Dillingham and Aleknagik; PO Box 563 Dillingham , AK, 99576; 1-866-252-7335

Bristol Inn, P.O. Box 330 104 Main Street, Dillingham, AK, 99576;842-2240

Dillingham Hotel, 429 2nd Avenue West, Dillingham, AK; 842-5316

Fisherman's Hideaway, PO BOX 342 Dillingham, AK ; 842-1598

Lake Road Cottage, Private guest houses; P.O. Box 342, Dillingham, AK 99576; 842-2449

Thai Inn, Dillingham; 842-7378; www.thaiamerican.com

Westmark Hotel, Dillingham; 1-800-544-0970

Togiak River

Flyfishermen planning a trip to western Alaska tend to overlook the Togiak River. That can be a mistake. Caught between the fabled waters of the Nushagak drainage and the renowned fisheries of the Goodnews and Kanektok, the Togiak provides an opportunity to experience a remote and often underutilized fishery. Its lower stretches provide classic big-river salmon fishing, and its upper branches hold nice populations of trout and char. The Togiak is located 500 miles southwest of Anchorage and 55 miles from Dillingham, the nearest hub. It flows 60 miles from the outlet of Togiak Lake to the village of Togiak on Bristol Bay.

The Togiak system consists of the main stem and five large tributaries, each with a name that, even by Alaskan standards, is unpronounceable. Beginning about 16 miles from the outlet of the lake, the river is joined by the Ongivinuk River, the Kashaiak, the Narogurum, Pungokepuk Creek, and the Gechiak River. Much of the best fishing, at least for trout, is found in these tributary streams. The upper watershed is located within the boundaries of the Togiak National Wildlife Refuge. Below Pungokepok Creek, the river flows through native lands.

The Togiak is perhaps best known for its coho fishing. These thick-shouldered powerhouses range between 9 and 15 pounds, with a few larger ones taken every year. They flood into the river by the second week in August.

For anglers who like to brawl in the heavyweight class, the Togiak also gets a good run of king salmon. They arrive by late June and can be found staging on the upper river flats in Late July. The river also gets good runs of sockeye, chum, and pink salmon. Fishing for rainbows in the main stem is only fair, but there is good fishing for arctic char and grayling.

The first salmon to enter the river in June are the kings. These fish are serious tackle-busters, so come well armed. Ten- to 12-weight rods are not too heavy, and reels capable of holding 200 yards of backing may be needed if you get a fish that decides to go back to sea on you. The Togiak is a big river, and a spey rod will provide a big advantage in both distance and control.

Kings tend to hug the bottom and will hold in heavier currents than other fish. In order to hook them you need to slowly swing your fly directly in front of their noses. This means deep sinking lines, such a T-300 or Rio Dredger. Weighted flies may be necessary, but bring a range of weights in order to keep the fly at the proper depth in a variety of conditions. Tippets should be kept short—3 or 4 feet and at least 15-pound test.

Flies for kings are big and gaudy—lots of flash, bright marabou, and bunny fur. Sizes run from 2 to 5/0. Colors tend to be chartreuse, cerise, hot pink, silver, and purple.

The upper stretches of the Togiak are clear, gravel-bottomed, and full of char.

Some patterns, such as Alaskabous and Fat Freddies are designed specifically for chinooks, but any oversized bright steelhead fly is likely to work, and some saltwater patterns, like Deceivers and Clouser Minnows, have been adapted to searching for kings. Since these are Alaskan fish, an Egg-Sucking Leech is always appropriate. Although kings don't feed in freshwater, and no one really knows why they hit a fly or lure, they can be fickle. If you are on fish and they aren't hitting, keep trying different styles and colors of flies. Yesterday's secret may be today's bust.

Blind fishing for kings in a river the size of the Togiak is usually an exercise in futility. Always try to locate the fish. The guides and lodge owners usually have a good idea where they are at any given time, and fish will often give themselves away by rolling on the surface. To truly experience what it is like to catch a king, you need to hook one within a few miles of the sea. The explosions of these sea lice–covered chromers are a far cry from the lethargic fight you get from a colored-up fish taken far upriver. Once the kings are on the spawning beds, you should avoid harassing them and concentrate on the big char and rainbows that are holding just below each pair of spawners.

As powerful as the chinooks are, the flyrodder's real prize is the coho. Where a chinook may simply move into heavy water and slug it out, a hooked coho will go ballistic, expending every ounce of energy—in the water and in the air—in order to win its freedom. A fresh silver salmon is truly one of the world's great fly-rod quarries. An 8-weight rod with a floating or sink-tip line is usually the right system.

Cohos are aggressive fish that will not only move to a fly, but will take a skated dry fly on occasion. The Togiak is

Togiak and Izavieknik Rivers

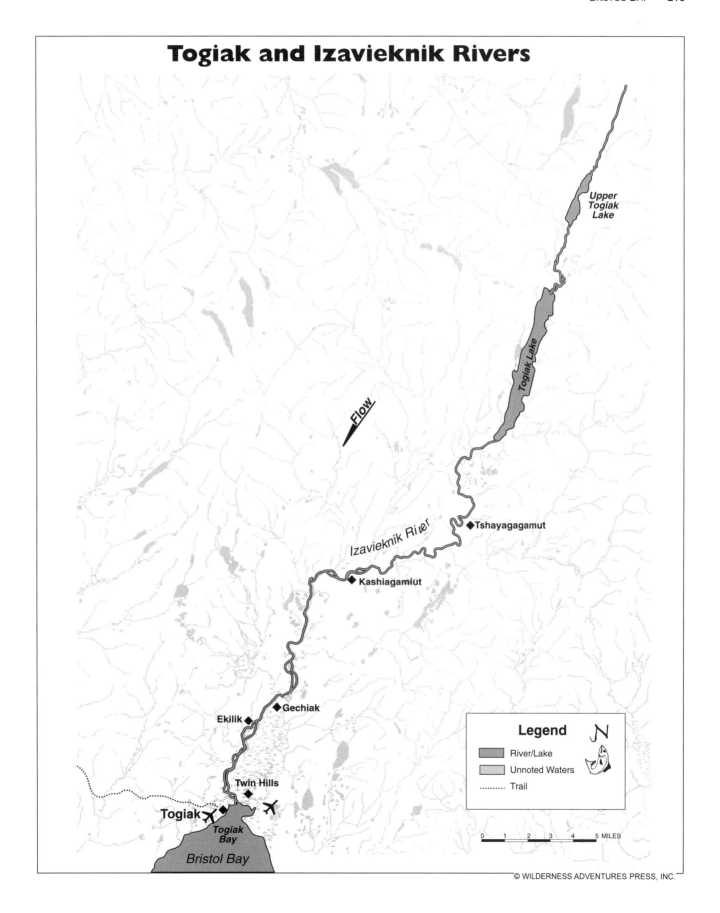

Upper
Togiak
Lake

Togiak Lake

Flow

Izavieknik River

◆Tshayagagamut

◆ Kashiagamiut

◆Gechiak

Ekilik ◆

Twin Hills ◆

Togiak

Togiak
Bay

Bristol Bay

Legend N

River/Lake

Unnoted Waters

.... Trail

0 1 2 3 4 5 MILES

© WILDERNESS ADVENTURES PRESS, INC.

Togiak Lake is a spectacular start to a float trip.

a great river for skating a fly. The classic pattern is a Pink Wog, but others will also take fish. Look for fresh fish holding in shallow water and strip the fly across the surface with short, sharp bursts. Cohos may follow the fly, water bulging over their backs, before inhaling it, or they may simply smash it without warning.

Egg-Sucking Leeches, Crystal Bullets, and Flash Flies are all good patterns for fish that aren't inclined to come to the surface. Use a deep drift with short strips. The strikes are usually more solid than the gentle takes of king salmon. Just remember that silvers often go through periods of lockjaw before suddenly turning on and hitting anything you throw at them.

Look for silvers in slow water. They tend to congregate in the deep part of pools, sloughs, and back eddies, and rarely hold in the main current like chinook. Perhaps the most memorable coho fishing I have experienced came on a 40-yard-wide pool on a Togiak back channel. It was jammed with a school of aggressive fish that would smack every fly thrown at them. We caught cohos till our arms gave out.

Like all salmon, silvers are at their best when caught close to salt water. Cohos are more likely to hit a fly that is swinging than other salmon, which means that you can cover more water effectively. Sight fishing is the ideal method and on the clear water of the Togiak, this is often possible.

There are rainbows in the Togiak, but they are neither numerous or easy to find. The best fishing for them is in the streams that flow into the main river, particularly Pungokepuk Creek and the Gechiak River. Both of these streams support large runs of sockeye salmon and the trout follow them upriver to feed on the eggs. Like most Alaskan streams, the best time for trout fishing is a brief period in June and again in August and September.

In the early season trout and char are feeding on salmon fry and smolt. Look for fish at the mouths of tributaries, where they wait to ambush the migrating bait. For fry patterns, try Thunder Creeks (size 10) fished on a floating line. Fish the edges of the slow water and grassy areas. Smolt run larger and are best imitated by Zonkers, white Woolly Buggers, and similar silvery-colored streamers. These fish are headed downstream and the flies should be fished accordingly.

By August the trout have moved upstream and are focused on eggs. They will still hit streamers, and occasionally you can find good dry-fly fishing, but a single egg pattern is the basic fly. Fish it on a floating line, dead drifted behind any holding salmon. Once the salmon start to die, the trout start their final pre-winter gorge on the carcasses. Flesh flies dead drifted through deep holes and behind snags are particularly effective.

The Togiak and its tributaries all host good populations of arctic char and grayling. Look for char in the same places you would expect to find rainbows. They will take egg patterns readily and will often slam an egg hanging in the current at the end of the drift. Grayling are the only consistent dry-fly fish in Alaska, so bring some size 14 Adams and Elk Hair Caddis. If you overpower them, they simply go stiff and put up little fight, but on light tackle they can be a lot of fun.

The Togiak is larger than most of the clear-water rivers of western Alaska. It flows from 18-mile-long Togiak Lake, which gives it stability and clarity even during periods of heavy rains. Mountains line both sides of the upper river, but even as the valley broadens out, the river hugs the western hills, making it one of the most scenic floats in this part of the state. The banks are willow-lined and brushy, without the frequent gravel bars found on rivers with more fluctuation. Ridges line one bank or the other for most of the length of the river.

At the outlet of the lake the Togiak is a manageable river—some 20 yards across and 3 or 4 feet deep, lined with tall willows and cottonwood. Below Kashiak River, it grows to 100 yards wide and 6 to 10 feet deep. The Togiak is a straightforward river to float, with no serious hazards. Although the current is fairly fast (3 or 4 mph), there is no whitewater and few sweeper-filled channels. The lack of gravel bars with sand can make camping difficult, though.

Unfortunately, the Togiak is not an easy river to fish effectively on a float trip. It is difficult to pull over quickly, and as a consequence, it is common to drift past fishable lies or rolling salmon without getting an opportunity to cast. Much of the river is too deep to fish with a fly rod, making spinning tackle almost a necessity. If you do float it, concentrate on the mouths of the tributary streams (hiking upstream when possible) and the occasional riffle section. The back sloughs should also be explored, particularly if the cohos are running.

Most floaters put in at the lake and float down to the end of the refuge at Pungokepok Creek, a four- to six-day float. The lower stretch of the river runs through private property (native lands), and camping is prohibited on the banks (although it is permissible to camp on gravel bars below the high water mark).

The most effective way to fish the river is with one of the lodges, which have boats that can run up the smaller streams. The guides also have a good idea of where to find the salmon, which move steadily upstream to their spawning beds. The Togiak is a beautiful and easy river to float on your own, but if you want to catch fish here, use a lodge.

One final note, particularly for floaters: Over the years, a certain amount of resentment has developed in the village of Togiak toward sport fishers. The tension stems from the fact that the salmon fisheries are the primary source of both food and cash for the village. In years of small runs, commercial fishing is often shut down, although sport anglers from distant places are allowed to continue to fish, albeit with little or no take allowed. From a biological viewpoint, it is an acceptable practice—from a sociological viewpoint, it epitomizes the source of Alaska's most significant racial conflict. Keep in mind that you are a guest on the villagers' land and that these fish constitute their food, their livelihood, and their culture. Treat both the people and the resource with respect.

Izavieknik River

The Izavieknik River (often referred to as the Upper Togiak) flows about 7 miles from Upper Togiak Lake to Togiak Lake. It is a study in contrasts with its larger brother—small and fast, winding so sinuously through the willows and cottonwoods that there are few long sight lines. Given the number of bears that fish this river, and the constant threat of sweepers blocking the channel, it is a float trip only for the experienced.

There is the constant threat of rounding a corner and finding yourself about to run over a fishing bear. Because this area sees very few people, these bears are not habituated to human presence, and their reactions are unpredictable. The sweepers may be more of a danger. If you float this section, carry a saw capable of cutting through a 10-inch cottonwood, and keep it handy. I once spent an uncomfortable 30 minutes balanced on a bobbing sweeper with a Sven saw, trying to cut an opening large enough for our overloaded kayak to squeeze through.

On the plus side, the scenery is even more spectacular than on the lower river, and the fishing is reputed to be very good for small char, although largely unexplored. The number of bears using the area is a good indication of the health of the salmon runs, and where there are salmon, there are trout and char. This is a late-summer float, which allows the salmon time to get through the lake and onto the spawning beds. The salmon will be too far gone to be worth fishing for, but they will have pulled the char up from the lake.

The price you pay for this float is the 18-mile crossing of Togiak Lake. It can be paddled in a collapsible kayak, but if you are floating in a raft, a small outboard is almost a necessity. The lodges don't fish this river, but if you are planning a float on the Togiak, and are experienced, prepared to take some risks, and do some work, it is a pretty little stretch of water.

Stream Facts: Togiak River

Seasons and Special Regulations

- King Salmon: May 1 to July 31. Limit 3 per day, 3 in possession, only 2 over 28 inches.

- Other salmon: open entire year; limit 5 per day, 5 in possession.

- Rainbow trout: Open entire year; limit June 8 to Oct. 31, 2 per day, 2 in possession only 1 over 20 inches; Nov. 1 to June 7, 5 per day 5 in possession, only 1 over 20 inches.

- Arctic char/Dolly Varden: Open entire year—June 8 to Oct. 31, 3 per day, 3 in possession; Nov. 1 to June 7, 10 per day, 10 in possession.

- Arctic Grayling: open entire year; 2 per day, 2 in possession.

Species

- King (chinook) salmon average 18 to 30 lbs. Enter river in early June, season closes July 31.

- Chum salmon average 8 to 15 lbs. Best fishing is in lower river. Enter river in late June, with the peak of the run in mid-July.

- Pink salmon run strongest in even-numbered years. Average 4 to 6 lbs. Enter river in July. Fish are in the best shape in lower river and at the beginning of the run.

- Sockeye (red) salmon average 5 to 7 lbs. Enter river in July and move through quickly.

- Silver (coho) salmon average 9 to 15 lbs. Enter river in early August, with run peaking by late August.

- Rainbow trout average 16 to 21 inches; present year-round. Best fishing is in the tributaries.

- Arctic char/Dolly Varden average 16 to 22 inches; present year-round. Best fishing is behind spawning salmon.

- Arctic grayling average 14 to 18 inches. Present year-round.

River Characteristics

- The Togiak is about 60 miles long, flowing from Togiak Lake to Bristol Bay. The village of Togiak is located at the mouth and is the only permanent settlement on the river. The river is fairly fast (3 or 4 mph), but it's flat water with no rapids and few sweepers. It is about 20 yards wide and 3 or 4 feet deep at the mouth of the lake, but grows to over 100 yards wide and 6 to 10 feet deep by the time the Kashaiak River enters. The slower pools at the lower end of the river may be 15 to 20 feet deep.

- It is mountain tundra country, with the banks lined with willows. The river runs clear with few gravel bars suitable for camping.

Outfitters and Lodges

- **Togiak River Lodge**, www.togiakriverlodge.com; lodge at lower end of river; P.O. Box 350, Togiak, AK 95678; 493-5464

- **Togiak River Fishing Adventures**, www.togiakfishing.com; weatherport camp run by

- **Tikchik Narrows Lodge and Bristol Bay Lodge**; (winter) 509-925-6606, P.O. Box886 Ellensburg, WA 98922; (summer) P.O. Box 370, Togiak, AK 99678; 493-5744

- **Mission Lodge**, 1-800-819-0750

- **Alaska Rainbow Adventures**, www.akrainbow.com; float trips; 1-877-235-2647, P.O. Box 456, Anchor Point, AK 99556

- **Ultimate Rivers**, www.ultimaterivers.com; float trips; P.O. Box 670534, Chugiak, AK 99567; 688-6535

Maps

- *Alaska Atlas and Gazetteer*, page 55

KUSKOKWIM BAY

Kuskokwim Bay is a land of long raft trips and dark-spotted trout. This is the country for anglers who think that life reaches its peak in a gravel bar camp next to a run full of spawning salmon and hungry trout. Floatplanes may ferry you to a headwater lake, and riverboats may buzz the lower stretches of the rivers, but for the most part fishing the streams of this area is a quiet and uncrowded wilderness experience.

These drainages are actually not part of Bristol Bay, lying just beyond its western border. But the boundaries in this chapter are drawn by fishing, not geography. This is the outer limits of the range of rainbow trout in North America—and what trout they are. Although they do not have the size of the Iliamna and Katmai fish, they have a wildness and color that is unsurpassed. Universally referred to as leopard 'bows, they are heavily marked fish that will chase down a rabbit leech, hammer a deer-hair mouse, or softly sip an egg pattern.

The rainbows are not the only target here, though. These streams have some of the best flyfishing available for king and coho salmon. Not only do they have good runs of fish, they are small enough to make a fly rod the perfect tool. There is excellent grayling fishing in all of the streams, and big runs of char follow the salmon in from the salt. In spite of the healthy runs of fish, there are fewer bears here than in the Katmai and Alaska Peninsula areas.

If you want great fishing in a remote environment, and don't mind sleeping in a tent, then this area may become your favorite spot in Alaska.

Kanektok River

Back in the '70s (a time that predates graphite rods and neoprene waders) there were rumors of a river in western Alaska with fishing that surpassed even the state's most fabled streams. Known by various fictitious names, including the Chosen River, it was reputed to support large populations of all five salmon species, grayling, Dolly Varden, and a stock of heavily spotted rainbows known as leopard trout. I learned its true name from a couple of wired-in friends who returned with tales of spectacular trout and a description of a great new fly they had discovered—the Woolly Bugger.

Secrets never last, though, and gradually people began to dig out the maps of the Kanektok. In spite of their lasting popularity, both the river and the fly have maintained their reputations over time.

The Kanektok is one of Alaska's premier float-fishing rivers. It flows for 90 miles from its headwaters in Kagati Lake (sometimes spelled Pegati Lake) to the Yu'pik village of Quinhagak. This is classic western Alaska terrain,

The Kanektok is a river that is meant to be floated. Spawning beds and gravel bars make for great fishing and camping.

storm-scoured mountains giving way to a flat coastal plain. The river itself is a true fish factory, with overlapping runs of salmon providing the nutrition base for trout, char, and grayling. A clear, gravel-bottomed stream, it is hard to imagine a river better suited to flyfishing.

The Kanektok is the crown jewel of the Togiak National Wildlife Refuge; a 4.7-million-acre wilderness located about 400 miles west of Anchorage. The Ahklun Mountains form the backbone of the refuge and provide the headwaters not only for the Kanektok, but also the Togiak and Goodnews Rivers. This is truly remote country. The refuge is immense in its own right, but it's also surrounded by vast lands that are equally as wild. Civilization here consists of a few villages huddled near the coast, each with a population numbering in the hundreds. The nearest town of any size is Dillingham.

Access to the Kanektok is by floatplane from Dillingham or Bethel into Kagati Lake. The only take-out point is at Quinhagak, at the end of the river. Wheelplanes can land there, which helps cut the cost a bit. Between put-in and take-out, you are on your own, with no options but to float all the way to the mouth.

Kagati Lake sits nestled in the mountains and is surrounded by tundra and rocky ridges. The shoreline is low willow, but beyond its immediate confines, little grows above knee-height. The stream empties from the western end of the lake as a shallow creek, only 20 yards wide. At times of low water, the constant gravel bars, riffles, and rocks may require lining or dragging the boat.

At Paiyun Creek the stream grows by about a third and begins to braid a bit. The terrain becomes more canyon-like, with tundra-covered ridges marking the path of long-retreated glaciers. Although there are a grayling and char at this altitude, the fishing doesn't peak until you reach the middle stretches of the river. This is a good place to

just float along and enjoy the scenery and, with luck, the wildlife. Grizzly bears, caribou, and wolves wander this high country.

As you get closer to Nakailingak Creek, trees begin to appear and the threat of sweepers increases. The Kanektok runs fairly swiftly, and although it has no rapids, the sweepers and brushpiles are a hazard. This is particularly true in June and after periods of heavy rain (they don't refer to August as the monsoon season for nothing), when the normally benign river can become dangerous. Be particularly cautious in the braids, where the entire force of the current might plunge under a fallen tree. Because the river cuts new channels every spring, the supply of fallen spruce and cottonwoods is never-ending, and the old quadrangle maps are of little help in identifying the main channel.

Campsites are plentiful at this altitude. Look for long gravel bars with a level patch of pea-sized stones, which you'll usually find at the lower end. Although it is still too high for large numbers of rainbows, there are good populations of arctic char. They like to hold in the riffles and bars that develop below the islands and along the inside of the bends. Fish the soft edges of the seams. The right gravel bar will offer both a comfortable campsite and good fishing.

At Klak Creek, the river enters the transition between the mountains and the coastal plain, and it is here that the river's fishing comes into its own. This is some of the best trout habitat in Alaska, with big leopard 'bows shadowing the salmon, hiding in the brushpiles, and hanging along the cutbanks. The river braids heavily here, making it difficult to beach the raft at will, but anywhere you can get out and work a run will yield trout or char. Don't neglect the smaller back channels—you can find some nice fish holding next to the banks and under the rootwads.

The scenic part of the float is essentially over by Klak Creek, with views limited to a shoreline choked with willow and cottonwood. As you get lower, the trees give way to a barren coastal plain, but the banks are usually too high to see over from the raft. It is impossible to take a compass bearing, and the maps are of little help in this constantly changing landscape. Without a GPS, you will be left with dead reckoning of the crudest kind. You will still reach Qunihagak, but it will be difficult to maximize your time in the most productive areas.

As you drop out onto the coastal plain, the river becomes deeper and more featureless. The current slows, and it often becomes necessary to row into the face of an upstream wind. The braided sections still hold trout, but the prime lies are fewer and farther between. This water is better suited to salmon fishing, and it can be crowded when the kings are running in late June through July.

Kanektok and Goodnews Rivers

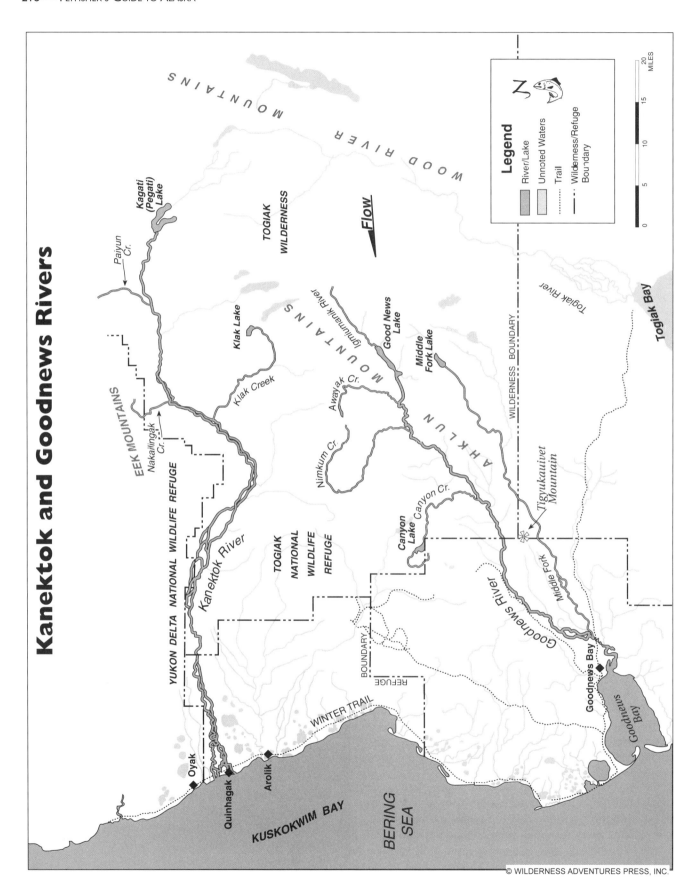

Legend

River/Lake

Unnoted Waters

Trail

Wilderness/Refuge Boundary

Flow

WOOD RIVER MOUNTAINS

Kagati (Pegati) Lake

Paiyun Cr.

TOGIAK WILDERNESS

Togiak River

Togiak Bay

Klak Lake

Klak Creek

Igmuimanik River

Good News Lake

Middle Fork Lake

EEK MOUNTAINS

Nakailingak Cr.

Awayak Cr.

AHKLUN MOUNTAINS

WILDERNESS BOUNDARY

YUKON DELTA NATIONAL WILDLIFE REFUGE

Kanektok River

Nimkum Cr.

Tigyukauivet Mountain

TOGIAK NATIONAL WILDLIFE REFUGE

Canyon Lake

Canyon Cr.

Goodnews River

Middle Fork

BOUNDARY

REFUGE

Goodnews Bay

WINTER TRAIL

Goodnews Bay

Oyak

Quinhagak

Arolik

KUSKOKWIM BAY

BERING SEA

© WILDERNESS ADVENTURES PRESS, INC.

20 15 10 5 0 MILES

The local Yu'pik rely on the salmon for subsistence, and the shoreline is dotted with fish camps. Drying racks are loaded with split salmon hung over poles, and riverboats move up and downriver. There are a few tent camps operated as sport-fishing lodges, sitting high on the gravel bars. This stretch of the river runs through private land and only the portion below mean high water is open to the public. The take-out point is the village of Quinhagak, whose residents are quite sensitive to the influx of foreign fishermen competing for a resource that they have claimed as their own for centuries.

One of the major draws of the Kanektok is the variety of species available. Depending on the season, that tug at the end of your line could be a rainbow, grayling, arctic char, king, chum, sockeye, or silver salmon (with the occasional pink salmon thrown in for good measure). Time your trip to coincide with whichever species you are most interested in.

The season begins in earnest with the arrival of king salmon in June. Fishing for kings closes on July 31 in order to protect spawning fish. These are big, strong fish, and the best shot at them is in the lower 10 miles of the river, where they are still chrome-bright and covered with sea lice. Bring some heavy gear for these tackle-busters—a 10- or 11-weight rod is about right.

Like all fish, kings will seek out shelter from the current to rest and you should work a fly along the edges of sloughs and behind snags and islands. Kings are so powerful, though, that much of the best fishing is found in deep lies right in the main stem of the river. Deep is the operative word. Kings will rarely move up to take a fly. Successful fishermen are those who bounce a fly right along the streambed. If you don't hit the fish on the nose, you aren't going to catch many.

A heavy sink-tip or shooting head will get your fly down, although you may still need weighted flies. Kings prefer big, gaudy flies. Alaskabous, Wiggletails, Fat Freddies, and Flash Flies in silver, chartreuse, fuchsia, orange, red, and purple are good. Tie them in sizes 2 through 5/0 and add some weight or lead eyes.

The Kanektok is one of the state's premier chum salmon fisheries. Many would consider this damning with faint praise, but in truth there are few fish that fight harder than a fresh chum. They move into the river in early July. Look for them in water with a moderate current that's 2 to 3 feet deep, or schooled up in side sloughs. Although chums can get much larger, most run between 8 and 12 pounds and an 8-weight rod will handle them. Brightly colored flies, smaller than those used for kings, will draw aggressive strikes. Fish them close to the bottom with short erratic strips.

The Kanektok gets a healthy run of sockeye salmon, but there is little sport fishing for them. Unlike kings, chums, and cohos, sockeyes are generally not aggressive in fresh water, and most catches on the Kanektok are accidental. Try small flies like Comets bounced behind a split shot. Takes are subtle so strike at any hesitation in the drift of your line.

Silver salmon provide some of the most exciting fishing on the river. Most of these fish run from 8 to 12 pounds and will take a fly aggressively. The river provides good habitat and good fishing for silvers well upstream, but the brightest fish are found in the lower stretches. A 7- or 8-weight rod with a sink-tip or shooting head is about right. Floating lines can be used in the slower sloughs. Silvers are more aggressive fish and will move to a fly, even taking waking flies from the surface on occasion. Try fishing leeches and Woolly Buggers tied in purple, chartreuse, fuchsia, and pink. Crystal Bullets are also effective.

Silvers prefer slower water than kings, and you will find them in protected channels, deep pools, sloughs, and eddies. Use a deep drift and short strip. Silvers are notorious for turning off and on. There are few things more frustrating than sight fishing to a huge pod of silvers with lockjaw, but keep at it and try changing flies. Sooner or later they will turn on and you will have all the action that your arms can handle.

Arctic char are the backbone of the Kanektok's fishing. They are numerous, inhabit most of the river, and will take a fly eagerly. Look for them along gravel bars and in tailouts. They will often lie in schools just where a pool begins to break into a riffle. A 5- or 6-weight will handle the char, trout, and grayling. Char will hit streamers, Woolly Buggers, and smolt patterns, but they are most effectively taken on egg imitations, particularly late in the summer when they are keyed into spawning salmon.

One of my most memorable evenings in Alaska

The rolling hills of southwest Alaska provide a background for the Kanektok.

occurred at the lower end of a gravel bar just above Klak Creek. A large school of char—all males—lay in a tailout. A friend and I spent several hours skating deer-hair mice over them, landing a fish on almost every cast. I use the word "landing" advisedly, because every time a fish would throw the hook another would grab it immediately. The fish would explode up from under the fly or roostertail across the surface after it or, on occasion, even launch themselves into the air and come down on top of the waking mouse. We moved 20 yards upstream and the same thing occurred, except these fish were all female. We finally quit for dinner, and when we went back for a few late evening casts, the fish wouldn't even look at the fly.

Like the char, grayling are abundant and eager. You will be overgunned for these fish with a trout rod, so if you have room for an extra rod, consider a 4-weight with a floating line. Grayling that are overpowered will simply quit fighting, and as a result Alaskans often treat them with disdain. On light tackle, however, they can give a good account of themselves, and they will readily take a dry fly. They are not selective and a collection of Elk Hair Caddis, Parachute Adams, and Yellow Humpies will suffice.

The Kanektok's real prize is its rainbows. They are not the bragging-size fish found in the rivers farther east, but they make up for it with their strength and beauty. Often referred to in publicity fliers as leopard rainbows, they are characterized by a deep crimson stripe and dark heavy spots. Most run in the 18- to 22-inch range, with larger fish tucked away in the cover. Drift an egg pattern behind every pair of spawning salmon you see. Bang Woolly Buggers and sculpin patterns into the banks or swing them through the riffles. The rainbows love those big piles of snags and rootwads, particularly if there are dead salmon carcasses caught up in the branches. Try a ginger Bunny Bugger, a flesh fly, or an Egg-Sucking Leech.

The Kanektok is perhaps the best river to fish Alaska's most famous surface pattern, the deer-hair mouse. You can buy these flies tied so realistically that you'd swear they eat cheese. The addition of ears and little beady eyes don't seem to have any effect on the trout, however, and a trimmed gob of deer hair with a chamois tail will do just as well.

Conventional wisdom has you toss the fly into the bank and then swim it as if it were a vole or lemming that has fallen in the water. In fact, it is far more effective to simply skate the fly midstream or even just let it hang in the current. It doesn't look much like a panicked mouse, but trout and char love it. The exception to this technique is in the slow back channels, where a realistic presentation will pull those big leopard 'bows up through 3 feet of crystal-clear water to suck in your fly. There are few sights in freshwater fishing more tantalizing than watching a big trout slowly drift up under a mouse.

There is a temptation when fishing remote areas such as this to believe that you cannot have an impact on the population. Fishermen who wouldn't dream of killing a rainbow at home are sometimes tempted to relive the trout dinners of their childhood, ignoring the catch-and-release regulations. But keep in mind that rainbows are at the edge of their range here and cannot take any significant pressure. Char and grayling are better adapted, but they should also be considered catch-and-release fish.

Salmon, on the other hand, are managed for harvest, including commercial, subsistence, and sport. Save that fish dinner for the lower stretches of the river, when fresh food is at a premium, and the salmon are in prime shape. You will never have a better streamside fish fry. Just be careful about drawing in a hungry bear and check the regs before you go—emergency closures may be instituted on some species during years with small runs.

There has been a lot written about the Kanektok over the past 30 years. The articles always include tales of big trout, massive numbers of salmon, and spectacular scenery. There is, however, another thread that seems to run through almost every article—lousy weather. The river is tucked up against the mountains and catches the full force of the Bering Sea storms. It is not uncommon to have a week of hard rain, stiff winds, and swirling fog, particularly in August. Three-season tents and plastic raingear that suffice in much of the Lower Forty-Eight are dangerously inadequate for Bristol Bay. If your gear won't keep you dry and warm through days of monsoon-like downpours, you had better upgrade before you venture into this country.

The Kanektok is one of those rivers that appear on every serious flyfisherman's wish list. Its popularity has perhaps tarnished its appeal, but it is still one of the world's premier flyfishing streams. And it's hard to think of a better western Alaskan destination.

Stream Facts: Kanektok River

Seasons and Special Regulations

- All species: unbaited single-hook artificial flies or lures. In all flowing waters downstream of the Togiak National Wildlife Refuge wilderness area, no person may sport fish from a boat or the riverbank within 300 feet of a legally operating subsistence gill net.

- King salmon: May 1 to July 25. The bag and possession limit is 3 fish over 20 inches only 2 of which may be over 28 inches. The bag and possession limit is 10 fish of 20 inches or less. King salmon tag required.

- Other salmon: open entire year; limit 5 per day, 5 in possession.

- Rainbow trout: open entire year; catch-and-release only June 8 to Oct. 31; limit 2 fish, only one over 20 inches Nov. 1 to June 7.

- Arctic char/Dolly Varden: the bag and possession limit is 3 fish, no size limit.

- Arctic grayling: the bag and possession limit is 2 fish, no size limit.

Species

- King (chinook) salmon average 18 to 30 lbs. Enter river in early June.

- Chum salmon average 8 to 15 lbs. Best fishing is in lower river. Enter river in late June, with the peak of the run in mid-July.

- Pink salmon run strongest in even-numbered years. Average 4 to 6 lbs. Fish enter river in late July and are in the best shape in lower river and at the beginning of the run.

- Sockeye (red) salmon average 5 to 7 lbs. Best fishing is mid-July.

- Silver (coho) salmon average 9 to 15 lbs. Enter river in early August, with run peaking by late August.

- Rainbow trout average 16 to 21 inches; present year-round.

- Arctic char/Dolly Varden average 16 to 22 inches; present year-round. Best fishing is mid-July to mid-September.

- Arctic grayling average 14 to 18 inches. Present year-round.

River Characteristics

- The Kanektok is about 90 miles long, flowing from Kagati Lake to Kuskokwim Bay. The village of Quinhagak is located at the mouth and is the only permanent settlement on the river. The river is moderate-sized with flat water and no rapids. There are sweepers in the braids.

- The upper river is high tundra, with the banks lined with willows. Trees (and sweepers) appear in the middle, braided section. The coastal plain is wet tundra. The river runs clear and, except at high water, there are plenty of gravel bars suitable for camping.

Weather can be severe, particularly late in the season.

Lodges and Guides

- **Alaska West**, www.anglersadventures.com/akwest; tent camp;
(winter) 200 W, 34th Ave., Ste. 1170, Anchorage, AK; 563-9788;
(summer) P.O. Box 129, Quinhagak, AK; 556-8146

- **Kanektok River Safaris**, tent camp, Annie Friendly, P.O. Box 9, Quinhagak, AK; 556-8211

- **Kanektok River Wilderness Camp**,
www.royalcoachmanlodge.com;
(winter) 1062 West Ridge Road, Cornville, Maine 04976
(summer) P.O. Box 450 Dillingham, AK 99576; 868-6033

- **Ultimate Rivers**, www.ultimaterivers.com; float trips; P.O. Box 670534, Chugiak, AK 99567; 688-6535

Maps

- *Alaska Atlas and Gazetteer*, pages 54, 55

Goodnews River

It's hard not to like a river with a name like the Goodnews, especially when it's surrounded by numerous waters with unpronounceable names. And there is a lot to like about the Goodnews. It is a scenic beauty with good fishing for silvers, rainbows, and Dolly Varden. The upper river cuts through a wilderness area, and there is not a lot of wilderness left as wild as what you'll find in southwestern Alaska. It is intimate in size, crystal-clear, and moves at a moderate pace. The caribou are once again beginning to wander here, and the bear population, although healthy, is not unreasonable. And the Goodnews is a river made to be floated.

The Goodnews actually consists of several branches, all flowing out of the Ahklun Mountains into lower Kuskokwim Bay about 375 miles southwest of Anchorage. In a part of the state characterized by flat and marshy tundra, the Ahkluns are a picturesque bright spot. These are old eroded mountains covered in green (or the brighter colors of autumn tundra), and they're reminiscent of some areas in the Brooks Range. Access is by floatplane from either Dillingham or Bethel. The upper stretches of all the branches are small and may require dragging the raft at low water, so the vast majority of fishermen float the main stem of the river, beginning at Goodnews Lake.

There is a little-used alternative to the main stem, though. The Middle Fork is formed by two small branches

The Goodnews is well known for its heavily spotted rainbows—usually referred to as leopard 'bows.

that join about 15 miles downstream of their respective headwater lakes. Both are shallow and rocky at the top, and you have to travel about a day and a half before you hit fish. From the confluence of the branches, the Middle Fork (sometimes referred to as the Kukaktlik) remains smaller than the main river, but it has the same populations of fish. It joins the main river a few miles from the ocean, making it a distinctly separate river for floating purposes.

Assuming that you choose the main river, the plane will land you on a gravel beach at what may technically be the outlet of Goodnews Lake, but it's little more than a narrow neck in the lake. The rolling hills and dry tundra ridgelines that surround the campsite provide such a tempting invitation to explore that it is not easy to begin the float. The first stretch of the trip is slow going, so unless you arrive early, this is a good spot to set up camp, relax, and shift gears.

The row across the lower section of the lake is a mile-long grind if the usual headwind is blowing, and that pace continues until you reach Awayak Creek, about 2½ miles farther downstream. The current moves quickly enough, but it is still a small stream, and at low water the raft will be dragging bottom. The silver salmon get this high and sockeye move all the way into the lake, but there are very few kings in this upper stretch. There are no rainbows, but the Dollys will follow the salmon all the way up from the ocean.

No good campsites are available in this stretch, so you must make it at least to Awayak Creek, where most people make their first river camps. If there are other rafters at the mouth of the creek, you can move on down. There are several campsites over the next 4 miles.

You will begin to find rainbows at Awayak Creek, but don't let the quickening speed of the river determine your pace. The best scenery and fishing are in the wilderness area, so don't be in a hurry to reach the bottom. (Just make sure you leave enough time to row through the very slow stretch near the mouth of the river.) Chuck Ash, one of Alaska's premier float-trip guides, know the Goodnews intimately. He prefers to travel only 6 to 8 miles a day in the stretch above the wilderness boundary.

Nimgun Creek comes in about 4 miles below Awayak. There is good Dolly and rainbow fishing in this stretch. The Goodnews is famous for its leopard 'bows, one of the most beautifully marked populations of rainbows in the world. They are heavily spotted, with bright colors, and most run 3 or 4 pounds. The Dollys can match them in size and color, if not in leaping ability. In August, the silvers are moving through, and with the river only 60 miles long, they are still in good shape even this close to the top.

Below Nimgun Creek the river enters a shallow canyon. The water moves a little faster through here, and there are a few rocks that need to be avoided. However, there are no sweepers and no whitewater of consequence. The kings and sockeyes spawn in this stretch. Look for trout and Dollys lying behind paired-up salmon. You will also find fish in the pockets just above and below the rocks. The canyon is about 7 miles long, and there is very little camping within its confines. The only places available are a few tundra benches, with their inherent problems of roots and bugs.

The river continues its pace below the canyon, running about 100 feet wide for the next 7 or 8 miles. The fishing for silvers improves, with a few deeper, slower stretches that allow the fish to pause in the migration. Watch for flashes or rolling fish. If the pool is not too deep, sight fishing will be the most productive method of getting your fly in front of the fish's nose. Just don't spook them by getting too close. Most salmon flies will work, but Ash says that it is always difficult to beat an Egg-Sucking Leech for silvers. Fish them deep with a slow strip.

A couple of miles above Canyon Creek, the river enters a wet tundra flood plain, and begins to braid up, with willow- and cottonwood-covered islands breaking the flow into classic small-stream fisheries. The braids continue all the way to the outlet, becoming more predominant as you move downstream. Without a GPS you will almost certainly be lost in this stretch most of the time, although the river does swing by the occasional low hill that may give you a position on the map. There are some sweepers in here, but the channels are all large enough that they do not pose a problem. There are plenty of gravel bars in the braids, and camping is easy.

As you pass through the sometimes narrow, brushy channels, you need to remember that these are the same waters in which local bears are looking for salmon. It is easy to drift right up on an unsuspecting bruin without either you or the bear realizing it until the last minute. My closest encounters have come in exactly that situation. Most bears faced with fight-or-flight proximity will run, but if you float into a sow with cubs, you have a big problem. The only way to survive an attack by a mother bear is by protecting your vital areas and playing dead. This is probably not an option if the bear is suddenly in the raft with you in the middle of the river. The easiest prevention tactic is to talk loudly to each other if you are drifting through brushy braids with a short sight line.

The fishing for both salmon and trout can be very good in this stretch. Bright silvers can be found along the edges of sloughs and in slow, deep water. Spend some time exploring the back channels, particularly around the logs and snags that provide cover for rainbows. Look for spawning chums in the shallows, and the brick red logs that denote king salmon in the main flow. The rainbows and Dollys will be lying behind them. This is also a good place to try a deer-hair mouse, at least if you are there before or after the spawning season. Once the salmon start to spawn, the trout will be focused on a steady diet of eggs.

The wilderness area designation ends at Tigyukauivet Mountain. The remainder of the river is within the Togiak National Wildlife Refuge, but there are a number of private inholdings along the banks (native allotments). In order to avoid any conflicts from this point down you should camp only on the islands or the gravel bars below mean high water.

The braids last for about 25 miles until you reach the confluences with the middle and the south forks. There is a sport fishing camp on the left bank, and the river splits here. Take the channel on the river's left—it has more water.

It's very slow going in here, and you need to have someone from the village of Goodnews meet you with a powerboat and tow you back across the tidal flats. The alternative is a truly ugly row into a constant headwind, with the prospect of the tide going out and stranding you on some exposed mudbar. Having floated the Goodnews before such pickups were available, I can assure you it is worth the extra expense. Freshwater Adventures, the air taxi service in Dillingham, can arrange a pickup for you.

As with all Alaskan rivers, timing is everything if you hope to catch fish. Chums and sockeyes move into the river in late June and early July. The kings come in just a bit later in the Goodnews than in other rivers, just behind the early chums. The Dollys are sea-run char and enter the river about mid-July. Most fishermen come for the great runs of silver salmon, which means that mid-August is prime fishing, but also the busiest time on the river.

Although the Goodnews is not a large river, the fish are big, wind can be a problem, and some of the best holes are deep. You need tackle that can handle those conditions. Ash recommends a 6-weight for trout and Dollys. You can muscle a big rainbow with that rod, which is easier on the fish. You will need a floating line and a sink-tip. If you have a heavy sink-tip, such as a Teeny 300, throw it in the bag. If the river is high, it will help get the fly down into some of the deeper holes.

Fly selection is pretty standard. Woolly Buggers, Egg Sucking Leeches, and other streamers will work on the rainbows and Dollys until the salmon start to spawn. Once that happens, an egg pattern is almost mandatory. Ash ties his Glo-Bugs with a $5/16$ tungsten bead in front. This often is enough to get the fly down without additional weight, which makes it easier to detect a strike. You may also want to throw a few size 14 Adams into the box. A mayfly hatch comes off in late August and early September, and there is a chance for some dry-fly action.

The Goodnews receives its heaviest usage during the coho run—about the middle of August. An 8-weight is the rod of choice for silvers. A sink-tip is usually the best way to get the fly down to the salmon's level. Use a short leader of about 12-pound test. Egg-Sucking Leeches, black and chartreuse Woolly Buggers, and bunny flies in various colors will cover most of your fly pattern needs.

For anglers with the necessary wilderness experience, the Goodnews is one of Alaska's finest float trips. For those who are not equipped to do it themselves, but don't mind sleeping on gravel bars and packing up their tents, guides like Chuck Ash will show you Alaska as it was meant to be enjoyed. And if all that sounds too rigorous, there are outfitters with permanent camps near the mouth that will take you upstream in a jet boat and bring you back for a hot shower in the evening.

Stream Facts: Goodnews River

Seasons and Special Regulations

- All species: Open year-round except king salmon.

- King salmon: May 1 to July 25. The bag and possession limit is 3 fish over 20 inches only 2 of which may be over 28 inches. The bag and possession limit is 10 fish of 20 inches or less. King salmon tag required.

- Other salmon: open entire year; limit 5 per day, 5 in possession.

- Rainbow trout: open entire year; limit two fish, only one over 20 inches.

- Arctic char/Dolly Varden: the bag and possession limit is 3 fish, no size limit.

- Arctic grayling: the bag and possession limit is 2 fish, no size limit.

Species

- King (chinook) salmon average 18 to 30 lbs. Enter river in early June, season opens June 15, closes July 31.

- Chum salmon average 8 to 15 lbs. Best fishing is in lower river. Enter river in late June, with the peak of the run in mid-July.

- Pink salmon run strongest in even-numbered years. Average 4 to 6 lbs. Fish enter river in late July and are in the best shape in lower river and at the beginning of the run.

- Sockeye (red) salmon average 5 to 7 lbs.; best fishing is mid-July.

- Silver (coho) salmon average 9 to 15 lbs. Enter the river in early August, with run peaking by late August.

- Rainbow trout average 16 to 21 inches; present year-round.

- Arctic char/Dolly Varden average 16 to 22 inches. Fish enter river in June. Best fishing is mid-July to mid-September.

- Arctic grayling average 14 to 18 inches. Present year-round.

River Characteristics

- The Goodnews is a small crystal-clear wilderness river. It holds good populations of rainbows and char and has a strong run of silver salmon. It is very remote, but has few obstacles to rafting. One of Alaska's finest floats.

Lodges and Guides

- **Brightwater Alaska**, www.brightwateralaska.com; float trips with independent guide Chuck Ash; P.O. Box 112796, Anchorage, AK 99511; 344-1340

- **Alaska River Adventures**, www.alaskariveradv.com; float trips; 1-888-836-9027, 235-2647, P.O. Box 725, Cooper Landing, AK

- **Goodnews River Lodge,** www.epicfishing.com; weatherport camp; 4066 Wolf Lake Dr., Lewiston, MI 49756; 1-800-274-8371

Maps

- *Alaska Atlas and Gazetteer*, pages 54, 55

Aniak River

The Aniak, and its sister river the Kwethluk, flows from the Kilbuck Mountains through forests and muskeg across the coastal plain into the Kuskokwim. Although the fishing can be good, and at times excellent, these streams receive much less pressure than many other rivers. They are very remote, subject to blowing out in heavy rains, and possess a number of obstacles ranging from bears to sweepers and huge logjams. Nevertheless, if you possess the necessary experience, and are looking for a wilderness river on which you will see few other people, the drainages of the lower Kuskokwim may be the ticket.

The largest of these rivers, the Aniak, is the most popular. A few outfitters float it from its upper stretches, and several lodges near the village of Aniak run jet boats upstream. It has good runs of king and silver salmon and healthy populations of char, grayling, and rainbows. It is not an easy river, and there are sweeper-choked stretches that are dangerous, but most of it is pure wilderness.

There are two places from which it is possible to begin a float trip on the Aniak. You can put in at Aniak Lake and float the main river, or you can start on the Salmon River and float down to its confluence with the Aniak. The latter is the better choice for most people.

Salmon River floats begin with a wheelplane landing at a dirt airstrip at Bell Creek—the product of some old mining activity in the area. The strip can handle a Beaver or a 206, which determines how much gear you can carry. Be careful if you are flying with someone not familiar with the strip—it can get soft after heavy rains. Most people fly in from the village of Aniak, which has scheduled air service from Anchorage.

From the Bell Creek strip, it's about a quarter-mile

Don't be afraid to explore the back channels for rainbows, as they will follow the spawning chums into shallow water.

Aniak and Kwethluk Rivers

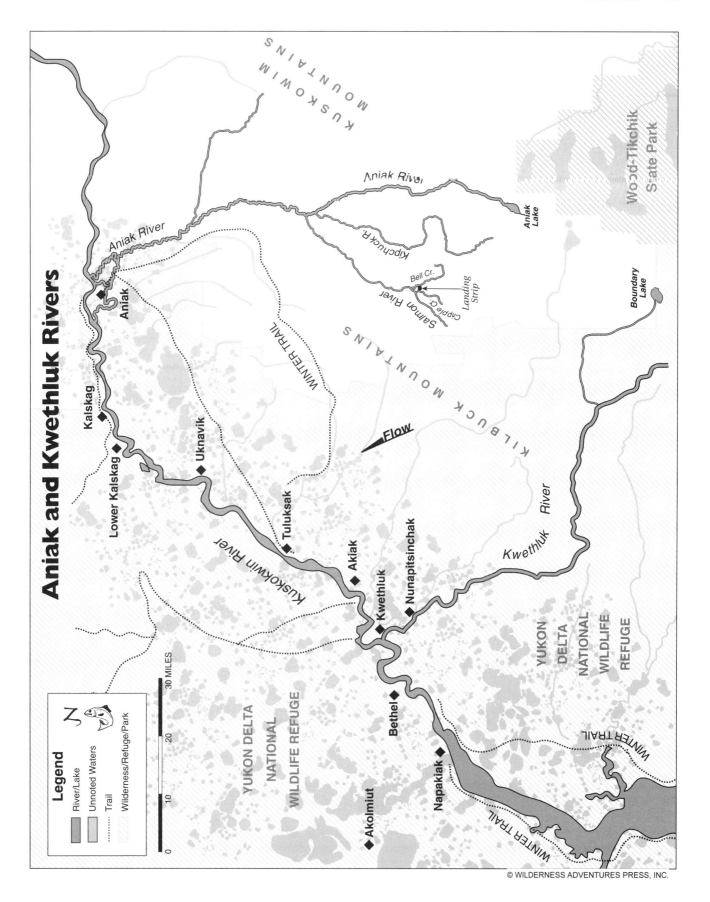

KUSKOWIM MOUNTAINS

Aniak River

Aniak River

Kipchuck R.

Aniak Lake

Wood-Tikchik State Park

Bell Cr.

Landing Strip

Salmon River

Cripple Cr.

Boundary Lake

Aniak

Kalskag

Lower Kalskag

Uknavik

WINTER TRAIL

KILBUCK MOUNTAINS

Flow

Kwethluk River

Tuluksak

Kuskokwin River

Akiak

Kwethluk

Nunapitsinchak

Kwethluk

YUKON DELTA NATIONAL WILDLIFE REFUGE

Bethel

YUKON DELTA NATIONAL WILDLIFE REFUGE

WINTER TRAIL

Akolmiut

Napakiak

WINTER TRAIL

Legend

N

| River/Lake
| Unnoted Waters
| Trail
| Wilderness/Refuge/Park

0   10   20   30 MILES

descent down a steep trail to Cripple Creek, a small tributary of the Salmon. A short float brings you to the confluence, which has king and silver salmon, as well as grayling and char, the resident species found at higher altitudes. This is subalpine country with scrub spruce and open ridges. The scenery is delightful, and there is a fair amount of wildlife.

The first 10 miles or so of the river flow through open country. It is small, fast, and clear with riffles and pools. There can be good dry-fly fishing during the first part of the summer. Below this stretch, the river drops down into heavier timber, and it begins to twist and wind. Sweepers and logjams appear and some scouting is required to avoid being swept into (or under) fallen trees. King and chum salmon spawn here, beginning in late July, and the fishing for char is very good. Fish the seams and ends of the islands. As you drop down the river, rainbows begin to appear and the fishing continues to improve.

The Salmon represents about half of the total float. There is good camping, particularly at the upper end. The last 15 to 20 miles are the most productive. It braids up in the lower section and has a few back channels that deserve fishing. The river returns to a single channel just before the confluence, but enters the Aniak in a small tripartite delta.

Sweepers and logjams become common, but are less of a problem than on the main river below the confluence. The Salmon is one of the few rivers in this part of the country that remains clear after heavy rains. Some of the best fishing comes as it joins up with the Aniak and the Kipchuck (a third branch).

The float down from Aniak Lake is much more problematic than the Salmon. The river begins in high tundra among the Kipchuck Mountains. The upper stretch is slow, thin, and straight, but it soon enters spruce forest. Rafters encounter frequent logjams and heavy sweepers.

The tangled pools of the Aniak hold some beautiful, heavily spotted rainbows.

Multiple difficult portages around obstructions are required. A saw is a necessity to cut your way through snags and brushpiles.

The river is fast enough that there is a real risk of being trapped under a sweeper. You need to scout heavily to avoid being swept into a dangerous situation. There are also a lot of bears (both black and grizzly) in this area, and frequent confrontations are usual. There are a lot of spawning areas, though, and the fishing above the confluence can be very good.

Once the three rivers come together, the Aniak swells to a major river. It braids up into a maze of side channels and islands, with back sloughs and oxbows. Sweepers and logjams become even more frequent, making navigation difficult even for the experienced. There are numerous gravel bars and camping is excellent. The river flows due north, winding through cottonwood forest.

Because the channels change dramatically every winter, the downed trees collect at current bottlenecks, the very places that the river wants to take a raft. Jet boats reach up into this area, probing the back channels. Even for them, though, this is a challenging and sometimes dangerous stretch of river. To make matters worse, the river is susceptible to blowing out in bad weather, a common occurrence in August. High water may simply sweep over the banks, with the entire river flowing through the trees, a nightmare for rafters. Make no mistake, this is a fast, big river best fished with a guide.

The same collection of sweepers and snags that make the river a navigational challenge provide cover for its big leopard-spotted rainbows. The sloughs and back eddies provide holding places for migrating silvers, and the strength of the main channel makes it a great king salmon river. Much of the best fishing is found in the numerous backwaters. These old sloughs and oxbows often have a section with enough current to provide spawning habitat for chums, with their attendant rainbows and char. Unless it has rained heavily, the side channels, which roared through the forest during spring runoff, have dropped by August and provide prime fishing.

As the river approaches its confluence with the Buckstock, it begins to slow. Below the Buckstock it becomes a deep meandering stream that has little in the way of fishing beyond pike and the occasional sheefish in the spring. Most rafters avoid a long row by being picked up by jet boat before they enter this stretch.

So, given these difficulties, why do people continue to rave about the Aniak? Simply put, the fishing is superb. The kings begin to arrive in early summer, and the last week of June and early July provide good fishing. They prefer the main channel of the river, but also move up the Salmon and into the upper Aniak, where they are accessible to a flyrodder. Don't wait too long if you are targeting kings, though. They are on their spawning beds by mid-July and should not be harassed. A 10-weight rod is about right for these fish.

Fishing for kings requires getting deep in heavy water, a perfect place for a heavy sinking line. Unfortunately, it is a river bottom full of snags, and the risk of losing an entire fly line is high. Most experienced anglers prefer a floating line with lots of weight. The usual collection of king flies will work here.

Silver salmon enter the river during the first week in August. It takes them two to three weeks to make it to the upper river. The numerous areas of slow water are perfect for silvers, which will use the edges and current seams for resting areas. An 8-weight will handle the silvers here. Take both heavily and lightly weighted flies. You will need to go deep, but in some stretches the water is slow enough that a big lead-eyed leech will simply snag on the bottom. Leeches and Flash Flies work well. The water is often colored up, and bright flies are most effective.

The Aniak is one of the most distant outposts for rainbows, but it grows them big. The river's resident fish (rainbows, char, and grayling) provide excellent fishing, particularly in late summer when the salmon are spawning. Marty Decker, of Frontier River Adventures, has been rafting the Aniak for about eight years. He recommends looking for rainbows in the back channels and up the sloughs, where they will follow the chum salmon.

For the main river, Marty is adamant that heavily weighted flies are a necessity. This is a fast, deep river, and you need to get the fly down quickly if you are to have a shot at the best holding water. A strike indicator can be used, but it is often more effective to use heavy split shot and keep a tight line. These are not sophisticated trout, and a perfect dead drift is not often necessary. You should probably not go lighter than a 6-weight for rainbows. These are tough, heavy fish and there's a lot of current and plenty of cover to dash into. The faster you can land them, the better shape they are in when you release them.

Marty tells his clients to bring lots of terminal tackle and heavy tippet, regardless of the species being targeted. The river bottom is littered with snags, and the fish lie in among them. If you are going to catch fish, you are going to lose flies. With all the snags and sweepers, a broken rod is always a possibility, so take spares.

The Aniak is a difficult river with big rewards for those who venture there. It can make a challenging float trip for an experienced rafter or an exciting guided float for the adventurous or for those staying at one of the comfortable lodges on the river, an opportunity to fish country seen by very few.

The day may come when it has the same crowds as its more accessible cousins, but in the meantime it remains a wilderness gem.

Stream Facts: Aniak River

Seasons and Special Regulations

- All species: In all flowing waters upstream of Doestock Creek, only unbaited single-hook artificial flies or lures.

- King salmon: May 1 to July 25. The daily aggregate bag limit for salmon is three fish, of which no more than two can be king salmon, including pink, sockeye, and coho salmon. King salmon limit is two daily more than 20 inches long, and two annually more than 20 inches long.

- Sockeye, pink, and coho salmon: open entire year; three fish, no size limit.

- Chum salmon: no retention or possession year-round. All chum salmon must be released immediately.

- Rainbow trout: open entire year; no retention or possession year-round. All rainbow trout must be released immediately.

- Arctic char/Dolly Varden, arctic grayling, lake trout, sheefish, northern pike, and burbot (in combination): the bag and possession limit is three fish, in aggregate—but only one of each species may be retained. No size limit.

Species

- King (chinook) salmon average 18 to 30 lbs. Enter river in late June.

- Pink salmon run strongest in even-numbered years. Average 4 to 6 lbs.; fish enter river in late July. Fish are in the best shape in lower river and at the beginning of the run.

- Sockeye (red) salmon average 5 to 7 lbs.; best fishing is mid-July.

- Silver (coho) salmon average 9 to 15 lbs. Enter river in early August, with run peaking by late August.

- Rainbow trout average 18 to 22 inches, with larger fish common; present year-round.

- Arctic char/Dolly Varden average 16 to 22 inches; present year-round. Best fishing is mid-July to mid-September.

- Arctic grayling average 14 to 18 inches. Present year-round.

River Characteristics

- The Aniak is a big, fast river with lots of sweepers and brushpiles. It is a difficult and sometimes dangerous float and is best done with an experienced guide. Fishing can be excellent for king and coho salmon, as well as large rainbows and arctic char.

Lodges and Guides

- **Frontier River Guides**, www.frontierriverguides; float trips; 929-3244

- **Alaska Dream Lodge**, www.alaskadreamlodge.com; lodge; P.O. Box 289, Aniak, AK 99557; 1-888-850-2555

- **Aniak River Lodge**, www.aniakriverloadge.com; lodge; (winter) 295 Kelly Rd., Bellingham, WA 98226; 1-800-747-8403

- **Aniak Air Guides**: www.worldwidefishing.com/alaska; fly-outs, guided and unguided float trips; P.O. Box 93, Aniak, AK 99577; (winter) 495-9001; (summer) 675-4540

- **Ultimate Rivers**, www.ultimaterivers.com; float trips; P.O. Box 670534, Chugiak, AK 99567; 688-6535

Maps

- *Alaska Atlas and Gazetteer*, page 131

Kwethluk River

Remote and rarely traveled, the Kwethluk provides an alternative to its more renowned neighbors. For the wilderness diehard who wants to catch some fish, this is one of the last streams to provide isolation and rainbow trout. It takes about a week to float down to the take-out point, and you may not see another person.

The float trip begins on a small tundra lake located at the edge of the Togiak National Wildlife Refuge, known appropriately enough as Boundary Lake. There is a short portage (50 yards) from the lake to the river. The flat glacial plain that encompasses the river makes for good hiking, but make sure you have your bug dope accessible when you land.

The upper river is tiny, and at low water will require some dragging. This is a riffle-and-pool section, but holds nothing other than a few small grayling. The best thing to do is keep the rods in the cases and enjoy the float. There is a lot of wildlife in the edge of the mountains, particularly caribou and bear. You may also be lucky enough to spot a wolf.

Unlike many rivers in western Alaska, the Kwethluk does not go through a canyon section as it descends from the mountains. As a consequence, there are no portages or rapids to contend with. There is some spruce, but it is primarily open country, making it a trouble-free float.

The good rainbow fishing begins above Elbow Mountain and continues on down to Three Step Mountain. Look for fish in cover and behind the spawning salmon. Most of the fishing takes place in the main stem of the river, rather than the braids and backwaters common on some streams. John McDonald, of Kuskokwim River Adventures, likes sculpin patterns and ginger bunny flies with a little red or green flash in the tail.

The Kwethluk gets a good run of silvers, but they are not always easy to find. Look for them in deeper holes and at creek mouths.

Traditional subsistence culture is still the dominant use of salmon on many Kuskokwim Basin rivers.

BETHEL

Population: Approx. 5,471
Alaska Area Code: 907
Zip Code: 99559

GUIDES AND LODGES

Kuskokwim Wilderness Adventures, P.O. Box 1225, Bethel, AK 99559; 543-3900; www.kuskofish.com

Rainbow Wilderness Lodge, Nugashak River; P.O. Box 85022, Fairbanks, AK 99708; 458-8515; www.rainbowwildernesslodge.com

ACCOMMODATIONS

Bethel Slough Bed & Breakfast, Bethel, AK; 1-888-543-4334; www.bethelhotel.com; grantfbx@unicom-alaska.com

Pacifica Guest House, P.O. Box 1208, 1220 Eddie Hoffman Highway, Box 1208; Atmautluak, AK 99559; 543-4305

Sandbar Suites, Bethel, AK 99559; 543-2861

Lynnette's Bed and Breakfast, 4401 Larson; 543-7730

Bentley's Porter House B & B , 26 rooms; 624 1st Ave.; 543-3552

Delta Cottage, 124 Gunderson Ct.; 543-3610

Bethel Longhouse Hotel, 543-4612

RESTAURANTS

Dimitri's Riverfront Restaurant, Greek/American food

Datu's Snack Shack, burgers

Northern Lights, breakfast

CAR RENTAL

Payless Car Rental, 3340 Airport Road, Bethel, AK 99559; 543-3058

Emerald Car Rental, 3580 State Hwy. Bethel, AK 99559, 543-1990

AIR TAXIS

Papa Bear Adventures/Ptarmigan Air, P.O. Box 2509, Bethel, AK 99559; 543-5275; www.pbadventures.com;

BEAR ESSENTIALS

By Dan Busch

Bears are an important part of the Alaska ecosystem. There are over 80,000 brown, grizzly, and black bears in the state, and your chance of sighting or encountering bears increases when traveling river and lake systems. Remember, you are on the river for the same reason the bears are—to fish. With some prior knowledge of their habitat and behavior, your time in Alaska's bear country can be safe and pleasant.

Alaska has around 30,000 brown and grizzly bears. Technically, they are classified as the same species. Generally, the term "brown bear" is used to identify the species found along the coastal areas, and the term "grizzly" to identify species found in the interior and northern areas. The coastal brown bear is generally larger, most likely because of the rich food sources available and the milder, shorter winter. Mature male brown bears average about 700 pounds, but a large mature male can reach as much as 1,400 pounds.

There are also 50,000 or so black bears, including all the subspecies and color phases. Mature male black bears average about 200 pounds, but a large mature bear can be more than double that size.

When planning your fishing trip to Alaska, I recommend you contact either the ADF&G, National Park Service, or U.S. Fish and Wildlife Service offices for the area you are considering. They can provide you with accurate and current information regarding bear densities on river and lake systems in the area at various times of year. In addition, they can provide you with complete field guides to bear behavior and guidelines for hiking, camping, and fishing in bear country.

These guidelines should be familiar to everyone in your group, and each person should know the appropriate response to different bear encounter and sighting scenarios. Remember that being informed and respecting bears will reduce the risk of either the bear or you suffering from an unpleasant experience.

The suggested guidelines below for travel in bear country by no means represent a complete field guide to bear behavior or for hiking, camping, and fishing in bear country. Be sure to contact local game managers in the area you plan to fish for complete information.

AVOID ENCOUNTERS. Avoid bears if you can and give them an opportunity to avoid you. Most bears are only interested in protecting their own space, cubs, and food. When selecting a campsite, keep it away from obvious bear trails along riverbanks and lakeshores, as these are natural travel routes for bears. It's nice to have the river visible and audible from your camp, but by doing so you only increase your odds of an unpleasant bear experience.

If a bear approaches while you are fishing, stop immediately. If you have a fish on, break it off immediately. One technique that has become popular in recent years is the use of portable electric fence systems to protect cabins and campsites from uninvited guests. Motion-activated devices that emit high volume sounds have also become popular for detecting approaching bears, especially at night.

DO NOT SURPRISE BEARS. Make your presence known by talking, traveling in a group, and avoiding thick cover. Using bear bells seems to be popular, but bears respond best to human voices.

DON'T INVITE BEARS FOR DINNER. Keep a clean campsite. Keep all food and garbage in bear-proof and odor-proof containers away from your campsite and avoid preparing smelly foods. Accumulated garbage on multi-day trips can be a problem, but you can reduce this accumulation by avoiding disposable paper or plastic products. Reusable dishware and utensils should be used. Wash all can, plastic, and paper food-packaging products with hot soapy water before storing them.

DO NOT ATTEMPT TO BURN YOUR GARBAGE. You can't get a fire hot enough to eliminate all of the food odors, and the burn pit will only become an attraction for bears. Attempting to bury garbage also causes problems. Bears have a very keen sense of smell and will locate and dig up trash regardless of how deep it's buried. If you have fish carcasses, dispose of them in the river or lake far from your campsite. Every possible effort should be made to discourage bears from associating humans and food. Pack out what you pack in.

ENCOUNTERS. Help the bear recognize you by talking, moving your arms, and standing abreast if you are with a group. Move away slowly, and move off a trail if you are on one. Do not attempt to outrun a bear. Frequently, curious bears will stand up on their hind legs to get a better view or smell. This is generally not threatening and should not be confused with other bear postures such as a frontal position or vocalizations like woofing, jaw-popping, growls, or roars. Other aggressive bear behaviors may include yawning, excessive salivation, or false charges. Bears frequently make false charges, but then break off before contact is made.

CONTACT. If a bear does make contact with you, fall to the ground and play dead, curling up in a ball with your hands protecting the back of your neck. It's easy to give this advice, of course, and something else all together to carry it out. But try to remain motionless and quiet for as long as possible. If a bear sees you move or hears you, it may continue or resume its attack. In some cases, especially with black bears, a bear may perceive you as food. If a bear continues an attack after you have assumed a defenseless position, fight back.

PROTECTION. Aerosol sprays that contain red pepper extract have become popular in recent years and have been used with some success. The sprays have an effective range of less than 15 feet, but they are handy and easy to use. Airlines prohibit packing these pepper sprays in your luggage, but they can be purchased in most destination communities.

The state of Alaska allows you to kill a bear in self-defense, but the hide and skull must be salvaged and turned over to the state. A 12-gauge shotgun with rifled slugs or a .300-caliber magnum rifle is an appropriate firearm for bears, but only in the hands of someone well schooled in their use. Heavy-caliber handguns are not adequate, even at close range in emergency situations.

In most situations bears are not a threat, but they do require your attention and respect. Keep alert and follow the guidelines developed by game managers for bear behavior, hiking, camping, and fishing in bear country. Learn how to share Alaska's rivers and lakes with the bears and enjoy your Alaska experience.

Not every angler you meet on the river will be a fly angler.
(*SHOT IN THE DARK Photography*)

Kodiak Archipelago

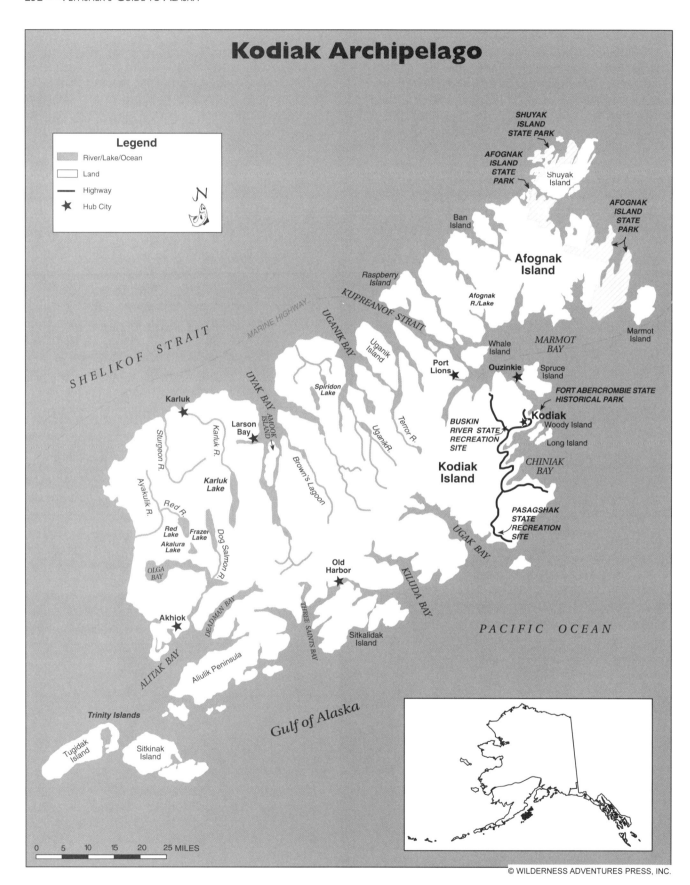

Legend
River/Lake/Ocean
Land
Highway
★ Hub City

N

SHUYAK
ISLAND
STATE PARK

AFOGNAK
ISLAND
STATE
PARK

Shuyak
Island

AFOGNAK
ISLAND
STATE
PARK

Ban
Island

**Afognak
Island**

Raspberry
Island

Afognak
R./Lake

Marmot
Island

SHELIKOF STRAIT

MARINE HIGHWAY

UGANIK BAY

KUPREANOF STRAIT

Uganik
Island

Whale
Island

*MARMOT
BAY*

Spruce
Island

UYAK BAY

Spiridon
Lake

**Port
Lions**

Ouzinkie

Karluk

AMOOK ISLAND

**Larson
Bay**

Karluk R.

Terror R.

Uganik R.

**BUSKIN
RIVER STATE
RECREATION
SITE**

FORT ABERCROMBIE STATE
HISTORICAL PARK

Kodiak

Woody Island

Sturgeon R.

Brown's Lagoon

*Karluk
Lake*

Long Island

Ayakulik R.

Red R.

**Kodiak
Island**

*CHINIAK
BAY*

Red
Lake

Frazer
Lake

Dog Salmon R.

Akalura
Lake

OLGA
BAY

UGAK BAY

PASAGSHAK
STATE
RECREATION
SITE

DEADMAN BAY

**Old
Harbor**

KILUDA BAY

Akhiok

THREE SAINTS BAY

Sitkalidak
Island

PACIFIC   OCEAN

ALITAK BAY

Aliulik Peninsula

Trinity Islands

Gulf of Alaska

Tugidak
Island

Sitkinak
Island

0   5   10   15   20   25 MILES

Kodiak Archipelago

By Dan Busch

Kodiak Island Archipelago is a group of islands in the Gulf of Alaska about 40 miles east of the Alaska Peninsula coast. This landmass covers over 5,000 square miles and extends over 175 miles north to south. Kodiak Island, the largest in the group, is about 3,500 square miles, and Afognak Island covers nearly 1,200 square miles.

Glaciers once covered much of the archipelago, carving out the irregular landscape as they receded. What remained were vast bays, mountains, valleys, and the island of Kodiak, with over 900 miles of coastline. No part of Kodiak Island is more than 15 miles from the ocean. The mild maritime climate tempers the area from the mainland extremes, and the 70 inches or more of annual rainfall keep the islands lush during the summer months and moist year-round.

Kodiak's early inhabitants date back over 7,000 years. They survived on the rich marine life around the island. At times, their numbers were double the current population of Kodiak. Russian colonization began in the mid-1700s. A fur-trading center was established on Kodiak, and the native population was enslaved to hunt the sea otter. One of the early fur warehouses still stands and is now the Baranov Museum.

Today, the island is known for its large commercial fishing port and fleet. Kodiak is ranked as one of the top fishing ports in the United States, with millions of pounds of salmon, crab, and bottom fish leaving the island each year bound for various parts of the world. Kodiak is also well known as the home of the Kodiak brown bear. The ADF&G estimates that between 2,800 and 3,500 of these large carnivores roam the archipelago.

The city of Kodiak is the population and economic center for the area. There are around 13,000 people here, with another 1,000 in the six surrounding villages. The island is easily reached via commercial air carrier. Both Alaska Airlines and ERA Aviation have direct daily flights from Anchorage. Schedules vary with the seasons and range from six to eight flights a day.

The Alaska Marine Highway system also provides passenger and vehicle service to Kodiak City and the village of Port Lions. The ferry departs from Homer or Seward, and it's a 10- to 14-hour trip depending on the weather. Service varies with the season, with four or five weekly trips during the summer months. Kodiak Island has a very limited road system, with less than 100 miles of road, and only a small portion of the northeast end of the island can be reached by vehicle. The outlying villages can only be reached by boat or plane. While Port Lions is the sole village with scheduled ferry service, all villages have weekly plane service and charter flights can be arranged.

Good fly-casting skills will increase your catch rate.

A happy angler with a fall coho.

KODIAK GENERAL FISH RUN TIMES

Species	Jan	Feb	Mar	Apr	May	Jun	Jul	Aug	Sep	Oct	Nov	Dec
King Salmon	-	-	-	+	++	+++	+++/++	++/+		-	-	-
Sockeye Salmon	-	-	-	-	-/+	++/+++	+++	+++/++	-	-	-	-
Coho Salmon	-	-	-	-	-	-	-	-/++	+++	++/-	-	-
Pink Salmon	-	-	-	-	-	-	++	+++	++/-	-	-	-
Chum Salmon	-	-	-	-	-	++	+++	+++/+	-	-	-	-
Dolly Varden	+	+	+	+++	++/+	+	+/+++	+++	+++	+++	+	+
Rainbow Trout	+	+	+	-	-	-/++	+++	+++	+++	+++	+	+
Steelhead Trout	+	+	+	-	-	-/+	+	+	+++	+++	++/+	+

+++ Excellent   ++ Good   + Fair   - Nonexistent/Closed Season

A happy angler with a fall coho.

"Chance favors the prepared angler."

LAND USE, ACCESS, AND OWNERSHIP

Access to most areas on Kodiak, Afognak, and Shuyak Islands can be difficult. However, along the road system many bays, river systems, and lakes can be reached by vehicle, and access can be extended with some hiking. Travel to the more remote areas requires the use of a boat or plane. Kodiak has a number of charter plane companies that provide wheel and float-plane service for remote travel.

Charter plane service can be costly, with limited weight capabilities, so plan carefully. Remember that you pay for the plane in both directions, the time it takes to get to your destination and the time it takes for the plane to return to its base. The reverse is also true on your pickup. Wheelplane landing areas are limited to the remote village airstrips and beaches. Travel to remote lodges and areas is done by floatplane. Some charter boat services can also provide transportation to remote coastal locations around the islands.

Kodiak, Afognak, and Shuyak Islands have several major public and private landowners, including the state of Alaska, the federal government, and several private native corporations. Some of these landowners require use permits and fees for specialized activities within their boundaries. Knowledge of the land ownership is a necessity before traveling around the Kodiak and Afognak areas. The ADF&G, Kodiak National Wildlife Refuge, and native corporations all have maps available to the public that show land ownership and permit requirements.

The Kodiak National Wildlife Refuge, established in 1941, is made up of over 1.6 million acres across Kodiak, Afognak, and Ban Islands. Hunting, fishing, and other recreational activities are permitted on refuge land. Permits are required in some areas, and there are limits on the number of anglers allowed on some systems at a given time.

These regulations and requirements change regularly, so contact the refuge prior to arriving in Kodiak for the current regulations.

The refuge has seven rental cabins available for public use, and many of these are on excellent salmon systems. The popular ones are booked in advance, and user selection is done by a quarterly lottery, four months prior to use. The cabins are well equipped and maintained and rent for $30 per night. Camping is also permitted within refuge boundaries. The refuge can also be a great source for information regarding fish availability and run timing on its lands.

The state of Alaska operates and maintains over 120,000 acres of parkland on Kodiak, Afognak, and Shuyak Islands. The most popular is the 47,000-acre Shuyak State Park. It covers most of Shuyak Island, located off the north end of Afognak Island. The park has four cabins available for public use and has a resident park ranger in the field during the summer season. These cabins are scattered throughout the island, and several are within a short walk of some very productive salmon systems.

Afognak Island State Park encompasses 75,000 acres and is on the northeast side of Afognak. Here the park has two cabins available for use. Cabin reservations can be made up to six months in advance and are on a first-come, first-served basis. The park service charges $50 per night for use of their cabins, and camping is also permitted within the park.

Buskin River State Park is on the road system just a few miles from the city of Kodiak, near the airport. It has improved campsites and toilet facilities and is within 100 yards of the Buskin River. The Pasagshak River State Park is also on the road system about 30 miles from the city. It has toilet facilities and camping areas and is located on the banks of the Pasagshak River. Fort Abercrombie State Park is 4 miles from the city center. It has improved campsites and toilet facilities and serves as the headquarters for the area.

Inquire about land ownership before traveling to remote sites.

Two of the larger private landowners are Koniag and Afognak native corporations. Much of Koniag's land is located on the southwest end of Kodiak, with the Afognak corporations on the northwest end of Kodiak and on Afognak Island. Both of these corporations require land-use permits to trespass on their lands. Day-use and year-long permits can be purchased by phone or directly from their offices in Kodiak at a rate of $35 per day, per person or $125 per year, per person. Several of the other native corporations in the area also require use permits.

Before you venture out into the remote areas of Kodiak and Afognak Islands, be sure you know who the landowners are and whether or not permits are required. If you are using a guide, outfitter, or going out to one of the many remote lodges in the area, they should be aware of any required permits.

Buskin River weir.

FISHING KODIAK WATERS

Fishing the waters of the Kodiak Archipelago takes some planning (around species run timing) and preparation (gear and equipment). If you will be fishing with a guide, then some of the pre-trip ground-work will be done for you. But if you are doing the trip on your own, then some in-depth research is necessary to assure yourself a quality experience. Allow for some weather days and some time to familiarize yourself with the area. Remember, the trip begins when the planning starts.

Accurate information in regard to run timing is essential. The chart at the beginning of this chapter should get you in the ballpark, but keep in mind that in most cases you will be targeting migrating fish rather than a resident population. The ADF&G monitors about 15 weir sites on Kodiak and Afognak, where they count and identify all the fish entering that system on a daily basis. With this detailed, current information, an angler can plan a trip date that corresponds to the peak return period of a specific species. This data is public information and is available through the ADF&G office in Kodiak or from their website at www.state.ak.us/adfghome.htm.

Personnel from the Kodiak office can also provide information regarding other river systems that are not monitored daily with a weir. By looking at return dates and fish return numbers for several previous years, some average return dates and numbers can be established. Return time varies from system to system, so if you are doing a trip on your own, you should concentrate on systems you hope to fish.

Doing a trip on your own requires some additional effort. If you are going to be fishing off the road system, be sure to familiarize yourself with the information provided for remote fishing. Know who the landowners are and whether or not you need a land-use permit. Since you will likely fly out to a river system, be sure to make arrangements with a flight service prior to your arrival in Kodiak.

Shop around if you are going to book with a guide or lodge. Fishing out of a lodge with a guide is no guarantee you will have great fishing, good guiding, or outstanding accommodations. Inquire about the lodge's return rate and talk to previous guests. Be sure that the operator's idea of an ideal fishing week is the same as yours. Have them supply you with a recommended tackle list and suggested fly patterns or fly samples.

Some lodges may claim they are a flyfishing service, yet don't have qualified or experienced staff to back it up. They may have a person who can flyfish and has done some local flyfishing, but that may be the extent of their experience. And try to avoid lodges where you have a mix of gear types being used. Be sure your fishing partners have the same philosophy as you. One angler's goal on an Alaskan fishing trip may be to take home a cooler of salmon, while others in the group may prefer other aspects of the angling experience. Talk it out before you go.

Fly patterns and fishing techniques here are similar to what you'll need for the rest of Alaska, but many anglers seem to have their own favorite patterns. The area sport shops carry an excellent selection of local patterns and can provide you with samples before you arrive in Kodiak. It is not necessary to be encumbered with dozens of fly patterns. Make sure you have a few productive styles and profiles that can be tied in a variety of colors and weights. Be versatile and flexible in your fly angling approach and tackle selection. I find that my fishing guests who have the most diverse fly angling experience are more adept and comfortable with new methods. You may find fish on the surface or holding in a fast, 6-foot-deep run. Be prepared to present a fly at whatever level the fish are holding.

Do not compromise with your gear. With the harsh weather conditions that an angler may encounter, only the best quality gear can give you the necessary service. Nothing can ruin a week of fishing faster than a rain jacket that can only keep you dry for the first hour or two of the day. And don't find out on the first day of a weeklong trip that your waders leak because they were not repaired or tested after the last outing. The same goes for any camping gear. When you are camping in a remote area, the last thing you want to experience is gear that does not meet your expectations or the claims by the manufacturer.

Rod sizes vary with the species around Kodiak. Five-weight rods work well for trout and pink salmon. For steelhead, coho, chum, and sockeye salmon, an 8-weight is a good selection. For chinook salmon, a 10-weight is the rod of choice. Depending on the quality of the rod, your experience, and the fishing conditions at the time of your visit, you may wish to go up or down a weight. Be familiar with the rod size you are going to be using. If you are accustomed to fishing with a 5-weight, do not buy an 8- or 10-weight the day before your trip without casting with it to see if it meets your needs and casting ability.

Learn how to fly cast, and be able to double haul. All your trip planning and gear preparation is of little value if the fish are 70 feet out and your casting limit is 50 feet. If you are not able to shoot a line out 80 feet or more with a few false casts, then learn how. Many anglers are good with dry flies or nymphs at 40 feet, but when the conditions require casting a weighted fly 80 feet or more, they begin to struggle even on calm days.

Often, I see fly anglers losing valuable fishing time and opportunities by false casting a dozen times or more just to get their flies out 50 feet. Their flies spend more time in the air that they do in the water. Nothing is more frustrating for an angler than to spend a week watching other anglers catch fish, while their own casting skills limit their success.

Guides can help you improve your skills and teach you how to cast, and that is fine if it is part of the objective of your trip. However, if your main objective is to catch fish, then learning how to fly cast is something you should accomplish before you reach your fishing destination. Most fly shops and major sporting goods stores will have fly casting lessons and classes at some time during the year. Take advantage of them. There are also several good videos available on fly casting that can be helpful. Fishing conditions can be challenging at times regardless of where you fish. By being able to handle the wind, wet, cold, heavily-weighted flies, sinking lines and have the ability to shoot your fly out 8 feet with a few false casts, you will be aready for whatever the day may bring or require.

Fishing Along the Road System

The road system on Kodiak is limited, but it does provide opportunities for the angler who doesn't want to fly out to remote destinations or lodges. However, one must keep in mind that because of the easy access, many of the popular river systems and bays can get crowded at times, especially during the coho season. Although you may not experience the density that other road-accessible areas of Alaska do, you will not be fishing alone.

The road-accessible waters account for nearly 70 percent of the total angler days in the entire Kodiak regulatory area. The run timing on these rivers is similar, and all of the road system rivers are closed to salmon fishing from August 1 through September 15 above the highway bridges to allow for fish escapement. On the Buskin River the closure begins at Bridge #1, the first bridge from the ocean.

Depending on the returns, some of the rivers can have extended closures if runs do not materialize or are late. Many of these are short river systems, 5 miles or less in length. Consequently, a rainfall of a half-inch or more can have a dramatic effect on the number of fish entering a system, run timing, holding areas, and fishing. Anglers must realize that fish entering these systems are migrating fish, and their location in a river can change daily. It is not uncommon to have large numbers of fish holding in a tidal zone one day and a few miles upriver the next, simply because of a rain shower or a cloudy day. However, because the rivers are short, they do clear up and drop quickly, unless the area receives an excessive amount of rain.

Although not every river on the Kodiak road system is discussed here, most streams that have some flowing water will have a few salmon or Dolly Varden in the system. Also, do not overlook the many bays and inlets. Most will have salmon within reach from the shoreline at some time in the salmon season. Look for showing fish as you travel along the road system. And pay close attention to areas where fresh water is flowing into salt water.

Remember, too, that just because you may be in sight of the road or near the road does not mean that bears are absent. Keep alert and watch for signs that bears are in the area. Always know the guidelines for bear behavior and fishing in bear country.

Buskin River

The Buskin River is the most popular river on the road system, and for good reason. It offers more diverse fishing opportunities and a greater variety of fish species than any other road-accessible fishery. You can stay right in the city of Kodiak and just take an easy 4-mile drive to excellent fishing each day.

The river exits Buskin Lake 4 miles up the Buskin River valley and flows into Chiniak Bay a few hundred yards from Kodiak State Airport. A road parallels most of the river, offering plentiful and easy access. The river has a variety of runs, riffles, and pools and is a friendly river to fish. It has heavy brush and high grass cover along some of its stable banks and varies in width from 30 to 100 feet, excluding the tidal zone areas.

The system supports a small population of resident rainbows, a small steelhead run, and healthy runs of pink, coho, and sockeye salmon. In addition, a few incidental chum salmon enter the river each year, but they are not of adequate number to make them a target species. Buskin Lake is also a winter holdover area for many Dolly Varden.

The tidal beach directly in front of the river's outlet offers good opportunities for anglers as fish first enter the system. If water levels are low in the river, huge buildups of salmon can occur here. Even with normal water levels you will find salmon staging.

To reach this area, follow the road to the Kodiak National Wildlife Refuge. From there, the road will take you to the beach parking area. There are also public toilets and shelters here. The beach is relatively shallow, and on low tide an angler can walk out several hundred yards on the tidal flats and fish the incoming tides. The shorelines on both sides of the outlet offer opportunities for anglers to intercept fish as they make their way to the river. This is the place to be during the early stages of a run, and it can also be very productive at times throughout the season. However, the beach can develop large waves and swells from any easterly wind, making it unfishable at times. Also, be aware of the rising tide. Once the tide starts to build up in the river, the tidal zone water depth is unwadeable, and a few miles of walking may be necessary to get back to the vehicle parking area. The tidal zone waters extend up to Bridge #1, which is about half a river mile from the outlet.

From Bridge #1, where only a few remnants of a bridge still remain, to Bridge #2, the river riffles along at a modest depth and rate. There are two sweeping bend holes just above Bridge #1 that are fishable before the river straightens. A few hundred yards below Bridge #2 the river passes through Buskin River State Recreational Site. Here there are improved campsites, public toilets, and shelters. The site also has a handicapped fishing platform

along a section of the river, and there are some excellent moderately deep runs. This is an appealing area for sockeye and coho.

The fish weir is located directly above Bridge #2. When it is in place, fishing is prohibited within 100 yards on either side of it. From here several hundred yards upstream, the river shallows and widens and the gradient increases. At Bridge #2 a trail parallels the true left side of the river for several hundred yards up to the Pump House Hole. This is a great holding area for salmon and steelhead making their way upriver. This long, deep hole, and the heavy run below it, is one you don't want to pass up. From here to the highway bridge the river shallows with riffles, but still offers good fishing at normal water levels.

From the highway bridge to Bridge #4 the river deepens, with many excellent pools, runs, and some whitewater. The salmon will stage here for a longer period as they make their way upstream. A road parallels the true left side of the river, and the turnoff is right at the highway bridge. This road provides easy access and has off-road parking.

At Bridge #4 there is a turnoff road up the true left side of the river, which leads to an area called the Beaver Pond. This area is about an acre in size, off the main stem of the river but still bordering the main flow. Migrating salmon use this area heavily, especially coho, which hold here for extended periods. It is also a good spot for Dolly Varden, when they make their spring exit from the lake.

Directly below the Beaver Pond to Bridge #4 there are some nice stretches of deep riffles and a nice sweeping corner run. From here upstream for several hundred yards, the river narrows again and deepens slightly, with heavy alder brush overhanging the banks.

At Bridge #5, the river is closed to access downstream

Handicapped-access fishing platform at Buskin River State Recreational Site.

Buskin and Red Cloud Rivers

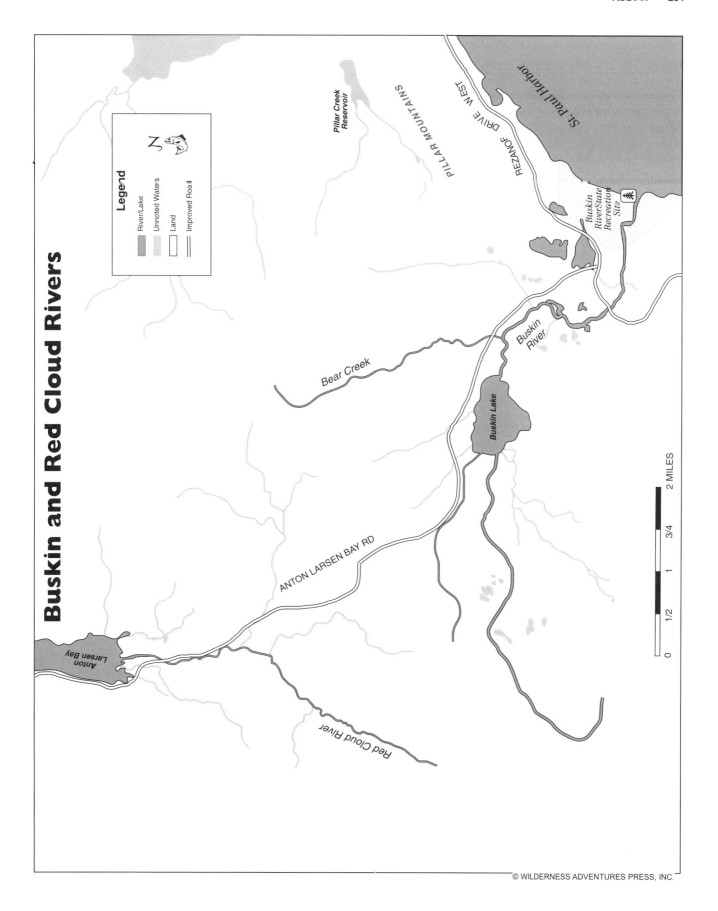

Legend

River/Lake
Unnoted Waters
Land
Improved Road

N

Pillar Creek
Reservoir

PILLAR MOUNTAINS

St. Paul Harbor

REZANOF DRIVE WEST

Buskin River State Recreation Site

Bear Creek

Buskin River

Buskin Lake

ANTON LARSEN BAY RD

Anton Larsen Bay

Red Cloud River

0   1/2   1   3/4   2 MILES

for a few hundred yards as it passes through U.S. Coast Guard property, but just two hundred yards upstream is Buskin Lake. This stretch of the river is riffled, with some deeper holding water directly below the lake.

The outlet of Buskin Lake is also a weir site. Usually it is only in place during the sockeye run, at which time fishing is prohibited within 100 yards on either side. The lake holds many angling opportunities, as well. The north shoreline is excellent for coho when they first enter the lake, and Dolly Varden congregate at the outlet.

It can be fished from shore or from a float tube at higher water levels. The west end has several small streams coming in. Fishing for Dolly Varden is excellent here in the spring and good for coho later in the season. Bears frequent this area and the lower stretches of the river throughout the salmon season. Be alert for signs of their presence.

You can usually find fish where you see other anglers or you can just explore the river on your own. Generally, the lower reaches of the river are most productive during the early stages of a run, and the upper reaches and lake improve as the season progresses. With the river's extensive access and fishable runs, there is space for many anglers.

The Buskin River escapement average for major species during the past 10 years is as follows:

- 12,250 sockeye salmon, with a mid-June peak
- 66,000 pink salmon, with a mid-August peak
- 9,000 silver salmon, with a mid-September peak

Outlet of Buskin River.

Russian Creek and Sargent Creek

Russian and Sargent Creeks are small streams that drain into Womens Bay. They both offer good fishing between the highway and bay, where their shorelines are accessible. Once you get above the bridge, Sargent Creek becomes narrow and shallow, varying in width from 5 to 10 feet. The banks are densely covered with alder brush, which makes fishing difficult.

Russian Creek is a bit wider at 10 to 20 feet and offers more holding water above the highway. The best fishing here is below the bridge and the saltwater flats, where the salmon are still fresh and prime. The beaches in these areas are very shallow, and an angler can walk hundreds of yards out into the tidal flats and follow the salmon as they meander in and out with the tides. Good Dolly Varden fishing can be had here in spring and summer months.

The combined escapement for these two systems is about 12,000 pink salmon and a few hundred coho.

Salonie Creek

Salonie Creek is a more substantial and fishable system that also drains into Womens Bay. The river extends up the Salonie Creek valley for over 3 miles, with the first mile offering the best water. The entire river is prone to flooding, with washouts changing the course and character of the river periodically.

The lower river varies in width from 10 to 30 feet and has many riffles, runs, and holes. Beyond a mile or so upstream, the river braids out, loses depth, and has an unstable streambed. Here you are more likely to find salmon in a spawning condition. However, the Dolly Varden fishing is great up here, as they follow spawning salmon upstream to feed on the eggs.

There are a few pools near the highway bridge and within the first few hundred yards upriver. Much of the riverbanks are heavily covered with alder brush, making access difficult in places. Bears frequent the river during the salmon runs, and with the dense cover and limited sight lines, it's easy to encounter bears at close quarters. Make your presence known as you fish up this river.

The better salmon fishing is generally found on the lower reaches, from a short distance upstream of the bridge and down to the salt water. The beach at the outlet is relatively shallow, and at low tide the surrounding area is exposed for more than a quarter-mile out into the bay. Great fishing can be had here as the salmon make their way to the river and drop back out on low tide.

The average estimated escapement for major species in Salonie Creek is as follows:
- 35,000 pink salmon, with an early August peak
- 600 chum salmon, with a mid-August peak
- 600 coho salmon, with an early September peak

American River

The American River is a popular stream that offers a variety of salmon and trout fishing opportunities. It extends up a scenic valley over 5 miles from the ocean, draining streams from the surrounding mountains into Middle Bay. With the large runoff area on the river, it's very prone to flooding, but it generally clears and drops in a few days after a heavy rain.

You'll find the best fishing in the first few miles upstream from the ocean. The area directly in front of the river outlet has some nice tidal flats that are fishable on low water. The ¾ mile of river between the bay and highway bridge is very defined and stable, with a steady water flow. It varies in width from 25 to 40 feet and has holes up to 6 feet or more in depth.

The first quarter-mile is tidal and a great place to fish when the salmon first enter the system. This is a good area in which to target chum salmon, and other salmon species and Dolly Varden will hold here. There are many deep pools and holding areas along this lower reach of the river. The salmon enter the system on an incoming tide, and as the tide recedes they hold and stage in the deeper water. Much of this part of the river is very fishable regardless of the tide stage. From this point up to the highway bridge, the river loses some of its depth but still offers numerous holding areas. And its grass-covered banks are easy to fish and very accessible.

Upstream from the highway, the river changes character as its banks become overhung with alders. It also lacks the stability of the lower river. Here you will find more riffles, runs, and long glides between intermittent pools. Fishing for Dolly Varden is good along here before the salmon enter the system and again later in the fall after most of the salmon have spawned and died off.

By the time pink salmon have reached this part of the river they are in poor condition and in their spawning ritual. However, prime coho salmon can still be found here. A few miles above the highway the river braids out and becomes less stable, composing the system's prime spawning grounds. An unimproved road parallels the true right side of the river for several miles and continues 9 miles over the pass to the Saltery River.

The road is not drivable with a standard passenger vehicle. A couple of visiting anglers once attempted to drive the lower part of this road. When they opened the doors of the vehicle after becoming stalled, the water came into the vehicle up to the dashboard. The engine was submerged, and they ended up with a very costly charge from the rental agency. The road does provide walking access to the upper reaches of the river, though.

The approximate average escapement for major species on the American River is as follows:

- 66,000 pink salmon, with a mid-August peak
- 6,000 chum salmon, with an early August peak
- 2,000 coho salmon, with a mid-September peak

Angling for Dolly Varden on the American River.

Saltery River

The Saltery River is a pleasant 2½-mile-long stream that exits Saltery Lake. Access to the river is from an unimproved 10-mile-long road that parallels the true right side of the American River for about 5 miles before crossing the pass to Ugak Bay. Most travel on this road is done by all-terrain vehicles or by larger 4-wheel-drives when road conditions permit. You can also charter a floatplane and fly into the lake or bike or hike in.

There is easy access to most of the river from the unimproved road that parallels the left bank up to the lake and Saltery Lake Lodge. Along with salmon, steelhead, and Dolly Varden, the system has a small population of resident rainbow trout.

The river varies in width from 25 to 40 feet for most of its length, with some wider areas near the lake outlet. Much of the river can be fished from the banks as it twists and turns its way to the outlet in Saltery Cove. It has a moderate gradient with nice holding water, scattered pools, and some good runs.

Directly below the lake the river widens, with some sweeping corners that provide a stretch of great holding water. The coho congregate and hold here for extended periods before they enter the lake. There are also some major river bends and holes throughout the river, especially in the upper portions. The lower reaches, just up from the salt water, offer exceptional opportunities for sockeye when they first enter the system.

The tidal reaches are also great during the early stages of the salmon runs, especially for coho. This lower region of the system is certainly the place to be as salmon move and hold with the tide stages, waiting to make their upstream run. If you are in the Kodiak area you do not want to pass up an opportunity to fish the Saltery.

Average escapement for major species on the Saltery River is as follows:

- 47,000 sockeye salmon, with a mid-July peak
- 30,000 pink salmon, with a mid-August peak
- 1,000 chum salmon, with a mid-August peak
- 8,000 coho salmon, with a mid-September peak

Fishing the lower reaches of the Olds River.

Olds River and Kalsin Creek

The Olds River is a heavily fished system that drains into Kalsin Bay. Most of the fishing pressure on this system takes place just below the highway bridge and where it spills into the bay. The river is narrow, riffly, and shallow at the outlet on low tide, with an extensive tidal zone that extends hundreds of yards into the bay. This area provides good fishing with the rising tide.

The entire mile-long stretch of beach to the west of the outlet is also a fine place to intercept salmon as they make their way to the river mouth. The shorter beach to the east of the outlet has good opportunities, as well. An inland flood plain parallels the beach for over a mile, and in places it is several hundreds yards wide. This flood plain has a soft bottom, however, and caution should be taken when fishing this area.

Once the tide is up the character of the area changes. The tidal zone in the bay is covered, and the shallow, defined river at the outlet is 50 to 80 feet wide and unwadeable. The inland flood plain becomes a lake. Fishing can be good throughout this entire area as the salmon follow the rising tide up to the more defined river a quarter-mile below the highway bridge.

From the bridge downstream to the tidal area, the river has numerous holding pools and slow-flowing water of moderate depth. This is an excellent staging and holding area for salmon when they first enter the freshwater flow. The Olds River also provides some excellent Dolly Varden fishing from mid-July through the fall months.

The first mile of river upstream from the highway has deep, scattered pools and moderate riffles, and the banks are lined with dense alders in many places. The river varies in width from 25 to 40 feet, with a slightly steeper gradient than the lower reaches. Many of these pools are filled with run-off debris such as tree limbs, stumps, and brush, which make fishing difficult. However, there is still plenty of good fishing for coho salmon and Dolly Varden. Beyond this first mile of water the river braids out, with numerous feeder streams and a maze of beaver ponds. The river is prone to flooding, but it usually settles out and drops quickly.

The Olds River is also the outlet for Kalsin Creek, which flows through the tidal area and into the Olds a few hundred yards from the bay. The creek can be completely dry on low-water years. It is a very unstable system, but does get a return of salmon in years with solid flows.

Kalsin Pond also drains into the Olds River. The pond is about a half-mile long and several hundred yards wide and is located about a half-mile from the Olds River outlet on the east side of the highway. The pond drains through a culvert, with salt water flowing into the pond on high tide. It is very weedy, with a muddy bottom, and is best fished from a float tube. It provides some good fishing for coho salmon during the month of September.

The approximate average escapement for major species on the Olds River is as follows:
- 53,000 pink salmon, with an early August peak
- 3,000 chum salmon, with an early August peak
- 3,000 coho salmon, with a mid-September peak

Fishing from a float tube can place you within range of the fish.

Roslyn Creek

Roslyn Creek drains a wooded valley south of the highway before flowing into Chiniak Bay. The river is small, 15 to 25 feet wide near the highway with some wider, slower stretches as it gets closer to the bay. It narrows as you go upstream, and the rate of flow increases. Its banks are heavily wooded with large spruce trees, making fishing a challenge.

The best fishing can be found in the lower tidal areas near the bay. Salmon entering this system will hold and stage in water and are easily spotted. The beach directly in front of the outlet also has good fishing when salmon enter the river. The beach is very exposed to the weather, and huge swells can develop that make it unfishable at times.

The approximate average escapement for major species on Roslyn Creek is as follows:
- 20,000 pink salmon, with a mid-August peak
- 200 chum salmon, with a mid-August peak
- 500 coho salmon, with a mid-September peak

Chiniak Creek

Chiniak Creek also drains a small valley on its way to Chiniak Bay. It is a gravel-bottomed stream, 15 to 30 feet in width, with a moderate flow that braids and shallows as you go upstream. The prime fishing here is in the salt water directly in front of the river's outlet. The beach is rocky, but has ample open areas from which to fish. Once the salmon start moving upstream, this small creek actually becomes too choked with fish for easy fishing.

The approximate average escapement for major species on Chiniak Creek is as follows:
- 36,000 pink salmon, with an early August peak
- 200 coho salmon, with a mid-September peak

Myrtle Creek

Myrtle Creek flows into Kalsin Bay. It's a boisterous little stream with good spawning habitat and varies in width from 10 to 15 feet. This stream is best fished in the tidal zone directly in front of the outlet. There is usually a good number of Dolly Varden lingering off the mouth until early August, when they disperse and start following the salmon upriver.

Myrtle Creek has a yearly escapement of a few thousand pink salmon.

Pasagshak River System

The Pasagshak River is a flat-water outlet for Lake Rose Tead. It is about a mile and a half long and varies in width from 60 to 300 feet. Its entire length is influenced by the various stages of the tide, which change the depth, width, and direction of water flow.

Wading this flat-water area can be difficult in places, with its soft muddy bottom and fluctuating water depth. Fishing is good right at the mouth of the river for both sockeye and coho. When the surf is at a moderate level or less, the beach on both sides of the mouth can be fished, and there is a beach on the west side where fish can be intercepted.

You can easily spot the sockeye and coho in the narrow stream mouth and follow them upstream a short distance until the river widens and deepens. Once the salmon move out of the lower river, they can be difficult to locate in the expansive waters. Most of the holding areas between the ocean and lake change from year to year. Some years you will find coho holding for several weeks in the midsection of the system, other years they move directly up to the lake.

One small area that consistently holds a few fish is a section midway to the lake below an old bridge site. There is a nice corner pool here and directly below it you'll find a straight run about a hundred feet in width and several hundred yards long where fish will sometimes linger. The lake outlet is another area where fish can sometimes be found.

Lake Rose Tead, named after a 1940s USO performer, extends up the valley about 2 miles and widens to over ½ mile in places. Once fish enter the lake they can be difficult to find unless they are showing. If fish cannot be seen, then some extensive prospecting may be necessary. You can wade the shoreline here when the lake is at a normal or low water level or you can bring a float tube. The coho are generally found in the lower end of the lake early in the season and in the mid and upper sections as the season progresses. Once the coho leave the lake and enter some of the feeder streams, they are usually past prime condition.

The approximate average escapement for major species on the Pasagshak River is as follows:
- 9,000 sockeye salmon, with a late June peak
- 2,000 pink salmon, with a mid-August peak
- 5,000 coho salmon, with a mid-September peak

Red Cloud River

The Red Cloud River is a picturesque little stream that tumbles out of the foothills surrounding Anton Larsen Bay. The river itself has limited fishing opportunities because of its size and holding water. However, the bay at the river's outlet has extensive tidal flats that are productive on various tide stages. The river braids out as it flows into the bay, and on low tide salmon hold up in these braided areas. They can be tracked as they move with the rising and falling of the tide.

The approximate average return for major species in Red Cloud River is as follows:
- 4,000 pink salmon, with an early August peak
- 700 chum salmon, with an early August peak

Pillar Creek

Both Pillar and Monashka Creeks drain reservoirs that are part of the city of Kodiak's water supply. Pillar Creek is closed year-round to fishing above the high-tide line. However, at its outlet there is beach of several hundred yards that offers good fishing for pink salmon.

The approximate average return for major species in Pillar Creek is as follows:
- 11,000 pink salmon, with an early August peak
- 100 chum salmon, with an early August peak
- 100 coho salmon, with a mid-September peak

Monashka Creek

Monashka Creek is a small meandering stream, 10 to 30 feet in width, which flows into Monashka Bay. There is only about a mile of sparsely fishable river below the reservoir dam. Most of the water below the highway bridge is tidal. There are extensive tidal flats at the outlet that can be fished on low water when salmon are holding and waiting for a rising tide.

The Sport Fish Division of the Alaska Department of Fish and Game is in the process of developing a chinook salmon enhancement program for Monashka Creek. The brood stock for this program are from the Karluk River. The smolt are reared in the Pillar Creek Hatchery for two years before their release into Monashka Creek. This has been an ongoing project for several years, and in June 2005 thousands of adult chinook salmon should be returning to this system. This should provide some outstanding road-accessible chinook salmon fishing in the tidal area of the river and in the saltwater bay.

The approximate average return for major species in Monashka Creek is as follows:
- several thousand chinook salmon starting in 2005, with a mid-June peak
- 7,000 pink salmon, with an early August peak
- 100 coho salmon, with a mid-September peak

Landlocked Lakes

Kodiak Island has a total of 23 lakes, many of which are stocked with rainbow trout or coho fingerlings on a regular basis by the ADF&G. Although they are considered landlocked, most have a runoff outlet of some type. These lakes are the most overlooked fishery on the island and offer endless opportunities for the adventurous angler. Seldom do you ever see another angler on these lakes. A great way to fish some of the more remote lakes is to pack in and camp for a few days. This will give you time to explore the lake and enjoy the remoteness and solitude.

All have reasonable road access, with a few requiring some hiking or a short boat ride. The lakes sit in a variety of pristine locations, ranging from thick forests to alpine settings. Some of the lakes can be fished along the shoreline or by wading, but many of them have soft, muddy bottoms. The most efficient way to fish is by float tube. You can explore an entire lake and not be hindered by shoreline obstacles or water depth.

Generally, you will find that the fish in these lakes are concentrated in one or two areas, and some exploring is usually necessary to locate them. Look for shoreline irregularities, overhangs, and fish movement in the shallows. Occasionally, you will see a few sporadic rises, which always helps. At times throughout the warmer months, some very good hatches can occur.

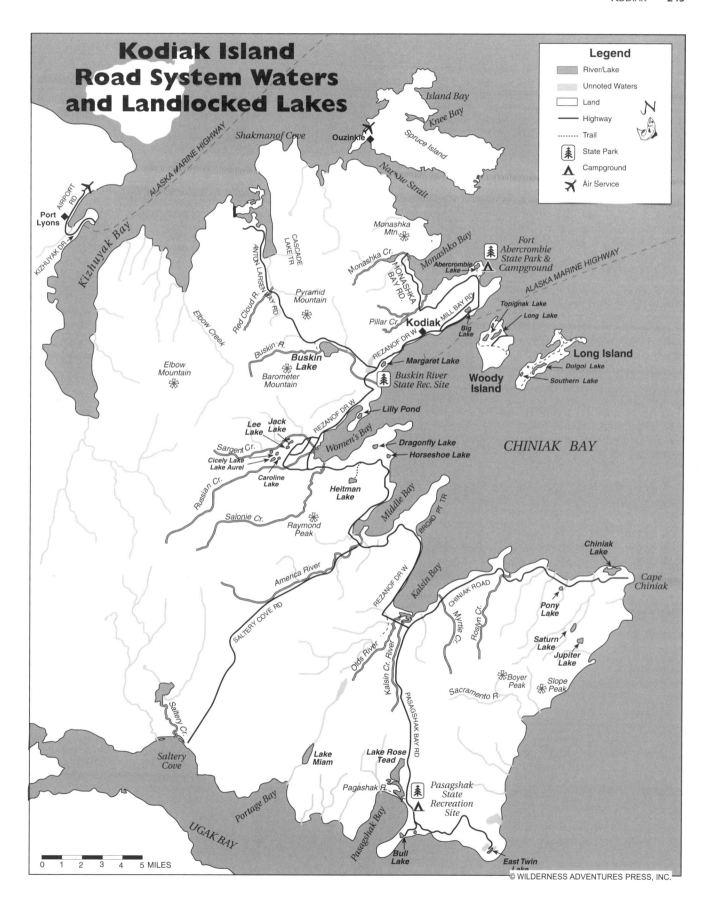

Kodiak Island Road System Waters and Landlocked Lakes

Legend
- River/Lake
- Unnoted Waters
- Land
- Highway
- Trail
- State Park
- Campground
- Air Service

N

Island Bay
Knee Bay
Spruce Island
Shakmanof Cove
Ouzinkie
Narrow Strait

Port Lyons
AIRPORT RD
ALASKA MARINE HIGHWAY
KIZHUYAK DR
Kizhuyak Bay

CASCADE LAKE TR
Monashka Mtn.
Monashka Cr.
Abercrombie Lake
Fort Abercrombie State Park & Campground
Monashko Bay
MONASHKA BAY RD.
ALASKA MARINE HIGHWAY

ANTON LARSEN BAY RD
Red Cloud R.
Pyramid Mountain
Pillar Cr
Kodiak
MILL BAY RD
Big Lake
Tonignak Lake
Long Lake

Elbow Creek
Buskin R.
Buskin Lake
Barometer Mountain
Elbow Mountain
REZANOF DR W
Margaret Lake
Buskin River State Rec. Site
Woody Island
Long Island
Dolgoi Lake
Southern Lake

REZANOF DR W
Lilly Pond
Lee Lake
Jack Lake
Sargent Cr.
Cicely Lake
Lake Aurel
Caroline Lake
Women's Bay
Dragonfly Lake
Horseshoe Lake
Heitman Lake
CHINIAK BAY

Russian Cr.
Salonie Cr.
Raymond Peak
Middle Bay
BROAD PT TR
Chiniak Lake
Cape Chiniak

America River
Kalsin Bay
CHINIAK ROAD
Myrtle Cr.
Roslyn Cr.
Pony Lake
Saturn Lake
Jupiter Lake

SALTERY COVE RD
REZANOF DR W
Olds River
Kalsin Cr. River
Boyer Peak
Slope Peak
Sacramento R.

Saltery Cr.
Saltery Cove
PASAGSHAK BAY RD
Lake Miam
Lake Rose Tead
Pagashak R.
Pasagshak State Recreation Site

Portage Bay
UGAK BAY
Pasagshak Bay
Bull Lake
East Twin Lake

0 1 2 3 4 5 MILES

© WILDERNESS ADVENTURES PRESS, INC.

Dolgoi Lake on Long Island.

As the stocked fingerlings mature and develop, they take on all the characteristics of wild fish. The survival of these fingerlings varies from year to year, as does the fishing and fish size. The majority of the rainbows will vary in size up to 18 inches, with fish up to 20-plus inches not uncommon, and an occasional 4- or 5-pounder. Some of the lakes have some natural reproduction. You may wish to check with the Sport Fish Division of the ADF&G in Kodiak to see which lakes are currently considered quality fisheries.

The following lakes are stocked with rainbows:

Abercrombie Lake. Located at mile 4.0 on Monashka Bay Road in Fort Abercrombie State Park. Elevation is near sea level, with a maximum depth of 25 feet and a surface area of 18.7 acres.

Aurel Lake. Located off the Chiniak Highway at mile 9.6. Take a right on Sargent Creek Road and go 0.4 mile to Salmonberry Road and 0.2 mile to Middle Bay Road. Take a left on Middle Bay Road and continue 1.3 miles to the trailhead. It's 0.75 mile to the lake. Elevation is 280 feet, with a maximum depth of 19 feet and a surface area of 15.2 acres.

Big Lake (also known as Lilly). Located at mile 1.3 off Mill Bay Road. Elevation is 110 feet, with a maximum depth of 6 feet and a surface area of 18.3 acres.

Bull Lake. Located at mile 30.1 off the Chiniak Highway. Take a right on Pasagshak Bay Road and go 10.1 miles to the gravel road on the right, and continue 1.2 miles to the lake. Elevation is 200 feet, with a maximum depth of 7 feet and a surface area of 9.9 acres.

Caroline Lake. Located off the Chiniak Highway at mile 9.6. Take a right on Sargent Creek Road and go 0.4 mile to Salmonberry Road and 0.2 mile to Middle Bay Road. Left on Middle Bay Road 1.3 miles to the trailhead. It's 1 mile to the lake. Elevation is 280 feet, with a maximum depth of 22 feet and a surface area of 6.6 acres.

Cicely Lake. Located off the Chiniak Highway at mile 9.6. Take a right on Sargent Creek Road and go 0.4 mile to Salmonberry Road and then 0.2 mile to Middle Bay Road. Left on Middle Bay Road 1.3 miles to the trailhead. It's 1 mile to the lake. Elevation is 350 feet, with a maximum depth of 12 feet and a surface area of 5.6 acres.

Dolgoi Lake. Located on the south end of Long Island, 3 miles from the city of Kodiak. Elevation is 40 feet, with a maximum depth of 15 feet and a surface area of 51.6 acres.

Dragonfly Lake. At mile 14.1 on the Chiniak Highway, take a right on Cliff Point Road 0.5 mile to the trailhead on the left. It's 0.3 mile to the lake. Elevation is 170 feet, with a maximum depth of 12 feet and a surface area of 7.6 acres.

Heitman Lake. The trailhead is on the right side of the road at mile 14 on the Chiniak Highway. It's 1.25 miles to the lake. Elevation is 950 feet with a surface area of 32.4 acres.

Horseshoe Lake. The trailhead is on the right side of the road at mile 15.1 of the Chiniak Highway. It's 0.5 mile to the lake. Elevation is 150 feet, with a maximum depth of 16 feet and a surface area of 4.8 acres.

Jack Lake. Located off the Chiniak Highway at mile 9.6. Take a right on Sargent Creek Road and go 1.7 miles to the trailhead on the left side of the road. The trail to the lake is 0.25 mile. Elevation is 220 feet, with a maximum depth of 8 feet and a surface area of 4.7 acres.

Jupiter Lake. At mile 41.6 on the Chiniak Highway state road maintenance ends. Continue on the gravel road 4.8 miles to the trailhead on the left. It's 0.75 mile to the lake. Elevation is 450 feet, with a maximum depth of 15 feet and a surface area of 17.5 feet.

Lee Lake. Located off the Chiniak Highway at mile 9.6. Take a right on Sargent Creek Road and continue 1.7 miles to the trailhead on the left. It's 0.33 mile to the lake. Elevation is 270 feet, with a maximum depth of 17 feet and a surface area of 14.3 acres.

Lilly Pond. Located off the Chiniak Highway at mile 6.3. Take a left onto the U.S. Coast Guard Station. Follow Windriver Drive 1.7 miles to Seafarer Drive, then take a left and go 0.8 mile to the lake. Elevation is 3 feet, with a maximum depth of 8 feet and a surface area of 7.9 acres.

Long Lake. Located on Woody Island, 1.5 miles from the city of Kodiak. From the dock, follow the trail across Outlet Spit to the lake. Elevation is 20 feet, with a maximum depth of 20 feet and a surface area of 36 acres.

Lupine Lake. Located off the Chiniak Highway at mile 30.1. Take a right on Pasagshak Bay Road and continue 10.1 miles to the gravel road on the right. Follow the gravel road 0.5 mile to the trailhead on the left. It's 0.25 mile to the lake. Elevation is 100 feet, with a maximum depth of 7 feet and a surface area of 7.5 feet.

Margaret Lake (also known as Boy Scout). At mile 3.3 of the Chiniak Highway, you'll find the lake on the left side of the road. Elevation is 70 feet, with a maximum depth of 22 feet and a surface area of 7.9 acres.

Saturn Lake. At mile 41.6 of the Chiniak Highway state road maintenance ends. Continue on the gravel road 4.8 miles to the trailhead on the left. The trail passes Jupiter Lake and continues 1.25 miles to Saturn Lake. Elevation is 450 feet, with a maximum depth of 12 feet and a surface area of 11.7 acres.

Tanignak Lake. Located on Woody Island 1.5 miles from the city of Kodiak. At the end of Ice House Lake Road, take a trail 0.25 mile to the lake. Elevation is 50 feet with a surface area of 29.7 feet.

East Twin Lake. At mile 30.1 of the Chiniak Highway, take a right on Pasagshak Bay Road 16.8 miles to the lake, which is located on the left side of the road. Elevation is 10 feet, with a surface area of 17.3 acres.

The following lakes are stocked with coho salmon, which run 14 to 20 inches:

Pony Lake (also known as Sawmill). The lake is located on the south side of the road at mile 36.7 of the Chiniak Highway. Elevation is 10 feet, with a maximum depth of 11 feet and a surface area of 14.3 acres.

Southern Lake. Located 3 miles from the city of Kodiak, this is the southernmost lake on Long Island. Elevation is 10 feet, with a maximum depth of 12 feet and a surface area of 17.3 acres.

Chiniak Lake. At mile 42.3 on the Chiniak Highway an abandoned WWII airstrip crosses the road. Drive north on the airstrip. The lake is located at the end of the runway near the beach. This is usually a consistent lake for catching coho, and it's the largest of the stocked lakes.

REMOTE RIVER SYSTEMS

With hundreds of rivers and streams in the Kodiak area, the opportunities for remote wilderness fishing are endless. The systems described here include some of the major rivers in the Kodiak Archipelago, but there are many others, as well. Visiting anglers can explore these systems on their own or take advantage of one of the many remote lodges, guides, or outfitters in the Kodiak area.

If you explore on your own, keep in mind that you are in a remote wilderness environment where medical assistance of any kind may be hours or even days away. Some prior outdoor experience is essential, and you may want to select a location where you are less likely to be isolated from other anglers. Cell phones do not work in these remote areas, but you can purchase or rent a satellite phone for use in an emergency.

Another factor to consider is the timing of the salmon runs into each system. The return of a particular species can vary by as much as a month or more from system to system. By reviewing past weir counts and records, an angler can estimate a reasonable timeframe for peak fishing in a system. The Sport Fish Division of the ADF&G and the Kodiak National Wildlife Refuge will have this information. They will also have additional local knowledge about various systems. It is essential that before you go through the expense and time to reach a fishing destination, you will have some assurance that there will be fish in the system when you arrive.

If the river you want to fish is near the coast and a reasonable distance from the city of Kodiak, it may be accessible by one of the local charter boats. This

The Kodiak National Wildlife Refuge is your source for land use and ownership information.

method of transportation would be considerably more time consuming than flying, but the cost per pound for transporting you and your gear may be less. But for many of the inland destinations and distant coastal locations this isn't a practical option.

The most convenient and reliable method of transportation is a local flight service. Via floatplane, you can be dropped off at your destination regardless of whether it is inland or on the coast. However, careful planning is important when selecting your gear and supplies. Flight services operate under very strict guidelines regarding load capabilities. You, along with your gear and supplies, will be carefully weighed before a flight to be sure you are within the load limits of a particular plane. It is not an uncommon sight to see outbound anglers repacking to eliminate some of their gear and supplies at the floatplane facility. When inquiring about charter flights be sure to obtain load limits for each plane model so you can plan your flight, costs, gear, and supplies accordingly.

In addition to the considerations previously mentioned, be sure you are knowledgeable about the land ownership. Many of these systems are on private lands owned by one of the several local native corporations. In most cases, access to their land is allowed, but you must first purchase a land use permit from them. There are also areas where the number of anglers is limited during certain times of the year. The Kodiak National Wildlife Refuge or the Sport Fish Division of the Alaska Department of Fish and Game can be contacted for current information regarding restrictions and necessary permits for the Kodiak area.

There are hundreds of archeological sites in these remote areas, and many are located along the banks of some popular river and lake systems. Federal law prohibits the taking of any artifacts and the disturbance of any sites. Before selecting a campsite, be sure the location isn't a site that was used by ancient inhabitants of the area.

If you fish these remote areas with the use of a lodge, guide, or outfitter, then it should be their responsibility to provide you with the information regarding run timing, transportation, gear and load limit restrictions, and land ownership. However, be sure to ask them about these considerations before you book a trip—and certainly before you arrive in Kodiak.

Karluk River

The Karluk River is the signature fishing destination on Kodiak Island and known throughout the angling community as one of the top sport-fishing systems in Alaska. It has everything an angler could want: classic water, abundant fish and wildlife, and a striking setting. Fishing the Karluk is always a memorable and rewarding experience.

The river flows out of Karluk Lake about 22 miles from the Karluk Lagoon and village. The lake extends another 12 miles up a valley and is surrounded by a range of 3,000-foot mountains and rolling hills. This area has one of the highest densities of bears on the island. So always be alert and adhere to the guidelines for traveling and fishing in bear country.

The Karluk has some very complex land ownership and management issues. There is a period of time in June and July, during the chinook salmon run, when the number of anglers on the system is limited. In addition, there are some campsite and access restrictions. Be sure to check with the Kodiak National Wildlife Refuge regarding these issues before arriving in Kodiak.

Numerous small tributary streams flow into Karluk Lake, and most offer some splendid rainbow and Dolly Varden fishing opportunities. Thumb, O'Malley, Halfway, and Meadow Creeks are a few of these. The lake also has a resident population of char that range from 15 to 20 inches. Meadow Creek is consistently the hot spot for these, but they can be taken in most of the lake's inlet streams and in the main stem of the Karluk at the lake outlet. Where these streams flow into the lake, you will generally always find some trout and char. By the time the salmon reach the upper regions of this system, they are usually in spawning condition and no longer sought after.

The salmon will generally hold at the lake outlet, which is an excellent area to fish. The first half-mile downriver has some noteworthy riffles and shallow runs that offer excellent trout and char fishing.

Steelhead can also be taken in these upper reaches of the river. And it's a prime area for sockeyes and cohos, although most of the time you can expect the bears to be fishing right along with you.

From here the river slows and meanders its way down to the next noteworthy area, a place called the Oxbow. It's within walking distance of the lake, and most anglers will stop and fish here on their float downriver. There is a series of deep, sharp bends here that nearly always hold

Fall steelhead fishing on the Karluk River.

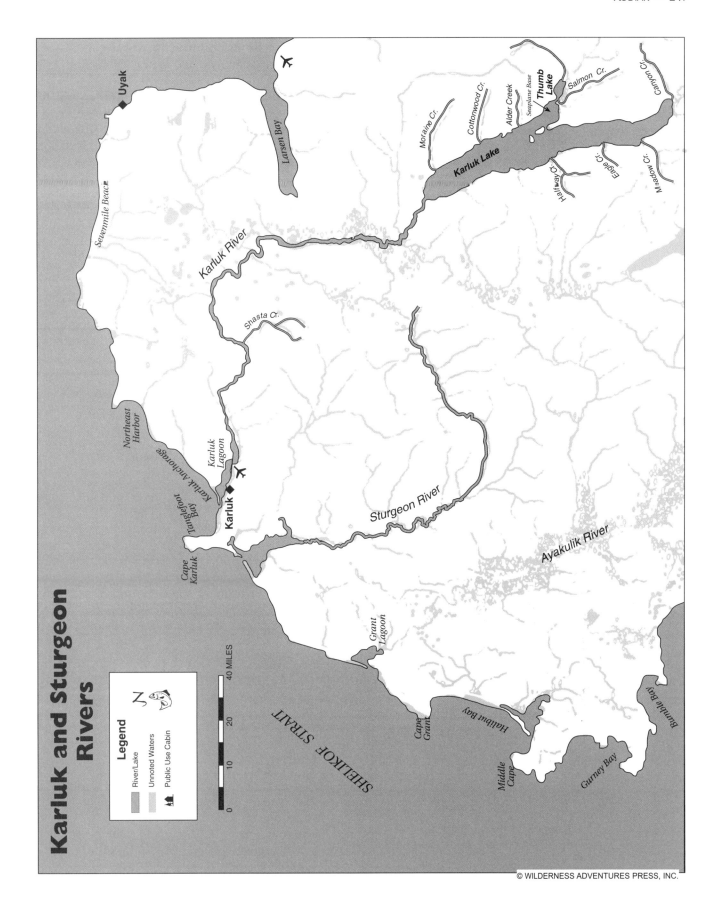

Karluk and Sturgeon Rivers

Legend

N

River/Lake
Unnoted Waters
Public Use Cabin

40 MILES
0   10   20

Uyak

Larsen Bay

Sevenmile Beach

Karluk River

Shasta Cr.

Northeast Harbor

Karluk Anchorage

Karluk Lagoon

Tanglefoot Bay

Karluk

Cape Karluk

Grant Lagoon

SHELIKOF STRAIT

Cape Grant

Halibut Bay

Middle Cape

Gurney Bay

Bumble Bay

Sturgeon River

Ayakulik River

Moraine Cr.

Cottonwood Cr.

Alder Creek

Seaplane Base

Thumb Lake

Salmon Cr.

Canyon Cr.

Karluk Lake

Halfway Cr.

Eagle Cr.

Meadow Cr.

© WILDERNESS ADVENTURES PRESS, INC.

Author with Karluk River steelhead.

salmon. It's a place you don't want to pass up if you are in the area. Beyond here, the river shallows and widens, making a float trip difficult under low-water conditions. There are also fewer holding areas in this section of the river.

The next landmark is a place referred to as Portage. For a mile or more directly above this location the river deepens, and there is a stretch of water where floatplanes can provide access. Many anglers will start their float trip here. Fish hold in this slow water, but the river is deep and over 150 feet wide in places. And it has a soft bottom, making wading and fishing difficult. Upstream there is an excellent deep and fishable run for salmon and steelhead at the base of the first mountain on the river's left bank. The spot is marked by the remnants of several old beaver lodges.

For a few miles below Portage, the gradient increases and the river narrows slightly. It becomes a series of long runs and whitewater rapids for the next few miles. Some of the lower reaches of this area are tricky to wade because of the heavy flow and rocky bottom. This is all great water for steelhead and coho and chinook salmon. It is very easy to fish and can be crossed for much of its length under normal water conditions. The flat, shallow water just below Portage has phenomenal Dolly Varden fishing during the fall months.

Next, the river widens, with shallower riffles and runs for a mile or so before it narrows and deepens again. Here again, you will find some exceptionally good holding water for steelhead, coho, and chinook. The reference location here is known as Canoe Rock. The area above and below this spot has several miles of continuous deep runs and riffles, with bank and corner holes. This is a popular fishing and camping spot for anglers floating the river.

The river continues to narrow and the gradient increases as it goes through an area known as the Canyon.

The water is deep and fast along here, with some high banks making fishing difficult in places. Beyond the Canyon, the river widens and slows for about a mile before it flows into the Karluk Lagoon.

There are opportunities for fishing throughout the lagoon. At the head of the tidal area where the river enters, salmon stage and move with the tide cycle. The area is very wadeable, and fish can be followed upstream with the incoming tide. This is an ideal spot for coho, sockeye, and chinooks as they first enter this system. On low-water years, salmon will prolong their stay here, offering weeks of great fishing. Salmon will also hold in other areas of the lagoon, but these are best fished from a boat or float tube. Andrew Airways has a cabin near the head of the lagoon, which it rents to anglers.

The Karluk River average escapement for major species during the past 10 years is as follows:

- 12,000 chinook salmon, with a mid-June peak
- 770,000 sockeye salmon, with a mid-July peak for the early run and a mid-August peak for the late run
- pink salmon 106,000 odd years, 785,000 even years, with a mid-August peak
- 27,000 coho salmon, with a mid-September peak
- 8,000 steelhead, with a late September peak

Ayakulik River

The Ayakulik River is located on the southwest side of Kodiak Island. It is one of the major salmon systems on the island, located about 80 air miles from the city of Kodiak. Two major tributaries merge to form the main branch of this system. The northern arm winds its way more that 15 miles through a low, wet muskeg area before merging with the 4-mile-long Red Lake tributary. These branches are the primary spawning grounds for this system—and fishing grounds for the area bears.

The main branch extends another 12 miles before spilling into a saltwater lagoon at the outlet. The river is within the Kodiak National Wildlife Refuge, and maps are available to help anglers locate recommended campsites and private lands in the lagoon area.

The best angling begins at the confluence of the two main branches. There is some enticing fishable water for sockeye salmon here, but bears also heavily use the area. From the confluence, the river meanders about 2½ miles downstream, maintaining a consistent depth until it reaches an area known as Bare Creek. The flat water above Bare Creek is an area floatplane operators use to drop off and pick up anglers. From this spot anglers will generally hike down to the Bare Creek area and camp or float and camp their way down to the lagoon for a pickup.

From the confluence to its outlet in the lagoon, the river will vary in width from 50 to over 100 feet. In the Bare Creek area, the Kodiak National Wildlife Refuge maintains an angler monitoring station during the June chinook salmon run. To help discourage bears from becoming regular dinner guests, they set up an electric fence around an area in which campers can store their food and garbage.

At Bare Creek the river begins to develop more character as the gradient increases. For a mile or so directly below this point the river has delightfully long and moderately deep runs, ideal holding water for steelhead, coho, and chinook. Intermixed with these runs are riffles where holding chinook can be sight fished.

A deep run known as the Guide Hole is in this first mile below Bare Creek. Below this, the river slows and develops a series of large, deep, sweeping corner pools with names such as Swallow, Catfish, Oxbow (also known as Horseshoe), and Bird Island. Many of these pools are only fishable from the inside of the corners because of the high steep outside banks.

As you near the lagoon, the gradient increases and you encounter heavier riffles and pleasant runs. Directly below the weir site, and above the lagoon, is an outstanding long run where salmon first hold as they make their way upriver. This is the most fishable stretch of water on the lower reaches of the Ayakulik. The river supports a population of resident rainbow trout, and Dolly Varden are generally present.

The Ayakulik River average escapement for major species during the past 10 years is as follows:

- 13,000 chinook salmon, with a mid-June peak
- 327,000 sockeye salmon, with an early July peak
- pink salmon, 450,000 even years, 16,000 odd years, with a mid-August peak
- 25,000 coho salmon, with an early September peak
- 2,000 steelhead, with an early October peak

Outlet of Ayakulik River.

Sturgeon River

The Sturgeon River is located on the southwest side of Kodiak Island, about 65 air miles from the city of Kodiak. If you want to target chum salmon this is the river for you. No other system in the Kodiak area has a larger return of chums than the Sturgeon. In addition, the run peaks in mid-June, before most other salmon are in the river.

The challenging part of fishing this system is the access. Before the river exits into the Shelikof Strait, it flows into a large tidal lagoon about 3 miles long and over a mile wide in places. Because of the large tide range on the west side of the island, much of the lagoon area doesn't maintain sufficient water for a floatplane to operate throughout an entire tide cycle. This is especially true at the upward end of the lagoon where the river enters. However, there is a window of a couple hours on either side of a high tide when a floatplane can access this area. Take-outs and pickups in this location have to be planned accordingly.

Two major stems merge about 8 miles from the outlet in the lagoon. Above this confluence are the major spawning grounds for thousands of chum salmon that return each year and a major feeding area for bears. Because this system has such an early run, it's an area where bears get their first opportunity of the year to feed on salmon. It is not uncommon to fly over this area in June and see 50 or more bears at a time feeding along the river.

The Sturgeon picks up several smaller tributaries as it nears the outlet, and the flow and gradient increases. The frequency of moderate-depth runs increases, and the lower 3 or 4 miles of river offer almost continuous fishable holding water with multiple holes and deep runs. The majority of the river varies in width from 30 to 80 feet, with some wider spots in the lower reaches.

The midsection has a few short braided areas where the river still maintains depth and offers some pleasing corner water. The lower half of the river has some of the system's best holding water for steelhead.

For chum and coho salmon, concentrate your efforts in the lower tidal areas of the river and the upper lagoon. As the river enters the lagoon it widens and varies in depth with the tide cycle. Chum and coho follow the tide flow and can be pursued throughout the tide cycle as they enter the lower river on the incoming tide and then drop back into the lagoon as the tide falls. Most of this area has wadeable depth water with deeper channels where salmon will hold on low tide. There are very few places anywhere in Alaska that can rival the Sturgeon for chum salmon fishing.

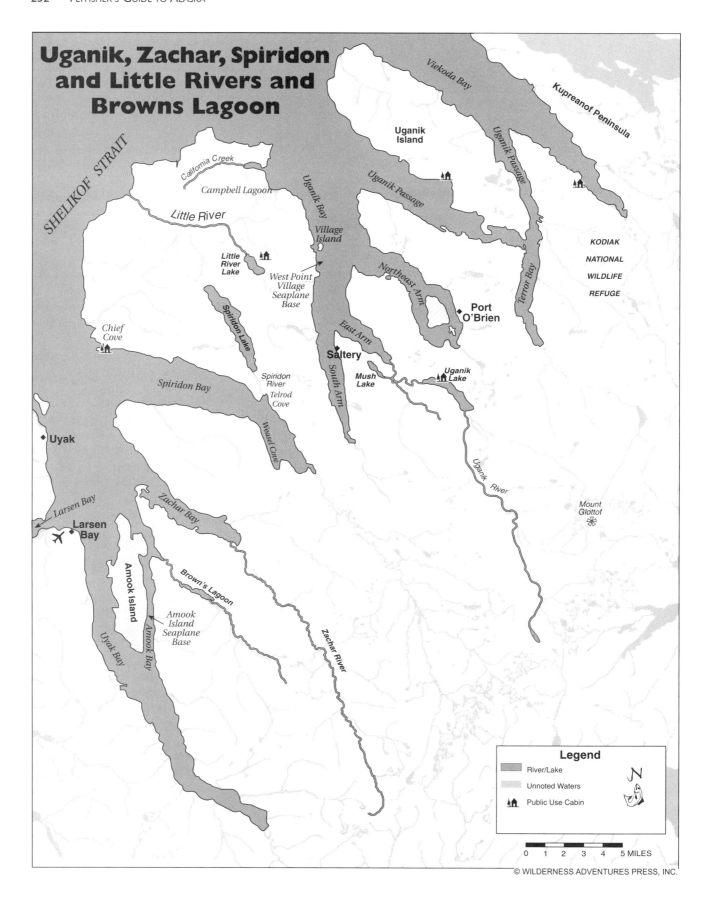

Uganik, Zachar, Spiridon and Little Rivers and Browns Lagoon

SHELIKOF STRAIT

Viekoda Bay

Kupreanof Peninsula

Uganik Island

Uganik Passage

Uganik Passage

California Creek

Campbell Lagoon

Little River

Uganik Bay

Village Island

Little River Lake

West Point Village Seaplane Base

Northeast Arm

Terror Bay

Port O'Brien

KODIAK NATIONAL WILDLIFE REFUGE

Chief Cove

Spiridon Lake

East Arm

Saltery

South Arm

Mush Lake

Uganik Lake

Spiridon Bay

Spiridon River

Telrod Cove

Weasel Cove

Uyak

Uganik River

Larsen Bay

Zachar Bay

Larsen Bay

Mount Glottof

Brown's Lagoon

Amook Island

Amook Island Seaplane Base

Amook Bay

Uyak Bay

Zachar River

Legend

	River/Lake
	Unnoted Waters
🏠	Public Use Cabin

N

0 1 2 3 4 5 MILES

© WILDERNESS ADVENTURES PRESS, INC.

The Sturgeon River estimated average escapement for major species is as follows:

- 50,000 chum salmon, with a mid-June peak
- 6,000 coho, with a late September peak
- 800 steelhead, with an early October peak

Uganik River

The Uganik River is located inside the Kodiak National Wildlife Refuge on the west side of Kodiak Island, about 30 air miles from the city of Kodiak. It has about 4 miles of pleasant, classic water below Uganik Lake before it braids out and flows into Uganik Bay. The lake is nestled between some thousand-foot mountain ridges, several of which drop off sharply to the lakeshore.

Above the lake, the river extends 10 miles up an expansive valley where it drains the surrounding mountains and the Mount Glottof glacial areas. This glacial runoff can color the lake and river for several weeks or more after a heavy rain. At the lake inlet, the Kodiak National Wildlife Refuge has a rental cabin available to anglers and hikers visiting the area. The system is best accessed by floatplane directly into Uganik Lake.

The lake and inlet and outlet rivers offer excellent fishing opportunities. The outlet river, which varies in width from 60 to 100 feet, and much of the lake and its inlet system are surrounded by large cottonwood trees. The inlet, where the braided water flows into the lake, is an excellent spot for early and late season Dolly Varden and staging salmon. The lake outlet offers similar opportunities and also has some nice protected camping areas.

Immediately below the lake there is a long straight stretch of river of almost a mile that has a mixture of excellent intermittent deep runs, riffles, and some rapids. This water is best approached from the true right bank. When the river is at a lower than normal level you can cross in several locations along this first mile. At normal or high water levels, be sure to descend the river along its true right side. If you don't you may find yourself over a mile downstream and unable to cross. You will be hemmed in by a high, steep riverbank and bluff densely covered with brush, which many anglers won't be able to negotiate.

After this straight run, the river takes a long sweeping left turn with a high, steep bank on its outside corner and then a sharp right. A trail leads you up and around this area on the true right side of the river. At this right turn, there's a long, deep pool with a heavy, deep tailout that extends several hundred feet. For the next mile or so the gradient increases, and the river has some rapids and runs that end in slower pools.

Beyond this, the river slows and becomes more placid, with some occasional moderate-depth runs and riffles. At the outlet, the river braids out before flowing into Uganik Bay. This tidal area is a great spot to fish as the salmon enter the system.

Along with the abundance of salmon in this system, there's also a healthy population of medium-sized resident rainbow trout. The Dolly Varden fishing is excellent throughout the system, especially in the early spring and again in the late fall. Five-pound or larger Dollys are not uncommon, and there are a few incidental steelhead in the system. Along with the great fishing in classic water, this is just a wonderful area to visit.

The Uganik River average escapement for major species is as follows:

- 90,000 sockeye, with an early July peak
- 150,000 pink salmon, with a mid-August peak
- 10,000 chum salmon, with a mid-August peak
- 11,000 coho, with a mid-September peak

Olga Bay Systems

Olga Bay is located on the southwest end of Kodiak Island about 75 air miles from the city of Kodiak. It's a large inland saltwater bay, extending about 17 miles east to west. The narrow inlet restricts the tidal flow, which results in a tidal fluctuation of only a few feet. This means that there is some excellent tidal zone fishing at the river outlets, where you can fish by wading or from a float tube or boat.

The bay has many excellent salmon systems and a variety of fishing opportunities. This area has a very heavy concentration of bears, and although they are accustomed to people, one must be alert at all times to avoid unpleasant encounters.

Dog Salmon Creek

Dog Salmon Creek, also known as Frazer River, is the most popular system in the area. The river exits Frazer Lake and flows about 7 miles before entering Olga Bay. It offers a variety of fishable water and supports a consistent run of fish. The Kodiak National Wildlife Refuge has two rental cabins on Frazer Lake.

There is a healthy population of resident rainbows, with the larger fish generally found in the waters above the falls. The Dolly Varden fishing is excellent, especially in the lower reaches of the river, and there's a run of a few hundred steelhead in the fall. The river usually gets an escapement in excess of 350,000 salmon through the lower weir each year.

About a mile below the lake outlet there is a large falls.

Olga Bay Area Rivers and Lakes

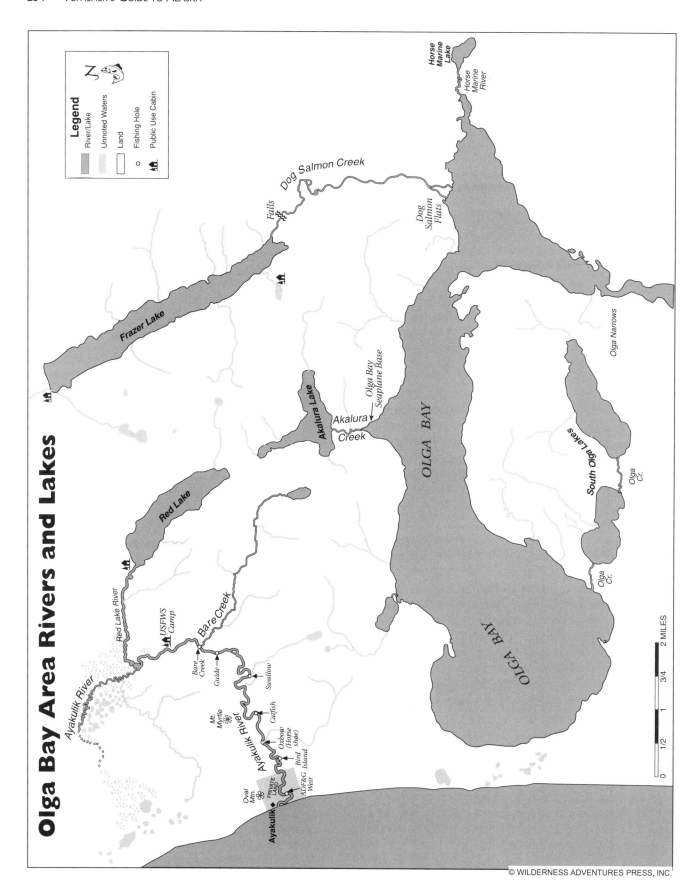

And the ADF&G has constructed a series of fish ladders that allow the salmon to ascend the 30-foot waterfall. The water from the falls to the lake outlet has a moderate gradient with deep runs and varies in width from 50 to 100 feet. The river is very fishable here, with easy access, but it does have plenty of high grassy and alder banks.

This is prime holding water for fish on their way to the lake and a resting spot for fish that have just ascended the fish pass. Bears use the river directly below the falls as a feeding area, and it's not uncommon to see a dozen or more here at one time. Several flight services use this site as one of the stops in their bear viewing programs.

Below the falls, the river widens and changes character. The gradient increases, with shorter, faster runs and deeper rapids. Access also becomes a little more difficult as heavy brush lines much of the bank. As you near the bay the gradient decreases, and about a mile above the outlet the river forks into two major flows. Here the river widens to over 100 feet in places, with lots of moderately deep riffles that make wading and access easier. This is delightful water to fish when salmon first enter the system.

The tidal zone where the river enters the bay is a prime fishing location for salmon as they stage before making their run upstream. If you are in the Olga Bay area you don't want to miss a shot at this tidal zone.

Dog Salmon Creek escapement for major species during the past 10 years is as follows:

- 213,000 sockeye salmon, with an early July peak
- 3,000 chum salmon, with a late July peak
- 250 chinook salmon, with a late July peak
- 142,000 pink salmon, with an early August peak
- 5,000 coho salmon, with an early September peak
- 250 steelhead, with an early October peak

Olga Creek

Olga Creek, sometimes referred to as Upper Station, is a mile-long river extending from South Olga Lake to Olga Bay. The system also has an additional mile of river between South Olga Lake and North Olga Lake. There's a good run of salmon, as well as a small run of steelhead.

The river varies in width from 40 to 50 feet, with scattered brush and high grass along its stable banks. Both sections are of low gradient with long moderately deep pools and runs. They each offer reasonable access and are comfortable to wade. The mile of river between the lakes has a healthy population of rainbows in the 12- to 18-inch range, and Dolly Varden can be found in both sections.

The migrating salmon will sometimes congregate and stage at the outlet of Olga Creek where it flows into South Olga Lake. This area can be especially good for coho salmon. The lower reaches of the river just above the bay and the outlet are usually dependable spots for both coho and sockeye salmon.

Olga Creek average escapement for major species during the past 10 years is as follows:

- 250,000 sockeye salmon, with a mid-July peak
- 9,000 pink salmon, with an early August peak
- 3,500 coho salmon, with an early September peak

Akalura Creek

Akalura Creek is a pleasant stretch of water running about a mile in length between Akalura Lake and Olga Bay. It has a healthy population of resident rainbow trout 10 to 12 inches in length, Dolly Varden, a few incidental steelhead, and a moderate return of salmon.

It varies in width from 25 to 30 feet and has a moderate flow. Some of the wider, softer sections are just below the lake. It has long, gentle runs and riffles and low, stable banks. The upper reaches have some sections of heavy brush, but the lower section is open, with scattered brush and moderately high grass. The lagoon where the river enters Olga Bay is the ideal spot for coho salmon as they enter the system. With Olga Bay's small tidal change, fish will hold in this area throughout the tidal cycle. This is a great spot to hit coho while they're still in the salt.

Akalura Creek average escapement for major species during the past 10 years is as follows:

- 20,000 sockeye salmon, with a late August peak
- 9,000 pink salmon, with a late August peak
- 3,500 coho salmon, with an early September peak

Horse Marine Creek

Horse Marine is a relatively short system. Starting at the bay, you will encounter a narrow entrance that leads into a large tidal lagoon about a mile in length and about a quarter-mile wide. This is a prime fishing area for coho salmon—another great spot in the Olga Bay area that you don't want to miss.

The coho will sometimes stage in this lagoon for several weeks before they make their run upriver. This staging period can be even longer under low-water conditions. Because of its narrow entrance, the lagoon has relatively little tidal fluctuation and can be fished from shore or by float tube.

Horse Marine Creek is a small stream, 20 to 30 feet in width and about a mile long, flowing out of Horse Marine Lake. It has a moderate gradient with some nice riffles and short runs. At normal water levels you'll find salmon holding in the lower reaches, along with some resident rainbow trout.

This system has a moderate escapement of sockeye and pink salmon. The coho salmon escapement will range from 3,000 to 4,000 fish annually.

Silver Salmon River

Silver Salmon River is also a short system flowing into Olga Bay. It varies in width from 15 to 25 feet, with a moderate flow and low gradient. It exits Silver Salmon Lake about a half-mile from the bay. This system has another extensive saltwater lagoon where salmon stage, and it's an ideal spot to intercept coho, the primary quarry here with an annual escapement of several thousand fish.

Additional Kodiak Island Systems

The west side of Kodiak Island has many other appealing systems for sockeye and coho salmon. The **Zachar River**, **Spiridon River**, and **Browns Lagoon** are a few that have excellent coho salmon escapements of around 5,000 to 6,000 fish. They offer fine fishing opportunities in the tidal waters and lower reaches.

Little River is a good option for sockeye salmon and has a fishable run of steelhead and coho salmon. It also has some nice rainbow trout fishing at the lake outlet. The Kodiak National Wildlife Refuge has a rental cabin available to anglers on Little River Lake.

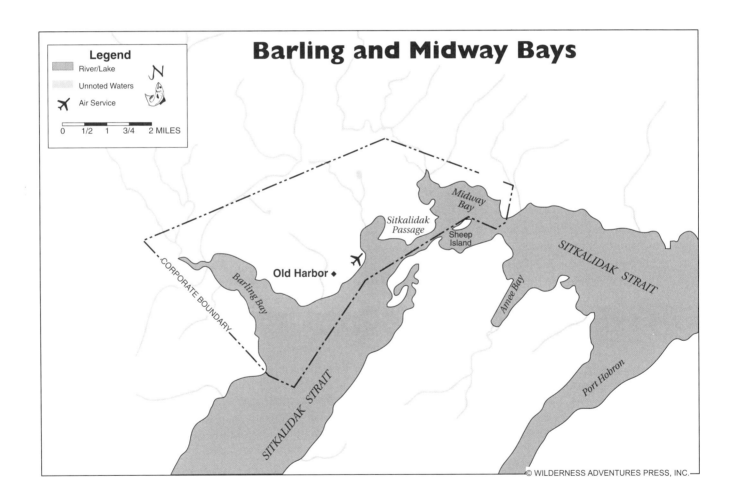

These systems can be fished on a daily fly-out basis from the city of Kodiak or by using some of the guides and outfitters that work these areas. The timing of the runs for these systems is similar to what you'll find in other west-side rivers.

On the east side of Kodiak Island there are a couple of fine coho salmon systems in the vicinity of **Old Harbor**. Day trips out of Old Harbor into **Barling Bay** and **Midway Bay** will place you within reach of several outstanding coho salmon rivers.

The north end of Kodiak Island has some small salmon systems in the vicinity of Port Lions in **Kizuyak** and **Sharatin Bays**. These are less popular rivers, but they can be fished by anglers using Port Lions as a base for accommodations and transportation.

For the adventurous angler there is also **Lake Miam**. This system drains into Portage Bay, a small bay within Ugak Bay. It can be reached with a two- or three-hour hike out of the Kalsin Bay area or the Pasagshak Bay area. You can also access the lake with a short floatplane flight out of the city of Kodiak. Lake Miam receives a small escapement of sockeye salmon and pink salmon. The escapement for coho is usually about 4,000 fish, with an early September peak.

DeHavilland Beaver, the backcountry taxi.

Salmon can often be intercepted in saltwater bays before they reach freshwater rivers.

AFOGNAK ISLAND

Pauls Bay System

If you are looking for a remote place in the Kodiak area with easy access to sockeye or coho salmon, then the Pauls Bay system should be at the top of your list. This system is located on the northeast end of Afognak Island about 40 air miles from the city of Kodiak. A half-hour floatplane trip will put you on the water. This is a great place to spend a week fishing and enjoying the surroundings.

The system consists of a chain of three lakes and rivers that flow into Pauls Bay. The entire area is densely wooded with large Sitka spruce trees, which form an impressive setting that few areas can equal. The land on the east side of this system is in Afognak State Park. Camping is openly permitted here, and the park has a rental cabin available on the lower end of Laura Lake.

The system develops inland at Gretchen Lake, about 8 miles from the outlet at Pauls Bay. Gretchen is a small lake, less than a mile in length, and its outlet stream is the major spawning area for coho and sockeye. The stream is a pleasant flow of water that opens up into an expansive meadow in its lower half-mile. This lower section has some nice fishing for rainbow trout in the 10- to 15-inch range early in the summer before the spawning salmon take over the water. Dolly Varden are usually present here and at the outlet into Laura Lake. By the time salmon reach this point they are usually past prime condition.

Laura Lake is about 3 miles long and is made up of numerous small bays and islands. The rainbow trout fishing can also be good here at times, but it usually takes a lot of exploring to find the fish. The same goes for coho. You'll see them jumping and showing, but they are generally on the move, and it's difficult to stay in reach of them. The best place for salmon on the lake is a few hundred yards from the outlet. The lake narrows to less than 100 feet here, and the salmon—especially the coho—will hold for extended periods of time.

Laura Creek, which flows into Pauls Lake, is a boisterous, picturesque little stream with a steep gradient and a good flow of water. It varies in width from 20 to 30 feet, and its banks are heavily lined with trees and brush, making fishing difficult at best. There is a very good trail down the true right side of the river.

A few hundred yards downstream from the Laura Lake outlet, there is a 40-foot falls. There are a series of diversion weirs and fish ladders here that help the salmon ascend. This is also a great spot for bear viewing, as the bears feed on the pooled-up salmon at the base of the falls.

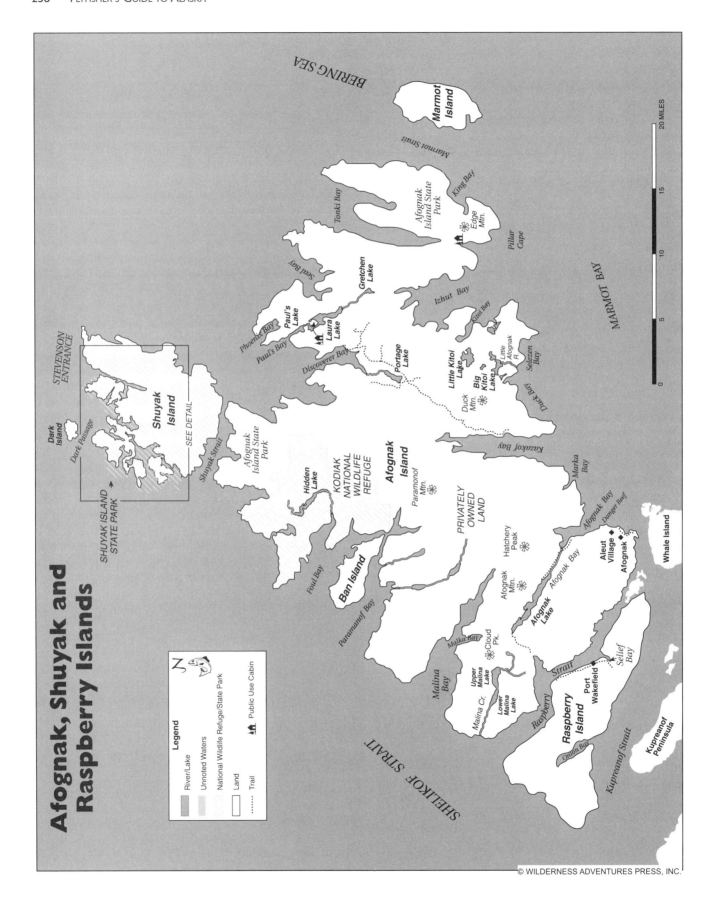

Afognak, Shuyak and Raspberry Islands

Legend

- River/Lake
- Unnoted Waters
- National Wildlife Refuge/State Park
- Land
- Trail
- Public Use Cabin

BERING SEA

Marmot Island

Marmot Strait

Afognak Island State Park

King Bay

Edge Mtn.

Pillar Cape

MARMOT BAY

Tonki Bay

Seal Bay

Izhut Bay

Kitoi Bay

Gretchen Lake

Paul's Lake

Phoenix Bay

Paul's Bay

Laura Lake

Discoverer Bay

Portage Lake

Little Kitoi Lake

Big Kitoi Lake

Little Afognak R.

Selezen Bay

Duck Mtn.

STEVENSON ENTRANCE

Dark Island

Dark Passage

Shuyak Island

SEE DETAIL

Shuyak Strait

SHUYAK ISLAND STATE PARK

Afognak Island State Park

Hidden Lake

KODIAK NATIONAL WILDLIFE REFUGE

Afognak Island

Paramonof Mtn.

PRIVATELY OWNED LAND

Duck Bay

Kazakof Bay

Marka Bay

Afognak Bay

Danger Reef

Aleut Village

Afognak

Whale Island

Ban Island

Foul Bay

Paramanof Bay

Hatchery Peak

Afognak Mtn.

Afognak Bay

Afognak Lake

Malina Bay

Malka Bay

Cloud Pk.

Upper Malina Lake

Lower Malina Lake

Malina Cr.

Raspberry Strait

Selief Bay

Port Wakefield

Raspberry Island

Onion Bay

Kupreanof Strait

Kupreanof Peninsula

SHELIKOF STRAIT

0   5   10   15   20 MILES

Pauls Lake is the first staging area for salmon leaving the saltwater bay. Fish will sometimes stay for a short time at the lower end of the lake before working their way up to the Laura Creek inlet. At the upper end there are several small bays and islands where both coho and sockeye will hold for extended periods. At times, you can encounter thousands of fresh, ocean-bright coho and sockeye in this area. Depending on the water level, this holding period can be for a month or more, but a heavy rain can move the majority of the fish out and up to Laura Lake in a few days.

The area where Laura Creek enters Pauls Lake can be fished from the bank, and it's a great spot for sockeye salmon. The coho salmon will disperse more into the bays and around the islands and are best fished from a small boat or float tube. There is an island about two acres in size in this area that is an ideal camping location. The coho will school up and hold by the thousands around this island. The lake is best fished for coho from mid-August to mid-September.

Pauls Bay itself is a prime location for fishing coho in salt water. They are still actively feeding and will eagerly take a fly. You can fish yourself out in a few days here with these aggressive and acrobatic fish. It's not uncommon to see 5,000 coho schooled up in the area where Pauls Creek enters the bay. This bay is best fished by small boat or float tube. It is adequately protected from most winds, and it's not necessary to venture more than a hundred yards from shore.

The fish are easily spotted here with all their jumping and finning. There is an island of several acres in the immediate area that is a perfect place to camp. It is heavily wooded, with large spruce trees providing good protection from the elements, and close to the fishing.

The Pauls Lake average escapement for major species during the past 10 years is as follows:

- 20,000 sockeye salmon, with a late June peak
- 5,000 pink salmon, with a mid-August peak
- 15,000 coho salmon, with a mid-August peak
- a few incidental steelhead

Portage Lake System

The Portage Lake drainage is another system on Afognak Island that offers excellent fishing for coho salmon. This system is on the northeast end of the island, about 6 miles from Pauls Bay.

The lake is about 2 miles long and has a short shallow stream of less than a mile, which flows into Discoverer Bay. The best fishing takes place in the tidal zone where the stream enters the bay. This tidal zone is over three-quarters of a mile in length and several hundred yards wide. It can be fished by wading the shoreline, but a more produc-

tive approach would be to use a float tube. A small inflatable boat allows you to access more of the bay and follow the fish when they back out on low tide.

There are some good camping locations here, and a boat also permits you to set up away from the outlet and areas frequented by bears. Discoverer Bay itself is about 3 miles long and narrow for its length, with several large islands. These features protect the fishable tidal zone from windy weather and rough seas. Ouzinkie Log Cabins has a rental unit in Discoverer Bay available to anglers. Do not overlook this location for a week of coho or sockeye fishing.

This system has an annual escapement of about 10,000 sockeye salmon and 6,000 coho salmon. There are a few resident rainbow trout in the stream, and Dolly Varden are usually present. The system also supports a small run of steelhead.

Malina Lakes System

The Malina Lakes system is also a fine location on Afognak for coho and sockeye. Malina Lakes are located on the lower southwest side of the island, about 40 air miles from the city of Kodiak. Unlike many other Afognak systems, Malina doesn't have an easily fished tidal-zone lagoon at its outlet. Instead, it flows directly into the Shelikof Strait. You can fish the outlet here, but large ocean swells can make it difficult at times.

The 3-mile-long river is narrow but fishable, and there is some nice scattered holding water throughout. You will also find fish holding at the outlet and inlet of Lower Malina Lake and in the stream between Lower and Upper Malina Lakes.

This drainage has an annual escapement of about 10,000 sockeye salmon and 5,000 coho salmon. Dolly Varden are usually present, and there are a few resident rainbows. This system also has a fishable run of steelhead.

Outlet of Laura Creek into Pauls Lake.

Afognak River

The Afognak River is located on the southeast end of Afognak Island, about 25 air miles from the city of Kodiak. (The area is locally called Litnik.) The river flows about 4 miles through a densely wooded area of large Sitka spruce before reaching the tidal lagoon. This is some of the most scenic water in the Kodiak and Afognak areas.

At the lake outlet there is a short section of river with some nice holding water. The coho and sockeye will usually stage here for a short time before moving through the lake and into its tributaries to spawn.

The next several miles of river have shallow riffles and runs, with few good holding areas. Migrating salmon and steelhead will pass through here quickly, even under normal water conditions.

The lower reaches offer better holding water for both salmon and steelhead. The river is deeper here with a heavier flow and a steeper gradient, but the steep, high banks make access and fishing difficult in places. The river maintains a width of 40 to 60 feet for most of its length, and there is a well-defined trail up the true left side of the river. There is also a picturesque waterfall in the lower reaches that fish have to negotiate before they can make their way to the lake.

The large tidal lagoon and bay at the river's outlet provide good fishing as salmon first enter this system. Dolly Varden are usually present in the river, along with a small population of rainbow trout.

The Afognak River average escapement for major species during the past 10 years is as follows:

- 70,000 sockeye salmon, with a late June peak
- 38,000 pink salmon, with a mid-August peak
- 12,000 coho salmon, with a mid-September peak
- 500 steelhead, with an early October peak

Additional Afognak Island Systems

Afognak Island has numerous other destinations where you'll find some exceptional coho salmon fishing. Many of these systems are relatively short, but offer some very good opportunities for taking these exciting sport fish in salt water. There are also some nice bays and lagoons where coho stage that are available to anglers. The run timing in these systems is similar to that of other Afognak waters.

Hidden Lake and Paramanof Bay are both notable fisheries along the west side of Afognak. On the south end of the island, Marka Bay and several systems at the head of Danger Bay are worth exploring.

Also in this area is the Little Afognak River. It's a delightful system that has a nice protected lagoon at its outlet into Duck Bay. Pink, sockeye, and coho salmon and a small population of resident rainbow trout are present here, along with a few incidental steelhead. The best fishing is for coho staging in the lagoon. Much of the lagoon can be fished by wading from shore or you can venture upriver and fish some of the deeper holding runs. Ouzinkie Log Cabins has a rental cabin on Little Afognak Lake.

Kitoi Bay is the site of a commercial terminal harvest fisheries and fish hatchery operated by the ADF&G. The hatchery only rears fish for the first year or two of their life cycle. They are then released into the ocean and return to the site to spawn. Prior to the terminal harvest, Kitoi Bay is alive with returning chum salmon in June, pink salmon in August, and coho in September. The area provides excellent opportunities for taking these salmon in salt water. But you'll need a boat to fish this bay. Ouzinkie Log Cabins has a rental unit here, which provides anglers with a good base to explore area fisheries.

Raspberry Island is located near the southwest end of Afognak Island. Here you will find Selief Bay, a sheltered little body of water that gets a moderate escapement of coho salmon. The small system that drains into this bay is also fishable in its lower reaches and has a small population of resident rainbow trout. The bay itself is best fished from a small boat or float tube.

Public-use cabin on Shuyak Island State Park.

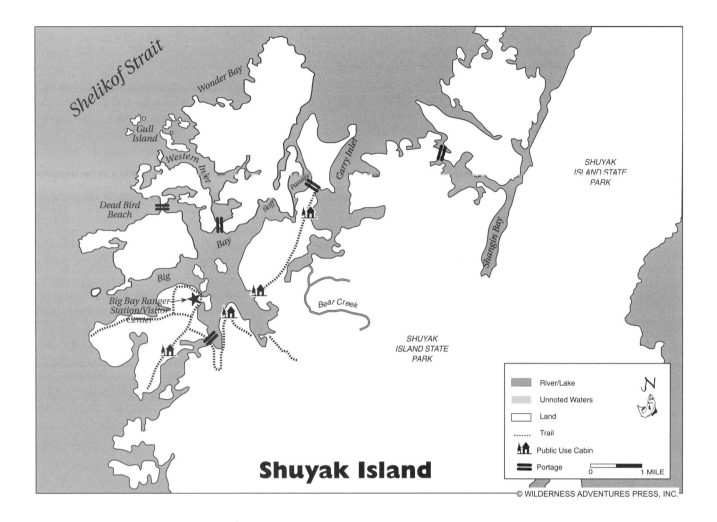

Shuyak Island

River/Lake
Unnoted Waters
Land
Trail
Public Use Cabin
Portage

0   1 MILE

N

© WILDERNESS ADVENTURES PRESS, INC.

SHUYAK ISLAND SYSTEMS

Shuyak Island is just a few miles off the north end of Afognak Island, about 55 air miles from the city of Kodiak. Most of the island's 47,000 acres are within Shuyak Island State Park. The island has a dense covering of old growth Sitka spruce trees, which form an enchanting setting in which to fish and explore. Camping is permitted, and the park system has four well-maintained and equipped public-use cabins available on a rental basis. A park ranger is based on the island during the peak of the cabin rental season. And a commercial vender, Mythos Expeditions out of Kodiak, has kayaks available in the park on a rental basis.

The area has two systems that offer excellent opportunities for coho salmon fishing in salt water during their mid-August peak. Bear Creek is a relatively short system at the head of Carry Inlet. It receives an annual escape-ment of about 2,000 pink salmon and 2,500 coho. It also gets a few incidental sockeye and has a small resident population of rainbow trout and some Dolly Varden.

Coho are best fished in the salt. They will school up in Carry Inlet and stage before making their way up Bear Creek. In low-water years this staging period can be quite lengthy. You can fish from shore, but a small inflatable boat or float tube will put you onto better fishing. Upper Carry Inlet is very well protected from wind and heavy seas. Deer Haven is the nearest state park public-use cabin to Bear Creek.

The other Shuyak system is Big Bay. It is very compa-rable to Bear Creek and can be fished in a similar manner. It has an escapement of about 3,000 pink salmon and 2,000 silvers. It also has a few resident rainbow trout and some Dolly Varden. Salmon Cove and Eagle's Nest are two state park public-use cabins within a mile of Big Creek's outlet.

OFFSHORE SALTWATER FISHING

Very few fly anglers take advantage of Kodiak's offshore saltwater fishing opportunities. Whether your interest is salmon or one of the many other saltwater species, the challenge and excitement is all part of a new adventure for most fly anglers. And fishing offshore extends the short season of availability for many species. Salmon, for example, can be taken offshore a month or more before they arrive in bays and rivers.

You will, of course, need transportation to take you to the fishing grounds. Kodiak has a fleet of over 25 charter boats that work out of Kodiak City Harbor. They all do conventional offshore fishing, so when selecting a boat be sure the captain knows and understands exactly the type of fishing you are interested in.

Try to get an exclusive charter, without a mixture of gear types and techniques being used. Write out how you want to fish and what you want to fish for. That way when you are looking for a charter boat you can hand the boat captain your expectations for the day and avoid any later misunderstandings. If, after you get out on the water, you find the captain not living up to these written expectations, you can have him take you immediately back to the harbor.

Most captains have limited or no flyfishing experience, but they do know where the fish are and how to find them. Some are willing to attempt new fishing methods, but be cautious when selecting a charter boat service. Captain Tony Chatto with Pearson Cove Charters has some flyfishing experience and is receptive to fly angler requests. Give him a call when you start your search.

Chinook salmon are certainly the most sought after species by offshore anglers. You will find saltwater chinook a much different fish than when they are in fresh water. Here they are a fast, strong, acrobatic fish, willing to put your 10-weight tackle to the test. They can be taken throughout the year, with May through September being the most productive months. These salmon are located with the use of electronic fish finders or by observing birds working on bait or through the general knowledge of your boat captain.

Your fishing can take place from near surface to over 100 feet down. However, once you start fishing at depths of 50 feet or more, it becomes a matter of just jigging a fly rather that using conventional flyfishing techniques. Be sure to have a selection of sinking lines and a variety baitfish patterns before you venture offshore in search of any saltwater species.

Chum, coho, and pink salmon are also species that aggressively take flies in offshore saltwater situations. They are more likely to be found at shallower depths, where normal flyfishing techniques can be effective. Generally, these fish show more on the surface by jumping and finning, and consequently are easier to locate. Plus, there are a lot more of them. These salmon are still aggressively feeding, and baitfish imitations are usually the best choice when it comes to pattern selection.

Taking halibut on a fly can also be quite sporting when you can find them at moderate depths. Here again, once you start trying to present a fly to bottom-dwelling fish at 50 feet or more all conventional flyfishing methods can be disregarded. You will need heavy fast-sinking lines to reach fish at their level and a stout rod to bring up a 50-pound or larger halibut in a reasonable amount of time. Not all halibut fishing has to take place in deep water, though. You can experience some good fishing in shallower water by looking for shallow reefs and ledges. Halibut will work their way up out of deeper water to areas that may only be 20 to 30 feet deep.

Numerous other species of rockfish, greenlings, cod, and flatfish can be taken in shallow water. Fishing into rocky shorelines and kelp beds is usually productive and can also be done with a pontoon-style float tube. But be sure the device is seaworthy, wear a personal flotation device, be aware of the tides and wind, and never venture out alone. Additional care must also be taken when attempting to land any large fish in this situation. Bringing them into the beach may be the safest option.

This chinook salmon was caught offshore.

CITY OF KODIAK

Population: 13,000
Area Code: 907
Zip Code: 99615

HOTELS

Best Western Kodiak Inn, 236 Rezanof Drive; 486-3430, 1-800-563-4254

Buskin River Inn, 1395 Airport Way; 487-2700, 1-800-544-2202

Inlet Inn Guest Rooms, 1315 Mill Bay Road; 486-4004, 1-800-423-4004

Russian Heritage Inn, 199 Yukon Street; 486-5657

Shelikof Lodge, 211 Thorsheim Street; 486-4116

BED AND BREAKFASTS

AAA Bayview & River Inn, 2915 Bayview Drive, 481-2882, 1-888-568-2882

AAA Channel's End, 1213 Larch Street, 486-4773, 1-888-254-1485

A Bear Country, 161 Seabreeze Circle, 486-4908

A Captain's Quarters, 4149 Woodland Drive, 486-6444

A Eider House, 782 Sargent Creek Road, 487-4315

A Lake View, 1720 Larch Street, 486-8519, 1-888- 922-8519

A Smiling Bear, 2046 Three Sisters Way, 481-6390

A Wintel's, 1723 Mission Road, 486-6935

Alaska Townhouse, 307 High Street, 486-4424

An Island Suite, 720 Rezanof Drive East, 486-2205

Beachside, 1421 Yanovsky Street, 486-4941

Bear and the Bay, 216 Rezanof Drive East, 486-6154

Beaver Creek Lodge, 11572 South Russian Creek Road, 487-4636

Berry Patch, 1616 Selief Lane, 486-6593

Buoy Bell, 1124 Stellar Way, 486-3377

Distant Loon Guest House, Mile 37.2 Chiniak Highway, 486-1789

Emerald Island Suite, 362 Shahafka Circle, 486-2967

Emerald Isle, 1214 Madsen, 486-4893, 1-866-486-4893

Four Seasons, Box 3750, 486-5380, 1-800-575-5380

Harbor Side, 414 Marine Way, 486-4438

Harborview, 310 Rezanof Drive West, 486-2464, 1-888-283-2464

Ismailoft, 1324 Ismailoft Street, 486-3638

Kaplan's, 418 Lilly Drive, 486-1711

Kodiak, 398 Cope Street, 486-5367

Kodiak Bear's Den, 1817 Simeonoff, 486-6954

Kodiak Island River Camps, 363 Bay Circle, 486-5310

Kodiak's Sunrise, 810 Rezanof Drive, 486-4145

Lagoon Side, Mile 36 Chiniak Highway, 486-5445

Lakeview Terrace, 2426 Spruce Cape Road, 486-5135, 1-866-250-5135

Ocean's Edge, 3594 Spruce Cape Road, 486-2524, 1-888-482-2524

On the Cape, 3476 Spruce Cape Road, 486-4185

Sea Otter, 1723 Rezanof Drive East, 486-3682

Shahafka Cove, 1812 Mission Road, 486-2409, 1-888-688-6565

Spruce Haven, 2109 Mission Road, 486-5171

The Teal House, 3300 Wilton White Way, 486-3369

The Village Connection, 1818 Mission Road, 481-3035

Woodland, 3974 Woodland Drive, 486 8428

VACATION RENTALS

AAA Bayview & River Inn, 2915 Bayview Drive; 481-2882, 1-888-568-2882

Kodiak Winery Cottages, Mile 36.4 Chiniak Highway; 486-6129

Parkside Guesthouse, 1165 Abercrombie Drive; 486-9446

Pasagshak River Accommodations, Box 8095; 486-6702

CABINS & CAMPGROUNDS

Alaska State Parks, 1400 Abercrombie Drive; 486-6339

Homestead Cabin, P.O. Box 946; 487-2566

Kodiak National Wildlife Refuge, 1390 Buskin River Road; 487-2600

Ouzinkie Log Cabins, P.O. Box 946; 487-2566

RESTAURANTS

Chart Room Restaurant, 236 Rezanof Drive West; 486-8807

Eagle's Nest Restaurant, 1395 Airport Way; 487-2700

El Chicano Mexican Restaurant, 103 Center Avenue; 486-6116

Eugene's Chinese Restaurant, 202 Rezanof Drive East; 486-2625

Henry's Great Alaska Restaurant, 512 Marine Way; 486-8844

Kalsin Bay Inn, Mile 29 Chiniak Highway; 486-2659

Kings Dinner, 2009 Mill Bay Road; 486-4100

Kodiak Island Winery, Mile 35.9 Chiniak Highway; 486-4848

Kodiak Mongolian BBQ, 1247 Mill Bay Road; 486-4414

Mill Bay Coffee & Pastries, 3833 Rezanof Drive East; 486-4411

Shelikof Lodge, 211 Thorsheim; 486-4141

2nd Floor Japanese Restaurant, 116 Rezanof Drive West; 486-8555

CAR RENTAL

Avis, State Airport; 487-2264

Budget Rent A Car, State Airport; 487-2220

Rent-a-Heap, 508 Marine Way; 486-8550

OUTDOOR EQUIPMENT RENTAL

Kodiak Kamps, 311 Upper Mill Bay Road; 486-5333

Mythos Kayak Rentals, Box 2084; 486-5536

MUSEUMS
Alutiiq Museum & Archaeological Repository, 215 Mission Road; 486-7004

Baranov Museum, 101 Marine Way; 486-5920

Kodiak Military History Museum, Fort Abercrombie State Park; 486-7015

AIRLINES
Alaska Airlines, 1200 Airport Way; 487-4363, 1-800-252-7522

Era Aviation, 1200 Airport Way; 487-4363, 1-800-866-8394

Island Air Service, 2191 Mill Bay Road; 486-6196, 1-800-478-6196

AIR CHARTERS
Andrews Airways Inc., 1522 Devils Creek Road; 487-2566

Harvey Flying Service, 5279 Airport Way; 487-2621

Island Air Service, 2191 Mill Bay Road; 486-6169, 1-800-478-6196

Kingfisher Aviation, 477 Shahafka Circle; 486-4120, 1-800-693-2333

Kodiak Air Service, 415 Mill Bay Road; 486-4446

Maritime Helicopters, State Airport; 486-4400

Sea Hawk Air, 505 Trident Way; 486-8282, 1-800-770-4295

MARINE HIGHWAY
Alaska Marine Highway, 100 Marine Way; 486-3800, 1-800-526-6731

SPORTING GOODS
Bear Country Sports, 3833 Rezanof Drive East; 486-6480

Cy's Sporting Goods, 117 Lower Mill Bay Road; 486-3900

Mack's Sport Shop, 212 Lower Mill Bay Road; 486-4276

Orion's Sports, 1247 Mill Bay Road; 486-8380

58 Degrees North, 1231 Mill Bay Road; 486-6249

FLYFISHING GUIDES
Flyfish Kodiak, 1221 Madsen; 486-4206

Fly Fishing Kodiak, 3344 Spruce Cape Road; 486-3366

Kodiak Island River Camps, 350 Bay Circle; 486-5310

LODGES/CAMPS WITH FLYFISHING SERVICES
Rohrer Bear Camp, 486-5835

Silver Salmon Lodge, 680-2230

Saltery Lake Lodge, 486-7083

Zacher Bay Lodge, 1-800-693-2333

Aspen View Wilderness Lodge, 486-5373

Kodiak Island River Camps, 486-5310

Salty Fly Safaris, 486-1439

Karluk Wilderness Adventures, 1-866-686-2527

CHARTER BOATS
Chazman, 486-6930

Dutchman, 486-2955

Gunnar's, 486-8128

Happy Hooker, 486-2524, 1-888-482-2524

Hidden Falls, 486-1068

Kodiak Fish Konnection, 486-2578

Kodiak Island, 486-5380

Magnum, 486-7600, 1-888-330-7600

Mythos Expeditions, 486-1771

Person Cove, 486-5301

Pristine, 486-3474

Runnamuck, 486-3802

Sea Otter, 486-3682

Shoot The Breeze, 486-2409

Three Sons, 486-6824

Tim's Trips, 487-2529

Woodland, 486-8428

MEDICAL
Providence Kodiak Island Medical Center, 717 Rezanof Drive East; 486-3281

NATIVE CORPORATIONS
Afognak Native Corporation, 215 Mission Road; 486-6014, 1-800-770-6014

Koniag Inc, 202 Center Street; 486-2530

PUBLIC LAND AGENCIES
Alaska State Parks, 1400 Abercrombie Drive; 486-6339

Kodiak National Wildlife Refuge, 1390 Buskin River Road; 487-2600

ADDITIONAL INFORMATION SOURCES
Kodiak Island Convention and Visitors Bureau, 100 Marine Way; 486-4782, 1-800-789-4782

Alaska Department of Fish and Game, 211 Mission Road; 486-1880

AKHIOK

Population: 80

Kodiak Island's southernmost community, Akhiok is about 75 air miles from the city of Kodiak. It's located on the southwest end of Kodiak Island in Alitak Bay. From June through September, it has daily flight service from the city of Kodiak. There are no commercial services available in the village of Akhiok.

KARLUK

Population: 27

The village of Karluk is about 70 air miles from the city of Kodiak. It's located on the southwest side of Kodiak Island on the banks of Karluk Lagoon and the Karluk River outlet. From June through September it has daily flight service from the city of Kodiak.

CABIN RENTALS
Homestead Cabin, P.O. Box 946, Kodiak; 487-2566

LARSON BAY

Population: 115

Larson Bay is about 60 air miles from the city of Kodiak and is located on the west side of Kodiak Island. Daily flight service from the city of Kodiak is available year-round. The village has a small grocery, but few other services. It's in an ideal location for access to the middle reaches of the Karluk River. Several fine lodges are located in the village.

LODGES

Black Tail Point Lodge, P.O. Box 41, 847-2212
Larson Bay Lodge, 847-2239, P.O. Box 92; 847-2238, 1-800-748-2238
Sprit of Alaska Wilderness Adventures, P.O. Box 123; 1-800-677-8641
Uyak Bay Lodge, P.O. Box 7; 847-2350

ADDITIONAL INFORMATION

Kodiak Island Convention and Visitors Bureau, 101 Marine Way, Kodiak; 486-4782, 1-800-789-4782

OLD HARBOR

Population: 237

Located on Sitkalidak Strait on the east side of Kodiak Island is the village of Old Harbor. It's about 50 air miles from the city of Kodiak and the location of many historic sites. Nearby you'll find the location of the first Russian settlement on Kodiak Island and the site of the last American commercial whaling station. There are daily flights into the village from the city of Kodiak. A variety of services are available, including a small grocery store, café, lodges, and charter boats.

LODGES

Sitkalidak Lodge, P.O. Box 155; 286-9246

CHARTER BOATS

Kodiak Combos, P.O. Box 14; 286-2252

ADDITIONAL INFORMATION

Old Harbor Native Corporation; 286-2286
Kodiak Island Convention and Visitors Bureau, 101 Marine Way, Kodiak; 486-4782, 1-800-789-4782

OUZINKIE

Population: 225

Ouzinkie is located on the southwest side of Spruce Island about 8 miles from the city of Kodiak. It is nestled among large spruce trees, and the 10-square-mile island has an excellent trail system. The village has daily flight service from the city of Kodiak. You can also reach Ouzinkie by charter boat service from Kodiak. There is a small grocery store, and several charter boats work out of the village.

CHARTER BOATS/LODGES

Spruce Island Charters, P.O. Box 189; 680-2332, 1-888-680-2332
Spruce Island Lodge and Charters, P.O. Box 3219, Kodiak; 654-8067, 1-866-777-8235
Marmot Bay Excursions, 680-2203

ADDITIONAL INFORMATION

Ouzinkie Native Corporation, 680-2208
Kodiak Island Convention and Visitors Bureau, 100 Marine Way, Kodiak, 486-4782, 1-800-789-4782

PORT LIONS

Population: 256

The village of Port Lions is about 15 air miles from the city of Kodiak. It's on the north end of Kodiak Island in Kizhuyak Bay and Settlers Cove. The village was relocated here from Afognak Island, where it was destroyed by the 1964 tsunami. The new village was named after the service group that helped relocate it, Lions Club International. Port Lions is served by the Alaska State Ferry system and has daily flights from the city of Kodiak. It can also be reached by charter boat from Anton Larson Bay and the city of Kodiak. The village has a well-stocked grocery store, several B&Bs, lodges, and charter boat services. It's a great place to spend a week fishing and exploring.

BED AND BREAKFASTS

Settler's Cove, 137 Kizhuyak Drive; 454-2573
Wilderness Beach Adventures, 431 Main Street; 454-2301

LODGES

Port Lions Lodge, 454-2264, 1-800-808-8447
Kodiak Wilderness Outfitters, P.O. Box 29; 454-2418, 1-888-454-2418

CABIN RENTALS

RAK Outfitters, P.O. Box 63; 454-2333

CHARTER BOATS

Kodiak Sports and Tour, 111 Ptarmigan Street; 454-2419
Nelson Charters, 324 Hillside Drive; 454-2554
Pete's Trophy King Salmon Fishing, P.O. Box 63; 454-2333

ADDITIONAL INFORMATION

Kodiak Island Convention and Visitors Bureau, 100 Marine Way, Kodiak; 486-4782, 1-800-789-4782

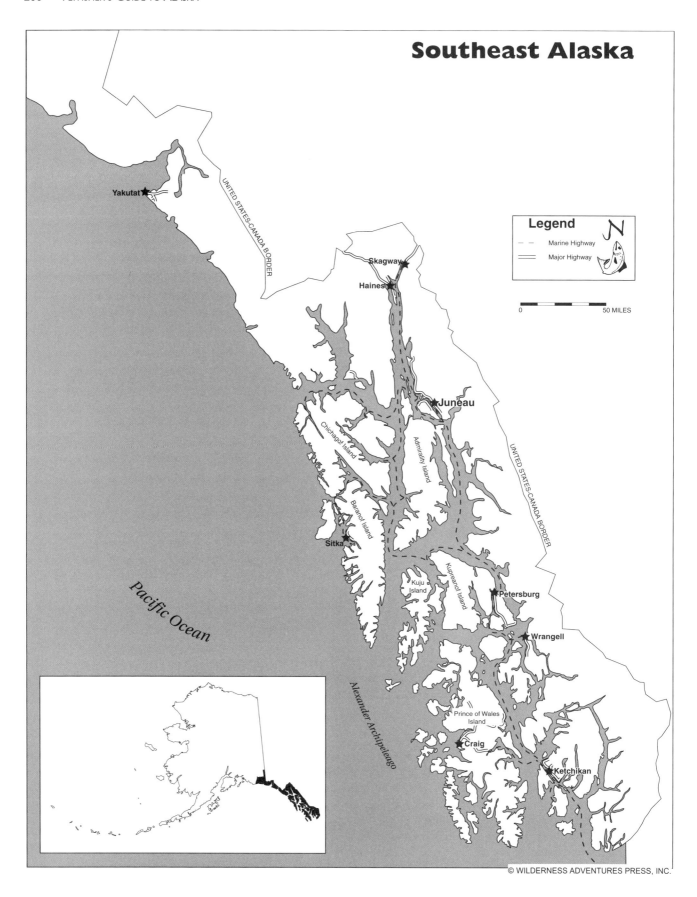

Southeast Alaska

Legend
- - - Marine Highway
——— Major Highway

0   50 MILES

UNITED STATES-CANADA BORDER

UNITED STATES-CANADA BORDER

Yakutat

Skagway

Haines

Juneau

Chichagof Island

Admiralty Island

Baranof Island

Sitka

Kuju Island

Kupreanof Island

Petersburg

Wrangell

Pacific Ocean

Alexander Archipelago

Prince of Wales Island

Craig

Ketchikan

© WILDERNESS ADVENTURES PRESS, INC.

Southeast Alaska

By Scott Haugen

GENERAL RUN TIMING FOR SOUTHEAST ALASKA

Due to the extensive north/south distance occupied by the Southeast Alaskan archipelago, the freshwater run timings of fish can vary. For this reason, two run-timing charts are provided. The first chart takes in southern Southeast Alaska, including the featured regions in and around Ketchikan, Prince of Wales Island, Wrangell, and Petersburg. The boundary line dividing northern from southern Southeast Alaska runs from Frederick Sound west and south into the Pacific Ocean. North of this line, including all of Baranof and Admiralty Islands and the mainland north of Frederick Sound, the northern Southeast Alaska run timings are in effect. The featured areas covered in the northern chart include Sitka, Juneau, Haines, Skagway, and Yakutat.

Of all the vast regions covered in this book, Southeast Alaska is the most challenging to represent on paper. With more than a thousand islands, numerous fjords, endless miles of shoreline, thousands of rivers, creeks, and lakes, and tough-to-access topography, this area remains one of the most unexplored in the state.

Despite the fact that Southeast Alaska—which stretches for more than 500 miles from south of Ketchikan to north of Yakutat—sees an exorbitant number of tourists each season, very few people explore beyond the beaten path. One reason is because there's such good fishing close to many towns, some within walking distance of the ferry terminals or a few minute's drive from the airports.

To attempt to list each and every fishable piece of water in Southeast Alaska would be extremely difficult. Instead, we will focus on the top fisheries near each port town and the best fly-in opportunities. Fly anglers should note, however, that more than any other region in the state, Southeast Alaska is a saltwater fishery. Every hub city listed in this chapter offers prime ocean fishing for salmon right from town. Many even offer bottom fishing directly from the docks.

Southern Southeast Alaska

Species	Jan	Feb	Mar	Apr	May	Jun	Jul	Aug	Sep	Oct	Nov	Dec
King Salmon	-	-	-	-	+/++	++/+++	+++	+++/++	-	-	-	-
Sockeye Salmon	-	-	-	-	-	++	+++	+++	+/-	-	-	-
Coho Salmon	-	-	-	-	-	+	++	++/+++	+++	++	+	-
Pink Salmon	-	-	-	-	-	-	+/+++	+++	+++	+	-	-
Chum Salmon	-	-	-	-	-	-	++	+++	++	+	-	-
Steelhead Trout	+	+	+	+++	+++	+	+	+	+	+++	+++	+
Rainbow Trout	+	+	+	++	+++	+++	++	++	++	++	+	+
Cuttrout Trout	+	+	+	++	+++	+++	++	++	++	++	+	+
Brook Trout	+	+	+	+	+	+	+++	+++	+++	+	+	+
Dolly Varden	+	+	+	+	++	++	+++	+++	+++	+++	+	+
Arctic Grayling	+	+	+	+	+	+	+	+	+	+	+	+

+++ Excellent   ++ Good   + Fair   - Nonexistant/Closed Season

Northern Southeast Alaska

Species	Jan	Feb	Mar	Apr	May	Jun	Jul	Aug	Sep	Oct	Nov	Dec
King Salmon	-	-	-	-	++	++	+++	++	-	-	-	-
Sockeye Salmon	-	-	-	-	-	++	+++	++	++	-	-	-
Coho Salmon	-	-	-	-	-	-	-	-/+	++/+++	+++/++	++	-
Pink Salmon	-	-	-	-	-	-	+++	++	++	-	-	-
Chum Salmon	-	-	-	-	-	++	+++	++	++	+	-	-
Steelhead Trout	+	+	+	+++	+++	+	-	-	+	+++	++	+
Rainbow Trout	+	+	+	+	++	++	++	++	++	++	+	+
Cuttrout Trout	+	+	+	+	++/+++	+++	+++	++	+	+	+	+
Brook Trout	+	+	+	+	+	+	+	+++	+++	+	+	+
Dolly Varden	+	+	+	++	+++	++	+++	+++	++	+++	+	+
Pike	+	+	+	+	+	+	+++	+++	+	+	+	+

+++ Excellent   ++ Good   + Fair   - Nonexistent/Closed Season

The fact that halibut can be caught off local piers is one indication of just how rugged the terrain is in Southeast Alaska. Less than a half-mile from shore, many mountains rise 3,000 feet. Such a drastic change in elevation means that high lakes are tough to reach and rivers and creeks have extreme gradients. This is a major reason why so much stream fishing here is done in estuaries, at the mouths of streams, and only a short distance upstream from the mouth.

You'll see a wide mix of anglers here: some hauling their own vehicles on the ferry in order to fish as much of the road system as possible; others hopping off cruise ships, rods in hand, running to the nearest stream to wet a line before their vessel once again sets sail; anglers traveling the famed Alaska Marine Highway looking to score on fish at each of the portages; adventurous types heading out to sample remote fly-in fishing opportunities by way of helicopter or floatplane; and finally, anglers staying at one of the many lodges operating throughout the vast archipelago.

Be prepared for rain in Southeast Alaska. No matter where you go or what time of year you're here, bring raingear. Annual rainfall averages 90 inches, with more than 200 inches drenching some towns. Throw in another couple hundred inches of snow and you can see why this is one of the wettest regions in America. But the overall climate is surprisingly mild compared to the rest of the state, due in large part to warm ocean currents.

During the summer, temperatures average 60°F, rarely exceeding 70°F. Even in the middle of summer, weather can vary greatly. Travelers should be prepared for rain, fog, clouds, and low visibility at any time. For anglers intent on fly-in trips, know that delays as a result of bad weather are routine.

Due to Southeast Alaska's moist, warm climate, rich flora exists throughout the region. Within the rainforest environment, Sitka spruce, cedars, and hemlock grow to magnificent proportions. Beneath the canopy a lush carpet of green covers the forest floor, with mosses and ferns dominating the scene. Huckleberries, blueberries, and the pain-inflicting devil's club are also present. Above tree line, where many high-lake fisheries are located, you'll find typical alpine terrain.

Three-quarters of Southeast Alaska is covered in dense forest. In fact, the Tongass National Forest, the largest forest in the United States, covers 16.9 million acres here, over 73 percent of the land that constitutes Southeast Alaska. In addition, the world's highest coastal range, the Saint Elias Mountains, are here, towering more than 18,000 feet into the sky.

Because the environment is so wet and temperate, biting insects like mosquitoes, no-see-ums, and white-sox (black flies) can be thick, especially if you're fishing away from the coastline. Protective head nets, gloves, and insect repellent are all requirements, particularly if you're hitting boggy lakes or working your way along the wooded trails of forest streams.

Travelers should also be cognizant of bears, particularly brown bears. Due to the thick foliage surrounding many waters, bear encounters can take place at distances measured in feet, not yards. Anglers need to be prepared for such a chance occurrence. Bear densities are very high around some coastal towns, and many of the bruins have no fear of humans. Be prepared at all times and if you see a bear, maintain your composure.

A final word of warning for anglers working along tidal zones: Southeast Alaska is home to tidal fluctuations that can reach up to 23 feet in just a few hours. Two high and two low tides occur each day, with 6.5 hours between the maximum and minimum tides. With so much water moving in and out of an area in such a short time, and the many islands, bays, and passages through which the water must move, anglers need be aware of what's happening at all times. The beach you hiked along to reach the mouth of a stream may be 15 feet underwater by the time you need to leave. A river mouth you waded across earlier in the morning may be over its banks on an extreme high tide, making it impossible to forge until the tide drops. When wade fishing in estuaries with fast tidal movements, don't wade too far out. These tides can rip through an area and pick up astounding power, wiping out everything in their path.

While ocean fishing for salmon is the primary draw for hardware anglers, fly anglers can expect to find a wide variety of fish that can be pursued in bays, estuaries, streams, and lakes. There are also stocked ponds near many of the hubs. But steelhead and Dolly Varden are the primary targets of most of the longrodders who visit this region. From late April through May, steelhead can be had as they move into their natal streams, while Dolly Varden are caught in estuaries where their home waters empty into the ocean. In the spring, Dollys are migrating to sea for a couple of months, feeding on out-migrating salmon smolt. The fishing here for Dollys is the best in Alaska, with fish in the 1- to 3-pound class average.

All five salmon species can be caught in Southeast Alaska, although king salmon fishing is prohibited in most streams. In late summer, pink, red, chum, and coho salmon attract many anglers. In fact, many people travel to this part of the state specifically to target feisty silvers as they make their way into coastal streams.

Though arctic grayling are not indigenous to Southeast Alaska, they have been planted in some lakes and offer excellent fishing opportunities, especially for dry-fly enthusiasts. Rainbow, cutthroat, and brook trout can be found throughout much of the region too, rounding out a wide range of freshwater fishing possibilities. Combine these fish with the halibut and other bottom fish available, and the list of fish one angler can reasonably expect to catch on a single trip hits double digits.

If you're serious about spending time in some of the coastal communities and maximizing your lake fishing experience, consider bringing along a float tube and a mountain bike. A mountain bike will allow you to more quickly negotiate some of the rugged trails, while a float tube will get you away from brush-choked shorelines and into better fishing.

Due to a recent downturn in the U.S. and world economy, there's been somewhat of a decline in travel to this area. If you're an angler, this is good news, as it means less overall pressure on the waters you want to fish. For example, Forest Service cabins in Southeast Alaska are traditionally very difficult to secure. But as a result of the lack of travel, many of these cabins have gone unclaimed recently, and making reservations is a cinch.

We'll begin our discussion with the fishable waters in the southern portion of the region, starting with Ketchikan and working our way north, ending at Yakutat. Eight of the nine major port towns highlighted here can be reached by plane or boat. Yakutat, the northernmost town, is accessible only by air; all other towns mentioned are on the Alaska Marine Highway and can be reached by ferry or cruise ship. Haines and Skagway are the only fishing towns that can be reached by road off the highway, and Sitka, Juneau, and Haines/Skagway are by far the most frequented towns.

Stream mouths offer some of the best fishing in Southeast Alaska, especially on a low tide when the fish stack up. (Photo Cameron Hanes)

Ketchikan

While Ketchikan is one of Southeast Alaska's most visited port towns, it has only about 18 miles of road system. This means a great many of the fisheries in the area are accessible only by boat or plane, though there are some roadside systems worth hitting that are fairly easy to reach.

There are many charter companies working from Ketchikan that specialize in fly-in fishing. Up to 65 percent of the fly-in drop-offs center around Forest Service cabins located on lakes around the Ketchikan area. Cabins need be reserved well in advance—six months is not too early. Most Forest Service cabins come with skiffs, a real boon to fly anglers who would otherwise be forced to cast from brushy shorelines.

As with all regions of Alaska, be sure to check current fishing regulations prior to wetting a line in any area waters.

The following is a look at the roadside fisheries around Ketchikan, working north to south. Next, we'll look at some of the top remote fisheries.

Settlers Cove and Lunch Creek

The northernmost roadside fishery lies 18 miles above Ketchikan on the Tongass Highway. Settlers Cove is easy to reach, and there's a day-use state park here.

Settlers Cove is a tidal zone, and its gradual beach lends itself well to flyfishing for pink and chum salmon. Though the area can be fished from the bank, chest waders will be a big help, particularly during tide changes. As you should for most tidal fishing zones in the area, concentrate on incoming tides, which often bring strong surges of fish. The tides can be big and fast, however, so don't get caught out too deep on an incoming tide.

Casting and stripping along the shores where the salmon often travel can be very effective here. Look for salmon jumping just offshore. Good casts may get you into some large schools of fish waiting to venture upstream.

Lunch Creek feeds into Settlers Cove, and though it's only about 15 feet wide and a couple of feet deep, it can offer good fishing in its lower stretch. The mouth of the stream has the best fishing, with some good fishing also available at the barrier falls. The falls are within easy walking distance of the mouth. Due to the narrow, brushy nature of the stream above the falls, there's no reason to fish there. Instead, if it's a freshwater experience you yearn for, stay close to the creek mouth, where fish often slow down as they make their way in from the salt water. Like most creeks in Southeast Alaska, Lunch Creek is tannic stained.

One word of caution when fishing this area: There are some native-owned lands where fishing access isn't permitted. Pay attention to posted areas and abide by all "no trespassing" signs.

Second Lakes

Sixteen miles north of Ketchikan on the Tongass Highway, you'll come to a trailhead leading to Second Lakes, a fairly remote hike-in fishery. The hike is 4 miles long on a primitive trail, some of which is tough to negotiate.

But if you're in good shape and are up to the physical challenge, this is a good place to escape the crowds. If you're feeling really energetic, pack a belly boat into the lake to give yourself some additional fishing opportunities. Don't expect anything spectacular on the lake, however, as rainbows up to 12 inches are the only species present.

The area in and around the lake has been impacted by logging, so the scenery may not be what you'd expect when you think of a remote Southeast Alaska lake. There's a good bear trail around the lake, which makes it easy to cover the entire ¾-mile shoreline. There are a few places where you can cast from shore, but the best places to fish are the inlet and outlet. There are also some windfalls around the lake that provide structure for the rainbows.

Though rainbow trout don't grow as large in Southeast Alaska as in the Iliamna or Kenai regions, they are still premier fish to battle on the fly.

Ketchikan
and Surrounding Water

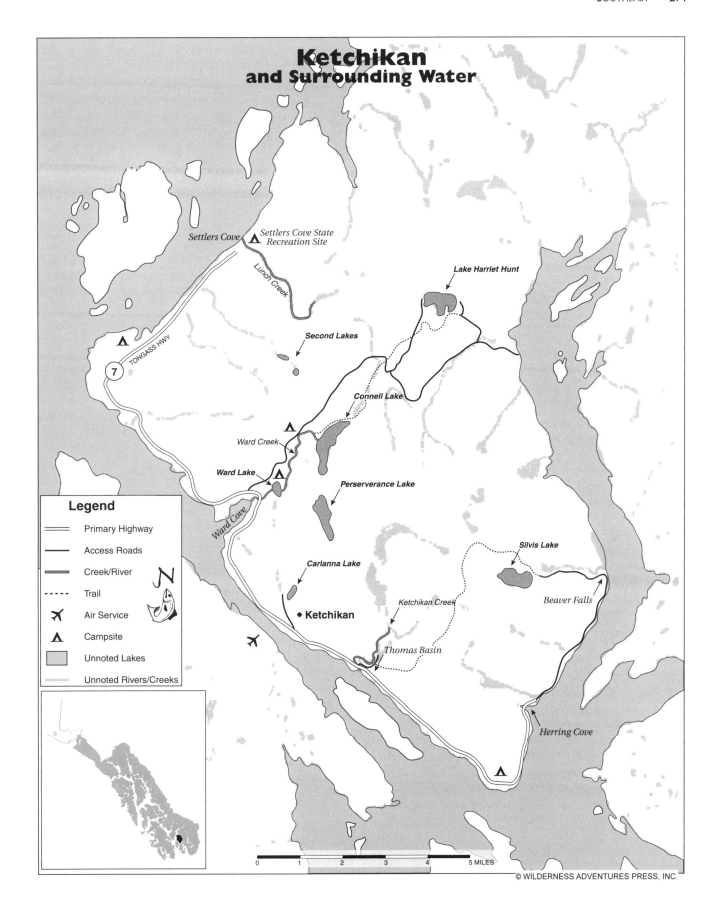

Settlers Cove

Settlers Cove State
Recreation Site

Lunch Creek

TONGASS HWY

7

Lake Harriet Hunt

Second Lakes

Connell Lake

Ward Creek

Ward Lake

Ward Cove

Perserverance Lake

Silvis Lake

Beaver Falls

Carlanna Lake

Ketchikan Creek

◆ Ketchikan

Thomas Basin

Herring Cove

Legend

═══	Primary Highway
────	Access Roads
━━━	Creek/River
- - - -	Trail
✈	Air Service
⛰	Campsite
▨	Unnoted Lakes
∿∿	Unnoted Rivers/Creeks

N

0 1 2 3 4 5 MILES

© WILDERNESS ADVENTURES PRESS, INC.

Harriet Hunt Lake

Eighteen miles north-northwest of Ketchikan, at the end of the Ward Creek road system, you'll find Harriet Hunt Lake. Access to the lake is off an old logging spur road, from which a small canoe or raft can be launched. Though the lake is fairly large, and up to 300 feet deep in some sections, anglers are wise to work the shallows.

Harriet Hunt Lake is stocked with hardy triploid rainbows, and though there is a five-fish limit on the lake, there were no size limitations on the fish themselves at the time of this writing. Trout will range from 6 to 15 inches and fight hard for their size.

The best fishing lies near the inlet and outlet streams of the lake, both of which are the color of root beer. Anglers working from the bank can expect good success, while those working from a raft or belly boat can do even better. In some shallow stretches, there is natural structure that bank anglers can fish around.

Connell Lake

Because Connell Lake was once the primary storage reservoir for a pulp mill that used to operate here, it's not a fishery on which you'll see many local anglers. The dam to the lake was constructed in the 1950s, and current anglers are left to negotiate a huge stump patch with lots of hangups.

In addition, because the mill is no longer running, the dam does not hold back water like it used to. Thus, the lake is very low and tough to fish from shore. Anglers willing to make the 11-mile drive from Ketchikan up the Ward Creek logging spur will find a primitive boat ramp from which a canoe or raft can be launched. This is the best way to negotiate the stumps and get into some fair fishing around structure. Cutthroat, rainbow, and brook trout inhabit this lake, some growing up to 15 inches.

Ward Creek and Lake

The most popular roadside fishery in the entire Ketchikan area is Ward Creek, which is located 8 miles north of Ketchikan off a marked logging spur road on the North Tongass Highway.

Many trails on both sides of the creek allow easy access to prime fishing water. And except when high, it's an easy creek to wade. Ward averages about 50 feet across and around 3 to 4 feet deep. It's tannic colored and rises rapidly with the onset of a rainstorm. From where the road hits the creek, there's a good 3 miles of bank fishing available, and anglers can work from either bank, wading midstream in most places.

This creek is one of the few on the road system large enough to have deep holes and large pools where incoming fish can congregate. Silver, red, and pink salmon, along with steelhead, can often be found staging in these pools for a day or two after leaving salt water, acclimating to the fresh water before continuing upstream. Dolly Varden and cutthroat trout can also be found here. And all these species can be caught in various riffles and tailouts, too.

A Forest Service trail follows the upper third of the creek, leading anglers to Ward Lake. There are three Forest Service cabins on the lake, and with skiffs available at each.

A 1.3-mile trail circles the lake, but the best fishing is at the lake's inlet and outlet. In addition, there is good fishing around the blowdowns that pack the shore areas. Spend time working the shoreline, as fish often move in to forage on food. As usual, a float tube will give you a better chance at tagging fish.

Ward Cove

Below Ward Creek, fly anglers in search of saltwater opportunities can try Ward Cove. The Tongass Highway crosses over Ward Creek 6 miles north of Ketchikan. For good intertidal fishing, park at the bridge, the only real access to the lower water.

The action heats up during the summer and fall runs of coho salmon. Starting in the middle of July and continuing for the rest of the summer, then again in mid-September through October, silver salmon filter into the cove, offering anglers a good chance to battle these fish on the fly. The summer months are also good for pink salmon.

You'll have to hike down to the cove from the bridge, as access is limited farther downstream due to an old pulp mill that doesn't grant trespass requests. But from the bridge as far down as you can walk there is plenty of fishing opportunity. The beach is rocky here and can be very slippery, so felt-soled wading boots are advised. Anglers should also pay extremely close attention to the tide changes. As 20-foot tide swings are common, be certain to consult a local tide book to make sure you don't get caught in a fierce, incoming tide.

This area is definitely worth hitting when the fish are in.

Perseverance Lake

Another hike-in lake can be reached by driving 8 miles north of Ketchikan on the Ward Creek logging spur. From the marked trailhead at Ward Lake, a hike of 1.5 miles leads you to Perseverance Lake, where there are two Forest Service cabins. Each cabin comes with a skiff, and given the steep sides of this lake it's almost imperative to

Pink salmon runs can be immense, offering nonstop catching action all day long.

have some sort of watercraft to get you to good fishing for brookies and rainbows.

Another option is to pack in a small inflatable raft or float tube, which is fairly easy to do on the well-maintained trail that leads from the road to the lake. In fact, because the trail is so easy to access, this is a popular summer lake for local anglers, so make your cabin reservation well in advance.

Though Perseverance Lake is a long, narrow body of water—1.5 miles long by ¾-mile wide—it runs 150 feet deep in places. Concentrate your fishing along edges that are tough to reach from the bank, the inlets and outlets, and around areas of structure.

Carlanna Lake

Located at the west end of Ketchikan, Carlanna Lake is another hike-in fishery anglers may want to explore. There is a gravel road leading into the lake, but it's gated, so you'll have to make a half-mile hike in.

Access is tough due to the steep-sided, brush-choked banks. Most of the fishing on Carlanna takes place at the

outlet near the dam. The target species here is planted triploid rainbow trout, of which the daily bag limit is five with fish ranging from 6 to 12 inches long. Due to the lack of structure in and around the lake, it's best to carry in a float tube and concentrate most of your efforts around the inlet stream, which offers good fishing.

Silvis Lake and Beaver Falls

Silvis Lake is situated 16 miles southeast of Ketchikan off the Tongass Highway and is part of the city power system. A 3-mile hike up a gravel road is required to reach the lake, which does offer some shoreline fishing. Again, a float tube will get you into better fishing.

Silvis was planted with rainbows before Alaska even became a state, and the fish population continues to thrive. Fish up to 15 inches long reside in Silvis, and due to the fact that it receives very little pressure, trout can be caught throughout the entire lake.

Silvis Lake is set amid a fairly industrial-looking area, though, so it's not as pristine as some tourist anglers may envision. In addition, the lake gets drawn down in the summer to meet city power needs, but it still remains fishable.

Beaver Falls, where the power plant is located, is located below Silvis. Below the falls there is a saltwater fishery, which offers limited opportunities for anglers to take pink and chum salmon. As it's located at the southern end of the road system, getting here is simple, but native-owned land does block a good deal of access. Extreme tidal changes also make this a challenging and somewhat dangerous place to fish, but if you're in the area, it's worth wetting a line on a low tide.

Ketchikan Creek

Ketchikan Creek flows south of the town of Ketchikan. Though it's normally closed to sport fishing from the middle of May to the middle of September, when there is a surplus of any salmon species there may be special regulations temporarily opening the river. It's a hit-and-miss, and you can learn if it's open to angling at the time of your visit by phoning the local ADF&G office or by paying a visit to the stream yourself. It is, however, open to angling from mid-September to mid-May.

Ketchikan Creek is a clear stream with a private hatchery on it. Even if it's not open to angling at the time of your visit, it's worth visiting to observe the migrating and spawning fish. You'll see silver salmon, king salmon, and pink salmon, along with steelhead. Dolly Varden and cutthroat trout are also present in the creek. There's a fee for touring the hatchery, and the proceeds go to keep the hatchery functioning and to support other projects.

Thomas Basin

At the mouth of Ketchikan Creek, there are year-round angling opportunities for all the species that enter the creek in what's known as Thomas Basin. Saltwater regulations apply here. There is no snagging, bait is prohibited, and only single hooks can be used. These rules make for a more enjoyable fly angling experience.

Thomas Basin is actually a boat harbor, open to anglers seaward of the Steadman Street bridge. In fact, many tourists find fantastic fishing right off the bridge. You can also find good fishing off the docks, just be aware of the fact that many boats use the area as a moorage.

Thomas Basin is a place where you can step right off the cruise ship and be fishing within minutes. In some years you can look off the bridge and observe upwards of 200,000 pink salmon moving by, with a mix of king and silver salmon thrown in.

This area is worth a visit, and it's one of the easiest fisheries to access in the Ketchikan area.

Herring Cove

Nine miles south of Ketchikan there's a bridge on the Tongass Highway that crosses over Herring Cove. The water above the bridge is closed to angling year-round, but below the bridge you can fish for king, silver, and pink salmon from August 10 to January 31.

Every year this area is loaded with pink salmon, and king salmon ranging from 12 to 50 pounds are regularly taken. There are both hatchery and wild strains of king and silver salmon entering this fishery, and anglers may keep both varieties.

From the bridge you can park and walk down to the mouth, where you'll see three ADF&G markers. This is a fantastic flyfishing area, but pay close attention to incoming tides and privately owned land. If you hit the low tide just right, you can maximize your fishing time on the water, working ahead of the incoming tide as it moves back in. However, once the tide hits private property, your fishing becomes very limited. Trespassers misusing private lands is a major problem here, so be sure you know where you are at all times.

Roadside parking is also limited, and there is no parking allowed on private property. Combine this with the Alaska state law that no vehicle can be parked within 10 feet of any highway, and it's easy to see why so many people receive citations in this area. As long as you know where you are and abide by posted signs you'll have a good time chasing these salmon on the fly.

Remote Fishing Destinations

There are many remote fisheries out of Ketchikan that can only be reached by floatplane or boat. While they are far too numerous to list, what follows is a look at some top destinations you may want to consider.

McDonald Lake is 43 miles north of Ketchikan and can be reached by floatplane or boat. There is a Forest Service cabin and skiff on the lake. Due to the popularity of this lake, however, be sure to reserve the cabin early, preferably for the middle of the week. Every Pacific salmon species but kings inhabit this water, as do steelhead, Dolly Varden, and cutthroat trout. The inlet and outlet are the best places to fish, although there is some structure in and around the lake. If you're unable to book the cabin, you can fly in for a single day of fishing and head back to town that same afternoon.

There are countless bodies of water that can only be reached by floatplane in this region of Alaska.

Wilson Lake sits 42 miles southeast of Ketchikan and can be reached only by floatplane. There are two Forest Service cabins on the lake, both with skiffs. Cutthroats here must be 25 inches or longer to keep, though catch and release is a sound practice in this true trophy cutthroat fishery. No bait is allowed on this beautiful lake, which is part of the Misty Fjords National Monument, and you should again concentrate on the inlet and outlet. Anglers sometimes fish off the floatplanes that bring them into the lake. You could also work a float tube around the lake's inlet and outlet, but the rest of the water is pretty big for such a craft.

Ella Lake lies 25 miles east of Ketchikan and can be reached by plane or boat and trail. This is another trophy cutthroat fishery on which no bait is allowed. Two Forest Service cabins are located here, and both come with skiffs. Again, the inlet and outlet of the lake offer the best cracks at bruiser cutts, though there is also good fishing to be had along the shoreline if you have access to one of the skiffs or bring your own float tube.

KETCHIKAN

Population: 14,070
Alaska Area Code: 907
Zip Code: 99901

TOURIST INFORMATION
Alaska Department of Fish and Game, 2030 Sea Level Drive, Suite 205; 225-5195
Ketchikan Visitors Bureau, 131 Front Street; 1-800-770-3300; www.visit-ketchikan.com
Southeast Alaska Discovery Center, 50 Main Street; 228-6220
U.S. Forest Service Cabin Information, Ketchikan-Misty Fiords Ranger District, 3031 Tongass Avenue; 225-2148

GUIDE SERVICES
Adventure Charters & Marine Services, P.O. Box 23602; 225-2628; www.chartertheboat.com
Classic Alaska Charters, P.O. Box 6117; 225-0608; www.classicalaskacharters.com
Ketchikan Fishing Reservations; 1-800-928-3308; www.ketchikanfishing.com

FLY-IN CHARTERS
Carlin Air, P.O. Box 5542/ 1-888-594-3036; www.carlin-air.com
Family Air Tours, P.O. Box 23514; 1-800-380-1305; www.familyairtours.com

Southeast Aviation, 1249 Tongass Avenue; 225-2900; www.southeastaviation.com

TACKLE SHOPS
Bob's Guns & Sporting Goods, 685 Pond Reef Road North; 247-8139
Wal-Mart, 4230 Don King Road; 247-2156

ACCOMMODATIONS
Backpackers Hostel Eagleview, 2303 5th Avenue; 225-5461
Best Western Landing Hotel, 3434 Tongass Avenue; 1-800-428-8304
Blueberry Hill Bed & Breakfast, P. O. Box 9508; 1-877-449-2583
Captain's Quarters Bed & Breakfast, 325 Lund Street; 225-4912
Gilmore Hotel, 326 Front Street; 1-800-275-9423
Naha Bay Outdoor Adventures, P.O. Box 7482; 247-4453; www.nahabayoutdooradventures.com
Nichols Passage Bed & Breakfast, 3032 South Tongass; 225-4698
Salmon Falls Resort, P.O. Box 5700; 1-800-247-9059
The Classic Stop Bed & Breakfast, 216 Madison Street; 225-3607
The Narrows Inn, Restaurant & Marina, 4871 N. Tongass Avenue; 1-888-686-260
West Coast Cape Fox Lodge, 800 Venetia Way; 1-866-225-8001

CAMPGROUNDS AND RV PARKS
Clover Pass Resort and R.V. Park, P.O. Box 7322; 1-800-410-2234; www.cloverpassresort.com

RESTAURANTS
Bar Harbor Restaurant, 2813 Tongass Avenue; 225-2813
Dockside Diner, 1287 Tongass Avenue; 247-7787
The Edge, #5 Salmon Landing Market; 225-1465
Good Fortune Restaurant, 4 Creek Street; 225-1818
Steamers on the Dock, 76 Front Street; 225-1600

FISH PROCESSING
Alaska General Seafoods, 930 Stedman Street; 225-2906

BOAT RENTALS
Alaska Wilderness Outfitting/Alaska Kayak Rentals, 3857 Fairview; 225-7335; www.lattitude56.com

RENTAL CARS
Alaska Car Rental, 2828 Tongass Avenue; 1-800-662-0007
Budget Car Rental, 4950 N. Tongass Hwy.; 1-800-478-2438
Payless Car Rental; 225-6004

AIR SERVICES

Alaska Airlines, 1200 Airport Terminal; 1-800-426-0333;
www.alaskaair.com

L.A.B. Flying Service Inc., 247-5220; www.labflying.com

Promech Air, 1515 Tongass Ave.; 1-800-860-3845;
waterfront office 225-3845, airport office 225-4494;
www.promechair.com

AUTO REPAIR

Carriage Works Auto Repair, 6633 Roosevelt Drive
South; 225-9344

R D Mechanics, 6012 Dotson Lane South; 225-3206

LOCKSMITHS

Ketchikan Lock & Key Company, 2711 Tongass Avenue;
247-4107

Romine's Locksmith, 225-4795

MEDICAL

Ketchikan General Hospital, 3100 Tongass Avenue;
225-517

VETERINARY CLINICS

Ketchikan Veterinary Clinic, 97 Eichner Avenue North;
225-6051

TOURIST ATTRACTIONS

Deer Mountain Hatchery and Eagle Center, 1158
Salmon Road, Ketchikan City Park

Saxman Totem Park, Mile 2.5 South Tongass Hwy.;
225-4846

Totem Heritage Center, 601 Deermount Street;
225-5900

Native art near Ketchikan.

PRINCE OF WALES ISLAND

Prince of Wales Island encompasses more than 2,200 square miles. It has perhaps the world's most numerous array of steelhead streams, with over 300 known streams, some of which aren't even officially named. Some 2,000 miles of road meander across the island, the result of large scale logging operations that are more or less finished. An angler could spend a lifetime exploring all the fishing to be had on this island and still not see it all. In this section, we'll address the top streams, which still leaves plenty for anglers to explore on their own.

Prince of Wales Island can be reached daily by plane or via the ferry from Ketchikan. It's common for anglers on an extended trip to put their vehicle on the ferry so they can delve into the fishing opportunities at their own pace. While logging has scraped much of the beauty from the landscape, it has also opened pathways to innumerable fisheries. Most of the roads are gravel, though paved sections do exist on the road from Craig to Thorne Bay and from Craig to Hollis.

It should be noted that due to the extensive logging, runoff is high during rainstorms and streams can rise rapidly. Instead of being absorbed by trees and their root systems, much of the water flows over the land and directly into streams. As a result, streams can quickly become unfishable, though they do recover rapidly. And during periods of intense rainfall, some streams that are usually easy to wade may become inaccessible. Pay close attention to weather systems when fishing on this island and understand that you're often at the mercy of Mother Nature.

As time goes on, look for more roads to be paved, opening up even more access to fisheries. With the logging boom over, resident human populations are declining as people move out of the area. As a result, sport fishing is going to become an even larger part of this island's economy.

Here is a look at the premier fisheries on the island's road system, running north to south, followed by some of the top remote fisheries adventurous anglers may want to consider.

Red Lake and Red Creek

You'll find Red Lake and Red Creek on the north end of Prince of Wales Island, halfway between Baker Point and Whale Pass. There is a Forest Service cabin on Red Lake, and if you're looking at spending any time here, it's worth reserving. Bank access on this small lake is limited, and the cabin's skiff will get you into a lot more fishing.

Red Creek is a small stream that's easy to wade fish. A

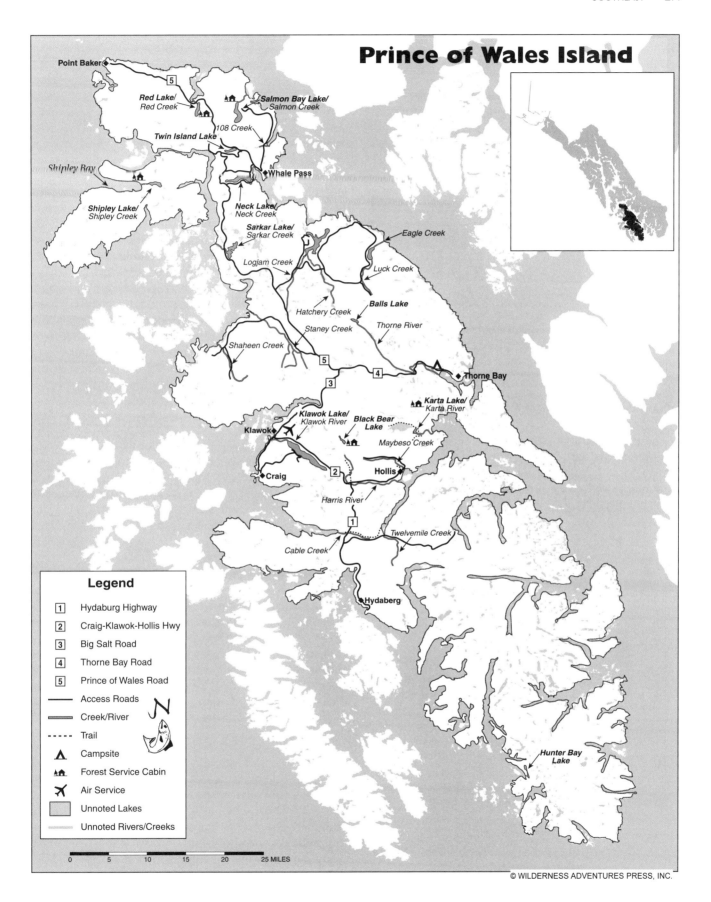

Prince of Wales Island

Point Baker

Red Lake/
Red Creek

Salmon Bay Lake/
Salmon Creek

108 Creek

Twin Island Lake

Whale Pass

Shipley Bay

Shipley Lake/
Shipley Creek

Neck Lake/
Neck Creek

Sarkar Lake/
Sarkar Creek

Eagle Creek

Logjam Creek

Luck Creek

Hatchery Creek

Balls Lake

Staney Creek

Thorne River

Shaheen Creek

Thorne Bay

Karta Lake/
Karta River

Klawok Lake/
Klawok River

Black Bear
Lake

Klawok

Maybeso Creek

Craig

Hollis

Harris River

Twelvemile Creek

Cable Creek

Hydaberg

Hunter Bay
Lake

Legend

1 Hydaburg Highway
2 Craig-Klawok-Hollis Hwy
3 Big Salt Road
4 Thorne Bay Road
5 Prince of Wales Road
— Access Roads
— Creek/River
---- Trail
▲ Campsite
🏠 Forest Service Cabin
✈ Air Service
Unnoted Lakes
Unnoted Rivers/Creeks

N

0   5   10   15   20   25 MILES

© WILDERNESS ADVENTURES PRESS, INC.

Due to a rich food supply, Dollys grow nice and plump in many estuaries throughout this part of the state.

bridge crosses over the creek, and you can wade about a half-mile downstream and about a mile upstream. Wading directly in the creek as you fish you way up or down or hopping on one of the bear trails that parallels the creek is a good way to cover ground. The creek is small enough to wade across in most places. Hit the holes and prime holding water, which you'll have no trouble identifying in this creek.

As with 95 percent of the streams in Southeast Alaska, Red Creek runs dark in color due to staining by tannic acids released from the surrounding vegetation. All salmon species but kings can be pursued here, but the creek is most noted for its red salmon, Dolly, and cutthroat fishing.

108 Creek

Located near Whale Pass, 108 Creek is famous for its silver and pink salmon fishing. The area around this creek was once logged down to the banks, and as a result, the regrowth has created a brushy habitat that can make it tough on fly casters.

However, at 20 to 30 feet wide and 2 or 3 feet deep, the creek can easily be waded for most of its length. I'd advise wading midstream, roll casting as you go. Hit the deep holes in which salmon congregate and work close to the banks where fish often travel.

Twin Island Lake

Twin Island Lake sits northwest of Whale Pass. Home to Dolly Varden and cutthroat trout, this small, half-mile-wide lake is easy to access, as a road follows it. While the fishing at the outlet is perhaps the most productive, there is actually good fishing to be had throughout much of the

lake. Bank access is generous, and the fishing from shore can be fast-paced. If you're hauling a canoe or float tube you can launch off the side of the road and get into even more prime fishing water.

Neck Lake and Neck Creek

You'll find another Dolly and cutthroat fishery at Neck Lake just south of Whale Pass. There's a small boat ramp here that's easy to reach as the road borders the southern shoreline of the lake for 1.5 miles. There is good fishing throughout the lake, but it's recently been overshadowed by Neck Creek, which you'll find downstream of the bridge.

Wade fishing is good for a half-mile downstream in the creek, though it's all influenced by the tides. There is a barrier falls at the lake's outlet, where red and chum salmon have been planted. As a result, the creek is a great place to pursue these salmon. Neck Creek averages about 20 feet wide, and it's easy to wade along and fish here. Because this creek is just beginning to be recognized as a viable fishing destination, there are a few guides in the area who offer bank-fishing trips.

Sarkar Lake and Sarkar Creek

You'll find Sarkar Lake roughly halfway between Whale Pass and the village of Naukati. Access to the lake is limited, as it's best reached from the creek by canoe or raft. Most of the fishing in this area takes place right at the Forest Service bridge that crosses over Sarkar Creek. This area is intertidally influenced and offers anglers every salmon species but kings.

Sarkar Creek averages about 30 feet in width—though it's quite deep—and drains four different lakes in the area. Anglers should stick to the shore here, though the stream can be waded across at a few spots. There's only about a third of a mile of fishing on this creek, but the deep holes create ideal staging areas for newly arriving fish. Concentrate on the holding zones, as these are where salmon will stop for a few days to acclimate to their new freshwater environment prior to continuing upstream and into the lake and other tributaries.

Logjam Creek and Hatchery Creek

Logjam Creek and Hatchery Creek are located northeast of Naukati, and both streams feed into Sweetwater Lake. A Forest Service road crosses the creeks, providing easy access. Logjam Creek has about 6 miles of prime wade fishing. It's about 30 feet wide and has a couple falls. The chum salmon and spring and fall runs of steelhead make it over the falls, while the pink salmon often get caught in the lower falls. As you would expect, the foot of the falls is a great place to spend some serious fishing time. There are also classic pools spread throughout the prime water, all of which can hold fish. This stream can easily blow out with heavy rains, though, which makes it difficult to wade.

Hatchery Creek is just to the west of Logjam Creek. A Forest Service trail leads from the bridge to the creek. Hatchery is similar in physical appearance to Logjam Creek, and there is good fishing throughout. But one unique aspect of Hatchery Creek is that you can launch a canoe here and follow the drainage all the way to Thorne Bay. The journey takes a minimum of three days to complete, but it's an easy float that offers productive fishing for pink, silver, and chum salmon, along with Dollys, steelhead, and cutthroat trout.

Eagle Creek and Luck Creek

Eagle Creek and Luck Creek are situated just south of Coffman Cove on the northeast end of Prince of Wales. Both are located right on the road. Eagle Creek flows out of Luck Lake and Luck Creek flows into Luck Lake.

Wade fishing these creeks can be very productive for all salmon species except kings. A spring and fall run of steelhead, along with Dolly Varden, rainbow, and cutthroat trout, also call these waters home. There are nearly 8 miles of streamside fishing here. It's definitely worth spending a day or two here when the salmon are in, as the catching can be nonstop. If you get tired of wading through the streams, you can get on the bear trails that border each.

Luck Lake also hosts some good fishing opportunities. At 4 miles long and over a mile wide, this lake is best explored by canoe or small skiff. Most of the fishing on Luck Lake is near the mouth, though a small outboard motor will allow you to explore more of the lake's fringes.

Staney Creek

South of Naukati a Forest Service road crosses Staney Creek in four places. This means access is generous on this 50-foot-wide creek. When the creek is low, it's easy to wade fish. And with 15 miles of water to explore, there's no shortage of fishing opportunities.

Many tributaries feed into Staney Creek, and the fishing at the mouths of these streams, as well as farther up, can be very productive. Every salmon but kings and reds can be caught here. Though heavy logged has left the scenery less than pristine, the fishing can be excellent.

Because the stream is so exposed, it rises rapidly and darkens when it rains. This leaves the creek unfishable, and given its size and the number of tributaries flowing into it, some time is needed for it to recover. But when it's not raining, it's safe and easy to wade fish and can be crossed in several places. In addition to the confluences of the tributaries, hit the deeper holes and pockets of water; they will hold large numbers of several fish species.

Shaheen Creek

Farther along the road that takes you to Staney Creek, you'll find Shaheen Creek. The road crosses this creek in a couple of different places, so you can simply park at the bridge and walk directly to the stream below, where approximately 5 miles of very good fishing water awaits.

Shaheen Creek averages about 25 feet wide and 2 to 3 feet deep. All but king and red salmon inhabit the creek, and the steelhead run takes place in the spring, typically throughout the month of May.

The drainage has been clearcut, but offers wader-friendly fishing both up and downstream of the bridges (when not blown out by storms). Focus on the deeper pools, as the riffles are usually too shallow to hold fish.

Scott Haugen loves spring steelhead fishing.

Thorne River

The Thorne is the largest river on Prince of Wales Island, meandering 25 miles from its headwaters to where it eventually dumps into the sea at the town of Thorne Bay. The river, along with several of its tributaries, can be reached from numerous roadside access points. On average, the Thorne is about 75 feet wide and ranges from 3 to 20 feet deep, though it can be waded across in some spots. Its tannic-stained waters flow swiftly in some spots and just poke along in others.

There are many bank fishing opportunities along the Thorne River, and all fish species but king salmon can be pursued. Cutthroat ranging into the mid-20-inch class are a big draw, as are the sheer number of salmon caught on this closed-to-bait river.

There's one Forest Service cabin in the drainage, along with a big Forest Service campground. In addition, there are many places along the river to pull off, camp, and fish near the road. The Thorne River runs entirely on Forest Service land, though accessing the upper river is difficult as the road in this area is closed to motor vehicles. Those willing to walk or mountain bike the upper river will likely have the water all to themselves.

The lower section of river is easy to access and offers abundant fishing opportunities, and many anglers believe this stretch has better fishing than the upper end. Several guides operate on the Thorne River, and a couple of lodges were also in place at the time of this writing. As the area becomes more geared toward tourist fishing, look for the number of guides serving this river to increase.

But this is an easy stream to fish on your own, and one of the most productive and rewarding fisheries on the entire island.

Balls Lake

Located at the head of the Thorne River drainage, Balls Lake has a day-use picnic facility you can drive to and a boardwalk/gravel 300-yard trail leading to its shores. The lake is 1.5 miles long and a half-mile wide; large enough that you might want to consider bringing a canoe or raft. The well-maintained trail makes it easy to get your boat in the water.

Balls Lake is easy to fish from shore, too. Work along the shallow edges and amid blowdowns that have toppled into the lake, where you'll often find trout seeking sanctuary and food. For silver, red, and pink salmon, focus your efforts around both the inlet and outlet, where oxygenated waters attract these species.

Klawock River and Klawock Lake

Near the village of Klawock, you'll find the Klawock River and Klawock Lake. The river flows near the village and is a big fishery, both in size and popularity. All salmon species but kings run here, and there are spring and fall steelhead, rainbows, cutthroat, and Dolly Varden.

Much of the land surrounding the river is native-owned, and while the lower mile of the stream is open to the public at the time of this writing, there has been some speculation that this may change. Check posted areas or, better yet, contact the Klawock Native Corporation to make sure access is still being granted to the lower river.

The Klawock River averages about 60 feet wide, and in some places it's shallow enough to wade across. However, there are lots of deep slots, so watch your step when wade fishing. There is easy and plentiful streamside access along the highway side of the river.

Silver salmon runs are plentiful throughout much of Southeast Alaska, and they are definitely underfished.

Though the river is very dark in color, it's extremely popular among fly anglers, especially during the silver salmon and spring and fall steelhead runs. Anglers should note that the entire river is currently closed to sockeye salmon fishing. In addition, this river receives intense subsistence fishing pressure.

Klawock Lake is the largest lake on the island; too big to fish unless you have a boat. The road parallels the lake for some 5 miles, and there is a private hatchery at the lake's outlet, where both silver and red salmon can be taken. The fishing can be good here for hatchery-raised and wild fish.

Maybeso Creek

Near the town of Hollis, Maybeso Creek flows from the west on its way to the bay. The entire drainage has been logged, and the banks are very brushy. Combine this with high waters resulting from rainfall, and Maybeso can be tough to fish. When rain has affected the water, fish as near the bridge as possible, as this is where you'll find the most bank access.

When little precipitation has fallen, though, Maybeso is only about 30 feet wide and easily waded. If this is the case, you can cover about 4 miles of good fishing water upstream of the bridge. You'll find quite good silver and pink salmon fishing, with a smattering of chum salmon, spring steelhead, Dollys, rainbows, and cutthroat trout.

Harris River

The Harris River flows just south of Maybeso Creek. This is a bigger body of water, averaging about 75 feet in width. This is a river worth fishing, though, as it's one of the few on the entire island that runs clear. The sight fishing for steelhead and pink, silver, and chum salmon can be excellent.

The road leading from Hollis to Hydaburg crosses the Harris River three-quarters of the way up the drainage and offers access to great wade fishing for a long way upstream. This is a nice stream in a pretty setting, and it's very flyfisher-friendly. This river recovers quickly from a rain; it's capable of dropping in excess of 3 feet in a day. This makes the fishing for silver, chum, and pink salmon quite dependable.

Cable Creek

Cable Creek is located approximately halfway between Hollis and Hydaburg and is home to silver, pink, and chum salmon, along with spring steelhead, Dollys, and cutthroat trout. From where the road crosses the river, you'll find 3 miles of easy bank fishing. Averaging 25 feet

wide, this tannic-stained stream is tough to access when rain falls.

A Forest Service trail leads down to the lower drainage, about a third of a mile above the intertidal zone. From here, there's good fishing all the way down to the tidal waters. Many anglers choose to hike to the mouth on a low tide, then fish their way back upstream, hopefully following a surge of fresh fish on the head of an incoming tide. If your timing is right, the coho and pink fishing at the mouth can be some of the hottest action around.

Twelvemile Creek

To the southeast of Cable Creek, Twelvemile Creek is another stream you'll want to fish. Twelvemile Creek is accessed from a Forest Service road that leaves the Hydaburg Highway. One major bridge crosses the river, and from here anglers can park and hike 1 mile downstream to the salt water or 4 miles upstream. With so much ground to cover, there's no shortage of fishing.

Silver, pink, and chum salmon are on the menu, along with Dollys, cutthroat, rainbows, and a small spring run of steelhead. Silvers are the most popular fish on the creek, followed by the humpies.

Twelvemile is very tannic in color. It's about 30 feet wide and flashy when rains fall. If you're fishing this stream shortly after a rain, prepare to battle the brush to reach the prime fishing holes. When the water is in good condition, there are good riffles to fish and plenty of 10- to 12-foot-deep pools that hold salmon.

Remote Fishing Destinations

Despite the immense number of roadside fisheries on Prince of Wales, there are also innumerable remote fisheries on this large island. If you're seeking a change of pace from road-accessible fishing, consider hitting one of the following bodies of water.

Black Bear Lake is located near the town of Craig. This pristine fishery hosts rainbow trout up to 15 inches. There is a Forest Service cabin on the lake, which sits in the alpine zone at 1,200 feet above sea level. The thing that makes Black Bear Lake so attractive is its proximity to Craig, meaning the flight in and out is not as costly as other lakes on the island. And it's located in a beautiful setting, complete with a major falls at the lake's outlet. There is a bit of low-profile industrial development on the lake, though, as it is a source of power for both Craig and Klawock.

Karta Lake and the **Karta River** drainage are located between Hollis and Thorne Bay. Three Forest Service cabins are located here, and a Forest Service trail running from salt water all the way to the end of the upper lake

(**Salmon Lake**) provides all the fishing an angler could ask for. The system is home to all species of salmon except kings and is very popular among anglers traveling by boat from Hollis. A floatplane can also get you to the lake, which makes a nice day trip. Managed as a semi-wilderness area, the river hosts plenty of fish, as do the many lakes in the drainage.

Shipley Bay and **Shipley Lake** are located on the northwest end of the island, due west of Whale Pass, and can be accessed by floatplane or boat. There's also a Forest Service cabin on the 3-mile-long, 1-mile-wide lake. The lake is tannic colored, as is **Shipley Creek**, which connects the lake to the bay. The creek is about 25 feet wide and can be wade fished for its entirety. Outstanding saltwater action can be had on the fly for all salmon species except kings.

Salmon Bay Lake and **Salmon Creek** are located on the northeast tip of Prince of Wales and can be reached by either floatplane or boat. A Forest Service cabin is present on the lake, and a good trail leads to the salt water. The bay is noted for its bountiful run of silver salmon, and it's a good setup for flyfishers. Pink, red, and chum salmon can also be pursued in the salt.

Hunter Bay Lake sits on the southwest edge of the island and can be reached only by floatplane. The 2-mile-long, half-mile wide lake has 2 miles of stream that can also be fished, above and below the lake. All species of salmon except kings can be taken here. Both streams average about 30 feet wide, are tannic colored, and offer outstanding wade fishing. The hiking along the streams is confined to well-used bear trails. This lake is a good place to set up camp for a few days of stream and lake fishing.

Southeast Alaska has numerous Forest Service cabins available for public use. Just be sure to book your reservations early, as these are popular getaway sites.

CRAIG

Population: 2,125
Alaska Area Code: 907
Zip Code: 99921

TOURIST INFORMATION

Alaska Department of Fish & Game, 225-5195 (office located in Ketchikan)

Prince of Wales Chamber of Commerce, 826-3870; www.princcofwalcscoc.org

U.S. Forest Service, Craig Ranger District; 826-3271

U.S. Forest Service Cabin Information, Thorne Bay Ranger District, P.O. Box 19001, Thorne Bay, AK 99919; 828-3304

GUIDE SERVICES

Alaska Best Fishing, Inc., 2.5 Port St. Nicholas, Craig; 1-888-826-8500; www.alaskabestfishing.com

Doug Wilhite Fishing Expeditions, 503-472-2657

El Capitan Lodge, P.O. Box 1174, Craig; 1-800-770-5464; www.elcapitanlodge.com

J&J Charter Service, 109 Sea Otter Drive, P.O. Box 18015, Coffman Cove, AK 99918; 329-2009; www.coffmancove.org/jandjcharter.html

Shelter Cove Lodge, P.O. Box 798, Craig; 826-2939; www.sheltercovelodge.com

Sonny's Skookum SE Alaska Adventures, P.O. Box 19151, Thorne Bay, AK 99919; 828-8879; www.skookumadventures.com

Southeast Retreat, P.O. Box 282, Klawock, AK 99925; 755-2994; self and fully guided package options, lodging and car rental

Sunnahae Lodge, P.O. Box 90, Craig; 826-4000; www.sunnahaelodge.com

FLY-IN CHARTERS

Promech Air; 1-800-860-3845; www.promechair.com

Scott Air, LLC, P.O. Box 1174, Craig; 846-5464; www.Scott-Air.com

TACKLE SHOPS

Black Bear Store, P.O. Box 22, Klawock, AK 99925; 755-2292; gas, ice, bait, groceries, fishing licenses and fishing supplies; open 4:00 a.m. to midnight every day

Jim's Lures, P.O. Box 19248, Thorne Bay, AK 99919; 828-3470

Log Cabin Sporting Goods, 1 Easy Street, Craig; 826-2205; fishing, hunting and camping supplies, apparel; canoe and kayak rentals

Naukati Connection, P.O. Box NKI #430, Naukati, AK 99950; 629-4104

Riggin' Shack, P.O. Box 18101, Coffman Cove, AK 99918; 329-2213; fishing/hunting licenses, tackle, ice, bait and snack foods

Tackle Shack, Thorne Bay, AK 99919; 828-3333

ACCOMMODATIONS

Bayview Inn, P.O. Box 263, Craig; 826-3623

Dreamcatcher B&B, P.O. Box 702, Craig; 826-2238; www.AlaskaOne.com/dreambb

Hansen's 4-Mile Beach Cabin, P.O. Box 724, Craig; 826-3888

Lupine Pension, 607 Ocean View Drive, Craig; 1-888-546-3851

Northend Cabins, Box WWP, Whale Pass, AK 99950; 846-5315; rooms with kitchen, license vendor, walking distance to salmon streams and freezer

Oceanview B&B, P.O. Box 929, Craig; 826-2543

Overflow B&B, P.O. Box 945, Craig; 826-3382

Ruff It Bayside Cabins & General Store, Box WWP, Whale Pass, AK 99950; 846-5221;flyfishing in the bay, beachfront cabins, boat & motor, freezers, hot indoor showers, BBQs, crab cookers; www.ruffitresort.com

CAMPGROUNDS AND RV PARKS

Log Cabin Resort & RV Park, P.O. Box 54, Klawock, AK 99925; 755-2205; 14 full hookup sites, showers, laundry, phone, condos, beach cabins, boat and canoe rentals, charter fishing, whale and bird watching, pets allowed; www.logcabinresortandrv.com

Oceanview RV Park and Campground, Coffman Cove; 329-2015; 14 full hookup sites,showers, laundry, phone, tent space and bunkhouse, pets allowed; www.coffmancove.org/rvpark.html

Rain Country Recreation RV Park, P.O. Box 79, Craig; 826-3633; 11 full hookup sites, pets allowed

RESTAURANTS

Dockside Cafe, P.O. Box 1054, Craig; 826-5544

Papa's Pizza, P.O. Box 702; located in the Westwind Plaza, Craig; 826-2244

Rhonda's Drive-In, P.O. Box 1054, Craig; 826-2400

Ruth Ann's, P.O. Box 645, Craig; 826-3292

FISH PROCESSING

Jody's Seafood Specialties, P.O. Box 376, Klawock, AK 99925; 755-8870

Wildfish Smokery, Klawock; 755-2247

BOAT RENTALS

Alaska Rentals, 826-2966; www.alaskarentals.com

RENTAL CARS

Alaska Rentals, 826-2966; www.alaskarentals.com

Wilderness Car Rentals, 1-800-949-2205; www.wildernesscarrental.com

AIR SERVICES

Alaska Airlines, 1-800-426-0333; www.alaskaair.com

L.A.B. Flying Service, Inc., P.O. Box 517, Craig; 826-5220; www.labflying.com

AUTO REPAIR

Bayview Fuel & Tire Station, Thorne Bay; 828-3345

NAPA Auto Parts, 123 Easy Street, Craig; 826-3950

Shaub-Ellison Tire & Fuel, Craig; 826-3450; Mechanics on duty, car rentals, towing and 24-hour fuel

MEDICAL

Craig Clinic-Seaview Family Medical Center, 826-3433

TOURIST ATTRACTIONS

Prince of Wales Hatchery Association, P.O. Box 554, Craig; Mile 9 Craig-Hollis Hwy.; 755-2231

Haugen admires a nice coho.

WRANGELL ISLAND

Seventy-five miles of road allow anglers to discover many of Wrangell's popular fisheries. With the exception of the remote destinations touched on at the end of this section, all the waters mentioned here can be reached by road. As with many places on Alaska's Marine Highway, anglers often opt to put their vehicles on the ferry, setting out on their own to see what fishing in the Wrangell region is all about.

Pat Creek and Pat Lake

Located 10 miles south of the town of Wrangell, Pat Creek is a tannic-stained system not worth fishing for anything other than Dolly Varden. It's a short stream that receives a small run of steelhead, but they are so few in number and very few local anglers even spend time chasing them. However, transient populations of Dollys visit this creek all summer long. Because these fish are visiting from other area waters, they can be in and out quickly, so be sure to at least check it out when passing through.

The creek can have good fishing all the way to salt water. On the south side of the creek mouth, a big shelf allows you to wade quite a ways out, where you can expect Dolly Varden along with silver salmon and pinks. Flounder, a saltwater bottom fish, will also chase a fly here.

Pat Lake is very easy to reach as the road leads directly to it. The road parallels the north shore of the lake, and footpaths allow you to reach a great deal of shoreline. However, a canoe or float tube is the best way to fish this lake, which has a maximum depth of about 30 feet. From late summer through November, there is tremendous sea-run cutthroat trout and Dolly Varden fishing in the lake. Coho can also be fished here in the fall.

The cutts and Dollys can be taken with a variety of methods. If it's windy, troll a sink-tip line. If it's calm, cast and strip the shorelines, where fish can often be seen working the aquatic plant growth that rims the lake.

Pat Lake is one of the premier lakes in the area, with cutthroat up to 20 inches and Dollys measuring into the high teens. It's easy to fish, close to town, and receives most of its pressure on the weekends. During the weekdays in September and October, you'll have the lake to yourself.

Salamander Creek

Salamander Creek receives one of the best spring steelhead runs around. Though roughly 200 steelhead may not sound like many, when they keg up in this small stream it can appear as if there's more than enough steelhead for everyone. Cutthroat trout up to 18 inches are also present.

Located 18 miles southeast of Wrangell, Salamander Creek's best fishing lies below the road that crosses it. Hit every inch of water from the bridge down to salt water, which is about 3 miles. There are large gradients in some places, particularly following a rain, so proceed with caution.

You'll be impressed by the amount of classic steelhead water on this 25-foot-wide stream; one plunge pool after another presents itself. Short riffles are also worth covering. The entire stream can be waded from the bridge all the way to the mouth, but be sure of your wading ability when the water runs high, as it's tough to see where your steps will fall in the stained water.

Wide-open banks make this stream a line-whipper's paradise. Just be sure to stick to the downstream side of the bridge. Upstream, the water is too shallow and the fish hold beneath hard-to-reach cutbanks.

Mike Gallen shows why so many anglers are obsessed with Southeast Alaska's steelhead.

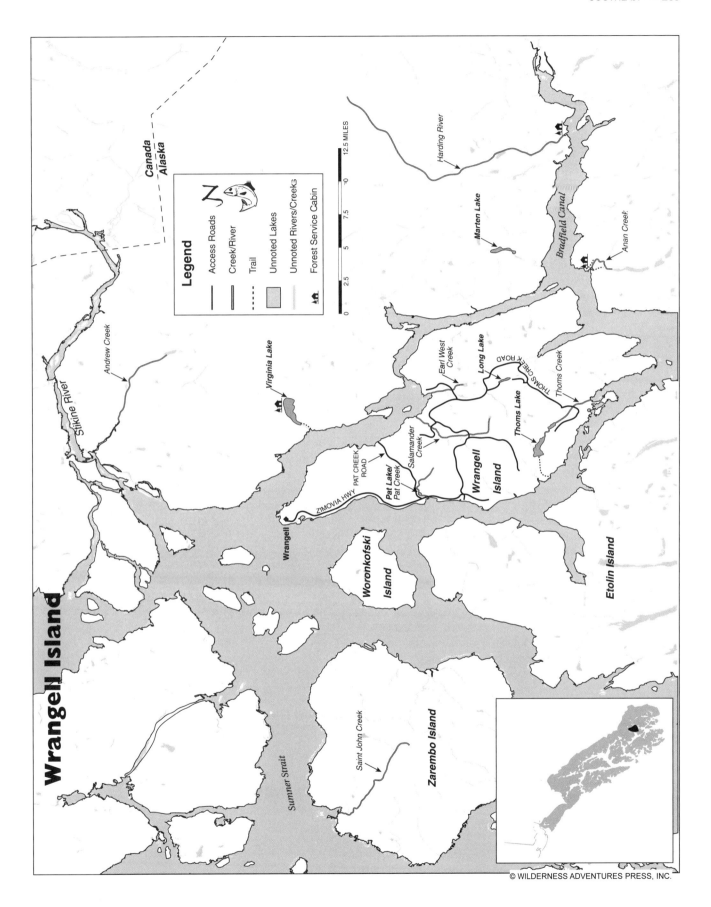

Wrangell Island

Legend

——	Access Roads
——	Creek/River
······	Trail
▨	Unnoted Lakes
	Unnoted Rivers/Creeks
🏠	Forest Service Cabin

0   2.5   5   7.5   10   12.5 MILES

Canada
Alaska

Stikine River

Andrew Creek

Virginia Lake

Harding River

Marten Lake

Bradfield Canal

Anan Creek

Earl West Creek

Long Lake

THOMS CREEK ROAD

Thoms Creek

Salamander Creek

Thoms Lake

PAT CREEK ROAD

Pat Lake/ Pat Creek

ZIMOVIA HWY

Wrangell Island

Wrangell

Woronkofski Island

Etolin Island

Sumner Strait

Saint John Creek

Zarembo Island

© WILDERNESS ADVENTURES PRESS, INC.

Earl West Creek

Driving 25 miles southeast of Wrangell will put you at Earl West Creek and what's known to the locals as Earl West Marsh. About 4 miles up from salt water, the marsh can be seen from the road, but you have to drag a canoe for five minutes or so to the edge of a slough, then paddle a mile upstream to reach it. The going is not as difficult as it may sound, and the effort can be well worth it.

There is good fishing for resident cutthroat trout within the marsh pond. Earl West Creek, interestingly enough, gets a run of sea-run cutthroat, none of which make their way into the pond. A strong number of coho also inhabit the creek, which is easy to wade fish. The mouth of the creek (where it dumps into the ocean) can offer very good coho fishing, and you can reach it with a 10-minute hike down from the trail.

There is a boat landing and campsite on Old West Road. From here it's easy to reach the estuary, where pinks, chums, and Dollys can also be caught in the salt. Flounder are also a common incidental catch for anglers using bright patterns.

Long Lake

Long Lake is located 28 miles southeast of Wrangell, and the road takes you right to a boardwalk path that connects to the lake. The half-mile walk to this mid-sized lake is easy. A shelter with a Forest Service boat is available on this lake on a first-come, first-serve basis.

The cutthroat that inhabit this lake are small, and it's mostly a fun place to go with the family. Unless you have the skiff to get help you get away from the banks, tossing lures is about the only way you can reach the fish from shore. If the kids are eager for some simple fishing in a nice setting, this is a fine place to spend part of the day.

Southeast Alaska has a strong population of both brown and black bears—proceed with caution.

Thoms Lake

Thoms Lake is considered the premier lake fishery on Wrangell Island. It receives good runs of most everything but king salmon and hosts outstanding fishing for cutthroat trout and red salmon. The lake sits 21 miles south of Wrangell, though it can seem a bit longer than you think to get to, as the road meanders around the south end of the lake. There are actually two lakes in the area, Big Thoms Lake and Little Thoms Lake.

Big Thoms Lake is a 1.3-mile hike up the trail. Take a float tube so you can cover more fishable water. There is a state-owned cabin on the lake, but it's falling apart and not worth staying in. There's also so much brush—and an abundance of temperamental bears—that you won't want to pitch camp in the area, especially during the height of the salmon runs.

Big Thoms is about 2 miles long and a half-mile wide, making it one of the bigger lakes on the island. It's tannic in color, yet fairly clear overall. Cutthroat trout are in abundance in the summer, with some 20,000 pink salmon making their way into the system later on, along with a good run of red salmon. Dollys and cutthroat measuring into the upper teens follow the salmon in, feasting on their loose eggs.

Little Thoms Lake has no developed trail leading into it, but footpaths that lead through muskeg bogs can get you there. It takes about 20 minutes to walk the primitive trail.

Little Thoms Lake is darker in color than Big Thoms and is ranked as a world-class cutthroat fishery. You're just about assured of catching 18-inch sea-run monsters in the fall, with a good chance of latching into something much larger. This short, narrow lake responds to what the rain is doing in the area.

If you're serious about seeing all this lake has to offer, you'll need a float tube or canoe. Either craft can easily be dragged to the lake from the road and will allow you to reach the best fishing sites. There are well-defined weed beds growing around the edges of the lake, so concentrate your efforts around these spots. Actually, the entire lake has great fishing, so don't get caught up on casting or trolling in a small area.

You'll likely see moose, bears, and an array of other wildlife around this lake, which makes for a special experience you won't soon forget. Combine the cutthroat fishing with the excellent run of silver salmon in the fall—with fish up to 15 pounds—and you'll soon see why many experienced locals rank this among the top fisheries in the area.

Thoms Creek

Thoms Creek drains from Little Thoms Lake. Thoms Creek Road crosses over the creek near its midway point, and you can park here and walk to the stream. The upper section of the 5-mile-long creek is slow and meandering. About halfway down it changes to a fast, rocky stream with lots of pools that consistently hold fish.

Cutthroat and steelhead are the primary species sought by anglers on Thoms Creek. Among the local anglers, there are well-known pockets of traditional steelhead water. Due to the high gradient of the creek, salmon shoot upstream quickly, making them tough to target.

Though it's a long hike down to the estuary from the bridge, the coho fishing can be very good. However, be extremely careful when the water is high, as it can be taxing on even the most seasoned wade anglers. Due to the 2-hour drive necessary to reach Thoms Creek, not many locals fish it on weekdays, so you can have outstanding fishing action all to yourself.

Forest Service cabins allow anglers to experience the Alaskan outdoors on their own.

Remote Fishing Destinations

As with most of the hard-to-reach waters in Southeast Alaska, the remote fisheries with reach of Wrangell area can only be accessed by charter plane or large boat. If you don't have your own seaworthy boat, the only other option is to hire a guide or outfitting service to take you to a remote area. While there are several such areas around Wrangell, here's a look at the more noteworthy fisheries you may want to consider visiting.

Bradfield Canal can be reached with a 30-minute boat ride due southeast of Wrangell. Six large drainages feed into the canal, all of which are unique. From big rivers to small lakes, there's no shortage fishing diversity in this area, which is one of the top remote fishing destinations in this part of Alaska.

The upper end of Bradfield Canal (the east end) is home to one of two blue-ribbon cutthroat fisheries in the area, Eagle Lake. There is a Forest Service cabin on Eagle Lake, which can be accessed only by floatplane. Due to dense timber and rugged country, pitching a tent is not advised. It's almost a must to reserve the cabin. The skiff that comes with the cabin will give you a huge advantage when you take a crack at landing landlocked cutthroat trout in excess of 5 pounds here.

Some say these are the most beautiful cutthroats in all of Alaska, but you have to work deep for them. Sinking lines are a prerequisite, as the trout avoid the streams where the bears roam, meaning you have to look for them in deeper, more protected waters. Expect to catch fish all day long in the 12- to 14-inch class, which should occupy your time between big fish. The best fishing on the lake is near the tributaries that feed into the lake. There is also a native population of kokanee, which offer good fishing (and one explanation for why the cutts grow so big).

The **Harding River** is across the bay from Eagle Lake. This river can be reached by boat directly from Wrangell and has a Forest Service cabin at its mouth, on salt water. You'll need to reserve the cabin if you come here, as it's too brushy to camp, fish, and hike in the area. This is primarily a saltwater fishing experience, with a great run of silvers, chums, and kings averaging 25 pounds making their way into the estuary. It's easy to wade along the shore, casting flies into the tidal-dependent waters. Your best bet of catching fish lies in working from a boat for a few days, as you have the freedom to move to where the fish are most active.

Moving to the west within Bradfield Canal, **Anan Creek** receives the third largest run of pink salmon in Southeast Alaska. But the creek is situated in a specially designated bear area and sees a tremendous number of bruins. There is a Forest Service cabin located on salt water, and there are good trails leading to the creek.

The bear observatory lies a mile upstream from the cabin and is worth visiting late in the salmon season, when the stream is closed to fishing to allow the bears to feed naturally on the spawning fish. Early in the season Anan Creek is a great steelhead stream, seemingly made with the fly angler in mind. May is the best time to fish Anan for steelhead. And you can work the pocket water, deep pools, and classic riffles that make up this great stream.

Cutthroat trout are also abundant in Anan, which receives very little pressure. The stream is easy to wade fish, as you can either wade in the stream itself or hop on one of the many bear trails bordering the creek to reach new waters.

Almost directly across the Bradfield Canal from Anan Creek is **Marten Lake**. There is a Forest Service cabin here, complete with a boat. While there is a small strain of land-locked cutthroat trout in Marten Lake, the best thing here is the boat you have access to. Once in the boat, head to the outlet of Marten Lake and take a short little walk to Clay Lake. Clay has loads of resident cutthroat as well, and though they're not big, you can catch them from just about anywhere all day long.

Closer to the town of Wrangell is **Virginia Lake**. Because this lake is so easy to reach, and due to the fact it houses the premier recreation cabin in the district, it's a popular spot for locals on the weekends. A 10-minute flight will take you to this lake, where cutthroat trout up to 18 inches can be had with a bit of work. The action is non-stop for cutts in the 10- to 12-inch range. There is also a small run of red salmon, but it's the stunning beauty of the cabin and its tranquil setting that will make your journey here worthwhile.

The world-famous **Stikine River** lies north of Wrangell Island. Though it's too silted to fish in Alaska, it's the fastest free-flowing river in all of North America and a wonder to behold.

Just up from the where the Stikine dumps into the Pacific Ocean, you'll find **Andrew Creek**, one of the few clear streams in the whole area. The lower section of the creek is simply gorgeous. Though there's a Forest Service cabin at the mouth of Andrew, there's no boat. Renting a canoe to take with you would be a good idea. And it's just a 30-minute charter boat ride from Wrangell. Fish around the mouth, where the creek flows into the Stikine River. This is one of the few places in the region where you can get Dolly Varden up to 4 pounds.

Everything but red salmon inhabits the estuary, and the cabin is a popular spot for locals on the weekend. If you want to go here, reserve the cabin well in advance and go in the middle of the week, when there's less competition.

Saint John Creek is on the northwest corner of Zarembo Island, just to the west of Wrangell Island. It can be reached with a 45-minute boat ride from Wrangell. There's a well-maintained dock here, but you'll need to bring your own camping gear. A great run of spring steelhead makes its way up Saint John Creek, and the bay is absolutely crammed with Dolly Varden. Halibut have even been caught off the dock here.

In this combination fresh and saltwater fishery, silver and pink salmon can be caught in the creek as well as the bay. The stream is easy to wade fish, though don't get too caught up in chasing fish upstream. For steelhead, stay in the lower stretch and wait for the fish to pass by you. If you feel the urge to wade upstream, hit the pockets and holding slots on the edges of fast water. For Dollys, stay in the tidewater, and for fall salmon runs, hit the bay as well as the creek. The diversity of fishing here is what makes it so appealing, both to locals and traveling anglers.

Because run numbers aren't abundant in many streams, it's important to handle steelhead with care and release them as soon as possible.

WRANGELL

Population: 2,308
Alaska Area Code: 907
Zip Code: 99929

TOURIST INFORMATION

Alaska Department of Fish and Game, 772-3801
(office in Petersburg)
Wrangell Convention & Visitors Bureau,
1-800-367-9745; www.wrangell.com
U.S. Forest Service Cabin Information, Wrangell
Ranger District, P.O. Box 51; 874-2323

GUIDE SERVICES

Alaska Waters, Inc., P.O. Box 1978; 1-800-347-4462;
www.alaskawaters.com
Timber Wolf Enterprises, P.O. Box 1987; 874-2893

FLY-IN CHARTERS

Alaska Peak & Seas Flyfishing Division, P.O. Box 301,
Mile 25 Zimovia Hwy.; 874-2590;
www.flyfishingwrangell.com
Alaska Vistas Company, P.O. Box 2245; 1-866-874-3006

TACKLE SHOPS

Ken's Reel Repair, P.O. Box 201; 874-3443

ACCOMMODATIONS

Bruce Harding's Old Sourdough Lodge, P.O. Box 1062;
1-800-874-3613; www.akgetaway.com/HardingsLodge
Fennimore Bed & Breakfast, P.O. Box 957; 874-3012
Grand View Bed & Breakfast, P.O. Box 927; 874-3225;
www.grandviewbnb.com
Helen's Place, P.O. Box 133; 874-3168
J & W Apartments, P.O. Box 606; 874-3954
Stikine Inn, P.O. Box 990; 1-888-874-3388
Zimovia Bed & Breakfast, P.O. Box 1424; 874-2626

CAMPGROUNDS AND RV PARKS

Alaska Waters RV Park, 241 Berger Street; level sites, full
hookups, restrooms, showers and tour desk

RESTAURANTS

Diamond C. Café, P.O. Box 110; 874-3677
Marine Bar & Hungry Beaver, P.O. Box 1677; 874-3005
Waterfront Grill, P.O. Box 1573; 874-2353
Zak's Cafe, P.O. Box 1929; 874-3355

FISH PROCESSING

G & G Alaska Smokery, Inc., P.O. Box 11;
1-800-874-3950

RENTAL CARS

Practical Rent-A-Car; 874-3975

AIR SERVICES

Sunrise Aviation, Inc., P.O. Box 432; 1-800-874-2319;
www.sunriseflights.com

AUTO REPAIR

Stikine Auto Works, 1329 Peninsula Avenue; 874-2468

MEDICAL

Wrangell Medical Center, 310 Bennett Street; 874-7000

TOURIST ATTRACTIONS

Wrangell Museum, 318 Church Street; 874-3770

PETERSBURG

Just north of Wrangell, you'll find the town of Petersburg. There's not as much roadside fishing here as there is in other places in Southeast Alaska, but good opportunities do exist.

When you hear talk of fishing in Southeast Alaska, the topic of catching fish in the bay, right off the docks, often comes up. This is precisely what happens at Petersburg. Due to the number of canneries processing fish, there's something in the water that attracts Dolly Varden and keeps them here. All around the harbor, big, fat Dollys can be had from many of the docks. Due to their high protein diet, these fish are robust and about the hardest fighting Dollys for their size you'll find anywhere.

If you're really strapped for time, but want to catch a fish in this pretty port town, then head to the bay with a shiny smolt pattern and hang on. But if you do have the luxury of time, there's more to fishing Petersburg than staying in the harbor.

Bear Creek

If spring steelhead get you fired up, Bear Creek is a good place to visit while you're in the Petersburg area. A 9.5-mile drive from the city puts you on the creek, by way of Three Lakes Loop Road. Park where the bridge crosses the creek and fish on the downstream side.

Bear Creek has a low gradient, but contains some ideal pocket water for steelhead. Once the steelhead run fizzles out, cutthroat become the main attraction through the summer months. As fall approaches, coho and pink salmon start to arrive.

Bear Creek is a tannic system, though quite small when not impacted by rainfall. It's easy to wade fish the whole thing from the bridge down to salt water. Some of the best water is located near the mouth, which takes about three hours to reach if you're fishing your way downstream. When the fish are in, you could easily spend an entire day on this creek.

Sand, Hill, and Crane Lakes

Near the mouth of Bear Creek there is a trio of lakes that can be accessed by hiking a half-mile to a mile along the marked trails off Three Lakes Loop Road. Sand Lake has saltwater access, so it receives a solid run of sea-run cutthroat and loads of silver salmon in the fall. Both Hill and Crane Lakes hold resident populations of cutthroat trout. All three lakes are connected by a series of trails.

There is a Forest Service boat available on a first-come, first-serve basis. Flyfishing from shore is difficult here due to the brush. But these lakes are great for families. If you're serious about catching good numbers of cutthroat, pack in a float tube so you can reach more water.

Blind River and Blind Slough

Blind River and Blind Slough are located 15 miles southeast of Petersburg on the Mitkof Highway. A hatchery on the river produces king and silver salmon, and though the king fishing sounds inviting, don't attempt it with fly gear. This is combat fishing in the purest sense, and the water is open to snagging. The locals pile in here to fill their freezers, meaning there's little room for fly anglers.

There is good sea-run cutthroat fishing in the spring, but if you really want to see what fishing this stream is all about, come for the silver salmon in late August. Fish in the lower river, as the stream is tidally influenced all the way to the hatchery. The farther downstream from the hatchery you are, the more likely you are to have the water all to yourself.

Pay close attention to the tidal changes, as it's easy to get stuck on the opposite shore. There is also a good run of pink salmon that offers solid flyfishing opportunities in the upper end of the slough.

Upstream from the estuary, a boardwalk trail leads from the road right to Blind River Rapids. And the fishing at the foot of these rapids is excellent, especially when the tide goes out, which leaves a few prime holding pockets that the salmon really pack into. They often hold here throughout the entire low tide and through the slack. As the tide comes in, the river swells to a few hundred feet across and becomes unwadeable, so be sure to time your arrival to coincide with the low tide.

Ohmer Creek

To the southeast of Blind River, some 21 miles out Petersburg, you'll find Ohmer Creek. This creek can be reached off the Mitkof Highway and holds a variety of fish. However, this is not an ideal stream for fly enthusiasts due to a dense forest canopy and brushy banks. It is a good place to take the family for some lure tossing from footpaths along shore, though. Ohmer Creek is tannic in color, too mucky to wade, and not good for float tubing. There is fine fishing to be had at the outlet, which is a good place to get a child hooked up with a decent cutthroat trout.

Petersburg Area Water

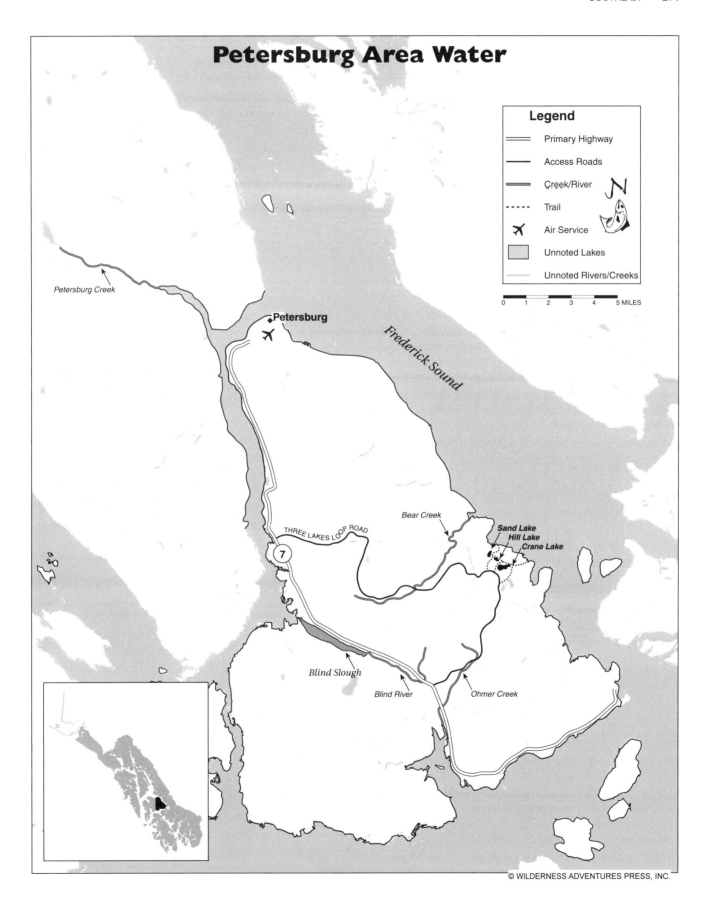

Petersburg Creek

Petersburg

Frederick Sound

THREE LAKES LOOP ROAD

7

Bear Creek

Sand Lake
Hill Lake
Crane Lake

Blind Slough

Blind River

Ohmer Creek

Legend

Primary Highway
Access Roads
Creek/River
Trail
Air Service
Unnoted Lakes
Unnoted Rivers/Creeks

N

0 1 2 3 4 5 MILES

Remote Fishing Destinations

There are several remote fishing experiences around the Petersburg region. Some can only be reached by plane, others by boat. But there's one that can be reached by kayak, right out of Petersburg through the Wrangell Narrows.

Petersburg Creek is directly across the harbor from the city and is the premier steelhead stream in the area. Because it's so easy to access by boat—or even by paddling a rented kayak—it does receive a good deal of pressure. About 600 steelhead make their way into the creek each spring, which is pretty good for this area. The fall run of coho is also outstanding and sees much less pressure. In addition, cutthroat and Dollys are present. There are 7 miles of creek and the low gradient and wide banks make for easy wade fishing. Be sure to hit the pools and pocket water, where steelhead and silvers often gather.

Over on the northwest corner of Kupreanof Island, south of the community of Kake, you can try **Irish Creek**. This stream hosts one of best coho runs in the area. This is a very rich habitat, and the annual return of silvers is abundant. Many anglers fly out to Irish Creek, spend the day fishing at the mouth, and then return to Petersburg that evening. The tidal area can be fished for about a mile upstream, near the fish pass. It's easy to work around the shorelines of this creek, hitting the pools at low tide. The entire lower section can be waded, while the upper stretch gets too nasty to even attempt it. Dolly Varden and cutthroat are also present, as are a high number of black bears. Pay close attention the bears, but don't panic, they are easier to fish around than brown bears.

An easy air charter from Petersburg lands you at **Duncan Salt Chuck** southeast of the city. This is one of the most diverse fisheries in the area. There's a Forest Service cabin here, but the boat is often lost due to heavy tidal changes. At low tide, fish the mouth of the chuck for some of the best cutthroat trout in the area. In the fall, a huge run of coho infiltrates the chuck, where they often stage for a week at a time. Time your trip for the last week in August and you'll likely catch silvers all day long; some anglers actually get tired of catching so many fish. Once the fish shoot upstream, they're not worth chasing, as too many fallen trees make for extremely tough fishing.

A creek you won't likely find listed on any maps, but one that offers excellent coho and sea-run cutthroat trout fishing is **Slippery Creek**. This is a fly-in destination, located on Kuiu Island between Rocky Pass and Port Camden. It got its name from the extensive algae growth at the mouth, which makes for tough wade fishing. A fish pass was installed in Slippery Creek in 1985, and since that time the coho have really taken off. The mouth of the creek offers the best fishing, and toward the end of August you can expect to catch fish all day long.

PETERSBURG

Population: 3,224
Alaska Area Code: 907
Zip Code: 99833

TOURIST INFORMATION

Alaska Department of Fish and Game, State Office Building, Sing Lee Alley; 772-3801

Petersburg Chamber of Commerce, P.O. Box 649; 772-3646; www.petersburg.org

Petersburg Visitor Information Center, P.O. Box 810; 772-4636; located at the corner of First and Fram Streets

U.S. Forest Service Cabin Information, Petersburg Ranger District, P.O. Box 1328; 772-3871

GUIDE SERVICES

Alaska Sea Adventures, P.O. Box 542; 1-888-772-8588; www.yachtalaska.com

Hook & Eye Adventures, P.O. Box 847; 772-3400

Sea Trek Charters - Ed Jones, P.O. Box 897; 772-4868; jjones@alaska.net

Terry's Unforgettable Charters, P.O. Box 114; 772-2200; www.terrysfishing.com

FLY-IN CHARTERS

Nordic Air, P.O. Box 1752; 772-3535

Pacific Wing Air Charters, P.O. Box 1560; 772-4258; pacwing@alaska.net

TACKLE SHOPS

Ace Hardware, P.O. Box 489, located in the Trading Union; 772-3881; sporting goods, tackle and insulated, airline approved fish boxes

True Value Hardware, located on Main Street; 772-4811

ACCOMMODATIONS

Heather and Rose Guest Hus, 14 Birch Street; 772-4675

Nordic House Bed & Breakfast, 806 South Nordic Drive; 772-3620; www.nordichouse.net

Petersburg Bunk & Breakfast, 805 Gjoa Street; 772-3632; www.bunkandbreakfast.com

Rainsong Bed & Breakfast Guest Home, 1107 Wrangell Avenue; 772-3178

Scandia House, Box 689; 772-4281; car and boat rentals available; reservations: 1-800-722-5006; car and boat rentals available

The Broom Hus Bed & Breakfast, 411 South Nordic Drive; 772-3459

Tides Inn, P.O. Box 1048; 1-800-665-8433; www.tidesinnalaska.com

Yurtsville Retreat, P.O. Box 2134, 415 Mitkof Hwy.; 772-2921

CAMPGROUNDS AND RV PARKS

LeConte RV Park, P.O. Box 2133; located on 4th Street and Haugen Drive; 772-4680; full hookups, laundry, showers and tentsites

Tent City, P.O. Box 329; 772-3392; located near Sandy Beach Park; elevated tent pads, bathrooms, showers, firepit area and firewood

Twin Creek RV Park, P.O. Box 90, Mile 7.5 Mitkof Highway; 772-2950; full and partial hookups, showers, laundry, groceries, tackle shop, and fishing licenses

RESTAURANTS

Alaskafe Espresso & Eatery, located on Nordic and Excel; 772-5282

Joan Mei, 1103 Nordic Drive; 772-4221

Helse Restaurant, 13 Sing Lee Alley; 772-3444

Northern Lights Restaurant, 203 Sing Lee Alley; 772-2900

Pellerito's Pizzeria; 772-3727

FISH PROCESSING

Coastal Cold Storage, 306 North Nordic Drive; 772-4177

Northern Lights Smokeries, P.O. Box 1083; 772-4608

Tonka Seafoods Inc., 22 South Sing Lee; 772-3662; www.tonkaseafoods.com

BOAT RENTALS

Tongass Marine, Inc., P.O. Box 1314; 772-3905

RENTAL CARS

Tides Inn, 307 N 1st Street; 772-4716; www.avis.com

AIR SERVICES

L.A.B. Flying Service Inc.; 722-4300; www.labflying.com

AUTO REPAIR

Petersburg Motors, Inc., P.O. Box 87, located on Haugen Drive and Second Avenue; 772-3223

Stikine Services, Inc., 904 South Nordic Drive; 772-2800

MEDICAL

Petersburg Medical Center, 103 Fram Street; 772-4291

VETERINARY CLINICS

Mitkof Island Veterinary Clinic, P.O. Box 773; 772-3191

TOURIST ATTRACTIONS

Clausen Memorial Museum, 203 Fram Street; 772-3598

Crystal Lake Fish Hatchery, Mile 17.5 Mitkof Hwy.

Swan Observatory, Mile 16 Mitkof Hwy.

Fishing the mouths of creeks and rivers will allow you to take several anadromous species.

SITKA

Sport fishing in Sitka centers around salt water. While there are lakes, rivers, and numerous creeks around Baranof and Chichagof Islands that offer good fishing, many of these out-of-the-way fisheries go virtually untouched. Even on the road system that branches north and south of Sitka, there is little pressure from local anglers, even on the best of waters.

For tourists seeking easy access to fishing, minus the crowds, Sitka is a great place to be. The Forest Service, with its many dedicated Sitka-area volunteers and eager staff, maintains some of the best foot trails in all of Alaska, making for easy, enjoyable access to creeks, rivers, and lakes. For anyone hopping off a cruise ship and looking to wet a line, there's good fishing close to town.

Unlike other areas in Southeast Alaska, the Sitka watershed is not laden with glaciers. As a result, the streams and lakes run clear, meaning fly anglers should be optimistic. For anglers with more than a day to spend on the island, there are numerous fly-in options to lakes, rivers, and bays.

Because so many streams in the Sitka area descend rapidly from the hills, some of the best fishing is in the bays, where the mouths of rivers and creeks feed into the ocean. Here, salmon will stage prior to entering their natal streams and migrating Dolly Varden will cruise the shore in the spring and fall.

Anglers should note that most of the streams in the area rise and turn chocolate in color within an hour or two of a good rain. However, due to their steep gradients, the streams also recover quickly, and the higher water usually brings an influx of fish moving upstream in the freshet. This is when freshwater stream fishing it at its best.

If you're looking to stock the freezer with fresh salmon fillets, pink salmon are the main draw here, with a few coho, chum, and kings in the mix. If it's king steaks you want, consider chartering a boat for some saltwater fishing.

What follows is a look at the bodies of water easily accessed from the town of Sitka, moving north to south, along with a few prime fly-in locations. Not many people come to Sitka to spend a couple thousand dollars to charter a plane for small trout on an inland lake when right in front of them, in Sitka Sound, there is prime ocean fishing for giant king salmon.

Starrigavan Creek and Bay

North of the town of Sitka, Halibut Point Road runs a mere 7 miles before reaching its terminus at Starrigavan Creek. You can pull off the road at the bridge and walk to the creek or follow the signs to Starrigavan Creek Campground.

Starrigavan Creek is closed to all salmon fishing, but pink, silver, and chum salmon can be picked up in salt water at the mouth of the creek. There is a small closed area of water right in front of the bridge, but that doesn't impact the quality of fishing to be had in the bay. Salmon are found in this area from July into September. The peak time for silver salmon is early to mid-September, with chum and pinks hitting high points in early to mid-August.

In 2002, some 80,000 pinks made their way into Starrigavan Creek, and the bay was crammed with fish in late summer. Seeing 20 fish in the air at a time is common, and fly anglers can wear out their arms on these salmon while fishing from shore. With a fresh supply of pinks constantly moving into the area, nabbing chromers is easy.

Anglers casting streamer patterns from the beach will have no trouble figuring out where to fish. Search for jumping salmon and go to them. If you tire of catching pinks, switch to weighted pink rabbit leeches. Cast out and let the fly settle, waiting to strip until it has dropped below most of the suspended pink salmon. Strip quickly to trigger coho bites and hang on.

There are also good numbers of Dolly Varden cruising the beach in the spring, feeding on pink salmon fry flushed out of Starrigavan Creek. Anglers looking to score on the sea-run Dollys should flip smolt patterns from late March into June. If you happen to be spin-fishing, cast any small, silver lure into the bay for Dollys, which don't start making their way into the creek until July.

If you want to follow the Dollys up the creek you'll find good action. You'll also see loads of salmon, but remember this stream is closed to all salmon fishing. If you're one of the half-dozen or so lucky anglers who hook a rare steelhead in the spring, then you'll really have something to brag about.

The creek is a small and tannic-colored but easy to wade. From the bridge, you can wade upstream on either bank for about 2.5 miles. Except where deep pools are present, wading across the 30-foot-wide stream is simple. There are many riffles laced with pools, making for ideal fish habitat.

Due to the small nature of the creek, it's tough to keep from spooking salmon, which will inevitably affect the Dollys. There is some braiding on this creek, but stick to the main channel and deeper holes. One of the primary reasons nearly all the fishing is done at the mouth of this creek is because of the dense bear population in the area. Only brown bears are present on Baranof Island, and the ones roaming around Starrigavan Creek are infamous for their tempers. Be prepared for bear encounters when fishing this stream, especially in the fall.

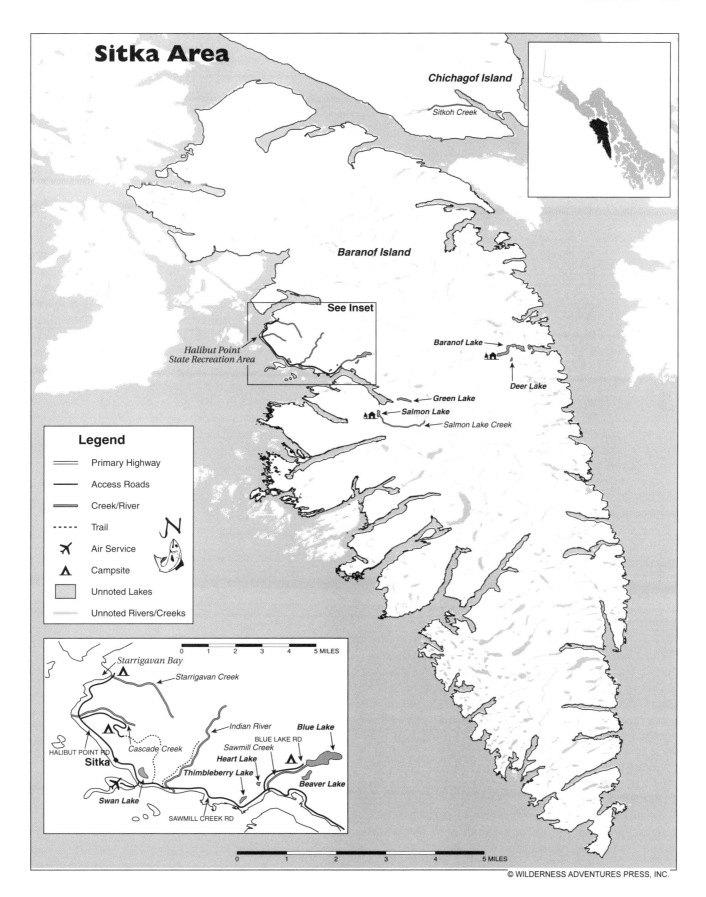

Sitka Area

Chichagof Island

Sitkoh Creek

Baranof Island

See Inset

*Halibut Point
State Recreation Area*

Baranof Lake

Deer Lake

Green Lake

Salmon Lake

Salmon Lake Creek

Legend

═══	Primary Highway
───	Access Roads
━━━	Creek/River
┈┈┈	Trail
✈	Air Service
▲	Campsite
▨	Unnoted Lakes
┉	Unnoted Rivers/Creeks

N

0 1 2 3 4 5 MILES

Starrigavan Bay

Starrigavan Creek

Indian River

Blue Lake

BLUE LAKE RD

Sawmill Creek

Heart Lake

HALIBUT POINT RD

Cascade Creek

Sitka

Thimbleberry Lake

Beaver Lake

Swan Lake

SAWMILL CREEK RD

0 1 2 3 4 5 MILES

© WILDERNESS ADVENTURES PRESS, INC.

Southeast Alaska is noted more for its saltwater fishing than freshwater opportunities. Anglers may want to consider heading to a bay to try their luck at massive king salmon, which are off limits in many streams.

Cascade Creek

At the Halibut Point Recreation Area, more bay-fishing opportunities await at the mouth of Cascade Creek. In the spring, Dollys from 1 to 3 pounds can be caught here, while pink salmon dominate the scene starting in July. This is a great place for flyfishing, as the gently sloping rocky bottom makes for easy wading.

Try hitting the low to middle tides here, so you can fish a shelf where the fish hold tight. Because Cascade Creek is bordered by much private land and becomes choked with alders not far upstream from the mouth, nearly all the fishing here is done in the estuary. Up to 20,000 pinks visit this spot in the fall, and when they're in thick, it's not uncommon to hook a salmon on nearly every cast.

Swan Lake

The first lake fishery we come to in the Sitka region actually sits within the city limits. Cutthroat up to 12 inches can be had here, as well as smaller rainbow trout and some Dolly Varden. If you're here in the spring, before the lilies start taking over, this is a fun lake to hit with dry flies.

Once the lilies crowd out the bank fishing, switch to nymphs. Though there are no motors allowed on this lake, it's good for small skiffs, rubber rafts, and belly boats. The rainbows are planted here as part of a local kids fishing derby held in May. The kids catch only about half the trout so there's plenty left. And as you will see with all the freshwater fisheries around Sitka, there are very few people fishing this lake, despite its central location.

Indian River

On the south end of Sitka, a Forest Service trail takes off at mile 0.6 on Sawmill Creek Road. For 5.5 miles the trail parallels the Indian River, taking you on a striking journey through old-growth rainforest. Indian River Trail is complete with a boardwalk in many places, making for easy walking.

While the river is closed to all salmon fishing (salmon can be fished for at the river mouth on the bay) there are some good Dollys to be had here in April and May, then again in late July and into the fall months. A healthy number of spawning char keep this a quality Dolly fishery. Due to the rugged, boulder-strewn nature of the stream 4.5 miles up the trail, there's little point in fishing upstream. Truth is, you'll likely find all the Dolly action one person can handle within the first 2 miles of water.

The Indian River is a small stream, 20 to 25 feet wide in most places. The deepest pools run about 12 feet, with the prime wading sections less than 2 feet deep. With no lake feeding this river, it runs very clear. There are small braids in some stretches, but none big enough to warrant exploration; stick to the main channel. Fish your way upstream with stealth, as you'll be sight fishing.

This is one of the most popular Dolly streams in the Sitka area, but I'd still be surprised if you see more than one or two people while fishing. For safety's sake, it's not a bad idea to check in at the marked trailhead at the parking area. There's a check-in form you can fill out to let Forest Service personnel know where you're going and when you expect to return. This is a wise precaution given the number of bears in the area.

Thimbleberry and Heart Lakes

Two hike-in lake fisheries just south of Sitka offer gorgeous scenery and are worth hitting if you don't mind small fish. A ½-mile-long trail at mile 3.7 off Sawmill Creek Road will take you to Thimbleberry Lake. Another mile past Thimbleberry and you'll be at Heart Lake. The trail is well maintained.

In the late 1920s, brook trout were planted in both of these lakes, and their numbers have held solid since that time. These fish grow to a maximum of about 14 inches, with 8-inchers the average. But if brookies interest you, this is the best place in the Sitka area to catch one. Nymphs and small white bucktail flies are effective brookie patterns on these lakes.

Sawmill Creek

Sawmill Creek is located 5 miles southeast of Sitka. Though a small number of steelhead make their way into the creek in early May, the fishing is slow. It's rainbow trout that draw anglers here, along with a few Dollys and pink, chum, and silver salmon.

Anglers lucky enough to be in town in July and August should check for emergency orders granting a season on king salmon in this creek. Some stray hatchery kings enter this creek, and in an effort to keep them from disturbing wild salmon runs ADF&G authorities will issue an emergency opening. Given the strong hatchery returns projected in coming years, this could be an exciting bonus fishery. Battling kings in the 20- to 40-pound class in this stream is a thrill. You'll forget all about the Dollys and bayside pink fishing.

Upstream from where Sawmill Creek Road crosses the creek is where you'll find the best fishing for salmon. However, you'll only be able to make it as far as the steep-sided cliff and barrier falls. Because there is a dam on this creek, it has more flow than other area streams, making it tough to wade in some places. For salmon, hit the slots, riffles, and holding pockets, all of which are easy to identify. Sawmill Creek usually runs clear, and wearing waders will allow you to fish a good bit of water.

While rainbows can be had throughout the entire creek, the best fishing comes above the barrier falls. To reach this area drive up Blue Lake Road to Sawmill Creek Campground. From here you can walk down and fish the pools below the dam, where average-sized rainbows await.

Beaver Lake

For the only shot at arctic grayling in the entire Sitka area, consider taking a ½-mile walk to Beaver Lake while you're at Sawmill Creek Campground. There's a footbridge crossing Sawmill Creek, and you can follow the marked trail for 45 minutes to the lake. As is the case with many hiking trails in the area, this one is in super condition, complete with boardwalks and benches. For the first 20 minutes you'll be going up a fairly steep, winding hill, but then the path flattens out.

In addition to a dandy trail, the Forest Service provides a boat at the lake, available to anglers on a first-come, first-serve basis. However, the oars for this craft sometimes disappear, so you may want to take a paddle along, or better yet, a float tube. Though there are some bigger fish, the typical grayling will run 9 to 12 inches.

Working dry fly patterns like Mosquitoes and Black Ants early in the morning and through the evening can yield fast action. Look for rising grayling. A trail borders much of the lake and there's some good bank fishing, but much of the shoreline has have trees and brush growing to the water line, making it tough to work flies. At the same time, the muddy, steep edges of the lake are not ideal for wading. A float tube will definitely be to your advantage here.

Beaver Lake just shy of 7 acres, and its boggy surroundings mean that biting insects can be a problem, so come prepared. The north end of the lake is best for wade fishing, offering more room for casting. The walk in to the lake is scenic, so take your time and your camera.

Blue Lake

Blue Lake is the source of Sawmill Creek. This lake has a dam on its lower end and serves as Sitka's main water supply. As you would expect, the lake is big and deep—more than 3 miles long and over 350 feet deep. Thus, it's not an ideal fly lake, but it is one of the better trout lakes on all of Baranof Island, holding some dandy rainbow trout that were originally planted here in the late 1930s.

However, there are some flyfishing opportunities at the lake's outlet and especially at the mouths of the inlet streams. Seven different feeder streams flow into the upper end of the lake, and fishing here can pay off in big rainbows. Nonetheless, because the fish can hang deeper than your sinking lines will reach, bringing along some lures and a spinning rod isn't a bad idea. If you have a boat, there are some windfalls at the upper end of the lake worth trying. The winds can be dangerous on this lake, so if you're in a skiff or raft, pay attention to the weather.

To reach the lake, turn off at the 5-mile marker south of Sitka on Sawmill Creek Road. Turn on Blue Lake Road and follow it 1.5 miles north. The final 300 yards or so down to the lake should be walked, as it can be tough even for 4x4s to negotiate.

When the outlet dam on Blue Lake overflows, rainbows are flushed over the spillway. This explains why rainbows are present throughout Sawmill Creek, and why the fishing is especially good in the creek pools below the dam.

Green Lake

Though the road leading to Green Lake is blocked, anglers who are up to a 4.5-mile hike, or who may have brought their mountain bike along, can get into some good fishing. The other option for reaching this lake is to take a boat into Silver Bay and hike in from there. Brook trout are the only fish in Green Lake, and your chances of seeing anyone else here are small, especially with Salmon Lake nearby. But if you're looking for a secluded fishing experience for brookies, this is the place. Green Lake can also be reached by floatplane.

Salmon Lake Creek and Salmon Lake

If you do make the 11-mile-long boat ride into Silver Bay south of Sitka, you're in for some of the best fishing around. Boat moorage is available at the mouth of Salmon Lake Creek, and if you don't have your own boat, charters can often deliver you there. Rather than quickly embarking on the 1-mile hike to Salmon Lake, spend time wetting a line in Salmon Lake Creek.

Salmon Lake Creek is a small, tannic-colored creek that you can wade right up, fishing as you go. All five salmon species, steelhead, Dolly Varden, and cutthroat can be found in the creek, making it one of the most popular streams in the Sitka region. But because it requires a bit of effort to reach, you'll still find very few people here. The ADF&G has a weir on this creek, and only rarely do they see anglers working the creek.

One of the key attractions is the number of stray hatchery king salmon that invade Salmon Lake Creek. Combine the opportunity to battle 40-pound kings with high numbers of pinks, silvers, and other species, and it's easy to understand the appeal of this creek. Perhaps the best fishing is right at the mouth, although the entire stream can produce fish.

This creek is buffered by the lake above it, which means that when rains come it takes a good six hours for the creek to rise and become turbid. If you arrive to find the creek blown out, stick close to the mouth. As soon as the stream starts dropping, hit it hard, for fish will be moving against the surge of fresh water.

You can hike in to Salmon Lake come by floatplane. There's a Forest Service cabin at the lake, and a skiff is provided. The salmon fishing can be excellent at the mouth of the lake. This is also a traditional site for bears, and they are thick in this region. Give the big browns a wide berth and you'll have an unforgettable fishing experience in this special place.

Deer Lake

If there is a sleeper lake in this region, Deer Lake is it. Located on the southeast corner of Baranof Lake, you aren't likely to find it on any maps. The biggest rainbows in all of Southeast Alaska call this lake home, with trout up to 15 pounds being caught. And plenty of fish in the 8- to 10-pound class are present.

There are no lodges on this lake, and a floatplane is the only way in. Once there, you may find a Regional Aquaculture project going on, where they are working with coho salmon. As a result of this project, they are eager for anglers to help control the rainbow population, which are believed to be devouring the coho.

Bringing an inflatable raft is your best bet for reaching good water, although the edges can be worked in a float tube. Zonkers and other small baitfish imitations fished on a sinking line are what you'll need, as the rainbows are keyed on the small coho cruising the lake.

You may also want to stop at Baranof Lake while you're in the area. This lake is home to cutthroat trout up to 14 inches, with many 11-inchers present. A Forest Service cabin and skiff are available here, making for a quaint lake-fishing experience. The best fishing is at the head of the lake, along the alluvial fan, and along the shoreline.

Sitkoh Creek

Located 30 air miles northeast of Sitka, Sitkoh Creek is situated on the extreme southern corner of Chichagof Island. If steelhead are your favorite species, then Sitkoh Creek is where you want to go when you're in Sitka.

Periodic weir counts have been taken here since the mid-1930s, and numbers have averaged around 700 fish per counting season. The middle of April to early May is considered prime steelheading time. Sitkoh is easy to wade, though it does have some blowdowns you'll have to negotiate. It does meander through a rugged canyon, and when you see it, you'll know why many people advise against fishing there. Stick to the Forest Service trail that borders the creek and you will have access to the best steelheading action on the creek. A few guides work Sitkoh Creek, but the likelihood of seeing anyone while fishing here is fairly small.

In some areas of Southeast Alaska, fish can be caught right off the dock, even on a fly rod. (Photo Cameron Hanes)

SITKA

Population: 8,835
Alaska Area Code: 907
Zip Code: 99835

TOURIST INFORMATION

Alaska Department of Fish and Game, 304 Lake Street, Room 103; 747-5355

Greater Sitka Chamber of Commerce, P.O. Box 638; 747-7413; www.sitkachamber.org

Sitka Convention and Visitors Bureau, P.O. Box 1226; 747-5940; www.sitka.org

U.S. Forest Service Cabin Information, Sitka Ranger District, 204 Siginaka Way; 747-4420

GUIDE SERVICES

Denny's Guide Service; 1-888-847-3659; www.sitkafishcharters.com

Dragon Lady Charters, P.O. Box 6174; 1-866-747-8414; www.dragonladycharters.com

Excursions Unlimited, P.O. Box 1603; 1-800-747-6477; www.excursionsunlimited.com

Eyak Adventures, P.O. Box 6273; 747-6344; www.eyakadventures.com

FLY-IN CHARTERS

Frontier Charters & Lodge - Frontier Flying, 511 Airport Drive; 966-2728

TACKLE SHOPS

Fly Away Fly Shop, 300 A Harbor Drive; 1-877-747-7301; www.alaskanflyshop.com

Mac's Sporting Goods, 213 Harbor Drive; 747-6970

Murray Pacific Supply Corp of Alaska, 475 Katlian Street; 747-3171; all sport and commercial fishing needs from gear to licenses; www.murraypacific.com

ACCOMMODATIONS

Alaska Ocean View Bed & Breakfast Inn, 1101 Edgecumbe Drive; 1-888-811-6870

Anglers' Landing Bed & Breakfast, 206 Lance Drive; 747-6055

Baranof Wilderness Lodge, P.O. Box 3107; 1-800-613-6551; world-class flyfishing streams; www.flyfishalaska.com

Cascade Inn & Boat Charters, 2035 Halibut Point Road; 1-800-532-0908

Sitka Hotel, 118 Lincoln Street; 747-3288; www.sitkahotel.com

Westmark Shee Atika/Totem Square Inn, 330 Seward Street; 1-800-544-0970

Where Eagles Roost, 2713 Halibut Point Road; 747-4545

CAMPGROUNDS AND RV PARKS

Sawmill Creek Campground, Mile 1.5 Blue Lake Road; 11 tentsites

Sitka Sportsman's Association RV Park, Halibut Point Road; one block south of the ferry terminal; 747-6033; 16 sites, water and electrical

Shoreline RV Bed & Breakfast, 3301 Halibut Point Road; 1-800-327-5131

RESTAURANTS

The Backdoor Cafe, 104 Barracks Street; 747-8856

Bayview Restaurant, 407 Lincoln Street; 747-7177

Captain's Galley, 1867 Halibut Point Road; 747-6266

Mojo Cafe, 203 Lincoln Street; 747-0667

Twin Dragon, 201 Katlian Street; 747-5711

FISH PROCESSING

Seafood Producers Cooperative, 507 Katlian Street; 747-5811

BOAT RENTALS

Baidarka Boats, 320 Seward Street; 747-8996; www.kayaksite.com

RENTAL CARS

North Star Rent-a-Car, 600 C Airport Road; 1-800-722-6927; www.allstarsitka.com

A & A Car Rental-Baranof Motors Inc., 1209 Sawmill Creek Road; 747-8228

AIR SERVICES

Frontier Flying, 511 Airport Drive; 966-2728

AUTO REPAIR

Al's Automotive Repair, 110 Jarvis Street; 747-8498

LOCKSMITHS

Locksmith, 134 Wolff Drive; 747-5888

MEDICAL

Moore Clinic, Inc., 814 Halibut Point Road; 747-3024

VETERINARY CLINICS

Sitka Animal Hospital, 209 Jarvis Street; 747-7387

TOURIST ATTRACTIONS

Alaska Raptor Center, 1000 Raptor Way; 1-800-643-9425; www.alaskaraptor.org

Isabel Miller Museum/Sitka Historical Society, 330 Harbor Drive; 747-6455

Sheldon Jackson Museum, 104 College Drive; 747-8981

Southeast Alaska Indian Cultural Center, 106 Metlakatla; 747-8061

JUNEAU

Juneau is the state capital and Southeast Alaska's most visited city. Visitors can spend time walking around this quaint harbor city or touring glaciers. For anglers looking to wet a line, there are several options fairly close to town that can be highly productive if your timing is right.

While there are remote lakes and streams accessible by floatplane or helicopter, it's the waters closer to town and along the road system that we'll discuss here. Anglers who have only a little time in the area, say an afternoon, will often rent a car or call a cab to haul them to a local fishing hole. Some of these fisheries have a surprisingly remote feel to them, despite their proximity to town.

Anglers should note that while some waters look appealing on paper, they may be hard to get to or may not have good fishing available. For instance, Antler Lake and Berner's Bay are north of town, but few people actually travel to Antler as it's accessible only by plane, and due to its elevation it is shrouded in clouds most of the time. Berner's Bay looks attractive, and some of the locals will spend time here, but it's tough to access unless you have a boat and know exactly where to fish in this big body of water. Thus, we'll concentrate only on the primary fish-producing waters within easy reach of Juneau, working from north to south.

Echo Cove

The northernmost fishery above town is located at the end of Glacier Highway, 40 miles from Juneau. Here, Echo Cove offers outstanding saltwater fishing for pink salmon during the month of July. The salmon stage here before entering local freshwater streams, and they can gather in mind-boggling numbers. Working the shoreline at low tide is especially productive.

Echo Cove itself is large, a few miles long, but anglers should concentrate on the inside edge of the cover. Here, near the highway, there's a deep drop-off where fish gather.

If you're here at the height of the pink run and want some solitude, consider walking out to the point of the peninsula. Though this will take an hour or so, you'll find it worth the effort. At the mouth of the bay there's a narrow gap through which the tide runs. Due to the large tidal changes, you have to fish this funnel more like you would a river than a bay, which makes it especially appealing to fly anglers.

If there are fish showing at the head of Echo Cove, then fresh fish should continue moving in through the mouth. Where you choose to fish—the mouth or back in the bay by the highway—will be determined by how much

Shoreline view of Juneau.

walking you want to do, as you should find good numbers of fish in both areas. You can often see these fish breaking the surface, which is an obvious sign for where you should be fishing.

Cowee Creek

If fishing the salt isn't appealing to you, try Cowee Creek at mile 39 on Glacier Highway. This is a glacial river with some clear, freshwater tributaries that help dilute the flow. Though Cowee receives a very small run of steelhead, it's not worth targeting them.

Coho salmon are the main attraction at Cowee Creek, making it the second most popular silver stream in the entire Juneau area. During the peak of the fall run, many cars can be found parked by the bridge, but with so much fishable water within easy walking distance, don't let the crowds dampen your enthusiasm.

Cowee Creek is a fast stream, and though it has limited visibility, it's clear enough to work a fly, especially upstream where smaller tributaries enter. The best fishing on the creek can be found directly beneath the bridge, as there's a good gravel bar that lends itself to bank fishing, and the river is clear of debris at this site. From the bridge, continue wade or bank fishing your way downstream.

If you want to break away from other anglers, consider hiking upstream, where you can hit some decent pools where fish gather. You can also make your way farther downstream, where a 45-minute to 1-hour walk will put you in big, lush meadows. This estuarine environment is beautiful to see, and the open flats make for easy casting. But because the bottom is so stable and fairly shallow, be sure to hit the flats at high tide. You'll have a bit more depth to work with and the fish will be traveling in to the tidal flats. There is a private land retreat area here belonging to Echo Ranch, and though they allow anyone to fish, please treat the area with respect.

Juneau Area

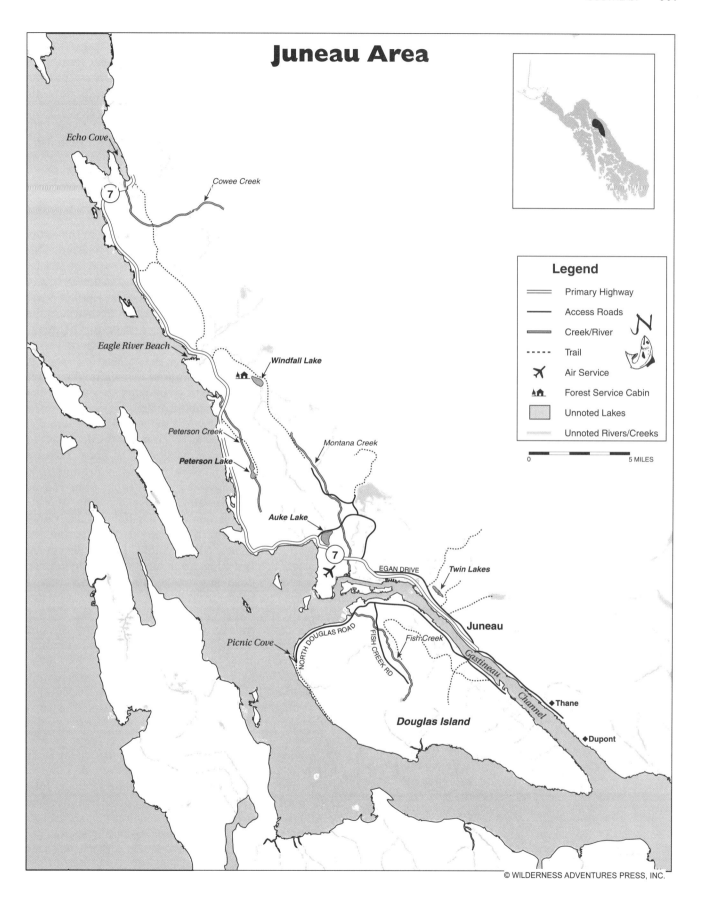

Echo Cove

Cowee Creek

⑦

Eagle River Beach

Windfall Lake

Peterson Creek

Peterson Lake

Montana Creek

Auke Lake

⑦

EGAN DRIVE

Twin Lakes

Juneau

Picnic Cove

NORTH DOUGLAS ROAD

FISH CREEK RD

Fish Creek

Gastineau Channel

◆ Thane

Douglas Island

◆ Dupont

Legend

	Primary Highway
	Access Roads
	Creek/River
- - - -	Trail
✈	Air Service
⌂	Forest Service Cabin
	Unnoted Lakes
	Unnoted Rivers/Creeks

0   5 MILES

© WILDERNESS ADVENTURES PRESS, INC.

In the spring months, Dollys and cutthroat, along with the occasional steelhead, can be picked up on the upper end of the meadows at high tide. Pink salmon also work their way into Cowee Creek in early August, but they receive very light pressure as most people pursue them in Echo Cove. Incoming fish will hold and mill about where the fresh water from Cowee Creek meets the salt, acclimating to the new environment.

As a final word of warning, you may want to bring the bear spray with you on this creek, as both brown and black bears can be thick, especially in the fall. There have been few problems with bears here, though, due to the fact that people are prepared for them and proceed with caution.

Eagle River Beach

While the Eagle and Herbert Rivers are unfishable due to heavy glacial silting—and few fish ascend the streams anyway—the outlet area at Eagle River Beach is worth fishing for sea-run Dolly Varden. At mile 27 on Glacier Highway north of Juneau, you'll come to a nice day-use park area where you can walk down to the beach and fish.

Dollys heading to sea travel close to the shore in this area, and hitting them on high tides can be very productive. If there on a low tide you can also tie into fish, but you'll need to cruise the exposed shoreline and do a bit more searching with smolt patterns. To find char ranging into the middle and upper teens, focus on the edge of the alluvial fan, along the outside of the point on the little peninsula. Don't spend too much time at the mouth of Eagle River; there's a shallow bench that keeps fish from running close to shore. Once on the point, you'll find a nice sandy beach and a grassy area, which make for comfortable fishing. There are some private buildings out here, but the area is not restricted.

Scott Haugen with a chum salmon taken in an estuary. There are many such opportunities for chum anglers along the coast.

Fishing for Dollys does not open here until June 1, with early June the best time for big fish. There is a 2-fish limit on Dolly Varden throughout the Juneau area. Sport anglers once largely depleted Dolly numbers, and the ADF&G is trying to rebuild their population. Back in the 1970s, Dollys received a great deal of pressure in this area, as they served as sustenance for many families. Now, with sound management and an improving run of hatchery king salmon to absorb the pressure, the Dollys are starting to reestablish themselves.

Windfall Lake

The outlet of Windfall Lake is the only place in the entire Juneau area where red salmon can be harvested. This hike-in fishery can be reached from mile 26 on the Glacier Highway. Take a right on a gravel road called the Spur Road some 200 yards before reaching the Herbert River bridge. You'll be able to see the bridge from where the Spur Road takes off, so you can't miss the turn. Drive ¼ mile and park at the end of the road, where the trail leads to Windfall Lake.

Though it takes about an hour to walk in, the trail is easy, with a boardwalk installed in many places. There is a nice Forest Service cabin on the lake.

The trail brings you to the outlet stream on Windfall Lake, and this ½-mile section of stream is the best place to tie into some good sockeye salmon. The narrow stream runs clear and is quite shallow throughout. In addition to reds, silver salmon, Dollys, and cutthroat trout can be found in this stretch of water.

Anglers should note that the Windfall Lake outlet stream and the portion of the Herbert River within 100 yards of the confluence of the Windfall Lake outlet stream are closed to all fishing from June 1 through July 31. However, fishing is allowed on Wednesdays and Saturdays during the month of June. Windfall Lake and all streams flowing into the lake are closed to the retention of sockeye salmon year-round. In the outlet stream, there is a one fish per day, one fish in possession limit on red salmon.

Near its mouth at the confluence of the Herbert River, the Windfall outlet stream averages about 2 feet in depth, with a 5-foot hole being deep. Sight fishing is popular here, as targeting fish in pools can be addicting. The water flowing out of Windfall Lake is quite warm compared to the Herbert River.

In Windfall Lake itself there is good fishing for Dolly Varden and cutthroat trout. But there's a wide band of lilies bordering the edge of the lake, so bring a float tube to reach the best fishing. At the time of this writing, there were a few places where anglers could find open pockets to fish from shore, but as more vegetation encroaches against the shoreline, bank opportunities will likely decrease.

One of the most popular places to float tube is at the upper end of the lake, which is littered with old beaver dams. As this area is quite marshy, walking and wading are impossible, but you can pick your way through in a belly boat. Once you've made it through the maze of beaver huts and marshland, search for the inlet, where big fish congregate near a good drop-off. This shelf can be tough to find, as beaver huts change the area each year, but it's worth the effort.

Peterson Creek and Peterson Lake

Peterson Creek is the best place on the entire Juneau road system to try your luck on steelhead. Though the run it receives is very small, the creek sees a lot of local anglers. The peak time to pursue steelhead in Peterson Creek is during the months of April and May.

In addition to steelhead, silvers, Dollys, and cutthroat, Peterson Creek is home to a small resident population of rainbows. At mile 24 on the Glacier Highway, you can park along the road and walk to good fishing. You can also take the road to Amalga Harbor, which leads to the mouth of the creek. This road crosses the creek again, offering even more roadside access. At the mouth of Peterson Creek, there is a little body of water called Salt Lake, what locals refer to as the "salt chuck," which offers good fishing.

Back up on Glacier Highway, you can easily wade the creek in many areas or fish from either bank. But the farther you head upstream, the more you'll find yourself wading in the middle of the creek, roll casting as you go.

At its widest point, Peterson Creek is only about 25 feet across, and it runs clear to tea colored. Due to the steep grade, the creek narrows down quickly, offering only about a mile of good wade fishing upstream from the main highway. Below where the bridge crosses, you'll have another mile of good fishing downstream, all the way to the salt chuck.

At mile 24 on the Glacier Highway, there's a marked trailhead leading to Peterson Lake. Years ago this lake was stocked with rainbow trout, and today the fishing for 9- to 13-inch fish can be pretty good. The trail moves slightly uphill as you make your way over the 1-mile trail. You can bank fish or carry in a belly boat.

Montana Creek

Montana Creek is the number-one fishery on the Juneau road system, and the lower stretches run right through the famed Mendenhall Valley. Though half the population of Juneau lives around Montana Creek, there is a good greenbelt bordering the creek, making it an attractive fishery that's also easy to get to.

The best fishing is at the mouth, where it flows into the Mendenhall River. To reach the mouth, take the Glacier Highway to where the bridge crosses the Mendenhall River near mile 10. Park at the Brotherhood Bridge parking lot and follow the paved walkway to the mouth, where you'll find the best coho and char fishing on the stream.

Montana Creek is about 30 to 35 feet wide at the mouth and runs pretty clear. Because it's a shallow stream, only 2 to 4 feet deep in most places, rains can turn it muddy in a hurry. There are some deeper holes scattered about, and these are worth exploring if you have a set of waders along. Also, work behind any trees that have fallen into the river, as these create small backwaters that fish love.

Montana Creek can also be accessed from Montana Creek Road, which is connected to Back Loop Road off the Glacier Highway. The water is much clearer up here, with a higher gradient and more cobbled rocks. This section is very pleasing to the eye and worth fishing if fast water appeals to you. You'll have to pick your way from hole to hole as you wade up the middle of the creek, but hip boots will suffice.

Auke Lake

Auke is a very accessible lake that offers coho and cutthroat trout, as well as catch-and-release fishing for red salmon and Dolly Varden. At mile 12 on the Glacier Highway (before you reach Auke Bay) there is a parking lot on the right side of the road. You can actually fish right off your front bumper if you wish, though the catching will be slow.

Unfortunately, there is a great deal of private property around the lake, so there's little chance to explore. Where public lands do exist, too many windfalls make navigation by foot all but impossible. However, there is hope.

On Back Loop Road there is a public trail off Fish Creek. The marked trail leads about 200 yards to the lake, where Fish Creek dumps in. Cutthroat gather around the ledge and delta created by the creek, and this area offers the best fishing on the lake. It takes determination to find good fishing at Auke Lake, but it can be worth the effort.

Twin Lakes

Another fishing option awaits anglers at Twin Lakes, 3 miles north of Juneau on the Glacier Highway. You can access these long, narrow manmade lakes off Egan Drive, and there is a city park and day-use area. If you're traveling with a family, this is a nice place to have a picnic and just take in the scenery. It's also popular among the locals.

Each year king salmon in the 8-inch range are planted

Dolly Varden are among the most popular freshwater fish in Southeast Alaska.

in the lakes, and they don't have a chance to grow much before being caught. The lake is open to bait year-round, making it tough for fly anglers to compete. Because the highway parallels the lakes along their entire west side, it's also a noisy area to fish. To get away from the traffic, stick to the park and work the banks from there.

Picnic Cove

Heading across Gastineau Channel to Douglas Island will put you on some of the best king salmon fishing in the Juneau area. To hit the salt water from shore, drive 9 miles out North Douglas Road and park at the paved pullout. From there, you can walk straight to the beach.

Wild runs of king salmon make their way to Picnic Cove beginning in late April and carrying into the middle of May. Though many anglers work the area in boats, shore-bound fishermen seem to land the greatest percentage of kings. But be prepared, this is a very popular fishery and the competition can be tough. This is a bait-fishing show, with most anglers suspending cured salmon eggs beneath a bobber or trolling herring offshore.

If you're patient, you might be able to wait for an opening among the anglers, then slip in for some fly casting. Or you might be able to find a quiet spot by walking the beach. The best time to hit the cove is midday on a weekday, when most of the locals are at work.

Fish Creek

Perhaps a better place to spend your time chasing king salmon is back at mile 8 on North Douglas Road. Park on the side of the road and walk a half-mile to the mouth of Fish Creek, where you'll find the best fishing. This is one of the more popular streams in the Juneau area, receiving an astounding number of chum salmon, as well as a good return of hatchery kings.

Beginning in late June and early July, king salmon begin gathering at the mouth of Fish Creek. Later in the summer the chums start making their way into the creek, though they adopt their spawning colors quite rapidly.

Because Fish Creek is intertidal, it's better to fish here on a low tide, right at the mouth. The fishing can actually be pretty good during anything but a high tide. Due to the small nature of the creek, it's easy to wade despite its high gradient. The mixture of bedrock and cobbled bottom structure is easy to negotiate in hip boots, but the rounded rocks are more slippery the farther upstream you go. The creek runs very clear and is only about knee-deep.

The kings that return to the creek were planted here as smolts, and represent one of the area's best put-and-take fisheries.

If you're lucky enough to hit an outgoing tide, go to the mouth, where fish nose up against the current. The tide will be moving out so rapidly, that it's more like fishing a river than an estuary. It should only take a few casts to learn why this is one of the hottest spots in the Juneau area.

Gastineau Channel

Gastineau Channel is a very large body of water located in the industrial part of town. If you're hopping off a cruise ship and searching for a quick fix, this might be the place you're looking for. Be prepared for some serious meat fishing by the locals, though. The water is open to snagging, and with so many fish gathering here, there's never a dull moment.

In September coho salmon stage here, while kings, pinks, and chums come in later in June and through July. Directly beneath the bridge there's an excellent spring Dolly fishery. These fish cruise the shoreline in search of smolt flushed into the channel from area streams.

There is a salmon hatchery 3 miles up Egan Drive and this is where many of the salmon are headed. A city-managed fishing dock adjacent to the hatchery offers good access to thousands of salmon milling about right in front of you. Because this dock sits at the base of the fish ladder, it's a popular spot for anglers.

Fly anglers will likely want to avoid the dock, and a nearby gravel beach allows them to do so. You can work streamers here for any salmon species that may be in the area. This can be a crazy angling experience, but the chances of catching fish on a fly are surprisingly good here.

JUNEAU

Population: 30,710
Alaska Area Code: 907

TOURIST INFORMATION

Alaska Department of Fish & Game, 465-4320

Alaska's Marine Highway, 6858 Glacier Hwy.; 1-800-642-0066; www.alaska.gov/ferry

Juneau Convention & Visitors Bureau, 101 Egan Drive; 586-2201; www.traveljuneau.com

U.S. Forest Service Information Center, 101 Egan Drive; 586-8751

U.S. Forest Service Cabin Information, Juneau Ranger District, 8465 Old Dairy Road, Juneau, AK 99801; 586-8800

GUIDE SERVICES

Alaska Fly 'n' Fish Charters, 9604 Kelly Court, Juneau, AK 99801; 790-2120; www.alaskabyair.com

FLY-IN CHARTERS

Alaska Seaplane Service, 1873 Shell Simmons Drive, Juneau, AK 99801; 789-3331; www.akseaplanes.com

Coastal Helicopters, Inc., 8995 Yandukin Drive, Juneau, AK 99801; 1-800-789-5610; www.coastalhelicopters.com

Era Helicopters, P.O. Box 21468, Juneau, AK 99802; 1-800-843-1947; www.eraaviation.com

NorthStar Trekking, P.O. Box 32540, Juneau, AK 99803; 790-4530; www.glaciertrekking.com

Temsco Helicopters, Inc., 1-877-789-9501

Ward Air, Inc., 8991 Yandukin Drive, Juneau, AK 99801; 1-800-478-9150; www.wardair.com

TACKLE SHOPS

Fred Meyer, 8181 Old Glacier Hwy., Juneau, AK 99801; 1-800-478-9944

Juneau Fly Fishing, 175 South Franklin Street, Suite 207, Juneau, AK 99801; 586-3754

Polks Net & Gear Sales, 8752 Trinity Drive, Juneau, AK 99801; 789-0438

ACCOMMODATIONS

Alaska Fireweed House Bed & Breakfast, 8530 North Douglas Hwy., Juneau, AK 99801; 1-800-586-3885; www.fireweedhouse.com

Aurora View Inn, 2917 Jackson Road, Juneau, AK 99801; 1-888-580-8439

Frontier Suites Hotel, 9400 Glacier Hwy., Juneau, AK 99801; 1-800-544-2250; close to the airport and ferry terminal, courtesy van, fitness center, playground, laundry, RV parking and internet access; www.frontiersuits.com

Juneau Super 8 Motel, 2295 Trout Street, Juneau, AK 99801; 1-800-800-8000; www.super8.com

Mountain View Bed & Breakfast, 9719 Trapper's Lane, Juneau, AK 99801; 1-877-552-2647; one mile to glacier and trails; www.mountainviewbb.com

Prospector Hotel, 375 Whittier Ave., Juneau, AK 99801; 1-800-331-2711; www.prospectorhotel.com

The Driftwood Lodge, 435 Willoughby Ave., Juneau, AK 99801; 1-800-544-2239; close to downtown and convention center, courtesy shuttle, laundry; www.Driftwoodalaska.com

CAMPGROUNDS AND RV PARKS

Auke Bay RV Park, 11930 Glacier Highway, Juneau, AK 99801; 789-9467

Auke Village Campground, Mile 15.4 Glacier Hwy.; 13 campsites, flush and pit toilets, water, tables and fire rings

Forest Service Cabins, National Recreation Reservation Service (NRRS); 1-877-444-6777; www.fs.fed.us/r10/tongass/recreation/recreation.html

Mendenhall Lake Campground, turn off Glacier Hwy. at Mile 9.4, and continue to Montana Creek Road; 68 sites, basic to full service, dump station, showers, flush toilets, tables and firepits; 586-8800

Spruce Meadow RV Park, 10200 Mendenhall Loop Road, Juneau, AK 99801; 789-1990; 64 full-service sights, showers, cable, Internet, laundry and tour desk; www.juneaurv.com

RESTAURANTS

El Sombrero Mexican, 157 South Franklin Street, Juneau, AK 99801; 586-6770

Fiddlehead Restaurant & Bakery, 429 West Willoughby Ave., Juneau, AK 99801; 586-1042

Hangar on the Wharf, #2 Marine Way, Suite 106, Juneau, AK 99801; 586-5018

Heritage Coffee Company & Cafe, 174 South Franklin Street, Juneau, AK 99801; 1-800-478-5282; www.heritagecoffee.com

Mount Roberts Tramway, 490 South Franklin Street, Juneau, AK 99801; 1-888-461-8726

FISH PROCESSING

TAKU Smokeries Fisheries, 550 South Franklin Street, Juneau, AK 99801; 463-5312

BOAT RENTALS

Alaska Boat & Kayak, 6105 Thane Road, Juneau, AK 99801; 789-6886; www.juneaukayak.com

Spring and fall steelhead runs can be fished in many areas of Southeast Alaska. Here, Mike Bogue prepares to free a prized catch.

JUNEAU, CONT.

MOTOR HOME RENTALS

Rent-A-Wreck, Juneau, 2450-C Industrial Blvd., Juneau, AK 99801; 789-4111

RENTAL CARS

Chrysler Rent-A-Car, 8725 Mallard Street, Juneau, AK 99801; 789-1386

Evergreen Motors Inc., 8895 Mallard Street, Juneau, AK 99801; 1-888-267-9300; www.evergreenmotorsjuneau.com

AIR SERVICES

Alaska Airlines, 1-800-426-0333; www.alaskaair.com

L.A.B. Flying Service Inc., 789-9160; ww.labflying.com

Wings of Alaska Airlines, 8421 Livingston Way, Juneau, AK 99801; 789-0790; www.wingsofalaska.com

AUTO REPAIR

Alaska Auto Repair & Sales Inc., 1115 3rd Street, Douglas, AK 99824; 364-3400

Auto Haus, 2315 Industrial Boulevard, Juneau, AK 99801; 789-2228

Frank's Service & Repair, 1750 Mendenhall Peninsula, Juneau, AK 99801; 789-4037

LOCKSMITHS

Paladin Locksmithing, 8201 Dogwood Lane, Juneau, AK 99801; 789-9581

MEDICAL

Bartlett Regional Hospital, 3260 Hospital Drive, Juneau, AK 99801; 586-2611

VETERINARY CLINICS

Veterinary Clinic, 7691 Glacier Highway, Juneau, AK 99801; 789-7551

Veterinary Hospital Juneau, 8367 Old Dairy Road, Juneau, AK 99801; 789-3444

TOURIST ATTRACTIONS

AJ Mine, P.O. Box 34105, Juneau, AK 99803; 463-5017; travel underground and see miners operating historic mining equipment

Alaska State Museum, 395 Whittier Street, Juneau, AK 99801; 465-2901; www.museums.state.ak.us

Juneau-Douglas City Museum, 155 South Seward Street, Juneau, AK 99801; 586-3572

Macaulay Salmon Hatchery, 2697 Channel Drive, Juneau, AK 99801; 1-877-463-2486; www.dipac.net

Mendenhall Glacier, 789-0097

The road system in Southeast Alaska gives anglers access to some of the best fishing in the region. By putting your car on a ferry, you can explore on your own.

HAINES AND SKAGWAY

One of the few regions in Southeast Alaska that can be reached by road is the corner of the panhandle where the hub towns of Haines and Skagway are situated. The beautiful setting, wildlife viewing opportunities, and tourist attractions draw travelers from around the globe, but there is some good fishing around these towns, as well.

Haines and Skagway sit at the northern terminus of the Alaska Marine Highway, and are two of the three towns in all of Southeast Alaska that can be reached by road. The Haines Highway starts in the town of Haines and runs 152 miles north to its junction with the Alaska Highway at the town of Haines Junction in the Yukon Territory. Though Haines is only 15 miles from Skagway, the two are not directly connected by road.

To reach Skagway travelers can take the Alaska Marine Highway by ferry or drive in from Canada. Conceivably, one could drive to Skagway from Haines, but the 360-mile journey makes taking a ferry the only reasonable option. If you're on the Alaska Highway, you can also turn off on the Klondike Highway to reach Skagway. The Klondike Highway runs 108 miles, connecting Whitehorse, Yukon Territory with Skagway.

Due to their proximity to Canada, Haines and Skagway draw many sport anglers from across the border, especially during the peak of the fall salmon runs. Combine these visitors with local anglers and tourists, and some of the more popular fisheries in the area can become quite crowded. Mind you, that's crowded by Southeast Alaska standards, not Kenai Peninsula standards. Even at peak fishing times, anglers should have little trouble finding a comfortable place to dunk a fly.

Big rivers, bays, and lakes constitute the primary fishing opportunities in this part of Southeast Alaska. While roads lead to good river fishing—and, to some extent, bay fishing—your legs will have to carry you into some of the area lakes, if that's the type of fishing you're after. If you desire a high lake experience but don't feel comfortable with some of the arduous hikes required, you can hire a helicopter charter in Skagway. As for bay fishing, the options are sometimes limited for fly anglers, as trolling plug-cut herring in deep waters infested with cruise ships, ferries, charters, and private crafts is the norm.

Nonetheless, there is some excellent flyfishing to be had. Anglers should note that rainstorms can turn rivers off-color at any time, making it difficult to fish with flies. As with much of Southeast Alaska, it's a good idea to carry a spinning rod with an assortment of lures, just in case.

In this section we'll detail the fishable waters northwest of the Haines area, continuing east into the Skagway region. There is good Dolly Varden fishing in April and May, then again from September through November. The salmon runs are fairly late in this area, with the majority of fish showing up in September and October. Most freshwater streams are closed to king salmon angling, though there is one exception at Pullen Creek, in Skagway.

Kelsall Landing

On the upper end of the Chilkat River, north of the villages of Klukwan and Wells, you'll find Kelsall Landing. Take the marked turnoff for Mosquito Lake on a logging road heading north from the Haines Highway. Just before reaching Mosquito Lake, turn left on a gravel road. The road winds a couple of miles through hill country before ending on the banks of the Chilkat.

If you're pulling a sled, this is one of the best places to launch and explore the fishing both up and downstream from the landing. However, if you're limited to bank fishing, this is a prime location for that, too. From the landing, a good 100 yards of wading water can be reached upstream, though there's not much in the way of downstream fishing action.

Fall salmon love holding in this backwater area, with the best bank angling coming right at the landing. Casting streamers, pink bunny hair leeches, or Flash Flies is just

You'll be amazed at the number of Dollys that can be pulled from a good pool.

Haines/Skagway Area

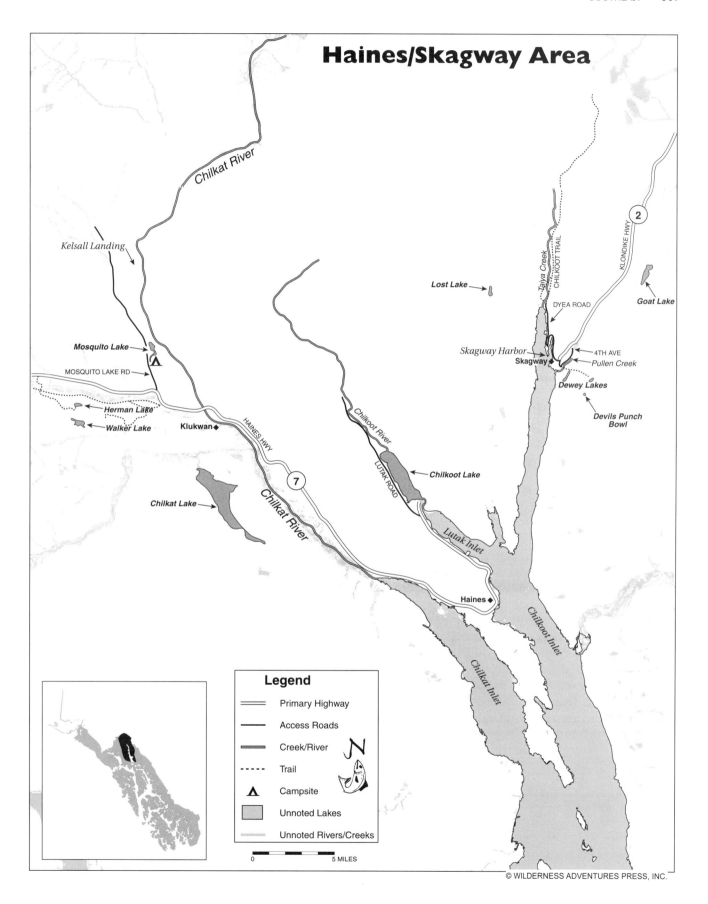

Chilkat River

Kelsall Landing

Lost Lake

Taiya Creek

CHILKOOT TRAIL

KLONDIKE HWY

2

Goat Lake

DYEA ROAD

Mosquito Lake

MOSQUITO LAKE RD

Skagway Harbor

4TH AVE

Skagway

Pullen Creek

Dewey Lakes

Herman Lake

Walker Lake

Klukwan

Devils Punch
Bowl

HAINES HWY

Chilkoot River

LUTAK ROAD

Chilkoot Lake

7

Chilkat Lake

Chilkat River

Lutak Inlet

Chilkoot Inlet

Haines

Chilkat Inlet

Legend

══════	Primary Highway
──────	Access Roads
──────	Creek/River
‑ ‑ ‑ ‑	Trail
Λ	Campsite
▓	Unnoted Lakes
░	Unnoted Rivers/Creeks

N

0   5 MILES

the ticket for fooling fall coho, which are in here from September through the month of October. While the silver salmon are the big draw here, attracting many anglers from the Whitehorse area, there are also a few red and chum salmon, as well as Dolly Varden and some cutthroat trout.

By the time the silvers hit the Chilkat in the fall, it's usually flushed of glacial sediments and running clear. Water levels should remain consistent, with the river averaging about 50 feet wide where you'll be fishing. However, heavy rains can change this in a matter of hours, so have a backup plan in mind, and return here a day or two later when the water is back in shape.

During the height of the fall salmon runs, this will be one of the most visited fisheries in the area, simply because it's road accessible. But anglers with a good pair of insulated waders can often escape bank fishermen by working their way around the brushy banks to find fish. The water should be clear enough for good footing, but keep an eye out for some deeper holes amid the slower sections of water. There is a campground here that is worth staying in if the fish are in thick.

Mosquito Lake

Back downstream of the river, Mosquito Lake Road leads to some good fishing at Mosquito Lake. This is a clear lake that's fairly shallow around the edges, with the middle dropping to around 70 feet. In recent years some of the shallower sections along the bank have been taken over by vegetation.

While there used to be good bank fishing at Mosquito Lake, it's now tough to cast anything beyond the weed beds. An angler with a float tube or canoe will have the best luck, working the fringes of the vegetation from deeper water. If you're hauling a small cartopper with a kicker, you can motor around the lake and get into even more fish.

There's a state campground here and a boat launch. The primary targets are Dolly Varden and cutthroat, which can be fished year-round. The lake also receives runs of silver and red salmon, though these are tough to coax into biting. Heavy timber surrounds much of the lake, except the northwest corner, and this protects the surface from high winds.

Chilkat River

The Chilkat River parallels the Haines Highway from the town of Klukwan down to its mouth. And there are numerous roadside fishing opportunities along this stretch. Lots of Dollys overwinter in the river, as well as in Chilkat Lake, which means the fishing here can very productive from late March into mid-May. Around mid-May, meltoff of mountain snows and glaciers makes the water turbid, high, and unfishable.

But earlier in the spring, the Chilkat runs low and clear, making it easy for wading anglers to move up and downstream. Because Dollys are feeding on outgoing salmon fry, small smolt patterns can be the ticket here.

It's late September before the river settles and drops back into shape. However, with such a late run of coho, the fishing can actually be good into the month of November. There is also a good late run of chum salmon in the Chilkat. Chums are a thrill to battle on a fly rod and seem to love green streamers.

It's easy to dump a canoe in off the highway and float downstream to where someone is waiting to pick you up, or you can hitch a ride back to the truck. There are no developed ramps here so simply slide the canoe down from the highway and take off. This is a slow, gentle river from Klukwan down to the intertidal waters near the Haines airport, but keep an eye out for the occasional sweeper.

If you're lucky enough to be here in the fall, have a camera handy. As spawning salmon litter the banks of the Chilkat, one of the world's largest populations of bald eagles gather for an easy meal. Even if the fishing is slow, seeing such a huge concentration of bald eagles is something you'll never forget.

Anglers should be aware that the Chilkat River receives a run of king salmon, but the season is closed year-round.

As for the Chilkat Inlet, there's not much fishing here other than right at the mouth during the spring months for cutthroat trout that migrate out of the river. In Chilkat Inlet itself—as with Letnikof Cove—most of the fishing is for king salmon in the spring, but the most effective angling methods include trolling and mooching herring. There is also some good bottom fishing in the area, and anglers looking to score on some meat for the freezer should look into hiring a charter boat.

At Chilkat State Park, there's little if any flyfishing, but the campground is at a good central location.

Stream Facts: Chilkat River

Seasons

- Closed to king salmon fishing.

Special Regulations

- Silver salmon 16 inches or more, 3 per day, 6 in possession.

- Chum and sockeye salmon 16 inches or more, 6 of each species per day, 12 of each species in possession.

- Dolly Varden, 10 per day, 10 in possession, no size restrictions.

- Cutthroat trout, 2 per day, 2 in possession, between 11 and 22 inches.

Fish

- Silver, chum, and red salmon, Dolly Varden, cutthroat trout

River Characteristics

- In the early spring and late fall months, the river runs fairly clear. Its gentle flow allows for safe wade fishing from the bank, as well as from a canoe. From mid-May to September, heavy silting makes the river unfishable.

Fishing Access

- Kelsall Landing 2 miles upstream from Mosquito Lake and along the entire stretch of Haines Highway from Klukwan down to the airport.

Maps

- *Alaska Atlas and Gazetteer*, page 37-38

Resident rainbows abound in many Southeast area rivers, creeks, and lakes.

Herman Lake

West of the Chilkat River, three lakes offer unique fishing experiences for those up to the task. At approximately mile 26 on the Haines Highway, you'll cross a big steel bridge. Just past the bridge, turn right on Porcupine Road, which heads to the old mining town of Porcupine. Go past the old town to Sunshine Mountain Road, following it up the hill for 5 or 6 miles.

This is a steep, winding, rough logging road; one on which you won't want to pull trailers or traverse in a motor home. Be on the lookout for Herman Lake below on the right side of the road. Because it's nestled amid the timber, it can be easy to miss.

From the logging road, a very steep, crude trail makes its way a half-mile down to the lake. This is not a developed, or even marked, trail and only fit anglers should consider giving it a go.

Herman Lake is also referred to as Cave Lake by the locals, as its outlet flows through a cave. As a result, the water can back up during spring meltoff, causing the level of the lake to rise some 20 feet. By late July or early August, the water has dropped and casting flies from shoreline is not a problem.

Herman Lake is small enough to walk around in an hour. For the best results, though, consider hauling a float tube down to the lake, keeping in mind that there will be a steep hike back up to the vehicle.

Arctic grayling are the only fish in this lake, having been stocked in the 1970s. The fish took off from that effort and today thrive in the lake. Grayling up to 11 inches are the norm, but you'll likely be fishing this beautiful, isolated lake all by yourself. Working dry flies early in the morning and in the evening will just about guarantee you fish.

Walker Lake

Continuing along Sunshine Mountain Road will bring you to the trailhead for Walker Lake. Though this trailhead is usually marked with a little signpost, souvenir seekers often make off with it—in other words, don't count on the sign being there. The trailhead is on the left side of the gravel logging road.

Though this trail is not as physically demanding as the one leading to Herman Lake, it is a bit rough in places. The 2-mile hike in can be taxing, especially when you're hauling a belly boat. But anyone in fair shape should be able to make it. You will, however, want to bring a belly boat, as the shoreline around this lake is brushy.

Resident Dolly Varden are the quarry here, with 10- to 12-inch fish the average. While the fish are nothing to brag about, the secluded experience is. This lake is in a glorious setting tucked into the woods and surrounded by alders, and it receives hardly any pressure. Floatplanes occasionally visit the lake, but even these make a beautiful sight against the stunning hills in the distance.

Chilkat Lake

The largest lake in the area is Chilkat Lake, which can be reached only by flying in. Though experienced locals do access the lake by jet sled, this is advisable for anyone who isn't familiar with every inch of the way. There are lodges and air services working the area, and these are your best bet for getting to the big lake.

The fishing for cutthroat and Dollys is good here, and silver and chum salmon also make their way into the lake. For its size, Chilkat Lake is not very deep, and the fishing can be good along the shoreline. But to really experience good fishing on Chilkat, you'll need a boat, and that means you'll probably have to hire an outfitter.

Lutak Inlet

Turning our focus to the north of Haines, where the ferry terminal is situated, we come to Lutak Inlet. Though this is a saltwater fishery, the action for pink salmon can be very good in July and August. The road runs right along the inlet, and finding a place to fish on low tide is not a concern. Simply pull off the road and make your way down to the water.

Dolly Varden also cruise around the inlet in the fall, and working tight to shore will turn up both Dollys and pink salmon. Lutak Inlet doesn't offer the secluded experience one envisions when dreaming of Alaska, but the fishing action is a great consolation.

Chilkoot Inlet

Chilkoot Inlet offers more urban bay fishing right in the town of Haines. Portage Cove is the name of the area you'll be fishing, and it can be seen from just about everywhere in Haines. Driving directly to the campground is easy, though it's currently designated for tent campers only, with no overnight parking.

The shoreline here is quite rocky, and it drops off rapidly. As a result, the fishing for pink salmon and Dolly Varden can be excellent on low tides. Hopping out on exposed rocks will get you near the fish, and with no brushline behind you there's no worrying about backcasts.

Chilkoot River

If you only hit one stream in the Haines/Skagway area, it should be the Chilkoot River. Second only to the Situk River in popularity in all of Southeast Alaska, the Chilkoot is home to excellent coho fishing from late September through October, pink salmon from late July through August, and a few chum salmon and Dolly Varden, which are available year-round, but sockeye salmon are the main attraction.

From June through August sockeye salmon anglers come from all over to take part in this phenomenal fishery. In addition to a good turnout from Canadian anglers, this is where many tourists and Haines residents spend time. If you're hopping off at the ferry terminal and looking to kill a few hours, grab a taxi or rent a car and get on Lutak Road and drive a few short minutes to the Chilkoot.

Lutak Road parallels the river, which can easily be seen from the road. Between Lutak Inlet, where the ferry docks, and the outlet of Chilkoot Lake, there is about a mile of easy-to-access, prime fishing to be had right from the bank. Above Chilkoot Lake, the river is closed to all salmon fishing, though some boaters head up that way for Dolly Varden.

About halfway between the lake and the salt, the ADF&G has a weir across the river. From June through early September, all fishing within 300 feet of this weir is usually prohibited. During the summer months, the best salmon fishing occurs below the weir.

The only other thing anglers need be aware of in this area is the brown bears. With so many salmon around, anglers aren't the only ones routinely visiting this river. People actually travel great distances just to come observe the bears feeding on the Chilkoot. If you do encounter a bear, give it space. If you're fighting a fish and a bear approaches, break it off and give way to the bear. Respect their natural domain and expect to see a bear at any given moment so you'll be ready to react when the time comes.

During the peak summer months, the Chilkoot can get fairly silted, making it challenging to fish. But overall it runs clearer than other rivers in the area, and flyfishers should have no trouble finding action. This river also runs a bit faster than most others, so anglers should hit the seams, pockets, and holding zones commonly associated with such water. Those with hip boots or waders will be able to get away from the bank a bit more easily and reach more fish. But there are spots where line-whippers can stay dry and still catch fish.

In the spring, Dolly Varden are the main attraction on the Chilkoot, as out-migrating fish that have overwintered in the lake begin heading to the ocean. Anglers working smolt patterns close to shore will do well on Dollys, as they're keyed on the salmon smolt being flushed downstream. Because these smolt often hold tight to shore, this is where you'll find the best fishing. When the Dollys move back up the river in the fall, fishing again becomes productive for them.

Stream Facts: Chilkoot River

Seasons

- Open year-round.

Special Regulations

- Dolly Varden limit is 2 per day, 2 in possession.
- Coho salmon 16 inches or more, 2 per day, 2 in possession.
- The possession for all other salmon species is equal to the daily bag limit.
- The use of bait is allowed year-round.

Fish

- Silver, red, pink, chum salmon, Dolly Varden

River Characteristics

- The Chilkoot is a relatively fast, clear river. It can carry quite a bit of glacial silt during midsummer, but cleans out fairly quickly. The best fishing during the summer is below the ADF&G weir. Wade fishing along the shore is safe, but be on the lookout for bears.

Fishing Access

- Between Lutak Inlet and Chilkoot Lake, Lutak Road borders the river. There are many roadside pulloffs here, making for easy bank fishing for about 1 mile.

Maps

- *Alaska Atlas and Gazetteer*, page 38

Chilkoot Lake

Though it may look attractive on a map, Chilkoot Lake is a huge, deep body of water that's very tough to fish from shore. Some fishing can be had by canoe, but high winds develop quickly on this 7-mile-long lake.

If you do dump a canoe in, or better yet, a motor boat, head to the western shore, where Dolly Varden are found. Incoming sockeye salmon spawn here in the fall, and ravenous Dollys can be caught on egg patterns and beads. In April and May, after the lake thaws, the lake's inlet is also good for Dollys.

All inlet streams, including the upper section of the Chilkoot River, which flows into Chilkoot Lake, are closed to all salmon fishing, though Dollys can be fished year-round. During and following the salmon spawn, the Dolly action is good. And there are a few cutthroat trout in these streams, too.

Skagway Harbor

A one-hour ferry ride transports you from Haines to the town of Skagway, through breathtaking Taiya Inlet. For travelers enjoying the Alaska Marine Highway, this is the most common way to reach Skagway. However, road warriors can drive to Skagway off the Alaska Highway, by traveling 108 miles along the Klondike Highway from Whitehorse.

Unlike Haines, there is virtually no flyfishing in the salt water around Skagway, as both Taiya Inlet and Skagway Harbor are packed with cruise ships, private ferries, and charter boats. But there is excellent bait trolling in these areas for hatchery-raised king salmon, and if you're looking to take a cooler of frozen salmon home, hire a charter here.

Southeast Alaska has hundreds of steelhead streams.

Lost Lake

If you feel like stretching your legs once you hop off the ferry, and don't mind working for a few undersized rainbows, then consider hiking in to Lost Lake. Planted with rainbows in the 1950s, these trout have been able to establish a self-sustaining population over the years. In 2003 the slot size for keepers dropped from 11 inches to 9, which is a good indication of the size fish we're talking about.

You'll need a float tube here, as the wooded perimeter of the lake offers very limited bank fishing. However, if you just want to fish this lake to say you did it, there are a few holes along the shoreline from which you can likely pull out a small rainbow or two.

Lost Lake is accessed off a marked trailhead at the head of Taiya Inlet. Drive to the trailhead at the end of Dyea Road, which leads through the old mining town of Dyea. From there it's a 2-mile hike to Lost Lake. This is a rough trail, and only fit anglers should go for it. If you have reservations about fishing here, hold off; there are more productive, easier-to-reach waters near Skagway.

Goat Lake

Perhaps the best lake fishing in the Skagway area is found in another tough-to-access body of water about 4 miles north of town. There is no developed trail leading to Goat Lake, but it can be reached by boarding the White Pass Train, then hopping off at Pitchfork Falls. From there, scramble up the mountainside to the outlet of the lake, which sits at nearly 3,000 feet.

This high alpine lake is well above tree line and is locked in ice from October through the middle of June. But when the ice clears, the fishing for grayling into the 15-inch class can be spectacular. Goat Lake was stocked with grayling in the 1980s and the fish are doing well thanks to a lack of fishing pressure.

The banks around Goat Lake are fairly steep, but can be fished. For the best results, concentrate on the inlets and outlets of the lake, where grayling seem to congregate.

You can also charter a helicopter out of Skagway to reach Goat Lake. There are a few high lakes just a short flight from town that won't drain your pocketbook. These charter services can drop you off and pick you up at a designated time. Temsco Helicopters Incorporated is the outfit most anglers use out of Skagway, and they can be reached toll-free at 1-877-789-9501. They can take you to Goat Lake, as well as some of the lakes mentioned below.

Lower and Upper Dewey Lakes

To the south of Skagway you'll find two more hike-in lakes, Lower and Upper Dewey Lakes. One is easier to access than Lost and Goat Lakes, the other is a bit more of a challenge. Several years ago both Lower and Upper Dewey Lakes were stocked with brook trout and the fish are doing well. In addition, Lower Dewey has a solid population of Dolly Varden.

Both lakes are reached by a trail taking off on the south side of town, east of 4th Avenue and just across the railroad tracks. Head toward Pullen Pond and you should be able to find the marked trailhead nearby. If you're having trouble, simply ask any of the locals, as they will be happy to point you in the right direction.

Lower Dewey Lake sits only a half-mile up the trail, which is rated easy going. There are a few places to fish from shore, but if you're serious about finding some of the 14-inch brook trout swimming around in this shallow lake, you're best bet is a float tube. Brook trout here love leech patterns tied on size 2 to 6 hooks. One of my favorite brookie leeches has a black marabou body with a whisk of purple, along with four or five strands of purple Flashabou. Woolly Buggers are also good, especially in green and brown.

Continuing on the Lower Dewey Lake trail for another mile or so will connect you with Upper Dewey Lake. The payoff for this uphill climb will be realized once you reach the beautiful lake, which sits above tree line. As a result, there is a great deal of shoreline to walk and fish, and brook trout cruising close to shore make for good fishing. Though the brookies will only average 10 inches or so, the seclusion you'll experience here may make it well worth the effort.

Southeast Alaska has some of the most extreme tidal changes in the world. Pay close attention to the tides when fishing bays, estuaries and tidally-influenced streams. (Photo Cameron Hanes)

If you made it to Upper Dewey Lake with no problems, you may wish to continue along the trail yet another mile to Devil's Punch Bowl. This lake was stocked with brook trout in the late 1980s, and they now average about 10 inches. The open shoreline provides plenty of fishing, and you're nearly assured of having this tough-to-reach lake to yourself. The only anglers you might encounter are ones who chartered a helicopter to drop them here for the day.

Pullen Creek

The best, and only, opportunity for landing a king salmon in a stream in Haines or Skagway is at Pullen Creek, thanks to a hatchery run that has taken root.

Pullen Creek winds through the town of Skagway, so you're not going to have the water to yourself. However, because several roads cross the creek, and given the large number of creekside pulloffs, finding a place to fish is rarely a problem, even during the peak of the king run.

Pullen Creek is quite small and you can cross it in chest waders in many places. There is some glacial influence on this stream, but not enough to impede the fishing. The banks are ideal for fishing, and though they can see lots of pressure, there's plenty of room to roam and find your own holes.

Once the spawning quota of king salmon has made its way into the hatchery on Pullen Creek—situated about a mile upstream from the mouth—the stream is open for sport fishing. The quota is usually reached around the middle of July. The earlier you can be on the creek once the quota has been reached, the brighter and fresher the fish will be. By the end of July or the first week in August, the salmon are turning quite dark and aren't worth fishing for. Battling 30- to 40-pound salmon on a fly in this shallow creek is something you won't want to miss.

Pullen Creek is also home to good Dolly Varden fishing, as well as pink salmon. Pullen Creek Park is a nicely manicured area offering day-use facilities. There is also a private campground near the park. Anglers with good timing can hop off the ferry or a cruise ship and be catching fish in Pullen Creek in a matter of minutes. Because the creek is located on the south end of town, between the harbor and town of Skagway, it's within easy walking distance.

Taiya River

The Taiya River is another popular stream fishery in the Skagway area. Drive north from Skagway on Dyea Road to where it meets the river. The roadside access connects you with the hottest fishing, with the best results coming near the mouth of the river. The famed Chilkoot Trail moves along the river, but deviates from its banks in several places, making access to the river difficult.

The most productive fishing will come to anglers wearing chest waders and working through the grassy tidal flats. Here, you'll find Dolly Varden and pink, chum, and a few coho salmon. The Dolly action is good in early spring and again in the fall, while the salmon bite occurs from late July on. With Dollys running up to 2 pounds, this area is worth spending time in.

The Taiya River is a glacial stream, and there's not much fishing here during midsummer when silt infiltration cuts visibility to a few inches. In appearance, the Taiya looks similar to the Chilkoot River. Where the road leads to the river it's about 100 feet across during prime fishing times. The medium flow rate means wading is safe, as long as you pay attention to where you're stepping.

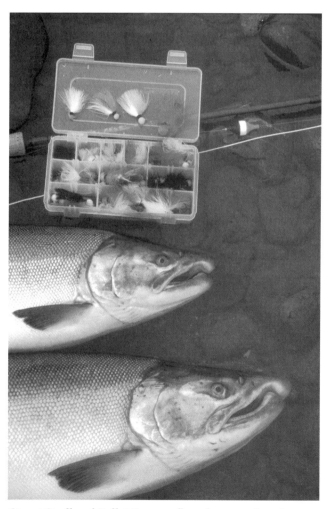

Stuart Steelhead Bullet Jigs on a fly rod can produce fast action for coho anglers.

HAINES

Population: 2,800
Alaska Area Code: 907
Zip Code: 99827

TOURIST INFORMATION

Alaska Department of Fish & Game, 766-3638
Alaska Inter-Island Ferry Authority, P.O. Box 495; 1-866-308-4848; www.Interislandferry.com
Haines Chamber of Commerce, 219 Main Street; 766-2202; www.haineschamber.org
Haines Convention and Visitors Bureau, P.O. Box 530; 766-2234
Visitor Information Center, 122 2nd Avenue; 1-800-458-3579; www.haines.ak.us

GUIDE SERVICES

Salmon Run Charters, Mile 6.5 Lutak Road; 723-4229; www.salmonrunadventures.com

TACKLE SHOPS

Alaska Sport Shop, 420 Main Street; 766-2441; camping and fishing supplies, licenses available; douglas@alaskasportsop.net
Outfitter Sporting Goods, Mile Zero Haines Hwy.; 766-3221; fishing, camping and hiking products, bait, licenses and outdoor clothing

ACCOMMODATIONS

Bear Creek Cabins, Mile 1.5 Small Tracks Road, P.O. Box 908; 766-2259
Cabin Fever, Mile 8 Mud Bay Road; 766-2390; solar-powered log cabins
Captain's Choice Motel, 108 2nd Avenue N; 1-800-478-2345; www.capchoice.com
Chilkat Eagle Bed & Breakfast, 69 Soap Suds Alley; 766-2763
Eagles Nest Motel, Mile 1 Haines Hwy.; 1-800-354-6006; courtesy van, pets allowed; www.eaglesnest.wyt-bear.com
Fort Seward Condos, 3 Fort Seward Drive; 766-2425
Summer Inn Bed & Breakfast, 117 2nd Avenue; 766-2970
Weeping Trout Sports Resort, Chilkat Lake, P.O. Box 129; 766-2827

CAMPGROUNDS AND RV PARKS

Chilkat State Park, Mud Bay Road; 32 RV sites, 3 beach front tentsites, fire rings, toilets, water pump, tables hiking trails and boat launch

Chilkoot Lake State Recreation Site, Lutak Road; 32 sites, fire rings, toilets, water pump, picnic tables and boat launch
Haines Hitch Up RV Park, 851 Main Street; 766-2882; 95 sites, 20 pull-thrus, cable, showers, laundry, gift shop and tour desk; www.hitchuprv.com
Oceanside RV Park, 10 Front Street, Park on the beach; 766-2437; full-service RV park
Portage Cove State Recreation Site; 0.5 miles past Fort Seward on Portage Cove; 9 tentsites, toilets, fire rings, water pump, picnic tables; walk-in and bicyclist camping only
Port Chilkoot Camper Park, 13 Ft. Seward Drive; 766-2000; full and partial hookups, showers, laundry, walking distance to town
Salmon Run Adventures Campground & Cabins, P.O. Box 1582, Mile 6.5 Lutak Road; 766-3240 or 723-4229; private sites, RV parking, restrooms, showers, hiking trails and boat ramp; www.salmonrunadventures.com

RESTAURANTS

Bamboo Room, 11-13 2nd Avenue; 766-2800
Chilkat Restaurant & Bakery, 5th and Dalton; 766-3653
Grizzly Greg's Pizzeria, 126 Main Street; 766-3622
"Just For The Halibut" Fish & Chips Cafe & Deli, 142 Beach Road; 766-3800
Lighthouse Restaurant, 101 Front Street; 766-2444
Mama Bear's Fudge Factory & Bakery, 118 Main Street; 766-3255
Mountain Market Deli, 151 3rd Avenue S; 766-3340
South of the Border, 31 Tower Road; 766-2840

FISH PROCESSING

Bell's Store, 18 2nd Avenue, N; 1-800-446-2950

BOAT RENTALS

Alaska Kayak supply, Deishu Expeditions and Boat Rentals, 425 Beach Road; 1-800-552-9257; www.seakayaks.com

RENTAL CARS

Avis Rent-a-Car, Halsingland Hotel; 766-2733
Rental Car, Captain's Choice Hotel; 766-3111
Eagles Nest Car Rental; 1069 Haines Hwy.; 766-2891

AIR SERVICES

L.A.B. Flying Service Inc., 390 Main Street; 766-2222; www.labflying.com

Skagway Air Service, 211 Willard Street; 766-3233; www.skagwayair.com

Wings of Alaska Airlines, #1 Airport Road; 766-2030; www.wingsofalaska.com

AUTO REPAIR

Bigfoot Auto Services, Inc., 987 Haines Hwy.; 1-800-766-5406

Bushmaster Auto Service, 130 4th Avenue N; 766-3217

Parts Place, 104 3rd Avenue S; 766-2940; auto, RV, and marine

MEDICAL

Searhc Haines Medical Clinic, 131 1st Avenue S; 766-2521; after hours 766-2121; www.searhc.org

TOURIST ATTRACTIONS

Alaska Chilkat Bald Eagle Preserve, Mile 17 Haines Hwy.; 465-4563

Alaska Indian Arts Inc., 13 Fort Seward Drive; 766-2160

Sheldon Museum & Cultural Center, 11 Main Street; 766-2366; www.sheldonmuseum.com

Tsirku Canning Company, 5th and Main Streets; 766-3474; www.cannerytour.com

Some area lakes and streams are tough to fly fish, and spinning gear is often the best option for catching fish.

YAKUTAT

Even by Alaska standards, the village of Yakutat is situated in a unique setting. There is still some debate about which region Yakutat belongs in. Some feel it is part of Southeast Alaska, others believe it's part of Central Alaska, while a few insist it should be classified as its own region. Most people, though, are comfortable with calling it the extreme northern border of Southeast Alaska.

Once you arrive in Yakutat, you'll understand why there's some confusion on this point. Set along a glacial outwash plain and uplifted seabed known as Yakutat Foreland, the streams in this region flow much more gently than those in other parts of Southeast Alaska.

The lakes in this region receive little if any attention, as a floatplane or helicopter is needed to reach most bodies of water. The fees required to access these remote lakes is only one reason they receive little pressure; the other factor is that one of Alaska's premier steelhead and silver salmon streams, the Situk River, lies near the town of Yakutat.

There are other streams to fish beyond the Situk, however. A few of these can be reached by vehicle, others must be accessed by floatplane. The area boasts a run of all five Pacific salmon species—farm-raised Atlantic salmon have even been verified in the area—as well as Dolly Varden, rainbow, and cutthroat trout. There's no disputing the fact that Yakutat is one of the state's premier freshwater game fisheries, ranked by many people as the second most popular and productive salmon and steelhead destination behind the Kenai system.

While in Yakutat, don't overlook the excellent ocean fishing for halibut, lingcod, and rockfish. The average size for halibut in Yakutat Bay is the best in the state, and with lings going into the 40-pound class, there's no shortage of excitement.

The village of Yakutat is rather spread out. At the time of this writing, three lodges cater to freshwater sport fishers. Yakutat Lodge is situated right next to the airport. You can literally get your luggage, walk 30 yards, and be in the lobby of this lodge. Leonard's Landing is located on the opposite end of town, near the harbor. Glacier Bear Lodge is situated off the main highway leading into Yakutat, near Forest Highway 10, which leads to Nine Mile Bridge.

Though I've visited all three lodges, I've only stayed in Glacier Bear (1-866-425-6343). In addition to excellent food, the lodge has plenty of rooms, can arrange for driftboat and car rentals, and can even help plan a saltwater fishing trip. Owner Martha Donohue has lived here her whole life and knows the area and the river extremely well. In addition, she is well connected with the local biologist and can provide anglers with the hottest fishing tips on the Situk.

Let's look at what this unique section of the state has to offer traveling anglers.

Situk River

The first time I fished the Situk River I was more pleased with the ease of getting there than I was with catching fish. Less than three hours of flying time from my Oregon home found the plane setting down on Yakutat's runway. Checking into Glacier Bear Lodge, I tossed my bags in a room, gathered my fishing gear, and was on the river two hours later. Before I knew it, I was preparing to release a 16-pound Situk steelhead and pondering how simple it all seemed.

The Situk is justifiably the most famous steelhead stream in the state. Nowhere else had I ever gazed into a pool to see more than 200 steelhead milling about, many of which exceeded 20 pounds. Hooking steelhead in the 30-pound range isn't rare, though landing them is. When the river is running low, it can be nearly impossible to handle these hot fish on even the most substantial gear, and that's what makes fishing this river so addicting.

The main stem of the Situk River winds 22 miles to the ocean from its headwaters at Mountain Lake. Averaging about 70 feet in width and a mere 3 feet in depth, this stream drains an area of 125 square miles and has two major tributaries, the Old Situk River and the West Fork Situk River. Because both tributaries are too choked in brush to fish, the mainstem Situk receives almost all the attention.

The lower 14 miles of river are the most popular with anglers. Many like to concentrate their efforts around the Nine Mile Bridge on Forest Highway 10, which runs east of Yakutat. Anglers can launch a boat directly beneath the bridge to take the 14-mile drift to the first and only take-

Camping and fishing along the Situk River is a great way to experience this incredible region.

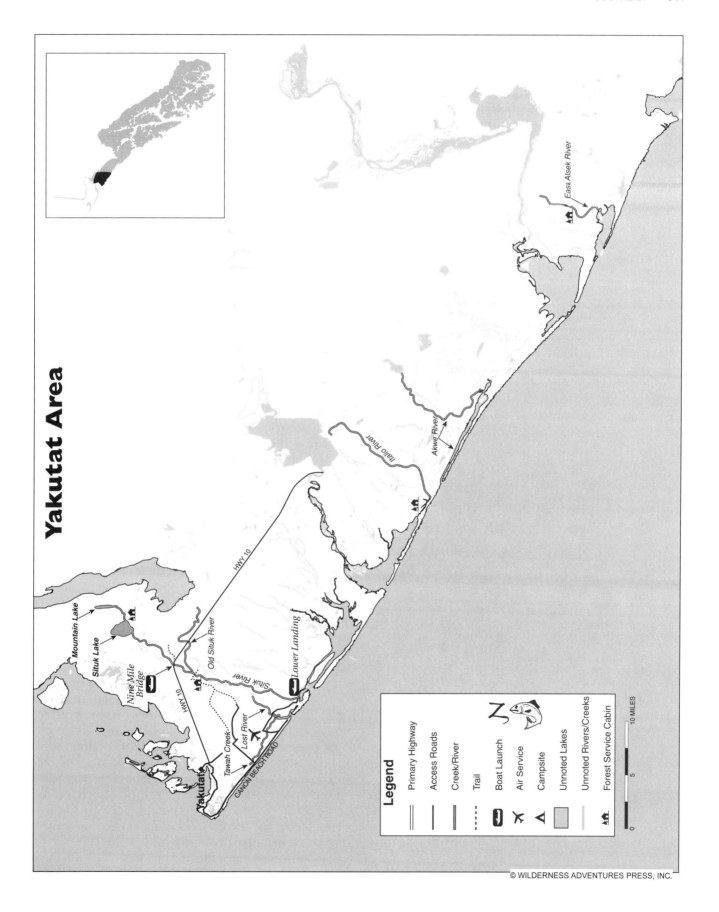

Yakutat Area

East Alsek River

Akwe River

Italio River

HWY 10

Mountain Lake

Situk Lake

Nine Mile Bridge

Old Situk River

HWY 10

Lower Landing

Situk River

Tawah Creek

Lost River

CANON BEACH ROAD

Yakutat

Legend

Primary Highway	
Access Roads	
Creek/River	
Trail	
Boat Launch	
Air Service	
Campsite	
Unnoted Lakes	
Unnoted Rivers/Creeks	
Forest Service Cabin	

N

0   5   10 MILES

out or try their luck from the bank. Nearly 4.5 miles of trail follow the river upstream and 3.5 miles of trail lead downstream from the Nine Mile Bridge. There are also a dozen or so unimproved campsites near the bridge, making it easy to settle in and enjoy your stay.

The take-out point for driftboaters, known as the Lower Landing, also offers excellent bank fishing. Well-maintained Forest Service trails skirt long sections of river, allowing anglers enough bank access to keep them busy for weeks. In fact, the first time I floated the Situk in a driftboat, it was so low that we opted to bank fish on our remaining days. We did well wade fishing up and downstream from the Nine Mile Bridge, but the fishing was especially good in the waters above the Lower Landing.

To reach the Lower Landing, turn on the gravel road just northwest of the airport, at the white sign that reads "To Situk Lower Landing." Continue on the gravel road until you reach Strawberry Point Road, then turn right and continue to the boat ramp. Just up from the ramp is an outhouse and plenty of parking. If you park here and walk upstream you'll find some of the best bank fishing on the entire river and far fewer people.

A great trail allows anglers to travel a couple of miles upstream, past the weir. Search for a good hole where fish are holding. Once you locate such a place, consider spending the entire day there. Because this stretch of river

Scott Haugen with a 17-pound Situk River steelhead. The Situk is to steelhead what the Kenai River is to king salmon.

is so near the ocean, fish will usually pull into holes and pockets and hold, acclimating to their new freshwater environment. Often, fresh fish can be observed moving into these holes all day long, which is why the precious spots are prized by local anglers, and why you might see a group of anglers staking out a hole for an entire day, if not longer.

As you travel the riverbanks, you'll see many shallow sections where fish push on through, as well as deep, dead-water holes in which steelhead suspend. There will also be prime holding slots along cutbanks and above and below riffles. Avoid wasting time targeting suspended fish; though it's inviting to try to coax a 25-pound steelhead finning 10 feet in front of you into biting, I've yet to see a suspended steelhead bite anywhere in the world, including on the Situk. Instead, concentrate efforts on prime holding waters, which usually include small riffles that break up the surface, allowing steelhead plenty of protection from direct sunlight and offering oxygenated water. Fish holding within 12 inches of the bottom will provide the most action.

When it comes to actually working water on this river, be it for steelhead or all five salmon species, there's one obstacle that will test your patience and your gear—downed trees. There's no way to prepare a traveling angler for the number of downed trees cluttering the banks of this stream. Because the Situk sits within a national park, the idea is to keep it as natural as possible, and trust me, this can be very frustrating when it comes to trying to catch big fish. When I took my first 14-mile driftboat float, I estimated that somewhere around 80 percent of the stretch was laden with trees. Due to excessive bank erosion, massive spruce trees are constantly being undercut and toppled into the river.

A few guides on the Situk have special permits that allow them to operate from a sled boat. These guys are often scorned by other anglers, yet they sometimes keep the river fishable. The day prior to my floating the river, three trees blocked the drift. Were it not for the jet boats cutting and hauling cut sections of these trees, no driftboat would have made it downstream.

Navigation aside, fishing amid all the downed trees can be a logistical nightmare. Because the top—if not the entire tree—is lying in the river, a back current is created on the downstream side. This means fish will congregate behind these trees, in a position that's virtually impossible to reach with any fishing gear. Even more frustrating, once you do reach a big fish behind these hideouts, they spool you into the trees before you know what's going on. I broke off three fish in the 20-pound range on one trip. Each one ran me into the trees, wrapping the line around limbs and snapping it.

In low water years, the tree factor can be even more

frustrating. In the spring of 2003 a group of friends and I traveled to the Situk for spring steelhead. It was the lowest the river had been in recent history. The 14-mile float in the driftboat took 15 hours. There were so many downed trees to negotiate, and so many shallow sections to yard the boat over, we devoted only around two hours to fishing. The next four days were spent fishing from the bank, and we did very well considering the low water.

When the water is running at an ideal level, the drift can be much more angler-friendly. Because it's such a long drift, however, I'd highly advise taking two days to make the run. You can either camp along the river on any of a number of exposed gravel bars or reserve one of two Forest Service cabins. When conditions are right there is good fishing along most of the 14-mile drift, and the last thing you want is to feel pushed for time.

Be sure to take a wide assortment of gear when fishing the river from a boat, no matter what species you pursue. There will be plenty of opportunities for flyfishers and anglers running plugs and jigs or tossing lures. However, in low water years, the angling approach can be very limited. For instance, on that 2003 trip, the river was so low and clear that the only setup that worked was a Glo-Bug presented beneath a 9-foot leader attached to a floating line. A few split shot kept the patterns tight to the bottom and in the steelhead's line of sight.

When it comes to flyfishing on this river, many anglers opt for a 20- to 30-pound mainline rather than using floating lines, sink-tip lines, or an intermediate Slime Line. The reason is because once you hook a big fish, it often has you into the backing before you can control it. It's not uncommon to have a monster steelhead spool you and wrap your fly line in the tangled trees, forcing you to snap the line somewhere in your backing. I've talked with experienced anglers who've lost multiple fly lines on a single trip here, and they are firm believers in going with a heavy monofilament or copolymer mainline. The choice is yours, of course, but when I go to the Situk I'm equipped with reels spooled with floating, sink-tip, and copolymer lines. Casting a monofilament mainline is not a problem because the stream is so choked in brush that roll casting is pretty much the rule.

Leaders are another issue you need to pay attention to here. I've talked with numerous anglers who've fished this river when it was low and clear, and because the fish were leader-shy, the anglers dropped to 8- and even 6-pound test lines. Such leaders are fine under the right conditions, but working amid fallen trees and beneath overhanging and partially submerged alders is not the place. Though you're more likely to latch onto a monster fish with such a light leader, the chances of landing it are nearly zero. I'd rather go heavy and have a chance to actu-

ally land the fish. This is where fluorocarbon leaders, with a refraction index nearly identical to water, come in.

I've fished beside many anglers who snapped off fish on light leaders, while I've been able to put 15-pound fluorocarbon to use landing fish that might otherwise get away. Granted, even this line won't stand up to being wrapped around trees, but it does allow you to put more pressure on the fish as soon as it's hooked. I've had the best luck with P-Line's fluorocarbon leader. Its strong, durable design is also quite abrasion resistant, outperforming everything else I've used. Given the pressure this river receives, trying something different, like a fluorocarbon leader, may be the ticket to success.

Though the Situk is one of the most heavily fished rivers in Alaska, if it still has one secret it would be the estuary fishing. This holds true for both steelhead and salmon. and if you're looking to escape the crowds, this is about your only hope. I have one person to thank for pointing me in the direction of the estuary fishing, and that's Martha Donohue, owner of Glacier Bear Lodge. "Tonight would be a great tide to hit the flats," Martha told me on my first night on the Situk. Reluctant to pass up a river opportunity for an unfamiliar estuarine experience, I opted to hit the upper river instead. That night Martha gave me a report of a few anglers who got into high numbers of steelhead at the mouth, and my buddies and I decided to give it a shot the following night.

Of all the steelhead fishing I've been fortunate enough to experience in my life, fishing the Situk estuary has been the most special. Perhaps it's because it was something new; maybe it's because sight fishing for sizzling steelhead in a foot of moving water, fresh from the ocean, made for a fight unlike any other.

To reach the estuary, go to the Lower Ramp. About 100 yards up from the ramp, just as it comes into view, an unmarked gravel road takes off to the right. Follow this road all the way to the scattered cabins and piles of driftwood along the shoreline. Locals use these cabins during the red salmon migration; they spend several days fishing and putting up meat for the winter.

Drive to the far south end, winding through the fish-camp cabins. Park up high, near the cabins, avoiding the tidal zone where the sand is deceptively soft. From here you can see the main river channel meandering down from the Lower Ramp. Fish the eastern and southern parts of the channel, which lies on the far side of the river. (It will be easy to spot at low tide.)

Though the water you'll be fishing is only 12 to 18 inches deep, chest waders are recommended as the wading can be muddy in places. The first time I hit the estuary was on an outgoing tide, through the low slack, and during the first hour of an incoming tide. It was amazing to sit there and watch the water level drop, then observe a surge of fish making their way upstream. We wouldn't wet a line until a wake of fish began moving against the tide, right in front of our feet. To see a wall of water stretching across the channel—the result of migrating steelhead making their way upstream—is a sight to behold, especially in the evening when the sun is setting over your shoulder, painting the snowcapped Saint Elias Mountains on the opposite horizon with a pastel of pink hues.

Anglers can spread out and wade to where the fish are moving. The anticipation is unlike anything in the steelheading world. You have only one crack at placing a cast on the nose of the fast-moving fish. A poor cast will spook the fish, often sending them in every direction, even back downstream.

We had our best luck casting and stripping flashy saltwater patterns, like 4-inch shrimp in either red or orange. Stripped leeches were also productive, and we did manage to nab a few fish on Glo-Bugs.

The second night we fished the estuary, Martha suggested we take our dinner down there, cook it on an open fire, and watch for the fish to move upstream. The experience couldn't have been more fulfilling. As we sat cooking halibut steaks on hot coals—from fish we'd caught in the ocean earlier that day—we watched as waves of steelhead made their way around the black sand point toward our location. We couldn't finish chewing the last bite before grabbing our rods and dashing into the river. Though the fish can be tough to coax into biting, once you hook one of these wild fighters, you'll soon realize that it's the quality of the fish not the quantity that makes the experience so special.

In addition to steelhead in the spring and fall, salmon can be taken this way in the estuary. Spey rods can be useful during high tides when you'll be casting over wide expanses of water to reach the main channel.

While the Situk hosts Alaska's strongest spring steelhead run, with annual returns ranging from 5,000 to 9,000 fish in good years, it hasn't always been this way. In the late 1980s and into the early 1990s, commercial fishing nets claimed a great many Situk steelhead. Habitat loss due to logging, as well as overharvest by sportsmen, also played a roll in declining steelhead numbers. However, strict regulations, both in the river and on commercial fishermen, have resulted in increased returns. Once again the Situk is regarded as one of the world's premier steelhead fishing streams.

Spring steelhead enter the river from March through June, with late April and early May traditionally the best times to be on the river. The fall run of steelhead starts in August and lasts well into December. As long as the area doesn't receive too much rainfall, the fall fishing can be outstanding from late October through November.

Dolly Varden and resident rainbow trout are also present in the Situk. Late summer and early fall offer the best trout and Dolly fishing, as the fish are feasting on a rich supply of salmon eggs rolling along the bottom of the river. The spring can be a good time to catch out-migrating Dollys, as they follow salmon smolt out to sea. Deep pools make the most productive Dolly holes.

Spring chinook are also in the river during late spring. The king run is very popular among local anglers. About 4,000 large fish—in the 25- to 35-pound class, with some going 55 pounds—make the run. The king season usually kicks off around June 15, winding down around July 10. The flyfishing for these kings can be very good, as no baits or artificial scents are allowed on the river.

Sockeye salmon will make their way into the river at roughly the same time as the kings. The Situk receives 40,000 to 60,000 sockeyes each year, with an annual sport angler harvest of 5,000 to 10,000 fish.

When it comes to fall fishing, coho take center stage. Coho runs in the Situk number about 40,000, which makes targeting the fall run of steelhead virtually impossible. Coho start showing up around the end of August, and the river is clogged into early October. While the fall fishing for steelhead typically commences around the middle of October, some years the river may freeze right on through the month of April, making fishing impossible. During mild winters, however, you can fish every week of the year.

While only a few chum salmon go up the Situk, there's no shortage of pink salmon. Between two hundred thousand and one million pinks enter the river from the middle of July and into August. Though these fish are on an even/odd year cycle, they show up in the river each summer, yet receive little pressure.

Some Atlantic salmon have even been caught by sport anglers in the Situk. Keep an eye out for these fish and promptly report them to local ADF&G agents. These salmon have escaped from fish farms and are not suited for life in this or any other river in Southeast Alaska.

Stream Facts: Situk River

Seasons

- All general seasons for Southeast Alaska freshwater streams and all species, as stated in the "Sport Fishing Regulations," apply to the Situk River.

Special Regulations

- Only unbaited artificial lures may be used year-round.

- From its mouth upstream to the railroad bridge ruins, the fishing is open from October 15 to June 14, though senior citizens (60 years or older) can fish in this portion of the river year-round.

- Upstream from the Middle Situk airstrip, the king salmon season runs September 1 to June 30.

- Upstream from ADF&G markers located 2 miles upstream from the Nine Mile Bridge on the Situk River to ADF&G markers 2 miles downstream from Situk Lake, is closed to fishing April 15 to May 15.

Fish

- Steelhead, king, silver, red, pink, and chum salmon, rainbow trout, Dolly Varden

River Characteristics

- Typically slow, clear water unless hampered by rainfall. The spring thaw and fall rains can force this river above its banks, with late spring, summer, and early fall offering the most ideal fishing conditions. The number of fallen trees greatly impedes the water that can be fished and dramatically limits bank access.

Fishing Access

- Nine Mile Bridge is the only place to launch a boat and offers the most popular bank fishing on the entire river. It can be reached by driving 9 miles out Forest Highway 10. The drift in a riverboat covers nearly 14 miles. Bank access is also available at the Lower Landing and near the mouth of the river. Along much of the river, Forest Service trails allow anglers to reach prime fishing holes.

Maps

- Check with local lodges upon arrival.

MOUNTING YOUR CATCH

More than any other section of the state, Southeast Alaska is home to catch-and-release fishing for trophy steelhead. As conservationists and sportsmen, it's our duty to perpetuate this species by quickly landing and releasing these wild fish in a proper manner. As with king salmon in the Kenai and trout in Bristol Bay, the steelhead of Southeast can be caught and released yet still preserved in the form of a quality trophy for the den. I have several fish species from Alaska gracing the walls of my trophy room, and nearly all were released.

To get an accurate graphite reproduction of a released fish, follow these three steps. Take a quick measurement of the fish's overall length by placing a tape alongside it while it's still in the water. Next, take a girth measurement by placing a flexible tape around the fish, gently snugging it across the front edge of the dorsal fin and the widest part of the belly. Don't pull the tape too tight, you don't want the soft belly to become misshapen, as this will throw off the proportions of your mount. The final step is to snap a few close-up photos of the fish. The objective is to capture spotting patterns and overall coloration. And if there are any unique qualities you want preserved, such as particular spotting or striping, be sure to get photos of it.

My fish taxidermist, Matt Yernatich of Artistic Anglers Taxidermy in Minnesota (218-721-4900), advises trying to get photos of the head and overall color of the fish. He notes that coloration can vary among individual fish and that capturing the colors with photos is essential for a quality customized job. But if for some reason photos are not available, Artistic Anglers and other expert fish taxidermists can match a fish pretty closely with a verbal description.

When taking photos, get as close to the fish as possible without blurring the image. Photos snapped from too far away may not capture the details necessary to create an accurate mount. The better your documentation, the better the quality of the mount.

Submitting the photos and two measurements to a taxidermist is the next step. Artistic Anglers has mounted all of my fish from Mexico to Alaska. They've kept their prices down to $10 an inch for several years, and the quality of work they do is tough to beat; just ask Cabela's, for whom Artistic Anglers has mounted numerous showroom fish in recent years.

Graphite replicas are economical and their durability lasts a lifetime, preserving memories like nothing else can. In addition, the finished product looks incredibly lifelike, as if the fish was just pulled from the river. And best of all, that amazing fish had a chance to continue its journey.

Lost River and Tawah Creek

The Lost River and one of its tributaries, Tawah Creek, offer very good angling for silver salmon. Situated between the Situk River and the town of Yakutat, the Lost River flows beneath the highway on its way to the sea. While steelhead enter the Lost River, there are too few to spend time fishing for them. The fall run of coho is the primary attraction, starting in late August and continuing through mid-October.

The Lost River can be fished from a boat or the bank. You can slide a boat with a small outboard over the bank at the bridge and motor your way to good fishing downstream.

The mouth of the Lost River changes position from year to year, and you can sometimes launch a small craft at this site. Canoes are a good way to go here, as you're never really certain how far you'll have to carry the boat. If you're planning to fish here from a boat, it's a good idea to phone the ADF&G office (907-784-3222) ahead of time to find out river levels and water conditions.

Don Newman traveled to Yakutat to catch this beautiful steelhead on a Glo-Bug.

The Lost River passes beneath Lost River Road about 6 miles from the airport. It's a slow, meandering stream that can be more than 100 feet across in places, though only 5 to 6 feet deep. The low gradient makes for easy wade fishing and you can cover a lot of ground. A good trail parallels the river to the mouth, offering numerous fishing opportunities. It's especially effective to time your arrival to hit the changing tides, when fishing at the mouth can be outstanding.

Tawah Creek flows along the coast for 5 miles before feeding into the Lost River. The creek can be reached off Canon Beach Road, and what the locals refer to as the "Broken Bridge," or by turning off the Lost River Road some 2 miles before the Lost River Bridge. These are the two best access points and they'll get you to the best fishing, much of it right along the roadside. A small trail off the left side of the road goes all the way to the confluence of the Lost River and Tawah Creek. The action at this spot can be nonstop when the fish are moving in.

Tawah Creek is about half the size of Lost Creek, averaging about 2 to 3 feet deep and about 70 feet across. This makes for safe and easy wading. Work your way along the cutbanks, hitting the deeper slots that silvers like.

You'll see three more rivers on maps of this region, but they aren't worth fishing. The Antlen River is extremely brushy, making for frustrating and dangerous bank angling. It's too small to float, and though the place where it feeds into the Ahrnklin River is good for silvers, it's not worth the effort it takes to get there.

Similarly, the Ahrnklin River, though it crosses Forest Highway 10, is even more problematic. It's a glacial-colored stream with a high gradient, making it tough to negotiate. Don't attempt drifting this river unless you're with a professional guide or unless you're very experienced in whitewater boating. Downed trees along this river make for tough boating and limited bank fishing. It's about twice the size of the Situk, and though it receives runs of red and silver salmon and some steelhead, along with Dolly Varden, the fishing doesn't warrant spending time here.

The Dangerous River is located at the end of Forest Highway 10, and it's the last road-accessible stream in the Yakutat area. Though this river receives all five Pacific salmon species, it's glacial character makes for tough fishing. As it's also closed to the use of bait, virtually nobody fishes it.

Italio River

A 15- to 20-minute bushplane flight down the coast from Yakutat brings you to a popular stream called the Italio River. Here, anglers have the luxury of pitching their own camp or hiring a guide who has a camp already in place.

Though the Italio gets a small run of steelhead from time to time, don't depend on these fish to provide fast action. Instead, target coho salmon and Dolly Varden. When flying to the river, you'll pass over the Old Italio River, which has a series of potholes bordering the beach. When flying over these potholes, search for schools of silver salmon. If the fish are in, have the pilot land the plane and start fishing right there.

Since changing its course in the mild-1980s, the Middle Italio River runs east of the main channel. The new tributary, known as the New Italio River, also changed course at this time and instead of flowing to the west and joining the Middle Italio, it shifted east and now empties into the mouth of the Akwe River.

Due to these shifting flows, the Forest Service cabin is now situated three-quarters of a mile from the river and about two miles from the mouth of the Akwe River. If you want to reserve this cabin, check to see where the river channel is currently located or if the cabin has been relocated near the river. If the cabin is still too far from the river, you may just want to pitch a tent. Due to these recent geographic changes, be aware that the Italio may not be accurately portrayed on maps.

The Italio is a clear stream that averages about 50 feet across and 2 to 3 feet deep in most places. It generally flows crystal-clear, though it's occasionally stained by muskeg vegetation. The gentle nature of this stream, and the fact that few people come here, make it appealing for anglers eager for some solitude.

Akwe River

The Akwe River drains into the Italio right near the ocean. After taking a drastic turn from the uplands from which it flows, the Akwe parallels the coast for 5 miles before feeding into the Italio. The best place to fish is at the river's mouth, where cutthroat trout, a few resident rainbows, and king and sockeye salmon can be pursued. You'll find some of the best cutthroat fishing in the area on this river, with fishing especially productive at the 5-mile bend, where clear tributaries flow into the Akwe.

The Akwe is a glacial-colored river, running milky during the prime summer fishing months, so fly anglers need to pick their spots carefully. The clearer the water you can target, the greater the chances of fish finding your presentation. At its confluence with the Italio, the water is swirling and a good deal of the sediment is filtered out, which makes this one of the best places to fish on the entire river.

There are a few outfitters working this river, or you can take a tent and go it alone. The best place to camp is near the mouth, on the Italio side of the river. Set up in the brush to escape the wind, which can be relentless along this section of coastline. However, be sure to have bear spray handy and keep a clean camp, for there are a good number of brown bears roaming this area.

Most anglers get dropped off at the mouth and fish from a base camp there or head 5 miles upstream to the big bend. When little rain has hampered the area the Akwe is an easy river to get around, giving anglers plenty of casting opportunities from shore. It's easy to fish your way from the mouth up to the big bend or vice versa.

East Alsek River

One of the most productive king salmon streams in the Yakutat area is the East Alsek River. Unfortunately, it's quite expensive to get there by chartered plane, so few people experience the thrill of fishing this river.

Towards the end of May and into the first three weeks of June, the king salmon fishing in the East Alsek is nothing short of phenomenal. All of the fishing is done at the mouth of the river, about 300 yards from the surf. As soon as you hook these hot chinook, they go screaming right back out to sea. And as they weigh in at 20 to 45 pounds, they're a handful.

The kings pull into the mouth of the river and stage there to ripen up for spawning when the water registers 50 degrees this time of year. The main stem of the Alsek is too cold, running 38 to 40 degrees, which explains why the fish hold in the mouth of the East Alsek. Toward the middle of June, this spot can be kegged with fish, offering all the action an angler could dream of.

A run of sockeye salmon also makes its way into the river, but for some reason they are tough to make bite.

A 45-minute flight from Yakutat will put you at the mouth of the East Alsek River, and if a group of anglers pitches in they might be able to swing the cost.

YAKUTAT

Population: 680
Alaska Area Code: 907
Zip Code: 99689

TOURIST INFORMATION

Alaska Department of Fish and Game, Sport Fishing Division, P.O. Box 49; 784-3222

National Park Service Visitor Center, Yakutat District Office, P.O. Box 137; 748-3295

Yakutat Chamber of Commerce, P.O. Box 234; 1-888-925-8828

U.S. Forest Service Cabin Information, Yakutat Ranger District, P.O. Box 327; 784-3359

GUIDE SERVICES

Glacier Bear Lodge, 1-866-425-6343;
 www.glaciarbearlodge.com
Leonard's Landing, 1-877-925-3474;
 www.leonardslanding.com
Yakutat Lodge, 784-3232; www.yakutatlodge.com

FLY-IN CHARTERS

Alsek Air Taxi's, P.O. Box 326; 784-3831
Yakutat Coastal Air; 784-3232; www.yakutatlodge.com

TACKLE SHOPS

Leonard's Landing, 1-877-925-3474;
 www.leonardslanding.com
Middle Of Nowhere, 784-3155
Yakutat Hardware Store, 784-3203
Yakutat Lodge, 784-3232; www.yakutatlodge.com
Yakutat Marine Store, 784-3386

ACCOMMODATIONS

Blue Heron Inn Bed & Breakfast, P.O. Box 254; 784-3603
Copperhouse Bed & Breakfast, 784-3598
Glacier Bear Lodge, 1-866-425-6343;
 www.glaciarbearlodge.com
Leonard's Landing, 1-877-925-3474;
 www.leonardslanding.com
Moose Mansion Birds & Breakfast, 784-3600
Red Roof B&B, 784-3131
Shirley's Bed & Breakfast, P.O. Box 478; 784-3650
The Moorings Lodge, 1-888-551-2836
Yakutat Lodge, 784-3232; www.yakutatlodge.com

RESTAURANTS

Leonard's Landing Restaurant, P.O. Box 282; 784-3592
Ret's Place, 784-3440
Yakutat Burger Barn, 784-3037

FISH PROCESSING

Ravens Table, 784-3497

BOAT RENTALS

Glacier Bear Lodge, 1-866-425-6343;
 www.glaciarbearlodge.com
Leonard's Landing, 1-877-925-3474;
 www.leonardslanding.com
Situk Leasing, 784-3316
Yakutat Lodge, 784-3232; www.yakutatlodge.com

RENTAL CARS

Situk Leasing, 784-3316
Yakutat Auto Leasing, 784-3698

AIR SERVICES

Alaska Airlines, 1-800-426-0333; www.alaskaair.com
ALSEK Air Taxis, P.O. Box 326; 784-3831

MEDICAL

Yakutat Community Health Center, 784-3275

THE ALASKA MARINE HIGHWAY

(See Southeast Overview Map)

Anglers can access Southeast Alaska by air or sea. Air travelers usually have a single city as their destination. They can then fish around the city or hire an air taxi to get them to more remote waters. Those on a tight schedule often opt to stay at a fishing lodge.

But if time is on your side, and you want to see what the Inside Passage is all about, consider taking the Alaska state ferry. The Alaska ferry begins as far south as Bellingham, Washington, and runs north to the terminus port in Skagway. While the majority of travelers hop on the ferry at points south and head north, if you want to avoid the crowds, think about driving or flying to Skagway or Haines, and then catching the ferry on its trip south when it's less occupied.

Traveling the Alaska Marine Highway is the best way to see what this unique part of the state has to offer. And traversing the Inside Passage is safe and easy, as numerous islands and fjords protect against rough seas.

Ferries in British Columbia also serve the Inside Passage. These take passengers and their vehicles from Port Hardy on the north end of Vancouver Island to Prince Rupert at the west end of the Yellowhead Highway. Prince Rupert serves as the southern port for three Alaska state ferries and nearly four-dozen BC ferries.

Most passengers travel in only one direction on the Alaska Marine Highway, either north or south. You can board a ferry at a southern port, travel north to Haines or Skagway, then get on the road system, or vice versa.

The Marine Highway offers travelers a chance to do some whale watching.

Depending on your road route and overall travel plans, you can cut anywhere from 700 to more than 1,500 miles of highway travel by taking the ferry.

The summer schedule for the Alaska state ferry typically runs from May 1 through September 30. Travelers should note that the state reserves the right to cancel or revise schedules and rates at any time and takes no responsibility for any delays or expenses incurred through such changes. At the time of this writing, nine vessels served the Southeast Alaska ferry system. Ships range in size from those able to carry 190 passengers and 28 standard vehicles to ones that accommodate 1,000 passengers and 180 vehicles.

Keep in mind that these are Marine Highway vessels not elaborate cruise ships. You won't find swimming pools, weight rooms, casinos, or room service. But you will be offered access to some of Alaska's most breathtaking scenery, looked after by top-notch crews, and delivered to the doorstep of world-class fishing, and all for a fraction of the cost you'd pay on a cruise ship.

The atmosphere on board a ferry is carefree and casual. Many people who travel the ferry keep coming back because of the vacation-like feeling it instills. Due to the time between dockings, travelers are forced to sit back and enjoy the journey.

For information on Southeast ferry schedules, passenger, vehicle, and cabin rates, contact the main office of the Alaska Marine Highway System at 6858 Glacier Highway, Juneau, AK 99801-7909 or call them toll-free at 1-800-642-0066. They also maintain a very detailed website at www.alaska.gov/ferry that allows easy access to the latest scheduling changes and other pertinent information.

The table below shows approximate run times between the major Southeast Alaska hub cities. Travelers seeking to explore other islands and smaller towns and villages can also do so by way of the ferry system.

Inside Passage Route Times

Bellingham to Ketchikan	37 hours
Prince Rupert to Ketchikan	6 hours
Ketchikan to Wrangell	6 hours
Wrangell to Petersburg	3 hours
Petersburg to Juneau	8 hours
Petersburg to Sitka	11 hours
Sitka to Juneau	8.75 hours
Juneau to Haines	4.5 hours
Haines to Skagway	1 hour

Well-maintained Forest Service trails grant increased fishing opportunities throughout much of Southeast Alaska.

U.S. FOREST SERVICE CABINS

There are currently over 150 recreational cabins available for public use within the Tongass National Forest, which is the largest national forest in the country. These rustic cabins offer a unique and comfortable experience for anglers and are a great value in comparison to other alternatives. Ranging from $25 to $45 per night, the cost per night is negligible if you share the cabin with a small group.

The Forest Service cabins are primarily accessible by floatplane, helicopter, and boat, though some are reached by way of roads and hiking trails. Traditionally, between the dates of April 1 and September 30, cabin use is limited to seven consecutive days per party. Between October 1 and March 31, 10 consecutive days of use are the norm. Note that a few select cabins do have a limitation of less than seven nights.

Reservations for these cabins are granted on a first-come, first-serve basis and are accepted up to 180 days prior to the intended date of use. Guides and outfitters cannot reserve cabins for commercial operations, and anyone 18 years of age or older is allowed to reserve a cabin.

Cabins come equipped with bunks, tables, benches, wood or oil-burning stoves, and pit toilets. Anglers need to supply their own cooking and bedding items. In cabins with wood stoves, an ax or splitting maul is furnished, but it's a wise idea to bring your own small ax, in case the cabin's tool has disappeared.

If you're staying in a cabin with an oil-burning stove, you'll need to supply your own oil. Use #1 stove oil. Five to 10 gallons of diesel oil will usually last seven days, though this can vary depending on weather conditions at the time of your stay. For cooking purposes, it's advised to bring along a small camping stove.

Most of the cabins located on lakes come with a skiff and oars. You'll need to bring your own life vests and motors (some areas may prohibit the use of motors), and in some lakes near populated areas it's a good idea to bring a spare set of oars, as they have a tendency to disappear.

Though the cabins were built for public use, visitors are still on their own when it comes to knowing how to take care of themselves. Be prepared to deal with anything from bears to bugs to broken legs to being weathered in. Every season a few anglers get stranded for extra days because bad weather halts all travel. Always bring a little extra food.

First-aid kits, waterproof matches, bear repellent, bug spray, compass or GPS, maps, quality raingear and boots should top the list of essential items. The more prepared you are for a remote, wilderness adventure, the more positive the overall experience will be.

To make cabin reservations, call the United States Forest Service (USFS) at 1-800-444-6777 or log on to www.reserveusa.com. To learn more about individual cabins log on to www.fs.fed.us/r10/tongass.

The listings below provide general information for Forest Service cabins based on the hub city fisheries detailed throughout this chapter. These are the cabins most likely to be visited by traveling anglers.

Ketchikan Cabins

Anchor Pass: 50 air miles north of Ketchikan; accessible by floatplane or boat; wood stove, mooring buoy; king salmon in Unuk River, salmon, halibut, shrimp, and red snapper in area.

Blind Pass: 40 air miles north of Ketchikan; accessible by floatplane or boat; wood stove, mooring buoy; king salmon in Unuk river, salmon, halibut, red snapper, shrimp, in area, trout in lake upstream.

Fish Creek: 20 air miles east of Ketchikan; accessible by floatplane or boat; oil stove; salmon, steelhead, trout in Fish Creek, halibut, salmon, and crab in area.

Heckman Lake: 15 air miles north of Ketchikan; accessible by floatplane or 6-mile trail from Naha Bay; steelhead, salmon, trout and Dolly Varden in Naha River.

Helm Creek: 24 air miles northwest of Ketchikan; accessible by floatplane or boat; wood stove, mooring buoy; trout and Dolly Varden in Helm Lake, salmon, red snapper, halibut, and crab in area.

Jordan Lake: 15 air miles north of Ketchikan; accessible by trail only; wood stove, skiff; steelhead, salmon, trout, and Dolly Varden.

McDonald Lake: 50 air miles north of Ketchikan; accessible by floatplane or 1.5-mile trail from Yes Bay; wood stove, skiff; steelhead and salmon in Wolverine Creek and trout and Dolly Varden in lake.

Patching Lake: 20 air miles north of Ketchikan; accessible by floatplane; wood stove, skiff; cutthroat trout.

Plenty Cutthroat-Orchard Lake: 35 air miles north of Ketchikan; accessible by floatplane or boat or 1-mile trail from Shrimp Bay; oil stove, skiff; cutthroat trout and kokanee.

Rainbow Lake: 27 air miles northwest of Ketchikan; accessible by floatplane; wood stove; rainbow trout.

Reflection Lake: 50 air miles north of Ketchikan; accessible by floatplane or boat or 2-mile hike from Short Bay; wood stove, skiff; salmon and steelhead in Short Creek, trout and Dolly Varden in lake.

Prince of Wales Island Cabins

Barnes Lake: 70 air miles northwest of Ketchikan; accessible by floatplane or boat; wood stove, skiff; silver salmon.

Black Bear Lake: 50 air miles west of Ketchikan; accessible by floatplane; wood stove, skiff; rainbow trout.

Control Lake: accessible by car and small boat; wood stove, skiff; cutthroat, Dolly Varden, and silver salmon.

Essowah Lake: 65 air miles southwest of Ketchikan; accessible by floatplane; wood stove, skiff; cutthroat, Dolly Varden, steelhead and four salmon species.

Honker Lake: 54 air miles northwest of Ketchikan; accessible by floatplane or canoe; wood stove and skiff; cutthroat, rainbow trout, Dolly Varden, sockeye, and silver salmon.

Karta Lake: 34 air miles northwest of Ketchikan; accessible by floatplane or boat and 1.5-mile trail from Karta Bay; oil stove; winter and spring steelhead, cutthroat and rainbow trout, Dolly Varden, and four salmon species.

Karta River: 34 air miles northwest of Ketchikan; accessible by floatplane or boat; oil stove; winter and spring steelhead, cutthroat and rainbow trout, Dolly Varden, and four salmon species.

Red Bay Lake: 84 air miles northwest of Ketchikan; accessible by floatplane; wood stove, skiff; steelhead, cutthroat and rainbow trout, Dolly Varden, and four salmon species.

Salmon Bay Lake: 84 air miles northwest of Ketchikan; accessible by floatplane or trail from Salmon Bay;

wood stove, skiff; cutthroat, Dolly Varden, steelhead, and four salmon species.

Salmon Lake: 36 air miles west of Ketchikan; accessible by floatplane or 5-mile trail from Karta Bay; wood stove; cutthroat and rainbow trout, Dolly Varden, and three salmon species.

Sarkar Lake: 76 air miles northwest of Ketchikan; accessible by floatplane or road and canoe or boat; wood stove, skiff; cutthroat and rainbow trout, Dolly Varden, and four salmon species.

Shipley Bay: 85 air miles northwest of Ketchikan; accessible by floatplane or boat; wood stove, skiff; cutthroat and rainbow trout, Dolly Varden, steelhead, and three salmon species in stream and lake.

Stanley Creek: 68 air miles northwest of Ketchikan; accessible by floatplane, boat or road and trail; propane heater; cutthroat and rainbow trout, Dolly Varden, and four salmon species.

Sweetwater Lake: 63 air miles northwest of Ketchikan; accessible by floatplane or road and trail; wood stove; trout and silver salmon.

Petersburg Cabins

Beecher Pass: 17 air miles south of Petersburg; wood stove; salmon and halibut in Duncan Canal.

Big John Bay: 28 air miles west of Petersburg; oil stove; trout, pink and silver salmon in Hamilton and Big John Creeks.

Breiland Slough: 15 air miles southwest of Petersburg; oil stove; silver salmon, crab, and shrimp.

Cascade Creek: 16 air miles north of Petersburg; oil heater, wood stove, skiff; steelhead and silver salmon.

Castle River: 16 air miles southwest of Petersburg; wood stove, skiff; steelhead, silver and trout.

DeBoer Lake: 20 air miles north of Petersburg; oil stove, skiff; rainbow trout.

Devil's Elbow: 40 air miles west of Petersburg; oil stove; silver salmon.

Harvey Lake: 18 air miles south of Petersburg; wood stove, skiff; cutthroat in lake and silvers near the mouth of Harvey Creek.

Kadake Bay: 39 air miles west of Petersburg; oil heater, wood stove; steelhead, cutthroat, Dolly Varden, silver and pink salmon in Kadake Creek.

Kah Sheets Bay: 24 air miles southwest of Petersburg; oil heater, wood stove; steelhead, trout and three salmon species.

Kah Sheets Lake: 22 air miles southwest of Petersburg; oil stove, skiff; steelhead, cutthroat, Dolly Varden, and three salmon species in lake and stream.

Petersburg Lake: 9 air miles northwest of Petersburg; oil heater, wood stove, skiff; steelhead, cutthroat, silver and sockeye salmon.

Portage Bay: 15 air miles northwest of Petersburg; oil stove; steelhead, trout, silver and pink salmon in Portage Creek, halibut in Portage Bay.

Salt Chuck East: 15 air miles northwest of Petersburg; wood stove, skiff; steelhead and silver salmon.

Spurt Cove: 16 air miles north of Petersburg; oil heater, wood stove; trout in beaver ponds, halibut and king salmon near the cove.

Swan Lake: 18 air miles north of Petersburg; oil stove, skiff; rainbow trout.

Towers Arm: 16 air miles west of Petersburg; wood stove; steelhead and silver salmon.

Wrangell Cabins

Anan Bay: 31 miles southeast of Wrangell; accessible by boat or floatplane; oil stove, outdoor grill, mooring buoy; cutthroat, Dolly Varden, and pink salmon.

Anna Lake: 31 air miles southeast of Wrangell; accessible by floatplane; oil stove, skiff; steelhead, cutthroat, silver and pink salmon.

Berg Bay: 22 miles southeast of Wrangell; accessible by boat or floatplane; oil stove, outdoor grill; steelhead, crab, and three salmon species.

Eagle Lake: 44 air miles south of Wrangell; accessible by floatplane; wood stove, skiff; cutthroat trout.

Frosty Bay: 36 miles south of Wrangell; accessible by boat or floatplane; oil stove; king, pink, and silver salmon, crab and halibut in salt water.

Harding River: 31 air miles southeast of Wrangell; accessible by boat or floatplane; oil stove, mooring buoy; silver and chum salmon in Harding and Eagle Rivers, crabbing in Bradfield Canal.

Marten Lake: 25 air miles southeast of Wrangell; accessible by floatplane; wood stove, skiff; cutthroat and Dolly Varden in Marten and Clay Lakes, steelhead in Marten Creek.

Mount Flemer: 32 miles northeast of Wrangell; accessible by shallow boat; oil stove; cutthroat and Dolly Varden.

Mount Rynda: 18 miles northeast of Wrangell; accessible by shallow boat; oil stove; cutthroat, Dolly Varden, and three salmon species.

Shakes Slough #1: 25 miles northeast of Wrangell; accessible by shallow boat or floatplane; oil stove; cutthroat and Dolly Varden.

Shakes Slough #2: 25 miles northeast of Wrangell; accessible by shallow boat or floatplane; oil stove; cutthroat and Dolly Varden.

Steamer Bay: 25 air miles west of Wrangell; accessible by boat or floatplane; wood stove, outdoor grill; Dolly Varden, three salmon species and halibut in bay and Porcupine Creek, clams and crabs in bay.

Twin Lakes: 18 air miles northeast of Wrangell; accessible by shallow boat; oil stove; cutthroat and three salmon species.

Virginia Lake: 10 air miles east of Wrangell; accessible by boat or floatplane; handicap-accessible cabin; wood stove, fire ring, floating dock, skiff; cutthroat, Dolly Varden, and sockeye salmon.

Sitka Cabins

Appleton Cove: 50 miles north of Sitka; accessible by boat or floatplane; oil stove; rainbow trout, pink and silver salmon.

Avoss Lake: 30 miles southeast of Sitka; accessible by floatplane; oil stove; rainbow trout and Dolly Varden.

Baranof Lake: 20 miles east of Sitka; accessible by floatplane; wood stove, skiff; cutthroat and rainbow trout and Dolly Varden.

Davidof Lake: 40 miles southeast of Sitka; accessible by floatplane; wood stove, skiff; rainbow trout, Dolly Varden, and silver salmon.

Goulding Lake: 60 miles northwest of Sitka; accessible by floatplane; wood stove, skiff; cutthroat, steelhead, and silver salmon.

Kanga Bay: 12 miles south of Sitka; accessible by floatplane or boat; wood stove; sockeye and silver salmon.

Kook Lake: 45 miles northwest of Sitka; accessible by floatplane; wood stove, skiff; cutthroat, Dolly Varden, and silver salmon.

Lake Eva: 27 miles northeast of Sitka; accessible by floatplane; handicap-accessible dock; oil stove, outdoor grill, skiff; cutthroat, Dolly Varden, steelhead, silver and sockeye salmon.

Moser Island: 48 miles north of Sitka; accessible by floatplane or boat; wood stove; silver, pink, and chum salmon.

North Beach: 20 miles northwest of Sitka; accessible by helicopter or boat and trail; wood stove; Dolly Varden, silver and pink salmon.

Plotnikof Lake: 45 miles southeast of Sitka; accessible by floatplane; oil stove, skiff; steelhead, rainbow trout, and silver salmon.

Redoubt Lake: 10 miles south of Sitka; accessible by floatplane or boat and trail; wood stove, skiff; Dolly Varden, silver and sockeye salmon.

Salmon Lake: 11 miles south of Sitka; accessible by floatplane or boat and trail; wood stove, skiff; cutthroat, Dolly Varden, sockeye and silver salmon.

Shelikof: 20 miles northwest of Sitka; accessible by helicopter or boat and trail; wood stove; Dolly Varden and silver salmon.

Sitkoh Lake East: 30 miles northeast of Sitka; accessible by floatplane or boat and trail; wood stove, skiff; cutthroat, steelhead, Dolly Varden, pink and silver salmon.

Sitkoh Lake West: 30 miles northeast of Sitka; accessible by floatplane; wood stove, skiff; cutthroat, steelhead, Dolly Varden, pink and silver salmon.

Suloia Lake: 30 miles northwest of Sitka; accessible by floatplane; wood stove, skiff; rainbow trout and Dolly Varden.

White Sulphur Springs: 65 miles northwest of Sitka; accessible by boat and trail; wood stove; cutthroat trout and silver salmon.

Juneau Cabins

East Turner Lake: 20 miles east of Juneau; accessible by floatplane; oil stove, skiff; cutthroat, Dolly Varden, and kokanee.

Peterson Lake: 24 miles north of Juneau; accessible by road and trail; wood stove, propane heater; Dolly Varden and cutthroat in lake, steelhead, trout, silver and pink salmon in creek below falls.

West Turner Lake: 18 miles east of Juneau; accessible by floatplane or boat; oil stove, skiff; cutthroat, Dolly Varden, and kokanee in lake, pink salmon in Turner River.

Windfall Lake: mile 26 on the Glacier Hwy.; accessible by road or floatplane; wood stove, propane heater; sockeye salmon.

Yakutat Cabins

Eagle: 8 air miles east of Yakutat; accessible by trail, boat or wheelplane; oil stove, outdoor grill; rainbow trout, Dolly Varden, steelhead, and four salmon species.

Italio River: 30 air miles southeast of Yakutat; accessible by wheelplane; oil stove; rainbow trout, Dolly Varden, steelhead, and four salmon species.

Raven: 8 air miles east of Yakutat; accessible by trail, boat or wheelplane; oil stove, outdoor grill; rainbow trout, Dolly Varden, steelhead, and four salmon species.

Situk Lake: 14 miles northeast of Yakutat; accessible by floatplane or trail; wood stove, skiff; rainbow trout, Dolly Varden, steelhead, and four salmon species.

Square Lake: 40 miles southeast of Yakutat; accessible by floatplane; oil stove, skiff; cutthroat and silver salmon.

Interior Road System

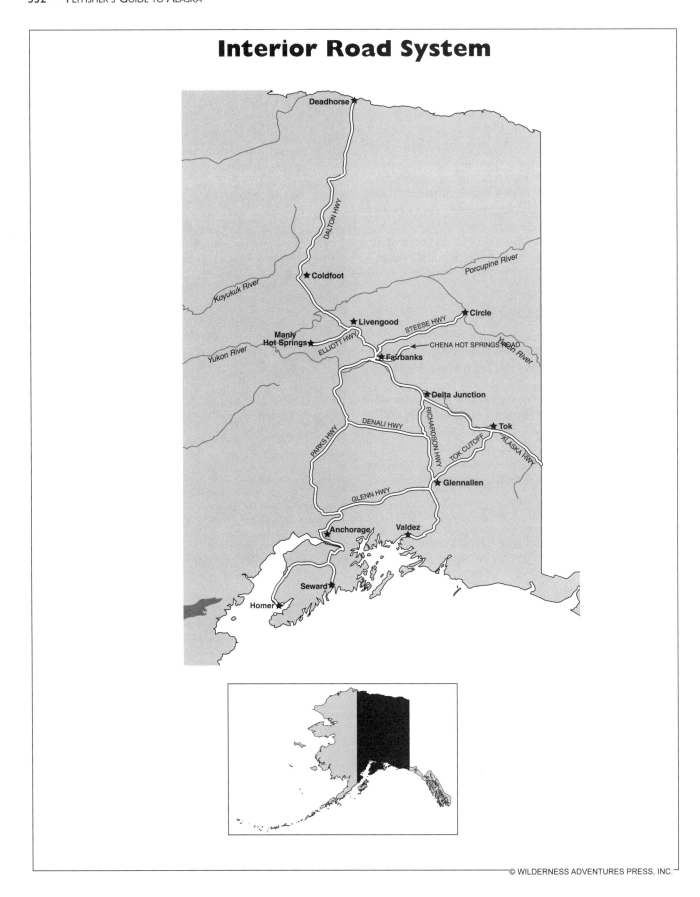

Fishing Alaska's Road System

By Scott Haugen

Taking your time and camping as you go is one of the best ways to experience all the road systems have to offer.

While fly-in trips around the state and the famed Kenai Peninsula are regarded as Alaska's premier fishing attractions, the vast road system should not go overlooked. More than a dozen highways lead to thousands of roadside lakes, rivers, and creeks, and Alaska's roads can transport you to just about any type of fishing you desire. When it comes to angling diversity, the roads link you to unique habitats in a way nothing else can. Each summer, many traveling anglers choose to spend two or three months following the road system, fishing for everything from king salmon to burbot.

In this chapter, we will look at what Alaska's 10 most popular road systems have to offer. It would be a Herculean task to list every single fishery accessible by road, and such an undertaking would leave little room for anglers to explore on their own, so we'll focus on the best waters in each area. But not to worry—there are plenty.

Stay flexible if you are designing a fishing trip around Alaska's road system, as your plan might have to be adapted as you go along. Foul weather, mining, or any one of a number of factors can spoil a stream's fishing for a day or more, and you should always be in position to reach other fishable waters.

Few anglers traveling by road are looking to drive to one destination and spend a week hiking and fishing in a remote area, although this could easily be done. The strength of the state's roadside fisheries lie in the fact that there are so many easily accessed waters with so much outstanding fishing. And the many cities, towns, and villages along most of these roads make travel comfortable.

This book offers plenty of information on Alaska's fisheries, but don't be afraid to chat with folks at roadside pullouts and campgrounds, as this is an excellent way to attain the latest fishing report. They may have information that leads you to a local hotspot the few anglers know exists. At the same time, what you discover along the way might just make the day of fellow anglers you meet.

Seeking out and sharing information with other anglers will help you take full advantage of the road-system fisheries. The only drawback is that you'll find yourself running short on time, no matter how many months are allocated for such a trip.

GENERAL RUN TIMING FOR ROAD-SYSTEM FISHERIES

Because the road system covers such a vast amount of land, grouping the run timings into one table is impossible. Instead, what follows is a detailed look at the run timings from the northern part of the state at Prudhoe Bay to the southernmost point highlighted in this section, Valdez.

Elliott, Steese, Alaska, and Northern Parks Highways

Species:	Jan	Feb	Mar	Apr	May	Jun	Jul	Aug	Sep	Oct	Nov	Dec
King Salmon	-	-	-	-	-	-	+++	-	-	-	-	-
Coho Salmon	-	-	-	-	-	-	-	-	+/+++	+++	+/-	-
Chum Salmon	-	-	-	-	-	-	+++	++	+	++	+++	-
Rainbow Trout	+	+	+	+	++	++	+++	+++	+++	++	+	+
Dolly Varden	+	+	+	+	++	+++	+++	+++	+++	++	+	+
Lake Trout	+	+	+	+	+++	+++	++	+	+++	+++	++	+
Pike	+	+	+	+	+++	+++	+	+	+++	+++	++	+
Grayling	+	+	+	+++	+++	+++	+++	+++	+++	++	+	+
Sheefish	+	+	+	+	+	+++	+++	+++	+++	+	+	+
Burbot	++	++	++	++	++	++	++	++	++	++	++	++

Glenn, Denali, and Southern Parks Highways

Species:	Jan	Feb	Mar	Apr	May	Jun	Jul	Aug	Sep	Oct	Nov	Dec
King Salmon	-	-	-	-	++	+++	++	++	-	-	-	-
Coho Salmon	-	-	-	-	-	-	++/+++	+++	++	+	-	-
Sockeye Salmon	-	-	-	-	-	++	+++	+++/++	+/-	-	-	-
Pink Salmon	-	-	-	-	-	-	++/+++	++/-	-	-	-	-
Chum Salmon	-	-	-	-	-	-	++/+++	+++/++	+	-	-	-
Rainbow Trout	+	+	+	+	++	++	++	++/+++	+++	++	++	+
Lake Trout	+	+	+	++	+++	+++	+	+	+++	+++	++	+
Dolly Varden	+	+	+	+	++	++	++	++/+++	+++	++	++	+
Pike	+	+	+	++	+++	+++	+	+	+++	+++	++	+
Grayling	+	+	+	+++	+++	+	+	+++	+++	+	+	+
Burbot	+++	+	+	+	+	+	+	+	+	+	+	+++

Richardson Highway and Tok Cutoff

Species:	Jan	Feb	Mar	Apr	May	Jun	Jul	Aug	Sep	Oct	Nov	Dec
King Salmon	-	-	-	-	-	-/++	+++	-	-	-	-	-
Coho Salmon	-	-	-	-	-	-	-	-/+++	+++/+	-	-	-
Sockeye Salmon	-	-	-	-	-	-/+++	+++	+++	-	-	-	-
Rainbow Trout	+	+	+	+	++	++/+++	+++	+++	+++	++	+	+
Cutthroat Trout	+	+	+	+	+++	+++	++	++	++	++	+	+
Dolly Varden	+	+	+	+	++	++/+++	+++/++	++	++	++	+	+
Lake Trout	+++	+++	+++	+++	+	+/+++	+++/+	+	+	+	++	+++
Steelhead	+	+	+	+	+	+	+	+	+++	++	+	+
Grayling	+	+	+	+	++	+++	+++	+++	+++	++	+	+
Burbot	+++	+++	+++	+++	+	+	+	+	+	+	+	+++

+++ Excellent   ++ Good   + Fair   - Nonexistent/Closed Season

WHERE TO BEGIN?

With so many miles of road to cover, determining where to start may be the most critical decision of your trip. For example, if you're after salmon, stick to the southerly road systems. Or if it's grayling you desire, head north. Study the run-timing charts in this chapter to get a better understanding of the peak periods for the species you'd like to catch.

Once you decide which fish species to pursue, you can select the highways with the best opportunities. If you're driving from the Lower Forty-Eight and have no time constraints then your options are many, especially if you have a 4x4. And if you're pulling a boat or hauling a canoe or float tube, your fishing options dramatically increase. Just be sure you have honed your skills before floating anywhere in Alaska, as the extremely cold water, multitude of obstacles, and distance from populated areas make boating an adventure here.

If you're flying into one of Alaska's two main cities along the road system, Anchorage or Fairbanks, you can rent a vehicle.

Be sure to discuss with the agency which roads you plan on traveling. Very few—it used to be zero—agencies rent vehicles for use on gravel roads. If you're driving your own vehicle, be advised that some highways do have tracts of gravel, complete with potholes and washboards that will pound the heck out of your car frame and its passengers; paint chips are inevitable.

The more prepared you are to deal with the plethora of water types and fish species along Alaska's roads, the more rewarding your trip will be. And wherever you decide to fish, apply common sense, stay alert for bears, heed all posted signs, and get ready to have the time of your flyfishing life.

THE GEORGE PARKS HIGHWAY

The Parks Highway is the most popular road system detailed in this chapter. The 362-mile highway connects Anchorage to Fairbanks and is the primary gateway to Denali National Park. Formerly known as the Anchorage-Fairbanks Highway following its completion in 1971, it was renamed the George Parks Highway in 1975.

The Parks Highway offers spectacular views throughout its length, but is especially inviting the closer you get to Denali. The two-lane highway is paved for its entire length, but passing lanes are few and far between and some winding sections slow traffic flow. During the summer months, dense foliage impedes motorists' views, so proceed with caution and be certain to travel with your headlights on at all times. And keep a watchful eye out for moose and pedestrians.

Due to the number of towns with services along the highway, travel is comfortable and easy. On the other hand, fishing pressure on easily accessible bodies of water can be extreme around populated areas. In most of these fisheries, king salmon draw the most attention, followed by early arriving silver salmon. If you find yourself here during the peak of the king and silver runs, you'll have little choice but to be aggressive and muscle your way in with the rest of the crowd. In some instances, you can partially escape the hordes, which may allow you to more comfortably work your fly rod, but the fishing will likely not be as fast-paced as in the honey holes in which the majority of anglers gather.

If I could choose one period of time to fish the Parks Highway, it would be in late August through the middle or end of September. Late arriving silvers, big Dollys, rainbows, and nice grayling are present, but more importantly, there is very little fishing pressure. This tourist traffic will have dramatically decreased, the local kids will be back in school, and hunting season will be in full swing. For resident Alaskans, hunting trumps fishing throughout the state. So streams that only months earlier were choked with people can be virtually void of anglers.

A pull-out on the George Parks Highway.

George Parks Highway

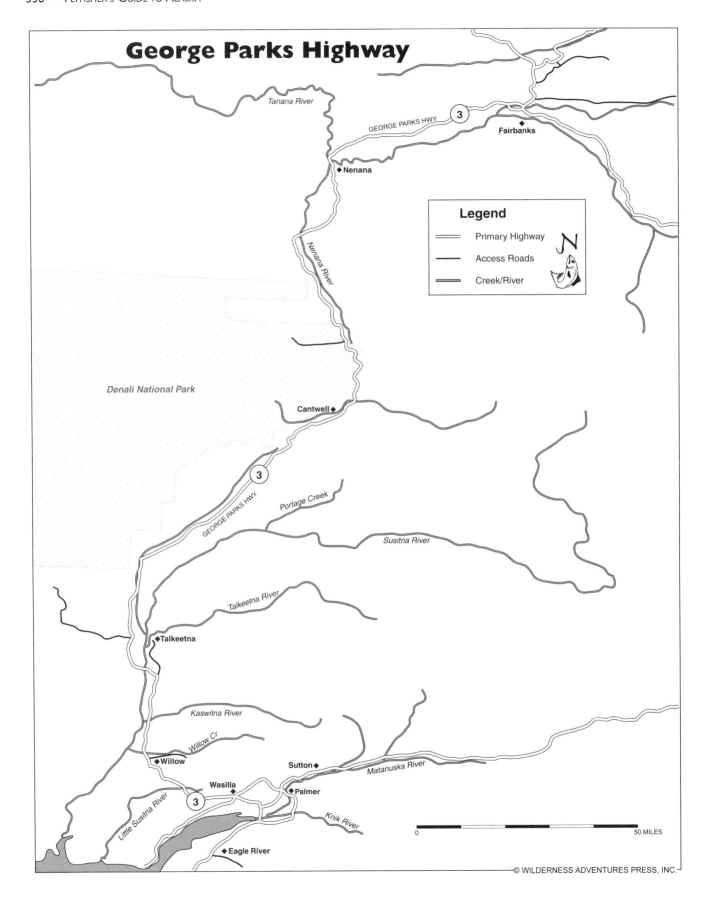

Legend
Primary Highway
Access Roads
Creek/River

Tanana River
GEORGE PARKS HWY ③
Fairbanks
Nenana

Nenana River

Denali National Park

Cantwell ◆

③

GEORGE PARKS HWY

Portage Creek

Susitna River

Talkeetna River

◆Talkeetna

Kaswitna River

Willow Cr

◆Willow

Sutton ◆

Matanuska River

Wasilla

◆ Palmer

③

Little Susitna River

Knik River

0   50 MILES

◆ Eagle River

© WILDERNESS ADVENTURES PRESS, INC.

The stretch of we'll discuss here begins at the junction with the Glenn Highway, 35 miles north of Anchorage. We'll count miles from here north to Fairbanks. (To learn more about the fishing opportunities along the first 30 miles of the Parks Highway, refer to the chapter on the Anchorage area.)

There are countless streams and lakes in this region, so we'll concentrate on the fishing locales that are most user-friendly and relatively painless for the traveling angler to reach. By this I mean waters that are easy to access, hold good numbers of fish, and fairly stable throughout the fishing season.

Consult the latest sport-fishing regulations when you fish in this area. Many of the streams see ever-changing tackle regulations or special closures that range from a few days to nearly two weeks.

Wasilla Area Lakes

Overrun with jet skis, recreational boaters, and swimmers, **Wasilla Lake** and **Lucille Lake** are two of the many lakes situated near the town of Wasilla that are stocked with rainbow trout. These aren't lakes I'd recommend to anglers, however.

If you find yourself staying in the Wasilla area for a few days and want to wet a line in a lake, there are other options. If you're here early in the spring, **Cottonwood Lake** and **Finger Lake** are worth spending time on. Leech patterns cast and stripped close to shore can get you into rainbows up to 5 pounds. To reach these lakes, turn north off the Parks Highway onto Wasilla Fishhook Road in the town of Wasilla. Then turn right on Bogard Road and follow the signs to the lakes. If you beat the summer crowds, the fishing here is worth the effort.

An aerial view near Wasilla, Alaska.

Big Lake

Heading out of Wasilla on the Parks Highway, numerous lakes and ponds can be seen on both sides of the highway. Detailing these lakes would be an injustice to the higher quality fisheries in the area, and few traveling anglers spend time fishing these "urban" waters.

However, Big Lake, at mile 52.3 on the Parks Highway, may be worth a look. Turn west on Big Lake Road, then access the lake and wayside parks off either North Shore Drive or South Big Lake Road. This is a monstrous body of water, with a lot of human activity. But the number of fish makes it worthwhile.

The lake is home to some exceptional rainbow trout, nice Dolly Varden, and burbot, and fly anglers should concentrate their efforts close to shore early in the spring and late in the fall. As summer progresses, trolling weighted flies can produce some nice rainbows.

Fish Creek

Spilling out of the eastern edge of Big Lake, Fish Creek meanders south to Cook Inlet. While gravel roads follow the creek for more than 2 miles from the lake, the only good fishing is near the mouth.

The fishable portion of Fish Creek is accessed back at the town of Wasilla, by turning south on Knik Goose Bay Road. Stay on the road some 20 miles until it crosses Fish Creek. There's a roadside parking area right beside the best fishing area.

Given its proximity to town, Fish Creek is quite underfished. It receives a good silver salmon run, and locals speak of good red salmon action, as well. The mouth of this stream is influenced by extreme tidal changes, and flyfishing with streamers can be very productive. Just remember to keep a close eye on the incoming tide.

Little Susitna River

Continue west on the Knik Goose Bay Road and you'll find some of the best river fishing for magnum king salmon in the state—if your timing is right. The Little Susitna River, referred to as the Little Su, is world-renowned for its easy-to-access, quality king fishing. And with monsters up to 60 pounds—30 pounds being the average—the action can get heated.

Off Knik Goose Bay Road, head west on Point MacKenzie Road and follow it all the way to the end where you'll come to Burma Landing. There is a paved trail leading a mile or so from the parking area, which opens a lot of bank access. While rainbows, Dolly Varden, grayling, and all five salmon species are present, the main king salmon are the main draw, as usual.

Big Lake and Fish Creek

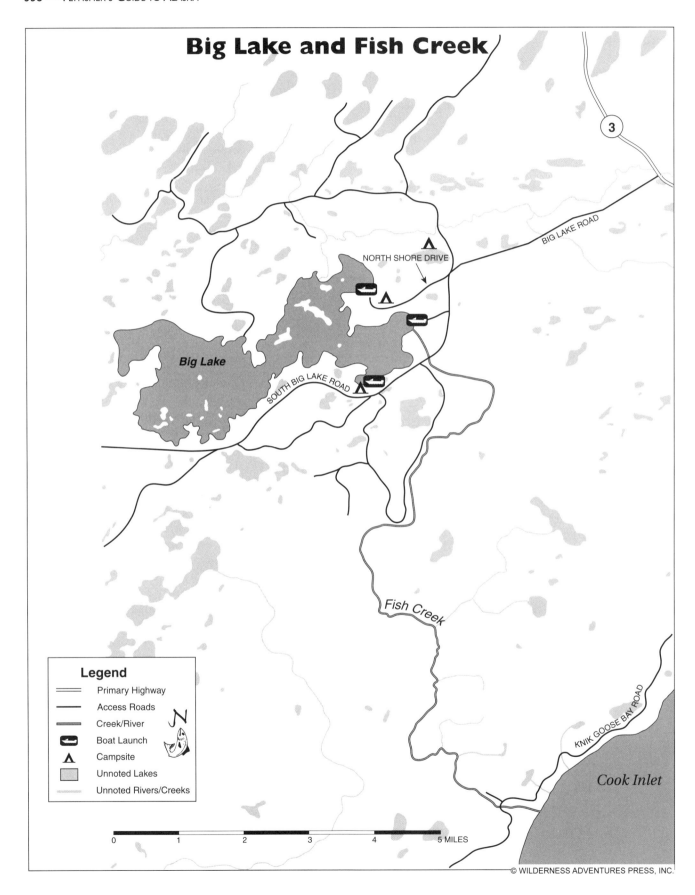

Big Lake Road

North Shore Drive

South Big Lake Road

3

Big Lake

Fish Creek

Knik Goose Bay Road

Cook Inlet

Legend

Primary Highway
Access Roads
Creek/River
Boat Launch
Campsite
Unnoted Lakes
Unnoted Rivers/Creeks

N

0   1   2   3   4   5 MILES

© WILDERNESS ADVENTURES PRESS, INC.

King salmon activity on the Little Su starts in mid-May and is good through the end of the season in mid-July. The chum, red, and pink salmon enter the river in mid- to late July and run through August, while the silvers begin appearing in good numbers early in August and run into October.

The Little Su is rated one of Alaska's best silver salmon streams, and this is a good place to stop for anglers looking to take some quality meat home. Coho limits are often raised to five or six per day, so be sure and check emergency orders regarding the regulations on this river. Rainbow, char, and grayling action is best in the fall, as these fish follow the spawning and dying salmon upstream.

The Parks Highway can connect anglers with some of the best coho fishing in the state.

After breakup in late April or early May, the Little Su typically runs fairly low and green in color, with a good 3 feet of visibility during the king season. Toward the end of May, warmer weather melts surrounding snow, causing the river to rise and silt up. Usually by mid-June the river recedes to its normal level and clears up. But remember, this is a big river influenced by rain and mountain storms; it can rise and turn off-color at any time, but recovers quickly as well.

At the same time, the Little Su is a gentle river that is easy and safe to float. There are no big rapids, and people routinely drift it in a canoe. In addition to a vast choice of prime riverbank from which to fish, there are many gravel bars for floaters to stop and fish. With waders—whether you're fishing from the bank or navigating in a boat—it's easy to wade beyond the brush to get plenty of room for lengthy casts.

The best float is off the Parks Highway, from Houston down to Burma Landing at the Little Susitna Public Recreation Use Site. This is a nice 2-day, 20-mile float, and there are plenty of places to camp. The best time to float the river is probably around mid-August, when several species of fish are in the river. Be patient when running the river, as the numerous meandering turns can wear on you. Also, be on the lookout for jet sleds, as they can create quite a wake.

There are many good holding pockets for salmon between the Parks Highway and Burma Landing. Hit these pools, pockets, seams, and deeper runs the entire way down and you will get into large numbers of fish. Also, be sure to hit any creeks that feed into the Little Su. Salmon often congregate here, and the fishing can be above average, especially at the Nancy Creek (Lake Creek) confluence. Some guide operations will actually meet you at the Parks Highway bridge, run you down to Nancy Creek, then return to pick you up at the end of the fishing day. Fishing at this confluence can be hectic, so you might want to get dropped a bit farther downstream.

King season can be a hectic time on this river, with shoulder-to-shoulder fishing the norm. If this is your only crack at a big king salmon while you're in Alaska, then go for it. But if you're here in late summer through fall, when other salmon species are in the river, the fishing pressure falls off, the action can be nonstop, and the overall experience is much more pleasurable.

Beware: The later in the year you're on the Little Su, the greater the likelihood of seeing bears. Bank anglers encounter bears about a third of the time on this river. Carry bear spray, especially if you're on the water overnight.

It should also be noted that in the upper section of the Little Su, near the town of Houston, fishing for king salmon upstream from the Parks Highway bridge is closed year-round, but open to other species of salmon. For further details look under the Knik Arm section of the "South-Central Alaska Sport Fishing Regulations."

Stream Facts: Little Susitna River

Seasons

- From its mouth upstream to the Parks Highway, the river is open to fishing for all species year-round, except king salmon 20 inches or longer. The open season for king salmon 20 inches or longer is January 1 to July 13.

- No retention of rainbow trout is allowed April 15 to June 14.

- Upstream from the Parks Highway, the river is closed year-round to fishing for king salmon 20 inches or longer, but is open for all other species June 15 to April 14.

Special Regulations

- From its mouth upstream to the Parks Highway, the bag limit for king salmon 20 inches or longer is 1 per day, 1 in possession.

- For salmon other than kings, the bag limit is 3 per day, 3 in possession, of which only 2 per day, 2 in possession may be silver salmon.

- Upstream from the Parks Highway, only one unbaited single-hook artificial lure is allowed.

- In waters open to king salmon fishing, no fishing is allowed between 11:00 p.m. and 6:00 a.m. from May 15 to July 13.

- After retaining a king salmon 20 inches or longer, a person may not fish on that same day anywhere in waters open to king salmon fishing.

Fish

- King, silver, red, pink, and chum salmon, rainbow trout, arctic grayling, Dolly Varden

River Characteristics

- A gentle meandering stream with many switchbacks and no big rapids below the Parks Highway. In spring, it runs green in color with some silting, clearing up as summer progresses. A safe river to bank fish or float. Beware of bears.

Fishing and Boating Access

- Off Goose Bay Road heading south out of Wasilla, turn west on Point MacKenzie Road and follow it all the way to the end where it meets the Little Susitna River at Burma Landing, home to the best bank fishing on the river. There is also bank access where the Parks Highway crosses the river. A canoe can be launched at the Parks Highway bridge for a 2-day float to Burma Landing.

Maps

- Alaska Road & Recreation Map, Parks Highway; *Alaska Atlas and Gazetteer*, page 82

Nancy Lake State Recreation Area

On the west side of the Parks Highway, a series of lakes runs from mile marker 64 north to the town of Willow near mile 71. Turning west at mile 66.5, just over the railroad tracks, will lead you to Nancy Lake State Recreation Site. Here, more than 30 campsites, picnic areas, toilets, and other facilities await the traveling angler.

Nancy Lake is a large lake stocked with rainbows, lake trout, and Dolly Varden. In recent years, this lake has been overrun with pike, so stocking efforts of other species may be curtailed in the near future. With pike up to 15 pounds, anglers may want to target these fish with large, flashy, saltwater streamers fished close to shore and near structure.

Northwest of Nancy Lake, covering more than 10 miles, you'll find over 100 lakes in the Nancy Lake State Recreation Area. There are 12 miles of canoe trails meandering through the area, with stocked rainbow trout the main target for anglers. To reach the canoe trailhead, turn off the Parks Highway at mile 67.2, on the Nancy Lake Parkway Road. The canoe trailhead is 4.7 miles down the road. The portages between lakes are well marked and the lakes fairly calm.

You could spend just a weekend camping along these trails or extend your journey. Follow the marked trail south to the southern outlet at Skeetna Lake. From here you can connect with the Little Susitna River and spend an extra day floating down to the Burma Park Landing. Make arrangements to have your vehicle shuttled or have someone meet you at the landing.

Willow Creek

Ranked by many anglers as the second hottest river for big kings in the state of Alaska, Willow Creek is to this part of the state what the Kenai River is to the Kenai Peninsula. Salmon nearing 80 pounds have been taken from Willow Creek, with fish in the 60-pound class coming to net annually.

Just north of the town of Willow, the creek flows beneath the Parks Highway at mile 71.5. Due to the number of streams feeding into Willow Creek, as well as the Susitna River, Willow Creek may become turbid after a rain or on warm days when the snow melts. When the

Little Susitna River

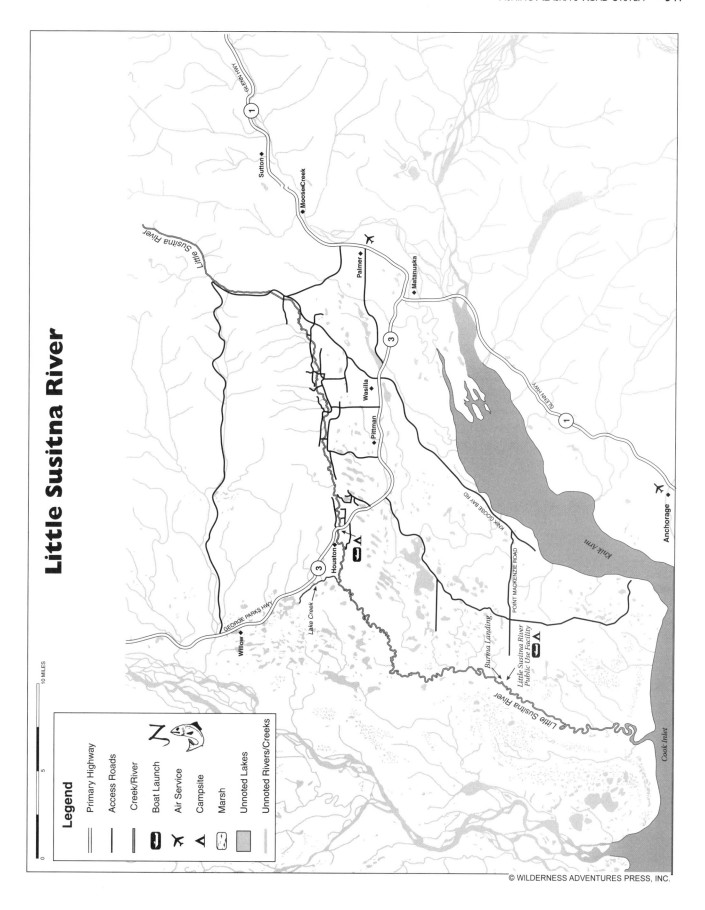

Legend

	Primary Highway
	Access Roads
	Creek/River
	Boat Launch
✈	Air Service
▲	Campsite
	Marsh
	Unnoted Lakes
	Unnoted Rivers/Creeks

Nancy Lake
State Recreation Area

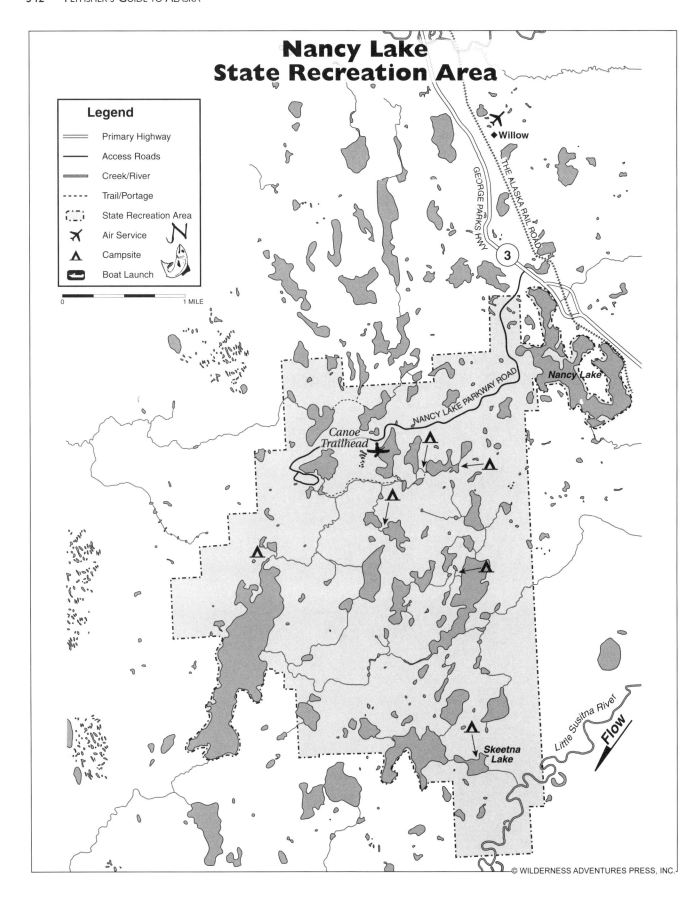

Legend

Primary Highway
Access Roads
Creek/River
Trail/Portage
State Recreation Area
Air Service
Campsite
Boat Launch

N

0   1 MILE

Willow

GEORGE PARKS HWY
THE ALASKA RAIL ROAD
3

Nancy Lake

NANCY LAKE PARKWAY ROAD

Canoe
Trailhead

Skeetna
Lake

Little Susitna River

Flow

© WILDERNESS ADVENTURES PRESS, INC.

Susitna swells it often backs up into Willow Creek, impacting the best fishing at the mouth.

Turn west on Willow Creek Parkway at mile 70.8 to access the hottest king salmon site on Willow Creek. Follow the road 3.5 miles to the Willow Creek Campground, where there are over 125 campsites. As you would expect, the fishing pressure can be serious here. In fact, local anglers claim the combat-style fishing for kings here is far worse than on the Russian River when the red salmon are running.

The end of June and the first part of July marks prime king salmon time. If you have access to a boat, or book a local guide, there's a nice float from the Parks Highway down to Willow Creek Campground. But it's not necessary to have a craft to experience the fishing between the mouth of Willow Creek and the highway.

Willow Creek is clear, easy to wade, and a pleasure to sight fish. You can usually wade the entire stretch from the mouth up to the highway, which is particularly good later in the season when the fish spread out. There will be some logjams and other obstacles to overcome, but these should pose no problems.

If you discover loose salmon eggs in a stream, find a bead to match and target Dollys and rainbows.

It should be noted that the lodge at Willow Creek rents boats for you to float down the creek on your own. At the end of the day, they will meet you at the landing and haul you, the boat, and your fish back up to the highway. They will also take you downstream in one of their sled boats, drop you off for however long you'd like, and pick you up later if you prefer.

If you're covering water on your own, the farther from the mouth you get, the greater the likelihood of a bear encounter. In fact, in the fall, you are just about guaranteed to bump into a bear, so proceed with caution and be alert at all times.

Around the end of July the silver salmon begin entering the creek, with the run peaking in mid-August. Pink and chum salmon are also in the river at this time, and the fishing action for all three species can be constant. In fact, you can expect to catch chum salmon literally all day long on green streamers. These are some of the hardest fighting fish around, and they grow larger than silvers in these waters. Fly anglers will be physically drained after battling dozens of dogs in a single day. When these salmon are in the river, there's no real need to go more than a mile upstream from the mouth, and with the number of bears in the area, you won't want to.

In addition to the salmon, Willow Creek has trophy-sized rainbow trout on tap. The rainbows follow the salmon upstream, feeding on eggs and flesh until freeze-up in early October. The redsides then back into the Susitna and make their way into big lakes where they spend the winter. As you would suspect, beads, Glo-Bugs, and flesh flies offer the best chance at a wall-hanger rainbow. Trout in excess of 10 pounds are taken here each fall. Dolly Varden are also present in the creek during this same period.

You'll find great bank access by following Hatcher Pass Road, which parallels the creek, east from the highway. This stretch has good rainbow action, and some nice grayling can be taken here, too.

Stream Facts: Willow Creek

Seasons

- From its mouth upstream to the Parks Highway, the stream is open to fishing for all species, including king salmon, from January 1 to June 17, June 22 to 24, and June 29 to July. From July 14 to December 31, this section is open for all species, except king salmon 20 inches or longer.

- There is no retention of rainbow trout or grayling year-round.

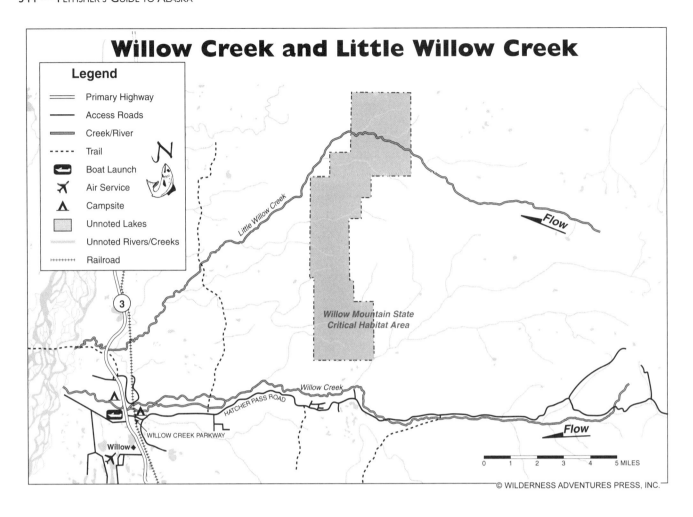

Willow Creek and Little Willow Creek

Legend

═══	Primary Highway
──	Access Roads
━━	Creek/River
- - -	Trail
🛥	Boat Launch
✈	Air Service
⛰	Campsite
▨	Unnoted Lakes
～～	Unnoted Rivers/Creeks
┼┼┼┼	Railroad

Little Willow Creek

Willow Mountain State Critical Habitat Area

Flow

③

HATCHER PASS ROAD

Willow Creek

WILLOW CREEK PARKWAY

Willow ◆

Flow

0   1   2   3   4   5 MILES

© WILDERNESS ADVENTURES PRESS, INC.

Special Regulations

- From its mouth upstream to the Parks Highway, the bag limit for king salmon over 20 inches is 1 per day, 1 in possession.

- Bag limits for all other species are as listed under the general limits in the fishing regulations booklet.

- Upstream from the Parks Highway bridge, one unbaited single hook artificial lure is allowed year-round.

Fish

- King, silver, chum, and pink salmon, rainbow trout, arctic grayling, and Dolly Varden

River Characteristics

- Willow Creek is a clear stream that is easy to wade fish all the way from the mouth to the Parks Highway. During heavy rains, the Susitna River backs up into the creek, spoiling the water temporarily.

Fishing and Boating Access

- At mile 71.5 on the Parks Highway, a turnout provides easy walk-in access. You can reach the creek mouth by turning west on Willow Creek Parkway at mile 70.8. Boaters can drift from the Parks Highway to the take-out at the Willow Creek Campground near the mouth of the river.

Maps

- Alaska Road & Recreation Map, Parks Highway; *Alaska Atlas and Gazetteer*, page 82

Little Willow Creek

For a miniature version of Willow Creek, head up the highway to mile 74.7, where you'll find the aptly named Little Willow Creek. This is a rocky stream, running a bit more tannic in color than its sister stream. Nonetheless, wade fishing is the rule here, and spot-and-stalk tactics can be highly effective.

The best angling on Little Willow is from the Parks

Highway bridge downstream to the mouth. Park in the designated pullout on the southeast corner of the bridge and make your way down to the creek. Silver and pink salmon dominate the late summer fishing here, followed by rainbow trout and grayling.

Caswell Creek

Because Kashwitna Lake is stocked with rainbows, and the Kashwitna River has a tendency to run off-color through the summer, I'd recommend moving to better waters to the north. One such fishery is Caswell Creek, situated at mile 84 on the Parks Highway. This creek hosts king, silver, and pink salmon and a run of rainbow trout.

Caswell Creek is small and clear, narrowing down to 6 feet across in some places, but there is plenty of water for king and silver salmon to migrate in. As you would expect in a stream this small, the best fishing is at the mouth, and there are ADF&G markers restricting how far upstream you can fish.

Due to its ease of access—you can drive down to the mouth—Caswell Creek receives considerable pressure during the king and silver salmon runs. However, it's worth checking out in September for late arriving silvers and incoming rainbows.

Sheep Creek

Up the road at mile 88.6 Sheep Creek crosses the Parks Highway. This is a popular king, silver, and pink salmon fishery, but its physical nature does not make it a viable flyfishing stream. In addition, only a very limited stretch of this creek is open to fishing, and the crowds make flyfishing difficult. If you do want to try your luck here your best bet is in September, when the angling hordes have thinned and rainbows and grayling are in the stream.

Goose Creek

Goose Creek crosses the highway at mile 93.5. A clear, narrow, shallow stream, Goose is ideal for wading and fishing. In fact, from the gravel turnout along the highway, you can navigate the stream all the way to the mouth.

Due to the minute stature of this creek, the salmon fishing can be hit or miss, as fish waste no time moving upstream. There are some good king salmon here, though, and they can be taken on a fly. If you're passing through the area from mid-June into July, it's worth stopping to see if there are any salmon around. And if you spot the salmon before anyone else does, you'll discover

one of the area's best-kept secrets. Also, check for rainbows if you pass through in late August or September.

Montana Creek

Mile 96.5 brings you to the last great king salmon stream on the Parks Highway and one of the most popular fisheries on the entire Alaskan road system. King salmon in excess of 70 pounds have been taken from Montana Creek, with 40-pounders fairly common. Silver, pink, and chum salmon are also present, along with rainbow trout and arctic grayling.

Due to the size of Montana Creek, it's almost exclusively a bank-fishing stream. From the highway, where there is plenty of parking and a campground, walking to the creek is easy. Montana has clear, shallow water with a good gravel bottom, so wading is not a problem. Most of the fishing takes place near the mouth, though hitting the pools and pockets can be good all the way from the bridge to the outlet.

There are many places to wade across this stream, providing you with the perfect angle for working that fly into prime holding water. If you hook a behemoth king on a fly in this small stream, you'd best make sure you have an exceptional drag and plenty of backing.

Several trails leading up and downstream can also be accessed near the highway. Even when the mouth is jammed with king salmon anglers, there is plenty of room to spread out upstream.

In addition to kings, the silver salmon action can be exceptional during the month of August. Pink and chum salmon make their way into this creek in late July and last through mid-August. The pink and chum numbers can be so dense around the mouth of Montana Creek that you can expect hookups on virtually every cast, all day long.

In May and September, the rainbow trout fishing can be very good, with redsides up to 10 pounds not uncommon in the lower river. Grayling fishing is good from June through September in the upper stretches of the creek.

Stream Facts: Montana Creek

Seasons

- From its mouth upstream to ADF&G markers ½ mile above the Parks Highway is open to fishing for all species, including king salmon, from January 1 to June 17, June 22 to 24, and June 29 to July 1. This section is also open July 14 to December 31 for all species except king salmon 20 inches or longer.

- No retention of rainbow trout or grayling year-round in the entire creek.

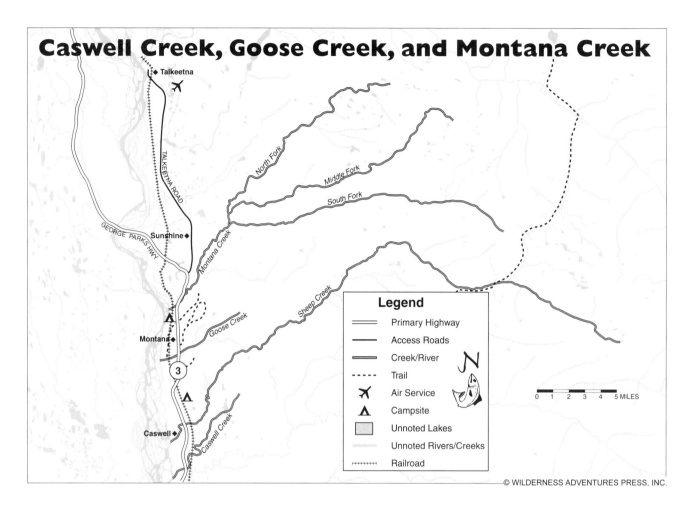

Caswell Creek, Goose Creek, and Montana Creek

Legend

══════	Primary Highway
──────	Access Roads
══════	Creek/River
- - - -	Trail
✈	Air Service
⚑	Campsite
▨	Unnoted Lakes
	Unnoted Rivers/Creeks
+++++++	Railroad

0 1 2 3 4 5 MILES

© WILDERNESS ADVENTURES PRESS, INC.

Special Regulations

- The bag limit for king salmon 20 inches or longer is 1 per day, 1 in possession.

- For all salmon species but king salmon, the daily limit is 3 per day, 3 in possession, of which only 2 per day, 2 in possession may be silver salmon.

Fish

King, silver, pink, and chum salmon, rainbow trout, arctic grayling

River Characteristics

Montana Creek is a very clear, gravel-bottomed stream with solid banks for wade fishing.

Fishing Access

- From a turnout of the Parks Highway at mile 96.5 you can follow the creek all the way to the mouth. Trails lead to water above the bridge, and for grayling in the upper river, take the Talkeetna Spur Road then follow the foot trails to the river.

Maps

- Alaska Road & Recreation Map, Parks Highway; *Alaska Atlas and Gazetteer*, page 93-94

Troublesome Creek

From this point, fishing along the Parks Highway becomes a small-stream affair, with arctic grayling the primary species. There are some streams and lakes that hold rainbows and Dollys, as well as some salmon, but most of these areas are closed to salmon fishing.

Because salmon target many of the little streams as spawning grounds, and because these streams are set amid brush and forests, bear numbers can run high. Be on constant alert for bears, particularly in the fall. I know of locals who won't set foot on any of these creeks unless they are with a partner.

Keep in mind that bears in this part of Alaska don't see as many humans as do bears in some areas, like the famous Brooks Camp. As a result, they aren't as "friendly" as bears that are used to human intrusion.

Due to the brushy nature throughout much of this

Troublesome Creek, Byers Creek, and Byers Lake

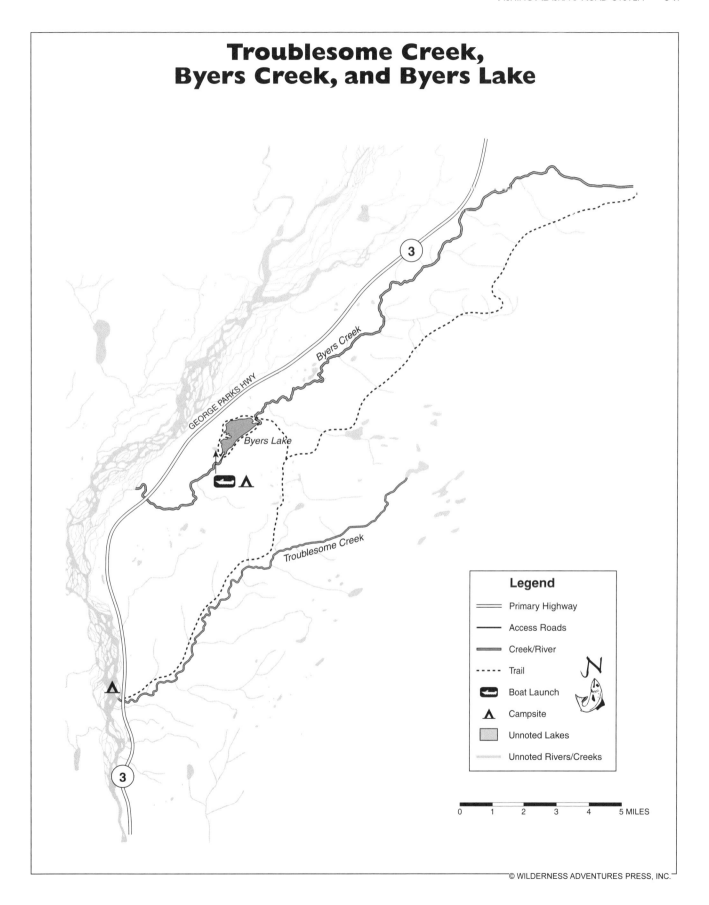

Legend

Primary Highway

Access Roads

Creek/River

Trail

Boat Launch

Campsite

Unnoted Lakes

Unnoted Rivers/Creeks

0 1 2 3 4 5 MILES

terrain, the chances of actually seeing a bear while fishing are quite slim, which makes it all the more dangerous. Having spent many years in bear country, I'd rather see what I'm getting into than catch one by surprise.

On the drive up to Troublesome Creek, you'll pass by the Susitna and Chulitna Rivers. In this region, these rivers are running big and choked with silt. Neither is fit for the flyfishing.

But Troublesome Creek is a pretty stream worth spending some time on. From July into early October, the rainbow fishing can be pretty good. However, this creek receives a run of king salmon late in the fall, and the bears can be thick. In fact, it's often closed during these times due to intense bear activity, so pay close attention to posted signs along the roadside at mile 137.5, the Troublesome Creek bridge and trailhead.

The creek runs fast and gin-clear, which is typical of many mountain streams up here, and is laden with slippery rocks. At first glance it may appear that the stream is too turbulent to hold fish, but the rainbow trout and grayling are in there.

Rubber knee boots are ideal for hiking along this creek. From the trailhead on the highway, you can fish about 7 miles of the creek before the trail turns off and heads 6 miles to Byers Lake.

Byers Lake and Byers Creek

If the 15-mile hike from the Parks Highway along the Troublesome Creek Trailhead doesn't appeal to you, you can drive to Byers Lake. At mile 147 on the Parks Highway, turn down the marked road for a quarter-mile and you're at the lake.

This is one of the more beautiful lakes in the area, and while the fishing is not the best, the view may be. There are rainbow and lake trout here, along with grayling, but I've never talked with anyone who has done very well here. Byers Lake Campground is a popular spot beside the lake, which likely results in above average fishing pressure.

When the weather is calm, you can work the edges of this lake in a float tube, though covering water in a canoe is more efficient. No matter how you fish Byers Lake, or how many fish you catch, this is one lake where it's simply a blessing to be a part of the pristine setting.

Byers Creek runs both into and out of Byers Lake and offers good rainbow trout fishing on the downstream side. This is a clear stream that's easy to wade and fish as you go. Brush can be a bit troublesome in some areas, so you'll need to pick your fishing spots. The creek ranges from 15 to 20 feet across, with some pools approaching 30 feet in width.

Spawning salmon make their way up this stream, which can be overrun with bears in the fall. Muddler patterns are popular here. The best access to the creek is where it flows beneath the highway. From there, you can hike and fish your way down to its mouth or up to the lake.

Honolulu Creek

Honolulu Creek is another clear stream that is surprisingly narrow. It flows under the highway at mile 178 and may appear too small to hold any fish. But there are some rainbows and arctic grayling here. The best fishing is between the highway and the mouth, with the best results right at its confluence with the Chulitna River.

A run of king salmon also makes its way into Honolulu Creek. From the mouth of the creek upstream ¼ mile, anglers can try their luck at what is considered to be quite good king salmon action. If your timing is right, this is a good place to latch into a king on the fly. Consult the current fishing regulations for the open king salmon days on this stream.

Broad Pass Lakes

As the highway climbs Broad Pass, the road breaks out into the open, offering what many believe to be the most picturesque view along the entire Parks Highway. Atop this drive there are a series of lakes offering easy road access between miles 198 and 206. Some of these are stocked with lake trout, and grayling are also present. At the main turnout, it's a quarter-mile from the road to the lakes, but if you're here in July, it's worth the hike.

Late July marks prime blueberry season, and you can wade your way through lush blueberry patches before crossing the railroad and hitting the lakes. Many anglers stop here to gather blueberries and skip the fishing.

Because there are few trees around these lakes, they can be tough to fish from a belly boat when the wind is whipping around. These lakes are better for bank fishing. Teasing a lake trout on the fly is tough, though, and the fishing is typically very slow here, which may explain why the blueberry picking is so popular.

Jack River and Carlo Creek

Driving north, you'll pass the town of Cantwell, and the Denali Highway junction. Though the Nenana River at this locale is not fishable due to its size and turbidity, two of its tributaries are worth hitting.

The Jack River flows into the Nenana near mile 216, and you can easily walk to the water from the highway. At mile 224, Carlo Creek feeds into the Nenana, and it's also easy to access on foot. The best fishing in both streams is at the mouth and on up through select pools, where trout and grayling reside.

Penguingue Creek

Despite its long, tongue twister of a name, Penguingue Creek is a tiny, shallow stream with miniature fish. It's a very clear creek, and narrow enough to jump across in most places. But if you're into outsmarting small fish in tight pools, give this creek a shot.

The creek flows under the Parks Highway at mile 252.5 and is easy to reach from the road. You can fish in either direction, but you'll likely find bigger fish at the confluence with the Nenana River on the east side of the highway. Grayling are present, but it's the dwarf Dolly Varden that purist fly anglers take interest in.

If you land a Dolly that stretches the tape to 7 inches, you have something to boast about here. The growing season is short, and the shallow water means that winter mortality is probably high. But if you want to put your spot-and-stalk fishing skills to the test, this is the place. The good part about this stream is that when you do catch a "trophy" Dolly, the taxidermy bill won't be too outrageous.

Scott Haugen admires a beautiful small-stream Dolly before sending it on its way.

Julius Creek

Though a few small creeks lie between Julius Creek and Penguingue Creek, they aren't noted fishing hotspots. At mile 285.7, Julius Creek flows under the Parks Highway, and while there is a gravel pulloff here where the fishing for grayling can be good, there's a better spot up the road if you don't mind a hike.

If you want to experience the creek's best grayling fishing, and what it has to offer in terms of silver salmon, head to mile 295 and turn west onto the gravel road. Follow it a half-mile or so to the railroad tracks and park there. It's a 2-mile hike to the mouth from this point. In late August and early September, the silver salmon are in and flyfishing for them where Julius Creek meets Clear Creek can be quite a thrill.

The water is shallow enough to wade across in many places, and the tea-colored stream is easy and fun to fish. There are some nice grayling in the lower stretch. As for the silver runs, some years are better than others, but regardless, if you're here during the peak of the run, it's worth the walk.

Fish Creek

The Parks Highway crosses Fish Creek a mile and a half up the road. Similar in size and structure to Julius, Fish Creek is easy to reach from the roadside pulloff. You can wade fish downstream as far as you care to go or try upstream.

The area around Fish Creek is a bit boggy, meaning hip boots or chest waders may be in order. Grayling are the sole target on this creek, where the pressure is usually light in the fall.

Chena River

After you pass through the town of Nenana, there's not much fishing until you hit Fairbanks. Though the Tanana River can be fair in its upper stretches, it's simply not fishable at this juncture. But what does await anglers is Fairbanks's most popular river fishery, the Chena River. And the river can be accessed from several spots off the highway.

Shortly after the Fourth of July, king salmon make their way into this river, and the town goes nuts getting after them. There is also a run of chum salmon later in July. Though the fishing pressure can be intense for the kings, fortunately there's enough access to spread people out. And many of the serious local anglers have their own boats.

The best place to tie into a king on the fly is at the mouth, right near the airport. You can park off the Chena

Pump Road and take a short walk through a wooded area to the river. There are huge sandbars here, affording plenty of room for fly anglers to spread out among the drift fishermen. Resist the urge to wade into this large, fast river; it can swallow an angler before he or she even knows what's happening.

The Wendell Street bridge and the Nordale bridge also offer good bank-fishing access, as do many roadside pulloffs throughout town. During the peak of the salmon run, just look for clusters of vehicles, as that's probably where the fish are. Pikes Landing provides boat launch access, and there's another ramp up near the Chena River Dam. Salmon fishing above the dam is prohibited, as this is protected spawning grounds.

The middle and upper sections of the Chena River, primarily grayling fisheries, are addressed with the Chena Hot Springs Road later in this chapter.

By the time king salmon reach some of the northernmost rivers along the road system, they have lost considerable weight and darkened up.

ANDERSON

Population: 517
Alaska Area Code: 907
Zip Code: 99744

TOURIST INFORMATION

Visitor Information, City Office, 582-2500

ACCOMMODATIONS

Fireweed 288 Roadhouse, 582-2224; mile 288.5 Parks Hwy.

Rochester Lodge, 582-2354; mile 280.1 Parks Hwy.; rooms, showers, RV parking, tent sites, meals

CAMPGROUNDS AND RV PARKS

Tatlanika Trading Co., P.O. Box 40179, Clear, AK 99704; 582-2341; mile 276 Parks Hwy. RV parking with hookups, tentsites, water, showers, dump station, authentic gift shop

Riverside Park, 582-2500; turn at mile 283.5 off Parks Hwy., continue west of town of Anderson; RV parking, some electrical hookups, campsites, picnic area showers, restrooms, dump sites

Summer Shades Campground, 582-2798; mile 289.8 Parks Hwy.; cabins, showers, dump station, playground

RESTAURANTS

Clear Sky Lodge, 582-2251; mile 280 Parks Hwy.; great dining, propane available

DENALI PARK

Alaska Area Code: 907
Zip Code: 99755

TOURIST INFORMATION

Denali Chamber of Commerce, P.O. Box 437, Healy, AK 99743; 683-4636; mile 0.5 Healy Spur Road

Denali Visitor Center, P.O. Box 688, Talkeetna, AK 99676; 1-800-660-2688; mile 99 Parks Hwy. and Talkeetna Airport; picnic and park area, knowledgeable staff; www.alaskan.com/talkeetnadenali

Denali National Park & Preserve, P.O. Box 9; 683-2294; www.nps.gov/dena

Talkeetna Ranger Station, P.O. Box 588, Talkeetna, AK 99676; 733-2231

ACCOMMODATIONS

Carlo Heights Bed & Breakfast, Box 86; 683-5212; mile 224 Parks Hwy.; spacious and secluded home

Denali Crow's Nest Log Cabins, Box 70; 683-2723; mile 238.5 Parks Hwy.; www.denalicrowsnest.com

Denali Hostel, Box 801; 683-1295; mile 1.3 Otto Lake Road; www.denalihostel.com

Denali Mountain Morning Hostel & Lodge, Box 208; 1-866-D-HOSTEL; mile 224 Parks Hwy.; log cabins, private or shared, kitchen, outdoor gear rentals; www.hostelalaska.com

Denali Princess Wilderness Lodge, 1-800-426-0500; mile 238.5 Parks Hwy.; luxurious accommodations, offering fine and casual dining

Denali River Cabins, Box 210; 1-800-230-7275, 683-8000 (local); located on banks of Nenana River next to park, outdoor grills, no pets; www.denalirivercabins.com

The Perch, 1-888-322-2523; mile 224 Parks Hwy.; cabins, dining; theperch@yahoo.com

CAMPGROUNDS AND RV PARKS

Denali Grizzly Bear Cabins and Campground, Box 7; 683-2696; on south boundary to park, full hookups, cabins, wooded campsites, laundry, propane

Denali RV Park & Motel, Box 155; 1-800-478-1501; mile 245.1 Parks Hwy.; 30 full and 60 partial hookups, pull-throughs, dump station, showers, laundry; www.denalirvpark.com

Denali Rainbow Village & RV Park, Box 777; 683-7777; mile 238.6 Parks Hwy.; 77 full and partial sites, electric, water, dump station, firepits, showers, laundry, tent sites, walk to stores, restaurants; www.denalirvpark.com

Denali Riverside RV Park, 1-888-778-7700; mile 240 Parks Hwy.; dry and pull-through sites, water, electric, propane, showers, toilets, laundry, picnic table, firepits

Morino Campground, mile 1.6 Denali Park Road; walk-in camping only, 60 sites, tents, pit toilets, fee

Riley Creek Campground, mile 0.4 Denali Park Road; 102 campsites, tents, trailers, toilets, water, dump station, fee, open year-round

Sanctuary River Campground, mile 22.5 Denali Park Road; 7 campsites, tents, pit toilets, water, fee

Savage River Campground, mile 12.5 Denali Park Road; 34 campsites, tents, trailers, toilets, water, fee

Teklanika Campground, mile 28.7 Denali Park Road, 53 campsites, tents, trailers, pit toilets, water, fee; driving of vehicle back and forth is prohibited except when checking in or out, shuttle bus avail.

RESTAURANTS

McKinley Creekside Cafe, Box 89; 683-2277; mile 224 Parks Hwy.

TOURIST ATTRACTIONS

Mount McKinley, 20,320 feet, tallest mountain in North America

EAGLE

Population: 152
Alaska Area Code: 907
Zip Code: 99738

TOURIST INFORMATION

Eagle Historical Society & Museum (Visitor Information), P.O. Box 23; 547-2325; eagleak.orgNational Park Service, P.O. Box 167; 547-2233

ACCOMMODATIONS

Falcon Inn B&B, P.O. Box 136; 547-2254; a log building with private baths on Yukon River, suites, TV, home-cooked hot breakfast; custom wilderness riverboat excursions

CAMPGROUNDS AND RV PARKS

Eagle Trading Co., P.O. Box 36; 547-2220; RV hookups, motel, public showers, groceries, cafe, fishing licenses

CANOE RENTALS

Eagle Canoe Rentals, P.O. Box 4; 547-2203; on the Yukon River, canoe rentals offered between Dawson City, Yukon Territory, Eagle and Circle; paddleak@aptalaska.net

MEDICAL

Eagle Village Health Clinic, 547-2243

TOURIST ATTRACTIONS

Yukon-Charlie Rivers National Preserve, National Park Service (Fairbanks Hqrts); Eagle Ranger Station (Field Office); P.O. Box 167; Eagle, AK 99738; 201 First Avenue; Fairbanks, AK 99701; Visitor Information; 907-547-2233 (EAA); email: YUCH_Eagle_Office@nps.gov

HEALY

Population: 889
Alaska Area Code: 907
Zip Code: 99743

TOURIST INFORMATION

Healy Chamber of Commerce, P.O. Box 437; 683-4636; mile 0.5 on Healy Spur Road

ACCOMMODATIONS

Denali Dome Home Bed & Breakfast, P.O. Box 262; 683-1239; mile 137 Healy Spur Road; close to park; wwwldenalidomehome.com

Denali EarthSong Lodge, P.O. Box 89; 683-2863; mile 4.1 on Stampede Road; www.eathsonglodge.com

Denali Lakeview Inn, 683-4035; mile 247 Parks Hwy.; open year-round; www.denalilakeviewinn.com

Denali Suites, P.O. Box 393; 683-2848; located on Healy Spur Road; www.alaskaone.com/densuites

Pat & Windell's Bed & Breakfast, P.O. Box 50; 1-800-683-2472; off Healy Spur Road on Sulfide Drive; pwindell@mtaonline.net

Totem Inn, 683-2384; mile 248.7 Parks Hwy.; full menu, deluxe and economy rooms,open year-round

Touch of Wilderness Bed & Breakfast, P.O. Box 397; 683-2459; mile 2.9 on Stampede Road

Valley Vista Bed & Breakfast, P.O. Box 395; 1-877-683-2841; www.valleyvistabb.com

White Moose Lodge, 1-800-481-1232; mile 248 Parks Hwy.; private wooded area, deck with grill, picnic tables; www.whitemooselodge.com

CAMPGROUNDS AND RV PARKS

McKinley RV and Campground, P.O. Box 340; 1-800-478-2562; mile 248.5 Parks Hwy.

Otto Lake RV Park, P.O. Box 195; 683-2100 (summer), 683-2603 (winter); mile 247 on Parks Hwy., turn west on Otto Lake Road, go 0.5 miles; RV and tentsites, firepits, picnic tables, water, toilets, dump station; www.ottolakealaska.com

RESTAURANTS

Bushmaster Restaurant, 683-2244; mile 248.8 Parks Hwy.

Crows Nest Bar & Grill, 683-2641; mile 238.5 Parks Hwy.

Lynx Creek Pizza, 683-2547; mile 238.6 Parks Hwy.

McKinley-Denali Cabins And Salmon Bake, 683-2258; 238.5 Parks Hwy.

The Bushmaster Restaurant, 683-2244; mile 248.8 Parks Hwy.

MEDICAL

Healy Clinic, 683-2211; Tri-Valley Community Center, 2nd floor, at mile 0.5 Healy Spur Road

HOUSTON

Population: I,202
Alaska Area Code: 907
Zip Code: 99694

GUIDE SERVICES

Alaska Explorers & Fishermen, P.O. Box 940213; mile 54.3 Parks Hwy.; guided fishing, can arrange cabin and boats

Fisherman's Choice Charters, P.O. Box 940276; 1-800-989-8707; specializes in fishing the Deshka, Little Susitna and Talkeetna Rivers, award-winning service; www.akfishermanschoice.com

Miller's Riverboat Service, mile 57.6 on Parks Hwy.; 891-6129; charters, drop-offs, boatlaunch

TACKLE SHOPS

Miller's Place, mile 57.6 on Parks Hwy.; 891-6129

ACCOMMODATIONS

Houston Lodge, mile 57.4 on Parks Hwy.; 892-6808

Miller's Place, mile 57.6 on Parks Hwy.; 891-6129; cabins, camping, RV parking, food

CAMPGROUNDS AND RV PARKS

Little Susitna River Campground, mile 57.4 on Parks Hwy.; 86 sites, picnic tables, water, restrooms, boat launch

Riverside Camper Park, P.O. Box 87; 892-9020; mile 57.7 Parks Hwy.; 56 full hookups,dump station, showers, laundry; bank fishing for king and silver salmon, riverboat charter service available; walking distance to post office, grocery store, service station, restaurant and bar

RESTAURANTS

Houston Lodge, mile 57.4 on Parks Hwy.; 892-6808
Miller's Place, mile 57.6 on Parks Hwy.; 891-6129

AUTO REPAIR

Houston Chevron, mile 57.5 on Parks Hwy.; 892-6211; full repair, wrecker, propane

NENANA

Population: 435
Alaska Area Code: 907
Zip Code: 99760

TOURIST INFORMATION

Nenana Visitor Center, 832-9953; located at Parks Hwy. and A Street junction
Alaska Department of Fish & Game, 459-7202 (Fairbanks office)

ACCOMMODATIONS

Alaskan Retreat Bed and Breakfast, 211 East 4th Street; 832-5431
Bed & Maybe Breakfast, 832-5272; located above the railroad depot next to the Nenana River
Colony Inn, 325 East Elmwood; 745-3330; a former teacher's dormitory converted to motel
Roughwoods Inn & Cafe, 2nd and A St., 832-5299, rooms with kitchenettes, open year-round; roughwoods1@juno.com
Skinny Dick's Halfway Inn, P.O. Box 88; 388-5770; mile 328 Parks Hwy.; rooms, camping
Tripod Motel, 832-5590; mile 304 Parks Hwy.; private bath, kitchenettes available

CAMPGROUNDS AND RV PARKS

Nenana Valley RV Park & Campground, 4th and C Streets; 832-5230; 30 large RV sites, electric hookups, pull-throughs, tentsites, restrooms, showers, laundry, dump station

RESTAURANTS

Two Choice Cafe, 832-1010; located on Main Street; soup and sandwich is the special here, along with ice cream and giant cinnamon rolls

AUTO REPAIR/LOCKSMITH

Parks Highway Service & Towing, P.O. Box 127; 1-800-478-8697; mile 313.6 Parks Hwy.; towing and emergency road services along the northern Parks Highway, 24 hours, including lockouts, recoveries, jump-starts, and tire changes

MEDICAL

Nenana Native Clinic, 802 Front, Nenana, AK 99760; 832-5247

TOURIST ATTRACTIONS

Alfred Starr Nenana Cultural Center, P.O. Box 270; 907-832-5520

TALKEETNA

Population: 363
Alaska Area Code: 907
Zip Code: 99676

TOURIST INFORMATION

Talkeetna Chamber of Commerce, P.O. Box 334
Alaska Department of Fish & Game, 746-6300 (Palmer office)
Talkeetna Historical Society Visitor Information Center, located at junction of Parks Hwy. and Talkeetna Spur Road
National Park Service, Talkeetna Ranger Station, P.O. Box 588; 733-2231

GUIDE SERVICES

Larson Lake Lodge, Inc., P.O. Box 984; 733-2394; remote fly-in fishing lodge east of Talkeetna; www.larsonlakelodge.com
Mahay's Riverboat Service, P.O. Box 705; 1-800-736-2210; wide range of offerings, fully guided, drop-off, all five salmon species; www.mahaysriverboat.com
Talkeetna Riverboat Service, P.O. Box 74; 733-2281; salmon, trout, grayling; www.gotalkeetna.com
Talkeetna River Guides, P.O. Box 563; 1-800-353-2677; trips range from 2 hours to several days; www.alaska.net/~trg

TACKLE SHOPS

Talkeetna River Adventures, P.O. Box 473; 733-2604; mile 14 on Talkeetna Spur Hwy.

ACCOMMODATIONS

Birchwood Cabins, P.O. Box 402; 1-866-247-2496; 3 miles from town, lake access
Chinook Wind Cabins, 733-1899; located on 2nd St
Denali Overlook Inn, P.O. Box 141; 733-3555; info@denalioverlook.com
Fairview Inn, P.O. Box 379; 733-2423; located downtown, rich in history
Grace & Bill's Freedom Hills B&B, P.O. Box 502; 733-2455; gmgermain@worlnet.att.net
Swiss Alaska Inn, P.O. Box 565; 733-2424; motel, restaurant; www.swiswsalaska.com
Talkeetna Alaskan Lodge, 1-888-959-9590, in Talkeetna 733-9500; mile 12.5 Talkeetna Spur Road; 203 deluxe rooms, full-service restaurant; www.talkeetna lodge.com
Talkeetna Cabins, P.O. Box 124; 1-888-733-9933; custom log cabins, kitchen, bath; www.talkeetnacabins.org

TALKEETNA, CONT.

Talkeetna Hostel International, P.O. Box 952; 733-4678; downtown location, private rooms available; wwwltalkeetnahostel.com

Talkeetna Motel, Box 115; 733-2323; 25 rooms, restaurant; open year-round; talkeetna@netscape.net

CAMPGROUNDS AND RV PARKS

Brown Bear Motor Court, 733-2211; ¼ mile up Talkeetna Spur Road; RV park, pull-throughs, tentsites; open May to September; located near good fishing

Christiansen Lake, mile 12 Talkeetna Spur Road; day-use only, toilets, picnic tables, firepits, swimming, fishing

His & Hers, 733-2415; ½ mile north of Talkeetna turnoff, mile 99.5 Parks Hwy.; RV sites, camping, cabins, rooms, fuel, laundry, RV dump site, showers

Talkeetna Camper Park, Box 221; 733-2693; 35 gravel spaces, RV dump, hot water, showers, laundry, full hookups, easy walk to town; www.talkeetnacamper.com

Talkeetna River Adventures, P.O. Box 473; 733-2604; mile 14 on Talkeetna Spur Hwy.; 60 wooded campsites, showers, restrooms, water, dump station, boat launch, fishing for salmon and trout

RESTAURANTS

Talkeetna Roadhouse, P.O. Box 604; 733-1351; located on Main Street, one of Alaska's most famous restaurants, noted for cinnamon rolls and homestyle cooking, rooms and bunks also available; www.alaska.net~rdhouse

AUTO REPAIR

Talkeetna Auto Care, 733-1996; mile 99 Parks Hwy.

Top of the World Auto Body; 746-1122; mile 5 Palmer-Wasilla Hwy.; www.topworldautobody.com

MEDICAL

Sunshine Community Medical Center, 733-2273; mile 4.4 Talkeetna Spur Road

TOURIST ATTRACTIONS

Museum of Northern Nature, Main St.; 733-3999

TRAPPER CREEK

Population: 345
Alaska Area Code: 907
Zip Code: 99683

GUIDE SERVICE

Trapper Creek Inn & General Store, P.O. Box 13209; 733-2302; fishing charters, tackle, license, good source of fishing information

ACCOMMODATIONS

Mary's McKinley View Lodge, P.O. Box 13314; 733-1555; mile 134.5 Parks Hwy.

Mount McKinley Princess Lodge, 733-2900; mile 133 Parks Hwy.

North Country B&B, P.O. Box 13377; 733-3981; on Petersville Road, 2.7 miles from Parks Hwy. junction; www.alaskan.com/northcountrybnb

Trapper Creek Bed & Breakfast, 733-2234; located near general store, museum and library; www.trappercreekbnb@gci.net

CAMPGROUNDS AND RV PARKS

Trapper Creek Inn & General Store, P.O. Box 13209; 733-2302; RV park, full hookups, dump station, showers, restrooms, laundry, fuel; innmaster@matnet.com

RESTAURANTS

Trapper Creek Pizza Pub, 733-3344; mile 115.9 Parks Hwy.; homemade pizza, salad, sandwiches, German beer, bread

WASILLA

Population: 5,213
Alaska Area Code: 907
Zip Code: 99687

TOURIST INFORMATION

Wasilla Chamber of Commerce, P.O. Box 871826, Wasilla, AK 99687; 376-1299; take Trunk Road exit to the Mat-Su Visitors Center

Alaska Department of Fish & Game, 746-6300 (Palmer)

GUIDE SERVICES

Eagle Talon Charters, P.O. Box 874506, Wasilla, AK 99687; 357-5873; salmon fishing and drop-offs; info@eagletaloncharters.com

Fisherman's Choice Charters, P.O. Box 940276, Wasilla, AK 99694; 1-800-989-8707; fishing the Little Susitna, Deshka and Talkeetna Rivers; www.akfishermanschoice.com

Rainbow River Expeditions, 373-2975; 90 minutes north of Anchorage; specializes in rainbow trout fly-fishing and Little Susitna River kings and silvers; www.fishingalaskasalmon.com

Salmon Ready, Box 5221, Wasilla, AK 99654; 1-077 355 2130j specialize in Little Susitna River; www.salmonready.com

Valley River Charters, Box 5167, Wasilla, AK 9965; 1-877-376-6583; specializes in Little Susitna River kings and silvers

TACKLE SHOPS

Fred Meyer, 1501 East Parks Hwy., Wasilla, AK 99654; 352-5000; basic fishing gear, along with complete one-stop shopping

Outdoors & More Sporting Goods, 455 West Parks Highway, Wasilla, AK 99654; 907-376-4464

Three Rivers Fly & Tackle, 390 E Railroad Ave., Wasilla, AK 99654; 373-5434; excellent gear selection and where-to advise

Wal-Mart, 1350 S Seward Meridian Pkwy, Wasilla, AK 99654; 376-9780; good supply of local fishing tackle

ACCOMMODATIONS

Alaskan View Motel, 2650 E. Parks Hwy.; 376-6787; mile 40 Parks Highway; 26 rooms in log motel, cable TV; akview@matnet.com

Kozey Cabins, 351 E. Spruce Ave., Wasilla, AK 99654; 376-3190; one mile from town of Wasilla; heated cabins, fully furnished, kitchens, baths; www.matnet.com/~kozeyac

Lake Lucille Inn, 1300 W. Lake Lucille Dr., Wasilla, AK 99654; 373-1776; situated on lake with watercraft rentals; www.bestwestern.com/lakelucilleinn

Mat-Su Resort, 1850 Bogard Rd., Wasilla, AK 99654; 376-3228; lakeside resort with restaurant and lounge; www.matsuresort.com

Yukon Don B&B, 1830 East Parks Hwy., Wasilla, AK 99654; located at 2221 Yukon Circle; 1-800-478-7472; www.yukondon.com

Shady Acres B&B, 1000 Easy St., Wasilla, AK 99654; 1-800-360-3113; www.home.gci.net/~sabnb

Windbreak Hotel, 2201 E. Parks Hwy., Wasilla, AK 99654; 376-4209; mile 40.5 Parks Hwy.; 10 rooms, excellent dining cafe and a great source of local fishing information and reports

CAMPGROUNDS AND RV PARKS

Alaska R & R Laundry & R V, 495 Park, Wasilla, AK 99654; 373-7286

Best View RV Park, P.O. Box 872001, Wasilla, AK 99687; 745-7400; 1-800-478-6600 (toll free in Alaska); mile 35.5 Parks Hwy.; 63 large spaces, full hookups, pull-throughs, dump station, showers, tent campers, laundry, firepits, picnic tables

RV Park & Country Store, 892-8200; mile 50.2 on Parks Hwy., full hookups, pull throughs, dump station, showers; gifts, food

RESTAURANTS

Black Dog Deli, 1830 East Parks Highway, Wasilla, AK 99654; 373-5291

Chepo's Fiesta Restaurant, 731 West Parks Hwy., Wasilla, AK 99654; 373-5656

Country Kitchen, 401 West Parks Hwy.; 376-6357; family dining, breakfast, homemade pies and cakes

Denali Steak House, 543 West Parks Highway, Wasilla, AK 99654; 357-9444

Great Bear Brewing Co., 238 N. Boundry St., Wasilla, AK 99654; dining in relaxed atmosphere; www.greatbearbrewing.com

Mead's Coffeehouse, 405 E. Herning Ave., Wasilla; 357-5633; soups, salads, sandwiches, email service; www.meadscoffeehouse.com

Meadow Lakes Pizza, 357-1400; mile 49 Parks Hwy.

Peking Chinese Restaurant, 500 East Railroad Ave., Wasilla, AK 99654; 376-4919

The Burger Shack, 4891 East Bogard Rd., Wasilla, AK 99654; 373-3033

The Windbreak Cafe & Lounge, 2201 E Parks Hwy., Wasilla, AK 99654; 376-4484; excellent food, mounted fish and fly displays every angler will want to see, one of the best sources of fishing information in the region

Tokyo Japanese Restaurant, 735 West Parks Highway, Wasilla, AK 99654

CAR RENTALS

Hall's Auto Rental, 1-877- 611-4255 or 746-4255; mile 4.4 Palmer-Wasilla Hwy.; late model cars, pickups, 4x4s; pick up and delivery available

AUTO REPAIR

Mr. Lube, 373-4654; downtown Wasilla behind McDonalds; lube, oil, tires, cooling systems, belts, dump station, transmissions, wheel bearings; open 7 days a week

WASILLA, CONT.

Northern Recreation, 376-8087; mile 40 Parks Hwy.; full line of parts and accessories for campers, motor homes, trailers

Suburban Propane, 745-4841; mile 37.5 Parks Hwy.; RV gas appliance repairs, motor fuel and cylinder filling

LOCKSMITHS

Chucks Lock & Key Service, 376-3184

Katz Towing & Recovery, 376-9257

Neils Lock & Safe, 373-0961

Wolverine Towing Services Limited, Wasilla, AK 99654; 373-2900

MEDICAL

Aic Urgent Care, 950 Bogard Rd., Wasilla, AK 99654; 352-2880

Valley Hospital, 515 East Dahlia, Palmer, AK; 745-4813

VETERINARY CLINICS

All Creatures Veterinary Clinic, 376-7930; mile 74 Palmer-Wasilla Hwy.

TOURIST ATTRACTIONS

Dorothy Page Museum and Visitors Center, 323 Main Street, Wasilla, AK 99654; 373-9071

Iditarod Trail Sled Dog Race Headquarters, P.O. Box 870800, Wasilla, AK 99687; 376-5155; mile 2.2 on Knik Road; www.iditarod.com

WILLOW

Population: 507
Alaska Area Code: 907
Zip Code: 99688

TOURIST INFORMATION

Willow Chamber of Commerce, 495-5858; mile 68 Park Hwy.; www.willowchamber.org

Alaska Department of Fish & Game, 746-6300 (Palmer office)

GUIDE SERVICES

Deshka Silver-King Lodge, P.O. Box 870910; 1-800-928-2055; lodge overlooks Deshka and Susitna Rivers, guided and unguided fishing provided

High Country Alaska, P.O. Box 512/ 495-5125; www.jeffpralle.com

Mat-Su Valley RV Park, Box 431; 495-6300; mile 90.8 Parks Hwy.; www.matsurvpark.com

Pioneer Lodge, P.O. Box 1028; 495-1000; mile 71.4 Parks Hwy.; bank fishing available at lodge; pioneer-lodge@gci.net

Ron's Riverboat Service, P.O. Box 670; 495-7700; www.ronsriverboat.com

Willow Island Resort, 495-6343; mile 71.5 Parks Hwy.

FLY-IN CHARTERS

Denali Flying Service, P.O. Box 1017; 495-5899; mile 70 Parks Hwy. at Willow Airport; www.denaliflying.com

Susitna Air Service, 495-6789; mile 76.5 Parks Hwy.

Willow Air Service, P.O. Box 42; 1-800-478-6370; mile 70 on Parks Hwy.; offers fly-in fishing guided or drop-offs

TACKLE SHOPS

Mat-Su Valley RV Park, Box 431; 495-6300; mile 90.8 Parks Hwy.; www.matsurvpark.com

Willow Island Resort, 495-6343; mile 71.5 Parks Hwy.

Willow True Value Hardware, 495-6275; mile 69 Parks Hwy.

ACCOMMODATIONS

Birch Pond Lodge, P.O. Box 370; 495-3000; mile 67.5 Parks Hwy.; www.birchpondlodge.com

Gigglewood Lakeside Inn, P.O. Box 1601; 1-800-574-2555; mile 88.1 Parks Hwy.

Pioneer Lodge, P.O. Box 1028; 495-1000; mile 71.4 Parks Hwy.; on banks of Willow Creek, private cabins, motel rooms, RV park, laundromat, fine dining; www.gigglewood.com

Susitna Dog Tours & Bed & Breakfast, P.O. Box 464; 495-6324; mile 91.5 Parks Hwy.; log cabin lodge; www.susitnadogtours.com

Willow Island Resort, 495-6343; mile 71.5 Parks Hwy.; cabins, camping, showers, laundry

Willow Trading Post, 495-6457; mile 69.6 on Parks Hwy.; lodging, RV park, showers, laundry, cafe

CAMPGROUNDS AND RV PARKS

Deception Creek Wayside, turn at mile 71.2 off Parks Hwy. and go 1 mile on Hatcher Pass Road to state campground; 17 campsites, toilets, water; good fishing

Mat-Su Valley RV Park, Box 431; 495-6300; mile 90.8 Parks Hwy.; full hookups, pull-throughs, RV dump station, showers, laundromat, camping, picnic sites; openMay to September; www.matsurvpark.com

Montana Creek Campgrounds, 566-CAMP; mile 96.5 Parks Hwy.; situated on good salmon and trout fishing stream

Nancy Lake Recreation Area, mile 67.2 Parks Hwy., 106 campsites, water, toilets, boat launch

Nancy Lake State Recreation Site, Mile 66.6 Parks Hwy., 30 campsites, picnic tables, toilets, water, boat launch

Nancy Lake Resort, 495-6284; mile 64.4 Parks Hwy.; cabins, camping, restrooms, showers, propane, fuel

Pioneer Lodge, P.O. Box 1028; 495-1000; mile 71.4 Parks Hwy.

South Rolly Lake Campground, at milepost 67 take the Nancy Lake State Parkway for 6.6 miles to the campground; 99 campsites, toilets, water, boat launch, rainbow trout fishing

Willow Creek Campground, turn at mile 70.8 off Parks Hwy. and go 3.6 miles on Willow Creek Parkway to state campground; 138 campsites, toilets, water; good salmon fishing

Willow Island Resort, 495-6343; mile 71.5 Parks Hwy.; RV park, full hookups, dump station, showers, laundry

RESTAURANTS

Pioneer Lodge, P.O. Box 1028; 495-1000; mile 71.4 Parks Hwy.

Rocky Ridge Cafe, 495-1312; on Parks Hwy.

Speedway Inn Restaurant & Liquors, 495-6420; mile 75.5 Parks Hwy.

CANOE & BOAT RENTALS

Nancy Lake Resort, 495-6284; mile 64.4 Parks Hwy.

AUTO REPAIR

Newmans' Hilltop Service, mile 68.8 Parks Hwy.; 495-6479; 24-hour wrecker service, gas, diesel, propane, RV water source; open June to September

Willow Creek Service, mile 69 Parks Hwy.; 495-6336; towing, mechanic, parts, batteries, propane, fuel oil, tires, water, full-service gas station

Fall runs of silver salmon receive little pressure, as most Alaskans are in hunting camp. Throughout the month of September, you can often have prime fishing sites all to yourself.

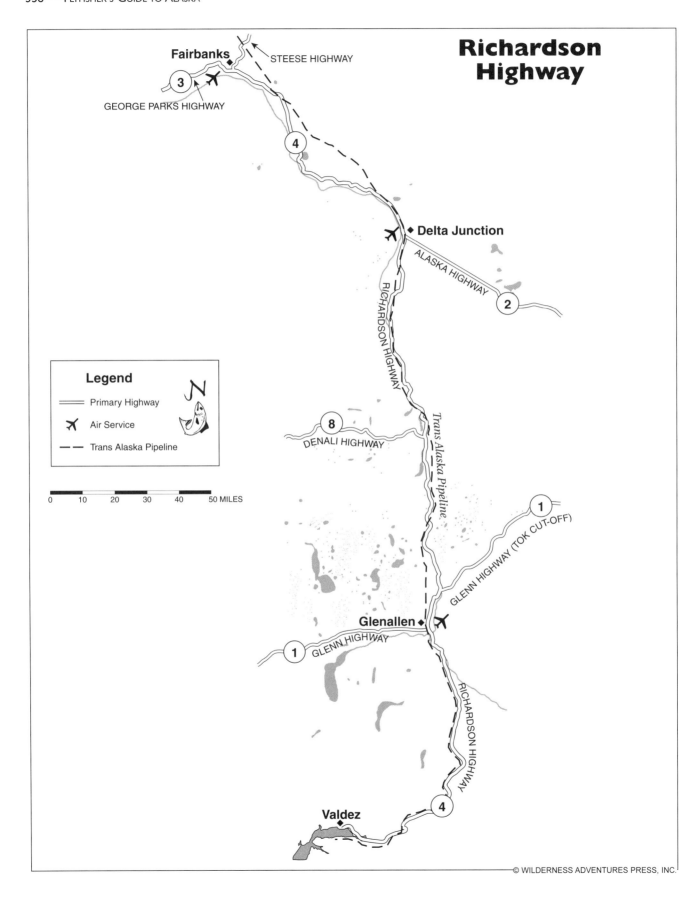

Richardson Highway

Legend

Primary Highway

Air Service

Trans Alaska Pipeline

0 10 20 30 40 50 MILES

Fairbanks

STEESE HIGHWAY

GEORGE PARKS HIGHWAY

Delta Junction

ALASKA HIGHWAY

RICHARDSON HIGHWAY

DENALI HIGHWAY

Trans Alaska Pipeline

GLENN HIGHWAY (TOK CUT-OFF)

Glenallen

GLENN HIGHWAY

RICHARDSON HIGHWAY

Valdez

© WILDERNESS ADVENTURES PRESS, INC.

THE RICHARDSON HIGHWAY

From the port town of Valdez, the Richardson Highway runs 366 miles north to Fairbanks, meeting the Alaska Highway at the 270-mile mark at Delta Junction.

Alaska's first road, the Richardson Highway actually started as a gold-rush trail in the late 1890s. By 1910 the trail was improved to accommodate wagons, and in the 1920s it became fit for vehicle traffic. In the late 1950s the road received its first hard surface, and today it's one of the nicer, more travel-friendly roads in the state.

Most people traveling the Richardson Highway are en route to Valdez, one of the premier port fisheries in Alaska. Others enjoy driving the Richardson Highway because it leads to so many other roads that head off to areas somewhat off the beaten path.

In addition to affording motorists a view of the Chugach Mountains and the Alaska Range, the highway offers an up-close look at the Alaska Pipeline, with formal viewpoints established at miles 64.7, 243.5, and 275.4.

We'll start our discussion of the top fisheries along this road in Valdez and continue on to Fairbanks. With options running from saltwater to high mountain streams, the only drawback is that there's rarely enough time to fish it all.

Please note: Because the Richardson Highway houses many delicate fisheries, anglers need be aware of current fishing regulations, regulatory changes, and emergency orders that may be put into effect on short notice.

Pink salmon are a popular draw on the road system.

Port of Valdez

Once you start discovering all the town of Valdez has to offer, you'll want to stay for as long as possible. As for the flyfishing, don't overlook the world-class salmon fishing to be had from shore, right in the bay. Valdez is renowned for its pink and silver salmon fishing, not close to town, as well as offshore. In fact, this is likely the best pink salmon fishing in the entire state, if not the world.

When you enter Valdez off the Richardson Highway, Dayville Road takes you south across the Lowe River and directly to Allison Point, where you can cast a fly from shore all day long. You can look across the bay and see salmon jumping everywhere, with the town of Valdez in the background.

Allison Point offers plenty of room for anglers to move about. There is no brush to impede casting, and if you wish, you can wade into the bay, further escaping the crowds.

What draws the salmon to this locale is the Solomon Gulch Hatchery. Millions of pink salmon return here each year, which explains why sport anglers take an estimated 50,000 from this area annually. The hatchery also produces silver salmon, with some 25,000 silvers taken near Valdez each season. Many fish hold at the mouth of the hatchery, while wild stocks are continually moving through.

According to Dave Winney of the Hook, Line, and Sinker sporting goods store in Valdez, the best time to fish the salt for salmon is the two hours before and after a high tide, with the high-slack being the most productive. Winney has worked at the Hook, Line, and Sinker since 1986 and is considered one of the area's top authorities on sport fishing, more specifically, flyfishing.

He says the best way to target these tidewater salmon is with a floating line and a variety of streamers. Winney prefers a tarpon fly, although he notes that anything weighted and flashy will catch fish here. The area you're fishing is fairly shallow, and both species of salmon run tight to shore. Long casts aren't as important as getting the fly down quickly to where the fish are.

Because the bay is brackish, incoming silver salmon quickly seek out fresh water. When the silvers are in, anglers can find success anywhere fresh water flows into the bay, from small culverts to bigger water. Once you experience the silver salmon fishing here, you'll see why many consider it Alaska's best-kept silver salmon secret. The fact that in 2003 the daily bag limit was an astounding six fish per day, per angler says it all. As always, when fishing any area in Alaska, make sure you're up to date on the current sport-fishing regulations.

Pink salmon start making their way into the Valdez Arm around late June. The peak of the pink run typically

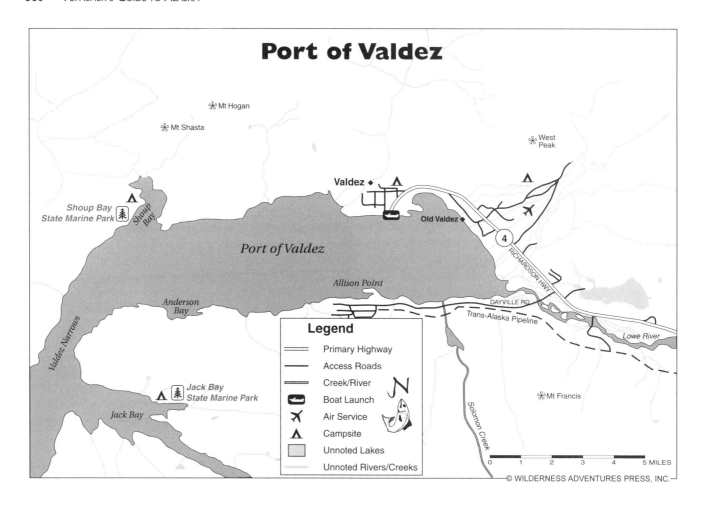

lasts from the first week in July through the end of the month. Silver salmon begin making their presence known in mid- to late July, with the peak fishing coming in the second or third weeks of August. The silver fishing can still be excellent through the first week in September.

If you'd like to earn some extra cash, you may want to put your fishing prowess to the test in one of several Valdez fishing derbies that go on throughout the summer. In 2003, the prize money totaled more than $65,000, including a first-place prize of $15,000 for the largest silver salmon caught. In 2002, the record silver salmon fell in the Valdez Silver Derby, with a fish of 21.76 pounds. Incidentally, this is the state's oldest silver salmon derby.

While the silver salmon derby normally runs from the first Saturday in August through the end of the month, the Valdez Halibut Derby lasts for more than three months, from Memorial Day weekend in May through the end of August. Derby tickets can be purchased at any store that sells fishing license for only $10.00 per day or $50.00 for the season for each derby.

If you're looking to take some fresh fish home for the winter, Valdez offers some of Alaska's finest bottom fish-

ing. Halibut are the main draw, though lingcod and several other bottom fish can be taken from these waters. With several charter boats operating out of Valdez, all you need to do is shop around locally and book your trip with whomever you feel most comfortable.

Robe River

You don't have to travel far from Valdez to get into some quality stream fishing. In fact, there are many streams and lakes within short driving distance of town, which is why it serves as an ideal base camp for anglers looking to do it all.

At mile 2.5 on the Richardson Highway, there's a roadside pulloff that allows easy access to the Robe River. From the highway downstream the water is designated flyfishing only, though there are hook and weight regulations anglers need to be aware of. The Robe River is currently open to Dolly Varden and silver, red, pink, and chum salmon fishing.

Where the Robe crosses the highway, the fishing can be tough due to excessive brush. You'll need chest waders to get into the middle of the stream so you can cast up or down in search of fish. The river is typically slow and quite clear, except after a rain when it acquires a tannic hue. At its widest spot, the Robe runs about 30 yards across.

If you have a float tube along, this is a good place to put in and work your way down to the mouth of the river. If you're on foot, you may want to consider driving back downstream, where the locals like to fish this river.

On the way out of Valdez, you'll see a few softball fields. Take what the locals refer to as the Ball Field Road, which runs behind these fields, and follow it to the river mouth. The wade fishing is much easier here, as there are no trees to inhibit your backcast, only lush grasses to wade through on your way to some great fishing.

Due to the variety of salmon in the Robe River, egg patterns work great early on, with flesh flies proving lethal later in the summer. Streamers are always a good bet, but make sure they carry at least a little bit of white in them. White streamers are a local favorite on this river.

Keep an eye out for bears, as they are thick here during the salmon runs.

Robe Lake

Despite the rich fishing offered by the Robe River, Robe Lake leaves something be desired. At mile 3.1 a roadside pulloff allows access to the lake, which holds the same fish species as the river. The lake is closed to all salmon fishing, though, which leaves only Dollys on the menu. The fishing is good only in the fall, during a small window of time in September.

The lake is shallow and the amount of dissolved oxygen is poor due to the fact that some of the lake's inflow has been diverted over time. This problem is being rectified, but until that time, it's not worth spending too much

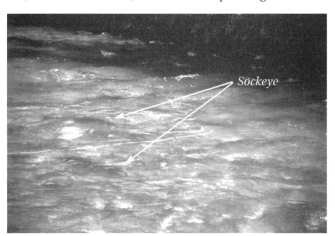

Rolling egg patterns below sockeye redds is a great way to find trout and char.

time at this lake. Some years the Dollys enter and spend the winter, some years they don't. Why is anyone's guess, but it attests to how spotty the action can be.

Lowe River

Though the Lowe River is presently closed to salmon fishing, it offers great Dolly Varden action, and on rare occasions, a steelhead or two. From where the river dumps into the Port of Valdez up to the 24-mile mark on the Richardson Highway, there are several places to pull over and fish. However, because the Lowe is a glacial stream, it runs quite silty, making it tough on fly anglers.

Still, there is good Dolly fishing where clear-running tributaries enter the river and give fish a chance to flush their gills of silt. The Lowe River is easy to wade and fish, with smolt imitations a good choice during the spring months. As the season progresses, switch to beads, Glo-Bugs, and flesh flies to target ravenous Dollys taking advantage of the variety of salmon proteins in the water.

Don't try to stick your float tube in this river. Many whitewater rafting companies based out of Valdez run this stream and it has some raging rapids. A few rafts are lost in this river each year.

The Lowe River flows into the bay near the Robe River, meaning access can be had behind the same softball fields. And the fishing can be good towards the mouth.

One of the signs Dave Winney depends on when fishing this river is bird activity. If you see gulls or eagles flocking together, it means fish are near, and an easy meal is only a matter of time. Because Dollys follow the migrating salmon, anglers can use the birds to their advantage, slipping in and pulling some fine char from the river before the bears arrive.

Thompson Lake

You can see Thompson Lake sitting below the highway at mile 23.3. Grayling, rainbow trout, and Dolly Varden are present. This is a very open lake with few hangups, seemingly designed with the wading fly angler in mind. The only drawback is the wind; once it kicks up, the bite seems to decline considerably.

Dave Winney likes to stir up the mud as he wades his way around the lake. This seems to kick up insect life and attract schools of grayling, which can be seen rolling for the food. Beadhead nymphs work great for grayling, but once you see them rising, waste no time switching to black, red, or brown surface patterns. Black Ants, Black Gnats, and Mosquito patterns are all top choices for surface-feeding grayling. The fishing can be good here all summer long.

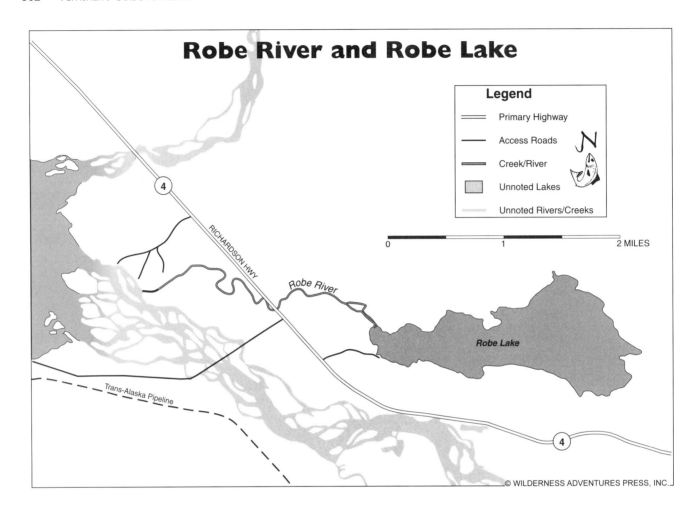

Blueberry Lake

A stocked rainbow lake located at mile 24, Blueberry Lake is a clear body of water that offers good fishing. The deeper spots are located in the middle of the lake, and the only fishing that can be done in waders is at the picnic area.

If you have a float tube, you'll be able to do a great deal more fishing, but watch out for the wind. When it blows hard, the bite on this lake subsides. A fun aspect of fishing Blueberry Lake is watching the rainbows feed, then coaxing them into a rise on a dry fly. There is an abundance of fallen timber, which makes the fishing a real challenge at times.

Even if you don't intend to fish this lake, check out the Blueberry Lake State Recreation Site. This is rated as one of Alaska's most attractive campgrounds, nestled in an alpine setting amid towering peaks. There are campsites, restrooms, firepits, and water here, and you can camp overnight for a fee.

Worthington Lake

Worthington Lake is a clear body of water situated in an alpine setting and commanding an open view of the surrounding area. You'll find the lake at mile 27 on the highway, near the top of Thompson Pass. You can park right at the lake's outlet, which is also where you'll find the best wade fishing.

Though Worthington is a stocked lake, it's not a closed system so the stocking program isn't very strong. Nonetheless, some good-sized rainbows hold over and catching trout up to 24 inches in not that rare. If you have a boat, make your way across the lake to deeper waters, where larger rainbows will hang out during the summer months. Nymphs and streamers can be very effective at fooling the hogs.

Tiekel River

Between miles 43 and 50, the Richardson Highway runs parallel to the Tiekel River. And though this is a very attractive stream, you're a master angler if you can tease a 12-inch Dolly from here. Dollys are the only fish present, with fish between 6 and 8 inches the norm.

The Tiekel looks like it should be teeming with fish, but a waterfall blocks it off from the Copper River, so no salmon make their way into the drainage. But if you want to try your luck on some of these pretty little native char, go small on the fly selection.

Knee boots suffice on this water, as there's little actual wading to do in the deep, slow water that is filled with logjams and beaver dams. It's behind these structures that the little Dollys reside.

Little Tonsina River

Another tough-to-fish river lies just past mile 64, where a roadside pulloff leads to the Little Tonsina River. Dolly Varden in the 3-pound class are fairly common, with some larger ones often taken.

The Little Tonsina is a clear, deep river, and anglers are forced to walk along trails carved atop its banks. If it's raining, hip boots are a wise choice, as the going can get rather mucky. The water moves at a good clip and there are a good many snags to deal with. If you approach the water with patience and persistence, you won't be disappointed, though, for once you tie into a hefty Dolly, all the hard work suddenly seems worth it.

Keep an eye out for schools of salmon when you're fishing here. Salmon do enter this stream, and though it is closed to fishing for them, the Dollys rely on them as a primary source of sustenance. Beads and egg patterns are good selections during the salmon spawn, with flesh patterns good shortly thereafter.

Tonsina River

Ten miles farther down the road brings you to the mainstem Tonsina River. Though this river receives a run of king salmon, the fast, heavily silted water is not conducive to flyfishing. If you want a shot at the kings here, you'll probably have to plunk bait, though there is one other option.

If you yearn to land a king on a fly in this river, the best chance lies near the mouth, on what is referred to as the Lower Tonsina River. To access this area, turn east on the Edgerton Highway at mile 82.5 and follow it 19.5 miles to the Tonsina River bridge near the mouth. This is pretty much the only place you can latch into a king on the fly.

Squirrel Creek Campground Lake

Squirrel Creek Pit, located at mile 80 on the Richardson Highway, is an old gravel pit that's been converted into a fairly good fishery. There's also a large, clean, attractive recreation site here, complete with a boat launch. The lake is generously stocked with grayling and rainbow trout and receives surprisingly little pressure.

Squirrel Creek Pit is a clear lake, and there's no real need for a boat to experience quality fishing. Fishing from a float tube works great according to Dave Winney. From a tube, you can cover a great deal of water. There are also many trails around Squirrel Creek Pit that make for easy access. If an easy-to-reach fishery with lots of action for trout and grayling in a small pond sounds good to you, give this water a try.

Edgerton Highway Lakes

If you turn east at mile 82.6 you'll be on the Edgerton Highway, heading toward the towns of Chitina and McCarthy. Between the Chitina airport and the town of Chitina, there are three lakes that offer great fishing opportunities for fly fans.

Third Lake, often referred to as Three Mile Lake, is located east of the highway at mile 29.7. A paved turnout leads to the lake, where grayling and rainbow trout await. **Second Lake**, or Two Mile Lake, sits on the west side of the highway at mile 30.7 and has a large gravel parking area on its southeast end. There are also good grayling and rainbows in this lake. **First Lake**, or One Mile Lake, is found east of the highway at mile 31.8 and has a boat ramp at the east end.

All three of these lakes are long and narrow and parallel the highway. First Lake is a bit brushier than the other two, but with a canoe or boat, anglers can choose the places they want to fish. All three lakes are fairly open, but they're so narrow that the wind isn't a major factor. Float tubes are also useful on these lakes. There are places to bank fish, especially around Second and Third Lakes, but the soil in the lakes makes for tough wade fishing.

As the lakes are nestled between the peaks of the Chugach and Wrangell Mountains, anglers can often spot Dall sheep foraging the hillsides or soaking up the sun.

Klutina River

Perhaps the best place to fight a king salmon on a fly rod thus far in the journey lies at the century mark on the Richardson Highway. Mile 100 is where the Klutina River flows beneath the road on its way to the Copper River. You can fish up or downstream here, though the river is fast and glacial fed.

Don't attempt to cross this stream or float it, as whole trees come barreling down on a regular basis. Stick to the banks and fish the seams and current lines for king salmon. One caveat to the king fishing: In the previous

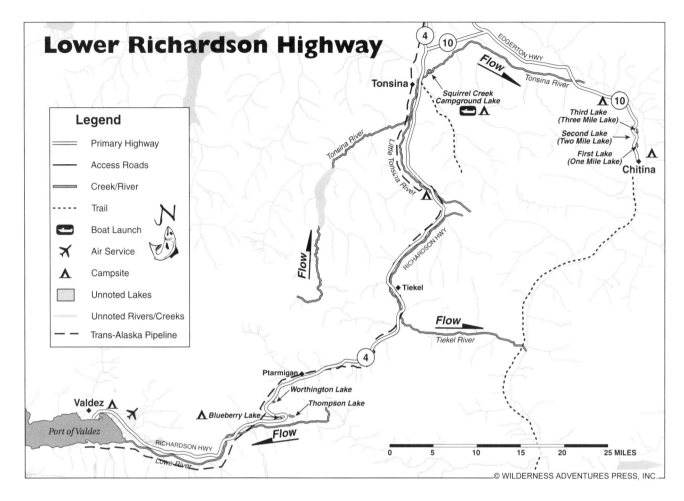

paragraph I stated that this is the best place to hook a king salmon. Landing it is another matter. The king salmon here are of a unique physical design—more like a torpedo than a typical fat Alaskan chinook—that allows them to more efficiently conquer the long distances required to reach their spawning grounds. This bullet-like frame, combined with a swift current and lots of large impediments, means the odds of landing a salmon are slim. Nevertheless, you can go with some heavy gear and at least give it a shot.

The Klutina is one of the best rivers in the area for sockeyes. As in most streams, migrating red salmon hug the bank, and this is where anglers should concentrate their efforts. Streamers fished tight to the shore are the key here.

Dolly Varden and grayling are also present, though they can be tough to find in the big, silty waters. If you don't mind a bit of a physical challenge, head up the marked road to Klutina Lake. If it's raining, you'll need a 4x4, and if there's been recent road slides, and it's bone dry, 4x4s are still helpful. This road leads to a primitive campsite, but because the road runs atop the bluffs, the

river is in a gorge a good distance below. You have to be in good shape to make this journey, but the fishing can be worth it. You'll also be required to pay a native land access fee as you make your way to the campsite.

Stream Facts: Klutina River

Seasons

- All flowing waters upstream from ADF&G markers at mile 19.2 on Klutina Lake Road to Klutina Lake are open to all salmon fishing January 1 to July 19.

- All flowing waters downstream from ADF&G markers at mile 19.2 on Klutina Lake Road to a line between the two ADF&G markers located at the confluence of the Klutina and Copper Rivers are open to king salmon fishing January 1 to July 31, and for all other salmon the season is open year-round.

Special Regulations

- One king salmon 20 inches or more, anglers are allowed 1 per day, 1 in possession.

Klutina River

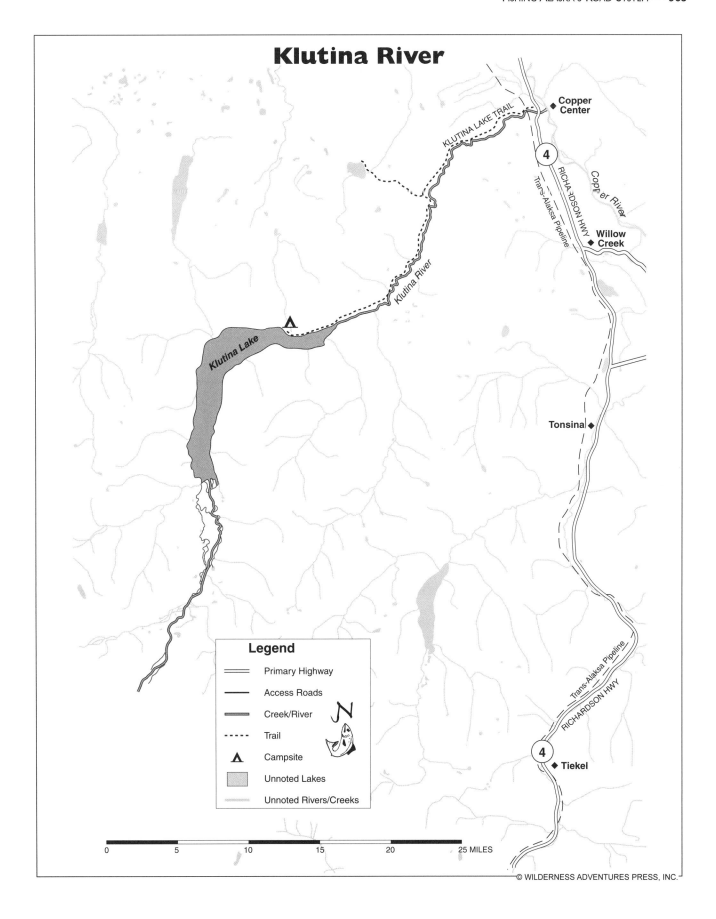

Copper Center

4

KLUTINA LAKE TRAIL

Copper River

RICHARDSON HWY

Trans-Alaska Pipeline

Willow Creek

Klutina River

⛺

Klutina Lake

Tonsina

Legend

	Primary Highway
	Access Roads
	Creek/River
- - -	Trail
⛺	Campsite
	Unnoted Lakes
	Unnoted Rivers/Creeks

Trans-Alaska Pipeline

RICHARDSON HWY

4 Tiekel

0   5   10   15   20   25 MILES

- Other salmon 16 inches or more, anglers are allowed 3 per day, 3 in possession.

- On all salmon species less than 16 inches in length, anglers are allowed 10 per day, 10 in possession.

Fish

- King and red salmon, Dolly Varden, arctic grayling

River Characteristics

- A fast, glacial stream that can be heavy with silt. Floating logs and large impediments make this a dangerous river to wade or float.

Fishing Access

- Mile marker 100 from Valdez on the Richardson Highway.

Maps

- *Alaska Atlas and Gazetteer*, page 86

Bear Creek

Continuing on the main highway, you'll see the Copper River to the east, and it will soon becomes obvious that this is not a fishable stream. Pushing on past the town of Glennallen and the junction with the Glenn Highway you'll soon come to Bear Creek at mile 127, another fishery that can be unforgiving in its own way.

Bear Creek offers fair spring and fall grayling fishing. This is a narrow, clear, little stream that is shallow in places and can be crossed in several spots, which helps you get around brushier areas along the bank. Due to the creek's location and easy access, it gets hammered pretty hard by the locals, meaning large grayling can be tough to come by.

The worst aspect about fishing Bear Creek, however, is its rampant mosquito population. Be certain to take plenty of bug repellent and a head net. It can be so mosquito-infested here that at times you literally can't take in a breath without inhaling a mouthful of insects. But if you don't mind dealing with the bugs, and keeping your eyes shut from time to time, a dry mosquito pattern can get you into fish (believe it or not).

Gulkana River

Considered the premier fishery of the entire Richardson Highway, the Gulkana River offers numerous prospects. Access is excellent, with many easy-to-reach locations between miles 128 and 148. In addition to the roadside pulloffs, there are fishing trails at miles 129, 136.7, 139.6, 141.4, and 146.5. There is also a user's site at mile 148.

Crimson sockeye salmon frequent many road system streams.

From mile 189 to 194, the upper section of the Gulkana offers excellent access and fishing opportunities, as well.

Downstream from mile 128, where the Gulkana flows under the highway, it's designated flyfishing-only water. Home to king and red salmon, along with grayling and rainbows, this section of river is ideal for wading. The Gulkana is a clear stream, except when rains dirty it temporarily. Though the river is up to 80 yards wide in places, there are still areas where anglers can cross. Native land access fees are required at some points below the bridge.

The Gulkana is clear enough to sight fish, and this tactic can greatly increase your catch rate. One good method to kickoff your fishing is to simply stand atop the bridge, locate fish, and wade your way to within casting range. Observe what the fish are doing. Are they on the move, schooling up, or holding individually in isolated pockets? Figuring out their behavior is one of the keys to success.

An interesting aspect of this river is one that's recognized more by resident anglers than tourists. It has to do with rainfall and the bite. The pattern seems to be that following a fairly heavy rain—though not intense enough to throw the water off-color—the bite turns off. In fact, though the stream may look like it's in perfect condition, it can take up to three days for the bite to resume once again. Dave Winney first brought this phenomenon to my attention, though no one seems to know why it happens. Perhaps it's a small change in temperature or a slight rise in river level or the release of natural elements into the river; we may never know.

The gravel banks of the Gulkana provide ideal wade fishing. Chest waders will allow you to wade out into the river, getting closer to fish, and they'll also help keep mosquitoes from devouring most of your body. Yes, the bugs are bad here, and if you can wade well into the river, a breeze often keeps them at bay.

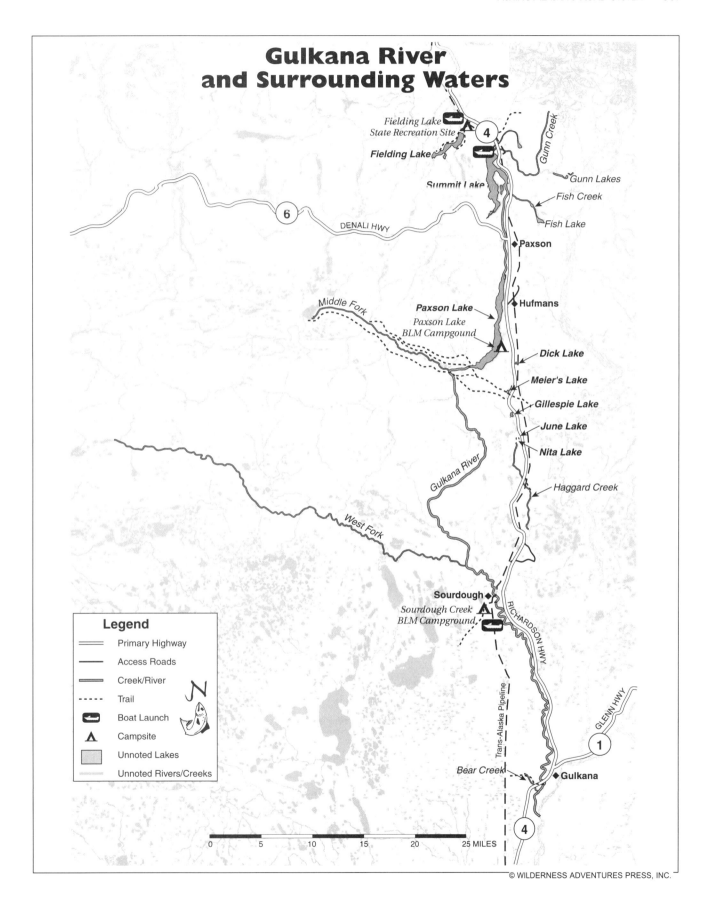

Gulkana River and Surrounding Waters

Fielding Lake
State Recreation Site

Fielding Lake

Summit Lake

Gunn Creek

Gunn Lakes

Fish Creek

Fish Lake

4

6

DENALI HWY

◆ **Paxson**

◆ **Hufmans**

Middle Fork

Paxson Lake

*Paxson Lake
BLM Campgound*

Dick Lake

Meier's Lake

Gillespie Lake

June Lake

Nita Lake

Gulkana River

Haggard Creek

West Fork

Sourdough ◆

*Sourdough Creek
BLM Campground*

RICHARDSON HWY

Legend

═══	Primary Highway
───	Access Roads
～～	Creek/River
‐ ‐ ‐	Trail
⛴	Boat Launch
⛺	Campsite
▮	Unnoted Lakes
～	Unnoted Rivers/Creeks

N

Trans-Alaska Pipeline

GLENN HWY

1

Bear Creek ◆ **Gulkana**

4

0   5   10   15   20   25 MILES

© WILDERNESS ADVENTURES PRESS, INC.

Rafting is easy on this river. Simply launch at one point along the road and drift to another, then walk back up the highway or hitch a ride to your car. The Gulkana runs a bit warmer than most rivers in the area, and its slow, meandering nature makes floating a pleasure.

Though it involves a steep trail and tough going unless you have some experience in packing in a raft and floating on your own, a good one-day trip is to hike to the river at Poplar Grove at mile 137 and float down to the bridge. The fishing for grayling and king and red salmon can be very good on this run. The river is shallow in many places in this stretch, which forces the fish to congregate in holding areas.

At mile 148 you'll find the Sourdough Creek BLM Campground and Sourdough Creek. The campground has numerous campsites, outhouses, picnic tables, grills, and a nightly camping fee is required. The creek holds some trophy-class grayling, approaching 18 inches. From early May through the month of June, yellow egg patterns are good grayling medicine, while standard grayling patterns work well from the middle of June to the start of winter.

There is also excellent bank fishing to be had on the Gulkana River right at the campground. The slack water and a deep hole offer salmon a great staging area. Because the current is so slow, you can actually put in a float tube, fish through the hole, and take out in the same place. The campground is also a good place to shove off in a raft for points downstream.

From Sourdough Campground, it's a comfortable two-day run to Poplar Grove. The river is slow and fairly deep compared to other sections, and the fall fishing for big grayling and rainbows up to 24 inches can be very good. When they're in, the action for king and red salmon can be brisk. With king salmon reaching 60 pounds here, you'll have your work cut out for you if you hook one of these monsters from a raft. If you want to extend the drift, and avoid a challenging hike out, consider floating down to the highway and taking out there.

The upper Gulkana River, between miles 189 and 194, is closed to salmon fishing, but fat, healthy grayling up to 16 inches can be expected with regularity. There are many places to wade and fish up here, but the big, slippery boulders require felt soles. The water runs clear here, and it's easy to see where you're going, so hip boots will get you by just fine. Salmon can be seen making their death march to the spawning grounds, and you'll often spot moose and bear. The river is within a quarter-mile of the road throughout this stretch, but it will feel more like a wilderness experience, which for many anglers just adds to the appeal.

Stream Facts: Gulkana River

Seasons

- King salmon season runs January 1 to July 19.
- All other fishing is open year-round.

Special Regulations

- On the mainstem Gulkana, downstream of the Richardson Highway bridge, only single-hook artificial flies can be used from June 1 to July 31 (gap between hook point and shank is not to exceed ¾ inch, and additional weight must be affixed at least 18 inches above the fly). From August 1 to May 31, only unbaited single-hook artificial lures can be used.

- On the mainstem Gulkana, upstream from the Richardson Highway bridge to the ADF&G marker 7.5 miles upstream from the West Fork confluence, bait and artificial lures are permitted (including treble hooks) from June 1 to July 19. From July 20 to May 31, only unbaited single-hook artificial lures can be used.

- For king salmon 20 inches or longer, anglers are allowed 1 per day, 1 in possession.

- For all other salmon 16 inches or longer, anglers are allowed 3 per day, 6 in possession.

- For rainbow trout, anglers are allowed 2 per day, 2 in possession.

- For grayling, anglers are allowed 5 per day, 5 in possession.

Fish

- King and red salmon, rainbow trout, arctic grayling

River Characteristics

- The Gulkana is a large, wide, clear stream when not hampered by rains. Up to 80 yards wide in areas, it's actually shallow enough to wade across in places. The clarity and ease of access make it a premier bank-fishing river. Chest waders give anglers the freedom to explore many miles of water, and sight fishing can be highly effective.

Fishing Access

- The Gulkana River can be reached from the highway at several places between miles 128 and 148. And there are many roadside pulloffs and trails in the area. There is also a user's site at mile 148. From mile 189 to 194, the upper Gulkana River can be accessed from the road.

Maps

- *Alaska Atlas and Gazetteer*, pages 86-87

Haggard Creek

At mile 161, Haggard Creek makes its way to the highway and offers good fishing for grayling, the only species present.

This clear stream can be waded on both sides of the highway, with a BLM trailhead located on the west side.

June and Nita Lakes

Lakes June and Nita are located to the west of the highway and are fairly easy to reach. There is roadside parking at mile 166 and it's a quarter-mile hike into either lake.

Both lakes hold grayling, and a float tube will help you reach the best fishing. There is some bank angling available, too, and fly anglers will have the best success targeting rising fish late in the day.

Gillespie Lake

More fishing awaits at Gillespie Lake, which is located at mile 169.5 on the highway. This lake can be reached by hiking a quarter-mile up the creek from the roadside. Though it's a tiny creek, persistent anglers can pull grayling from its waters.

If you don't feel like battling the stream to reach the lake, there are nice, open trails you can follow. Packing in a belly boat will definitely increase the amount of water you can fish. But the shores of this lake are fairly open, too.

Meier's Lake

Meier's Lake can be seen from the road near mile 171. It's a good-sized body of water for this area. If you're fishing from a float tube, stay close to the shoreline in case the wind picks up. If you want to cover a large amount of water, a canoe would be a better choice.

For bank anglers, the best fishing is at the lake inlet. Often, you can pull over and watch for rising grayling. If you detect action, throw on the hip boots and head to the lake with your favorite dry flies, as there are some big grayling in this lake.

Dick Lake

Dick Lake, located at mile 173, gives anglers the dubious honor of fishing within plain view of the Trans-Alaska Pipeline.

To reach the lake, take the narrow lane on the east side of the highway. (It's easy to miss if you aren't paying attention.) This will lead you to the small lake, where you can expect grayling up to 12 inches.

Paxson Lake

Paxson Lake is one of the larger roadside lakes in the area and can be reached at various places along the highway between miles 175 and 182. At mile 175, you'll find plenty of campsites and facilities at the Paxson Lake BLM Campground.

A boat is necessary to fish this lake thoroughly in search of grayling, lake trout, and burbot. To wet a line from shore look to the lake's outlet, where you'll find surprisingly good fishing.

Fish Lake and Fish Creek

It's a 2-mile hike into Fish Lake from the roadside pulloff on the west side of the highway near mile 192.

Fish Creek parallels the trail the entire way to the lake, and though it's closed to salmon fishing, spawning reds can be seen here in the fall. If you like catching grayling, Fish Lake is worth the walk in.

The best fishing can be found at the lake, but if high winds hamper your casting just slip back to the creek where you can sight fish for grayling. The creek is clear and shallow and you could easily wade fish it the whole way back to the highway.

Just how good is the grayling fishing in Fish Lake? You can expect to catch upwards of 50 fish an hour here, if your arm doesn't tire. At this writing, Fish Lake was a catch-and-release fishery and this, combined with a lack of pressure, makes it one of the premier grayling lakes in the region. Hefty grayling up to 16 inches are not uncommon here.

Later in the season the lake recedes from shore and the fish move to deeper water. At this time, wading the boggy shoreline is the rule. Watch closely for scavenging bears, though, and give them the right of way at all times.

Summit Lake

Summit Lake is a large lake tucked behind Fish Lake. At mile 194, anglers can pull off the road and walk to the lake. Grayling, lake trout, and burbot live in this massive lake, which can be tough to fish from a boat due to high winds.

For fly anglers, there are plenty of places to wade out from shore and get away from the brush. The best time to fish here is in mid-May, just as soon as the ice goes off. Search for rising grayling near shore.

Gunn Creek

If there's a diamond in the rough along this highway, Gunn Creek is it. I've yet to see anything published on Gunn Creek, despite the fact that it's the premier grayling

Some roadside lakes are planted with rainbows, offering good opportunities for family angling.

stream in this drainage. Anglers can expect to pull grayling from this stream that measure an honest 18 inches, about as big as you'll find anywhere in the region.

At mile 196, the creek flows from east of the highway, draining out of Gunn Lake. You can literally hike several miles up this clear stream, picking up large grayling as you go. There are a couple of nice holes directly under the bridge. But as is the case in most places, the farther you get from the road, the better the fishing will be.

These are the biggest, fattest grayling you'll find up here, and catch-and-release fishing is encouraged. Once you've battled a trophy or two from one hole, move on to the next sweet spot to allow the place to rest.

Gunn Creek has a gravel bottom with some exposed gravel bars, and there is plenty of room to cast around what few alders do exist. Chest waders are recommended here. In addition to hitting the usual holding pockets and tailouts, don't overlook the side channels, where big grayling often seek incoming food.

Fielding Lake

Fielding Lake is yet another large lake, situated at mile 200.5 off the Richardson Highway. Turn west off the highway and follow the gravel road for 2 miles to the lake. A limited number of primitive campsites are present at Fielding Lake State Campground.

Home to grayling, lake trout, and burbot, Fielding offers fairly good fishing for lakers. Bank anglers working the shoreline in low-light conditions early in the morning and late in the evening will often catch lake trout cruising the shallows, particularly in early spring when the ice leaves the lake for the first time. There's a two-week window when the action can be very good before the water heats up and the trout migrate to deeper waters.

If you're here in the fall, trolling a weighted streamer behind a sinking line can be productive if you have a boat. During the summer months, the best way to pull lake trout and burbot from the depths is with hardware and bait.

Quartz Lake

For the next several miles of highway, you'll see numerous creeks that offer limited fishing opportunities. The **Delta River** parallels the west side of the Richardson Highway, but this river is too large and packed with silt to fish. However, if you're intent on exploring this area, spend the majority of your time at the mouths of the river's many clear tributaries; you may learn a few secrets.

There are seven lakes at mile 240, known as the **Coal Mine Lakes**. Be warned, however, that a 4x4 is required to reach these lakes. A short drive down Coal Mine Road will connect you with the lakes, and some very beautiful country. Char, lake trout, and grayling are on tap in these lakes. It's also fun to explore some of the abandoned mines around the area.

Continuing on the Richardson Highway brings you to the town of Delta Junction, where the Alaska Highway ends. Clearwater Creek runs east of Delta Junction and is addressed at the end of the section on the Alaska Highway, as this is the best road from which to access the stream.

Moving north on the Richardson Highway, you'll cross the **Tanana River**, which borders the highway for many miles. There is some burbot fishing in the river between the bridge and Shaw Creek north of the town of Big Delta. Referred to as the "poor man's lobster" in Alaska's interior, burbot are worth catching just to taste. The only hitch is that you must have bait anchored to the bottom to tie into these freshwater relatives of the cod family.

Quartz Lake is the body of water most people head for on this stretch of road, and once you see it you'll understand why. Quartz Lake and the Quartz Lake Recreation Area are easily reached by taking the marked turnoff to the east at mile 278. A drive of 2.8 miles takes you to the lake and campground, which has numerous developed campsites, firepits, toilets, and running water. Though this is the most popular lake in the area for recreational use, an abundance of plant life on the surface restricts where jet skiers can travel.

Rated as the best stocked lake in the region, Quartz is also a visually appealing body of water with exceptional fish. Though it covers some 1,500 acres, more than three-quarters of the lake runs less than 15 feet deep, with 40 feet the maximum depth.

Quartz Lake
and Surrounding Waters

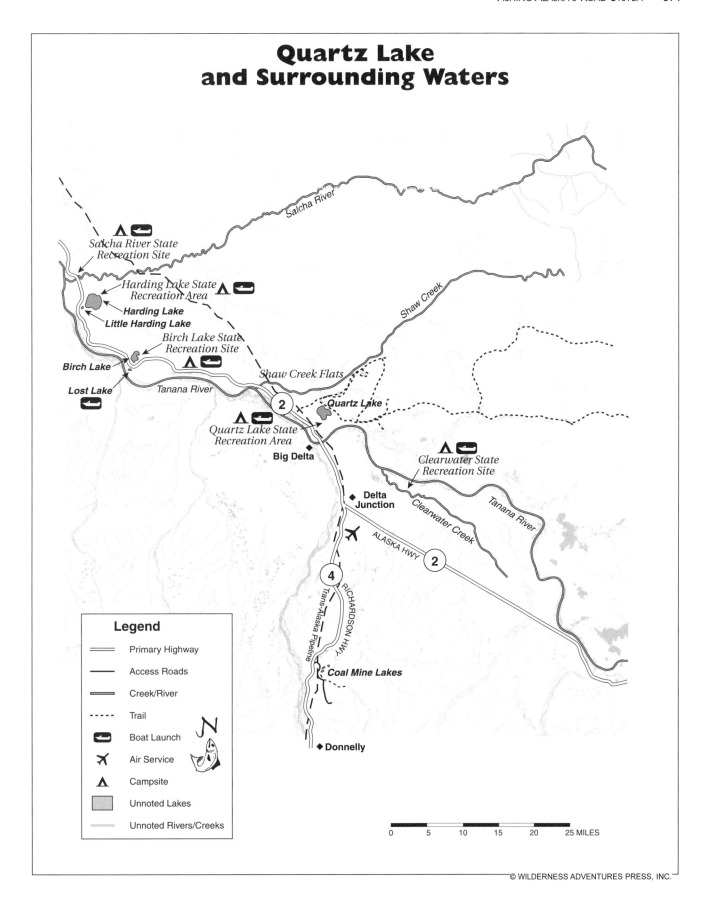

Salcha River

Salcha River State
Recreation Site

Harding Lake State
Recreation Area

Harding Lake
Little Harding Lake

Shaw Creek

Birch Lake State
Recreation Site

Birch Lake

Shaw Creek Flats

Lost Lake

Tanana River

2

Quartz Lake

Quartz Lake State
Recreation Area

Big Delta

*Clearwater State
Recreation Site*

Tanana River

**Delta
Junction**

Clearwater Creek

ALASKA HWY

2

4

RICHARDSON HWY

Trans-Alaska Pipeline

Coal Mine Lakes

Legend

	Primary Highway
	Access Roads
	Creek/River
- - -	Trail
⛵	Boat Launch
✈	Air Service
⛺	Campsite
▨	Unnoted Lakes
	Unnoted Rivers/Creeks

N

♦ Donnelly

0   5   10   15   20   25 MILES

Quartz Lake is stocked with rainbows, arctic char, undersized silver salmon, and occasionally small king salmon. With char up to 25 inches and rainbows in the upper teens, this lake is worth a visit.

There are two boat launches, and a small launch fee is required. A canoe or float tube can be used comfortably on this large lake, and some kind of boat is just about required to get beyond the groves of lilies. If you want to explore more water but don't have a motorboat, you can rent one at the lake.

Egg-Sucking Leeches fished around the edges of the lily pads can be very effective. Using a sinking line, cast close to the weeds, letting the fly sink among the stems. Vary your retrieval rate until you find what the fish like that particular day. Dark leeches tied with sparkling tinsel are also useful.

Shaw Creek

As you pass through Shaw Creek Flats, you'll find Shaw Creek flowing under the highway on the western fringes near mile 287. Because the mouth of the creek is so near the road, it's a good place to hit in early spring when the grayling begin their migration to the spawning grounds. The fall grayling fishing can also be good here.

Beyond the bridge there is a great deal of private land, and gaining access is tough.

Birch Lake

A pullout on the east side of the highway at mile marker 306 lands you at the next road-accessible lake. From this rest area, you can look over Birch Lake, plotting your plan of attack on this attractive body of water.

Though it's fairly large, Birch Lake can be fished from much of its shore or with a canoe or belly boat. This is a stocked lake that receives considerable pressure for the rainbows, char, and silver salmon it receives. But it can handle a lot of activity, as more than 60,000 fish are annually dumped into this 800-acre lake.

It's nice to fish the lake from a canoe, cruising around and working the fringes of lily pads. There are also some beaver huts in the lake, and the fishing is usually productive around these structures. The lake's outlet at the northwest corner is one of the better places to concentrate your efforts.

Across from the rest stop, there is a military recreation area, where retired military personnel have access to cabins and boats.

Lost Lake

Directly across the Richardson Highway from Birch Lake, you'll find Lost Lake. Stocked with rainbows and char, this lake is less than a half-mile drive from the highway.

A visually appealing lake, Lost Lake is a fun one to belly boat, and the fishing action can be fast at times. There's a small boat launch here, which makes it easy to put in a canoe or float tube.

There is an active Boy Scout camp here, and the lake also hosts the Becoming an Outdoors Woman program. Education classes on fly casting are held here throughout the summer, as well. With so many activities going on, this lake is kept well stocked with fish. And most are dumped into the water right at the boat ramp.

Little Harding Lake

If there is a lake in this area managed with flyfishermen in mind, it's Little Harding Lake, which is located at mile 321.5. Closed to all fishing from mid-September through mid-May, the lack of ice fishing allows winter survival rates to be maximized. Anglers are also restricted to single-hook artificial lures.

But don't be fooled into thinking the catching is easy on Little Harding Lake. Because it's a very boggy lake, a canoe or belly boat is required to reach prime fishing water. The lake is usually calm, and its small size means you can fish it thoroughly. You may see quite a few belly-boat anglers working around the lily pads and around a beaver house here at any given time.

Though the lake is too small to produce any record fish, there are some nice trout to be had. If you want to keep a rainbow for the frying pan here, it must be 18 inches or longer.

Harding Lake

Just beyond Little Harding Lake you'll come to Harding Lake, a considerably larger body of water that houses some enormous fish. But if you're a fly angler, you may find it difficult to fish here.

During the summer, this is a high-use recreational area, and water skiers, jet skiers, and swimmers are everywhere. Cabins ring the lake on three sides, while the fourth side has a state recreation area with some 80 campsites. Though there are arctic char up to 18 pounds and lake trout in the 30-pound class, they are tough to pull from the depths here. It's predicted that the next state-record char will come from Harding. The lake also has pike, but the fishing for them is currently closed.

Salcha River

At mile 323 the Richardson Highway crosses the Salcha River, offering the only road access to this clear mid-sized stream. For the first time in many miles, king salmon anglers can finally break out their 9-weights and start tossing big egg patterns. This is also one of the better grayling rivers in the area.

There is a state recreation site at the bridge with ample parking and a boat ramp. The presence of a picnic area, toilets, and running water tell you right away that this is a popular fishing locale, but there's very good fly-fishing for king and chum salmon.

The king salmon start to arrive sometime around the Fourth of July—it's difficult to say exactly when, as they are 1,000 miles from salt water at this point and have battled harsh element to get here. Though the kings average about 25 pounds, 50-pounders aren't uncommon. Later in July, the chums start to arrive.

Both salmon species are fairly battered by the time they reach this point. The kings have turned red and the chums metamorphosed into their pastel colors. I don't know anyone who eats the chums caught here, though I'm told the kings are still good when smoked.

Military Base Waters

As the highway enters the city of Fairbanks, you'll come to several stocked ponds that offer easy access and bank fishing for rainbow trout and char. There are also a number of stocked lakes situated on military bases, and all you need to fish them is an official permit.

To obtain an access permit for any of the three military base lakes in the Fairbanks region, call the Department of Natural Resources at 907-377-5182. Very few tourists spend time on these manmade lakes, though. There are plenty of other waters to fish in the area.

The lakes on Eielson Air Force Base, the northern-most full-operation base in the U.S., are all rock pit lakes. They were dug to obtain enough gravel to construct the massive runway on this base, which incidentally, serves as the third alternate runway for the space shuttle. The lakes you'll find here—Grayling, Moose, Scout, Pike, and Mullens—all hold stocked fish.

Just east of Fairbanks, Forth Wainwright Military Reservation holds a few ponds that also have stocked fish. Ghost, Chet, and Nickel Lakes are the main attractions here.

Back near the town of Delta Junction, Fort Greeley Military Reservation, off Meadow Lakes Road, grants access to the Fort Greeley Ridge Road Lakes. These consist of Bull Winkle, Sheefish, Bolio, Luke, Mark, North &

South Twin, No Mercy, Rock Hound, and Dock Lakes. As with the other bases, stocked fish are present here.

Chena Lake

One lake worth mentioning is located 15 miles from Fairbanks, just out of North Pole, Chena Lake is situated off the Richardson Highway at mile 346.5. Follow the signs 2.5 miles down Lawrence Road to the Chena Lakes Recreation Area, where you'll find 80 campsites, more than 90 picnic sites, pump water, and a wheelchair-accessible fishing dock.

Constructed by the Army Corps of Engineers, this 260-acre lake was superbly designed, making it easy to escape crowds. Plenty of islands and bays are present in this pretty lake.

Canoes can be rented at the lake, as can paddle boats. This is also a popular swimming hole among the locals. But this lake is definitely worth fishing, for with a canoe you can find many places that hold stocked rainbows, arctic char, grayling, and silver salmon. Annually, more than 50,000 fish are planted in this lake, so there's plenty to go around. Casting along the many points of land and working the islands will yield fish, as will trolling sinking lines through some of the deeper sections of the lake.

Fishing opportunities in the Chena River and waters located on the Chena Hot Springs Road are covered with the Parks Highway.

When hiking through brush-choked waters of the road system, be careful of devil's club, the needle-sharp bush will leave its mark.

VALDEZ

Population: 4,350
Alaska Area Code: 907
Zip Code: 99686

TOURIST INFORMATION

Valdez Chamber of Commerce, 208 Chitina; P.O. Box 512; 835-2330

Valdez Convention & Visitors Bureau, 200 Chenga St., P.O. Box 1603; 1-800-770-5954 or 835-4636 or 835-2984; www.valdezalaska.org

Alaska Department of Fish & Game, 822-3309 or 822-5224 (Glennallen office)

GUIDE SERVICES

Rugged River Guide Company, 835-9130; offers flyfishing in area waters, hike in or with families along the roadside

TACKLE SHOPS

Beaver Sports, 316 Galena St.; 835-4727

Hook, Line & Sinker, 200 Chitina Drive; 835-4410; located at corner of Chitina and Kobuk Streets; Dave Winney is one of the most knowledgeable sources of fishing information in the Valdez area and has been at this shop since 1986

South Central Hardware, 835-2300; located at corner of Meals and Galena Streets

The Valdez Prospector, 141 Galena St.; 835-3858

ACCOMMODATIONS

Aspen Hotels, 100 Meals Ave.; 1-800-478-4445; located in downtown Valdez

Blessing House B&B, P.O. Box 233 /835-5333; walking distance to the harbor and shopping

Downtown Bed & Breakfast Inn, 113 Galena Dr; 1-800-478-2791; close to town and harbor, private and shared baths

Guest House Inn, P.O. Box 365; 835-4445; has 78 remodeled rooms, complimentary deluxe continental breakfast

Keystone Hotel, Box 2148; 1-888-835-0665; located at corner of Egan Drive and Hazelet; 106 rooms, central locations, great dining; www.alaskan.com/keystonehotel

Wild Roses By The Sea Bed & Breakfast, Box 3396; 835-2930; central location, privatebaths; www.bytheseaalaska.com

CAMPGROUNDS AND RV PARKS

Bayside RV Park, Box 466; 1-888-835-4425; full and partial hookups, showers, laundry, restrooms, tour bookings

Bear Paw RV Park, Box 93; 835-2530; located next to Small-Boat Harbor; full and partial hookups, restrooms, showers, laundry, tour bookings; www.bearpaw-valdez.com

Captain Jim's Campground, Box 1369; 835-2282; located on Allison Point; 70 sites,restrooms, oceanfront

Eagle's Rest RV Park, 631 East Pioneer; 1-800-553-7525; full hookups, pull-throughs, tentsites, cabins, showers, laundry, dump station, tour bookings

RESTAURANTS

Alaska's Bistro, 100 Fidalgo St.; 835-5688; serving breakfast, lunch and dinner, offers fine dining near the harbor along with Mediterranean grill and oyster bar

Fu Kung Chinese Restaurant, 207 Kobuk Street; 835-5255; serving authentic Chinese food, including sushi

Harbor's Edge Restaurant, 107 N Harbor Dr; 835-5989; family-style restaurant that serves breakfast, lunch, and dinner

Keystone Seafood Grill, 1-888-835-0665; located at corner of Egan Drive and Hazelet; excellent selection of fresh seafood

Lunch Box Sandwich Shop, 103 Harbor Ct.; 835-9500; specializing in custom lunch sandwiches, ideal for the traveling angler, also serving soups

Pipeline Inn & Club, 112 Egan Drive; 835-4444; specializing in seafood and steaks, offering live entertainment

Mike's Palace, 201 N. Harbor Drive; 835-2368; serving Italian, Greek, Mexican, American food

The Rose Cache, 321 Egan St.; 835-8383; offers relaxed dining, specializing in homestyle cooking, this is a popular place so make dinner reservations

CANOE & BOAT RENTALS

Fish Central, 217 N Harbor Dr; 1-888-835-5002; www.fishcentral.net; rental boats and canoes available, along with bait, tackle, and gear

Valdez Harbor Boat & Tackle Rentals, 217 N. Harbor Drive; 1-888-835-5002; fishcentral.net; good source of fishing information, has boat rentals and equipment, offers access to state park cabins

AUTO REPAIR

Bell Tech Auto, 835-5668
Roosevelt Towing & Recovery, Inc., P.O. Box 687; 835-2030
Marks Repair, P.O. Box 3615; 835-2709

LOCKSMITHS

Valdez Lock & Key, P.O. Box 3702; 835-2482

MEDICAL

Valdez Community Hospital, 911 Meals Ave.; 835-2249

VETERINARY CLINICS

Valdez Veterinary Clinic, 321 Egan Street; 835-5280

TOURIST ATTRACTIONS

Jesse & Maxine Whitney Museum (PWSCC), 300 Airport Rd.; 1-800-478-8800; houses a wide collection of Alaska native art and artifacts along with natural history exhibits and wildlife mounts
Valdez Museum, 217 Egan Dr; 835-2764; saltwater aquarium and other bits of history

A highway near Valdez.

COPPER CENTER

Population: 550
Alaska Area Code: 907
Zip Code: 99573

TOURIST INFORMATION

Visitor Information Center and National Parks & Monuments Headquarters, P.O. Box 439; 822-5234; mile 105.1 Richardson Hwy.

GUIDE SERVICES

Grove's Klutina River Salmon Charters, 1-800-770-5822; mile 100.6 Old Richardson Hwy.; RV parking with hookups, laundry, shower, dump station; specializing in king and red salmon fishing on the Klutina River; alaskan.com/groves
Klutina Salmon Charters and Campground, P.O. Box 78; 822-3991; fully equipped campground, RV park with hookups, campers, trailers and tents welcome; all tackle furnished, specialty is salmon fishing on Klutina River, will fillet, freeze,and ship your catch; klutinacharters.com

ACCOMMODATIONS

Copper Center Lodge, Drawer J, Inner Loop Road; 1-888-822-3245; established in 1898 this road-house/lodge has 21 rooms, private/shared baths, restaurant serves breakfast, lunch, and dinner
Copper River Princess Wilderness Lodge, Brenwick Craig Road; 822-4000; mile 102 Richardson Highway; www.princesslodges.com

CAMPGROUNDS AND RV PARKS

Grove's Klutina River Salmon Charters, 1-800-770-5822; mile 100.6 Old Richardson Hwy.; RV parking with hookups, laundry, shower, dump station
Kenny Lake Mercantile & RV Park, P.O. Box 230; 882-3313; mile 7.2 Edgerton Hwy.; 10 electric sites and 10 pull-throughs, secluded RV and tentsites, hotel, cafe, fishing licenses
Klutina Salmon Charters and Campground, P.O. Box 78; 822-3991; fully equipped campground, RV park with hookups, campers, trailers and tents welcome
Grizzly Pizza & Gift Shop, 822-3828; mile 92.7 Richardson Hwy.; campground facilities

RESTAURANTS

Credit Union Burger Bus, P.O. Box 426; 822-4411
Kenny Lake Diner, P.O. Box 230; 822-3355
Grizzly Pizza & Gift Shop, 822-3828; mile 92.7 Richardson Hwy.

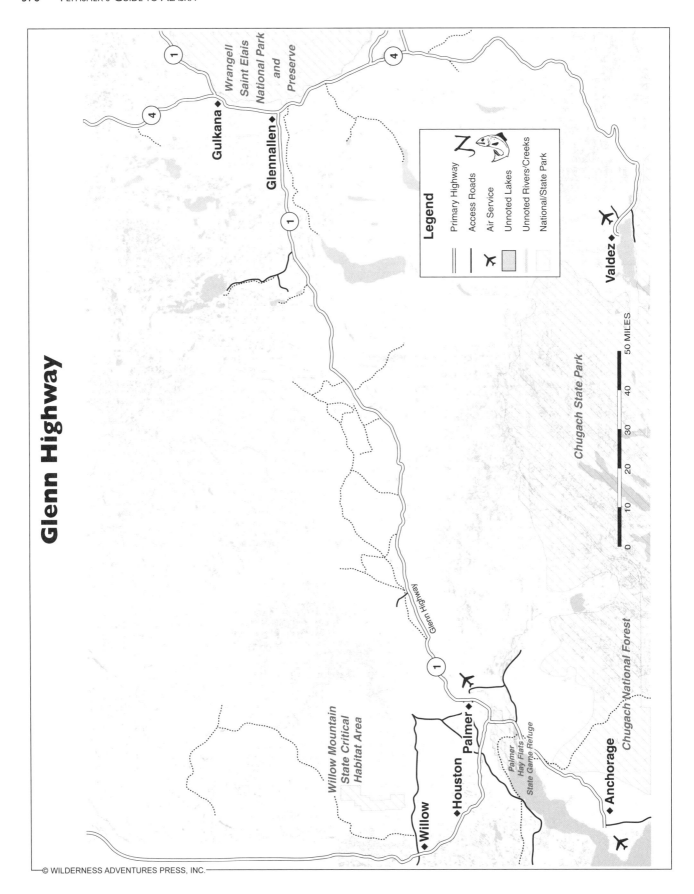

Glenn **Highway**

THE GLENN HIGHWAY

The Glenn Highway is the primary route traveled by tourists who enter the state via the Alaska Highway. From the Tok Cutoff Road 9 and Richardson Highway, Glenn provides the most direct access to Anchorage and the Kenai Peninsula. For angling purposes, we'll concentrate on the 147 miles of highway between Palmer and Glennallen.

Anglers should note that although this is an attractive highway on which to travel, the quality of the fishing leaves something to be desired. I know of several long-time residents in Anchorage, Palmer, and Wasilla who spend little time fishing the Glenn Highway, simply because there is superior fishing in virtually every other direction.

The problem with the streams on the Glenn Highway is that they offer no real place for trout, char, or grayling to winter. For the most part, these streams are very small and fast, rapidly winding their way out of very rugged country. The waters are usually crystal-clear too, which means that the fish you do find are very hard to coax into striking. But some of these streams are so small that not many fish even enter them.

Good friend, longtime Alaskan resident, and fishing fanatic Roy Roth, sums it up this way: "If a flyfisherman comes to Alaska and only targets the streams along the Glenn Highway, he'll likely be very disappointed."

And for stillwaters, even the most popular lakes on the Glenn are deep-water fisheries where downriggers are necessary to reach lake trout and burbot. For instance, Lake Louise, Susitna Lake, and Tyone Lake are all big bodies of water noted for their burbot and mackinaw but not their flyfishing. That's not to say that fly anglers can't cajole a laker or two from the shallows in early morning or late evening, it's just that the payoffs are few and far between. There are some opportunities for rainbow trout and grayling, though.

So let's take a quick look at the fisheries along the Glenn Highway, starting at Palmer and moving east to Glennallen.

Kepler-Bradley Lakes

If you're traveling from Anchorage there are a series of lakes that local anglers speak highly of (before you reach Palmer). Situated between the town of Palmer and the Glenn and Parks highway junction, Kepler and Bradley Lakes are only two of more than a half-dozen lakes offering respectable fishing for rainbows, Dolly Varden, and grayling. And a couple of lakes have stocked silver salmon.

The main access to these lakes is at mile 36.5 on the Glenn Highway, where you'll find a day-use recreation site. There is additional access at mile 37.3, which takes you to the Kepler Park office right between Kepler and Bradley Lakes.

Turn north at mile marker 38 to reach Canoe Lake, Irene Lake, and Long Lake. Canoe Lake is noted for its grayling, while Irene and Long Lakes hold rainbow trout. In Irene also has arctic char.

There is a commercial campground at Kepler Park, complete with a boat launch, boat rentals, and campsites. Anglers who work the shores from a raft or float tube during the spring and fall months have the best success on these lakes.

Streams at the West End of the Glenn Highway

The first attractive Dolly Varden and rainbow trout stream on the Glenn Highway is **Moose Creek**, at mile 54.5. Though it's a very attractive creek, it's so clear that fishing is difficult to totally frustrating for the small, finicky fish that live here. I'd recommend skipping this one.

Granite Creek, located at mile 62, is another beautiful stream. If you're itching to wet a line, you might latch into some small Dollys or even a few rainbows in Granite Creek. Not many people fish this clear little stream, simply because it's tough to get fish to strike. But dry flies can draw a rise from undersized Dollys, though the rugged terrain makes for tough going. There's a campground on the north side of the highway, and it makes for a nice setting if small native fish are what you desire.

At mile 66.5, the **Kings River** flows under the Glenn Highway. I know of no locals who spend time on this river, though it looks deceptively good. Rainbows and Dollys reportedly hang out here, but the fishing is not that good.

Another stream that appears fish-rich but falls short is the **Chickaloon River**, near mile marker 78. A few rainbows and Dolly Varden occasionally visit the Chickaloon, but this river, along with the Kings, tumbles down from the Talkeetna Mountains, dropping through rugged gorges and terrain unfit for angling.

When you glance at a map it appears that the **Matanuska River**, which runs south along the Glenn Highway, may be fishable; don't be fooled. The Matanuska is a very large, swift, heavily silted river. Though the mouths of some of the clear tributaries can offer fair fishing, this river isn't worth wetting a line in. This is a dangerous, fast river that is extremely cold and unfriendly to flyfishers.

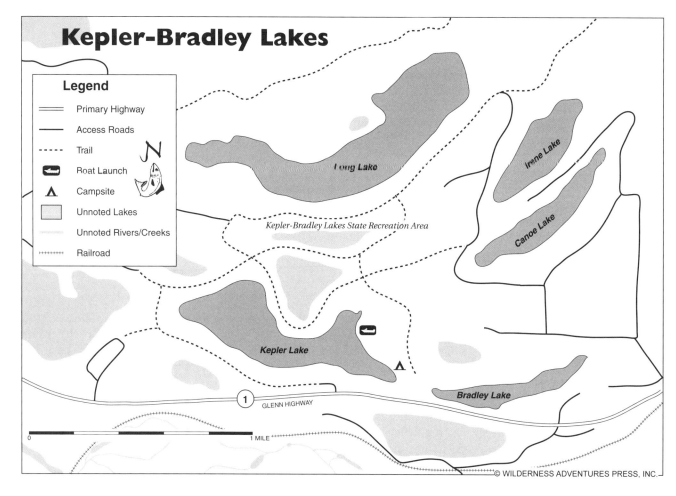

A Cluster of Small Lakes

Just past the Chickaloon River, you'll come to a cluster of small lakes on or near the Glenn Highway. These are easy to reach and offer good opportunities for grayling and rainbow trout. Both **Ravine Lake** and **Lower Bonnie Lake** are accessible from the Bonnie Lakes road turnoff at mile 83.2.

Ravine Lake is the smallest in this series of lakes, and it's the first one you'll come to on the access road. It is home to rainbow trout, and anglers can try their luck from the shore as well as a float tube.

Just over a mile up the dirt road you'll come to Lower Bonnie Lake on the north side of the highway. Motorists should note that this is a steep, winding road that is closed to motor homes and large vehicles pulling trailers. During periods of heavy rain, this road is not fit for any vehicle. However, if conditions are good, you'll be able to fish for wild rainbows and grayling, with the grayling proving most popular. There is a boat launch at Lower Bonnie Lake, along with a campground.

On the south side of the highway, at mile 85.3, you'll find **Long Lake** and the Long Lake State Recreation Site. Though there is no running water or garbage facilities here, there are nine campsites, toilets, and water. There is no fee to stay at this site.

This is a popular lake for grayling up to 18 inches. The waters seem most productive during early spring and fall. As waters warm in the summer, you'll have to go deeper for grayling during the day and search for rising fish in early morning and late evening. There are also some small burbot in this lake, but fishing bait off the bottom is about the only way to get them. A boat launch on the west end of the lake makes reaching prime fishing waters much easier.

A smaller version of Long Lake, **Weiner Lake** offers good fishing for stocked rainbow trout and grayling. This narrow lake sits at mile 87.5 on the Glenn Highway, on the same side as Long Lake. Bank fishing can be good here, as can working from a float tube, raft, or canoe. As with many lakes in the area, targeting rainbows with leech patterns and Woolly Buggers on a sinking line is a good bet.

Streams at West End
of Glenn Highway
And Small Lakes

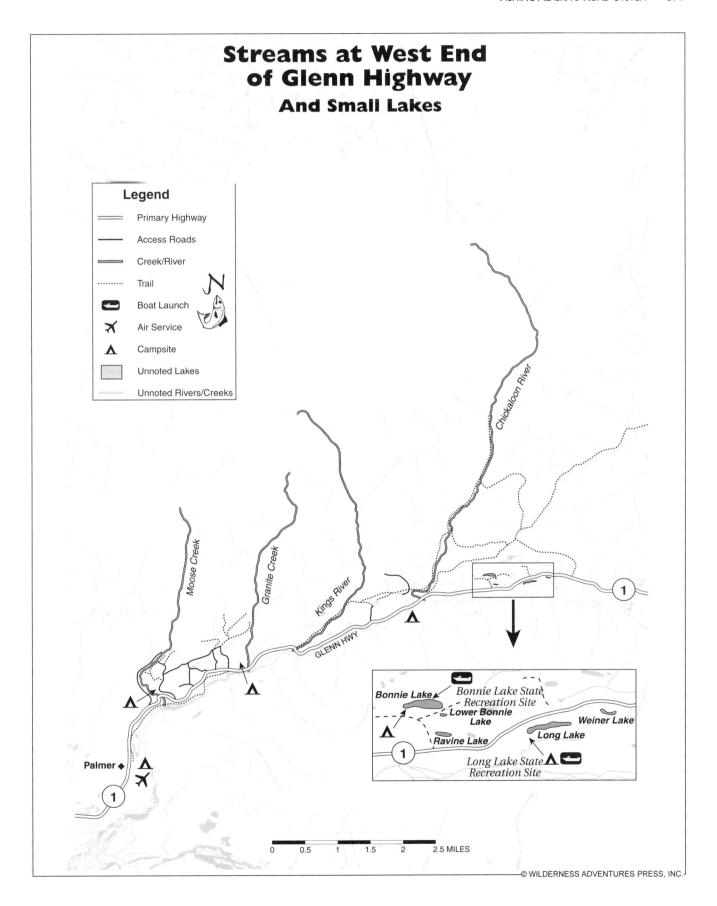

Legend

Primary Highway
Access Roads
Creek/River
Trail
Boat Launch
Air Service
Campsite
Unnoted Lakes
Unnoted Rivers/Creeks

N

Moose Creek

Granite Creek

Kings River

Chickaloon River

GLENN HWY

1

Palmer ◆

1

Bonnie Lake
Bonnie Lake State Recreation Site
Lower Bonnie Lake
Ravine Lake
Long Lake
Weiner Lake
Long Lake State Recreation Site
1

0   0.5   1   1.5   2   2.5 MILES

Leila Lake

There isn't much action for the next 25 miles until you come to Leila Lake on the south side of the Glenn Highway at mile 121. Fishing this lake requires a bit of a hike. From the small gravel pit parking area off the highway, follow the marked trailhead sign to the south. The trail winds on for about a mile, swinging around a smaller lake before ending up at Leila Lake.

The lake is known for its abundant grayling in the 8 to 14-inch class, and the fishing can be good from spring into fall. While it's possible to work the shoreline, a float tube will open up additional opportunities.

Mendeltna Creek and Nearby Lakes

One of the few streams so far on the Glenn Highway that offers good fishing is Mendeltna Creek, at mile 153. This creek has some big grayling.

Mendeltna crosses beneath the highway, and you can stand on the bridge in the fall and observe spawning salmon in action. Though the drainage is closed to salmon fishing, it's wide open for grayling that reach upwards of 18 inches.

There is plenty of bank access, and wade-fishing opportunities abound for fly anglers. You can walk up or downstream from the bridge, hitting pockets of water where grayling congregate. The bottom ends of riffles also hold grayling, and swinging a fly through can be productive.

You'll also find a campground, gas station, restaurant, and RV park here. The fishing here runs from May into November, but because salmon are in the system, remember to watch out for bears. If you're interested in floating the stream, inquire at any of the local public-use facilities for assistance.

At this point, it's also worth noting a few small lakes near the roadside that offer good angling opportunities. Back at mile 149, there's a road easement leading down to **Ryan Lake**, which is stocked with rainbows and has a good holdover of fish, with trout upwards of 18 inches caught regularly.

Arizona Lake is situated at mile 155 and has good fishing for stocked grayling in the 12- to 14-inch class. At mile 156 on the north side of the highway, **Buffalo Lake** provides good fishing for stocked rainbow, too. **Tex Smith Lake** at mile 162 is stocked with grayling and offers great public access. All of these little lakes are great for float tubes, especially Tex Smith.

Lake Louise Area Waters

Near Lake Louise Road, which heads north off the Glenn Highway at mile 160, there are several small lakes and streams that offer fair fishing. Most are too small to cover here in great detail, but it's worth knowing they are there due to the large grayling and stocked rainbows present. On the other hand, Lake Louise (home to the state-record burbot at 24 pounds, 12 ounces), Susitna Lake, and Tyone Lake are giant, deep lakes that are difficult to flyfish, so we'll pass over them.

As you make your way up Lake Louise Road, keep an eye out for **Junction Lake**, which is home to good grayling, right at the turnoff from the highway. A mile up the road, **Little Crater Lake** offers good stocked rainbow fishing, in addition to grayling. Five miles from the highway, **Round Lake** and **Old Road Lake** hold rainbows, while 2 miles farther puts you on some good grayling at **Forgotten Lake**.

At mile 6.5 on Lake Louise Road, Oilwell Road turns off to the west, leading to a series of lakes that sit on the south side of the road. **Tiny Lake** is the first in the series and offers fishing for rainbow trout. **Peanut Lake** is next and has stocked silver salmon and rainbow trout, while **40 Foot Lake** and **Teal Lake** hold grayling. Float tubes are ideal on all of these lakes. By the way, drive on by Stick Lake; it's void of fish.

Back on Lake Louise Road, mile 11.5 finds you at **Caribou Lake** and **Elbow Lake**. There is plenty of parking here, and grayling are present in both lakes.

Past Lake Louise, there are several other small lakes that can be fished. Many of the lakes mentioned here, as well as those not covered, can be fished from shore. Rafts and canoes can also be used in many lakes, and anglers with float tubes will also better their odds.

Tolsona and Moose Lakes

Eighteen miles west of Glennallen, and 170 miles from Anchorage, you'll come to a couple of good grayling fisheries, Tolsona and Moose Lakes. There are also rainbow trout and burbot in these lakes, but grayling up to 16 inches attract the most anglers. The fishing on these lakes can be good all summer long. Moose Lake has a boat launch, which opens up a lot more water.

Working your way along the shorelines of either of these lakes in a canoe can pay off, but it can sometimes get too windy for a float tube. In the evening, watch for rising grayling, and don't waste time trying to place a dry fly right in the middle of them. Mosquito patterns are popular for grayling here.

There's a campground at Moose Lake from which both lakes can be fished.

Tolsona Creek

If you stop at Tolsona Lake, you may wish to chase grayling in Tolsona Creek. Tolsona Creek flows under the Glenn Highway at mile 172, and parking is available near the bridge on the south side of the highway at a state recreation site. For anglers looking to get into some wade fishing, this stream is excellent for grayling up to 16 inches.

The first mile and a half upstream of the highway offers the best fishing. Fish around structure or search the clear pools for holding grayling and put that dry fly to work. Again, mosquito patterns are tough to beat for grayling.

Moose Creek

Moose Creek runs right through the town of Glennallen and can actually be seen out the back window of the ADF&G offices in town. But as you'd expect with most such streams, the fishing pressure can be heavy.

Moose Creek is noted for its grayling fishing. As a result of the creek's proximity to a human population, its easy roadside access, and the fact that it takes grayling so long to grow, the fishing is less than stellar here.

The best time to hit this creek is shortly after the ice melts when migrating grayling make their way to their spawning beds. Depending on the weather, though, the fishing can be hit or miss. If it's raining or exceptionally warm rapidly melting snow from the surrounding hills can blow out the water. But if it's clear and not too warm the fishing can be fair.

Don't go here expecting to catch large grayling. Though they may be plump, they aren't nearly the size you'll find in more remote fisheries. There is a pulloff where the creek flows under the highway, and a trail leads to the river, though it can be tough fishing when the water is up, as trees will snag your backcasts. Anglers should also note that there is a lot of private property and native-owned lands in the area, which greatly limits access to Moose Creek.

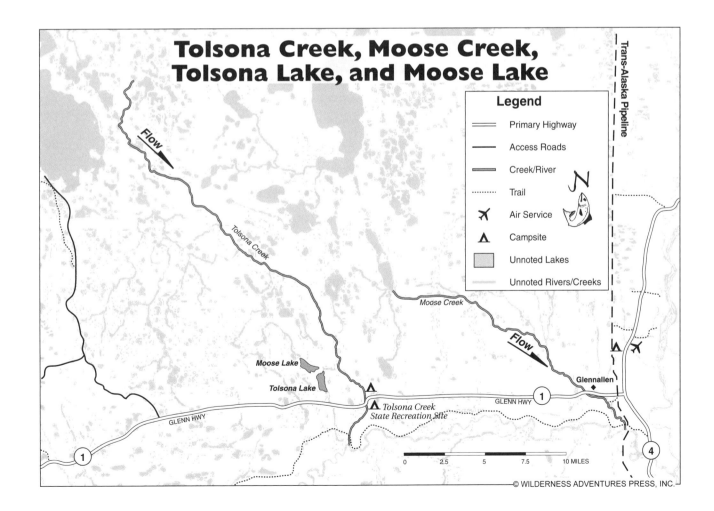

PALMER

Population: 4,385
Alaska Area Code: 907
Zip Code: 99645

TOURIST INFORMATION

Alaska Department of Fish & Game, 746-6300 (Palmer office)

Matanuska Susitna Convention & Visitors Bureau, mile 35.5 Parks Hwy.; 746-5000

Palmer Chamber of Commerce, P.O. Box 45; visitor information center located in log cabin at East Fireweed Ave., across South Valley Way

GUIDE SERVICES

Big Fisherman Charters, 7401 Eden Circle; 745-4965

Glenn Ventures Fishing, Palmer, AK; 746-4343

Sids Guide Service, Palmer, AK; 745-8872

Trophy Catch Charters, Palmer, AK; 745-4101

ACCOMMODATIONS

Alaska Gold Rush Bed & Breakfast, P.O. Box 691; 1-877-745-5312; cabins located 10 minutes from Palmer; www.alaskagoldrush.com

Caribou Cabins B&B, 10901 Center St.; 746-6881

Colony Inn, 325 E. Elmwood Ave.; 745-3330

Gold Miner's Hotel, 918 S. Colony Way; 1-800-7-ALASKA; www.goldminershotel.com

Moose Wallow B&B, P.O. Box 398; 745-7777; www.moosewallow.com

Peak Inn, 775 E Palmer Wasilla Hwy.; 745-8585

Pioneer Motel & Apartments, 124 W. Arctic Ave.; 745-3425

Tara Dells Bed & Breakfast, P.O. Box 6718; 1-800-745-0407; www.taradells.com

Valley Hotel, 606 S. Alaska St.; 745-3330; excellent cafe with complete all-day menu; www.valleyhotelalaska.com

CAMPGROUNDS AND RV PARKS

Finger Lake State Recreation Site, mile 0.7 Bogard Rd.; 69 acres, 41 campsites, fee, picnic tables, toilets, water, boat launch, daily parking fee, fishing

Fox Run RV Campground, P.O. Box 4174; 1-877-745-6120; mile 36.3 Glenn Hwy.; full hookups, pull-throughs, laundry, showers, restrooms; www.foxrun.freeservers.com

Independence Mine State Historical Park, mile 17.3 Hatcher Pass Rd.; 761 acres, picnic tables, restrooms, water, daily parking fee

King Mountain State Recreation Site, mile 76 Glenn Hwy., 20 acres, 22 campsites, fee, picnic tables, restrooms, water

Long Lake State Recreation Site, mile 83.5 Glenn Hwy.; 480 acres, 9 campsites, restrooms, boat launch, fishing

Matanuska Glacier State Recreation Site, mile 101 Glenn Hwy.; 229 acres, 12 campsites, fee, restrooms, water

Mountain View RV Park, Box 2521; 1-800-264-4582; located 3.7 miles from Palmer, off Old Glenn Hwy. on Smith Road; 83 full hookups, pull-throughs, bathroom, laundry

The Homestead RV Park, Box 345; 1-800-478-3570 or 745-6005; 6 miles south of Palmer on Glenn Hwy.; tentsites, water and electric hookups, showers, laundry, dump station

RESTAURANTS

Colony Kitchen, mile 43.5 Glenn Hwy.; 746-4600

Denali Steak House, 918 S. Colony Way; 745-6180

Fishhook Bar & Liquor, mile 6.5 Fishhook Rd.; 745-6374

Gold Rush Pizza, mile 3.5 Palmer-Wasilla Rd.; 745-7490

Inn Cafe, 325 E. Elmwood Ave.; 746-6118

La Fiesta Mexican Restaurant, 132 W Evergreen Ave.; 746-3335

Peking Garden, 775 W Evergreen Ave.; 746-5757

CANOE & BOAT RENTALS

Fox Run RV Campground, Box 4174; 1-877-745-6120; mile 36.3 Glenn Hwy.; fishing also offered

AUTO REPAIR

Matanuska Towing & Recovery, 745-5252

Wolverine Towing, 746-2980

LOCKSMITHS

Neils Lock & Safe, 4400 Engstrom; 746-0961

Valley Locksmith Services, 840 S Colony Way; 745-3408

MEDICAL

Valley Hospital, 515 E. Dahlia Ave.; 745-4813 or 746-8620

VETERINARY CLINICS

Palmer Veterinary Clinic, mile 39 Glenn Hwy.; 745-3219

TOURIST ATTRACTIONS

Musk Ox Farm, Box 587; 745-4151; located at mile 50 on Glenn Hwy.; one of the best places to get a close look at primitive musk ox; www.muskoxfarm.com

GLENNALLEN

Population: 495
Alaska Area Code: 907
Zip Code: 99588

TOURIST INFORMATION

Alaska Department of Fish & Game, 822-3309 (Glennallen office)

Copper River Valley Visitor Information Center, P.O. Box 469; 822-5555; located at the junction of the Glenn and Richardson Highways

FLY-IN CHARTERS

Evergreen Bed & Breakfast Lodge, P.O. Box 1709; 822-3250; located at mile 16.5 Lake Louise Road, overlooking Lake Louise; fly-in fishing and a remote cabin access

Silk Stocking Air, McCarthy No 4; 554-4469; offers glacier flight seeing, air taxi, and guided fly-in day hikes in Wrangell-St Elias National Park and Preserve

TACKLE SHOPS

Park's Place, 822-3334; mile 187.5 Glenn Hwy.; also has groceries, deli, produce

ACCOMMODATIONS

Evergreen Bed & Breakfast Lodge, P.O. Box 1709; 822-3250; located at mile 16.5 Lake Louise Road 25 miles west of Glennallen, overlooking Lake Louise; spacious rooms with private baths; fly-in fishing and a remote cabin access

Lake Louise Lodge, P.O. Box 1716; 1-877-878-3311; on Lake Louise Road at mile 159.8 on Glenn Hwy.; rooms with private baths, good food, hot tub, boat rentals; lakelouiselodge.com

Mendeltna Lodge Kamping Resorts of Alaska, P.O. Box 2560; 822-3346; mile 153 Glenn Hwy.; 100+ campsites, rustic cabins available, serving excellent pizza and giant cinnamon rolls; situated on banks of Little Mendeltna Creek; many nearby lakes with good fishing

The New Caribou Hotel, P.O. Box 329; 1-800-478-3302; mile 186.9 Glenn Hwy.; 55 rooms, 3 suites with full kitchens, large family restaurant, gift shop has Alaska-made items

The Point Lodge at Lake Louise, P.O. Box 1706; 1-800-808-2018; mile 17.2 on Lake Louise Road at mile 159.8 off Glenn Hwy.; serving home-cooked meals, boating and fishing; thepointlodge.com

CAMPGROUNDS AND RV PARKS

Brown Bear Rhodehouse, P.O. Box 110; 822-3663; mile 183.6 Glenn Hwy.; campground, cabins, restaurant specializing in steaks, seafood and pizza, RV parking, picnic sites

Northern Nights RV Campground, 822-3199; mile 188.7 Glenn Hwy.; pull-throughs, hookups, showers, firepits, dump station; nnites@yahoo.com

The Sports Page, 822-5833; mile 187 Glenn Hwy.; cabin rentals, tentsites, 22 RV sites with full hookups, showers, laundry, restaurant

Tolsona Wilderness Campground, P.O. Box 23; 822-3865; mile 173 on Glenn Highway; 80 creekside campsites, hookups, tentsites, showers, laundry, dump station; good fishing right at the campground

RESTAURANTS

The Great Alaskan Freeze, mile 187.5; excellent fast-food menu, low prices

The Hitchin' Post, mile 187.8; excellent fast-food, specializing in burgers, low prices

AUTO TOWING

Tesoro, 822-3555; located at junction of Richardson and Glenn highways, in Glennallen; 24-hour service

MEDICAL

Cross Road Medical Center, 822-3203; mile 186.6; clinic, pharmacy, emergency room

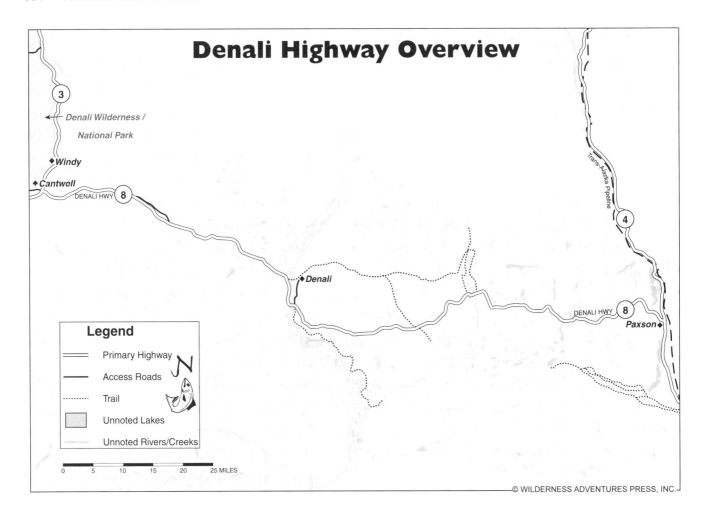

THE DENALI HIGHWAY

Until the completion of the Parks Highway in 1972 the Denali Highway was the only link to Denali Park, formerly called Mount McKinley National Park. At mile 185 from Valdez on the Richardson Highway, the Denali Highway takes off to the west. Starting at the town of Paxson, the highway connects motorists to the town of Cantwell at mile 210 from Anchorage on the Parks Highway. Today, this highway is little traveled by anglers, and a closer look shows why. The best fishing occurs close to Paxson, with little else available until you reach the opposite end of the road near Cantwell.

Traveling west from Paxson, the first 21 miles and the last 3 miles into Cantwell are the only sections of the Denali Highway that are paved. The rest of the road is gravel. And due to heavy snows in the region the road is closed during the winter, usually opening around the middle of May.

The condition of the gravel section varies depending on the time of year, weather, and maintenance activity. Though some of the gravel stretches are in good shape and quite smooth, others can be very rough. When conditions are dry, the road can be extremely dusty, and motorists should travel with their headlights on at all times. When conditions are wet, the road can rapidly deteriorate, so keep a sharp eye out for potholes and washboard areas. Motorists should also be on the lookout for mountain bikers, as this is a fairly common route for them.

Leaving the town of Paxson, it doesn't take long before a gradual climb leads motorists to Maclaren Summit, which at 4,086 feet is the second highest pass in the state's entire road system. While this is the only major grade on the Denali Highway, it does take a while to ascend and descend.

Although there isn't much, let's look at what angling awaits anglers on the 134-mile trip from Paxson to Cantwell.

Sevenmile Lake

Leaving the town of Paxson, you'll immediately cross the Gulkana River, but there's not much fishing at this site. (The better fishing on the Gulkana is described in the Richardson Highway section.) Moving over the river, a gradual climb of a couple miles transports motorists to the open tundra.

You'll have to travel 7 miles on the Denali Highway before you hit the first fishable lake, aptly named Sevenmile Lake. As with most lakes along this highway, the fishing is best early and late in the season. Due to long summer days, many of the area lakes heat up considerably, some approaching 70 degrees later in the summer. Fish seek deeper waters during these warmer periods, making it tough for fly anglers to connect with much of anything. But early in the season, shortly after the thaw, and later in the fall when water temperatures begin to cool the fishing can be good.

Sevenmile Lake is unique in that it's one of the few lakes in the area where anglers have a realistic shot at landing a lake trout on the fly. In fact, lake trout are the only species that inhabit this lake. The fish run on the small side for lakers, averaging about 20 inches. There is a two-fish limit on the lake.

To access Sevenmile Lake, turn off the Denali Highway at mile 6.8 and follow the gravel road for about ¾ mile to the lake. There is a campground and boat launch, and canoes work very well here. Belly boaters will also find success working the shorelines.

As with any lake trout fishery, the action from shore is only fair. Anglers with chest waders have the best shot at enticing a laker to bite early and late in the season. If you're fishing from a cartopper or a canoe, you can tow a sinking line with a weighted streamer around the lake.

Sevenmile sits in what's known as a frost pocket, and it's often the middle of June before the lake is ice-free. This is a prime time on the lake. If you stop here in July and August, at dusk when lake trout might be active and closer to shore.

Incidentally, the blueberry crop can be outstanding here in August.

Tenmile and Teardrop Lakes

A short drive farther along the Denali Highway leads to two lakes that sit side by side. Both Tenmile and Teardrop Lakes hold grayling, lake trout, and burbot. And a roadside pulloff affords easy access.

The fishing from shore can be productive for grayling, especially early and late in the year when they are cruising the shallows for food. Lake trout can also be taken close to shore soon after meltoff and late in the fall,

though this is a challenge that few traveling anglers have the patience or time for.

Tangle Lakes and Tangle River

Perhaps the most famous lakes on this side of the Denali Highway lie on the south side of the road at mile 22.5. Upper Tangle Lakes are a cluster of lakes that are easily accessed and popular among the local fishing fraternity. There's a BLM campground here, complete with picnic sites, restrooms, and water.

Several lakes compose the Tangle Lakes, and they are all connected by streams, so wading anglers can walk between each with little problem. Chest waders will allow you to travel in comfort as you search for grayling and lake trout. Fishermen can also find burbot in these lakes, but bait fished on the bottom is about the only way to get these fine-eating fish. Flyfishers will have the best luck on grayling and lake trout by concentrating at the inlets and outlets of each lake, where fish can often be seen rising.

When fishing the lakes in the evening—which can come late during the summer months this far north of the equator—search for dabbling fish and work your fly into the feeding schools. If you want to fish more than just the inlets and outlets, you'll need a canoe, as they are too big and can get too windy for fishing in a float tube. It should be noted that many fly anglers like to pursue whitefish in these lakes, as they are large and fight hard. Grayling will range from 6 to 14 inches.

From the road, you be able to see the Tangle River, the best flyfishing river in this section of Alaska. A narrow stream some 20 to 30 feet wide, the Tangle River carries tannic acids from the local vegetation. However, visibility into the river is quite good, and you can wade across in several spots. What's more, you can fish the entire length of the river, pulling out plump grayling up to 14 inches.

Be careful around the dark-colored algae on the rocks in this water. Though this is a very safe and easy river to wade fish, the algae can be slippery and tough to detect. Felt soles on your wading boots will help.

This system of lakes and the river are situated on state land, so you have freedom to roam and explore.

Rock Creek

Two miles past the Tangle Lakes BLM Campground, the Denali Highway crosses Rock Creek, which is fed by a series of lakes and flows into Upper Tangle Lake south of the highway. The only access to Rock Creek is right where the road crosses the stream.

As you would expect, the farther you walk from the road, the better the fishing will be, both for size and numbers of fish. You can walk upstream as far as your legs will

Tangle Lakes and Surrounding Water

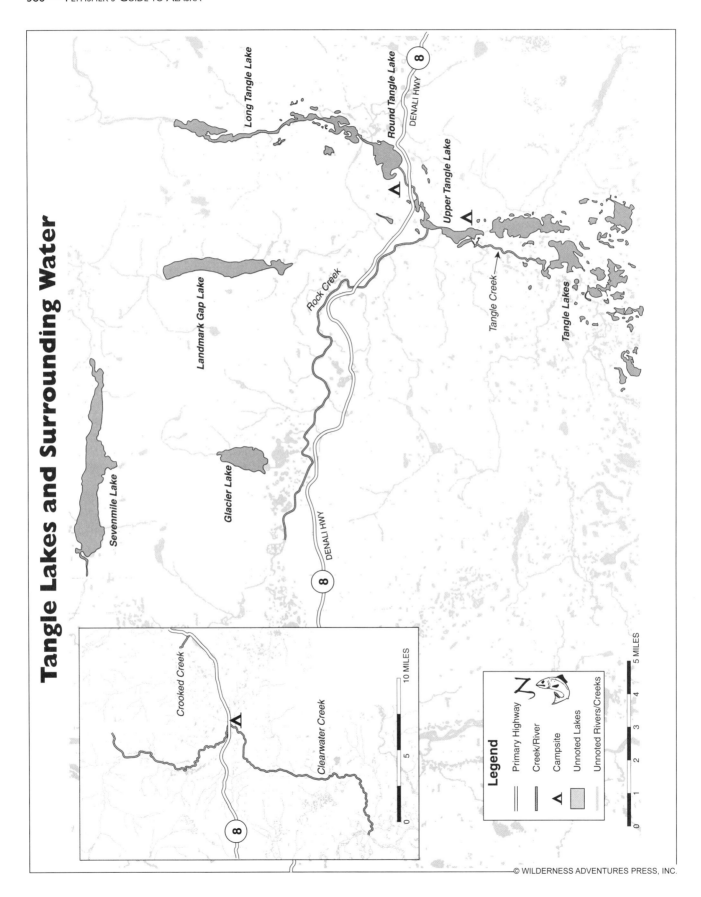

Long Tangle Lake

Round Tangle Lake

DENALI HWY

8

Upper Tangle Lake

Tangle Creek

Tangle Lakes

Rock Creek

Landmark Gap Lake

Sevenmile Lake

Glacier Lake

DENALI HWY

8

Crooked Creek

8

Clearwater Creek

10 MILES

5

0

Legend

Primary Highway

Creek/River

Campsite

Unnoted Lakes

Unnoted Rivers/Creeks

N

0   1   2   3   4   5 MILES

© WILDERNESS ADVENTURES PRESS, INC.

take you. Rock Creek flows clear, with a dark bottom. It's easy to see where you're going, and there are grayling throughout the creek.

There is quite a bit of brush along the creek, so practice your roll casts. Biting insects are also heavy along Rock Creek, even more so than in other waters in the region. In summer, mosquitoes dominate the bloodsucking scene, followed by biting gnats and whitesocks later in the summer and into fall. Don't set foot on this creek unless you have plenty of bug dope and a mesh head net.

Landmark Gap Lake

For anglers looking to get off the beaten path, Landmark Gap Lake provides great hike-in fishing. At mile 26 on the Denali Highway, a 4-mile hike from a roadside pullout will lead to good summer grayling fishing, with lake trout also on the menu. The hike takes place along an old cat trail, so the going isn't too difficult.

Those willing to pack in a belly boat will have better results, though there are plenty of places to wade and fish along the shoreline of this long, narrow lake. If you're here in the fall, keep an eye out for caribou and moose hunters.

Glacier Lake and Sevenmile Lake

Mile 31 marks the location of another hike-in lake. An arduous (especially when wet) 3-mile hike brings you to Glacier Lake, where grayling and lake trout await. Even when it's not raining, this trail can be muddy and slick.

Just north of Glacier Creek there is another Sevenmile Lake, this one much larger than the one near Paxson. At mile 40 on the Denali Highway, turn north on a gravel road and follow it almost a mile to Sevenmile. Summer fishing for lake trout can be excellent. But as you might expect, it's tough for fly anglers to get in on the action. Early and late in the season, and in late evenings, sinking lines and streamers might trick a few of these fish into biting.

Crooked and Clearwater Creeks

From Glacier Lake, the highway begins a gradual climb, and few of the streams in the area are worth fishing. You'll cross over the Maclaren River, but this glacial stream is not fishable.

But at mile 48 there is excellent grayling fishing to be had in Crooked Creek, a small stream that borders the north side of the highway. Wading and fishing this little creek can be productive, as most people simply pass it by.

The Denali Highway crosses Clearwater Creek at mile 56, and there is fair summer fishing for grayling here, along with a casual campsite and toilets. Anglers can wade on either side of the highway, searching for holding water where grayling congregate. The farther from the road you get, the better the fishing will be. But be careful not to overfish this delicate stream; once you've pulled an adult fish from a hole, continue on, preferably after you've released the fish.

Brushkana Creek

Near the end of the Denali Highway, a few small, roadside streams offer fair grayling fishing. Simply pick a stream that appeals to you, get your gear, and start walking. Most hold grayling, though you won't come away with any stories of giant fish.

One of the more popular streams for grayling is Brushkana Creek, located at mile 104.5. At the northwest corner of the bridge crossing the creek, you'll find a BLM campground with some 20 sites, firepits, toilets, and running water.

Brushkana is a small, clear stream with some brush around the edges. Still, it's easy to wade and fish, picking the spots you want to cast to.

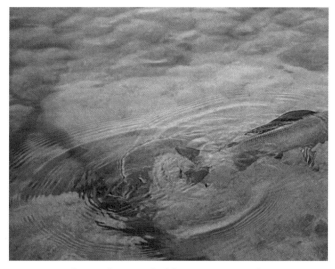

Lakes in this area hold many nice grayling.

CANTWELL

Population: 166
Alaska Area Code: 907
Zip Code: 99729

FLY-IN CHARTERS

Atkins Guiding & Flying Service, P.O. Box 22; 768-2143; 2.2 miles west of Parks and Denali Highway Junction; floatplane

ACCOMMODATIONS

Atkins Guiding & Flying Service, P.O. Box 22; 768-2143; 2.2 miles west of Parks and Denali Highway Junction; apartment and bunkhouse accommodations

Backwoods Lodge, 1-800-292-2232; 0.2 mile from the Parks and Denali Highway junction; backwoodslodge@hotmail.com

Cantwell Lodge, P.O. Box 87; 1-800-768-5522, in Alaska 768-2300; 2 miles west of Parks and Denali Highway junction; motel, camping, laundry, showers

Lazy J Lodge, 768-2414; mile 210.7 Parks Hwy.; log cabins, full-service

CAMPGROUNDS AND RV PARKS

Cantwell RV Park, P.O. Box 210; 1-800-940-2210; mile 209.9 Parks Hwy.; pull-throughs, dump station, water, showers, laundry, restrooms, electric sites, walking distance to fishing; open May 15 to Sept. 15; www.alaskaone.com/cantwellrv

Carlo Creek Lodge, 683-2576; mile 223.9 Parks Hwy.; cabins, RV park, tentsites, picnic tables, firepits, showers, water, dump station, bathrooms, propane, small store

RESTAURANTS

Lazy J Lodge, 768-2414; mile 210.7 Parks Hwy.; noted for their T-bone steaks, homestyle meals and pies

The Perch Restaurant, P.O. Box 53, Denali Park AK 99755; 683-2523; mile 224 Parks Hwy.; steaks, seafood, breakfast, cinnamon rolls; cabins also available

TOURIST ATTRACTIONS

Denali National Park and Preserve, P.O. Box 9, Denali Park, AK 99755; 683-2294; www.nps.gov/dena

The Tok Cutoff offers eye-popping scenery.

THE TOK CUTOFF

The fishing is pretty limited from Gakona to Tok on the Tok Cutoff road. Many private lands border streams and lakes, so access is restricted or completely lacking in many areas. If the private land restrictions aren't enough to thwart your fishing progress, the thick alders and spruce lining most streams will be. In the streams that are fishable, you'll often have to wade into the middle and roll cast directly up or downstream.

On top of that, the private native corporation lands aren't always posted, making it even more difficult to decipher where you can and cannot go. Even game offices struggle to stay current on what land is legal to fish and what's not. If you have questions about trespass law, call the ADF&G offices in Glennallen (907-822-3309) or Delta Junction (907-895-4632).

Some trails are marked with "no trespassing" signs. If in doubt, either call for the latest information or stay within the boundaries of the high-water mark for the stream you're fishing. While it is not legal to walk along the banks of rivers within private land holdings, it is perfectly legal to walk and fish within state and public waters.

All those caveats aside, what the Tok Cutoff does offer is eye-popping scenery. If you're looking for big fish in high numbers, I wouldn't spend too much time on this road. But if you're in no hurry and want to wet a line for a half-hour while enjoying a bite to eat, this road should work for you.

We'll start at the town of Gakona and move northeast to Tok.

Tok Cutoff

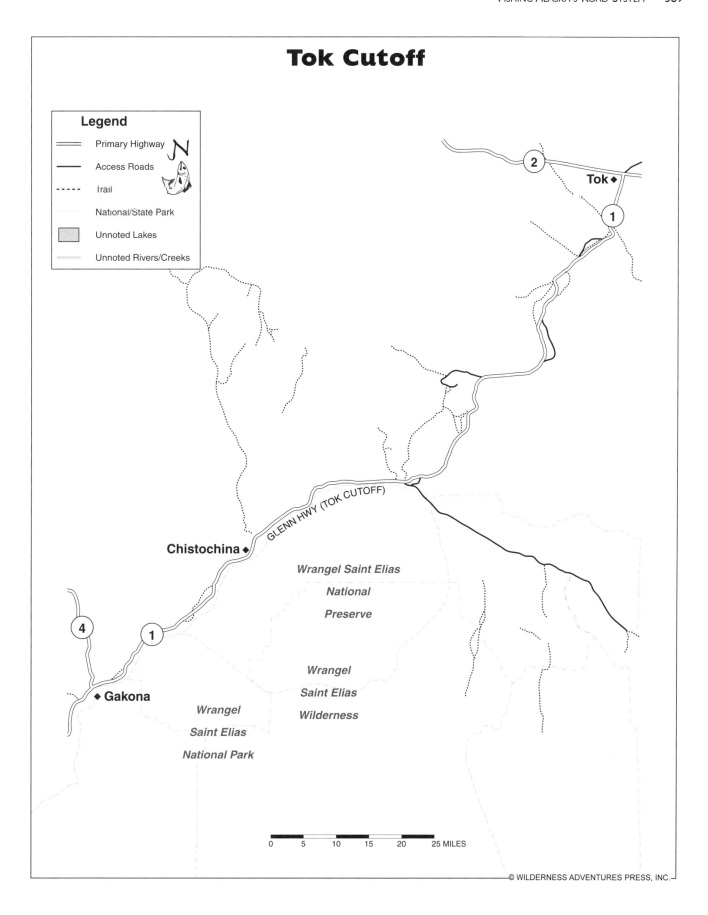

Legend

Primary Highway
Access Roads
Trail
National/State Park
Unnoted Lakes
Unnoted Rivers/Creeks

Tok ◆

GLENN HWY (TOK CUTOFF)

Chistochina ◆

Wrangel Saint Elias

National

Preserve

Wrangel

Saint Elias

Wilderness

◆ Gakona

Wrangel

Saint Elias

National Park

0   5   10   15   20   25 MILES

© WILDERNESS ADVENTURES PRESS, INC.

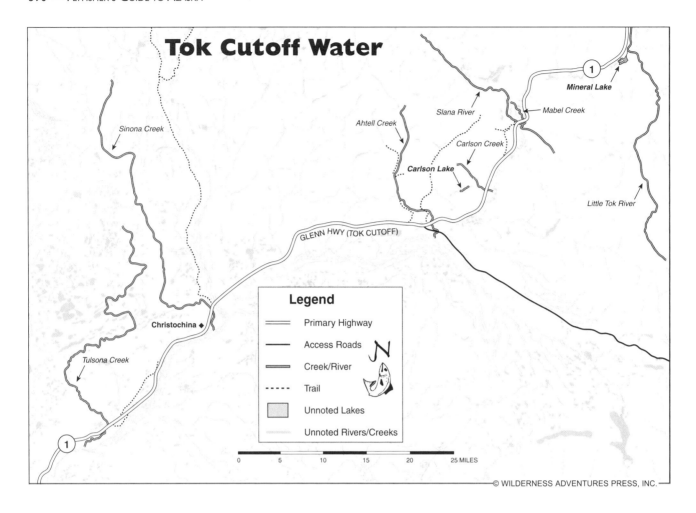

Tulsona Creek

From mile 15 to mile 18 along the Tok Cutoff, there are several places to pull over and fish. Tulsona Creek parallels the highway here, and reaching its banks is a cinch. Of all the waters on the Cutoff, this is perhaps the best one on which to spend some time.

Tulsona Creek is a clear stream, with a slightly tea-stained color due to the tannic acids from area vegetation. The creek is easy to wade and fish, and with so many places to pull off you can spend the better part of the morning here, trying your luck for average grayling, the only fish in this stream.

Sinona Creek

Sinona Creek flows near the town of Chistochina. As you would expect, there is a great deal of private land surrounding this creek, which is situated at mile 34 on the Tok Cutoff. Nonetheless, grayling, Dolly Varden, and king salmon inhabit these waters, where wade fishing is the norm.

The only real access to Sinona Creek is at the bridge where the creek flows beneath the road. You can wade in either direction, fishing as you go. There is a small run of chinook salmon in the creek, but they are fairly dark and ragged looking after their long journey. From spring into July, fly anglers can try their luck at these salmon, of which you're allowed to keep one per day, four in possession.

A series of beaver dams can make for tough going, and private land upstream limits how far you can go. And it's by no means a pristine creek, as there is a great deal of local pressure, and most of the big grayling have been weeded out.

Ahtell Creek

Continuing along the Tok Cutoff, you won't hit another fishing hole until mile marker 61. Here, a roadside pulloff near the bridge provides easy access to Ahtell Creek. (There has been some recent work on this section of road, so actual mileage may vary slightly.)

Grayling are the primary target here. Though there is

a small run of king salmon, the creek is closed to fishing for them. Stick with small grayling-type gear and you'll be okay.

Ahtell Creek runs bronze in color, but is fairly clear. The bottom is easy to see, so wading and fishing is the way to go. From the pulloff at the bridge, you can wade in either direction, hitting the pockets for grayling.

Carlson Creek

For more Dolly and grayling action, you can try Carlson Creek at mile 68. There is a pulloff on the shoulder of the road at the bridge. The best fishing is found under the bridge, though you can wade up and downstream. Similar to Ahtell Creek, Carlson is easy to wade and fish. As with many streams in this region, the Dolly Varden are small, averaging 8 to 14 inches. Grayling run in the 10- to 12-inch class.

If you're energetic and looking for a longer outing, you can hike 2.5 miles up the creek from the road. Stay within the banks of the stream, as there is a large spread of native lands along here. The going is not easy, though. Once you reach Carlson Lake, grayling and more Dollys are on the menu. But the fish aren't big, and the fishing can be slow.

Mable Creek

Mable Creek is a restricted fishery that crosses the Cutoff road at mile 76. Virtually the only fishing to be had here is directly beneath the bridge. There is a pool that offers fair grayling fishing, but as you'd expect, it doesn't take much pressure to ruin this hole. If you have a few minutes to spare, give it a shot; if not, keep moving.

The same holds true for the **Slana River**, which flows near the village of Mentasta. There are few pulloffs here and little wading available. Though it looks inviting, **Mentasta Lake** is another one you'll want to bypass, as increased private land restrictions are not worth fighting.

Mineral Lake

A beautiful small lake that's worth seeing—and fishing— is Mineral Lake, located at mile 89 on the Tok Cutoff. There is a roadside pulloff on the south of the road, which leads to a small lake. This small lake then feeds into Mineral Lake, where northern pike and grayling await anglers.

In the stream connecting the two lakes, there is some fair fishing, but you'll need chest waders because the going is muddy in this swampy terrain. If you feel ambitious, you can dump a canoe in the upper lake and fish your way down the stream and into Mineral Lake.

Mineral Lake is about a half-mile from the road, and you can actually see it from where you park. Walking in the marshy bog is taxing, though, and should only be tackled by anglers in good shape. The best fishing in this relatively shallow lake is found at the inlet and outlet. Fishing for grayling slows in the summer, but the pike fishing can be good from meltoff to late fall. Frankly, the fishing is tough here.

But if you're looking for a real floating adventure, continue through Mineral Lake in your canoe. Mineral Lake drains into the Little Tok River, which leads right back to the highway, where you can take out at mile 91 at what's called Broken Bridge. Due to the amount of private property throughout this area, floating it by canoe is the only way to really discover its beauty. The journey takes no more than a few hours, and the chance of seeing any other anglers is slim.

TOK

Population: 1,215
Alaska Area Code: 907
Zip Code: 99780

TOURIST INFORMATION

Alaska Department of Fish & Game, 822-3309 (Glennallen office)

Tok Civic Center/Main Street Visitor Center, P.O. Box 389; 883-5775; located at the Alaska Hwy. and Tok Cutoff junction

TACKLE SHOPS

The Bull Shooter Sporting Goods, P.O. Box 553; 883-5625; fishing tackle and licenses available

ACCOMMODATIONS

A Winter Cabin B&B, P.O. Box 61; 883-5655; individual log cabins, carpeted, breakfast-stocked refrigerator, microwave, tub/shower in separate/shared bathhouse

Cabins Outback B&B, P.O. Box 7; 883-4121; traditional sod-roofed log cabins with private bath

Tok Lodge, P.O. Box 135; 1-800-883-3007; 36 units, dining; www.alaskan.com/toklodge

Young's Motel, P.O. Box 482; 883-4411; 43 rooms, private bath, phone, satellite TV, connected to Fast Eddy's Restaurant

Westmark Tok Hotel, P.O. Box 130; 800 544-0970; 92 rooms, dining, adjacent to Tok

Visitor Center, open May 15 to September 15; www.westmarkhotels.com

CAMPGROUNDS AND RV PARKS

Eagle Trail State Recreation Site, mile 109.5 Tok Cutoff; 280 acres, 35 campsites, fee, picnic tables, restrooms, water

Golden Bear Motel Restaurant & RV Park, P.O. Box 500; 1-866-883-2561; 60-unit motel with private baths, phones, cable TV; full and partial RV hookups, showers, laundry

Moon Lake State Recreation Site, mile 1,332 Alaska Hwy.; 22 acres, 17 campsites, fee, restrooms

Rita's Campground RV Park & Cheryl's Old Fashion B&B Cabin, P.O. Box 599; 883-4342; pull-throughs, firepits, tentsites, picnic tables

Sourdough Campground, P.O. Box 47; 1-800-789-5543 or 883-5543; full hookups, pull-throughs, tentsites, picnic tables, showers, water, laundry, restrooms, dump station; open-air museum rich in area history; sourdough pancake breakfast; located 1.5 miles on Tok Cutoff

The Bull Shooter RV Park, P.O. Box 553; 883-5625; full and partial hookups, pull-throughs, water, showers, restrooms, dump station

Tok River State Recreation Site, mile 1,309 Alaska Hwy.; 9 acres, 43 campsites, fee, picnic tables, restrooms, water

Tok RV Village, P.O. Box 739; 1-800-478-5878 or 883-5877; 95 sites, full and partial hookups, pull-throughs, tentsites, showers, laundry, restrooms, dump station; gift shop, fishing licenses

Tundra Lodge and RV Park, P O Box 760; 883-7875; 78 sites, full and partial hookups, tentsites, showers, laundry, dump station, picnic tables, firepits

RESTAURANTS

Fast Eddy's Restaurant, P.O. Box 482; 883-4411; serving breakfast, lunch, dinner, specializing in steaks, seafood and pasta, salad bar, deserts; connected to Young's Motel; open year-round

Tok Gateway Salmon Bake, P.O. Box 577; 883-5555; specializing in flame-grilled salmon, halibut and BBQ ribs, also has buffalo burgers and reindeer sausage; wooded RV site with no hookups, water, showers, restrooms, dump station, tent sites, free overnight camping with dinner; www.tokalaska.com

Young's Cafe, 883-2233; located next to Young's Chevron at Tok Junction; full menu, homemade pies

BOAT RENTALS

Mineral Lakes Retreat, 1-866-244-3859; mile 89.5 Tok Cutoff; offers trophy pike and grayling fishing; boat rentals

AUTO REPAIR

James Enterprises, 883-5346 or 322-0427; towing service

Young's Chevron Service, 883-2821; located at Tok Junction; complete auto service

MEDICAL

Community Clinic, 883-5855; located across from the fire hall on the Tok Cutoff

TOURIST ATTRACTIONS

Tetlin National Wildlife Refuge, P.O. Box 779; 883-5312; one of only two road-accessible refuges in Alaska, located along the Alaska-Canada boundary between the Alaska Highway and Wrangell-St. Elias National Park and Preserve, high density of nesting waterfowl, moose, caribou, Dall sheep, grizzly and black bears, wolves, wolverine, lynx, and more

Mukluk Land, 883-2571; located 3 miles west of Tok Junction; indoor-outdoor museum, gold panning, open June through August

The southern regions of Alaska's road system host prime silver salmon action.

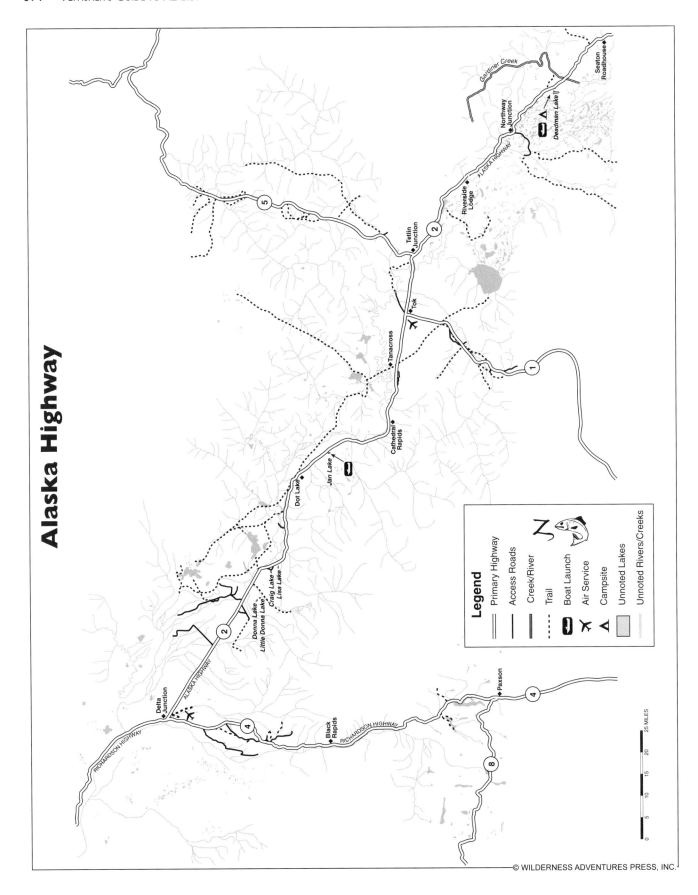

Alaska Highway

Legend

— Primary Highway
— Access Roads
— Creek/River
---- Trail
◨ Boat Launch
✈ Air Service
△ Campsite
▨ Unnoted Lakes
— Unnoted Rivers/Creeks

© WILDERNESS ADVENTURES PRESS, INC.

0 5 10 15 20 25 MILES

THE ALASKA HIGHWAY

The Alaska Highway enters the Last Frontier from British Columbia in a fairly central location and runs 1,390 miles to the town of Delta Junction.

Far removed from any oceans, the rivers in this area are often void of salmon. And the streams that do contain salmon are likely closed to protect fragile spawning grounds, but with fish so battered from their long death march this far north you wouldn't want to target them here anyway.

Anglers must also recognize that this portion of the state is not that rich in natural fisheries. The shallow lakes and streams and tough winter conditions make it difficult for fish to holdover from one season to the next, and the short growing season often equates to small fish. However, there is a saving grace, thanks to the ADF&G. Some 60 percent of the annual sport-caught fish taken from this part of Alaska have been stocked by the ADF&G.

Please note that the mileage listed for the fisheries below starts at Dawson Creek, British Columbia, the beginning of the Alaska Highway, and continues to Delta Junction at the highway's terminus.

Gardiner Creek

The lakes and streams that greet you in the Tetlin National Wildlife Refuge as you enter from Canada are spotty fisheries at best, which is why I'd continue 1,246.5 miles up the road to Gardiner Creek.

Gardiner Creek is a small stream that runs a bit dark in color due to the presence of tannic acids. Its color doesn't hinder flyfishing, however, and the stream can be waded or fished from shore. This is a seasonal fishery, with northern pike the main fish to target. The pike don't grow big here, but they can be aggressive during the summer months, striking flashy flies jerked across the surface or subsurface. A few grayling inhabit this pretty stream too, although they're not as large as what you'll find down the road.

Deadman Lake

The first fairly stable lake fishery can be found on the south side of the highway at mile 1,249, where a sharp turnout leads to Deadman Lake Campground about a mile down the gravel road. There are more than a dozen campsites here with toilets, firepits, and picnic tables.

This scenic lake has a boat ramp where you can launch a small craft to search for northern pike, the only fish in Deadman Lake. Though they average nearly 24 inches, the pike in this lake are very slender. Working a belly boat along the edges and aggressively stripping

flashy streamers is an effective way to attract these snaky fish, which can be caught from late spring into fall.

From this point on, there is a bit of fishing to be had along the **Tanana River** on the road from Northway Junction, but this can be very hit and miss. If the river looks clear and fishable when you pass through, it might be worth dabbling a fly for some roadside grayling.

You'll also pass **Midway Lake** on the south side of the highway. Though this lake looks attractive, it's very shallow and offers poor fishing. There are some pike in here, but I wouldn't devote much time to chasing them.

Once you pass the towns of Tok and Cathedral Rapids, more lake fishing is available. **Robertson Lake** is situated just west of the highway after you cross the Robertson River. Though this lake is stocked with rainbows, it's probably not worth the short hike in to try your luck. This is a pretty lake, but the low winter survival rate means that there aren't many big trout.

Excellent rainbow trout fishing can be found along much of Alaska's road system.

Jan Lake

At mile 1,353.5 on the Alaska Highway, you can turn south and follow the road about a half-mile to Jan Lake. Here you'll find a boat launch and toilets, though no overnight camping is allowed. Jan Lake is native owned, but permission to fish is granted.

This lake hosts good rainbow trout fishing thanks to stocking efforts by the ADF&G. The trout do well here through the winter, so there is a good holdover population of large rainbows. Though the lake goes down to 35 feet, it has good shallow margins for flyfishers to work. Fishing this lake from a float tube can be especially productive.

Lisa Lake

If you want to get out and stretch your legs, the walk to Lisa Lake may be just what you're looking for. There's a paved parking area on the west side of the road at mile 1,381, shortly after you cross the Johnson River. You can park your vehicle here and hike in about a mile to Lisa Lake.

This is another lake stocked with rainbows that offers good fishing. Anglers should note that lily pads line the shores of this lake, and casting beyond them from the bank can be difficult. If you pack in a float tube, though, you'll be able to work the edges of the lily pads from deeper water.

Craig Lake

Craig Lake requires a short hike and a belly boat. At mile 1,384 a turnout on the west side of the highway leads to the trailhead for Craig. A short half-mile walk takes anglers through a gorgeous birch forest to one of the most beautiful lakes in the region.

Craig Lake is stocked with rainbows, and there are also some lake trout that have held over in here since the late 1980s. Though they can be tough to catch on a fly, lakers up to 10 pounds are fairly common in Craig Lake.

As you might expect with lake trout present, Craig is fairly deep, descending down to 80 feet but just 40 acres in size. Sinking lines and weighted leech patterns prove most effective in bringing lake trout up from their depths, while Egg-Sucking Leeches and Woolly Buggers do the trick on the 'bows.

Once you stand along the banks of Craig Lake, you'll be glad you carried in a belly boat. Due to the steep banks around the entire lake, bank fishing is not an option. Fishing streamer patterns behind a sinking line is a productive method on this lake.

Donna Lake and Little Donna Lake

While there are many hike-in lake options along this stretch of highway, these two are worth noting for the quality of fishing they have to offer. And because they are set off the beaten path they receive light pressure. Both lakes are stocked by helicopter and the holdover rates are high, so there are some big rainbows to be had.

A parking area on the south side of the highway puts you at the trailhead for these lakes at mile 1,392. The trail is usually wet and muddy, making for tough travel. Only fit anglers should attempt this walk. Big Donna Lake is 3.5 miles in, and Little Donna Lake is a mile beyond that. While there is some bank access, a float tube will put you in position for the best fishing.

Delta Clearwater River

At the terminus of the Alaska Highway, where it meets the Richardson Highway in Delta Junction, you'll find one of the interior's best grayling fisheries. The Delta Clearwater River, referred to by locals as Clearwater Creek, flows into the Tanana River north of town.

Clearwater Creek is managed for trophy grayling, and it's a catch-and-release stream except for a one-month period in the summer, when fish under 12 inches may be kept. As a result, plump trophy grayling here run into the high teens.

The spring-fed creek runs crystal-clear, and the banks range from flat and open to thick with overhanging vegetation, creating good habitat. Due to the clarity, this is an easy stream to wade and fish. In places, it's shallow enough to wade across, though you will need chest waders.

Early in the summer, Clearwater Creek hosts an incredible array of insect hatches. Mayflies and caddisflies emerge in astounding numbers, and matching the hatch can lead to nonstop action.

While the majority of prime fishing is accessed by boat, good road access will also put bank anglers on super water. The best road access is upstream from the mouth, at river mile eight. At mile 1,414.8 on the Alaska Highway, prior to entering the town of Delta Junction, turn north on Clearwater Road. This road leads straight through farmland and forms a T-junction with Remington Road. Turn east on Remington Road and follow the signs to the Clearwater State Recreation Site, which has a campground with toilets and water.

There is a lodge nearby, situated on the banks of the river, that allows angler access, opening up even more water up and downstream.

DELTA JUNCTION

Population: 3,000
Alaska Area Code: 907
Zip Code: 99737

TOURIST INFORMATION

Alaska Department of Fish & Game, 895-4484 (Delta Junction office)

Delta Chamber of Commerce/ Visitor Center, P.O. Box 987; 895-5068; located at junction of Alaska and Richardson Highways

TACKLE SHOPS

Granite View Sorts & Gifts, 895-4994; located across from Visitor's Center

ACCOMMODATIONS

Alaska 7 Motel, P.O. Box 1115; 895-4848; 16 large rooms with bath/shower, kitchenettes available, open year-round; alaskan.com/ak7motel

Alaskan Steak House & Motel, P.O. Box 427; 895-5175; mile 265 Richardson Hwy.; breakfast, lunch, and family-style dinners, all-you-can-eat BBQ dinners, beer and wine are served, reasonable rates, in-room cable TV

Hines Site 20/20 Bed and Breakfast, Box 7195; 388-8299; mile 195 Richardson Hwy.; 5 rooms with queen beds and private baths, open year-round, full breakfast, goodfishing nearby

Kelly's Country Inn, 1616 Richardson Hwy., P.O. Box 849; 895-4667; open year-round, private baths, telephones, TV

Meier's Lake Roadhouse, P.O. Box 7190; 822-3151; mile 170 Richardson Hwy.; lodging, tenting, rustic cabins, restaurant, lounge and bar; fishing licenses, boat rentals

Rika's Roadhouse and Landing, P.O. Box 1229; 895-4201; mile 275 on Richardson Hwy. on banks of Tanana River; 24-hour RV parking, restaurant noted as one of the best on entire Alaska Highway

CAMPGROUNDS AND RV PARKS

Big Delta State Historical Park, mile 274.5 Richardson Hwy.; 11 acres; 25 campsites, fee, picnic tables, restrooms, water

Clearwater State Recreation Site, mile 1,415 Alaska Hwy.; 27 acres, 17 campsites, fee, restrooms, water, boat launch, fishing

Delta State Recreation Site, mile 267 Richardson Hwy.; 23 acres, 25 campsites, picnic tables, restrooms, water

Donnelly Creek State Recreation Site, mile 238 Richardson Hwy.; 46 acres, 12 campsites, fee, restrooms, water

Fielding Lake State Recreation Site, mile 200.5 Richardson Hwy.; 605 acres, 17 campsites, restrooms, cabins, boat launch, fishing

Lost Lake Campground, mile 277.8 Richardson Hwy.; 12 campsites, fee, picnic tables, restrooms, water, fishing

Quartz Lake Campground, mile 277.8 Richardson Hwy.; 80 campsites, fee, picnic tables, restrooms, water, fishing

Smith's Green Acre's RV Park & Campground, P.O. Box 1129; 895-4369; mile 268 Richardson Hwy.; full and partial hookups, tree shaded pull-throughs, tentsites, laundry, showers, restrooms, dump station; fishing for grayling, trout and pike nearby

RESTAURANTS

Buffalo Center, 895-5089; diner located next to post office, serving buffalo burgers and steaks, reindeer, pizza, breakfast, lunch, dinner; drive-in located next to Sullivan's Roadhouse, serving burgers, sandwiches, hot dogs

Packhouse Restaurant, P.O. Box 1229; 895-4201; mile 275 on Richardson Hwy., within Rika's Roadhouse & Landing; restaurant noted as one of the best on entire Alaska Highway, serving breakfast and lunch, salads, sandwiches, soups, pies

Pizza Bella Family Restaurant, 895-4841; located next to Visitor Information Center; full menu, American & Italian, steaks, seafood, wine, beer

BOAT RENTALS

Meier's Lake Roadhouse, P.O. Box 7190; 822-3151; mile 170 Richardson Hwy.; fishinglicenses, boat rentals

MEDICAL

Delta Rescue Squad, 895-4656

Steese Highway

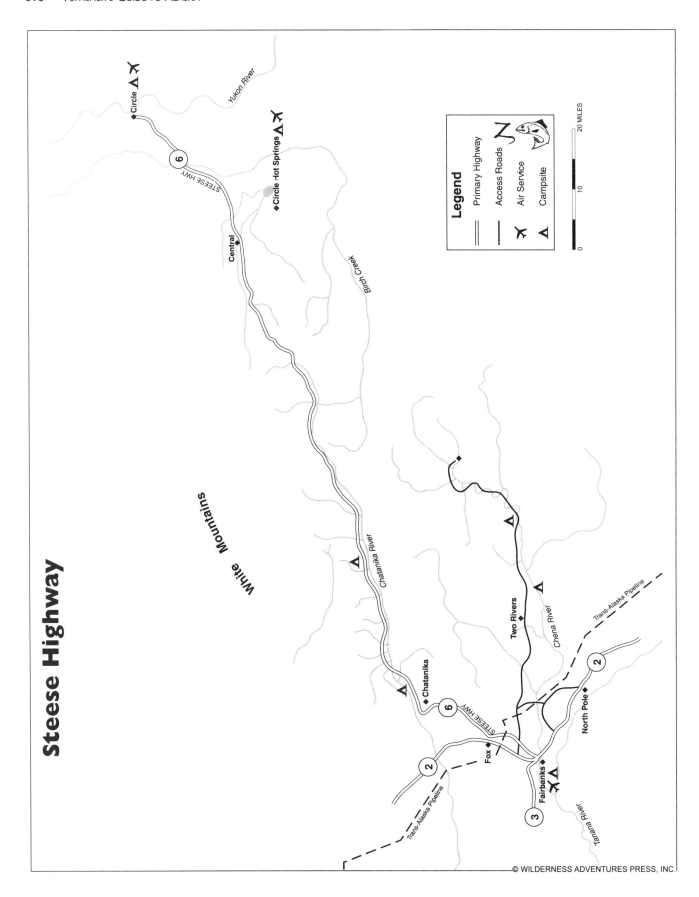

THE STEESE HIGHWAY

One of the state's most scenic drives can be had just out of Fairbanks on the Steese Highway, which leads 162 miles from Fairbanks to the town of Circle. The first 45 miles of the Steese are paved, with the rest gravel. The road is wide and makes for safe traveling. Near mile marker 128 and the town of Central, the road narrows and begins winding its way to Circle.

Many travelers—whether anglers or not—will take a day or two to drive the Steese Highway to sample what it has to offer. In addition to a close look at the Alaska Pipeline, there are commanding views of Fairbanks, access to camping and recreational-use areas, and hiking trails. And if it's fishing you're looking for, there's no shortage of that, either.

Anglers should note that while numerous creeks make their way toward the Steese Highway and the Chatanika River, which parallels the road for several miles, the fishing in these creeks is limited. Most of them are shallow spawning streams briefly occupied by grayling early in the spring when the water runs high. In the summer, the clear streams have little to offer in terms of fishing. However, at the mouths of many of these creeks—where they dump into the Chatanika—the fishing for grayling can be quite good. Larger grayling congregate at these confluences to gather food washed downstream.

Chatanika River

Of all the waters on the Steese Highway, the Chatanika River offers the best fishing and the most access. Grayling are the only fish pursued here, as the waters are closed to the taking of salmon.

The abundance of access is what makes fishing the Chatanika so popular. At mile 39, you'll find the Upper Chatanika River State Recreation Site on the north side of the highway, the first of the streamside campgrounds. More than two-dozen campsites await anglers at this pretty site, and a huge gravel bar leads directly to the river, where you'll find ample fishing opportunities.

If you're looking for a float-fishing adventure, this is the best place on the highway. At the campground you can launch a boat and float the river to where it crosses the Elliot Highway. Though the drift can be made in six to eight hours, it's worth spending the night on the river, taking in all the relaxing aspects this nice little float has to offer. Two items you won't want to forget are bug spray and sunscreen.

Due to the winding nature of the river here, and the fact that sweepers dropped into the river by beavers can pop up at any given moment, it's best to make the run in a raft. Don't attempt the run in a canoe unless you have strong river experience. Floating is a nice way to see the river and you'll tie into grayling in the 17-inch class.

The Chatanika River borders the road for the next 20 miles. There are numerous roadside pulloffs, and you have the freedom to park and fish wherever you'd like. The roadside grayling fishery is popular among the locals, and this is where they come to get fish for dinner, as trophy grayling can't be kept on the Chena River, which will be detailed with the Chena Hot Springs Road.

There is a 12-inch minimum on grayling here, and fish measuring into the upper teens are taken each summer.

Stream Facts: Chatanika River

Seasons

- From April 1 to May 31, grayling are catch-and-release only.

- From June 1 to March 31, a daily bag and possession limit of 5 grayling, all of which must be 12 inches or longer.

Because so much fishing takes place in salmon spawning streams, be particularly careful not to disturb any redds.

Chatanika River and Nome Creek

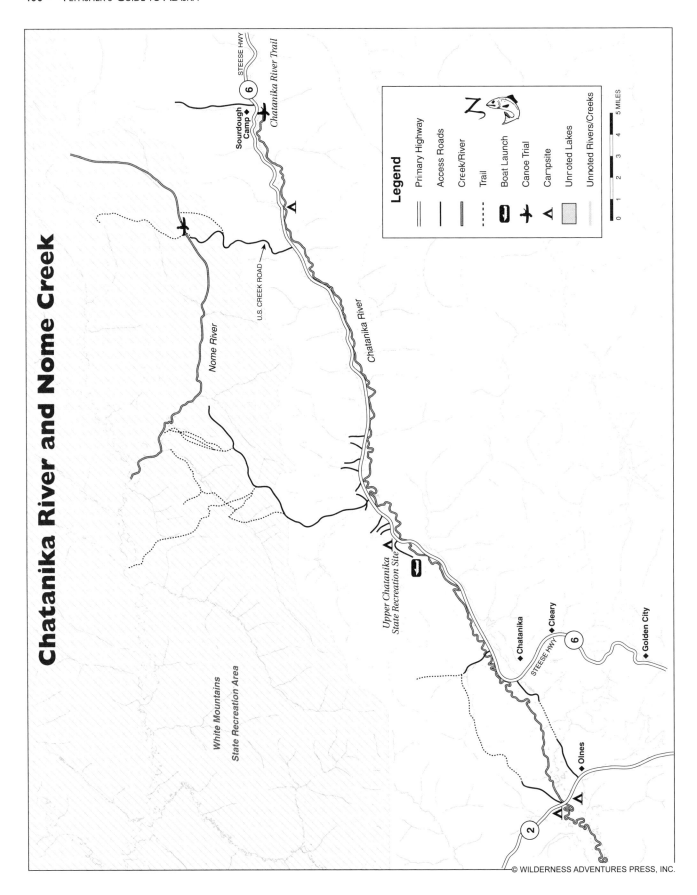

STEESE HWY

Chatanika River Trail

6

Sourdough
Camp ◆

Chatanika River

U.S. CREEK ROAD

Nome River

Upper Chatanika
State Recreation Site

White Mountains

State Recreation Area

◆ Chatanika

◆ Cleary

STEESE HWY

6

◆ Golden City

◆ Olnes

2

Legend

Primary Highway	
Access Roads	
Creek/River	
Trail	
Boat Launch	
Canoe Trial	
Campsite	
Unroted Lakes	
Unnoted Rivers/Creeks	

N

0 1 2 3 4 5 MILES

- From June 1 to October 14, the open season for northern pike allows for a daily bag and possession limit of 5 fish, only 1 of which may be over 30 inches long.

Special Regulations

- Upstream from the ADF&G markers located 1 mile upstream from the Elliott Highway bridge, only single hook unbaited artificial lures may be used April 1 to May 31.
- Closed to all salmon fishing upstream from the ADF&G markers located 1 mile upstream from the Elliott Highway bridge.

Fish

- King and chum salmon, arctic grayling, northern pike, sheefish

River Characteristics

- A clear river that picks up speed higher in the drainage. The flow rate slows below the Steese Highway bridge, and especially downstream from the Elliott Highway bridge. Plenty of gravel bars and solid banks make for excellent wade fishing.

Fishing and Boating Access

- At mile 39 the Upper Chatanika River State Recreation Site allows boat access and ample bank fishing. Floats can be made from here to the Elliott Highway bridge. The upper 20 miles of river offer numerous roadside pulloffs where anglers can park and fish.

Maps

- *Alaska Atlas and Gazetteer*, pages 124, 125, 126

Nome Creek

One creek that used to offer good grayling fishing but has been hit hard in recent years is Nome Creek. In an effort to revitalize this fishery, regulations are catch-and-release only, with single unbaited artificial hooks. This is a great stream to wade, and when the fish regain their large status, it should again be a noteworthy creek.

This area is rich in mining history and you can actually pan for gold here, so it's definitely worth seeing if that sort of thing interests you. Turn off the highway just past mile 57 and follow U.S. Creek Road west to the marked BLM Nome Creek Valley Gold Panning Area. The steep gravel road winds over the hills for 7 miles, ending at a parking area with signs informing prospectors of the mining rules. You'll also see remnants of early 20th-century mining activity.

Birch Creek

The road climbs in elevation along this stretch of the Steese Highway. If you're here in the fall, you'll likely see caribou hunters working the area. And Birch Creek is one of the better fishing locales this far up the drainage.

At mile 94, North Fork Birch Creek can be reached by following a little side road a quarter-mile to the creek. This turns into a major canoe route, and the upper end has good fishing for grayling up to 15 inches. The creek can either be fished by wading your way up or downstream or by canoe.

From where the creek leaves the highway, it makes a big bend to the east, away from the road. It then winds its way back to the road, where you can take out five to six days later. This is the only way to access these waters, as a hike in from the road is a long way and there are no trails.

In the mountains, Birch Creek is pretty swift and should only be run by experienced canoeists. I heard of one pair of anglers who, after hitting the big sweeping bend in the river, flipped their canoe and lost everything. They swam to shore and found an old trapper's cabin in the woods. They found some rice here that saved their lives. Because they'd lost their shoes, they fashioned sandals from old wood planks and some strips of hide. They barely survived the ordeal, as it was many miles of hard walking back to the road. So if you make this drift, be prepared.

The closer you get to the town of Circle, the more friendly Birch Creek becomes. You can put in at mile 140 or 147 and try your luck at what's reported to be good pike fishing.

When you arrive at the town of Circle you'll come to the banks of the Yukon River. There might be some burbot action here, but that's about it. The banks of the river are not conducive to angling, and the silty, fast water is the farthest thing from fly water you'll see.

If you'd like to try your luck at a stocked pond, there are some available along the Steese Highway. Most of these ponds have no formal names, but instead are identified by the mile marker. For instance, 29.5 Pond and 34.6 Pond can be found at those respective mile markers. Other such lakes can be found along the highway and are clearly marked. These ponds are stocked with rainbow trout one year, grayling the next. If you have a canoe or float tube, you might find a pond that appeals to you.

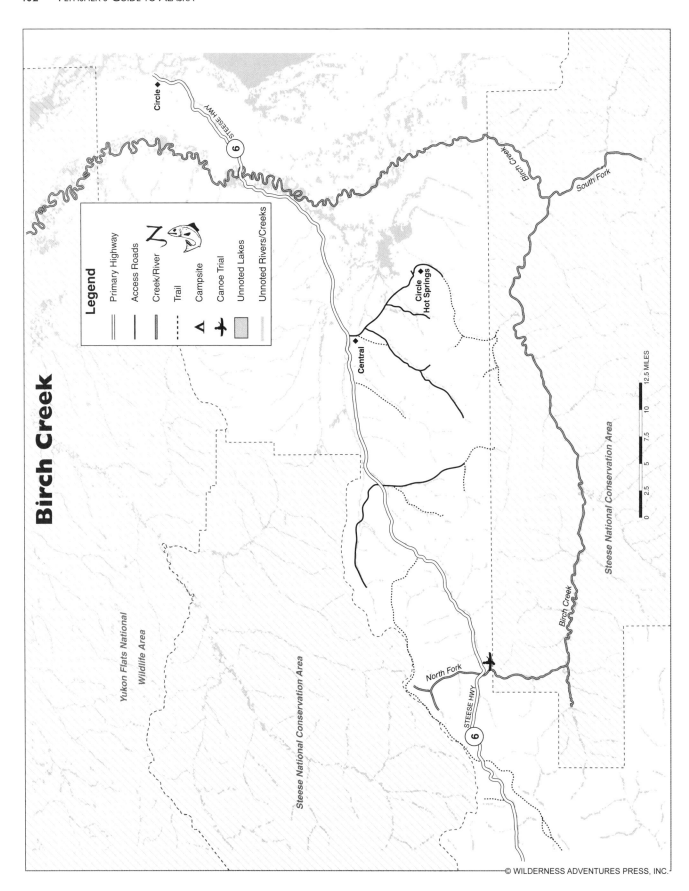

Birch Creek

Legend

Primary Highway	
Access Roads	
Creek/River	
Trail	
Campsite	◭
Canoe Trial	
Unnoted Lakes	
Unnoted Rivers/Creeks	

Circle

STEESE HWY

Birch Creek

South Fork

Circle Hot Springs

Central

Steese National Conservation Area

0   2.5   5   7.5   10   12.5 MILES

Yukon Flats National Wildlife Area

Steese National Conservation Area

North Fork

STEESE HWY

Birch Creek

FAIRBANKS

Population: 82,850
Alaska Area Code: 907

TOURIST INFORMATION

Alaska Department of Fish & Game, 459-7202
(Fairbanks office)
Fairbanks Visitor Information Center, 550 1st Ave.
(at Cushman St., at the end of the Alaska Hwy., mile
1,523); 1-800-327-5774; www.explorefairbanks.com

GUIDE SERVICES

Alaska Fishing & Rafting Adventures, Fairbanks;
455-7238
Arctic Grayling Guide Service, P.O. Box 83707,
Fairbanks, AK 99708; 479-0479
Coho Charters, Fairbanks; 474-0755
Hughes Sport Fishing Guide Service, 1-866-423-0474
or 479-3474; located below Arctic
Circle on the Koyukuk River; specializing in float
trips; bigalaskafish.com
Interior Alaska Adventures, Fairbanks; 455-8721
Ivory Gull Charters, 1713 Central Ave., Fairbanks, AK
99709; 322-3068
North Country River Charters, Fairbanks; 479-7116
Wilderness Fishing, Inc., P.O. Box 83707, Fairbanks,
AK 99708; 479-0479; specializing in Arctic grayling;
www.wildernessfishing.com

FLY-IN CHARTERS

Iniakuk Lake Wilderness Lodge, P.O. Box 80424,
Fairbanks, AK 99708; 1-800-479-6354;
www.gofarnorth.com
Marina Air, Inc., 1195 Shypoke, Fairbanks, AK 99709;
479-5684; provides boat and motor, cabins or tent
camps; www.akpub.com/fhwag.marina

TACKLE SHOPS

Alaska Fly Shop, 1875 University Ave., Suite 1,
Fairbanks, AK 99709; 456-3010; specializing in
quality flyfishing gear and information
The Fly Hatch, 16 Blanche Ave., Fairbanks, AK 99701;
457-3597
Fred Meyer, 19 College Rd., Fairbanks, AK 99701;
459-4200; basic tackle selection, excellent one-stop
shopping
J & L Sport Shop, 910 College Rd., Fairbanks, AK
99701/ 451-7210

ACCOMMODATIONS

7 Gables Inn, P.O. Box 80488, Fairbanks, AK 99708;
479-2229; central location, apartments, rooms, cottages, free canoe and bikes; www.7gablesinn.com
AAAA Care Bed & Breakfast, 557 Fairbanks Street,
Fairbanks, AK 99709; 1-800-478-2705; spacious and
private rooms, shared bath; www.aaaacare.com
All Seasons Inn, 763 Seventh Ave., Fairbanks, AK
99701; 1-888-451-6649; inn@alaska.net
Captain Bartlett Inn, 1411 Airport Way, Fairbanks, AK
99701; 1-800-544-7528 outside AK, 1-800-478-7900
in AK; famous for its Alaskan decor and hospitality
and cultural experience;
www.captainbartlettinn.com
Chena Hot Springs Resort, 1-800-478-4681, 451-8104
(local); located 60 miles from Fairbanks on Chena
Hot Springs Road; rooms, cabins, natural hot
springs, fishing, canoeing
Pike's Waterfront Lodge, 1-877-774-2400; located on
the Chena River in Fairbanks, near airport;
www.pikeslodge.com
River's Edge Resort, 4200 Boat St., Fairbanks, AK
99709; 1-800-770-3343; located in heart of city,
wooded, Chena riverfront setting, fine dining, tour
bookings; fishing for grayling and king salmon;
www.riversedge.net
Sophie's Station Hotel, 1717 University Ave.,
Fairbanks, AK 99709; 1-800-528-4916; excellent
hotel situated near prime shopping, one mile from
airport; www.fountainheadhotels.com
Super 8 Motel, 1909 Airport Way, Fairbanks, AK 99701;
1-800-800-8000 or 451-8888; www.super8.com

CAMPGROUNDS AND RV PARKS

Birch Lake State Recreation Site, mile 305.5
Richardson Hwy.; 48 acres, 28 campsites, fee, picnic
tables, restroom, water, cabin, boat launch, fishing
Chena Marina RV Park, 1145 Shypoke Dr.; Fairbanks,
AK 99709; 479-4653; drive-through sites, full and
partial hookups, showers, restrooms, laundry, reservations needed, April 15 to Sept. 15;
www.chenarvpark.com
Chena River State Recreation Site, located on
University Ave.; 27 acres, 61 campsites, fee, picnic
tables, restrooms, water, boat launch, fishing
Harding Lake State Recreation Area, mile 321.4
Richardson Hwy.; 355 acres, 81 campsites, fee, picnic tables, restrooms, water, daily parking fee, boat
launch, fishing
Lower Chatanika River State Recreation Area, mile
11 Elliott Hwy.; 400 acres, 12 campsites, fee, picnic
tables, restrooms, water, boat launch, fishing

Norlite Campground, 1660 Peger Rd., Fairbanks, AK 99701; 474-0206; RV and sites, full hookups, water, electric, laundry, dump stations, tourist information

Red Squirrel Campground, Mile 43 Chena Hot Springs Road; 5 campsites, fee, picnic tables, restroom, water, fishing

Riverview RV Park, 1316 Badger Rd., North Pole, AK 99705; 1-888-488-6392; located between Fairbanks and North Pole on Chena River; full and partial hookups, pull-throughs, shower, laundry, restrooms, groceries, salmon and grayling fishing

River's Edge RV Park & Campground, 4140 Boat St., Fairbanks, AK 99709; 474-0286; 180 sites, full and partial hookups, pull-throughs, tentsites, showers, laundry, dump station, close to shopping and groceries; www.riversedge.net

Rosehip Campground, mile 27 Chena Hot Springs Road; 37 sites, fee, picnic tables, restroom, water, fishing

Tanana Valley Campground, 1800 College Rd., Fairbanks, AK 99709; 456-7956; tent and RV spaces, showers, laundry, water, electric hookups, picnic tables, firepits; next to Creamer's Field bird sanctuary

Tors Trail Campground, mile 39 Chena Hot Springs Road; 24 campsites, fee, picnic tables, restrooms, water, fishing

Upper Chatanika River State Recreation Site, mile 39 Steese Hwy.; 73 acres, 35 campsites, fee, restrooms, water, fishing

RESTAURANTS

Alaska Salmon Bake, 3175 College Rd., Fairbanks, AK 99709; 1-800-354-7274; specializing in salmon, halibut, cod and prime rib; nightly shows at nearby Palace Theater & Saloon

Gambardellas Pasta Bella, 706 2nd Ave., Fairbanks, AK 99701; 456-3425 excellent Italian cuisine suitable for the whole family

Hot Licks Homemade Ice Cream, 3549 College Road, Fairbanks; 479-7813; the best ice cream in Alaska, I've tried every flavor

Pike's Landing, 1-877-774-2400; waterfront restaurant on Chena River, minutes from airport; outstanding seafood and steaks; www.pikeslodge.com

The Castle Restaurant & Lounge, 4510 Airport Way, Fairbanks, AK 99701; 474-2165; nice dining, nightclub and entertainment

The Pump House Restaurant & Saloon, 479-8452; mile 13 Chena Pump Road; great variety menu, from steaks to burgers

The Turtle Club, 457-3883; located 10 miles on Old Steese Hwy. in Fox, AK; famous for prime rib and prawns; call for reservations; get your name on the list, you'll want to spend an evening here

Two Rivers Lodge, 488-6815; located 16 miles on Chena Hot Springs Road; fine dining specializing in seafood, steak, prime rib, veal and chicken; rich in Alaskan character; need reservations

RENTAL VEHICLES

Affordable New Car Rental, 249 Alta Way, Fairbanks, AK 99701; 1-800-471-3101; one way rentals, 4x4s, vans, wagons, cars; www.nissan@polarnet.com

Aurora Motors, 1-800-849-7033; located at corner of Johansen Expressway and Danby Street; unlimited miles; www.auroramotors.com

Dalton Highway Auto Rentals, P.O. Box 82720, Fairbanks, AK 99708; one of the few agencies offering rental vehicles for traveling the gravel roads of the Dalton Hwy., fly-drive packages available, Arctic tour bookings

Denali RV, 100 Cornell Way, Fairbanks, AK 99709; 479-3764

Diamond Willow RV Rental, 350 Old Steese Hwy., Fairbanks, AK 99701; 457-2814

M-R Motor home Rentals, Fairbanks, AK 99701; 479-2605

Tanana Motor home Rentals, 2590 Shanks Mare Rd., Fairbanks, AK 99709; 452-2477

AUTO REPAIR

Arctic RV, 3013 Peger Road, Fairbanks, AK 99701; 451-8356; service, repair, parts and accessories, certified technicians

Gabe's Truck & Auto Repair, 456-6156; located on Frank Ave., off Airport Way; 24-hour towing, complete repair service on cars, trucks, RVs

LOCKSMITHS

Action Locksmiths, 516 Old Steese Hwy., Fairbanks, AK 99701; 451-7954

Larsons Locksmith & Security, Inc., 1249 Noble St., Fairbanks, AK 99701; 452-5625

MEDICAL

Fairbanks Memorial Hospital, 1650 Cowles St.; 452-8181

VETERINARY CLINICS

After Hours Veterinary Emergency Clinic, Fairbanks; 479-2700

Mt. McKinley Animal Hospital, 800 College Rd., Fairbanks, AK 99701; 452-6104; kind, friendly, and dependable service

TOURIST ATTRACTIONS

Alaskaland, P.O. Box 71267, Fairbanks, AK 99707; 459-1095; located at Airport Way and Peger Road; gold mining, paddle wheel boat, pioneer museum, frontier spirit, free admission

El Dorado Gold Mine, 1975 Discovery Drive, Fairbanks, AK 99709; 1-866-479-6673, 479-6673 (local); located 9 miles north of Fairbanks, on Elliot Hwy.; pan for gold, learn mining methods, a true taste of mining culture; www.eldoradogoldmine.com

Riverboat Discovery, 1-866-479-6673, 479-6673 (local); departs from Steamboat Landing, off Dale Road at 8:45 and 2:00 p.m., operates mid-May to September, rated among the nation's best riverboat tours; www.riverboatdiscovery.com

University of Alaska Museum, 907 Yukon Drive; 474-7505; on the UAF campus, one of the state's premier natural museums; they used to display the skull and one paw of the man-eating polar bear I killed in Point Lay in 1990

A shoreline near Fairbanks.

CHENA HOT SPRINGS ROAD

The 56-mile-long Chena Hot Springs Road is home to the mainstem Chena River and its forks and other tributaries. To access this road, head north out of Fairbanks on the Steese Expressway. At mile 5 on the Expressway, the Chena Hot Springs Road takes off to the east. This paved road offers safe travel and good fishing all the way to its terminus in Chena Hot Springs.

Anglers usually travel this road for one reason: world-class fishing for arctic grayling on the Chena River. Though there are several little creeks feeding into the Chena, there's little reason to explore beyond the Chena itself. You'd be hard pressed to find a trophy grayling fishery along any of Alaska's roads that would match the Chena.

Chena River

The Chena River borders the highway for some 30 miles along the Chena Hot Springs Road. There are actually too many access points to mention them all. All you have to do is drive until you find water you want to fish, pull over, and whip out the fly gear. In addition to easy roadside pulloffs, there are bridges and several recreation areas and campgrounds along the way.

What makes the Chena such a renowned grayling river is the way it's been managed. It's a catch-and-release river and has been restricted to single unbaited artificial lures for more than a decade. If you're looking for that magic 20-inch grayling, this is the place. Due to rich feed, these grayling are also plump, deep-bodied fish that put up a hard fight. An average grayling on the Chena runs about 14 inches.

In addition to grayling standbys like the Black Gnat and Mosquito, bring along some #14 Elk Hair Caddis, which sometimes drive trophy grayling nuts. In the evening, switch to gnat patterns, preferably ones that closely mimic the bugs you'll see here. If you hit the right spot in the evening, you'll observe so many grayling rising for bugs that it'll seem like the surface of the river is a giant vat of boiling water. The farther upstream you get, the larger the fish typically become.

The Chena is a clear river that is easy to wade and fish. If you want to slip into knee boots and drive from hole to hole, the banks are mostly flyfishing friendly.

Traveling up the Chena Hot Springs Road leads you to the headwaters of the North Fork Chena River and the South and Middle Forks. Here, the terrain opens up and the river gradient increases. More riffles are found in these waters, as are larger grayling. Set amid hill country, these beautiful streams offer solitude and phenomenal fishing for some of the world's most beautiful freshwater fish.

Of the three forks, the Middle Fork is the least explored. Hit the mouths of feeder streams and the lower ends of riffles and holding pools.

Wade fishing is still the rule in the upper forks, where you'll find clear water and generous bank access. The North Fork can be accessed at five different bridge crossings: miles 38, 39.5, 44, 49, and 55.3. Floating downstream from the first to the fourth bridge is a nice way to reach more water. Watch closely for logjams, as these can build

Chena Hot Springs Road

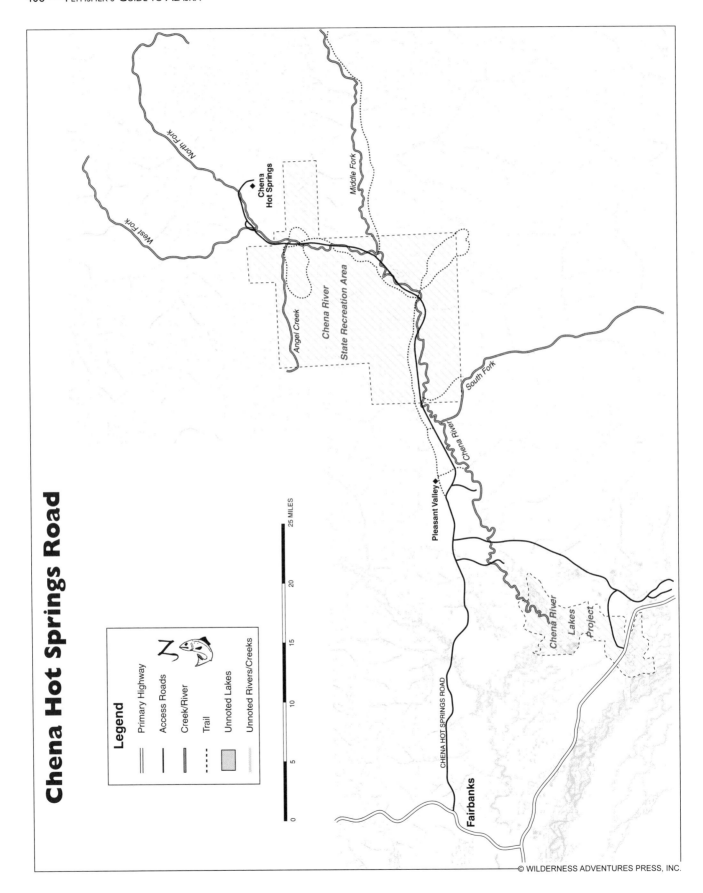

Legend

Primary Highway	
Access Roads	
Creek/River	
Trail	
Unnoted Lakes	
Unnoted Rivers/Creeks	

25 MILES

0   5   10   15   20

© WILDERNESS ADVENTURES PRESS, INC.

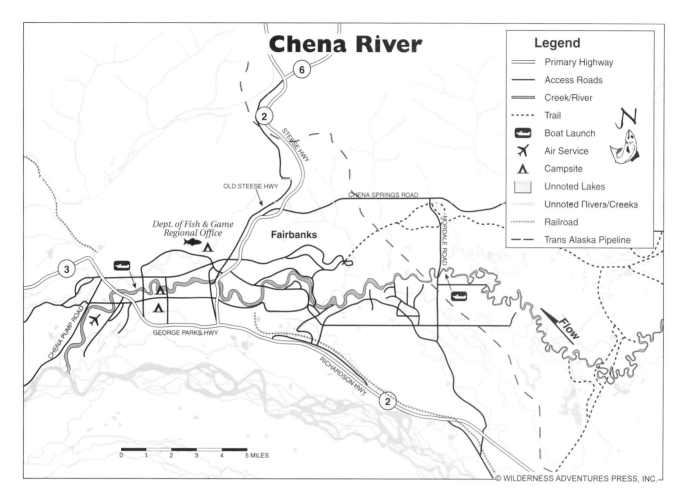

up across the entire river and may require a portage. Also, keep an eye out for sweeper logs motoring downstream. These are very cold, swift waters, so don't underestimate them.

The West Fork Chena River crosses the road at mile 52.3, offering yet another bank-fishing option.

Stream Facts: Chena River

Seasons

- Closed to all salmon fishing upstream from the ADF&G marker located 300 feet downstream of the Chena River Dam.

- Year-round, catch-and-release only fishing for grayling.

Special Regulations

- Upstream of the Chena River dam, only single-hook unbaited artificial lures may be used.

- Downstream of the Chena River dam, bait may be used only on single hooks with a gap larger than ¾ inch.

Fish

- Arctic grayling, king, chum, and silver salmon, northern pike, sheefish

River Characteristics

- A gentle river, the Chena makes its way out of the Steese National Conservation Area, bordering much of the highway on its downstream journey. Clear water makes for safe and easy fishing from the bank or when floating.

Fishing Access

- Roadside pullouts, day-use areas, and camping and recreation sites provide access to over 30 miles of river.

Maps

- *Alaska Atlas and Gazetteer*, pages 115, 116, 126

Angel Creek

At mile 50, Angel Creek is the last small stream with good grayling fishing before you enter the town of Chena Hot Springs 6 miles away.

Perhaps the best fishing on Angel Creek is at the mouth, where it feeds into the North Fork Chena River. But there's also great hike-in fishing on the north side of the highway. Hip boots will suffice here, as the creek can be waded with little effort. If you try your luck well upstream be sure to concentrate on pools that connect shallow sections of water. Grayling up to 17 inches are taken from Angel Creek, with most of the monsters falling to flies near the creek mouth.

THE ELLIOTT HIGHWAY

The Elliott Highway begins 11 miles north of Fairbanks at the junction with the Steese Highway at the town of Fox. From here, the Elliott Highway leads 152 miles to the town of Manley Hot Springs along the banks of the Tanana River.

The first 30 miles of the Elliott are paved, with the remainder gravel. The road is wide and provides excellent views as it passes through rolling hills in its way to the Dalton Highway junction. This stretch has a hard-rock base that makes for easy travel.

From the Dalton Highway junction to Manley Hot Springs, expect to find ruts, potholes, and washboard areas. The road also begins to narrow for the remainder of the journey. The condition of this part of the highway is weather dependent. If it's dry, expect easy traveling, if wet it can be slow going. In an effort to keep the dust at bay road crews often treat this section of road with calcium chloride, so at the end of your journey be sure to wash your vehicle.

The town of Fox has a general store and fuel. Your next fuel stop along the Elliott comes 5 miles down the road at Hilltop, then 60 miles farther down at North Country Mercantile. The town of Manley Hot Springs can also accommodate most of your needs.

Here is what to expect in terms of fishing as you make your way from Fox to Manley Hot Springs.

Olnes Pond

Ten miles into the journey on the Elliott Highway you'll come to Olnes Pond, a popular camping destination with very good grayling fishing. At mile 10.5 on the Elliott, turn off at the Lower Chatanika River State Recreation Area and Olnes Pond Campground. Continue 1 mile on a gravel road, which leads to more than four-dozen camp-sites and an open camp area around the pond. A water pump, picnic tables, and toilets are also available.

Because Olnes Pond is stocked by ADF&G, and because it's a common swimming hole, the number of people you might see on this lake may surprise you. However, the park has been experiencing financial setbacks in recent years, resulting in the closure of park facilities. Access was still granted, just no overnight camping. The result has been less fishing and recreational pressure.

This gravel-pit pond is home to grayling, rainbow trout, and burbot, and the fishing can be good for all three species. A bonus when fishing this lake is that a couple of short access trails lead through the woods to the banks of the Chatanika River, where the fishing can be pretty good for average grayling and king salmon in early to mid-July. Chum salmon are also available in late July, though they are a bit ragged by the time they reach their spawning stream.

Chatanika River

As mentioned above, the Chatanika River can be reached from Olnes Pond following a short, wooded walk. You can also access the river at the Elliott Highway bridge at mile 11. At the northwest corner of the bridge you'll find Whitefish Campground at the Lower Chatanika State Recreation Area. The upper Chatanika can be reached from the Steese Highway, which will be detailed in the following section.

King and chum salmon are the primary draw in this stretch, which is shallow and slow. A rocky bottom makes for safe and easy wade fishing, and the clear riffles dispersed throughout make ideal flyfishing water. At times the river runs the color of light root beer, but the visibility doesn't greatly impact the fishing.

From underneath the bridge, most people travel up and downstream in sled boats. Boats definitely remove anglers from the beaten path and get them into better salmon fishing. However, as these fish are on the move, there can be good fishing off the bank right at the bridge. In mid- to late July the kings typically begin to arrive, followed shortly by the chum salmon. Remember, these salmon have come a mighty long way from the ocean and they are a bit battered and well into the transitioning phase of their spawning colors. As a result, this is primarily a catch-and-release fishery.

There are also northern pike, sheefish, and grayling in the system. The grayling typically move quickly through on their way to summer feeding grounds in the upper river. The pike generally concentrate around the lower and middle section of the river, where they become

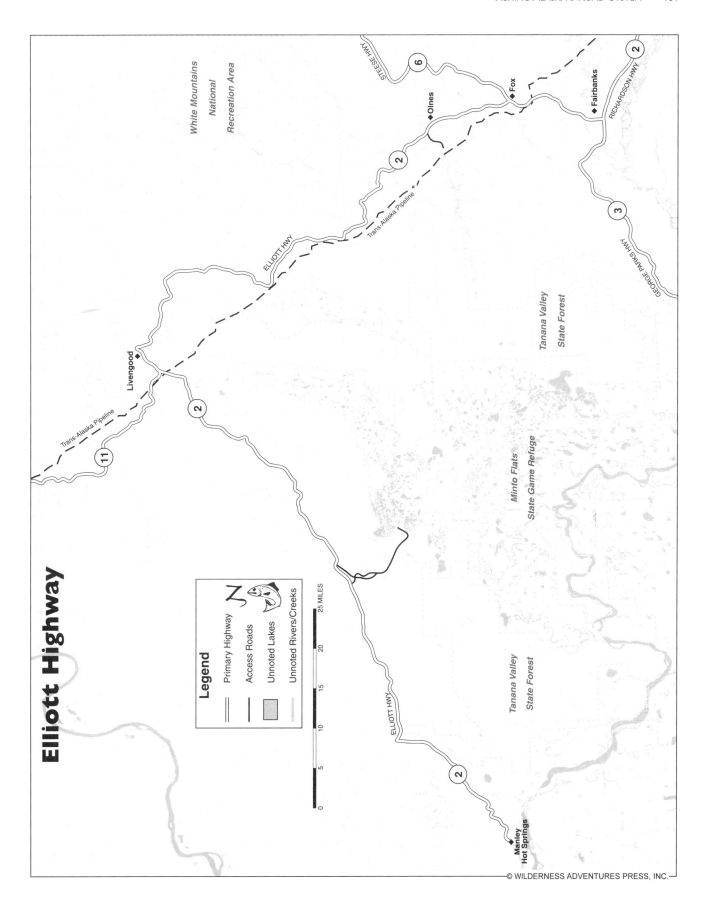

Elliott Highway

Legend

Primary Highway
Access Roads
Unnoted Lakes
Unnoted Rivers/Creeks

25 MILES
0 5 10 15 20

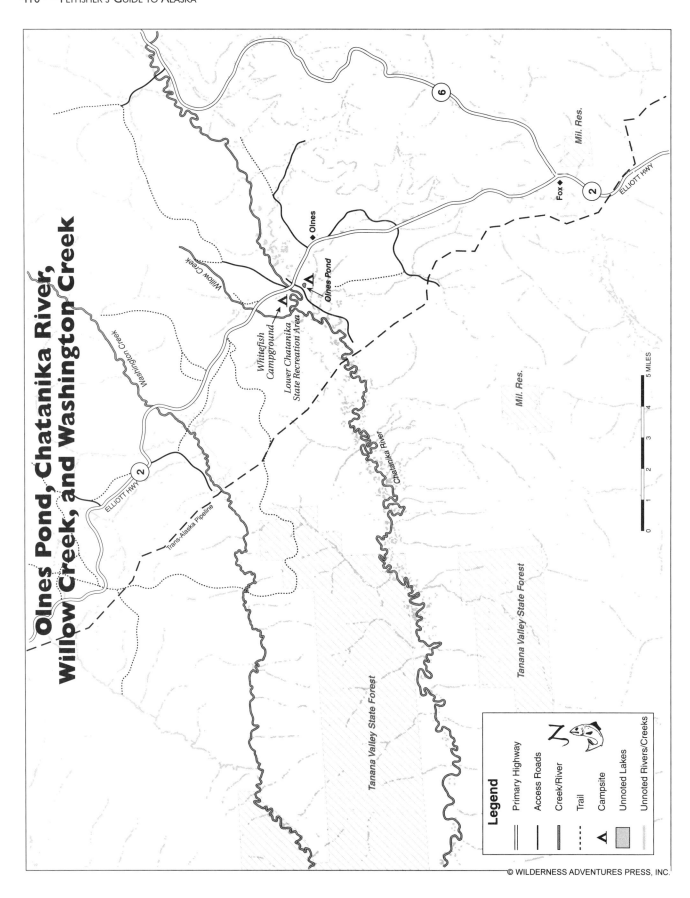

Olnes Pond, Chatanika River,
Willow Creek, and Washington Creek

6

2

Mil. Res.

Fox

ELLIOTT HWY

Olnes

Olnes Pond

Willow Creek

Washington Creek

Whitefish
Campground

Lower Chatanika
State Recreation Area

2

ELLIOTT HWY

Trans-Alaska Pipeline

Chatanika River

Mil. Res.

Tanana Valley State Forest

Tanana Valley State Forest

0   1   2   3   4   5 MILES

Legend

Primary Highway

Access Roads

Creek/River

Trail

Campsite

Unnoted Lakes

Unnoted Rivers/Creeks

© WILDERNESS ADVENTURES PRESS, INC.

Dolly Varden provide a great deal of action on roadside streams.

aggressive feeders from June through September. The sheefish action is best in September and October, when a small run of fish migrate upstream to spawning grounds. It should be noted that fishing for king salmon is closed 1 mile upstream of the Elliott Highway bridge (as marked by the ADF&G).

Willow Creek

A short distance up the road from the Chatanika, you'll find Willow Creek. The Elliott Highway crosses this nice little creek at mile 13.

The creek is a bit boggy where it crosses the highway, and its small stature and tea-colored water may make it appear as if it's void of fish. Not so. This is a good little grayling stream, and it can be fished in both directions. Few people fish Willow Creek due to its small size and brushy banks. However, with a pair of rubber knee boots—no need for waders—you can pick your way along, roll casting small dry flies for small grayling.

Tolovana River

Farther north on the Elliott Highway, you'll see where Washington Creek, Globe Creek, and the Tatalina River cross the road. The creeks are larger than Willow Creek, and run a tea color. All three streams wind their way through spruce and birch forests and are easy to wade and fish for grayling. Focus on pockets big enough to hold fish. During the summer months, the mosquitoes can be terribly thick along the Tatalina River, so be prepared.

At mile 57, the highway crosses the Tolovana River just south of the town of Livengood. Up the road, southwest of Livengood, the West Fork Tolovana River flows beneath the highway. On the mainstem Tolovana you can park right along the highway and make your way down to the river. The river has a little speed to it here, but working the banks can yield some good grayling action. There's little pressure on the main stem.

On the West Fork, pull off the highway at the bridge. There's a big, long sandbar on the river, where you'll find plenty of fishing. Though it's not a designated campground, people do camp right on the sandbar. The West Fork can be waded across in several places, and grayling up to 15 inches show up in the catch.

Minto Lakes

At mile 110, the Elliott Highway forms a junction with Minto Road, which leads south. From the town of Minto you can launch a boat where the Tolovana, Chatanika, and Tatalina Rivers come together. Following the Tolovana River to the Chatanika River drainage is the best way to access the Minto Lakes, often called the Minto Flats Lakes. This is strictly a boat fishery, and while a canoe will get you in and out of the waters, a motorized craft works best.

The area here is wide open, and incidentally, home to what is perhaps the best waterfowl hunting in Alaska. Due to the vastness of this marshy land, once you're in the labyrinth of lakes, sloughs, rivers, creeks, and ponds, navigation becomes a major concern. If you've never been to these lakes, I would highly recommend a GPS to get around. The willows and swamp grass will block your view of the surrounding country, and it's easy to lose sight of where you are during the day.

This boat fishery is noted for its exceptional pike fishing. With fish averaging 6 to 7 pounds or more, the action can be nonstop all day long. These waters also offer some of the best opportunities in the area to take sheefish. Big flashy flies resembling smolt work well on pike and sheefish. A friend who often fishes these lakes prefers a Lefty's Deceiver for these fish in summer and early fall.

Hutlinana Creek

For more small stream, small fish action, pull off the road where the bridge crosses over Hutlinana Creek at mile 129. This clear stream averages about 20 feet in width and can be waded across in most places. With hip boots you can wade up and downstream, concentrating on the pools where little grayling and beautiful little dwarf Dolly Varden congregate.

For a unique experience few tourists know about, pack a towel and fish your way upstream to the primitive hot springs. If it's not too overgrown, you should be able to see where the locals have made their way into the springs. Kick back and relax in this rich setting, then fish your way back to the vehicle

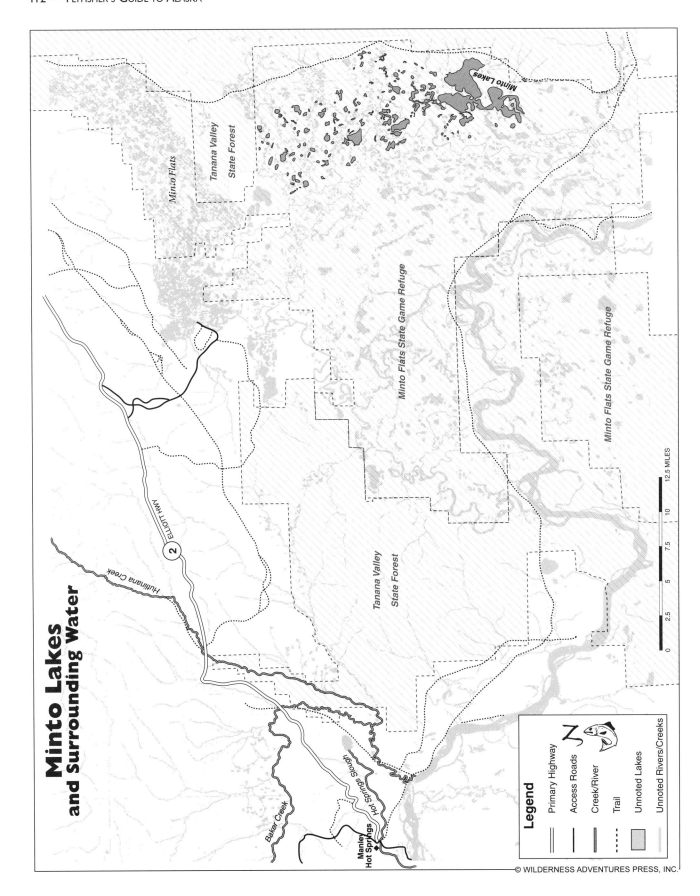

Minto Lakes
and Surrounding Water

Minto Lakes

Minto Flats

Tanana Valley
State Forest

Minto Flats State Game Refuge

Minto Flats State Game Refuge

Tanana Valley
State Forest

ELLIOTT HWY

2

Hutlinana Creek

Baker Creek

Hot Springs Slough

Manley
Hot Springs

Legend

Primary Highway
Access Roads
Creek/River
Trail
Unnoted Lakes
Unnoted Rivers/Creeks

N

0   2.5   5   7.5   10   12.5 MILES

© WILDERNESS ADVENTURES PRESS, INC.

Baker Creek

Though it may look appealing, don't spend any time fishing Eureka Creek, the next stream that crosses the highway. This creek freezes solid each winter, and there are no fish to speak of.

Instead, continue up the road to Baker Creek, where there are grayling up to 16 inches. Park near the bridge at mile 137 and make your way to the creek. Baker can be up to 40 feet wide in some areas, and hip boots or chest waders are required.

You can hike and fish up or downstream from the highway, and both directions offer good fishing. Downstream about a half-mile from the road there is a fishing hole that locals refer to as Cold Spring. Here, a coldwater spring bubbles up from the bottom of the creek, and the clear, chilled waters attract good numbers of fish. You can't miss the Cold Spring fishing hole, as the fisherman's trail leads right to it.

Anglers should note that there are some private native lands in this area. While access is usually not a problem along Baker Creek, ever-changing land acquisitions may mean that you run into posted land. Be sure to abide by all "no trespassing" signs.

Hot Springs Slough

At the end of the Elliott Highway you'll come to the unique little town of Manley Hot Springs. The tourist attractions here are worth a look, as is the fishing at Hot Springs Slough, which runs right through town.

Hot Springs Slough empties into the Tanana River and is home to some good pike fishing. The pike head up the river and into the slough, where they hold from May through September. There's a small ramp from which a canoe can be launched and paddled into the slough, which is up to 60 feet wide in areas. Work along the slough's banks for pike up to 36 inches and/or around 6 pounds. Paddle your way downstream to reach the better fishing. There is a great deal of private land surrounding the slough, so bank fishing is limited. A canoe is definitely the best way to explore this fishery.

Though it's not fishable due to heavy silting, the Tanana River is worth visiting just to observe the fish wheels and nets used to take salmon in the 40-pound class. From the Old Commercial Company Store, follow the dirt road out of town for 2.5 miles to the Tanana, where subsistence gatherers take king, silver, and chum salmon.

MANLEY HOT SPRINGS

**Population: 88
(unincorporated)
Alaska Area Code: 907
Zip Code: 99756**

AIRPORTS

Manley Hot Springs Airport, serves Manley Hot Springs and is owned by the state. The gravel runway extends for 2875 feet. The facility is at an elevation of 270 feet at a distance of about a mile or less from Manley Hot Springs, 907-451-5283

LODGING

Manley Roadhouse, Serving Alaska Since 1906. Many prehistoric and Alaskan artifacts are on display here in one of the state's oldest original roadhouses from the gold rush era. Single and double rooms with private baths, or choose one of our comfortable rustic cabins. Delicious home-style cooking, plus a liquor store, campground, general store, and more. The roadhouse is a favorite meeting place for local miners, dog mushers, trappers and fishermen, Single and double rooms at reasonable rates, Comfortable cabins for total privacy , Exquisit homestyle cooking (8 am to 8 pm) , A rustic, antique filled sitting room , The Roadhouse Bar, with 200 kinds of liquor , A general store, gas station, post office, liquor store and campground, 100 Front St, 907-672-3161

CONVENIENCE STORE

Manley Trading Post, sells fuel, av gas, groceries, liquor, gifts and includes the post office, 907-672-3221

Grayling are found in many creeks and lakes along the Elliot Highway.

Dalton Highway

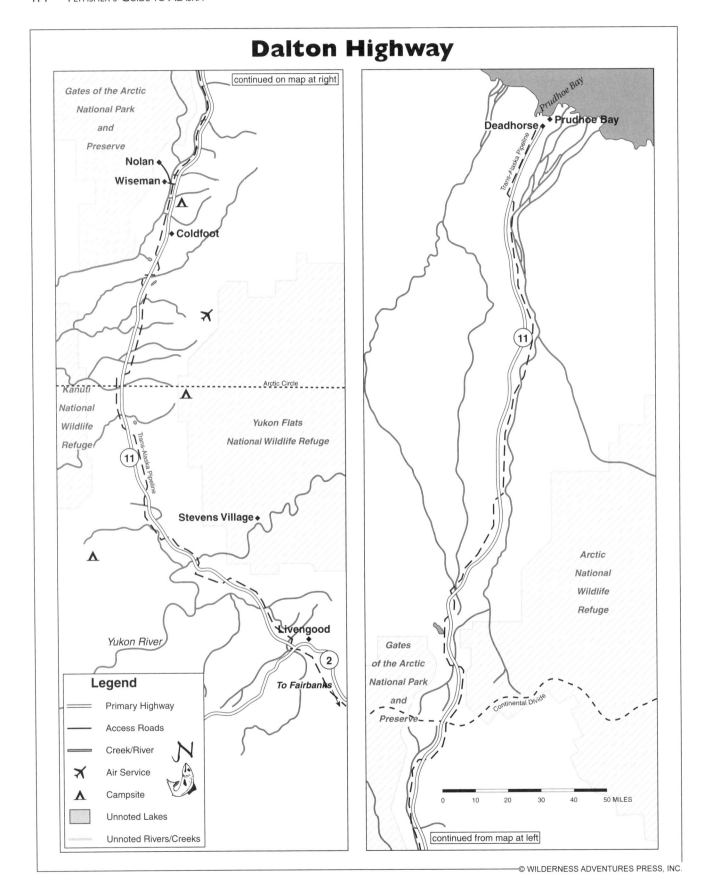

continued on map at right

Gates of the Arctic

National Park

and

Preserve

Nolan

Wiseman

◆ **Coldfoot**

Arctic Circle

Kanuti

National

Wildlife

Refuge

Trans-Alaska Pipeline

11

Yukon Flats

National Wildlife Refuge

Stevens Village ◆

Yukon River

Livengood

2

To Fairbanks

Legend

————	Primary Highway
——	Access Roads
═══	Creek/River
✈	Air Service
⛰	Campsite
▨	Unnoted Lakes
≈	Unnoted Rivers/Creeks

Prudhoe Bay

Deadhorse ◆ ◆ **Prudhoe Bay**

Trans-Alaska Pipeline

11

Arctic

National

Wildlife

Refuge

Gates

of the Arctic

National Park

and

Preserve

Continental Divide

0   10   20   30   40   50 MILES

continued from map at left

© WILDERNESS ADVENTURES PRESS, INC.

THE DALTON HIGHWAY

The Dalton Highway is the most rugged and remote of all the road systems. But the unique species of fish it leads to and the spectacular scenery above the Arctic Circle make it a popular destination for traveling sport fishers. Yet it's still the least traveled of the highways in this chapter, and if you're looking for secluded roadside fishing, this is the place.

Prior to setting off into God's Country, it's crucial to fully prepare yourself for travel on the Dalton Highway. First, no rental car agencies I know of allow you to drive one way from Fairbanks to Deadhorse and fly back. Given the fact that this journey covers 498 miles, you're looking at nearly 1,000 driving miles if you're determined to make it to the end of the road.

The actual Dalton Highway, or Haul Road, as it's affectionately referred to by many Alaskans, runs for 414 miles, starting at the Elliott Highway junction (84 miles north of Fairbanks) and terminating in Deadhorse, just south of the Prudhoe Bay oil fields. Built in 1974 to facilitate construction and maintenance of the Alaska Pipeline, the road was first opened to the public in 1981. Today, it offers outstanding fishing for grayling, char, pike, burbot, and even sheefish.

The Haul Road can be a rough ride if you're not mentally prepared. Steep grades ranging up to 12 percent are present on this route, which is mostly gravel over its entire length. During the summer months, the road can be very dusty and heavy with truck traffic. Keep your headlights on at all times. And there are limited pulloffs along the highway, so avoid stopping to snap pictures unless you can pull well off the road and allow room for two vehicles to pass.

Due to its gravel surface, the Haul Road can be a bumpy affair, with some teeth-jarring washboard sections. Practice on your patience and proceed with caution. Road construction is always underway on the highway in summer, as they try to pave approximately 10 miles of road each year. It's pure joy when you encounter these improved sections of road.

The Dalton Highway's rugged nature and remote setting require that you be self-sufficient. Once you get past Coldfoot, you're pretty much on your own. It is essential to carry extra food, water, fuel, flares, windshield wiper fluid, spare tires, and basic auto repair equipment. At a minimum, take two spare tires along. You can have damaged tires repaired in Coldfoot or Deadhorse.

It's also a good idea to get an update on road conditions. The Department of Transportation in Fairbanks can be reached at 907-456-7623. And you can call the Dalton Management Unit, Northern Field Office, in Fairbanks at 1-800-437-70211 or check out updates on their website www.aurora.ak.blm.gov/dalton.

If you're traveling this road from July through mid-August—prior to the first hard freezes—bring plenty of bug repellent. It's a good idea to take along a head net, or even a full-on mesh suit to keep bugs at bay. When the air is still, biting insects can be so thick that you literally will not want to be outside. Fortunately, the wind blows the vast majority of the time this far north. Though a brisk wind makes fly casting a challenge, it definitely keeps mosquitoes, whitesocks, and biting gnats away.

It should be also be noted that the Trans-Alaska Pipeline corridor runs 5 miles on either side of the Dalton Highway, beginning north of the Yukon River. The waters in this corridor are closed to all salmon fishing. Regulations on lake trout call for catch and release throughout the entire year, and there's a daily bag and possession limit of five grayling, all of which must be 12 inches or longer. For further angling guidelines, consult the ADF&G's "Region 3 General Sport-Fishing Regulations."

The best fishing on the Dalton Highway is from July through August. If snows don't arrive early, travel and fishing can be good well into September. Prior to July, snowmelt brings high, turbid water that cuts down on the fishing.

The 24 hours of daylight will allow you to get in all the fishing you desire. And if you're lucky enough to be on the Dalton in September, you'll be treated to the Northern Lights. But no matter when you find yourself on this secluded stretch of highway, you'll be amazed that a road can lead to such striking scenery and outstanding fishing.

The Alaska Pipeline near the Dalton Highway.

Hess Creek

The first noteworthy fishery on the Dalton Highway is 24 miles up the road from the Elliott/Dalton junction at Hess Creek, the largest stream between the junction and the Yukon River. Hess Creek is noted for its grayling fishing and is of special interest to fly anglers. The fall fishing in this crystal-clear, gravel-bottomed creek can be excellent.

There's plenty of roadside pulloff access here. And on the north end of the bridge that crosses Hess, there's a dirt access road that heads west toward a secluded little campsite on the creek. If this dirt road is wet, consider walking it rather than driving.

The best fishing will come to anglers willing to wade the creek. Working your way downstream from the highway and fishing the many pools with dry flies can be highly productive. Mosquito patterns and Beadhead Pheasant Tails top the list of local favorites on Hess Creek. Due to the clarity of this creek, sight fishing can also be productive.

Yukon River

At mile 55.5 on the Dalton Highway, you'll find the only bridge in Alaska that crosses over the mighty Yukon River. Unfortunately, the fishing in the Yukon is poor due to heavy silting. But if you're pulling a boat at least 14 feet long with a good motor, you can get into some fine fishing above the bridge.

There is a boat launch at the foot of the bridge, and you can run some 30 miles upstream from here to where the Little Dall River dumps into the Yukon on the west shore. You'll also see several other small tributaries emptying into the Yukon in this stretch. The clear water at the mouths of these streams holds some exceptional pike and sheefish.

For instance, at the confluence of the Dall and Yukon Rivers, you can expect to catch many pike over 10 pounds, with fish in the 20-pound class common. When fishing any of these turbid waters, be very aggressive with your presentation and retrieve. Mouse hair poppers and large, flashy saltwater flies are the top choices here, and the more noise and movement you can create, the more pike you'll catch.

Late July and into August is the best time to hit the Yukon, as silting will have leveled off within the river and in adjoining tributaries. But if you don't have a large boat with you, don't even bother with the Yukon.

Ray River

Just 5 miles past the Yukon bridge, you'll come to one of the few stopping points along the Dalton Highway, the Hot Spot Cafe (907-451-7543) at mile 60. This is a favored stop for long-haul truck drivers and local anglers alike, as the hamburgers, barbecued food, house specials, and homemade pies are a real treat after long days on the road. Overnight rooms are also available

Continuing up the Dalton Highway, 13 miles north of the Yukon River, you'll hit Ray Creek. This is only a mediocre fishery, and many people pass it by for the better fishing ahead.

But what makes the Ray River appealing is its ease of access and the variety of species available. From mile 69 to 74, the highway parallels the river, some ¾ mile to the east. There are plenty of pulloffs on both sides of the road, and grayling, sheefish, northern pike, and burbot are all present. Fishing is typically most productive late in the spring and into fall.

The various fish will require some diverse angling tactics. Dry flies on a light rod work for grayling when the water is clear, but sinking minnow imitations on a sinking line serve best for sheefish. The usual gaudy patterns fished on top are best for pike, with bait fished along the bottom the top choice for burbot anglers.

Like the Hess River, the Ray River runs a clear tea color. Flowing from the base of the Ray Mountains, the river is fairly fast and relatively deep. When storms hit, the Ray can be tainted with sediment flow, limiting visibility.

No Name Creek

Mile 80.5 on the Dalton Highway puts you at No Name Creek, a good little fishery offering grayling and burbot. To access this creek, turn off at the bridge that crosses the creek and make your way to the water.

This is a small creek, averaging only 10 to 15 feet wide in most places near the highway. The water runs shallow, making it a popular grayling stream for wade fishermen. As with many streams in the area, No Name Creek carries a clear tea hue, with visibility ranging up to a few feet. There are no deep holes to speak of, so wade fishing is easy upstream and down.

As with many of the streams carrying burbot in this region of Alaska, your best chance of catching fish comes on bait fished right on the bottom. Use a spinning rod and plenty of weight to anchor your bait in one place, allowing a scent trail to work its way downstream. Though fish parts work well on burbot, chicken livers are a favorite among local anglers.

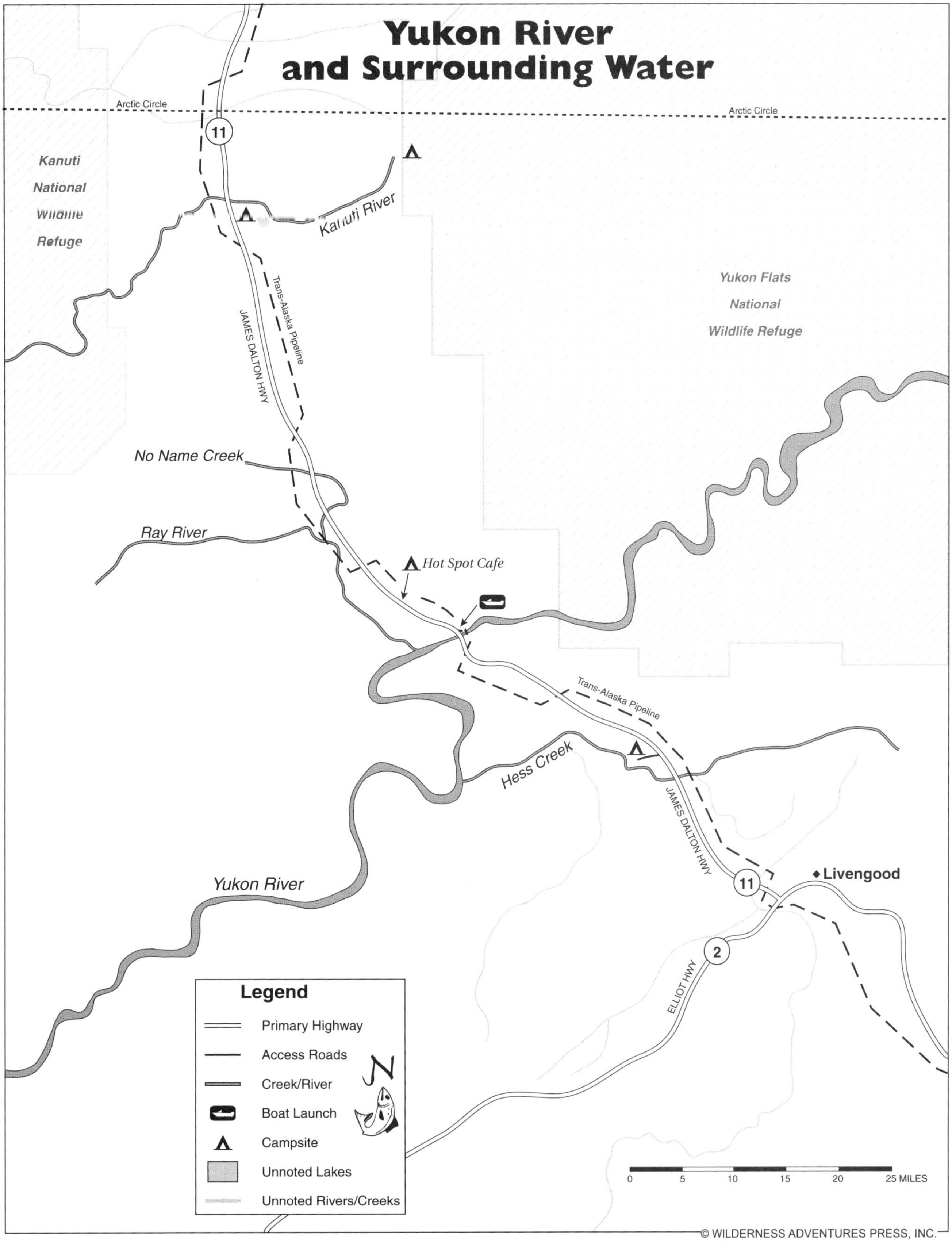
Yukon River
and Surrounding Water
Arctic Circle
Arctic Circle
11
Kanuti
National
Wildlife
Refuge
Kanuti River
Trans-Alaska Pipeline
JAMES DALTON HWY
Yukon Flats
National
Wildlife Refuge
No Name Creek
Ray River
Hot Spot Cafe
Trans-Alaska Pipeline
Hess Creek
JAMES DALTON HWY
11
Livengood
2
ELLIOT HWY
Yukon River
Legend
Primary Highway
Access Roads
Creek/River
Boat Launch
Campsite
Unnoted Lakes
Unnoted Rivers/Creeks
N
0
5
10
15
20
25 MILES

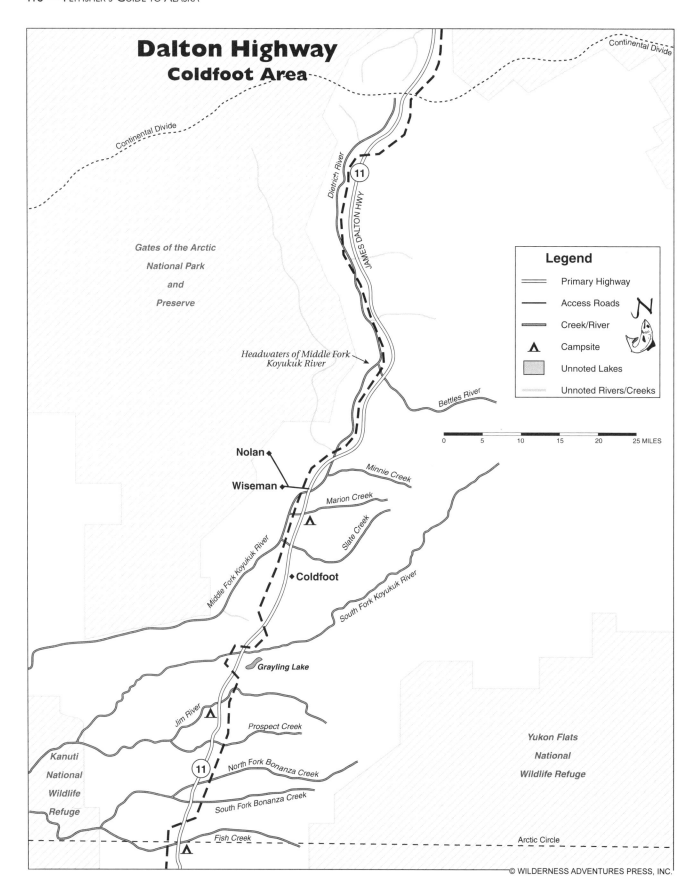

Dalton Highway
Coldfoot Area

Continental Divide

Continental Divide

Dietrich River

11

JAMES DALTON HWY

Gates of the Arctic

National Park

and

Preserve

Headwaters of Middle Fork
Koyukuk River

Bettles River

Legend

	Primary Highway
	Access Roads
	Creek/River
Λ	Campsite
	Unnoted Lakes
	Unnoted Rivers/Creeks

N

| 0 | 5 | 10 | 15 | 20 | 25 MILES |

Nolan

Wiseman

Minnie Creek

Marion Creek

Λ

Slate Creek

Middle Fork Koyukuk River

◆ Coldfoot

South Fork Koyukuk River

Grayling Lake

Jim River

Λ

Prospect Creek

Kanuti

National

Wildlife

Refuge

11

North Fork Bonanza Creek

South Fork Bonanza Creek

Yukon Flats

National

Wildlife Refuge

Fish Creek

Arctic Circle

Λ

© WILDERNESS ADVENTURES PRESS, INC.

Kanuti River

More burbot and grayling fishing can be found in the Kanuti River. Passing under the Dalton Highway at mile 106, the Kanuti is a good fall fishery. On the south end of the Kanuti River bridge, there is easy access and plenty of parking. There are also basic campsites here, though no facilities are available.

The Kanuti is one of the larger rivers we've encountered so far, running 20 feet wide in many places. It's a deep, slow, meandering river that wanders through the Kanuti Flats. As a result, there are many cutbanks and very few gravel bars. The deep holes tight to shore, combined with windfalls and overhanging tree limbs, make it a challenge to wade and fish.

Some locals like to put a canoe in the Kanuti, drifting through the middle of the river and fishing both sides. If you try this, though, be prepared for some work. Portaging over beaver dams and windfalls will make the going slow. Likewise, if you choose to wade fish this river, which is best done in chest waders, be prepared to make short, accurate casts. The fishing can be good within the first mile on either side of the road.

Fish Creek

For anglers looking to break the imaginary plane of the Arctic Circle, this next little creek is the place. Fish Creek lies at mile 115 on the highway, and turnouts on the north and south ends of the bridge make reaching the stream a cinch. Unimproved campsites are also available, though there are no facilities.

As for the fishing, this is a grayling show, with fish up to 18 inches taken with regularity. But the unique aspect of fishing this creek is that you can start at the road and work your way upstream, across the Arctic Circle. In fact, if you're willing to walk 2.5 miles upstream, the chance of hooking a grayling right on the Arctic Circle is quite good.

Fish Creek is tiny; in many places it's a stretch to claim that it spans 10 feet. However, it does have some exposed gravel bars and attractive riffles that are worth fishing. It's very shallow overall, making it simple to wade fish. Though the water runs a tea color, it's shallow enough to see the bottom throughout.

South and North Fork Bonanza Creek

The first stream above the Arctic Circle that's easy to reach is the South Fork of Bonanza Creek. A turnout at the bridge at mile 125 will lead you to the banks of the creek, where you'll find burbot and grayling.

Traveling another mile up the Dalton Highway puts you at the North Fork of Bonanza Creek. And the south end of the bridge crossing the creek offers the best pulloff access. Again, burbot and grayling are on the menu.

Both forks of Bonanza Creek are similar to Fish Creek. They're shallow tea-colored streams with some good-looking water, and both forks are popular among line-whippers. Burbot are typically taken on bait along cutbanks or in deeper portions of the middle of the creeks. Working dry flies for grayling will surely turn up some fish.

Prospect Creek

Just over 10 miles from the North Fork, you'll come to Prospect Creek at mile 135. Grayling and northern pike occupy this stream, where the fishing can be good from July through August.

Prospect is a small stream, and the fishing can be challenging at times. The water runs quite dark, with few riffles, and the overgrown banks make for a confining experience. The amount of heavy brush and lack of quality fishing water make this a stream you won't likely want to spend too much time on. However, there are fish to be caught, and your best chance lies in teasing pike and grayling to the surface—dries for grayling, flashy attractors for pike.

Jim River

Given the proximity of Prospect Creek to the Jim River, many anglers opt to bypass the former and head straight for the Jim. At times, it's not unusual to latch into grayling on every single cast on the Jim River. But as is the case with many grayling in these northern streams, fish tend to be long and slender. Grayling approaching 20 inches in length are not unheard of, though they will lack the mass of fish found in more southerly waters.

A unique feature of the Jim River is that it crosses beneath the Dalton Highway in three different places within a 4-mile stretch. This makes access simple. As noted by the locals, Jim River #1, where the river first crosses the highway at mile 140, provides access on the south side of the bridge. Rudimentary campsites are available here, though facilities are lacking.

Jim River #2, where the river crosses the highway at mile 141, also has a small turnout on the south side. At both turnouts, anglers have good success spot-fishing isolated holes, as well as covering water on foot.

Jim River #3, where the river crosses the highway at mile 144 near Pump Station 5 on the Alaska Pipeline, offers a large parking area at the south end of the bridge. There is also a nameless gravel access road that runs to the west. Follow this road for a couple miles and you'll come to a gravel bar that also serves as a primitive boat launch. If you're hauling a small boat and motor, fishing can be very good on this stretch of water. Once on the river, head downstream to the confluence of Prospect Creek and the Jim, where the fishing can be exceptional, with little competition from other anglers.

Measuring more than 30 feet across in many places, the Jim River is a bit faster than some of the surrounding streams. Its clear tea color and deeper, darker holes give way to a uniform gravel bottom. This is an easy river to wade fish, and targeting the deep cutbanks is productive. A word of caution for bank travelers: This is the beginning of bear country.

For travelers hauling a small raft, the Jim River offers some of the most relaxing float fishing on the Dalton Highway. My friend Troy Graziadei likes to launch at Jim River #3 and float to Jim River #1. For a shorter trip you can stop at Jim River #2 or float from #2 to #1. Depending on how much you stop to fish, the trip can take a few hours or eat up the better part of a day. Regardless of the route you choose, you won't be disappointed on this comfortable stream.

Grayling Lake

While there are numerous lakes in this portion of Alaska, Grayling Lake is situated right on the Dalton Highway at mile 150. There is plenty of parking at the wayside pull-out, which also offers an outhouse and trash bins.

The fishing is good from when the ice leaves this lake through September. Anglers working out of float tubes, canoes, or small boats have good luck casting and trolling for grayling, the only species in this lake. Dry flies like Gnats and Mosquitoes will produce rises here, though you should also have an assortment of subsurface patterns like Muddlers and Woolly Buggers for when the action is slow.

South Fork Koyukuk River

Another large river that meanders through the Alaskan Arctic, the South Fork of the Koyukuk is a river that may or may not be fishable. Because this river, located at mile 156 on the Dalton Highway, is so large and has a fair number of tributaries, it can run turbid during the spring and summer melting period. Grayling are the only sport fish worth pursing within the 5-mile corridor, and if the water is off-color don't waste your time.

But if the water looks clear, or has at least a few feet of visibility, it's worth wetting a fly here. The clearer the water is running, the better your chances of bringing grayling to the surface on dries. If the water is only slightly off-color, subsurface patterns can still elicit bites.

Work closer to shore than you would in the smaller streams encountered up to this point. Hit the inside edges of bends in the river where fish often congregate. Swinging flies over tailouts and through shallower riffles will also draw strikes.

A roadside turnout provides easy access to the South Fork. In addition to ample parking, there is an RV camping turnout, an outhouse, and trash bins. Even if you're pushing through to Coldfoot, this is a good place to stop and stretch your legs. If you're traveling all the way from Fairbanks to Deadhorse, this section of the South Fork Koyukuk is very close to the midway point of the journey.

Slate Creek

Before driving into the most remote stretch of highway in the entire state, there's one more stream to fish, and fortunately Slate Creek is located near Coldfoot (at mile 175), the last hub town on the Dalton Highway before you reach the terminus at Deadhorse. From this point, you're on your own more than at any other time on this journey. Because Slate Creek runs through town, the locals usually know just what is happening here. If the fishing for Dolly Varden or grayling is hot, they'll know it. Coldfoot Camp (907-678-3400) not only has local fishing reports, but road condition updates, a restaurant, lodging, and an RV park with hookups and dump station. There's also a general store, and if you have tires that need repair or an engine that needs a look, this is the place.

I flew into Coldfoot on several occasions while living in Anaktuvuk Pass. When you're traveling from the north, it's an especially welcome sight.

Marion Creek

From Coldfoot, it's only a 4-mile drive to the next fishing site at Marion Creek. This clear little stream, seemingly made for the wading angler, is noted for more than just its good Dolly Varden and grayling fishing during the summer months. It's also a very nice place for travelers to camp.

A gravel turnout leads to nearly 30 campsites, which can be used for a small fee, with firepits, grills, and other camp amenities. Later in the summer, the blueberry and cranberry picking can be excellent, something my wife and I used to always look forward to adding to our sourdough pancakes this time of year. The camp host and information center can point you in the direction of ripe berries—and good fishing holes.

Marion Creek is the first stream we've encountered within the mining district. In this area a stream that usually runs a clear tea color can turn turbid in a hurry when there is mining activity. Normally, Marion Creek is shallow enough that it's easy to wade fish. Some brushy areas near the bank make for tough going at times, but the fishing makes negotiating such obstacles worth the effort.

Minnie Creek

If you're tiring of catching grayling, Minnie Creek provides a change of pace, as you'll find good burbot fishing here. At mile 187, there's a parking area on the south end of the Minnie Creek bridge.

Displaying similar physical characteristics to Marion Creek, Minnie is a small stream lined with low brush that will test your patience at times. Bait fished on the bottom is the best bet for latching into burbot.

Middle Fork Koyukuk River

Up the road from Minnie Creek, you'll come to the larger Middle Fork of the Koyukuk River. At miles 188, 190, 204, and 204.5, the Dalton Highway crosses this river, paralleling it for much of this distance. There's plenty of roadside parking, and you can spend an entire day fishing for Dolly Varden and grayling in this stretch.

This is one of the bigger rivers in the region, large enough that jet boats have no trouble operating within its banks. Given the fact that it flows from higher in the mountains than most streams, it's usually silty. Nonetheless, it's easy to wade along the banks, and when the water is running gray to clear in color, the fishing can be very good. As with many streams, a day of rain can cloud the waters, making it tough for flyfishers to find success. Silver attractor patterns help, you might want to bring along a lightweight spinning rod with ½- to 1-ounce lures as a backup.

Bettles River

Near mile 205 on the east side of the highway, the Bettles River flows into the Dietrich River, forming the Middle Fork of the Koyukuk River. Wade fishing your way up the Bettles River can lead to good grayling fishing. This river receives little pressure from roadside anglers.

Dietrich River

At mile 207, the Dietrich River flows beneath the Dalton Highway, marking the halfway point between the start of this highway and the town of Deadhorse. The road parallels the river for approximately the next 25 miles and the fishing for burbot, grayling, and Dolly Varden can be fair to good.

There is parking on both sides of the Dietrich River bridge, and plenty of roadside pullouts. Wherever you choose to stop, be certain that the vehicle is completely off the road for safety reasons.

The Dietrich River is a fast stream with a nice gravel bottom. The fact that less brush occupies its banks makes it appealing to fly anglers, though there are still some low shrubs to be dealt with. The shallow edges and exposed gravel bars make this an easy and safe river to wade fish.

Atigun River

After you pass the Dietrich River, you'll come to a long, steep series of grades heading up to Atigun Pass. These grades run up to 12 percent, and remember as you ascend the steep hills that semi-trucks may be on their way down, often moving at fast speeds.

Within the Brooks Range, Atigun Pass tops out at 4,800 feet, making it the highest road pass in Alaska. Keep an eye out for Dall sheep feeding along the roadside cliffs as you top out on the pass. This is also a high-density grizzly bear area, and the chances of seeing wolves are good.

But when taking in the wildlife, stunning scenery, and excellent views of the pipeline, be sure to pay close attention to the road. Narrow roads without guardrails are the norm, and when wet the road can be muddy and very slippery. Also keep an eye out for rockslides, which can occur anywhere in next 30 miles or so. Resist the urge to stop in the middle of the road for a photo opportunity.

After descending the pass, you'll enter the Atigun River valley, officially putting you on Alaska's North Slope, one of my favorite regions on earth. The Atigun River crosses the Dalton Highway at mile 253. From here, the river parallels the highway, though at times it meanders a mile or so to the west of the road. At mile 271, the Atigun River again crosses beneath the Dalton.

The Atigun is a grayling stream, and when running clear or just slightly turbid it's worth fishing. Walking the banks and wade fishing with dry and wet patterns will draw strikes from these gorgeous little fish.

A clear river with a nice gravel bottom, the Atigun flows into the Sagavanirktok River. This means that late in the season you might chance into trophy-sized char heading for their spawning beds. Ranging up to 25 yards from bank to bank in places, and little more than 6 feet deep, this is a very open river. There are no trees here, making it easy to see what you're getting into. Exposed gravel bars, a variety of prime riffles, and deep holes make for enjoyable wade fishing.

Galbraith Lake

Anglers looking for a change of pace from stream fishing will find two of the better-known lakes above the Arctic Circle.

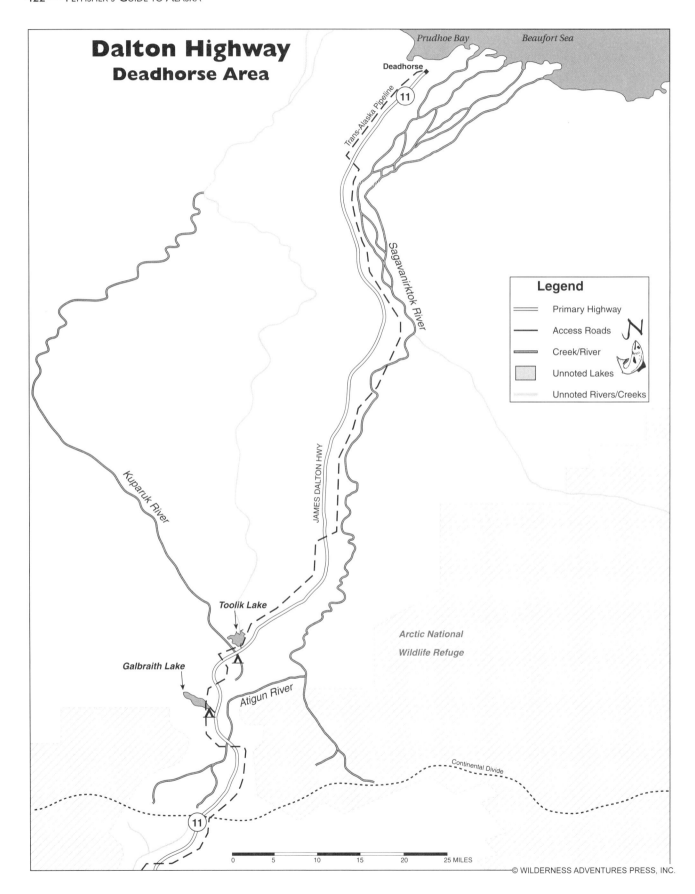

Dalton Highway
Deadhorse Area

Prudhoe Bay

Beaufort Sea

Deadhorse

11

Trans-Alaska Pipeline

Sagavanirktok River

JAMES DALTON HWY

Kuparuk River

Toolik Lake

Galbraith Lake

Atigun River

Arctic National

Wildlife Refuge

Continental Divide

11

Legend
- Primary Highway
- Access Roads
- Creek/River
- Unnoted Lakes
- Unnoted Rivers/Creeks

N

0   5   10   15   20   25 MILES

Galbraith Lake, the first of the two, holds lake trout, burbot, and grayling. There are also reports of arctic char inhabiting this body of water. To reach the lake, drive past it on the highway, and then turn west at mile 274. Galbraith sits just past Pump Station 4.

Five miles down the gravel road you'll find the Galbraith Lake Campground, which has an outhouse and trash bins but no other services. If you're not interested in stopping at the campground, which sits away from the lake itself, you can park and hike to the lake from the Dalton Highway. A short hike will take you to the shoreline and you can launch a raft or float tube to open up additional fishing opportunities.

Fishing on Galbraith Lake, which is situated at 2,600 feet in elevation, is best in late summer, when the water is completely free of ice. July and August are the prime months, and working sinking lines and flies near the generous shoreline is the best bet. Boaters may discover that trolling high-density sinking lines will produce strikes when nothing else will, especially from lake trout. Casting dry patterns in the evening can be the ticket for grayling.

Toolik Lake

At mile 284 on the Dalton a marked access road heads west to Toolik Lake. Take this road for approximately 1 mile to the lake, which appears to be set in a high desert. Technically, the North Slope's Arctic tundra is classified as a desert due to the lack of rainfall and snowfall it receives. It's the permafrost which keeps so much water above ground and misleads people into thinking the Arctic is a water-rich environment.

Nearing 100 feet in depth, Toolik is primarily noted for its lake trout, arctic char, and especially grayling fishing. Grayling in this lake approach 20 inches, and anglers willing to explore off the beaten paths should be well rewarded.

As with any lake up here, an angler with a raft or float tube will find it easier to access less pressured waters. Most of the fishing pressure in this part of the state comes from truckers and workers who travel the highway frequently. This means that fisheries with quick, easy access are usually the hardest hit. Even up here, a willingness to walk or launch a small craft will lead to better fishing.

As with Galbraith Lake, weighted minnow imitations fished beneath a sinking line can be effective for lake trout on Toolik. Woolly Buggers and nymph patterns are also good choices for grayling.

My friend Troy Graziadei of Fairbanks loves fishing this lake. Later in the summer, he can hammer grayling in the upper teens that are nice and fat.

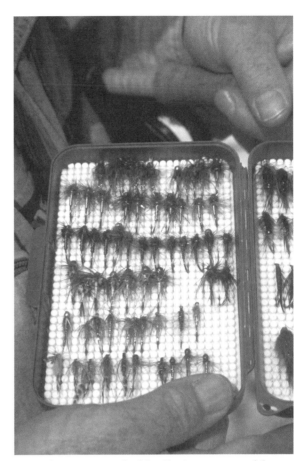

Nymph patterns are highly effective on some of the small streams you'll be fishing along the road system.

It should be noted that the University of Alaska Fairbanks currently has some long-term studies going on along the shores of Toolik Lake. The series of buildings, roped off sections of tundra for microenvironment studies, and an increased level of human activity may surprise you, but don't let it turn you away or mislead you into thinking you've found camping facilities or other services.

There are also many smaller lakes nearby that are easy to access and offer good fishing. Anglers willing to walk to some of these lakes will find grayling with a mix of lake trout and char. Burbot are also present in many of these waters, though you'll need spinning tackle and bait to catch these fish.

Kuparuk River

Traveling farther onto the North Slope and Alaska's Arctic tundra, you'll find two rivers that offer good fishing right off the Dalton Highway. The Kuparuk River flows beneath the highway at mile 290. There's a casual roadside campsite at the bridge, and if you're after big grayling, it's worth spending a day or two here.

Though it looks like little more than a creek here, the Kuparuk River is one of the regions best-kept secrets. It's a popular place for truckers to stop and fish because of its easy access and the number of large grayling. The Kuparuk is one of the North Slope's top-producing grayling rivers.

Many tourists pass by this river later in the summer, dismissing it as not large enough to harbor good fishing. But anglers who take the time to wade fish this shallow little stream will soon discover what makes it so special. There is good water both up and downstream, but upstream anglers will likely have the best results.

If you're into tossing a camp on your back and taking off, you'll get into world-class grayling fishing near the lake's headwaters, which lie on the south side of the Dalton Highway. In addition to superb grayling fishing, stunning beauty, and tranquility, you'll find good lake trout fishing at the mouth of Kuparuk Lake. It's about a 4-mile hike to the headwaters, and you should keep an eye out for grizzlies, especially sows with cubs.

Sagavanirktok River

Perhaps the best-known roadside fishery on the North Slope—if not along the entire Dalton Highway—is the Sagavanirktok River. Known affectionately as the Sag River, for obvious reasons, this stream first approaches the Dalton Highway at mile 298 and parallels the highway the rest of the way to Prudhoe Bay—more than 100 miles in all. Known for its oversized grayling, the Sag is also home to exceptional char fishing.

Because the Sag runs along the highway for such a great distance, there are many fishing holes to explore. Anywhere you find a roadside pullout, you'll likely find good fishing close by. This is a wide river that winds its way north en route to its terminus in the Beaufort Sea, and it's surprisingly clear when weather condition are good. In fact, the river is so clear at times that judging depths can be difficult.

If the water is running off-color, it's not worth pursuing grayling with a fly. However, tossing minnow patterns on sink-tip lines can be productive for char in turbid water conditions. Because rains and melting snow in the Brooks Range can cause the Sag to run dirty at any time, it's a good idea to bring some simple spin-fishing gear along. Vibrax spinners and flashy spoons will often pro-

duce bites when fly gear won't, and this is too long a drive to let purist ideals ruin your day.

Fish around cutbanks, where deeper holes hold both species of fish. Side pools and tailouts are also productive holding spots. In many places, the Sag is more than a mile wide, with many braided channels. The side channels are normally safe and easy to negotiate due to their high level of clarity, although the main channel is too deep to wade. Unfortunately, you may not be able to figure out which fast-flowing channel is the main one until you start wading.

Swinging flies through shallow riffles can also yield good grayling fishing. For char, the later in the season it gets, the farther upstream the bigger sea-run char can be found—in general. Keep an eye out for the many spring-fed tributaries that enter the Sag. These rich holding waters can attract large numbers of big fish.

Approximately 40 miles south of Deadhorse, the Franklin Bluffs area offers some of the purest Arctic experiences on the entire journey. Tourists often get to observe musk ox, grizzly bear, caribou, wolf, and rare falcon species unique to this part of the globe. This is also the best stretch for fishing due to the increased number of access roads put in place for North Slope workers.

Travelers can explore these access roads and get into exceptional fishing off the beaten path. Though the gated dike roads don't lead directly to the river, they get anglers one step closer to the Sag and are well worth exploring. You will often come across primitive campsites along these roadsides. These are nothing fancy, just simple pullouts that allow you to make sure your vehicle is out of the way. When the river is running clear, these little pullouts can lead to superb fishing.

Overall, the Sag is a wide, swift stream, heavily braided in places. But with 20-inch grayling and char in the 10- to 12-pound class not uncommon, it's worth spending some serious time on this water. The trophy char are normally taken at the bottom of the deeper holes, around 8 feet or more in depth.

Char make their way into the river to spawn in early August and from this time into the first part of September is the best time to latch into these trophy-sized fish. On occasion, lake trout are also taken from the Sag.

With its numerous access points, large fish, and captivating scenery, the Sag is rated among the favorite fisheries on the Dalton Highway for good reason.

COLDFOOT

Population: 15
Alaska Area Code: 907
Zip Code: 99701

TOURIST INFORMATION

Coldfoot Camp, 1-866-474-3400 or 678-3400; motel, 24-hour restaurant, laundry, general store, post office, phone, RV park with hookup and dump station

Coldfoot Interagency Visitor Center, operated by BLM, USFWS and National Park, all of whom have staff to assist tourists; maps, road and fishing information also available at this stop; aurora.ak.blm.gov/arcticinfo/

Coldfoot Services/Arctic Acres Inn, 678-5201

Coyote Air Service, P.O. Box 9053; 1-800-252-0603; flying to many remote Arctic regions throughout and to the north of the Brooks Range

ADDITIONAL LODGING IN WISEMAN

Boreal Lodging, 678-4566; located in Wiseman, 13 miles north of Coldfoot; 4 rooms, showers, laundry, kitchen; boreallodge@juno.com

Arctic Getaway Cabin & Breakfast, 678-4456; located at Pioneer Hall in Wiseman

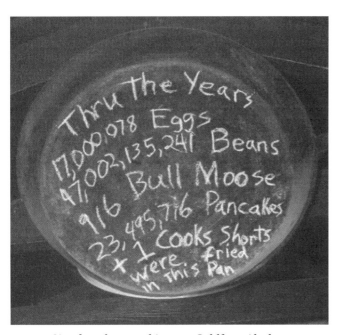

Sign found on a cabin near Coldfoot, Alaska.

DEADHORSE

Population: 25
(up to 5,000 part-time)
Alaska Area Code: 907
Zip Code: 99734

ACCOMMODATIONS

Arctic Caribou Inn, P.O. Box 340111; 1-877-659-2368; 75 rooms, RV parking, restaurant, tours to Arctic Ocean and Prudhoe Bay oil fields; arcticcaribouinn.com

Arctic Oilfield Hotel, 659-2614; located on Sag River Road and Spine Road; rooms with showers and laundry, buffet meals, RV parking

SERVICES

Deadhorse/Prudhoe Bay Tesoro, 659-3198; overnight parking, 24-hour gas, phone, restrooms

Prudhoe Bay General Store, 659-2412; located north of airport; offers snacks, supplies, fishing licenses, Deadhorse Museum, tour bookings

AUTO REPAIR

Arctic Oilfield Hotel, 659-3301; located on Sag River Road and Spine Road; wide range of repair work, large parts inventory, towing, body work

TOURIST ATTRACTIONS

Arctic Ocean; because tourists can't drive to the ocean, booking tours through a hotel is the only way to get there

Prudhoe Bay Oil Fields; field tours arranged by hotel is a must-see

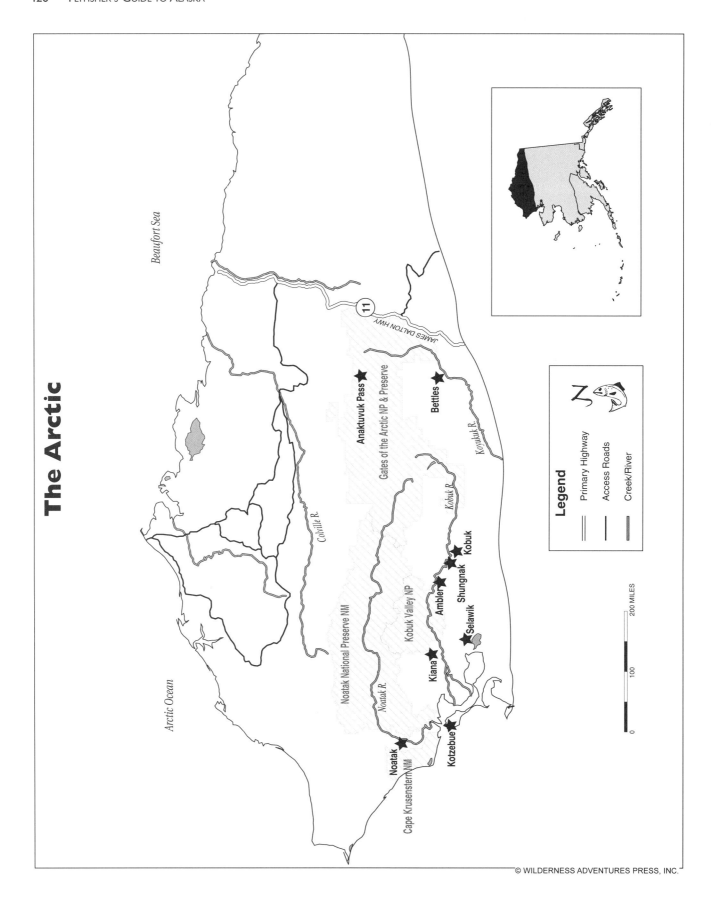

The Arctic

Beaufort Sea

Arctic Ocean

JAMES DALTON HWY

11

★ Anaktuvuk Pass

★ Bettles

Gates of the Arctic NP & Preserve

Colville R.

Koyukuk R.

Kobuk R.

Noatak National Preserve NM

Noatak R.

Kobuk Valley NP

★ Kobuk
★ Shungnak
★ Ambler
★ Selawik

★ Kiana

★ Noatak

Cape Krusenstern NM

★ Kotzebue

Legend

N

— Primary Highway
— Access Roads
▬ Creek/River

0   100   200 MILES

© WILDERNESS ADVENTURES PRESS, INC.

Fishing the Arctic

By Scott Haugen

I've had the good fortune to visit some of the most diverse habitat on the planet, from the Himalayas in Nepal and the savannas of Africa to the rugged rainforests of Indonesia and Australia's sweltering Outback. All of these locations are serene and beautiful, and I came away with new respect for the unique character of each, but somehow nothing quite compares with Alaska's Arctic. Perhaps I'm biased because I lived and worked in northern Alaska for many years, but most travelers who venture into this solitary setting agree it's unlike any place on Earth.

The Arctic is a land that commands respect. In winter, everything is locked in total darkness and subzero temperatures, and fishing opportunities for the traveling angler are virtually nil. True, there are some prime ice fishing locales, and I've spent my fair share of hours on frozen lakes and rivers up here. But battling weather and severe temperatures can often make even stepping outside a frustrating proposition.

So we'll focus on the more realistic fishing opportunities available during the months of July, August, and September, when the ice is off most lakes and conditions are more inviting in the 24 hours of daylight. The area being discussed takes in the land above the Arctic Circle, with Kotzebue the southwestern boundary, Bettles the south-central limit, and the Canadian border the eastern boundary. (Waters along the Dalton Highway were dealt with in the previous chapter, "Fishing the Road Systems.")

More than for any other area, anglers traveling to the Arctic must be prepared for any and every type of weather, even during summer. You may find temperatures ranging from 30°F to 80°F north of the Brooks Range, with snow, sleet, rain, high winds, and blue sky all possible in a short span of time. The southern slopes of the Brooks Range are less hostile, but travelers still shouldn't underestimate the elements.

As many of the adventures offered here are by way of drop camps or do-it-yourself excursions, being well prepared is the rule. Watertight tents capable of withstanding high winds, two layers of warm clothing, mosquito repellent, bear pepper spray, fire-starting supplies, and ample food supplies are essential. And it's a good idea to take extra food and clothing, as erratic weather can delay your plans no matter how thorough.

RUN TIMING FOR ARCTIC FRESHWATER FISHERIES

Species:	Jan	Feb	Mar	Apr	May	Jun	Jul	Aug	Sep	Oct	Nov	Dec
King Salmon	-	-	-	-	-	++	+++	++	-	-	-	-
Coho Salmon	-	-	-	-	-	-	-	-/+	++	+++	++	+/-
Chum Salmon	-	-	-	-	-	+	+++	++	++	++	+++	++
Rainbow Trout	+	+	+	+	++	++	+++	+++	+++	++	+	+
Dolly Varden	+	+	+	+	++	++	+++	+++	+++	++	+	+
Arctic Char	+	+	+	+	++	++	+++	+++	+++	++	+	+
Lake Trout	+	+	+	+	+	++	++	+	++	++	+	+
Pike	+	+	+	+	++	++	+	+	++	+	+	+
Grayling	+	+	+	+++	+++	+++	+++	+++	+++	++	+	+
Sheefish	+	+	+	+	+	++	+++	+++	+++	++	+	+
Burbot	+	+	+	+	++	++	+	+	++	++	+	+

+++ Excellent   ++ Good   + Fair   - Nonexistent/Closed Season

For example, two friends of mine once set out on an eight-week fishing and hiking journey from the summit of the Brooks Range north to the village of Kaktovik. They had figured on catching all the fish they'd need for meals, but such was not the case. They nearly starved before a bushplane finally dropped them a case of candy bars. Despite their many years of Arctic experience, they learned a hard lesson: Never take for granted the unforgiving demeanor of this land.

As to trip planning, the Arctic requires a unique approach. It sometimes takes months of research to put together a fishing trip to this part of Alaska. In planning your adventure, you'll probably be working directly with guides, outfitters, lodges, and other agencies that specialize in traveling and fishing the Arctic.

Anglers should note that river conditions can be greatly influenced by winter snowpack levels and spring runoff. Working closely with an outfitter who is familiar with the area you wish to fish is a major benefit. They can keep you abreast of current conditions, which will ultimately have an effect on where and when you'll fish.

The Arctic is a giant geographic region, and it would be impossible to list all the fishable lakes and streams it contains. The bodies of water covered here are fisheries commonly visited by anglers or ones known to provide good fishing opportunities. They should offer a great starting point for that "trip of a lifetime." As you delve into planning your trip, you'll likely hear names of lakes only the locals know about. Many waters up here remain nameless on even the most detailed maps, though veteran outfitters and pilots know where many of the fishable waters are and can often take you there. For the intrepid angling explorer, the Arctic will always hold a few secrets.

ARCTIC FISHING OPTIONS

You'll have two basic options when fishing the Arctic: going fully guided or hiring an air service for drop-off and pick-up service. Going it completely alone would be a third option, but this is unrealistic unless you are already very familiar with the region. Drop-camp services can supply you with all the gear necessary for your trip or you can bring everything yourself, including a raft. Most companies operating in the North Country offer a range of options depending on your desires and pocketbook.

Kotzebue and Bettles are the two primary travel hubs for Arctic fishing. Though there are several unnamed rivers, streams, and lakes in this region, air services operating out of Kotzebue and Bettles hit the ones that offer good fishing and safe travel in pristine habitats. Suffice it to say that if you see a body of water on a map that you'd like to fish, they can take you there if it's large enough to land a plane on. Your biggest concern, of course, will be whether or not there are fish present, which is why it's wise to hire a knowledgeable air service.

While many of the native villages in this region regard subsistence fishing as a mainstay in their daily lives, few offer sport fishers what they're looking for. Destinations like Barrow, Kaktovik, and Point Hope are interesting tourist sites, but an angler's time is better spent elsewhere. However, some villages are situated along prime waters and have people who can offer assistance in planning a trip.

If you see a body of water on a map that you'd like to fish, an air service can take you there if it's large enough to land a plane on.

ARCTIC FLY-IN COSTS AND SERVICES

For an example of what you can expect in fishing options and fly-in costs for the Arctic, let's look at the cost for a specific trip from a typical air service, Bettles Lodge. There are many other air services in the area that offer competitive prices and package deals, all the way down to the gear they provide. But Bettles Lodge has been in existence since the late 1940s and is one of the most reputable agencies operating in the Arctic. In addition to their own lodge facilities in Bettles, they have an air service and offer wilderness accommodations. I've not personally fished with this lodge, though when I lived in Anaktuvuk Pass I frequently met people on rivers and lakes who had been dropped off by Bettles Air Service.

If you want to fly into a lake, enjoy a short hike to a river, and float fish your way downstream to a pick-up point 10 days later (fairly close to the town of Bettles) it will run about $550 for one person, $300 each for three people, and $375 each for a party of five. If you want to fly a considerable distance from Bettles, say to the Kobuk River, and do a 14-day float, the costs will roughly triple.

It may seem odd that the price is high for one person, drops considerably for three people, then rises again as additional members join the party. But when you think about it from the point of view of the air service the cost fluctuation makes sense. In a small plane, it costs nearly the same to transport one person to a fishing site as it does two or three people. A slight additional charge will be added for three people due to the extra gear that adds weight and increases fuel consumption. There's also a time factor in terms of handling and meeting the needs of extra clients, which will add to the overall cost.

But why does the cost rise so much when five people make up the party? Simple. When you go with a bigger group the air service is forced to use a larger plane to transport the entire party to the fishing site or make two trips with a smaller plane. Either way, costs rise. If you know that a larger plane is going to be used, you can increase the size of your party from five to six or eight to again take advantage of the cost structure. If the overall cost of your trip is a major concern, be sure to ask your outfitter about transportation rates based on various party sizes early in the planning process.

If you want a fully outfitted adventure, they have rafts, kayaks, tents, stoves, stove fuel, USGS maps, waterproof bags, and fishing tackle, but the costs rise as well. They can also put together meal packages if you're not into packing your own food. But if you want to reserve a tent, no matter which agency you are working with, do it early as supplies are often limited.

Commercial airlines can get you to key Arctic hubs; a bushplane will get you to the fishing.

Whether you'd like to take a one-day guided fishing trip on a lake or stream, spend several weeks on a lake by yourself, or float a river for two weeks with a group of friends, it can all be done easily. Of course, the longer you choose to travel, the more costly the trip. In addition, the more people you have in your party, the more each individual typically saves-up to a point.

Another fly-in fishing option sometimes offered by outfitters in the Arctic is a flight into a lake where there's already an established campsite. These camps are typically fully equipped with wall tents, bedding, kitchen, and even boats and motors. If you want an experience that removes you from civilization but is easy on the body and doesn't require moving camp on a daily basis, this situation may suit you the best.

Pack as lightly as safety considerations allow when preparing for an Arctic fly-in trip. Though major airlines may allow two bags at 70 pounds each, bushplanes permit considerably less. Baggage regulations among air services vary based on the size of planes they operate. I've been on some that limit you to one checked bag weighing no more than 40 pounds. Check with the air service you're working with early on for regulations regarding the maximum amount of allowable weight for the trip you plan on taking.

When packing for bushplane flights, I like to put all I can in one small, soft-sided bag and carry on my fishing rods and camera. Any other fragile items will be placed in the middle of my duffle bag, surrounded by clothes that are tightly rolled up, not folded. Rolling up your clothes allows more to fit into a small bag, and a soft-sided bag lets you pack more efficiently and optimizes weight distribution in small aircrafts.

ACCESSING PRIVATE LANDS

Even in the remote Arctic, private lands border many rivers, especially where there are native communities. Even a river classified as wild and scenic may wind through a mix of parks and refuges and private land. On some rivers you may need to acquire permits from native corporations to be allowed access. Prior to booking any trip, contact local village corporations, park personnel, or the proper state agencies to see what access requirements may be in place.

In Alaska, waterways and land reaching the high-water mark are classified as public property, and it's legal to camp on gravel bars and river right-of-ways. But state and federal land management agencies offer maps depicting private lands, and these are easy to obtain.

It's also important to recognize that many villages still subsist off the fish that visiting anglers also pursue, so it may be wise to practice catch and release in some areas.

SOUTHWEST ARCTIC FISHING

The southwestern portion of the Arctic offers great fishing opportunities on some large river systems. Kotzebue is the hub for all travel in this area. As many of the prime rivers here flow into or very near Kotzebue Sound, you'll find good fishing close to town.

Established some 600 years ago, Kotzebue sits on a spit at the end of Baldwin Peninsula, 26 miles above the Arctic Circle, and carries a population of more than 3,000 people-making it one of the Arctic's largest towns. Kotzebue receives daily jet service from Anchorage 500 miles to the south and services several smaller native villages in the region. If you're not being met at the airport by a guide or outfitter, it's easy to get around by taxi cab, and you can make arrangements right at the airport.

Noatak River

One of the largest river drainages in this region of the Arctic and the eighth largest in Alaska, the Noatak offers excellent fall fishing opportunities for Arctic char. And from the middle of July through August you'll find chum salmon in the river, with pike, grayling, and pink, sockeye, and silver salmon also present.

You'll need an air charter from Kotzebue to reach this fishery. Both floatplane and wheeled aircraft service the Noatak, depending on where your drop-off and pick-up points may be. Rafts can be launched above the village of Noatak, near where the Aniuk River enters, on down to the village itself if current conditions permit aircraft to land. In fact, there is some fine char, pike, and grayling fishing to be had in the Aniuk River, too, as well as chum salmon if the timing is right.

If the village of Noatak is your starting or ending point, you'll be able to arrange for lodging. And if you're floating to the mouth of the Noatak River, you can arrange to be picked up by boat or plane.

When it rains the Noatak-like many Arctic rivers-can rise several feet in a few short hours. Err on the side of caution and plan to fish somewhere else under such conditions.

Wulik River

Like the Noatak, the Wulik River is located north of Kotzebue Sound and offers excellent fishing opportunities. The Wulik drains near the village of Kivalina, but no guiding outfits are in place here. However, this is a premier arctic char fishery, and Midnight Sun Adventures, situated 30 miles upriver from the village of Kivalina, can get you into prime fishing. There are also some grayling and chum salmon present.

Southwest Arctic Waters

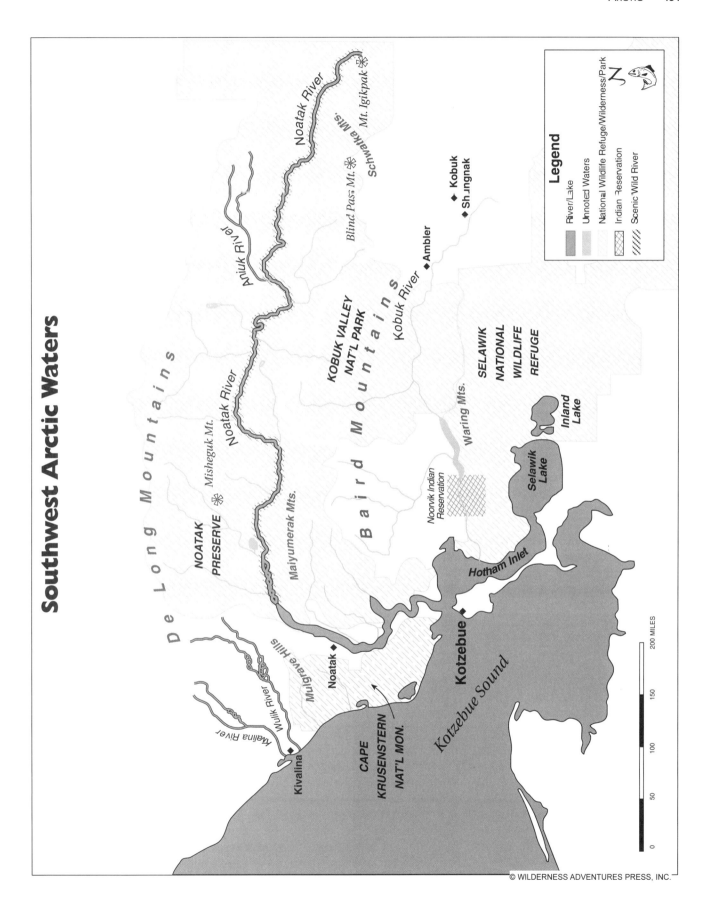

Kobuk River

The Kobuk River, Alaska's ninth longest, is another famed destination, offering world-class fishing for sheefish. Grayling, pike, and chum salmon are also mainstays on this wild river. The five villages spread out along the water make arranging float trips easy.

Anglers looking to add a little lake fishing can be flown into Walker Lake, within the Gates of the Arctic National Park on the southern slopes of the Brooks Range. It's possible to float the river from Walker Lake down to the village of Kobuk, but only highly experienced rafters should attempt it. Raging rapids, boulder patches, and extreme waters can wreak havoc here, and with so much other water to fish, there's no need to risk it, unless, of course, that's your style.

You can obtain a fishing license and the assistance of a native guide at the village of Kobuk. Boats can also be rented here, and air charter connections made. The culture and crafts in this village make it worth visiting. There is also a labyrinth of historic trails along the river here, making for enjoyable hiking.

Shungnak, the next village downstream, also offers guided fishing services, which can be arranged through the city office. You'll find some secluded campsites and even gold-panning opportunities if you float down from Shungnak. There is moorage available here for boats, and every type of fuel you'd need to restock. The town also offers marine engine repair services, making this a good stopover point for anglers continuing downriver.

Ambler is the next village in line. It sits on the north shore of the Kobuk, near where the Ambler River enters, and is surrounded by a beautiful spruce forest. Boat moorage is available here, as is mechanical repair and boat-rental services. A local fishing guide can be hired through the Ambler city office. The Ambler River offers anglers a shot at grayling and arctic char.

Floating downstream from Ambler, the next native settlement you'll come to is Kiana. Moorage facilities are available here, boats can be rented, and local guides arranged for. A unique feature of the Kobuk River in this area is the accessibility to burbot, North America's only freshwater cod. Though burbot can be caught in many locations throughout the Arctic, this is one of the more popular spots.

Just downriver from Kobuk Valley National Park, the banks of the Kobuk around Kiana feature a web of aged trading trails, still used today by subsistence hunters and fishermen.

You'll find a bonus fishery near Kiana in the form of the strikingly beautiful Squirrel River. The Squirrel flows by Kiana before dumping into the Kobuk, and this river holds good numbers of grayling, pike, chum salmon, and even burbot. A wheelplane can be hired to take you from Kiana to a designated drop point along the Squirrel. The 85-mile-long Squirrel River is also ideal for hikers. Though rafts and kayaks can get you into some good fishing, you may want to avoid the upper 15 or so miles of river, where the waters is rough. Water levels usually drop in the Squirrel in early August, cutting off rafting opportunities until the following summer.

Noorvik is the fifth and final village serving the needs of recreational anglers on the Kobuk River before it spills into Hotham Inlet. The town is situated on the southerly Nazuruk Channel of the Kobuk, and you can purchase a hunting license and sporting goods here, as well as find a marine engine repair service. Local fishing guides and boats are also available.

The fact that five villages on one river cater to sport fishing is a rarity in the Arctic and something anglers may want to capitalize on. With daily air service available from Kotzebue to all of these villages, getting in and out is not a problem.

Selawik River

The Selawik River runs more than 200 miles from its headwaters in the Zane Hills before dumping into Hotham Inlet, which feeds Kotzebue Sound. This is a large river, classified as a national wild river, with a number of sweeping rapids and boulders in the upper 60 or so miles. The closer you get to the mouth, the wider it becomes-and the more hammered it gets by driving winds off the Chukchi Sea.

You can have a floatplane drop you off on one of the nearby headwater lakes or fly in by wheelplane, which can drop you on exposed gravel bars between the village of Selawik and Shiniliaok Creek. A float down from Shiniliaok Creek covers more than 200 miles, requiring up to two weeks to navigate. Small to medium sheefish, arctic char, grayling, pike, chum salmon, and burbot are present in this river, which fishes well into mid-September. There are no local guides operating out of the village of Selawik, though overnight accommodations can be arranged at the school or in a private home by calling the city office.

If you're heading to any of the Arctic's southwestern villages on a do-it-yourself trip, make sure your plans are set well in advance of your departure date. You can't just show up in Kotzebue hoping to put together a game plan from there. Coordinating with village personnel is a crucial step in the planning process. (Village contact information is provided at the end of this chapter.)

Kobuk River

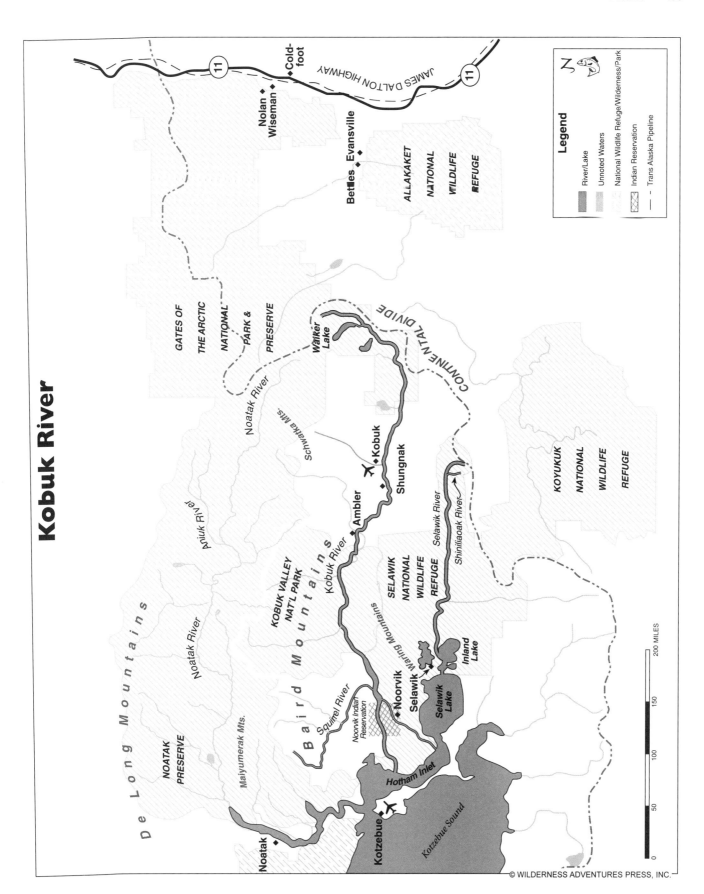

Legend

- River/Lake
- Unnoted Waters
- National Wildlife Refuge/Wilderness/Park
- Indian Reservation
- – – Trans Alaska Pipeline

JAMES DALTON HIGHWAY

Coldfoot

Nolan
Wiseman

Bettles Evansville

ALLAKAKET NATIONAL WILDLIFE REFUGE

GATES OF THE ARCTIC NATIONAL PARK & PRESERVE

Walker Lake

CONTINENTAL DIVIDE

Noatak River

Schwatka Mts.

Kobuk

Shungnak

Ambler

Aniuk River

KOYUKUK NATIONAL WILDLIFE REFUGE

Selawik River

Shiniliaoak River

De Long Mountains

Noatak River

KOBUK VALLEY NAT'L PARK

B a i r d   M o u n t a i n s

Kobuk River

SELAWIK NATIONAL WILDLIFE REFUGE

Waring Mountains

Maiyumerak Mts.

Squirrel River

Noorvik Indian Reservation

Noorvik

Selawik

Selawik Lake

Inland Lake

NOATAK PRESERVE

Hotham Inlet

Kotzebue

Kotzebue Sound

Noatak

0   50   100   150   200 MILES

© WILDERNESS ADVENTURES PRESS, INC.

Central and Northwest Arctic Fishing

The number of waters in the central and northwest regions of the Arctic is almost beyond imagination. I've fished many unnamed bodies of water in this region, though in all honesty, the fishing in other areas of Alaska is often better than what the extreme Arctic has to offer.

But what the Arctic provides in addition to some unique fishing opportunities is solitude unlike anywhere else on Earth. Many streams and rivers here host whitefish and cisco, with smelt, grayling, arctic char, and burbot rounding out the lot. Lake trout of magnificent proportions inhabit many large lakes, where fly-in access is the primary means of accessibility.

While I wish I could refer anglers to rivers near the villages of Point Lay, Wainwright, and Barrow, these areas are more for tourists interested in native culture. Point Lay, for instance, is one of the friendliest little settlements in Alaska, and one of the most isolated. I lived here for three years, serving as the sole high school teacher for the village school. I did a good deal of fishing here and came away with many fond memories, but for visiting anglers the fishing opportunities are nil. (In 1990 I tracked down and dispatched a man-eating polar bear, a most tragic encounter.)

And the fall whaling season in Barrow is a sight to behold, as the beach is lined with giant bowhead whales. These creatures, measuring upwards of 65 feet and weighing as many tons, are a subsistence mainstay. Unfortunately, few if any fishing opportunities exist out of Barrow, the northernmost city in the United States.

Still, there are some excellent bodies of water to fish, but they are scattered across the tundra and among the towering peaks of the Brooks Range. Anglers intent on battling 30-pound lake trout should realize that some lakes might not be free of ice until well into July.

As with southwestern Arctic fisheries, access is the key to good fishing up here. While Kotzebue serves the southwest region, Fairbanks, Bettles, and Anaktuvuk Pass are the gateways to the remainder of the Arctic. From Fairbanks you can take a bushplane directly to some waters, though flying into Bettles or Anaktuvuk Pass and then boarding a floatplane or wheelplane is a common way to reach many prime fishing areas.

Situated on the south shore of the Upper Koyukuk River, Bettles is a sparse community of about 50 people and is a primary stop for bushplanes en route to the region's remote native villages. There is daily flight service from Fairbanks to Bettles, where overnight accommodations and meals are available. Fishing licenses can be

Hiking and fishing remote Arctic waters is one of the most isolated fishing opportunities an angler can find anywhere in Alaska.

bought through the local trading post, and fly-out fishing trips can be booked from here. Both guided and drop-camp fishing is available or you can rent a boat. This is a popular jumping-off point for anglers.

Continuing north, the village of Anaktuvuk Pass is the next stop on the way to villages situated on the Arctic coastal plain. As with Point Lay, Anaktuvuk Pass holds special meaning for me, as my wife and I taught school here during the mid- to late 1990s. In fact, my first book, Hunting The Alaskan High Arctic, conveys many stories derived from this village, where hunting Dall sheep, caribou, moose, trapping wolves, hunting birds, and fishing were an integral part of our daily lives.

Anaktuvuk Pass is an Inupiat Eskimo settlement that hosts more than 1,000 tourists during the brief summer months. As it's just a two-hour flight from Fairbanks, many guides use this village as a meeting point with clients. While no fishing guides are based in Anaktuvuk Pass, overnight arrangements can be made at the school, the local camp, or in private homes by contacting the city office. Make it a point to visit the Simon Paneak Memorial Museum when you're in Anaktuvuk Pass. A one-of-a kind establishment rich in history, the local artifacts in this museum rival those found in the Smithsonian.

Anaktuvuk Pass is nestled in the heart of the Brooks Range, within Gates of the Arctic National Park and Preserve. Public access is granted to the parklands as well as across native regional and village lands. If you're interested in fishing rivers and lakes on foot, the park ranger and city personnel can assist you in planning your route.

The town sits on the Continental Divide, with the John River bisecting the village on its way south. The Anaktuvuk River runs northward, emptying into the Colville River, which then spills into the Arctic Ocean.

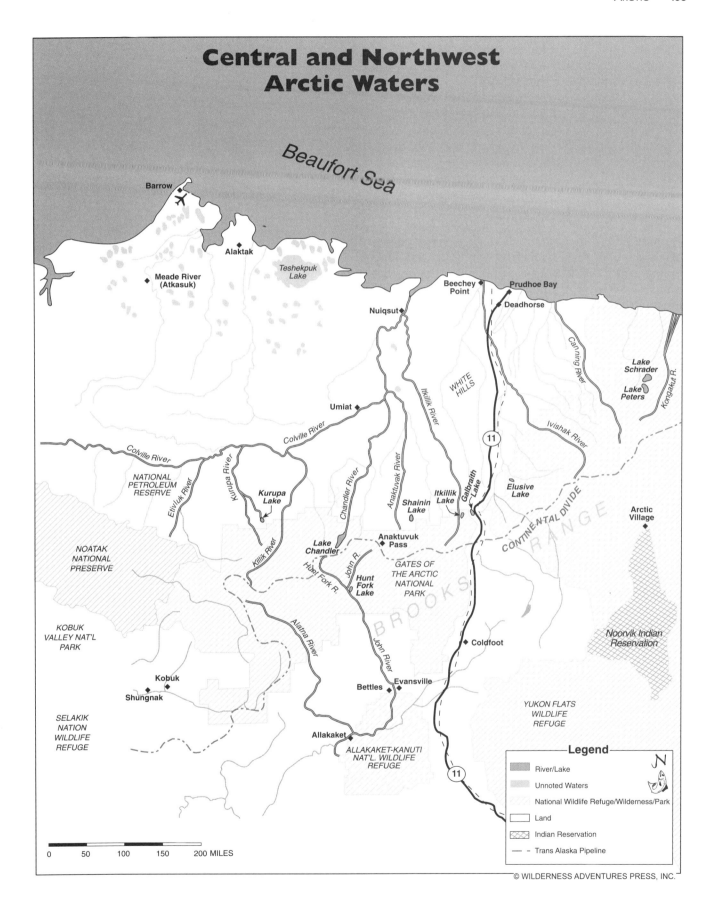

Central and Northwest Arctic Waters

Beaufort Sea

Barrow

Alaktak

Meade River (Atkasuk)

Teshekpuk Lake

Beechey Point

Prudhoe Bay

Deadhorse

Nuiqsut

Canning River

Lake Schrader

Lake Peters

Kongakut R.

White Hills

Ikillik River

Umiat

Colville River

Colville River

Ivishak River

11

Kurupa River

Etivluk River

NATIONAL PETROLEUM RESERVE

Kurupa Lake

Chandler River

Anaktuvak River

Shainin Lake

Itkillik Lake

Galbraith Lake

Elusive Lake

CONTINENTAL DIVIDE

RANGE

Arctic Village

NOATAK NATIONAL PRESERVE

Killik River

Lake Chandler

Anaktuvuk Pass

John R.

GATES OF THE ARCTIC NATIONAL PARK

BROOKS

Noorvik Indian Reservation

KOBUK VALLEY NAT'L PARK

Alatna River

Hunt Fork R.

Hunt Fork Lake

John River

Coldfoot

Kobuk

Shungnak

Bettles

Evansville

YUKON FLATS WILDLIFE REFUGE

SELAKIK NATION WILDLIFE REFUGE

Allakaket

ALLAKAKET-KANUTI NAT'L. WILDLIFE REFUGE

11

0 50 100 150 200 MILES

Legend

- River/Lake
- Unnoted Waters
- National Wildlife Refuge/Wilderness/Park
- Land
- Indian Reservation
- Trans Alaska Pipeline

N

© WILDERNESS ADVENTURES PRESS, INC.

During my time in the village, many anglers hiked and fished along both the Anaktuvuk and John Rivers.

One final note: The Arctic National Wildlife Refuge and Gates of the Arctic National Park and Preserve are remote and their rivers can undergo sudden changes due to rainfall and melting snow. July and early August are the safest months to float many of these rivers by boat, before they start dropping. To keep abreast of changing conditions, keep in touch with the outfitter or lodge you're working with and have a few backup fisheries in mind.

John River

The John River is built more for whitewater enthusiasts than anglers, but if you're into stunning beauty and snow-capped peaks, this is a great getaway. And the grayling fishing in this river can be outstanding, with the occasional burbot available along with a few pike from surrounding lakes.

There are easy-to-access drop points available from Bettles, which makes the river even more appealing to traveling anglers. From Bettles, air transport will take you and your raft to a predetermined launch site along the John River, usually near Hunt Fork Lake 5 miles below Bettles. The earlier in the summer you can float this river the better, as it drops considerably by early August.

The John River is a clear stream, and sight fishing for grayling in secluded pockets can be very productive. I lived very near the headwaters of this river and on several occasions stood along its banks during the spring breakup. When summer hits the Brooks Range, this river, like all others, turns into a torrent of chocolate water. But by midsummer, flows are stable and the water clear.

One of my favorite Arctic fishing experiences was to head out to the banks of the John River in search of grayling after work in the fall. From mid-August through September, the John runs crystal-clear, and the below average flow rates force grayling into little pockets, some no bigger than a bathtub. In fact, where it wraps around the village of Anaktuvuk Pass and heads south, the John River dries up. The onset of winter and lack of moisture result in nothing more than an exposed river bed. And freezing temperatures doom what fish that do happen to find miniscule pools in this area.

Though few people are likely to fish the John River so near its headwaters, late summer levels can lead to excellent dry-fly fishing throughout the system. Working mosquito patterns ahead of you or swinging them across the end of a riffle can lead to some impressive catches. The grayling aren't big high in the drainage, but the ice-cold waters yield some of the tastiest meat imaginable. And I'd often bring fish home for dinner.

The village of Anaktuvuk Pass, where the author lived through much of the 1990s, has several outstanding fisheries nearby.

Anaktuvuk River

The Anaktuvuk River offers excellent arctic char fishing and is one of the best-kept secrets for monster grayling in all of the Arctic. I caught several grayling in the 18- to 20-inch class from this river. Late August and early September are prime times for hauling in arctic char, but be aware of the fact that many subsistence hunters-as well as grizzly bears-are roaming the same area this time of year.

From where the Anaktuvuk River flows out of the Anaqtiqtuaq Valley, great schools of char can be seen milling about in pools in late summer and early fall. Given the intense clarity in the upper river, fish are easy to spot-you can even make out every bit of gravel on the riverbed. For this reason, small, subtle presentations with a weighted fly on a sink-tip line often work best.

From the village of Anaktuvuk Pass, you can hike 2 miles to the river. The trails are often wet, as you're slogging through low spots on the tundra, so hip boots or comfortable knee boots are advised. I prefer ankle-fit knee boots, not only for their support, but also for their added warmth and protection from mosquitoes.

The Anaqtiqtuaq Valley, from which the Anaktuvuk River flows, is my favorite valley on earth. I've taken grizzly bear, Dall sheep, caribou, moose, wolf, ptarmigan, and plenty of fish in this special place. In late summer, the grayling and char fishing is good, and the presence of moose feeding at river's edge and snow-white Dall sheep surveying the land from atop their lofty pinnacles makes for a rich experience.

The upper river runs a fairly straight course. You'll find some of the best, most accessible fishing from where the river enters the tundra and upstream for 15 miles. This stretch is ideal for fishing pockets along cutbanks, with some good riffles present, as well.

As the river carves its way out onto the open tundra toward the Arctic Ocean, it widens and meanders. You'll find deeper runs and chutes here, along with heavier riffles that are ideal for flyfishers.

However, as the Anaktuvuk River widens, it becomes more silted due to increased erosion of the fragile tundra. When fall rains come in late August, the river often runs off-color. But once things clear up, dead drifting a sinking line with weighted flies or nymphing on a dry line can be effective.

Colville River

The Anaktuvuk River eventually feeds into the Colville River, the largest river drainage on the North Slope and one of Alaska's most remote rivers. Approaching 430 miles in length, the Colville River drains an area of some 24,000 square miles. Flowing through a treeless landscape, this massive river has created some of the most valuable wildlife habitat on earth. Many captivating scenes depicting Alaska's vast caribou herds have been taken in this drainage. I've seen herds of caribou numbering over 100,000 in this region, something that makes a fishing trip here that much more special.

The Colville River can be reached either by floatplane or wheelplane. The most popular drop points for anglers brought in via wheelplane are near the mouths of the Etivluk or Killik Rivers, on exposed gravel bars. The ideal run is a float down to Umiat, where charters can pick you up and return you to Bettles or Anaktuvuk Pass. Some choose to be flown to Deadhorse instead, where there are tourist activities around the Prudhoe Bay oil fields. Arctic char and grayling are the primary targets on this journey, with the remote scenery and unique wildlife stealing the show.

Working the mouths of Arctic streams is a productive way to intercept incoming fish.

The Ivishak, Killik, and Nigu Rivers

The Ivishak River, a tributary to the Sagavanirktok River (covered with the Dalton Highway in the chapter on road systems), is another fly-in river that offers exceptional fishing for arctic char. Grayling also inhabit this crystal-clear river. Sight fishing for both species of fish can be a blast.

The Killik River runs north out of the central Brooks Range and into the Colville River, while the Nigu River flows north into the Etivillik River. Both the Killik and Nigu are clear streams that offer good fishing for char and grayling. The Nigu also has lake trout available in its system.

All three rivers can be run in rafts, with Class II rapids about as bad as it gets. If river levels are running high, you may encounter some Class II and III rapids. Trips to these three rivers are most commonly booked through Bettles, though bush flights from Umiat can also get you there. Floatplanes typically drop anglers at nearby lakes, with a short hike necessary to reach the rivers.

Kongakut and Canning Rivers

The Kongakut and Canning Rivers can also be accessed by floatplane or wheelplane out of Bettles, and they offer good fishing for arctic char and grayling. The Kongakut River is situated in the northeast corner of Arctic National Wildlife Refuge, while the larger Canning River slides through the western boundary of the refuge. Fishing with spoons or roe nets the best results here, as the fish can be finicky about flies.

Alatna River

The Alatna River, west of Bettles, is also a floatable river with good fishing for char, grayling, and pike. Boaters can take out at the village of Allakaket, with air service from here to Bettles and Fairbanks. Some anglers like floating the Alatna River to Helpmejack Lake, where they can be picked up by floatplane.

There are several lakes in this region of the Arctic with floatplane or wheelplane access-depending on the quality of the landing sites-available through Fairbanks and Bettles. Fishing from inflatable rafts or float tubes is the way to go on these lakes. However, it's a good idea to bring a spinning rod with lures and bait in addition to fly gear, especially if you're fishing big, deep water where flyfishing is difficult.

Chandler Lake

Perhaps the most famous body of water in this area is Chandler Lake, which sits some 25 miles west of Anaktuvuk Pass. When I saw old, tattered, black and white photos of native elders with 30-pound lake trout pulled from Chandler, I had to fish it. Though we took many good trout here over the years, we failed to connect with that wallhanger. But lakers in the 40-pound class are still said to be frequenting this body of water.

There are also some good arctic char in Chandler Lake, and flyfishing for grayling can be outstanding. As with most lakes up here, the trout fishing is best soon after the ice melts, while char and grayling fishing peaks in the fall, around mid-August into September. The caribou, Dall sheep, and wolves that frequent this magnificent area only add to the pleasure of fishing here.

Chandler Lake can be accessed by floatplane, and fishing from a rubber raft is easy. Unless you can work tight against the protection of the Brooks Range, I'd advise against a float tube. This big lake is susceptible to high winds. But the northeastern side of the lake, tight to shore, is a prime place to fish from tubes, rafts, and even from the bank.

There are many prime camping sites around this lake, used by hunters and anglers since the 1950s. In fact, you'll probably see traces left by past visitors in the form of fuel drums, old boats, and wrecked planes-all just part of the mystique surrounding this world-class angling destination.

Many anglers choose to combine hunting and fishing when traveling to the Arctic. The Brooks Range has much to offer such eager sportsmen. (Photo Cameron Hanes)

LAKES OF THE NORTHERN BROOKS RANGE

To the west of Chandler Lake-75 miles west of Anaktuvuk Pass-you'll find Kurupa Lake, a noted lake trout fishery. Fishing is at its best as soon as the ice breaks up, though it can continue to be good throughout the summer and into fall. There is fair grayling fishing here too, with mosquito patterns productive late in the summer.

Shainin Lake is located 22 miles northeast of Anaktuvuk Pass and holds some impressive lake trout and grayling. Sixty miles northeast of the village, Itkillik Lake is a prime lake trout fishery, with grayling also present. Just to the east of Itkillik Lake, Galbraith Lake offers similar fishing opportunities, as do Round Lake and Nanushuk Lake. About 80 miles northeast of Anaktuvuk Pass, you'll find good fishing for lake trout and grayling on the North Slope at Elusive Lake. Each of these lakes offers the kind of solitude anglers dream about but rarely experience.

In the extreme northeast corner of Alaska's Arctic, near the village of Kaktovik, there are two neighboring lakes noted for their fine fishing. Both Lake Schrader and Lake Peters are famous throughout the region for lake trout and arctic char. You'll also find respectable grayling in these lakes.

If you can get a raft into these lakes, you'll be able to cover a lot more water. In addition to basic casting and stripping, trolling with sinking lines can yield fish. Float-tube anglers working near shorelines can also experience excellent fishing in any of these waters.

LAKES OF THE SOUTHERN BROOKS RANGE

On the southern slopes of the Brooks Range, directly out of Bettles, there are numerous lakes accessible by bush-plane. In fact, there are too many to lakes to even attempt naming them all. The lakes covered here include some of the more popular angling destinations.

Lake Selby, located about 80 miles directly west of Bettles, is one of the better-known summertime fisheries in this region. Situated in Gates of the Arctic National Park and Preserve, Lake Selby kicks out lake trout, pike, and grayling all season long. And if you're willing to fish deep with big baits such as fish tails, heads, or fins, you'll also get into burbot.

On the eastern border of the park-about 45 minutes west of Bettles-Walker Lake has excellent fishing for lake trout throughout the summer. Northern pike and arctic char are also present in Walker. Between Lake Selby and

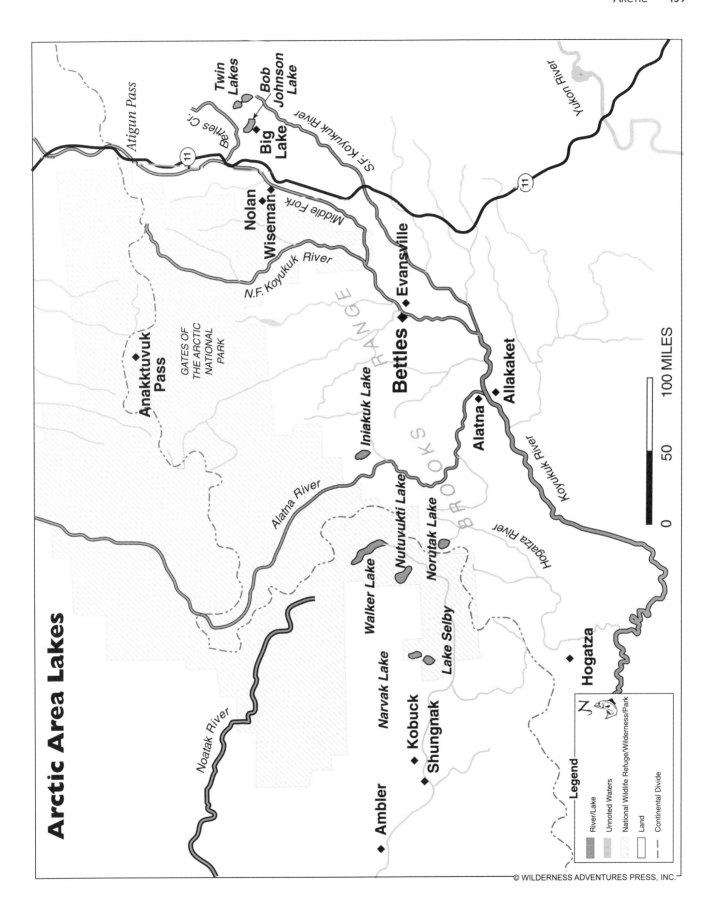

Arctic Area Lakes

Twin Lakes
Bob Johnson Lake
Atigun Pass
Battles Cr.
Big Lake
S.F. Koyukuk River
Yukon River
11
Nolan
Wiseman
Middle Fork
N.F. Koyukuk River
Evansville
GATES OF THE ARCTIC NATIONAL PARK
Anakktuvuk Pass
RANGE
Bettles
Iniakuk Lake
BROOKS
Alatna
Allakaket
Koyukuk River
Alatna River
Nutuvukti Lake
Norutak Lake
Hogatza River
Walker Lake
Lake Selby
Hogatza
Narvak Lake
Noatak River
Kobuck
Shungnak
Ambler

100 MILES
50
0

Legend
N

River/Lake
Unnoted Waters
National Wildlife Refuge/Wilderness/Park
Land
Continental Divide

© WILDERNESS ADVENTURES PRESS, INC.

Walker Lake you'll find Nutuvukti Lake. The fishing here is similar to what you'll find in Lake Selby.

Roughly a 30-minute flight west of Bettles, Helpmejack Lake and Iniakuk Lake offer good lake trout fishing from spring through fall. Pike are also available here well into the fall, and as with many lakes in this region, spoons and spinners may outperform flies. Whitefish are also abundant in these waters and respond well to flies.

A short flight northeast of Bettles puts you on Fish Lake, Twin Lakes, or Bob Johnson Lake, all of which offer good fishing. Lake trout are the main attraction early in the spring, with arctic char, pike, and grayling also available into the fall.

A Word on Arctic Villages

It may be difficult to conceptualize what traveling to the Arctic is like when you're sitting comfortably at home. The area is not that hard to reach, but once you're there the culture shock can be tremendous, especially for first-timers.

You'll be entering one of the world's last great subsistence-living regions. Here the lives of men, women, and children revolve around the outdoors, primarily hunting and fishing. At times, outsiders are seen as competitors. It's imperative to remember that you are a guest in the native communities and on their traditional lands.

The more removed you are from villages, the more tranquil your experience will be. But as you near villages, or as you work from one village to another when floating, you will likely bump into residents who aren't thrilled to see you there. Hunters usually have more confrontations than anglers, as the competition for big game is greater than it is for fish, but fishermen should still respect the waters near villages that are utilized by subsistence anglers.

If you fly into the village of Kotzebue, one of the larger communities in the Arctic region, getting around is easy. When you land-probably on an Alaska Airlines flight-simply pick up the phone and call for a cab. Chances are, though, you won't even have to make a call. Cabs will likely be waiting outside the airport. While I'm waiting for my luggage to be offloaded from the plane, I usually step outside and reserve a cab or make a phone call if necessary.

As for getting around the small hub of Bettles, it's a cinch, as the town is near the airstrip and can be reached on foot. The outfitter you contact to assist you with your fishing trip will probably meet you at the airstrip upon your arrival. If you're going to be dropped off at a lake, or if you're floating down one of the many area rivers, this is where you'll likely meet your contact.

Once you make your way from the hubs into smaller villages, things change. Everyone knows one another, and in most villages you can walk from one end to the other in 10 minutes or less. Many villages in this region of Alaska are constantly battling alcohol laws. Some prohibit the sale and importation of alcohol, while others are classified as dry, meaning possession of alcohol is illegal.

Having lived in and visited a large number of Inupiat Eskimo villages throughout the Alaskan Arctic, the best piece of advice I can give to travelers is to not treat the people like tourist attractions. Don't break out the camera and start snapping photos of the place or people until you've introduced yourself and made an effort to chat a bit. Smile and be friendly and sincere.

Whether you arrive by boat or plane, chances are that children will gather around to greet you. Some will come right up and start talking, others will hang back on the fringes. No matter how jet lagged you are or how hard a trip it's been to this point, smile and be friendly to them. Many children live rough lives, the likes of which outsiders have trouble even comprehending. Alcohol, neglect, and abuse are only the beginning. It's grim, but it's reality, and having lived in the middle of it all, I cannot stress enough the value of a smile, handshake, and friendly conversation from a warmhearted stranger.

A stroll through one of these villages is a cultural experience you'll never forget. Many have small stores, but few of these are reliable in terms of meeting your needs for a camping trip. Still, they may have a few items of interest, but don't let the cost surprise you. We once paid $17 for a gallon of milk and $5 for a head of lettuce. We were desperate and such things rarely made it into the village.

But what you can often find in villages are native crafts. These are the same ones you see in Anchorage, but for a more reasonable price. Many times you can chat with the artist, who is often an elder. The creation of arts and crafts is a dying pastime in many villages, carried on by elders but adopted by few members of younger generations. Some of my most cherished Inupiat Native possessions have come from elders who use their hands to make art for museums around the world.

So when you come here to fish, don't miss the opportunity to visit with and learn from the unique peoples of the Far North.

FLIES, TACKLE, AND GEAR FOR THE ARCTIC

Even if you're a dedicated fly angler, you should bring both fly gear and spinning tackle with you on most Arctic waters. Storms can quickly make mountain streams swell and run turbid, making lures and bait the only alternative to avoid a skunking.

Grayling, pike, lake trout, char, and sheefish are the primary species in the Far North. For pike, big, flashy flies will suffice. Weedless topwater patterns like mice are also good bets. You'll want something that moves a lot of water and captures a pike's attention. As for pike lures, anything big and bright that makes noise and throws water will attract fish. It would also be wise to have a few weedless lures along. If you're into topwater action, broken back and spinner-bladed plugs 4 to 7 inches long drive pike nuts.

Sheefish are more apt to hit baitfish patterns 2 to 3 inches long, with large, weighted, silver-bodied, flies the preferred choice of many anglers. A sink-tip or sinking line is a must. For lures, solid silver colors seem to produce the most strikes. A 1-ounce Luhr Jensen's Krocodile is an excellent sheefish lure.

For lake trout, leech, minnow, and sculpin imitations are good choices, with Zonkers particularly productive. The Gray Ghost and Black-Nosed Dace are also good patterns for lake trout up here. Fly anglers have the best chance of hooking into these fish early in the season, just after meltoff when the fish are cruising the shorelines in search of food. As waters warm, you'll need sink-tip and sinking lines to reach fish in deeper water.

Char will hit on patterns similar to what lake trout find appealing, with egg patterns being productive early in the fall. Krocodile, Daredevil, and Vibrax spinners and Pixee lures in the ¼- to 1-ounce range are good bets for both char and lake trout.

Grayling fishing can be exceptional on both wet and dry flies. Size 6 to 10 Woolly Worms, Beadhead Woolly Buggers, and attractor nymphs are good patterns to rely on. In addition, a variety of caddis patterns, the Parachute Adams, Mosquito, and Royal Wulff in size 10 to 16 should be in your vest. Roostertails from ⅟₁₆ to ¼ ounce in both black and white, along with small spinners, are excellent lure choices for grayling.

If you find yourself on waters where salmon are spawning, Polar Shrimp, Glo-Bugs, and other egg patterns can be the ticket.

Be sure to take at least one backup rod, as there are no repair shops to help you up here. Given the wet nature of the tundra, and the fact that you'll likely be wading a good deal of the time while fishing or lining your boat, hip boots are a must. Lightweight waders may be preferred, and of course, rain-stopping, wind-cutting raingear is essential. Depending on the nature of your journey, detailed topographical maps and a GPS may be useful. Regardless of where you go, make absolutely certain someone in a nearby destination knows your entire route of travel, when you'll be leaving, and when you'll be returning. I've seen too many lives lost in the Arctic due to such negligence.

Bug dope and a protective head net should also top the gear list. Continuous daylight during summer months finds the Arctic bursting with life. Not only do plants thrive at this time, but insects flourish; more specifically, mosquitoes. Once you see the size and number of mosquitoes inhabiting the water-laden land of the North Country, you'll understand why so many Alaskans regard them as the true state bird.

Swarms are so dense that even the locals remain indoors at times. A potent bug repellent is crucial, at least through mid-August when the first heavy freezes put the hurt on bug populations.

The best protection from mosquitoes and other biting insects is the wind. If you can stay in the wind, which isn't too difficult to do in the Arctic, your chances of having the life sucked out of you greatly diminishes. When the wind dies down, don't hesitate to apply healthy quantities of bug spray. Typically, the higher the percentage of DEET in your repellent, the better its effectiveness at keeping bugs at bay.

Sometimes it helps to have more than just a head net. I've been pleased with my Bug Out attire, but there are many specialized bug repellent suits on the market that serve their purpose well. Duct tape is another must-have item for the war against bugs. Wrapped around the cuffs of your pants and jacket, duct tape will seal off the pathways to your legs and arms, places biting insects seek out. It's also a good idea to talk with outfitters you'll be working with to learn what types of biting insects will be in the area you plan on fishing and what they recommend for repellent.

Raft Options

If you've booked a trip through a lodge, they should have quality rafts, canoes, or other boats available. And if you're only hitting small lakes, bringing your own float tubes is a good option. But if you're floating an Arctic river, make sure you know exactly what you're getting before you reserve a raft.

In the past, some anglers who have rented rafts from companies have had problems. Though the rafts were of ample size, they lacked internal frames. Bucking high winds and rough waters by paddling-one man up front, one in the rear-can be a nightmare. In fact, winds can be so powerful that they constantly kick up the front end of a frameless raft. I've heard horror stories of parties losing up to three days of fishing on a 14-day trip because of all the paddling they had to do.

Not only is paddling a raft on a large river dangerous, it's exhausting. Trying to make headway in horrible conditions can leave you soaking wet in perspiration. And after paddling all day, drenched from rain, spraying water, or sweat, it's imperative to dry out before the evening chill sets in. Even in summer, when it's daylight around the clock, hypothermia can be a concern in the Arctic. This is why dry, quality fire-starting gear should be kept close, even on your person, in case a raft gets away from you.

When you book a rental raft, just ask about the internal rowing frame. If companies don't have these available, I'd recommend taking your own. Even if there are only two of you on the trip, it will be worth the added cost of extra baggage. If you're traveling as a group of four, you can combine gear, often getting a raft into the hub villages without any excess baggage charge. Once in Bettles or Kotzebue, you will likely incur charges to transport the raft and frame to your drop point, but it's much better than being stuck with a less water-worthy craft.

The peacefulness of an Arctic river is something every angler should experience.

ARCTIC EQUIPMENT LIST

- Two complete sets of warm clothes, layers
- Raingear that's also windproof
- Warm jacket (wool or pile)
- Windbreaker
- Waterproof gloves
- Glove liners
- Hand warmers
- Wool hat
- Brimmed cap
- Sleeping bag (synthetic, not down)
- Sleeping mat
- Tent (wind and waterproof)
- Bear pepper spray
- Insect repellent
- Mosquito head net
- Sunblock
- Lip balm
- Sunglasses
- Hip boots
- Hiking boots
- Tennis shoes
- Wool socks
- Toilet paper
- Cooking kit and utensils (stove fuel)
- Water bottle (purification tablets or filter system)
- Lighter/waterproof matches
- Fire Starter
- Candle
- Pocket knife
- Signal mirror
- Toiletries
- Duct tape
- Dry bags
- Garbage bags (handy for many purposes)
- First-aid kit
- Space blanket
- Energy bars
- Fishing tackle
- Food supply
- GPS or compass and topographic maps

ALASKAN ARCTIC HUB CITY INFORMATION
Area Code: 907

GENERAL INFORMATION

Alaska Department of Natural Resources, 3601 C Street, Suite 1080, P.O. Box 107005, Anchorage, AK, 99510; 762-2251

Arctic National Wildlife Refuge, Room 266, Federal Building & Courthouse, 101 12th Avenue, Box 20, Fairbanks, AK 99701; 456-0405

Gates of the Arctic National Park & Preserve, 201 First Avenue, Fairbanks, AK 99701; 678-2004

AIR CHARTER COMPANIES, KOTZEBUE

Alaska Airlines, 442-3477
Baker Aviation, 442-3108
Bering Airlines, 1-800-478-5422
Cape Smythe Air Service, 442-3020
Hageland Aviation Service, 442-2936

AIR CHARTER COMPANIES, FAIRBANKS

Frontier Flying Service, 474-0014
Larry's Air, 474-9169
Wright's Air Service, 474-0502

ARCTIC ALASKA GUIDE SERVICES

Alaska Fish & Trails Unlimited, P.O. Box 26045, Bettles, AK 99726; 479-7630; www.alaskafishandtrails.com

Bettles Lodge, P.O. Box 27, Bettles, AK 99726; 1-800-770-5111or 692-5111; www.bettleslodge.com

Brooks Range Aviation, Box 10, Bettles, AK 99726; 1-800-692-5443; www.brooksrange.com

Iniakuk Lake Wilderness Lodge, P.O. Box 80424, Fairbanks, AK 99708; 1-800-479-6354; www.gofarnorth.com

Kiana Lodge, Larry & Starr VanMersbergen, P.O. Box 210269, Anchorage, Alaska 99521; 333-5866; www.alaskaoutdoors.com/Kiana/

Midnight Sun Adventures, 645-2203

Too-loo-uk River Guides, P. O. Box 106, Denali National Park, AK 99755; phone/fax 683-1542; www.akrivers.com

Vision Quest Adventures, P.O. Box 100965, Anchorage, AK 99510; 1-866-529-2525; info@alaskavisionquest.com

Wild Kobuk River Runners, P.O. Box 17, Kobuk, AK 99751; 948-2150; www.kobukriverrunners.com

Ambler
Population: 309
Location: N67°05' W157°52'
Zip Code: 99786

City of Ambler, P.O. Box 9; 445-2122; fax 445-2174
Ambler Traditional Council, P.O. Box 47; 445-2198; fax 907-445-2181; ambler@aitc.org

Anaktuvuk Pass
Population: 315
Location: N68°08' W151°45'
Zip Code: 99721

City of Anaktuvuk Pass, P.O. Box 21030; 661-3612; akp@gci.net
Nunamiut Corporation, P.O. Box 21009; 661-6026; fax 661-3025
Gates of The Arctic National Park, 661-3520

Bettles
Population: 43
Location: N66°44' W151°41'
Zip Code: 99726

Alaska Fish & Trails Unlimited, P.O. Box 26045; 479-7630; www.alaskafishandtrails.com
Bettles Lodge, P.O. Box 27; 1-800-770-5111or 692-5111; www.bettleslodge.com
Brooks Range Aviation, P.O. Box 10; 1-800-692-5443; www.brooksrange.com
Sourdough Outfitters, 692-5252
Brooks Range Aviation, 692-5444
City of Bettles, P.O. Box 26023; phone/fax 692-5191

Kiana
Population: 388
Location: N66°58' W160°26'
Zip Code: 99749

City of Kiana, P.O. Box 150; 475-2136; fax 475-2174; cityofkiana@aol.com
Kiana Traditional Council, P.O. Box 69; 475-2109; fax 475-2180; kiana@aitc.org

Kobuk

Population: 109
Location: N66°55' W156°52'
Zip Code: 99752

City of Kobuk, P.O. Box 20, Kobuk, AK 99752; 948-2217
Native Village of Kobuk, General Delivery; 948-2214, fax 948-2123; kobuk@aitc.org
Wild Kobuk River Runners, P.O. Box 17; 948-2150; www.kobukriverrunners.com

Kotzebue

Population: 3,082
Location: N66°54' W162°35'
Zip Code: 99752

HOTEL ACCOMMODATIONS

Bayside Inn, 442-3600
Drake's Camp, 442-2736
Lagoon Bed & Breakfast, 442-3723
Nullagvik Hotel, 442-3331
Sue's Bed & Breakfast, 442-3770

GOVERNMENT AGENCIES

City of Kotzebue, P.O. Box 46; 442-3401, fax 442-3742; www.cityofkotzebue.com
National Park Service, P.O. Box 287; 442-3890
Fish & Wildlife, 442-3799
Bureau of Land Management, 442-3430

REGIONAL NATIVE CORPORATION

NANA Regional Corporation, P.O. Box 46; 442-3301, fax 442-2866
Kikiktagnik Inupiat Corporation, P.O. Box 1050; 442-3165

RESTAURANTS

Bayside Inn Restaurant, 442-3600
Empress Chinese Restaurant, 442-4304
Hanson's Eagle Quality Center, 442-3101
Kotzebue Pizza & Deli, 442-3432
Shore Avenue Cafe, 442-3340

TAXIS

Polar Cab, 442-2233
The Cab Company, 442-3555
The Other Cab, 442-3001

TOUR & GUIDE SERVICES

Arctic Air Guides, Box 94; 442-3030; www.home.att.net/~maxson1
Arctic Alaska Safaris, 442-2505
Northwest Aviation, 442-3525
Quimikpak Tours, 442-3557
Tour Arctic, 442-3301

GENERAL STORES

Alaska Commercial Company, 442-3285
Bison Street Store, 442-2757
Uutuku Store, 442-3337

Noatak

Population: 428
Location: N67°34' W162°58'
Zip Code: 99761

Native Village of Noatak, P.O. Box 89; 485-2173, fax 485-2137; noatak@aitc.org

Selawik

Population: 772
Location: N66°36' W160°00'
Zip Code: 99770

City of Selawik, P.O. Box 49; 484-2132, fax 484-2209; cos1@gci.ne

Shungnak

Population: 256
Location: N66°52' W160°09'
Zip Code: 99773

City of Shungnak, P.O. Box 59; 437-2161, fax 437-2140
Native Village of Shungnak, P.O. Box 64, Shungnak, AK 99773; 437-2163, fax 437-2183; shungnak@aitc.org

Tips for Booking a Flyfishing Lodge

By Chuck Johnson (Publisher, Wilderness Adventures Press)

If you're going to shell out the money to stay at a remote fishing lodge, make sure you'll get the best possible service. My friend Alan Manas has taken 42 flyfishing trips to Alaska in the last 15 years, staying in a wide variety of fishing lodges. His experience as a traveling angler has led him to always ask the following fishing questions—knowing the answers can make the difference between a successful trip and an expensive bust.

- **Is this a flyfishing-only lodge?** Alan has found that flyfishing and fishing with conventional tackle do not mix well. If you are a flyfisher, it's usually best to book with a lodge that caters exclusively to flyfishing.

- **What is the maximum number of guests at the lodge?** Some lodges host 50 or more fishermen each week. To have the best fishing opportunities you should book with a lodge that has no more than 20 clients a week.

- **What are the primary fish species available in area waters and what are the top months for each?** It always pays to know what type of fishing you can expect.

- **How experienced are the lodge's guides?** Find out how long they've been guiding and how serious they are about flyfishing.

- **What is the ratio of guides to fishing clients?** The best ration is one to one or one to two. Anything above one to three can be a problem. Many people at the lodge will be first-time visitors or novice flyfishers. If the guide has to work with a couple of beginners, he may have very little time to assist you.

- **If this is a fly-out lodge, what is the ratio of airplanes to fishing clients?** You should make sure that you'll be able to fly out early each morning. If the lodge has more clients than its planes can carry in one trip, it may have to shuttle clients—meaning you could be sitting in the lodge drinking coffee until midmorning while waiting to get started. And with the famous rivers getting more crowded, getting a late start may mean losing out on some of the best fishing spots.

- **Will the airplane stay with you during the day?** If your plane drops you off and leaves, you could be sitting on the shore of a river that's flowing high and off-color or overcrowded. It's a good idea to have a few backup waters in mind each day and be able to reach them if needed.

- **On fly-out trips, does the lodge have boats cached at the rivers or lakes you fly into?** Boats can open up a whole world of additional opportunities, particularly on waters where flyfishing from the banks is difficult.

- **On no-fly days, does the lodge have a home river that offers good fishing?** Bad weather is always a possibility in Alaska, and it often grounds planes for hours or days. If you still want to fish on those days, you'll need to stay in a lodge near fishable waters that can be accessed by boat.

- **What types of boat does the lodge use and how many are available?** You'll probably want to be in the boat and on the way to the river by 8 a.m. Always avoid lodges where you may be shuttled in to fish with the second wave of clients. It wastes precious fishing time that you'll be paying for either way.

- **Does the boat stay with you all day?** You'll often need to move several times during the day to reach prime fishing, and you can't do that if the boat doesn't stay with your group.

- **How long does it take for the boats to reach prime fishing water?** Some lodges have great fishing as close as 15 to 30 minutes. Others require a trip of several hours, which can cut into fishing time.

Recommended Tackle

By Scott Haugen

FLY TACKLE

Depending on the species targeted, most flyfishers traveling to Alaska bring multiple rods and a wide range of flies and terminal tackle. Here's a general list of gear and flies you might want to consider.

Fly Rods and Terminal Tackle

- One 4- or 5-weight rod for small trout and pink salmon
- One 6- or 7-weight rod for silver, red, and chum salmon
- One 8- or 9-weight rod for silvers and kings
- One 9- or 10-weight rod for king salmon with Teeny T-Series fly lines in T-200, T-300, and T-400
- Floating line, weight-forward floating line, 8-foot, 300- and 500-grain sink-tip lines, sinking line, shooting-head line, 20-pound monofilament
- Strike indicators
- Tippet ranging from 0X to 6X; go with 20- to 30-pound tippet for kings

Flies for Rainbow Trout and Dolly Varden/Arctic Char (Sizes 4-16)

- Muddlers
- Sculpins
- Glo-Bugs
- Iliamna Pinkies
- Babine Specials
- Polar Shrimp
- Egg-Sucking Leeches
- Woolly Buggers
- Attractor nymphs
- Smolt patterns
- Flesh flies
- Beads, a variety to match color and size of salmon eggs
- Caddis, nymphs and dries
- Black Ants
- Stoneflies, nymphs and dries
- $1/32$- and $1/16$-ounce Stuart Steelhead Bullet Jigs

Flies for Arctic Grayling (Sizes 10-16)

- Elk Hair Caddis
- Parachute Adams
- Mosquito patterns
- Black Gnats
- Pheasant Tail Nymphs
- Hare's Ear Nymphs
- Beadhead Woolly Buggers (white and black)
- Woolly Worms
- Polar Shrimp
- Glo-Bugs
- Zug Bugs

Flies for Steelhead (Sizes 2-6)

- Polar Shrimp
- Hot Pink Sparkle Shrimp
- Egg-Sucking Leeches
- Babine Specials
- Glo-Bugs
- Sculpins
- Muddlers

Flies for Silver, Red, and Pink Salmon (Sizes 2-4)

- Zonkers
- Pink Streamers
- Popsicles
- Smolt Imitations
- Brassies
- Teeny Nymphs
- Sparkle Shrimp
- Pink Shrimp
- Comets
- Flash Flies
- Pollywogs
- Stuart Steelhead Bullet Jigs $1/32$ to $1/8$ ounce

FLY TACKLE, CONTINUED

Flies for King Salmon

- Popsicles in purple, pink, chartreuse, silver, or black tied on 3/0 to 7/0 hook

- Glo-Bug tied on 2/0 to 7/0 Gamakatsu Octopus hook fished below strike indicator

- Nymphs in black, dark green, ginger, natural, hot green, hot pink, purple and flame orange on size 2-4 hooks

Fly Selection for Other Species

- Lake Trout: Zonkers, general streamers, leeches, minnow, smolt and sculpin imitations

- Northern Pike: big, colorful flies similar to saltwater patterns such as a Dahlberg Diver, Lefty's Deceiver or Sea-Habit

- Sheefish: large streamers and flashy smolt patterns such as Zonkers and leeches

SPIN-FISHING TACKLE

Many flyfishers traveling to Alaska bring along spin-fishing tackle for situations where fly gear may not work as well, such as in heavily silted streams and rivers or in deep lakes. Here's a list of tackle you might want to consider.

Small Stream Trout and Grayling Gear

- Two ultralight to lightweight rods, 5 to 7 feet long

- 4-, 6-, and 8-pound lines

- 4-, 6-, and 8-pound P-Line fluorocarbon leader for clear streams

- A variety of beads, both in color and size, to match what's found in any given stream

- An assortment of lures ranging from $1/32$ to $1/4$ ounce, including but not limited to, Vibrax, Roostertails, Triple Teazers, Daredevils, Thomas Buoyants, Mepps Spinners. Colors and patterns imitating baitfish are good, as are red, chartreuse, silver and bronze

- Rubber egg imitations

- Size 6 and 8 hooks for bait (worms, grubs, larva, etc.)

- Size 12 snap swivels and size 10 barrel swivels

- A variety pack of split shot

Trophy Trout, Dollys, and Steelhead

- Two 8- to 10-foot medium-action rods

- 10-, 12-, 15-, and 17-pound test mainline and leaders

- 10-, 12-, and 15-pound P-Line fluorocarbon leader for clear streams

- A variety of beads, both in color and size to match what's found in any given stream

- Stuart Steelhead Bullet Jigs, $1/16$ to $1/4$ ounce, $1/8$-ounce floats and bobber stops

- An assortment of lures ranging from $1/16$ to $1/2$ ounce, including but not limited to Pixies, Vibrax, Roostertails, Krocodiles, Coyotes, Triple Teazers, Daredevils, Thomas Buoyants, Mepps Spinners. Colors imitating baitfish are good, as are red, orange, and chartreuse

- Size 7 barrel swivels and size 8 snap swivels

- A variety pack of split shot

Carrying bear spray is a wise idea for anglers, even in the Arctic.

SPIN-FISHING TACKLE, CONT.

Small Salmon Gear (pink, red, chum, coho)

- One 6- to 7-foot medium action rod

- One 8- to 8 ½-foot medium-action rod

- 10-, 12-, 15-, 17-, and 20-pound test mainline and leaders

- 10-, 12-, and 15-pound P-Line fluorocarbon leader for clear streams

- An assortment of spinners, wobble lures and spoons ranging from ⅛ to ½ ounce, including but not limited to Pixies, Vibrax, Coho-Bolo, Roostertails, Bang-Tails, Krocodiles, Flash-Glo Spinners, Wob-Lure, Needlefish, Bolo Spinner, FireMax, Vibric Rooster Tail, Daredevils, Hotrods, Thomas Buoyants, Mepps Spinners. Best colors include pink, pink/white, red, orange, chartreuse, silver, and gold

- Size 7 barrel swivels and size 8 snap swivels

- A variety pack of split shot

King Salmon (under 40 pounds)

- Two 8 ½- or 9-foot, stiff, medium-to-heavy-action rods capable of fishing up to 2 ounces of weight

- 20- to 30-pound mainline

- 17- to 25-pound leader

- 3/0 to 5/0 Gamakatsu hooks, octopus style for fishing roe

- Size 4, 2, and 0 Spin-N-Glos

- Size 6 and 4 Flashing & Spinning Cheaters

- Size 7 barrel swivels and size 2 or 4 three-way swivels to connect stout terminal gear

King Salmon (40 pounds and over)

- Lamiglass Kenai King Rods, 8 ½-foot, stiff

- 30-pound mainline

- 50-pound leader

- Magnum Jet Divers made by Luhr Jensen

- 7/0 Gamakatsu hooks, octopus style for fishing roe

- Size 000 and 00 Spin-N-Glos

- Size 2 Flashing & Spinning Cheaters

- An assortment of K-16 Kwikfish

- Large swivels and snaps to connect hefty terminal gear

Sunsets are spectacular in the Arctic, and even sweeter when you're fishing.

Alaska Tackle Shops

ANCHORAGE

Worldwide Angler, Inc., 510 West Tudor #3, Anchorage; 1-907-591-0662

6th Avenue Outfitters, 520 W. 6th Ave., Anchorage; 1-800-276-0233

Alaska Raft and Kayak, 401 W. Tudor Rd., Anchorage; 1-800-606-5950; raft, canoe, and camping gear rental

Boondocks Sporting Goods, Eagle River Loop Road, Eagle River; 694-2229

Fred Meyer,
1000 E Northern Lights Bl, Anchorage, AK 99508-4283; 907-264-9600
7701 Debarr Road; Anchorage, AK 99504-1872; 907-269-1700
2000 West Dimond Boulevar; Anchorage, AK 99515-1400; 907-267-6700
2300 Abbott Road; Anchorage, AK 99507-1400; 907-365-2000
13401 Old Glenn Hwy ; Eagle River, AK 99577; 907-689-4000

MacAfee's Fly Shop, 750 West Dimond Blvd., Anchorage; 344-1617; fully outfitted shop, a must-see for any fly angler traveling through Anchorage

Mountain View Sports, 3838 Old Seward Hwy., Anchorage; 563-8600; the most comprehensive collection of fishing tackle in town, source of fishing reports and other valued information

ANCHOR POINT

Anchor Angler, 235-8351; excellent local source for fishing reports and where-to information for fly anglers and campers

COOPER LANDING

Alaska Troutfitters, mile 48.2 on Sterling Hwy., P.O. Box 570; 595-1212; www.aktroutfitters.com

Cooper Landing Grocery & Hardware, Cooper Landing; 595-1677

Gwin's Lodge, 14865 Sterling Highway; 595-1266; www.ool.com/gwins

CRAIG

Black Bear Store, P.O. Box 22, Klawock, AK 99925; 755-2292; gas, ice, bait, groceries, fishing licenses and fishing supplies; open 4:00 a.m. to midnight every day

Jim's Lures, P.O. Box 19248, Thorne Bay, AK 99919; 828-3470

Log Cabin Sporting Goods, 1 Easy Street, Craig; 826-2205; fishing, hunting and camping supplies, apparel; canoe and kayak rentals

Naukati Connection, P.O. Box NKI #430, Naukati, AK 99950; 629-4104

Riggin' Shack, P.O. Box 18101, Coffman Cove, AK 99910; 320 2213; fishing and hunting licenses, tackle, ice, bait and snack foods

Tackle Shack, Thorne Bay, AK 99919; 828-3333

DELTA JUNCTION

Granite View Sorts & Gifts, 895-4994; located across from Visitor's Center

FAIRBANKS

Alaska Fly Shop, 1875 University Ave., Suite 1, Fairbanks, AK 99709; 456-3010; specializing in quality flyfishing gear and information

The Fly Hatch, 16 Blanche Ave., Fairbanks, AK 99701; 457-3597

Fred Meyer, 19 College Rd., Fairbanks, AK 99701; 459-4200; OR, 3755 Airport Way; Fairbanks, AK 99709; 907-474-1400; basic tackle selection, excellent one-stop shopping

J & L Sport Shop, 910 College Rd., Fairbanks, AK 99701; 451-7210

GLENNALLEN

Park's Place, 822-3334; mile 187.5 Glenn Hwy.; also has groceries, deli, produce

HAINES

Alaska Sport Shop, 420 Main Street; 766-2441; camping and fishing supplies, licenses available; douglas@alaskasportsop.net

Outfitter Sporting Goods, Mile Zero Haines Hwy.; 766-3221; fishing, camping and hikingproducts, bait, licenses and outdoor clothing

HOMER

Kachemak Gear Shed, Kachemak Drive; 235-8612

Slim's Alaska Fishing Lures, P.O. Box 2012; 235-1961

Sportsman's Supply & Rental, Boat Launch Road, under the big Alaska flag across from the boat ramp at Homer harbor; 235-2617

The Sport Shed, 3815 Homer Spit Road, Suite A; 235-5562

HOUSTON

Miller's Place, mile 57.6 on Parks Hwy.; 891-6129

KODIAK

Bear Country Sports, 3833 Rezanof Drive East; 486-6480

Cy's Sporting Goods, 117 Lower Mill Bay Road; 486-3900

Mack's Sport Shop, 212 Lower Mill Bay Road; 486-4276

Orion's Sports, 1247 Mill Bay Road; 486-8380

58 Degrees North, 1231 Mill Bay Road; 486-6249

NINILCHIK

Ninilchik General Store, P.O. Box 39434; 567-3378

PETERSBURG

Ace Hardware, P.O. Box 489, located in the Trading Union; 772-3881; sporting goods, tackle and insulated, airline approved fish boxes

True Value Hardware, Located on Main Street; 772-4811

SITKA

Fly Away Fly Shop, 300 A Harbor Drive; 1-877-747-7301; www.alaskanflyshop.com

Mac's Sporting Goods, 213 Harbor Drive; 747-6970

Murray Pacific Supply Corp of Alaska, 475 Katlian Street; 747-3171; all sport and commercial fishing needs from gear to licenses; www.murraypacific.com

SOLDOTNA

Fred Meyer, 43843 Sterling Hwy.; 260-2220; well stocked to meet all general fishing needs

Ken's Alaskan Tackle, P.O. Box 1168, Sterling Hwy.; 262-6870; one of the most complete tackle shops in the state, knowledgeable employees will put you on the fish and can recommend guides

The Fishin Hole, 139 B Warehouse St.; 262-2290; www.thefishinholealaska.com

TALKEETNA

Talkeetna River Adventures, P.O. Box 473; 733-2604; mile 14 on Talkeetna Spur Hwy.

TOK

The Bull Shooter Sporting Goods, P.O. Box 553; 883-5625; fishing tackle and licenses available

VALDEZ

Beaver Sports, 316 Galena St.; 835-4727

Hook, Line & Sinker, 200 Chitina Drive; 835-4410; located at corner of Chitina and Kobuk Streets; Dave Winney is one of the most knowledgeable sources of fishing information in the Valdez area and has been at this shop since 1986

South Central Hardware, 835-2300; located at corner of Meals and Galena Streets

The Valdez Prospector, 141 Galena St.; 835-3858

WASILLA

Fred Meyer, 1501 East Parks Hwy., Wasilla, AK 99654; 352-5000; basic fishing gear, along with complete one-stop shopping

Outdoors & More Sporting Goods, 455 West Parks Highway, Wasilla, AK 99654; 907-376-4464

Three Rivers Fly & Tackle, 390 E Railroad Ave., Wasilla, AK 99654; 373-5434; excellent gear selection and where-to advice

Wal-Mart, 1350 S Seward Meridian Pkwy, Wasilla, AK 99654; 376-9780; good supply of local fishing tackle

WILLOW

Mat-Su Valley RV Park, P.O. Box 431; 495-6300; mile 90.8 Parks Hwy.; www.matsurvpark.com

Willow Island Resort, 495-6343; mile 71.5 Parks Hwy.

Willow True Value Hardware, 495-6275; mile 69 Parks Hwy.

WRANGELL

Ken's Reel Repair, P.O. Box 201; 874-3443

Bruce Harding's Old Sourdough Lodge, P.O. Box 1062; 1-800-874-3613; www.akgetaway.com/HardingsLodge

Fennimore Bed & Breakfast, P.O. Box 957; 874-3012

Grand View Bed & Breakfast, P.O. Box 927; 874-3225; www.grandviewbnb.com

Helen's Place, P.O. Box 133; 874-3168

J & W Apartments, P.O. Box 606; 874-3954

Stikine Inn, P.O. Box 990; 1-888-874-3388

Zimovia Bed & Breakfast, P.O. Box 1424; 874-2626

YAKUTAT

Leonard's Landing, 1-877-925-3474; www.leonardslanding.com

Middle Of Nowhere, 784-3155

Yakutat Hardware Store, 784-3203

Yakutat Lodge, 784-3232; www.yakutatlodge.com

Yakutat Marine Store;,784-3386

Index